PLACE NAMES OF ALBERTA

VOLUME III

COMMITTED TO THE DEVELOPMENT OF CULTURE AND THE ARTS

This book has been published with the help of a grant from
the Alberta Foundation for the Arts.

PLACE NAMES OF ALBERTA
VOLUME III

Central Alberta

Edited and Introduced by
Tracey Harrison

Alberta Community Development
and
Friends of Geographical Names of Alberta Society
and
University of Calgary Press

© 1994 Alberta Community Development. All rights reserved.
ISBN 0-919813-91-7 (set)
ISBN 0-895176-44-1 (v.3)

University of Calgary Press
2500 University Drive N.W.
Calgary, Alberta, Canada T2N 1N4

Canadian Cataloguing in Publication Data

Main entry under title:
Place names of Alberta

   Vol. 3 edited by Tracey Harrison.
   Contents: v. 1. Mountains, parks and foothills - v. 2. Southern
Alberta - v. 3. Central Alberta

   ISBN 0-919813-73-9(v.1)
   ISBN 0-919813-95-X(v.2)
   ISBN 1-895176-44-1(v.3)

   1. Names, Geographical–Alberta. 2. Alberta–History, Local.
I. Karamitsanis, Aphrodite, 1961- II. Harrison, Tracey, 1963-
FC3656.P62 1990   917.123'003   C90-091236-7
F1075.4.P62 1990

Cover photo:
Edmonton viewed from North Saskatchewan River.
Photo courtesy of Government of Alberta, Photography Library.

Typography by Department of Communications Media,
The University of Calgary
Printed and bound in Canada by Jasper Printing Group Ltd.

♾ This book is printed on acid-free paper.

This book is dedicated to
Jeffrey Page and Elizabeth Alexandra Harrison

TABLE OF CONTENTS

ACKNOWLEDGEMENTS

The continuing compilation of this series remains an assisted project. Grateful acknowledgement is extended to Aphrodite Karamitsanis, without whose dynamic personality and perseverance the series would still be a hopeful concept. Penelope White significantly contributed to the publication once again with her search for historical photographs in various archives, and a special thank you is extended to this dedicated lady. These acknowledgements would be remiss if they did not once more recognize the pioneering efforts of Marie Dorsey, the first administrator of the Geographical Names Programme, and Randy Freeman, the second, whose contribution to the early stages of this series deserve mention, and Eric and Patricia Holmgren, the co-compilers of the first work of this kind in *Over 2000 Place Names of Alberta*. Martin Lynch, "resident Friend in B.C.," was of great assistance in the preliminary edit, for augmenting information and for pointing out some of the more obvious inconsistencies, and to him I extend my warmest thanks. The University of Calgary Press and its capable staff, especially Director Shirley Onn and Production Editor John King, provided large-scale assistance in the transition of this work from manuscript to publication. For their continued support and assistance, a special thank you is extended to Frits Pannekoek, Sandra Thomson, Dave Leonard and Michael Payne. Merrily Aubrey and Chris Robinson lent their time and talents by taking numerous photographs of features. A word of gratitude is extended to Elizabeth Falls, Donald Kumpf, Brad Rae and Kelly Kibblewhite, who provided support and research assistance. The Friends of Geographical Names of Alberta Society has remained a strong supporter of this project, and its membership, although relatively small, has participated in fund-raising projects to contribute substantial funds toward the publication of this volume. Under the strong and enthusiastic direction of its President, Ruth Groves, the "Friends" continue where many groups end, and grateful acknowledgement is extended to the rest of the executive and the general membership of the society.

lace names have come into being as a result of our
need to identify reference points – "to know where
you are going, you must know where you've been" – and a
natural extension of this idea may be – "you must know
what that where is called." The relationship between places
and names may be partly illustrated with a phrase from
Marcel Proust's *A la Recherche du temps perdu (Remembrance of Things Past)*, "place names the place – place
names the name;" Alberta's named landscape reflects
personal histories while providing a common reference
point for travellers and cartographers. As a result, the
study of place names reveals a great deal about the fascinating history and unique cultural heritage of any populated region. Even though toponymy is primarily concerned with the origins and meanings of place names, as a
key component of reliable maps and charts enabling
smooth navigation, a geographical name unlocks a valuable
store of information, in itself becoming significantly more
than the sum of its contributing parts.

Mutual sharing of information is the focus of Alberta's Geographical Names Program, and the purpose of this
publication, the third in the series *Place Names of Alberta*,
remains a twofold one. Over the course of several years,
archival and field research have been conducted in this area
of the province in order to provide accurate data for public
use. This volume makes that information accessible to
readers, even though the refinement process is continual.
Beyond presenting the most up-to-date information the
Geographical Names Program has collected, this volume
also invites those with additional information on individual names to assist in this research by making their
information public. Such individuals are a vital resource to
whom we owe a great debt and from whom co-operation
and help is always appreciated. Information may easily be
entered onto the geographical names database by contacting the Geographical Names Program, Alberta Community Development, Cultural Facilities and Historical
Resources Division, 8820 – 112 Street, Edmonton, Alberta,
Canada, T6G 2P8. Because of the guiding principles
behind Alberta's Geographical Names Program, it is not
surprising that the inventory of geographical names is
continually in a state of accumulation and revision.

The formal process of geographical naming is a
lengthy one, based on specific principles and procedures.
It should be noted that the first function of geographical
names is to ensure the most accurate identification of
places. Recognition of the importance of rendering a
correct spelling, use and translation of a geographical
name, as well as providing a generic definition (i.e., extent
of feature) of the type of feature being described, led to the
creation of the Geographic Board of Canada through an
Order-in-Council in 1897. Dedicated to the standardization of principles and procedures to be followed in naming
geographical features, the Board changed its centralized
approach very little over the years. A change of name in
1948 to the Canadian Board on Geographical Names still
left minimal provincial representation. In 1961, however,
the responsibility for geographical naming was transferred
to the individual provinces and territories, though the
necessity for coordination of activities at a national level
remained. Creation of the Canadian Permanent Committee on Geographical Names in that year provided the
opportunity for continued liaison between federal officials
and the naming authorities of each province and territory,
but provincial agencies like Alberta's Geographical Names
Program now conduct all research and maintain all information on proposed names, name changes and names
previously established.

Alberta's Geographical Names Program is part of
the Historical Resources and Cultural Facilities Division

of the Alberta Department of Community Development. Because of its focus on community participation and historical knowledge, its approach to geographical names research emphasizes the cultural dimensions of the province's geographical names. In addition to verifying local and historical usage through field research and archival materials, the Geographical Names Program maintains that to read a map is to read history.

Research has shown that the connection between geographical naming and the development of an area is very close: as individuals explore, survey and map a region, and settlement grows, the need to give places specific names increases. Indeed, geographical naming both affects and reflects the culture and heritage of a place. It also reveals significant cultural and environmental aspects of a community's identity. Names in Central Alberta reflect the multifaceted history of the region, and differ in important respects from other areas of the province. The First Nations of Alberta, the Metis, fur traders, surveyors and cartographers, railway engineers, missionaries and homesteaders all required familiar and common geographic points of reference, but in the choice of names for places each identified their landscape with their particular culture. It is not unusual to find names, in one form or another, of Aboriginal origin, or that refer to fur traders or their former homes, to missionaries or railway officials or to early settlers and homesteaders within the same area. The impact that these early arrivals had on the face and nature of the place names in the study area is therefore readily demonstrated. Not only are the pioneers reflected in the names in this area, but their endeavours may also be charted.

The specific area that this volume addresses (outlined on page xxv), contains the central areas of Alberta, south of the Athabasca River, north of Drumheller, along the Saskatchewan boundary, and as far west as Rocky Mountain House. The map located on this page is de-

signed to aid the reader in locating some of the features in a general way, relative to nearby populated places. Individual place names conjure images while maps invite exploration and discovery. Alberta's historical experience is comprised of many broad themes which are aptly reflected in place names in the study area. The following is an attempt to illustrate some of the main influences on Alberta's history and therefore its toponyms.

As with the other volumes, the earliest place names in this region were those used by aboriginal peoples, preserved and commemorated in translation or transliteration or the otherwise "anglicized" rendering of what are mostly descriptive names. It is not unusual to find several different native renderings and meanings of one place, as many groups may have occupied the same geographical area at different times. Long before fur traders, missionaries and explorers made their first forays into this vast land, it was inhabited by aboriginal groups. Many tribes used the area for hunting but tended to move south and east where game was plentiful and the winters were not as harsh. Central Alberta became a corridor for tribal groups going to the United States (Montana) and into Eastern Canada. Settlement patterns of the First Nations remain a broad and often speculative study. The nomadic nature of native groups is reflected in place names throughout *Place Names of Alberta Volume III: Central Alberta*, and cultural area overlaps are demonstrated in names such as Wetaskiwin (Cree: *wi-ta-ski-winik* - place of peace; Blackfoot: *inuststi-tomo* - peace hills; and Sarcee: *natzuna-atsi-klukee*) and Antler Hill (Cree: *was-ka-suk-is-kun ka-so-pit* - "the pile of elk horns;" Stoney: *pa-chi-di ha-ba jo-bi*). One therefore encounters a name such as Dogpound Creek (Cree: *mizekampehpoocahan* - wolf caught in Buffalo Pond; another Cree: *ko-ma-tas-ta-moin* - stolen horse (or dog) creek; Stoney: *so-mun-ib-wapta* - Edge Creek) and is initially perplexed that the meanings are so diverse. Native place names are most often descriptive, like

Tawayik, "in the middle of," or Kikino, "our home," but, on occasion, features that commemorate a special event, like Battle River, or an association with native lore, like Driedmeat Hill, are also recorded and housed within the inventory of the Geographical Names Program.

Native languages are diverse, dynamic and characteristic of an oral tradition and culture. In Alberta, there are eight distinct Native languages, and several dialects or regional variations exist among these. Transcription of these languages is a relatively recent phenomenon and begins with contact with European settlers. Missionaries seeking to convert Natives to Christianity developed a system of phonetic transcriptions using non-alphabetical symbols known as syllabics. Different religious denominations also created their own Romanized alphabetic writing systems, based mainly on English and French spelling rules. But early traders, settlers, and explorers who frequently referred to Native peoples and place names in their written documents and records used crude and inconsistent spelling that reflected their incomplete understanding of the languages as well as the lack of a formal system of transcription. It was not until the late nineteenth century that linguists in North America developed alphabetic systems intended for standardization of Native language transcription, although this was a standardization more for scholarly use than for Native communities themselves.

Currently, scholars in Native studies and linguistics have worked toward standardization of orthography of the more widely spoken Native languages. But standardization of usage is far from complete. Inconsistencies are common in present Native place name spelling, and this reflects a lack of consensus among communities and local authorities regarding the proper spelling of particular names. These inconsistencies can be accounted for by the overall lack of consensus and standardization (among non-natives, educators, local authorities and communities)

regarding the proper spelling of individual Native place names. It is because of this lack of standardization that throughout this volume many Native names are rendered with seeming inconsistency. The Cree word for "lake" has been spelled *sakahigan*, *saghahegan*, and *sagahegan*, depending on the time of naming and the individual who described and recorded it.

Much of the social and economic history of the Canadian fur trade took place within Alberta, where some 100 fur trading forts were established. The exchange of North American furs and provisions for European goods was a lucrative venture that expanded quickly west throughout Rupert's Land. In what would become Alberta, the first posts were established in the Lake Athabasca area, beginning with "Pond's Fort" (also known as The Old Establishment, Athabasca House and Pond's House, later known as Fort Chipewyan) of 1778.

Others followed in the next decade along the Athabasca and Peace rivers. However, by then, development was also occurring along the North Saskatchewan River. Fort Edmonton and Fort Augustus had appeared by 1795, and the fort at Rocky Mountain House was established by 1799. The name "Terre Blanche," bestowed on many forts along the North Saskatchewan River at that period, survives today as Whitemud, after which several features in the area take their names. Many of the posts, built for profit in favour of permanence, took on the names of features that were in close proximity, for example, Fort Assiniboine, established in 1824 was named after the Assiniboine River, and Lac La Biche, established in 1798 by David Thompson as "Red Deer Lake Post," took its name from the nearby lake. Other forts commemorated the home towns of the early factors and traders, for example, Greenwich House. The geographical names that are preserved in these sites remain a testimony to early contact between native peoples and the new inhabitants who were to transform the plains.

Another influence which figures prominently in the history, and hence the toponymy, of Central Alberta is that of early Catholic, Anglican and Methodist missionaries. The establishment of schools, colleges, hospitals and other social institutions was another means to expand their missionary role. Protestant missionaries and the early Catholic priests in Canada were often referred to by the people of the First Nations as the "Black Robes." Men like Robert Rundle, George McDougall, John McDougall and Father Lacombe added their unique presence to place names in Alberta. Throughout *Volume III*, the names of these early missionaries are commemorated in the names of towns and other features. The hamlet of Therien and the town of Lacombe are two examples of features commemorating early Oblates. The town of Vegreville takes its name from Father Valentin Vegreville, a missionary who began his work here in the early 1850s. Grandin is a former post office that commemorates Vital-Julien Grandin, the first Bishop of St. Albert. The name Mission Beach, a summer village 53 kilometres west north-west of Wetaskiwin, is taken from its proximity to the Rundle Mission. Commemorative naming was a norm throughout the missionary era, and one may find many examples of this practice. The Methodist missionary George McDougall established Victoria Settlement on the north-east shore of the North Saskatchewan River, naming it after the Queen, as naming features after royalty was another common exercise; hence, the name of the province, which was named after Louise Caroline Alberta, daughter of Queen Victoria.

In 1870, the fur trade empire of the Hudson's Bay Company passed to the Dominion of Canada. The North West Mounted Police was consequently sent on a mission to "Maintiens le droit – Maintain the right." In the summer of 1874 the North West Mounted Police made the long trek across the prairies, in part to prevent conflicts between the Natives and whites, but also to serve as a visible symbol of Canadian sovereignty in the newly acquired North West Territories. The first N.W.M.P. post in the region covered in this volume was established at Fort Saskatchewan in 1875 under Inspector W.O. Jarvis, at the junction of where the North Saskatchewan River crossed the survey line for the railway. Moonshine Lake was named after an incident which occurred circa 1920 during which a Metis settler was apprehended by the N.W.M.P. for manufacturing home brew. The Mounted Police forts were a precursor to permanent settlement and with law and order, the Mounties, in tandem with the railway and the Dominion Land Survey, also brought settlement after 1885, moving north by the mid-1890s due to the Klondike Gold Rush. Alberta's landscape was dotted with pack animals and amateur gold-seekers from Edmonton to the north-west, who left a small, but persistent legacy of place names along their way. Places such as the locality of Noyes Crossing, named after Daniel E. Noyes (1828-1910) who was a goldseeker, packer and businessman, and the locality of Busby which likely commemorates Edward Busby, Inspector of Customs in the Yukon during the Klondike Gold Rush, are examples of the influence that the Gold Rush had on place names in the study area.

Much of the information about the province of Alberta, information that was used by both the North West Mounted Police, as well as the railway companies in the later period, was the result of a British North American exploring expedition headed by Captain John Palliser (1817-1887) between the years 1857 to 1860 and known as the Palliser Expedition. The expedition collected vast amounts of data on the meteorological, geological and magnetic importance of this vast territory, and Palliser also collected information about the country's food supply, its flora, its inhabitants and its potential for settlement and routes of transportation. Palliser's published reports and especially his comprehensive map of 1865 were the main source of information about the lands in what is now

Alberta for some time and they became the basis for later railway routes and surveys of land. Since the vast majority of Palliser's treks involved routes through southern Alberta and the mountains, the expedition itself left few names in this study area. Palliser's Expedition, however, did pave the way for other surveyors and survey parties to make careful studies of the area, to take measurements, and to systematically divide the land. Other surveyors who arrived after the Palliser Expedition have their names associated with features and are commemorated in features such as Kitto Lake, Gough Lake and Seibert Lake.

Shortly after the transfer of Rupert's Land from the H.B.C. to the Dominion Government in 1870, arrangements were made for the new Territories to be surveyed into square townships. Surveyors marked boundaries for future farms and homesteads using equipment such as transits, rods and 66-ft. chains, which evolved as genuine folk symbols. Some of Alberta is still unsurveyed, but most of the completed surveying was done by the Third System of Township Surveys. Surveyors divided the arable prairie lands into square townships, each comprising 36 sections of 640 acres (259 ha.) with the basic homestead comprising one 160-acre (64.7 ha.) quarter section. Some features in Central Alberta have been named to reflect the influence of this type of survey, such as Fifteen Lake, a lake that is in section 15, township 48, range 4, West of the Fourth Meridian, Meridian Lake, on the Fourth Meridian, Point Thirteen, a point that extends into Buffalo Lake from section 13, and Town Lake, shortened from "Township Lake."

Priorities set by the Dominion Government in the east set the stage for the next major development in central Alberta, that of the railways. No other phenomenon in early western Canadian history so affected the toponymy of western Canada as railroad development. The Dominion Government hoped that the railway would improve transportation and communication lines across the prairies and between the east and west but, more importantly, they believed that the railway would open up a new economic hinterland for eastern and central Canada. The railroad builders entered Alberta in 1883, and an assortment of lines taken over from various operators who built lines north-west, north and north-east from Edmonton who wove their own names into the tapestry of the toponymy of central Alberta. Survey parties during 1890 marked the route of the Calgary-Edmonton Railway. The pace for settlement of the west was decided almost exclusively by the routes chosen for development by these various companies. The choice of names of the various stations that dotted the routes of the lines of these railways varied from strictly descriptive names to the commemoration of railway officials who directed or engineered the main and the branch lines. Still others were named after the companies that influenced the growth of an area, like **Antross** (a former station near Wetaskiwin), a combination of the names of the Anthony Lumber Co. and the Ross Board Lumber Co. Completed through modern Alberta in 1883, the transcontinental railway (C.P.R.) set the stage for the coming of settlement and the further development that followed very closely the main line westward across the prairies, and northward to new frontiers, heading toward Edmonton in 1890. By 1914, several main lines and spur lines criss-crossed the province.

The railways moved the farmers and the homesteaders toward their personal promised land, and with them, their toils and struggles, their hopes and aspirations, disappointments and successes. The Dominion Lands Act of 1872, modelled on American homestead legislation, provided the legal authority and policy under which lands were to be given to intending settlers in return for the payment of a $10 fee and the performance of specified settlement duties, eg., building a habitable residence within one year, and cultivating a certain area (30 acres) annually. This late 19th- and early 20th-century phenomenon called homesteading, provided newcomers with a clean start in life; however, despite their fresh beginning, there is evidence that many of the place names in the study area recall the ancestral homes of these early immigrants hailing from Ukraine, Germany, England, France, Finland, the United States, etc. Post offices were often named after the original postmasters or their places of birth; hence names such as Fribourg, Ispas, Lake Geneva, Ardrossan, Roras and Wostok. Throughout *Volume III*, the locations of post offices, former localities and localities are described at their last known spot. A variety of influences affected the locations of these places including, who volunteered to be postmaster/mistress, where the individual lived, railway line construction, or even political affiliation. It is therefore difficult to pin down a post office to a single location, as the locations changed regularly.

Place names in Alberta have been influenced by a number of developments and settlement patterns, as evidenced above, and have not escaped a degree of creative imagination in their selections over the years. While many of the geographical names reflect the names of the various people involved in many and a variety of ventures, others are more original. Prior to the establishment of official policies for geographical naming, features were often named for individuals or for companies or organizations that assisted in the development of industries in the various areas of the province. This practice has, however, been largely discontinued and geographical names are now chosen according to strict principles that govern the adoption of commemorative names. With the development of official naming procedures came the opportunity to accumulate extensive records on existing and proposed or local names. What follows is the geographical names history of central Alberta to the full extent of the Geographical Names Inventory to date. The intent of this overview of this area of the province is to provide a reference guide for the reader to accurately find locations using individual topographical map sheets as orientative tools. It is also intended to give readers information on the origin and significance of the place names of Alberta and to suggest the close connection between culture and heritage of the province and its citizens and the geographical names that describe and define the landscape.

EXPLANATORY NOTES

Individual place name entries in this volume may best be understood by considering the following example:

1. **Pigeon Lake** (lake)

2. **83 G/1 - Warburg**
3. **4-47-1-W5**
4. **53°01′N 114°02′W**
5. **Approximately 45 km west of Wetaskiwin.**

6. **The name for this lake has been in use since 1858 when Hector recorded it in his journal. It was known previously as "Woodpecker Lake," a translation from the Cree.**

1. Specialists in geographical nomenclature prefer to think of most place names as being comprised of two parts (both exemplified in the first line of this example): one part is called the *specific* (here "Pigeon"), whereas the other is referred to as the *generic* (here "Lake"). The generic identifies the type of feature, while the specific identifies the name of the feature of that type. Although generics very often form parts of place names (as in "Pigeon Lake"), many place names lack them. In this volume, the appropriate generics are always provided in parentheses at the end of the first line. The generics used here are consistent with those found in *Generic Terms in Canada's Geographical Names: Terminology Bulletin 176*, Minister of Supply and Services Canada, 1987; Catalogue No. S52-2/176-1987. An asterisk (*) preceding a place name indicates that the name has been rescinded or designates a former locality. A square box(■) at the beginning of an entry indicates that a colour photograph of the feature is to be found at the end of this volume.

2. The National Topographic System Grid Reference is a system that "blocks out" the country using map sheets of increasing scales. The second line of each entry identifies the map sheet corresponding to the described feature—in this case "83G/1-Warburg." Maps may be obtained from any Maps Alberta outlet in the province.

3. Where available, a legal description (here "4-47-1-W5") is given in the line that follows. It specifies the section, range, township, and meridian.

4. Next is the latitude and longitude location description, e.g., "53°01′N 114°02′W."

5. As a further aid to locating the described feature, the approximate distance to the nearest populated community (as the crow flies) is also provided.

6. The concluding sentence or paragraph of most entries summarizes any available descriptive or historical information concerning the feature or its name. Where a geographical name shares a specific with a number of entries, to avoid duplication the origin information for the common name is usually located under only one of the entries. Since the surrounding features are often named as a result of their proximity to the originally named feature, it seems appropriate to present the origin information under the feature that was named first. Wherever this is the case, the other entries conclude with a cross-reference.

Photo Credits

Geog Names — Geographical Names Programme,
Alberta Community Development

Red Deer — Red Deer and District Archives

P.A..A. — Provincial Archives of Alberta
12845 – 102 Avenue, Edmonton, Alberta T5N 0M6
A   Archives Collection
B   Ernest Brown Collection
P   Harry Pollard Collection
PA Public Affairs Bureau Collection

Feature Name	Number of Photograph	Location	Page
Astotin Lake	NCT-93-3-12	Geog Names	283
Athabasca Landing, 1898	B2590	PAA	10
Battle Lake	NCT-93-1-13	Geog Names	283
Battle River, 1907	A7679	PAA	16
Birch Lake	NCT-93-2-2	Geog Names	283
Blackfalds, 1894	P151 (373)	Red Deer	26
Blindman River	NCT-93-11-14	Geog Names	284
Bonnie Lake	MKA-93-4-1	Geog Names	284
Bonnyville Main Street, 1928	A3233	PAA	31
Near Bowden, 1890s	H815	PAA	32
Clover Bar, 1910	B335	PAA	54
Cold Lake Church and Director's Residence, 1920	UC41	PAA	55
Edmonton, Rossdale, c. 1904	B882	PAA	81
Edson, n.d.	B2788	PAA	81
Elk Island Park, 1940	B1306-4	PAA	83
Evarts, 1902	U32	Red Deer	87
Floatingstone Lake	MKA-93-4-5	Geog Names	284
Fort Saskatchewan, 1898	B3111	PAA	95
Frog Lake Settlement, 1885	B1686	PAA	97
Garner Lake	MKA-93-4-3	Geog Names	285
Gull Lake	NCT-93-1-19	Geog Names	285
Hairy Hill	NCT-93-3-7	Geog Names	285
Hanna Townsite, 1912	A11940	PAA	113
Innisfail, early 1900s	H486	PAA	127
Kehiwin Lake	NCT-93-2-20	Geog Names	285

*M*APS

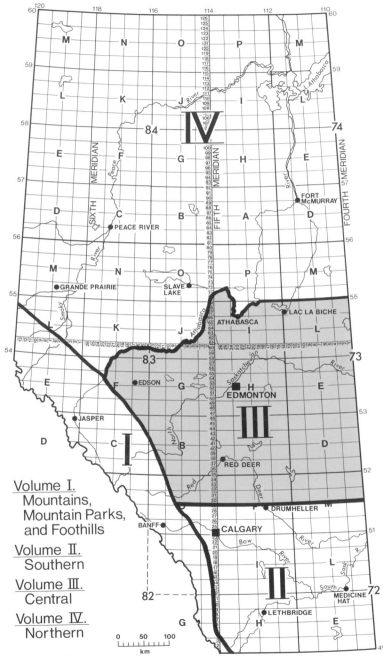

Volume I.
Mountains,
Mountain Parks,
and Foothills

Volume II.
Southern

Volume III.
Central

Volume IV.
Northern

Map showing study areas in the *Place Names of Alberta* series

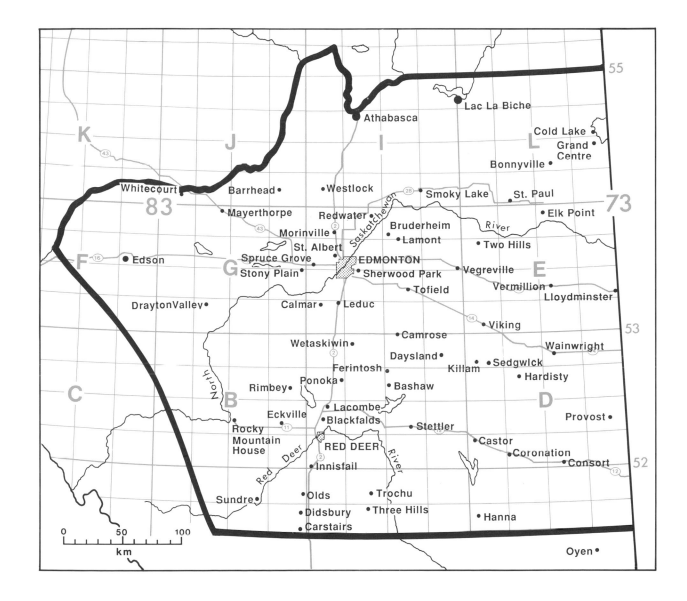

Map showing study area for Volume III

Abee (hamlet)

83 I/3 - Thorhild
1-61-21-W4
54°14′N 113°02′W
Approximately 86 km north north-east of
Edmonton.

The post office, which opened here in
January 1918, was named for A.B.
Donnelly, manager of the Northwest
Lumber Company, Edmonton.

Abilene (locality)

73 L/3 - Vincent Lake
18-59-10-W4
54°07′N 111°30′W
Approximately 18 km north-west of St.
Paul.

The name for this locality, whose post
office operated from August 1911 through
November 1956, was taken after a number
of places in the United States of the same
name. They were named after a province in
ancient Syria. The post office was originally
called "Clarksville," after the first postmaster, Lewis G. Clark.

Abilene Junction (railway point)

73 L/3 - Vincent Lake
19-59-10-W4
54°07′00″N 111°29′45″W
Approximately 18 km north-west of St.
Paul.

(see Abilene)

Abram Gates (gorge)

83 B/14 - Brazeau Forks
3-46-9-W5
52°56′03″N 115°13′05″W
Approximately 36 km south south-west of
Drayton Valley.

The name for this gorge was applied by Dr.
James Hector who writes in his journal
dated 4 January 1858: "the river became
hemmed in by lofty precipices of sandstone
about 150 feet high which I called Abram's
Gates after my guide."

Acheson (locality)

83 H/12 - St. Albert
4-53-26-W4
53°34′N 113°46′W
Approximately 9 km east of Spruce Grove.

The Grand Trunk Pacific Railway established a station here and named it after A.
Acheson Tisdale, assistant to the vice
president and general manager in Winnipeg.

Adamson Lake (lake)

83 H/10 - Elk Island Park
32-53-20-W4
53°37′N 112°55′W
Approximately 19 km south south-west of
Lamont.

This lake may be named after John
Adamson, an early homesteader in the area.
Many of the settlers in this area arrived
from Parry Sound, Ontario, and it is likely
that Mr. Adamson emigrated from there.

Adrian Lake (lake)

83 H/3 - Bittern Lake
3-48-22-W4
53°07′N 113°09′W
Approximately 25 km north west of
Camrose.

The name for this lake has been official
since at least 1958, but its origin is unknown.

African Lake (lake)

73 L/8 - Cold Lake
12-63-2-W4
54°26′N 110°10′W
Approximately 4 km south of Cold Lake.

The name for this lake has been official
since at least 1958, but its precise origin is
unknown.

* **Airways** (former post office)

73 D/3 - Coronation
34-37-8-W4
52°13′N 111°02′W
Approximately 32 km north-east of
Coronation.

Originally known as "Lakesend," this post
office was renamed after a railway survey
was made from the air by Colonel Birdseye
for the proposed line from Alliance,
Alberta, to Unity, Saskatchewan. The grade
for the railbed was actually completed, but
no line was ever laid and the post office
eventually closed in 1961.

Akasu Hill (hill)

73 E/5 - Innisfree
10-52-13-W4
53°28′N 111°50′W
Approximately 10 km east of Vegreville.

(see Akasu Lake)

Akasu Lake (lake)

73 E/12 - Two Hills
22-52-13-W4
53°30′N 111°50′W
Approximately 10 km east of Vegreville.

Akasu is the Cree Indian word meaning
"sick." The name for the lake is taken after
the nearby hill. There is no confirmation on
the precise origin of the name; however,
there is some evidence to suggest that the
name is taken after the smallpox epidemic

of the 1870s where many Indians died. There is also a story which involves a native who drank the alkaline water of the area, and it made him sick. Still another origin possibility suggests that this is the hill where old Indians came to die.

Akenside (locality)

83 H/11 - Edmonton
25-53-23-W4
53°36′N 113°15′W
Approximately 19 km north-east of Edmonton.

The Canadian Pacific Railway established a station here in 1950 and named it after Sir James Aikins (1851-1929), lieutenant-governor of Manitoba from 1916 through 1926. Aikins was born in Peel County, Ontario, the son of the Honourable James Cox Aikins. He practised law in Winnipeg, and from 1881 until 1911, he was the western solicitor for the C.P.R. It is not known why the spelling of Aikins' name was changed when the locality was established.

Alba Lake (lake)

73 D/16 - McLaughlin
6-44-3-W4
52°47′N 110°26′W
Approximately 30 km east south-east of the town of Wainwright.

The name for this lake has been in use since at least 1958, but the origin of the name is unknown.

Albert Lake (lake)

73 E/1 - Paradise Valley
25-48-4-W4
53°10′N 110°27′W
Approximately 31 km south-west of Lloydminster.

The name for this lake has been official since at least 1941, but its precise origin is

unknown. It is locally referred to as "The West Lake."

Alberta Beach (summer village)

83 G/9 - Onoway
22-54-3-W5
53°40′N 114°21′W
Approximately 60 km west north-west of Edmonton.

This summer village was incorporated as such 23 August 1920. It was originally named by the Canadian Northern Railway, after the province of Alberta, and the post office opened in July 1917. It is now a popular summer resort on the south-east shores of Lac Ste Anne.

Alcomdale (hamlet)

83 H/13 - Morinville
5-57-26-W4
53°54′N 113°50′W
Approximately 48 km north north-west of Edmonton.

This hamlet, whose post office opened in February of 1920, was named after Dr. Alcombreck, a dentist in Edmonton, who owned property in the area. *Dale*, a north England word for "valley," was used as a final syllable in place of "breck."

Alcurve (locality)

73 E/9 - Marwayne
27-52-1-W4
53°31′N 110°03′W
Approximately 26 km north of Lloydminster.

The name for this locality, whose post office operated from January 1938 through April 1968, is a combination of the first two letters of J.W. Alguire, the first postmaster, and the fact that the post office was originally located on a curve in the road.

Alder Flats (hamlet)

83 B/15 - Buck Lake
4-46-7-W5
52°56′N 114°57′W
Approximately 32 km south of Drayton Valley.

The post office, which opened here in November 1930, was descriptively named after the trees in the area.

Alexander Gate (gate)

73 D/11 - Hardisty
9-43-8-W4
52°41′50″N 111°05′30″W
Main entrance to the Canadian Forces Training Area on Hardisty Trail, 21 km south-west of the town of Wainwright.

Located in the Wainwright Regional Training Area, the name for this gate has been in use since at least 1909 when the Alexander family became the official gatekeepers. They lived a mere 270 metres south of the gate and the family name became firmly associated with the name for the gate.

Alexander Indian Reserve #134

(Indian reserve)

83 G/16 - Lac la Nonne
12-56-1-W5
53°49′N 114°01′W
Approximately 20 km west of Morinville.

This Cree Indian Reserve was formed in 1882 and was named after Chief Alexander Arcand (1845-1913). Arcand and his band moved to this reserve from Lac la Nonne.

Alexis Indian Reserve #133

(Indian reserve)

83 G/9 - Onoway
11-55-4-W5
53°44′N 114°29′W

Approximately 40 km south south-west of Barrhead.

This Stoney Indian reserve was formed in 1880 and was named after Chief Alexis.

Alexo (locality)
83 B/5 - Saunders
NE1/4-27-40-13-W5
52°28′N 115°48′W
Approximately 63 km west of Rocky Mountain House.

A post office operated here from April 1923 through July 1955 and was named after the Alexo Coal Mine. Alex Kelso discovered the mine.

Alhambra (hamlet)
83 B/7 - Rocky Mountain House
9-39-5-W5
52°20′N 114°40′W
Approximately 18 km east of Rocky Mountain House.

The post office, which opened here January 1916, was previously called "Horseguards," and was later named after the ancient fortress of the Moorish Kings in Spain. It is thought that the name was given by John T. Moore, president of the Alberta Central Railway, in a light-hearted attempt to connect his family with the Moors in Spain and their palace.

Alice Lake (lake)
73 E/4 - Viking
16-49-11-W4
53°13′N 111°34′W
Approximately 22 km north-east of Viking.

The well-established name for this lake was likely from Alice Tomlinson. Robert Burns Tomlinson came to Canada to file on a homestead on SE1/4, Sec 20-Tp49-R11-W4 in 1905. He brought his wife Alice and two children to Canada the following year.

Alix (village)
83 A/6 - Alix
36-39-23-W4
52°24′00″N 113°11′30″W
Approximately 45 km east north-east of Red Deer.

A post office opened here in June 1905 and was named for Alexia Westhead, an early pioneer and rancher whose name was shortened to Alix. She and her husband were reputed to be lavish hosts to visitors. Alix was incorporated as a village 3 June, 1907.

Alix Lake (lake)
83 A/6 - Alix
35-39-23-W4
52°24′N 113°12′W
Approximately 43 km east north-east of Red Deer.

(see Alix)

Alix South Junction (locality)
83 A/6 - Alix
23-39-23-W4
52°21′N 113°12′W
Approximately 45 km east north-east of Red Deer.

(see Alix)

Alkali Lake (lake)
73 E/12 - Two Hills
6-53-12-W4
53°32′N 111°46′W
Approximately 11 km north-east of Vegreville.

The name for this lake likely refers to the soluble mineral salts present in the water of many of the lakes in this area. Alkali water is not potable and is detrimental to the growing of most crops.

Allday Lake (lake)
73 L/3 - Vincent Lake
16-60-10-W4
54°11′N 110°27′W
Approximately 25 km north north-west of St. Paul.

The name for this lake has been official since 6 July 1950, but its precise origin is unknown.

Alliance (village)
73 D/5 - Alliance
15-40-13-W4
52°26′10″N 111°47′30″W
Approximately 45 km north-west of Coronation.

This village was named by Tom Edwards who had been charged with buying the right-of-way for the Canadian Northern Railway. He asked that the siding be named for his former hometown of Alliance, Ohio. The post office in the area, established in 1916, was originally known as "Galahad," but this post office was later moved and Alliance then received a new one. The village was incorporated 26 August, 1918.

Allingham (locality)
82 P/12 - Lonepine Creek
35-31-26-W4
51°42′15″N 113°36′00″W
Approximately 23 km west of Three Hills.

The post office operated at this location from August 1930 through November 1962, but the origin of the name is unknown.

Alma Creek (creek)
73 E/16 - Frog Lake
18-55-3-W4
53°45′15″N 110°26′00″W
Flows south-west into North Saskatchewan River, approximately 35 km south-east of Elk Point.

This creek drains Alma Lake. (see Alma Lake)

Alma Lake (lake)
73 E/16 - Frog Lake
28-55-3-W4
53°46'N 110°23'W
Approximately 62 km north north-west of Lloydminster.

This lake may be named after Alma Hasse, who married Clyde Rester Sr., an early homesteader.

Alness (locality)
72 M/12 - Hanna
13-31-13-W4
51°39'N 111°44'W
Approximately 17 km east of Hanna.

This former Canadian National Railway station takes its name from a place in Ross and Cromarty (now Highland), Scotland of the same name. It may derive from the Gaelic term, *ailean*, "green plain" or *ath 'n-innis*, "ford of the island."

Alpen (railway point)
83 I/7 - Newbrook
2-63-20-W4
54°26'N 112°55'W
Approximately 40 km south south-east of Athabasca.

The name for this railway point was officially applied in 1970 and was taken for its proximity to Alpen Siding. (see Alpen Siding)

Alpen Siding (locality)
83 I/7 - Newbrook
4-63-20-W4
54°26'N 112°55'W
Approximately 40 km south south-east of Athabasca.

A post office operated here from August 1930 through November 1970, and the name was suggested by W. Arason, administrative assistant and general manager of Northern Alberta Railways, but the precise origin is unknown.

Alpha Lake (lake)
83 G/14 - Mayerthorpe
22-55-9-W5
53°46'00"N 115°14'45"W
Approximately 32 km south south-west of Mayerthorpe.

The name for this lake has been official since at least 1958. *Alpha* is the first letter of the Greek alphabet; however, its connection to this lake is not clear.

Alsike (locality)
83 G/1 - Warburg
36-48-4-W5
53°11'N 114°29'W
Approximately 34 km east of Drayton Valley.

The name for the post office, which opened here in March 1933, is the Swedish name for a type of clover. Apparently, many Swedes settled the area.

Altario (hamlet)
72 M/16 - Grassy Island Lake
13-34-2-W4
51°55'N 110°09'W
Approximately 48 km south of Provost.

A post office opened at this site beginning in July 1919. The name is a combination of the names Alberta and Ontario, possibly reflecting the past and present homes of the early settlers. The post office was previously called "Wilhelmina."

Alvena Lake (lake)
73 D/9 - Chauvin
2-43-2-W4
52°40'45"N 110°12'30"W

Approximately 50 km east south-east of the town of Wainwright.

The origin for the name of this lake is not known although it has been in use since at least 1951.

Amber Valley (locality)
83 I/10 - Boyle
23-66-20-W4
54°44'N 112°55'W
Approximately 25 km east of Athabasca.

The *Concise Oxford Dictionary* defines amber as "yellow translucent fossil resin." According to Jeff Edwards, an old-timer in the area who was interviewed on the C.B.C. program "Hourglass" on 13 April 1973, the residents petitioned for a post office circa 1932, and the local teacher suggested the name Amber Valley from the colour of the land. The general area was originally called "Pine Creek" when its settlers arrived in 1911. When the post office opened in September 1931, the area and its community became more readily known by this name. The post office closed in October 1968.

Amelia (locality)
83 H/14 - Redwater
3-57-21-W4
53°54'N 113°03'W
Approximately 8 km south south-east of Redwater.

This locality, whose post office operated from June 1936 through March 1956, was named after the first baby girl born in the area.

Amisk (village)
73 D/11 - Hardisty
35-41-8-W4
52°34'40"N 111°03'25"W
Approximately 21 km south-east of Hardisty.

Originally established as a post office in 1908, subsequent to the survey conducted for the establishment of the Canadian Pacific Railway line, the name for this village derives from the Cree word for "beaver." The name was chosen presumably for the large population of beaver found around the Battle River area. One of the first residents of Amisk named the streets after local wildlife such as Gopher, Squirrel, Lynx and Badger.

Amisk Creek (creek)
83 H/7 - Tofield
34-50-18-W4
53°22′N 112°33′W
Flows north into Beaver Lake, approximately 10 km east of Tofield.

(see Amisk River)

Amisk Lake (lake)
83 I/10 - Boyle
2-3-65-18-W4
54°35′26″N 112°38′14″W
Approximately 47 km south-west of Lac La Biche.

This lake takes its name from the Amisk River which flows from it.

Amisk River (river)
83 I/8 - Victor Lake
11-19-63-14-W4
From 54°28′18″N 112°00′00″W
to 54°30′43″N 112°07′58″W
Flows east into Beaver River, approximately 36 km south of Lac La Biche.

Amisk is the Cree Indian equivalent of "beaver." The name is likely descriptive of this mammal's population in the area.

Analta (locality)
83 I/5 - Dapp
11-62-25-W4
54°22′N 113°38′W
Approximately 25 km north north-east of Westlock.

A post office operated here from February 1935 through September 1951, but the precise origin for the name is unknown.

* **Anatole** (former railway station)
72 M/9 - Esther
33-31-3-W4
51°42′N 110°22′W
Approximately 41 km north north-east of Oyen.

The precise origin for the name of this station is unknown.

Ancona (locality)
83 B/5 - Saunders
24-40-12-W5
52°27′N 115°36′W
Approximately 45 km west of Rocky Mountain House.

The Canadian Northern Railway established a station here in 1914. It was formerly known as "Pollock." The name Ancona is taken after a town in Italy, and there is also a place of this name located in Illinois.

Anderson Creek (creek)
83 B/16 - Winfield
27-44-4-W5
52°46′N 114°19′W
Flows east into Blindman River, approximately 65 km north north-west of Red Deer.

This creek was named in 1950 after Flight Lieutenant James Sangster Anderson, of Craigmyle, who was killed in World War II. (see Boyd Creek)

Andrew (village)
83 H/16 - Willingdon
32-56-16-W4
53°52′40″N 112°21′00″W
Approximately 29 km south south-east of Smoky Lake.

A post office opened here in March 1902 and was named for Andrew Whitford, one of the first settlers and a prominent farmer in the district. The village was incorporated 24 June 1930.

* **Angle Lake** (former post office)
73 E/15 - Elk Point
21-55-7-W4
53°46′N 110°58′W
Approximately 43 km north north-west of Vermilion.

The name for this former post office, which operated from February 1911 through January 1958, is taken for its proximity to the lake of the same name. (see Angle Lake)

Angle Lake (lake)
73 E/10 - Clandonald
9-55-7-W4
53°44′N 110°59′W
Approximately 43 km north north-west of Vermilion.

The name for this lake is descriptive of its shape: two long arms are at an angle to each other.

Angling Lake (lake)
73 L/1 - Reita Lake
23-60-3-W4
54°12′N 110°19′W
Approximately 31 km south south-west of Cold Lake.

The descriptive name for this feature has appeared on maps since at least 1950 and refers to the technique with which early natives fished on the lake, using a rod and line.

Ankerton (locality)

83 A/9 - Forestburg
25-43-17-W4
52°44′N 112°19′W
Approximately 46 km south-east of Camrose.

A Canadian Northern Railway station was established here in 1916. The post office opened the following year and operated from April 1917 through February 1970. The locality is named after Anker H. Lauritzen, the grandfather of the first postmaster, C.H. Lauritzen. It was previously called "Campbelton."

Annabel Lake (lake)

83 F/10 - Bickerdike
34-52-19-W5
53°32′N 116°43′W
Approximately 17 km west south-west of Edson.

The name for this lake was first submitted by R.J. Paterson, with the Department of Lands and Forests in November 1968. The well-established name was officially approved 21 March 1978, but its precise origin is unknown.

Anning (locality)

73 L/4 - Cache Lake
32-58-11-W4
54°04′N 111°41′W
Approximately 18 km west north-west of St. Paul.

The name for the post office, which operated here from September 1911 through June 1954, was taken after the first postmaster, S.H. Anning.

Ansell (locality)

83 F/10 - Bickerdike
12-53-18-W5
53°33′N 116°31′W
Approximately 8 km west south-west of Edson.

The Grand Trunk Pacific Railway established a station here in 1911 and named it after Albert Ansell, secretary to the vice-president of the railway.

Ansell Lake (lake)

83 I/11 - Athabasca
3-64-21-W4
54°30′15″N 113°06′00″W
Approximately 26 km south south-west of Athabasca.

The name for this lake has been in use since at least 1952, but its precise origin is unknown.

Anselmo (locality)

83 G/14 - Mayerthorpe
2-57-10-W5
53°53′N 115°23′W
Approximately 34 km south-east of Whitecourt.

The post office operated here from September 1913 through September 1964 and was named after the home town of the first postmasters, Rudolf and Maria Michalitscka, in Nebraska.

Anshaw (locality)

73 L/7 - Bonnyville
20-61-6-W4
54°17′N 110°51′W
Approximately 9 km north-west of Bonnyville.

The name for the post office, which operated here from July 1932 through July 1937, is a compound of the names Angus and Shaw. Angus Shaw was an early fur

trader with the North West Company who built a post on Moose Lake in 1789. It was also known as Fort Lac d'Orignal (moose in French) or Shaw's House, apparently the first house in Alberta.

Antelope Hills (hills)

72 M/12 - Hanna
17-32-14-W4
From 51°45′35″N 111°57′50″W
to 51°44′15″N 111°56′30″W
Approximately 10 km north of Hanna.

The hills are named due to the one-time presence of antelope in the area.

Antelope Lake (lake)

72 M/11 - Youngstown
20-31-9-W4
51°40′00″N 111°15′15″W
Approximately 48 km east of Hanna.

(see Antelope Hills)

Antler Hill (hill)

83 A/4 - Innisfail
2-36-28-W4
52°04′N 113°53′W
Approximately 5 km north-east of Innisfail.

According to the area's early settlers, it is thought that the local Indians piled the elk antlers here (atop the hill) as part of a particular religious ceremony. The name itself is an approximate translation of the Cree *was-ka-suk-is-kun ka-so-pit*, meaning "the pile of elk horns," and in Stoney, it is rendered *pa-chi-di ha-ba jo-bi* (Tyrrell).

Antler Lake (lake)

83 H/10 - Elk Island Park
23-52-21-W4
53°30′N 112°59′W
Approximately 25 km north-west of Tofield.

The name for this lake has been official since 1958, but its precise origin is unknown.

Antler Lake (hamlet)

83 H/7 - Tofield
24-52-21-W4
53°29'N 112°59'W
Approximately 35 km east of Edmonton.

This hamlet is on the east shore of Antler Lake. (see Antler Lake)

Antoine Lake (lake)

83 I/16 - Plamondon
12-4-67-14-W4
54°46'37"N 112°05'04"W
Approximately 9 km west of Lac La Biche.

The name for this lake has been in use since at least 1814, when a former employee of the North West Company, Antoine Desjarlais, trapped on the lake. Antoine Lake is referred by many local residents as "Little Egg Lake."

Anton Lake (locality)

83 I/3 - Thorhild
4-60-23-W4
54°09'N 113°24'W
Approximately 70 km north of Edmonton.

The post office operated here from January 1930 through May 1958 and was named after Anton Strilchuk, an early Ukrainian settler.

Antross (locality)

83 G/2 - Drayton Valley
22-47-4-W5
53°04'N 114°30'W
Approximately 88 km south-west of Edmonton

This name for this locality is a combination of the names of two sawmills in the district,

namely the Anthony Lumber Co. and the Ross Board Lumber Co.

Arcand Lake (lake)

73 E/2 - Grizzly Bear Creek
2-48-6-W4
53°06'N 110°47'W
Approximately 28 km south of Vermilion.

The name for this lake has been official since at least 1958, but its precise origin is unknown.

Archer Island (island)

83 H/10 - Elk Island Park
23-54-20-W4
53°40'N 112°50'W
Approximately 49 km east of Edmonton.

This island was named in December 1939 after the late Dr. A.E. Archer who owned a cabin in the Elk Island Park. He also took part in the 1909 Buffalo Round-Up.

Archie Hill (hill)

73 D/11 - Hardisty
33-43-8-W4
52°44'N 111°06'W
Approximately 12 km east north-east of Hardisty.

The name for this 668 metre hill has been in use since at least 1958 although the origin for the name is unknown.

Archie Lake (lake)

83 I/11 - Athabasca
2-64-21-W4
54°30'15"N 113°05'00"W
Approximately 28 km south-east of Athabasca.

The name for this lake has been official since at least 1952, but its precise origin is unknown.

Ardley (hamlet)

83 A/6 - Alix
16-38-23-W4
52°16'N 113°14'W
Approximately 40 km east of Red Deer.

This hamlet was named after a parish in Oxfordshire, England. It was previously called "Coalbanks," since much coal was mined in the vicinity. The post office operated from August 1912 through June 1961.

Ardmore (hamlet)

73 L/8 - Cold Lake
1-62-4-W4
54°20'N 110°29'W
Approximately 23 km south-west of Cold Lake.

One of the early settlers, Mr. Whilley, named the school district after his home in Ardmore, Oklahoma, which in turn was named after Ardmore, Ireland. There are many places in Ireland with this name, which means "great height." The post office opened in August 1913.

Ardrossan (hamlet)

83 H/11 - Edmonton
2-53-22-W4
53°33'N 113°08'W
Approximately 22 km east of Edmonton.

The hamlet of Ardrossan had its beginnings in 1909 with the coming of the Grand Trunk Pacific Railway. It was named after a holiday resort town in Ayrshire (now Strathclyde), Scotland, by Miss Edmiston, a local woman. The name is from the Gaelic, meaning "height of the little cape." The name was originally spelled as two separate words - *ard rosain* - meaning "the height of the little headland." The post office opened in July 1909.

Argentia Beach (summer village)

83 G/1 - Warburg
13-47-1-W5
53°03′N 114°01′W
Approximately 46 km west north-west of
Wetaskiwin.

The name for this summer village which
was incorporated 1 January 1967, is derived
from the Latin *argentum,* translating
"silver." The community was originally
named "Silver Bay," but this was changed
to avoid duplication with a Silver Beach on
Pigeon Lake.

Arm Lake (lake)

73 D/10 - Hughenden
36-43-5-W4
52°44′N 110°35′W
Approximately 21 km south-east of the
town of Wainwright.

The name for this lake, in use since at least
1958, was given because of a perceived
resemblance to an arm bent at the elbow.

Armena (hamlet)

83 H/2 - Camrose
12-48-21-W4
53°08′N 112°57′W
Approximately 13 km north-west of
Camrose.

The Canadian Northern Railway from
Edmonton to Calgary gave Armena its
beginning in 1911. Up to that time this
district had been called "Thodenskjold,"
but it was difficult to pronounce and to
spell, so a few men decided that they would
write to the department in Edmonton and
have them choose a name for the little town
that was about to sprout. It wasn't long
before they received word that this place
should, or could, be named Armena;
however, its origin is unknown. The post
office opened in May 1917.

Armistice (locality)

73 E/14 - St. Paul
7-57-7-W4
53°55′N 111°01′W
Approximately 20 km south-east of St.
Paul.

The post office operated here from August
1928 through November 1962, but its
precise origin is unknown.

Armstrong Hill (hill)

73 D/14 - Irma
28-44-8-W4
52°49′30″N 111°05′30″W
Approximately 16 km west of the town of
Wainwright.

The name for this 675 m hill located on the
Camp Wainwright Military Reserve was
proposed by Lieutenant Colonel M.R.
Gentles, C.D. in November 1980, was
officially adopted 13 March 1981, and
commemorates George Armstrong, a
Buffalo Park Rider from 1921 through
1939. (see Buffalo Park)

Armstrong Lake (lake)

83 I/5 - Dapp
26-62-25-W4
54°23′N 113°38′W
Approximately 30 km north north-east of
Westlock.

The name for this lake appeared on a
sectional map dated 1929 and was officially
adopted 8 December 1945, but its precise
origin is unknown.

Armstrong Spring (spring)

73 D/14 - Irma
26-44-8-W4
52°49′25″N 111°03′30″W
Approximately 10 km west of the town of
Wainwright.

The name for this spring has been in use
since 1926 when it first appeared on a map

produced by the Department of the
Interior. (see Armstrong Hill)

Arnault Lake (lake)

83 G/10 - Isle Lake
31-54-5-W5
53°42′N 114°44′W
Approximately 38 km south-east of
Mayerthorpe.

The name for this lake has been official
since at least 1950, but its precise origin is
unknown.

Arthur Lake (lake)

83 G/15 - Sangudo
22-55-5-W5
53°46′N 114°39′W
Approximately 50 km west north-west of
Spruce Grove.

The name for this lake is locally known as
"Little Jackfish Lake" due to its proximity
to Lessard Lake which is known to area
residents as "Jackfish Lake." The origin for
the name Arthur Lake is unknown.

Arthur Lake (lake)

83 I/11 - Athabasca
17-64-21-W4
54°32′N 113°09′W
Approximately 22 km south south-east of
Athabasca.

The name for this lake was officially
adopted in 1952, but its precise origin is
unknown.

Arthur Municipal District No. 48

(municipal district)

82 P/11 - Three Hills
28 to 34-21 to 27-W4
51°45′N 113°20′W
South of Red Deer.

The name for this municipal district was shortened from McArthur in 1918. (see Arthurvale)

* Arthurvale (former post office)

82 P/14 - Trochu
36-34-25-W4
51°58′N 113°25′W
Approximately 30 km north north-west of Three Hills.

The post office, which operated here from June 1905 through February 1910, was named after J.H. McArthur, the first reeve for the district. The municipal district takes its name from this feature.

Arty Hill (hill)

73 D/14 - Irma
9-44-8-W4
52°46′N 111°06′W
Approximately 17 km west south-west of the town of Wainwright.

The name for this hill has been in use since at least 1958. The name Arty is the shortened form for Artillery and was named by members of the Wainwright Regional Training Area.

Arvilla (locality)

83 G/16 - Lac la Nonne
12-58-1-W5
53°59′N 114°00′W
Approximately 20 km south south-west of Westlock.

The post office operated here from February 1911 through March 1967 and was named after Stella Arvilla Maxwell, daughter of a pioneer family.

Ashmont (hamlet)

73 L/4 - Cache Lake
27-59-11-W4
54°08′N 111°34′W
Approximately 55 km west south-west of Bonnyville.

The post office, which opened here in July 1911, was named after the hometown of its first postmaster, L. W. Babcock. Ashmont is a suburb of Boston, Massachusetts.

* Asker (former post office)

83 A/11 - Chain Lakes
4-14-43-23-W4
52°42′N 113°14′W
Approximately 20 km east of Ponoka.

A post office operated here from September 1900 through September 1915 and was named after a town in Norway.

Aspen Beach (locality)

83 A/5 - Red Deer
22-40-28-W4
52°27′N 113°56′W
Approximately 16 km west of Lacombe.

The origin for this name is taken from the poplar (aspen) trees on the shores of Gull Lake. A summer village was located here at one time. The post office name changed from "Wiesville" in 1916, and operated until August 1973. Esco Moore owned two quarter-sections on the lake at approximately the location where Aspen Beach Provincial Park extends west and the local name had been "Moore's Beach" since about 1913. The land has since been absorbed into Aspen Beach.

Aspen Beach Provincial Park

(provincial park)
83 A/5 - Red Deer
21-40-28-W4
52°27′30″N 113°58′50″W
Approximately 19 km west of Lacombe.

This is one of Alberta's most popular beaches. Visitors can swim, sunbathe or go boating on Gull Lake. Aspen Beach has more than 400 campsites in two campgrounds. (see Aspen Beach)

Asquith Municipal District # 52

(municipal district)
73 D/7 - Czar
36 to 42-1 to 9-W4
52°25′N 110°40′W
West of Provost.

This municipal district was named in 1914 after Herbert Henry Asquith, First Earl of Oxford and Asquith (1852-1928). Asquith was the Liberal Prime Minister of Britain between 1908 and 1916 and was responsible for the Parliament Act of 1911 that limited the power of the House of Lords. Asquith led Britain for the first two years of World War I and later accepted a peerage as Earl of Oxford in 1925.

* Astleyville (former post office)

83 H/14 - Redwater
23-56-23-W4
53°50′N 113°20′W
Approximately 30 km north north-east of Edmonton.

A post office operated here from May 1903 through October 1906 and was named after its first postmaster, H. Astley. The name was later changed to "Battenburg" and then to Gibbons.

Astotin Creek (creek)

83 H/15 - Lamont
12-56-21-W4
53°49′30″N 112°59′30″W
Flows north into Beaverhill Creek, approximately 7 km north of Bruderheim.

This creek flows out of Astotin Lake. (see Astotin Lake)

■ **Astotin Lake** (lake)

83 H/10 - Elk Island Park
22-54-20-W4
53°41′N 112°51′W
Approximately 9 km south south-west of
Lamont.

The name for this lake was made official in
1950 and is likely a corruption of the Cree
term *asteyotin*, "it ceases to blow." The
descriptive name likely refers to the fact
that the lake is calm and quiet most of the
time.

Athabasca (town)

83 I/11 - Athabasca
20-66-22-W4
54°43′N 113°17′W
Approximately 145 km north of Edmonton.

The name for this town, incorporated 19
January 1911 and whose post office opened
in January 1901, was originally "Athabaska
Landing." The Cree Indian name included
caupawin meaning "landing." In 1848, the
Hudson's Bay Company established a
trading post here as a distribution centre
and goods were shipped overland from
Edmonton and freighted down the river for
the North. During the era of the Klondike
Gold Rush and the decades of settlement
immediately following, this was an important route to the north with cargoes being
sent downstream by steamboat or scow to
the Mackenzie River or upstream by
steamer through Lesser Slave Lake for the
Peace River area, and Athabasca Landing
was a central transfer point. The town
grew, and took the name of the Athabasca
River, the spelling for which was officially
changed from "Athabaska" to "Athabasca"
in 1948. (see Athabasca River)

Athabasca County #12 (county)

83 I/11 - Athabasca
62 to 69-17 to 24-W4
54°40′N 113°10′W
North of Edmonton.

(see Athabasca)

Athabasca Landing

(undeveloped historic site)

83 I/11 - Athabasca
21-66-22-W4
54°43′N 113°17′W
Approximately 3 km north-east of
Athabasca.

(see Athabasca)

Athabasca Landing, 1898

Athabasca River (river)

83 I/15 - Grassland
12-8-69-19-W4
From 58°30′20″N 110°50′40″W
to 52°40′56″N 117°50′35″W
Flows into Lake Athabasca, passing
through Fort McMurray, Athabasca, etc.

The term "Athabasca" is usually said to be
a Cree word, although there is no evidence
for this translation in Father Lacombe's
Dictionnaire de la langue des Cris (1874).
The river has not always been recorded as

the Athabasca. In 1790, the lake was called
"Lake of the Hills" and the river "Great
Arabuska." In 1801 it was labelled
"Athapasco" or "Elk River." The
Arrowsmith map of 1802 shows a slight
variation as "Arthapescow" or Elk River.
In the late 18th century, the Beaver Indians
who lived along its banks called it the Elk
River, and it appears as the Elk on Alexan-
der Mackenzie's map dated 1801. David
Thompson and Peter Fidler, who explored
the middle section of the river in 1799-1800,
both referred to it in their journals as the
Athabasca. It seems most likely that
Mackenzie was using a translation of the
Athapaskan word for the river while
Thompson and Fidler were using the Cree
name. One possibility for the origin of the
name is that, since both the river and the
large lake into which it drains were Beaver
and Chipewyan territory in the 18th
century, the name derives from the name of
these Indian bands' common language,
Athapaskan. Colonel Henry Inman, who
journeyed down the Athabasca a year or
two before the Klondike rush, claimed in
Buffalo Jones' *Forty Years of Adventure*
(1899) that the Indian word means "without a spirit" or, "God-forsaken." Other
suggestions include a translation as "a chain
of prairies like the meshes of a net" and "a
low swampy piece of country with bare
patches." The most readily accepted version
of the name is that it is the Cree name
meaning "where there are reeds," referring
to the muddy delta of the river where it
falls into Lake Athabasca. Local residents
also refer to the river as simply "Big River."

Atim Creek (creek)

83 H/12 - St. Albert
22-53-26-W4
53°36′N 113°46′W
Flows north-east into Big Lake, approximately 11 km west south-west of St. Albert.

The name for this creek was made official in
1950 and is locally and historically known

as "Dog Creek" or "Dog Rump." The term *atim* is Cree for "dog."

Atim Lake (lake)
83 H/12 - St. Albert
19-53-26-W4
53°36′N 113°50′W
Approximately 8 km north-east of Spruce Grove.

The name for this lake was made official in 1963. (see Atim Creek)

Atmore (hamlet)
83 I/15 - Grassland
20-67-17-W4
54°49′15″N 112°33′00″W
Approximately 38 km west of Lac La Biche.

A post office opened here in April 1939 and may be named after the town of the same name in Alabama.

Auburndale (locality)
73 E/2 - Grizzly Bear Creek
18-47-6-W4
53°03′N 110°52′W
Approximately 24 km north of the town of Wainwright.

The name for this locality, whose post office operated from August 1907 through July 1944, commemorates the former home of the first postmaster, L.W. Crowe, in Auburndale, Massachusetts.

Auger Lake (lake)
83 I/10 - Boyle
4-21-66-17-W4
54°43′26″N 112°31′18″W
Approximately 36 km west of Lac La Biche.

The name for this lake has been official since at least 1948, but its precise origin is unknown. There is some mention in the records of the Lac La Biche Mission for the year 1853 of a Julie Auger, who was likely from a Red River Métis family. The name may have originated from this individual. The name is pronounced 'oh jay' and sometimes 'oh gee.'

Babette Creek (creek)
83 I/11 - Athabasca
26-65-21-W4
54°39′N 113°05′W
Flows south into Pine Creek, approximately 16 km east south-east of Athabasca.

The name for this creek has been official since at least 1958, but its precise origin is unknown.

Badger Hill (hill)
73 D/15 - Wainwright
29-44-7-W4
52°49′N 111°00′W
Approximately 10 km west south-west of the town of Wainwright.

The precise origin for the name of this feature is unknown.

Badger Hill (hill)
82 P/16 - Farrell Lake
9-14-34-16-W4
51°55′15″N 112°09′20″W
Approximately 34 km north north-west of Hanna.

This hill is named for its apparent resemblance to a badger. While the name appears to be well-established among the area's residents, no other information is available.

Bailey (railway point)
83 H/11 - Edmonton
13-53-24-W4
53°35′N 113°25′W
Immediately east of Edmonton.

(see Bailey Lakes)

Bailey Lakes (lakes)
83 H/10 - Elk Island Park
4-53-20-W4
53°33′N 112°54′W
Approximately 42 km east of Edmonton, in Elk Island National Park.

The name for these lakes has been official since at least 1958. They were likely named after John Bailey, an early homesteader who lived towards Ross Creek. One of his daughters married the first Park Warden, Frank McKellar.

Baird Lake (lake)
83 J/8 - Shoal Creek
5-62-3-W5
54°20′N 114°26′W
Approximately 24 km north of Barrhead.

The name for this lake has been official since at least 1958, but its precise origin is unknown.

Baker Lake (lake)
73 E/1 - Paradise Valley
9-47-2-W4
53°02′00″N 110°14′45″W
Approximately 31 km south south-west of Lloydminster.

The name for this lake appeared on sectional sheet #266, Wainwright, dated 1923, but its precise origin is unknown.

Ball Lake (lake)
83 H/11 - Edmonton
26-52-23-W4
53°32′N 113°17′W
Approximately 20 km east of Edmonton.

The name for this lake was made official in March 1950. It was named after George R. Ball (1872-1963), a pioneer and homesteader. He was born at Charlottetown, P.E.I., began homesteading 22 July 1896 on a section where the Hudson's Bay Company owned land. Older residents also remember calling it "Wood's Lake," after a farmer, J. B. Wood, who purchased the quarter from George Ball and lived on the north side of the lake.

Ballantine (locality)
83 G/15 - Sangudo
17-57-4-W5
53°55′N 114°34′W
Approximately 23 km south south-west of Barrhead.

The post office here was previously called "Wildhorse." This caused some confusion with mail directed to Whitehorse in the Yukon, so the Post Office Department in Ottawa notified early residents that a new name was required. There was no agreement on a new name, so a list of proposed names was sent to Ottawa, but none were selected. Then notification came that the name Ballantine had been chosen. The post office operated under this name from November 1914 through May 1952.

Balm (locality)
83 G/14 - Mayerthorpe
10-57-9-W5
53°55′N 115°16′W
Approximately 9 km south-west of Mayerthorpe.

A post office operated here from February 1914 through May 1952 and was named after the balsam poplar tree which grew abundantly in the area at the time. The balsam poplar (*Populus balsamifera*) was nicknamed the "Balm of Gilead" in Biblical times, and is from a small evergreen tree in an area north of the Dead Sea, and is noted for its medicinal balm.

* **Balmoral** (former locality)
83 A/5 - Red Deer
23-38-27-W4
52°17′N 113°46′W
Approximately 3 km north-east of Red Deer.

The name for this former locality was applied to the subdivision plan titled "College Park." The name College Park was also used in the 1966 Dominion Census listing with a population of 69. Its proximity to the Red Deer City boundary left it subject to annexation. The name was officially rescinded 12 February 1970.

* **Balsam Grove** (former locality)
83 I/7 - Newbrook
19-62-19-W4
54°23′N 112°50′W
Approximately 44 km south south-east of Athabasca.

The descriptive name for this former locality, whose post office operated from August 1932 through November 1954, refers to the number of balsam trees located in the area. The name was officially rescinded in July 1970.

Banana Lake (lake)
83 I/12 - Coolidge
22-66-26-W4
54°43′30″N 113°50′00″W
Approximately 38 km west of Athabasca.

The name for this lake has been official since at least 1958 and is likely descriptive of its shape.

Bangs Lake (lake)
73 L/3 - Vincent Lake
5,6-60-7-W4
54°09′N 111°02′W
Approximately 20 km east north-east of St. Paul.

The name for this lake has been official since at least 1958, but its precise origin is unknown.

Bank Bay (locality)
73 L/9 - Marie Lake
34-64-2-W4
54°34′N 110°13′W
Approximately 10 km north north-west of Cold Lake.

A post office operated here from October 1932 through December 1942, but the precise origin for the name is unknown.

Banko Junction (railway point)
83 H/12 - St. Albert
17-55-24-W4
53°44′45″N 113°32′00″W
Approximately 8 km north of St. Albert.

The junction was named for William Bence, a former Northern Alberta Railways employee. Mr. Bence was known by everyone as Bill Banko.

Baptiste Creek (creek)
83 I/14 - Sawdy
4-67-23-W4
54°46′N 113°27′W
Flows east into Athabasca River, approximately 13 km west north-west of Athabasca.

This creek was officially named in 1948 for its proximity to Baptiste Lake. (see Baptiste Lake)

Baptiste Lake (locality)
83 I/12 - Coolidge
17-66-24-W4
54°43′N 113°34′W
Approximately 20 km west of Athabasca.

This locality takes its name from Baptiste Lake. (see Baptiste Lake)

Baptiste Lake (lake)
83 I/12 - Coolidge
66-24-W4
54°44′N 113°33′W
Approximately 19 km west of Athabasca.

The name for this lake has been official since at least 1928 and was taken after Baptiste Majeau, an early settler.

Baptiste River (locality)
83 B/11 - Baptiste River
36-42-10-W5
52°40′N 115°17′W
Approximately 40 km north-west of Rocky Mountain House.

A post office operated here from February 1960 through July 1960 and was named for its proximity to Baptiste River. (see Baptiste River)

Baptiste River (river)
83 B/11 - Baptiste River
34-42-8-W5
52°41′N 115°05′W
Flows east into North Saskatchewan River, approximately 34 km north north-west of Rocky Mountain House.

The name for this river appears on Palliser's map of 1865. Its precise origin is unknown.

Barbara Lake (lake)
73 L/10 - Marguerite Lake
16-64-6-W4
54°32′N 110°52′W
Approximately 30 km north of Bonnyville.

The name for this lake has been official since at least 1958, but its precise origin is unknown. (see Elinor Lake)

Bard Lake (lake)
83 G/16 - Lac la Nonne
1-56-1-W5
53°49′N 114°01′W

Approximately 46 km north-west of Edmonton.

The name for this lake on the Alexander Indian Reserve has been official since at least 1958, but its precise origin is unknown.

Bardo (locality)
83 H/7 - Tofield
10-50-19-W4
53°18′N 112°41′W
Approximately 12 km south-east of Tofield.

A post office operated here from December 1904 through November 1914. It was known as "Northern" from March 1898 through December 1904. It was a Canadian Northern Railway station, named by Norwegians after the village of Bardu in northern Norway. The settlement of the Bardo community began in 1894, following an investigation by interested parties the previous year. Most of the original Norse settlers of this community who immigrated here in the mid-nineties came from Crookston, Minnesota, or the county nearby. However, a few years later, a great number of settlers came directly from Bardu, Norway.

Bargrave (locality)
82 P/11 - Three Hills
NE1/4-8-30-25-W4
51°33′N 113°28′W
Approximately 22 km south south-west of Three Hills.

A Canadian Pacific Railway siding was located here, but it closed in the 1940s. The origin for its name is unknown.

Barich (locality)
83 I/1 - Waskateneau
16-60-18-W4
54°12′N 112°38′W

Approximately 15 km west north-west of Smoky Lake.

The post office operated here from January 1917 through June 1921 and reopened from May 1935 through December 1968, but the precise origin for the name is unknown.

Barlee Junction (railway point)
83 H/2 - Camrose
14-47-20-W4
53°02′N 112°49′W
Immediately north of Camrose.

The origin for the name of this locality is unknown.

Barnegat (locality)
73 L/13 - Lac La Biche
8-67-12-W4
54°47′N 111°49′W
Approximately 10 km east north-east of Lac La Biche.

The Alberta & Great Waterways Railway established a station here prior to 1928. The post office operated from August 1952 through March 1963 and was named after a bay in New Jersey which was in turn named by Henry Hudson. The term "barnegat" is Dutch for "breakers inlet."

Barnes Lake (lake)
73 D/15 - Wainwright
1-44-5-W4
52°46′N 110°36′W
Approximately 20 km south-east of the town of Wainwright.

The precise origin for the name of this lake is unknown although it may at one time have been known descriptively as "Clear Lake."

Barnett Lake (lake)
83 A/5 - Red Deer
31-40-26-W4
52°29′N 113°45′W
Approximately 4 km north of Lacombe.

The name for this lake has been official since 1955 and commemorates Jack Barnett and his brother Ed, who lived near the Red Deer River crossing circa 1883. They came by rail and foot to Calgary, and from Calgary they travelled north by coach, and finally settled on the land north of this lake.

Barnett Lake (lake)

83 A/7 - Stettler
13-38-19-W4
52°16′N 112°35′W
Approximately 10 km south-east of Stettler.

This lake was named for Constable Ed Barnett (1858-1939), who joined the North West Mounted Police in 1878, and later took his discharge in 1881. He drifted north first to Red Deer and finally settled at Lacombe which promised to be a fine ranching area. Here he took up land which was given in recognition of his years of service. He kept a stopping place between Edmonton and Calgary which was at one time called "Barnett's Siding." Barnett Avenue in Lacombe is also named for him.

Barreyre Lake (lake)

73 L/7 - Bonnyville
16-61-5-W4
54°17′30″N 110°41′00″W
Approximately 4 km north-east of Bonnyville.

The name for this lake has been in use since at least 1908 when it was named for Alphonse Barreyre, an early squatter.

Barrhead (town)

83 J/1 - Barrhead
59-3-W5
54°08′N 114°24′W
Approximately 89 km north-west of Edmonton.

The post office was established here in January 1914 and was named after Barrhead, Renfrewshire (now Strathclyde),

Scotland, the birthplace of James McGuire, an early settler. The name was suggested by the directors of the Paddle River and District Co-operative Company. Barrhead is considered to be one area where the co-operative idea has been successful. Barrhead was incorporated as a town in November 1946.

Barrhead County #11 (county)

83 J/2 - Thunder Lake
57 to 62-1 to 7-W5
54°09′N 114°32′W
North-west of Edmonton.

(see Barrhead)

Barry Creek (creek)

82 O/15 - Sundre
25-33-8-W5
51°51′N 114°59′W
Flows south-east into Bearberry Creek, approximately 17 km west north-west of Sundre.

The name for this creek was officially approved in March 1937, but its origin is unknown.

Barton Lake (lake)

83 J/2 - Thunder Lake
29-58-4-W5
54°02′00″N 114°33′20″W
Approximately 16 km south-east of Barrhead.

The name was proposed for this feature by the Barrhead Historical Society to commemorate a Barrhead area pioneer, Robert Barton, and his family, who homesteaded by the lake in 1907, after arriving from England. The name was officially approved 6 March 1986.

Bashaw (town)

83 A/10 - Donalda
4-42-21-W4
52°35′20″N 112°58′00″W
Approximately 48 km south of Camrose.

Originally established as a post office in December 1910, this town was named for Eugene Bashaw, an early settler who owned land upon which the town now sits.

Bat Lake (lake)

73 L/12 - Beaver Lake
25-65-14-W4
54°39′N 111°58′W
Approximately 13 km south of Lac La Biche.

The name for this lake first appeared on a map dated 1918, but its precise origin is unknown.

Bat Lake (lake)

83 G/2 - Drayton Valley
16-49-4-W5
53°14′N 114°32′W
Approximately 30 km east of Drayton Valley.

The well-established name for this lake has been official since at least 1959, but its precise origin is unknown.

Bates Lake (lake)

73 L/1 - Reita Lake
24-60-1-W4
54°12′N 110°01′W
Approximately 26 km south south-east of Grand Centre.

The name for this lake has been official since at least 1958, but its precise origin is unknown.

* Bathgate (former post office)

83 H/8 - Ryley
10-51-17-W4
53°23′N 112°26′W
Approximately 18 km east of Tofield.

The name for the post office, which operated here from January 1906 through

May 1927, was taken after a town in North Dakota, the former home of the first postmaster, J.C. Morrison. There is also a Bathgate in West Lothian (now Lothian), Scotland.

* Battenburg (former post office)
83 H/14 - Redwater
23-56-23-W4
53°50'N 113°20'W
Approximately 30 km north north-east of Edmonton.

The post office operated here from October 1906 through September 1920, but the origin for its name is unknown. It was later changed to Gibbons.

Battensby Lake (lake)
73 D/15 - Wainwright
34-44-5-W4
52°50'N 110°39'W
Approximately 15 km east of the town of Wainwright.

The name for this lake has been in use since at least 1958, but its origin is unknown.

Batter Junction (locality)
72 M/12 - Hanna
8-31-13-W4
51°38'N 111°49'W
Approximately 9 km east of Hanna.

The precise origin for the name of this feature is unknown. It was previously known as "Medicine Hat Junction," likely because of its location as the turn off to Medicine Hat.

* Battle (former station)
83 A/15 - Ferintosh
5-46-20-W4
52°58'N 112°52'W
Approximately 10 km south of Camrose.

A Grand Trunk Pacific station was established here 22 June 1923. The precise origin for the name is unknown. The name was officially rescinded in 1960 since the station was no longer in use.

Battle Bend (locality)
73 D/6 - Brownfield
7-40-10-W4
52°26'N 111°27'W
Approximately 28 km south south-west of Hardisty.

The name for this post office and school district was suggested by Mrs. Main, an early resident, because the area was situated in the big bend of the Battle River. The post office opened in July 1906 and closed in August 1944.

Battle Butte (hill)
73 D/11 - Hardisty
17-43-8-W4
52°42'N 111°08'W
Approximately 12 km east north-east of Hardisty.

The name for this hill, in use since at least 1958, likely derives from the nearby Battle River.

Battle Creek (creek)
83 B/16 - Winfield
21-46-2-W5
52°59'N 114°14'W
Flows east into Battle Lake, approximately 58 km west of Wetaskiwin.

The name for this creek was officially approved in 1960 and flows into Battle Lake. (see Battle River)

■ Battle Lake (lake)
83 B/16 - Winfield
14-46-2-W5
52°58'N 114°11'W
Approximately 53 km west of Wetaskiwin.

(see Battle River)

Battle Lake (locality)
83 B/16 - Winfield
18-46-1-W5
52°57'45"N 114°08'30"W
Approximately 51 km west of Wetaskiwin.

A post office operated here from March 1908 through April 1968 and was named for its location near Battle Lake, in Battle River Country. (see Battle River)

* Battle Ridge (former locality)
73 D/6 - Brownfield
31-39-9-W4
52°24'N 111°17'W
Approximately 32 km south south-east of Hardisty.

Originally established as a post office, the name for this former locality is likely taken from the nearby Battle River. The post office opened in October 1914 and closed in October 1947.

Battle River (river)
73 D/16 - McLaughlin
1-45-1-W4
52°51'N 110°00'W
Flows south-east and north-west from the 5th Meridian into Saskatchewan, approximately 47 km south of Lloydminster.

The name for this river dates back to 1802 when it is labelled on Arrowsmith's map. It is a translation of the Cree *no-tin-to*. The Stoney equivalent is *kec-hi-sab-wapta*, and in Blackfoot it is rendered *kinok-kxis-sis-ughty*. Battles between the Blackfoot and the Cree Indian nations occurred near the watercourse.

Battle River (locality)
73 D/4 - Castor
4-38-14-W4
52°14'N 111°56'W
Approximately 5 km north-west of Castor.

---
*denotes rescinded name or former locality.

The Canadian Pacific Railway required a name for this locality, and the name was officially endorsed in November 1949. (see Battle River)

Battle River, 1907

Battle River Municipal District #61

(municipal district)

73 D/15 - Wainwright
41 to 47-1 to 10-W4
52°50'N 110°52'W
East south-east of Edmonton.

(see Battle River)

* Battleview (former post office)

73 E/2 - Grizzly Bear Creek
10-47-6-W4
53°02'N 110°48'W
Approximately 23 km north north-east of Wainwright.

The post office operated here from September 1908 through February 1929 and is located in Battle River Country.

Batty Lake (lake)

73 L/4 - Cache Lake
17-59-11-W4
54°06'N 111°37'W

Approximately 25 km north-west of St. Paul.

The name for this lake was officially adopted 28 July 1945, but its precise origin is unknown.

Bauer's Lake (lake)

73 E/6 - Mannville
1-50-8-W4
53°17'10"N 111°02'05"W
Approximately 14 km south-west of Vermilion.

The name for this lake derives from the Bauer family, who were the first to homestead the land upon which the lake is located. The name was officially approved 22 January 1992.

Bawlf (village)

83 A/16 - Daysland
31-45-17-W4
52°55'00"N 112°28'05"W
Approximately 27 km south-east of Camrose.

The post office, previously known as "Molstad," was officially established here with the name Bawlf in May 1907. Plans for the townsite were laid out in 1905, and it was incorporated in 1906. Nicholas Bawlf of Winnipeg was cofounder and president of the Northern Elevator Company and N. Bawlf Grain Company, and was long associated with the Winnipeg Grain Exchange.

Baxter Lakes (lakes)

73 D/15 - Wainwright
30-45-5-W4
52°53'N 110°43'W
Approximately 14 km north-east of the town of Wainwright.

These lakes were named for Mr. Baxter, the driver of the supply team of the survey

party who conducted a survey of the area some time around 1914.

Bayview Beach (hamlet)

73 L/4 - Cache Lake
NE-26-59-11-W4
54°08'N 111°32'W
Approximately 23 km north-west of St. Paul.

The descriptive name for this hamlet, which was established 14 February 1989, refers to the view of the bay on the lake upon whose shore it is situated.

Beach Corner (locality)

83 G/9 - Onoway
5-53-1-W5
53°33'N 14°07'W
Approximately 43 km west of Edmonton.

The descriptive name for this locality, whose post office operated from October 1937 through February 1970, refers to its location: it is at the corner where one turns off Highway 16 to go to Edmonton Beach. (see Edmonton Beach)

Beacon Corner (locality)

73 L/3 - Vincent Lake
9-60-8-W4
54°11'N 111°09'W
Approximately 27 km north north-east of St. Paul.

A post office operated here from July 1949 through October 1965 and was originally called "Nova Vukkournya" by the first Romanian settlers. It was later anglicized to Beacon. The name was endorsed by the Geographic Board of Alberta in June 1979.

* Beacon Heights (former post office)

83 H/12 - St. Albert
13-53-24-W4
53°35'N 113°24'W
Within the city limits of Edmonton.

The name for this post office was rescinded in September 1957. Its origin is unknown.

Beamer Junction (railway point)

83 H/14 - Bearhills Lake
18-56-21-W4
53°50′N 113°05′W
Approximately 13 km south of Redwater.

The origin for the name of this railway point is unknown.

Bear Hills (hill)

83 A/13 - Bearhills Lake
3-44,45-25-W4
52°52′N 113°33′W
Approximately 20 km south-west of Wetaskiwin.

The name for this hill appears in a report by James Hector of the Palliser Expedition, and is an approximate translation of *musquachis* or "Bear's Hill." Other native names for this feature include *mus-kwa-chi-si* in Cree, *kyo-etomo* in Blackfoot, and *o-zin-za-hen* in Stoney.

Bear Lake (lake)

73 L/1 - Reita Lake
16-58-2-W4
54°02′N 110°14′W
Approximately 43 km south-east of Bonnyville.

The name for this lake was officially adopted in 1950 on the suggestion of an unknown Métis who had killed a bear nearby.

Bear Lake (lake)

83 F/9 Edson
10-55-15-W5
53°44′45″N 116°09′00″W
Approximately 25 km north-east of Edson.

This has become a cottage lake and has been known as Bear Lake for many years. There

is also a recreational area called Bear Lake at the lake. The name was officially adopted 20 October 1983.

Bear Lake (lake)

83 J/2 - Thunder Lake
29-60-6-W5
54°13′N 114°52′W
Approximately 33 km west north-west of Barrhead.

The name for this lake has been official since 1958 and is likely descriptive.

Bear Valley (valley)

82 O/10 - Fallentimber Creek
14-31-6-W5
51°38′N 114°44′W
Approximately 24 km south-west of Sundre.

The name for this feature has been in use since at least 1937, but its precise origin is unknown.

Bearberry (post office)

82 O/15 - Sundre
27-33-7-W5
51°51′N 114°54′W
Approximately 21 km west north-west of Sundre.

A post office operated here from July 1909 through April 1968 and was named after the nearby creek. (see Bearberry Creek)

Bearberry Creek (creek)

82 O/15 - Sundre
3-33-5-W5
51°48′N 114°39′W
Flows east into Red Deer River, immediately south of Sundre.

The name for this creek is a translation of the Cree *a-chuk-i-si-pi*, and the Stoney *a-be-wap-tan*. It is descriptive of the berries

which grow along the banks of the creek and in the surrounding area. The post office and prairie take their names from this watercourse.

Bearberry Prairie (prairie)

82 O/15 - Sundre
27-32-6-W5
51°46′00″N 114°45′45″W
Approximately 18 km west north-west of Sundre.

The name for this feature was officially approved in March 1937 for its proximity to Bearberry Creek. (see Bearberry Creek)

Bearhills Lake (lake)

83 A/13 - Bearhills Lake
6-46-25-W4
52°56′N 113°37′W
Approximately 17 km west south-west of Wetaskiwin.

(see Bear Hills)

Beartrap Lake (lake)

73 L/2 - Muriel Lake
21-60-4-W4
54°12′N 110°32′W
Approximately 15 km south-east of Bonnyville.

The name for this lake has been official since at least 1958, but its precise origin is unknown.

Beaumont (town)

83 H/6 - Cooking Lake
34-50-24-W4
53°21′N 113°25′W
Approximately 20 km south of Edmonton.

This town, which was incorporated 1 January 1973, was named in 1895 because it is located on a hill with a view of the North Saskatchewan River. The descriptive name is French for "beautiful mountain."

Beauvallon (hamlet)

73 E/11 - Myrnam
14-54-10-W4
53°40′N 111°22′W
Approximately 26 km east south-east of
Two Hills.

The descriptive name for this hamlet, which
was established 1 October 1980, refers to
the beautiful view of the North Saskatchewan River valley. The term is French for
"beautiful vale." A post office opened here
in May 1909.

Beauvallon Lake (lake)

73 E/11 - Myrnam
10-54-10-W4
53°39′N 111°22′W
Approximately 25 km east south-east of
Two Hills.

The name for this lake was officially
approved 24 September 1991 for its
proximity to the hamlet of Beauvallon. (see
Beauvallon)

Beaver Bay (bay)

83 H/10 - Elk Island Park
15-14-54-20-W4
53°40′10″N 112°50′10″W
Approximately 40 km east of Edmonton, in
Elk Island National Park.

The name for this bay is likely descriptive
of the beavers that may, at one time, have
frequented the area. Since there are very
few residents in Elk Island National Park,
no local usage of the name was found as the
result of a field study. The name was
required by the Canadian Parks Service for
their administration of the Park and since it
seemed appropriate it was officially
approved 17 October 1991.

Beaver County # 9 (county)

83 H/1 - Holden
46 to 52-11 to 21-W4
53°10′N 112°13′W
East south-east of Edmonton.

(see Beaverhill Lake)

Beaver Creek (creek)

83 J/4 - Whitecourt
5-35-59-12-W5
54°08′40″N 115°41′45″W
Flows north-west into McLeod River at
Whitecourt.

The creek was previously officially
"Whitecourt Creek" because of its proximity to the town of Whitecourt. The name
Beaver Creek comes from the number of
beaver dams upon the creek. This name was
used by early settlers and is still used
locally. The name was changed in 1982 to
reflect local usage.

Beaver Creek (creek)

83 B/2 - Caroline
5-36-5-W5
52°04′N 114°41′W
Flows north into Raven River, approximately 38 km south south-east of Rocky
Mountain House.

The name for this creek has been official
since at least 1958 and is likely due to the
large beaver population in the area.

Beaver Creek (creek)

83 K/2 - Marsh Head Creek
2-58-20-W5
54°00′N 116°51′W
Flows north into Athabasca River, approximately 53 km north north-west of Edson.

The name for this creek has been official
since at least 1956, and likely refers to the
number of beaver in the area.

Beaver Crossing (hamlet)

73 L/8 - Cold Lake
15-62-2-W4
54°21′N 110°13′W
Approximately 6 km south of Grand
Centre.

This hamlet is named after the animal. The
post office, formerly Cold Lake Post
Office, operated from April 1910 through
July 1980.

Beaver Dam (hamlet)

73 L/1 - Reita Lake
24-60-3-W4
54°12′N 110°18′W
Approximately 23 km south south-west of
Grande Centre.

The post office operated here from July
1925 through January 1968 and takes its
name from the animal.

Beaver Lake (hamlet)

73 L/13 - Lac La Biche
32-66-13-W4
54°46′N 111°55′W
Approximately 10 km south-east of Lac La
Biche.

The name for this hamlet, whose post office
operated from September 1892 through
June 1928, is descriptive of the number of
beaver in the area.

Beaver Lake (lake)

83 B/2 - Caroline
16-35-6-W5
52°00′30″N 114°47′00″W
Approximately 26 km north north-west of
Sundre.

The name for this lake likely refers to the
abundance of beaver in the area.

Beaver Lake (lake)
73 L/12 - Beaver Lake
14-13-66-13-W4
54°43′02″N 111°50′10″W
Approximately 3 km south-east of Lac La Biche.

The name for this lake dates back to 1790 when it appears on the map by Philip Turnor. Alexander Mackenzie also names it on his map of 1793. It is also labelled on Daniel Harmon's map of 1820. It is presumably named for its location as the headwaters of the Beaver River.

Beaver Lake Indian Reserve #131

(Indian reserve)
73 L/12 - Beaver Lake
34-65-13-W4
54°40′N 111°52′W
Approximately 12 km south south-east of Lac La Biche.

This Chipewyan Indian Reserve was named for its proximity to Beaver Lake. (see Beaver Lake)

Beaver River (locality)

73 L/8 - Cold Lake
17-62-2-W4
54°22′00″N 110°15′15″W
Approximately 6 km south south-west of Grand Centre.

This station and locality was named by Father Laurent Le Goff (1840-1932), founder of an Indian Mission built on the banks of the Beaver River. (see Beaver River) The post office that services the locality is named Le Goff.

Beaver River (river)

73 L/12 - Beaver Lake
15-12-66-14-W4
From 54°43′18″N 111°57′54″W
to 54°39′16″N 112°00′00″W

Flows east into Beaver Lake, approximately 6 km south-east of Lac La Biche.

The local French inhabitants formerly called the feature "La Rivière au Castor." (see Beaver Lake)

Beaverdam (hamlet)

73 L/1 - Reita Lake
36-24-60-3-W4
54°12′N 110°18′N
Approximately 28 km east south-east of Bonnyville

(see Beaver Dam)

Beaverdam Creek (creek)

73 D/5 - Alliance
19-39-12-W4
52°22′N 111°43′W
Approximately 37 km north north-west of Coronation.

The name for this creek, though its precise origin is unknown, first appears on the Palliser map of 1865. The British North American Exploring Expedition headed by Captain John Palliser (1817-1887) between the years 1857 and 1860 was initiated by Palliser, but when he applied to the Royal Geographical Society for funding, the expedition grew and Palliser was instructed by the Imperial Government to expand the project into a scientific fact-finding mission. (see Introduction)

Beaverdam Creek (creek)

82 O/9 - Didsbury
10-30-3-W5
51°33′N 114°20′W
Flows north into Dogpound Creek, approximately 22 km south-west of Carstairs.

The name for this creek is taken after the many beaver found in it, and has been

associated with the feature since at least 1858.

Beaverhill (locality)

83 H/15 - Lamont
35-55-20-W4
53°48′N 112°52′W
Approximately 7 km north-east of Lamont.

A post office operated here from June 1894 through March 1918 and took its name from the nearby creek. (see Beaverhill Creek)

Beaverhill Creek (creek)

83 H/15 - Lamont
5-57-20-W4
53°54′N 112°57′W
Flows north into North Saskatchewan River, approximately 48 km north north-east of Edmonton.

The descriptive name for this creek and the lake appeared on David Thompson's map of 1814. The Cree name for the lake is *amisk-wachi-sakahigan*. The name refers to the population of beavers found in the area at one time.

Beaverhill Lake (lake)

83 H/8 - Riley
36-51-17-W4
53°27′N 112°32′W
Approximately 50 km north north-east of Camrose.

(see Beaverhill Creek)

Bell Lake (lake)

83 G/9 - Onoway
12-54-1-W5
53°39′00″N 114°00′15″W
Approximately 36 km west north-west of Edmonton.

The name for this lake was submitted for official approval in 1950 by Mrs. E.H.

Gostick, then secretary of the Geographic Board of Alberta. The name was made official 6 April of the same year. It is named for Mr. and Mrs. Benjamin Bell who came to Canada from England in June 1907 and lived in Edmonton for two years. They were one of the first families in a group of homesteaders that came to the Bilby district. In June 1909, Mr. Bell took up his homestead near the location of this lake.

Bellis (hamlet)
83 I/1 - Smoky Lake
34-59-15-W4
54°09′N 112°09′W
Approximately 23 km east north-east of Smoky Lake.

A post office was established here in April 1915, and the name is an approximation of the Ukrainian term *beei lis,* for white poplar, common in the area.

* **Bellcamp** (former post office)
73 E/9 - Marwayne
34-52-2-W4
53°32′N 110°13′W
Approximately 32 km north north-west of Lloydminster.

The name for the post office, which operated here from March 1915 through March 1927, was taken after George Campbell, an early settler. The two syllables in his name were reversed.

Bellevue, Lac (lake)
73 E/14 - St. Paul
6-56-9-W4
53°49′N 111°20′W
Approximately 20 km south of St. Paul.

The descriptive name for this lake is French for "beautiful view." The name has been in use since at least 1915.

Bellshill (locality)
73 D/12 - Lougheed
33-41-11-W4
52°34′N 111°31′W
Approximately 18 km south-west of Hardisty.

Originally established as a post office, this locality was named by Archibald Brown, the first postmaster, after his wife, Isabel, whom he called Bell. The post office operated from June 1907 through July 1930.

Bellshill Lake (lake)
73 D/12 - Lougheed
8-42-11-W4
52°36′N 111°33′W
Approximately 20 km south-west of Hardisty.

The name for this lake was taken from the nearby locality of Bellshill although it is also locally known as "Goose Lake" since Goose Creek flows into it. (see Bellshill)

Beltz Lake (lake)
83 A/2 - Big Valley
25-37-18-W4
52°13′N 112°35′W
Approximately 23 km south-east of Stettler.

The name for this lake is well known locally, and has been so since at least 1940. It may have been named by one of the early surveyors in the area.

Belvedere (locality)
83 G/16 - Lac la Nonne
10-58-3-W5
54°00′N 114°21′W
Approximately 15 km south of Barrhead.

The descriptive name for the post office, which operated near here from May 1905 through April 1952, refers to the view. A belvedere is defined as "a raised turret or summer-house to view scenery from." (*The Concise Oxford Dictionary*) The original site provided this type of vista. The post office was formerly called both "Pembina Crossing" likely after the river, and "Macdonald Crossing," after Gordon Macdonald, an early settler.

Benalto (hamlet)
83 B/8 - Sylvan Lake
31-38-2-W5
52°18′N 114°17′W
Approximately 32 km west of Red Deer.

A Canadian Pacific Railway station was established here in 1911 and was named by one of the C.P.R. surveyors when the rail line was built through to Rocky Mountain House. *Ben* is Gaelic for "hill," and *Alto* is Latin for "high"; hence the name Benalto is a hybrid of the terms, and describes its location on a hill overlooking the C.P.R. tracks. The post office opened in July 1916.

Benbow Junction (railway point)
83 K/2 - Marsh Head Creek
14-59-18-W5
54°06′N 116°35′W
Approximately 58 km north of Edson.

This point on the Canadian National Railways spur to the Chevron Standard plant was originally proposed as "Whistling Pine." This name was unacceptable, and the alternative suggestion, Benbow, after Private William N. Benbow (M100810) who was killed in action in 1945, was officially approved 18 January 1974.

Bennett Lake (lake)
73 E/16 - Frog Lake
27-56-1-W4
53°52′N 110°04′W

Approximately 65 km north of Lloydminster.

The name for this lake has been official since at least 1958, but its precise origin is unknown. Before 1958 it was misspelled "Bennet."

Bennett Lake (lake)
83 H/10 - Elk Island Park
35-52-21-W4
53°31'50"N 112°59'00"W
Approximately 32 km east of Edmonton.

The name for this feature was officially approved 11 August 1978, and came from the Bennett family who homesteaded there in the early 1900s. Albert Bennett has lived on his father's homestead since 1909. The homestead is situated on the south-east shore of a large shallow lake which in 1909 was still known by its native name, "Rat Lake." This name, however, was replaced by the name Bennett Lake shortly after that.

Bens Lake (lake)
73 E/12 - Two Hills
17-54-13-W4
53°39'N 111°52'W
Approximately 9 km south-west of Two Hills.

This lake appeared on sectional sheet #316, Surveyor General's Office, dated October 1928, but its precise origin is unknown.

Bentley (village)
83 B/8 - Sylvan Lake
26-40-1-W5
52°28'N 114°04'W
Approximately 28 km north-west of Red Deer.

This village, whose post office opened in April 1900, was named after George Bentley, an early settler. It was incorporated as a village 17 March 1915.

Bentley Lake (lake)
73 L/3 - Vincent Lake
25,36-58-8-W4
54°03'N 111°03'W
Approximately 18 km east north-east of St. Paul.

The name for this lake has been official since at least 1958, but its precise origin is unknown.

Berard, Lac (lake)
73 E/14 - St. Paul
4-57-10-W4
53°53'N 111°25'W
Approximately 14 km south south-west of St. Paul.

This lake may be named after one of the earliest homesteaders, Thomas Berard, a mixed-blood settler who filed on a special permit circa 1909.

Bergen (locality)
82 O/10 - Fallentimber Creek
3-32-5-W5
51°42'N 114°38'W
Approximately 10 km south of Sundre.

In 1907 J.T. Johannesen, with a group of his countrymen, founded a Norwegian settlement in this little valley beside Fallentimber Creek. This part of Alberta reminded them of their homeland and they named their settlement Bergen after the Norwegian city. Mr. Johannesen was the first postmaster when a post office was opened November 1907. The name Bergen is derived from *Bjorgvin*, translating, "meadow between the mountains."

Bergen Creek (creek)
82 O/10 - Fallentimber Creek
13-31-6-W5
51°39'N 114°42'W
Flows north-east into Highland Creek, approximately 12 km south of Sundre.

(see Bergen)

Berkinshaw (locality)
73 D/5 - Alliance
2-40-13-W4
52°25'N 111°46'W
Approximately 40 km south-west of Hardisty.

The name for this locality has been in use since at least 1951, but the origin is unknown.

* Berny (former post office)
83 I/16 - Plamondon
3-67-16-W4
54°46'N 112°21'W
Approximately 27 km west of Lac La Biche.

The post office operated here from November 1916 through April 1959, but the precise origin for the name is unknown.

Berry Lake (lake)
72 M/16 - Grassy Island Lake
12-34-4-W4
51°54'N 110°26'W
Approximately 55 km south south-west of Provost.

The precise origin for the name of this feature is unknown.

Berrymoor (locality)
83 G/7 - Tomahawk
1-50-6-W5
53°16'30"N 114°45'15"W

Approximately 16 km north-east of Drayton Valley.

A post office operated here from November 1910 through July 1985 and was descriptively named for the large numbers of berries which grew on low, wet ground.

Bessie Creek (creek)

83 J/4 - Whitecourt
11-60-14-W5
54°10′N 115°59′W
Flows north into Athabasca River, approximately 21 km west of Whitecourt.

The name for this creek has been official since at least 1958, but its precise origin is unknown.

Beta Lake (lake)

83 G/12 - Carrot Creek
9-55-11-W5
53°44′N 115°35′W
Approximately 36 km south-west of Mayerthorpe.

The name for this lake has been official since at least 1958. *Beta* is the second letter of the Greek alphabet; however, its connection to this lake is not clear.

Betty Lake (lake)

73 D/14 - Irma
36-44-8-W4
52°51′N 111°02′W
Approximately 12 km west of the town of Wainwright.

The name for this lake has been in use since at least 1958, but its origin is unknown.

Betula Beach (summer village)

83 G/10 - Isle Lake
4-53-5-W5
53°33′N 114°41′W
Approximately 40 km north north-east of Drayton Valley.

The descriptive name for this summer village that was incorporated 1 January 1960 refers to the number of birch trees in the area. *Betula* is the Latin term for "birch."

* **Beverly** (former locality)

83 H/11 - Edmonton
12-53-24-W4
53°34′N 113°24′W
A north-east suburb of the city of Edmonton.

The Canadian Pacific Railway established a station here in 1904. This former town was named after the Beverly township in Wentworth County, now Hamilton-Wentworth, Ontario. R.R. Jamieson, the general superintendent of the C.P.R., originally came from there. The town became a suburb of Edmonton in 1961.

Beyette Lake (lake)

83 J/9 - Flatbush
2-69-2-W5
54°35′N 114°11′W
Approximately 53 km north north-east of Barrhead.

The name for this lake has been official since at least 1958, but its precise origin is unknown.

Biche, Lac La (lake)

73 L/13 - Lac La Biche
13-32-67-13-W4
54°50′54″N 111°57′06″W
Approximately 170 km north north-east of Edmonton, immediately north of Lac La Biche.

The name for this lake, the French form of the name "Red Deer Lake," appears as far back as 1790. Philip Turnor, a surveyor from England, born circa 1752, was articled to the Hudson's Bay Company and published a map of the company's territories. It is on this map that the lake is recorded and named, due to the abundance of the animals found in the area. Literally translated, *lac la biche* means "lake of the red doe," so it is not as peculiar a translation as one might at first think.

Bickerdike (locality)

83 F/10 - Bickerdike
6-53-18-W5
53°33′N 116°38′W
Approximately 19 km west south-west of Edson.

A post office operated here from July 1911 through January 1957 and was named after Robert Bickerdike (1843-1919). Mr. Bickerdike was a livestock shipping and insurance agent, vice-president of the Bank of Hochelaga, member and later president of the council of the Montreal Board of Trade, and a Member of the Legislative Assembly of Quebec in 1897. In 1900 he was elected to the House of Commons in Ottawa and re-elected in 1904, 1908, and 1911, finally retiring in 1917. He was the M.P. for the St. Lawrence constituency of Montreal.

Big Beaver Creek (creek)

83 B/11 - Baptiste River
11-42-8-W5
52°36′N 115°03′W
Flows east into North Saskatchewan River, approximately 30 km north north-west of Rocky Mountain House.

The name for this creek has been official since at least 1958 and is likely descriptive.

---

*denotes rescinded name or former locality.

Big Eddy (eddy)
83 F/10 - Bickerdike
13-3-53-18-W5
53°33′15″N 116°34′30″W
Approximately 12 km west south-west of
Edson.

The descriptive name for this feature was
officially approved 5 September 1985.

Big Eddy (railway point)
83 F/10 - Bickerdike
4-53-18-W5
53°32′N 116°35′W
Approximately 13 km west south-west of
Edson.

(see Big Eddy)

Big Gap (gap)
73 D/2 - Neutral Hills
28-37-7-W4
52°12′41″N 110°57′20″W
Approximately 25 km north-west of
Consort.

The descriptive name for this natural pass
through the precipitous Neutral Hills was
officially approved 2 January 1991.

Big Gully Creek (creek)
73 E/8 - Lloydminster
35-51-2-W4
53°27′N 110°12′W
Flows west into St. Ives Lake, approximately 22 km north north-west of
Lloydminster.

The name for this creek has been official
since 1940, and is likely descriptive. It flows
between Big Gully Lakes in Saskatchewan
and St. Ives Lake.

Big Hay Lake (lake)
83 H/4 - Bittern Lake
29-48-22-W4
53°10′N 113°12′W
Approximately 28 km north-west of
Camrose.

The name for this lake was officially
approved in 1950, but its precise origin is
unknown. It is east of the village of Hay
Lakes.

Big Island (island)
73 L/13 - Lac La Biche
30-67-13-W4
54°50′N 111°58′W
Approximately 7 km north of Lac La
Biche.

The name for this island in Lac La Biche on
which Sir Winston Churchill Provincial
Park is located was officially adopted in
1951 and is likely descriptive.

Big Island (island)
83 H/5 - Leduc
32-51-25-W4
53°27′N 113°39′W
Approximately 15 km south-west of
Edmonton.

The name for this island in the North
Saskatchewan River is descriptive of its
size.

Big Johnson Lake (lake)
83 I/10 - Boyle
25-65-17,18-W4
54°38′N 112°35′W
Approximately 40 km west south-west of
Lac La Biche.

This lake, formerly known as "Chump
Lake" was officially named Big Johnson
Lake on 5 May 1987. It commemorates
Nick Johnson, a tie contractor who built a
cabin on the south side of the feature circa
1915 or 1916. His tie-cutting camp was near
his cabin. Another feature, Little Johnson
Lake, is south-east of this lake and is named
for its proximity to the larger feature.

Big Knife Provincial Park
(provincial park)
83 A/8 - Halkirk
34-40-16-W4
52°29′30″N 112°13′10″W
Approximately 40 km north-east of Stettler.

This provincial park was named for its
location on the Bigknife Creek/Battle
River. (see Bigknife Creek)

Big Lake (lake)
83 H/12 - St. Albert
24-53-26-W4
53°35′N 113°42′W
Approximately 14 km north-west of
Edmonton.

The descriptive name for this lake has been
in use since at least 1928 and is a translation
from the Cree *mistihay sakihan*, or "large
lake."

Big Meadow (locality)
73 L/7 - Bonnyville
27-62-5-W4
54°24′N 110°40′W
Approximately 14 km north north-east of
Bonnyville.

The name for this locality was officially
approved in 1950 and is likely descriptive.

* **Big Prairie** (former post office)
82 O/10 - Fallentimber Creek
4-30-5-W5
51°32′N 114°39′W
Approximately 28 km south of Sundre.

A post office operated here from November 1909 through December 1960. The

name is descriptive of the large flat area surrounding the post office.

Big Prairie Creek (creek)

82 O/10 - Fallentimber Creek
13-30-6-W5
51°34'N 114°38'W
Flows south-east into Little Red Deer River, approximately 29 km south of Sundre.

(see Big Prairie)

Big Valley (village)

83 A/2 - Big Valley
26-35-20-W4
52°02'N 112°46'W
Approximately 33 km south of Stettler.

The post office opened at this village in December 1907 and was descriptively named. Big Valley, as the name implies, is a valley extending in a southwesterly direction from Ewing Lake to the Red Deer River. It was incorporated as a village 14 March 1942.

Big Valley Creek (creek)

82 P/15 - Rumsey
29-34-21-W4
51°56'N 112°56'W
Flows south-west into Red Deer River, approximately 34 km north north-east of Three Hills.

The name is descriptive of the creek's locale. Originally, the creek was named "Mott's Creek," after an old pioneer who lived on it farther south. The name was changed later to coincide with the nearby village's name. (see Big Valley)

Bigknife Creek (creek)

83 A/8 - Halkirk
3-41-16-W4
52°30'N 112°12'W
Flows north-east into Battle River, approximately 38 km north-east of Stettler.

The name for this creek commemorates a confrontation between Big Man, a Cree, and Knife, a Blackfoot. Legend asserts that both of the men were killed during a fight with knives and tomahawks.

Bigoray River (river)

83 G/6 - Easyford
16-51-8-W5
53°24'N 115°07'W
Flows south-east into Pembina River, approximately 23 km north north-west of Drayton Valley.

This river was officially named in 1949 after Pilot Officer W.W. Bigoray, D.F.M. (1918-1944), a native of Redwater, Alberta who was killed during World War II.

Bigstone Creek (creek)

83 H/3 - Bittern Lake
12-47-24-W4
53°03'N 113°23'W
Flows north into Pipestone Creek, approximately 7 km north of Wetaskiwin.

The name for this creek has been official since at least 1958, but its precise origin is unknown.

Bilby (locality)

83 G/9 - Onoway
33-54-1-W5
53°42'N 114°06'W
Approximately 43 km west north-west of Edmonton.

A post office operated here from December 1918 through August 1961. It was presum-

ably named after a railway construction engineer whose name was corrupted from "Wilby" to "Bilby."

* Billos (former station)

83 I/9 - Hylo
11-66-15-W4
54°42'N 112°08'W
Approximately 14 km south-west of Lac La Biche.

This was an Alberta & Great Waterways Railway point, whose name was later changed to Venice in 1916, and was originally named after J.O. Billos who arrived in the area from Italy in 1902. (see Venice)

Bingley (locality)

83 B/7 - Rocky Mountain House
22-40-6-W5
52°27'25"N 114°47'30"W
Approximately 14 km north-east of Rocky Mountain House.

A post office operated here from November 1910 through April 1965 and was named after Bingley, Yorkshire, England. Mr. and Mrs. Tom Ogdesa, two of the early postmasters, suggested this name, after their birthplace.

Biollo Lake (lake)

83 I/9 - Hylo
33-65,66-14-W4
54°40'30"N 112°03'00"W
Approximately 7 km west of Lac La Biche.

This lake was named in honour of Oliver John Biollo (1883-?), pioneer farmer in this district, which he named Venice after his home city. He had been working with an early survey crew which happened to be plotting out a road in the vicinity of this lake, and the surveyors named the feature after Mr. Biollo in appreciation for his help.

Birch Cove (summer village)

83 G/16 - Lac la Nonne
W-27-57-3-W5
53°57′N 114°22′W
Approximately 20 km south of Barrhead.

This summer village was established by
Order-in-Council No. 223/89 effective 31
December 1988. The land was originally
owned by Anders and Ingeborg Anderson
and the area was locally known as "Norsemen's Cove." The Andersons sold the
subdivision to developers for resort lots and
the name of the subdivision was registered
as Birch Cove. Local residents believe that
the name is descriptive of the many birch
trees in evidence near the summer village.

Birch Creek (creek)

73 E/6 - Mannville
10-51-9-W4
53°23′N 111°15′W
Flows east into Vermilion River, approximately 27 km west of Vermilion.

This creek flows out of Birch Lake. (see
Birch Lake)

Birch Island (island)

73 L/13 - Lac La Biche
7-68-13-W4
54°52′N 111°59′W
Approximately 10 km north of Lac La
Biche.

The name for this island in Lac La Biche
was officially approved in 1951 and is likely
descriptive of the trees thereon.

■ **Birch Lake** (lake)

73 E/6 - Mannville
17-50-11,12-W4
53°19′N 111°35′W
Approximately 38 km south-east of
Vegreville.

The descriptive name for this large lake is a
translation of the Cree word *waskwai*.

Birch Lake (lake)

73 L/1 - Reita Lake
24-58-1-W4
54°02′N 110°01′W
Approximately 54 km south-east of
Bonnyville.

The name for this lake was officially
applied in 1950. An unidentified Métis
suggested the descriptive name referring to
the number of birch trees found along the
feature's shore.

Birch Lake (lake)

83 B/2 - Caroline
13-18-35-6-W4
52°00′42″N 114°51′11″W
Approximately 28 km north north-west of
Sundre.

The name for this lake is descriptive as it is
surrounded by a birch forest. The well-
established name was made official 29 July
1986. The proposal to have the name
officially adopted was forwarded by Fish
and Wildlife, as they have been stocking
this lake with trout for a number of years
and needed it named for management
purposes.

Birch Lake (lake)

83 G/15 - Sangudo
16-55-4-W5
53°45′N 114°32′W
Approximately 42 km south south-west of
Barrhead.

The name for this lake has been official
since at least 1958 and is likely descriptive.
Many features in the area take their name
from the abundance of birch trees.

Birchcliff (summer village)

83 B/8 - Sylvan Lake
19-39-1-W5
52°21′N 114°07′W
Approximately 23 km west north-west of
Red Deer.

The name for this summer village on the
north shore of Sylvan Lake is descriptive.
Many of the smaller subdivisions around
the lake take the name of trees. This
settlement was incorporated 1 January 1972
and the former hamlet of Sunnyside is
within its boundary.

Birkland Lake (lake)

73 L/13 - Lac La Biche
2-9-67-13-W4
54°46′35″N 111°55′13″W
Approximately 3 km east north-east of Lac
La Biche.

The name for this lake was officially
applied in 1951 and commemorates Flight
Lieutenant H. Birkland, M.I.D., of Calgary
who died in a prisoner-of-war camp in
1944. It is locally called "Frog Lake Two."

Birston Lake (lake)

83 J/9 - Flatbush
34-64-2-W5
54°35′N 114°13′W
Approximately 52 km north north-east of
Barrhead.

This lake appears on Sectional map No. 414
dated 1946, but the origin for the name is
unknown.

Bishop Hill (hill)

82 O/15 - Sundre
23-33-7-W5
51°51′00″N 110°53′42″W
Approximately 20 km west north-west of
Sundre.

This hill was officially named for the
Bishop family on 10 March 1991. Mr. and
Mrs. Luther Bishop and their son Reginald
came to the Bearberry area in 1907. Both
Luther and Reg each filed on a quarter-
section at the foot of this feature. From
1911 through 1918 the Bishops ran the

Bearberry Post Office. Two of their children, Reg and Maggie, remained in Bearberry until the 1950s.

* Bismark (former locality)

83 A/12 - Ponoka
19-43-27-W4
52°42′N 113°54′W
Approximately 23 km west north-west of Ponoka.

This post office, which operated from August 1903 through February 1922, was named by the Lutheran pastor, a Mr. Gruber, who was here at the time that the people asked for an office. The name honoured the German Chancellor. A large number of the early residents were of German origin.

Bissell (railway point)

83 H/12 - St. Albert
15-53-25-W4
53°35′N 113°37′W
Within the northwestern city limits of Edmonton.

The Canadian Northern Railway established a station here circa 1914. It may have been named after judge Herbert Porter Bissell (1856-1919), of Buffalo, New York, who took part in speeches in 1913 leading up to centennial celebrations of peace along the Canadian-U.S. border in commemoration of the ending of the War of 1812 on 28 December 1814.

Bittern Lake (lake)

83 H/3 - Bittern Lake
7-47-21-W4
53°03′N 113°04′W
Approximately 18 km east of Camrose.

The name for this feature is a translation of the Cree name *mokakasiu*, referring to the number of bitterns on the lake. A bittern is a genus of grallatorial birds allied to the heron, but smaller.

Bittern Lake (village)

83 H/3 - Bittern Lake
36-46-22-W4
53°00′30″N 113°03′00″W
Approximately 15 km west of Camrose.

The name for this village, whose post office opened in December 1899, was taken for its location on Bittern Lake. (see Bittern Lake) The original post office location was moved and renamed Halley in 1910, and at the same time, the Rosenroll post office was closed and reopened under the name Bittern Lake.

Black Creek (creek)

73 D/9 - Chauvin
11-43-3-W4
52°41′N 110°19′W
Flows north into Ribstone Creek, approximately 40 km east south-east of the town of Wainwright.

The name for this creek is likely descriptive of the colour of the water that flows through it, and the name has been in use since at least 1958.

Black Fox Island (island)

83 I/16 - Plamondon
4-68-14-W4
54°51′00″N 112°03′45″W
Approximately 10 km north-west of Lac La Biche.

The name for this island located in Lac La Biche has been official since at least 1958 and is likely descriptive. The Cree name for the feature is *Paskwaw Ministik*, or "Cow Island," referring to the fact that Mission cattle were pastured on the island circa 1860-80.

Blackett Lake (lake)

73 L/12 - Beaver Lake
10-22-66-11-W4
54°43′40″N 111°34′34″W
Approximately 26 km east of Lac La Biche.

The name for this lake has been pronounced "bracket" by nearly everybody in the district since at least March 1935. Rumours have circulated in the Fork Lake vicinity for many years that the first settlers in this area were Yukon prospectors one step ahead of the law, and it is after them that the lake is named. The lake is known locally as one of the *maniwansik* or "Egg" lakes.

Blackfalds (town)

83 A/5 - Red Deer
26-39-27-W4
52°23′00″N 113°47′30″W
Approximately 12 km north of Red Deer.

Blackfalds, 1894

A post office opened here in October 1902 and was named after a hamlet in Scotland, spelled *Blackfaulds*. The post office was previously known as "Waghorn," after the first postmaster, and before that was simply called "Eleventh Siding" by the Calgary & Edmonton Railway Company.

---

*denotes rescinded name or former locality.

Blackfalds Lake (lake)
83 A/5 - Red Deer
29-39-26-W4
52°23′N 113°42′W
Approximately 6 km east of Blackfalds.

(see Blackfalds)

Blackfoot (hamlet)
73 E/8 - Lloydminster
1-50-2-W4
53°17′N 110°10′W
Approximately 12 km west of
Lloydminster.

This hamlet had its origin in 1905 with the
coming of the railway, and its post office
opened in February 1909. It was previously
called Blackfoot Hills for its proximity to
the hills which were the hunting grounds of
the Blackfoot Indians, and which witnessed
many battles between the Blackfoot and the
Cree. (see Blackfoot Hills)

Blackfoot Creek (creek)
73 E/1 - Paradise Valley
36-46-1-W4
53°01′N 110°00′W
Flows south into Battle River in Saskatchewan, approximately 40 km south of
Lloydminster.

The name for this creek was officially
approved in 1940. (see Blackfoot Hills)

Blackfoot Hills (hills)
73 E/1 - Paradise Valley
47,48-2-W4
53°07′N 110°13′W
Approximately 22 km south south-west of
Lloydminster.

The Cree name for these hills is *ah-as-thi-
nioo-wa-chi*, and, according to one story,
five Blackfoot Indians were killed by the
Cree here. The Blackfoot Indians – the
Peigan, Blood and Blackfoot proper – when
combined, make up the Blackfoot Confed-
eracy. It is commonly believed that they
derived their name from the discoloration
of their moccasins from the ashes of prairie
fires. One interesting legend regarding the
origin of the Blackfoot tribe is as follows:
Three sons were born to a mighty chief.
One he named Kainah, or "the blood," the
second he named Peaginour, or "the
wealth" and the third he left nameless. This
third lad was scorned by all because of his
lack of skill in the buffalo hunt, and came to
his father asking for help. Touched by his
son's predicament, the old man blacked the
young man's feet with a charred stick from
the fire and stated: "My son, you have
suffered long, today I will make you a
mighty hunter." As such, Sastquia (or
Siksika) the Blackfoot became a successful
hunter and mighty leader. His descendants
formed the Blackfoot tribe, while the
descendants of his two brothers established
the Blood and Peigan tribes.

Blackfoot Lake (lake)
83 H/10 - Elk Island Park
30-52-19-W4
53°32′N 112°48′W
Approximately 46 km east of Edmonton.

The name for this lake was officially
approved in 1950. (see Blackfoot Hills)

Blackmud Creek (creek)
83 H/5 - Leduc
22-52-25-W4
53°27′N 113°33′W
Flows north into North Saskatchewan
River, within the city limits of Edmonton.

The descriptive name for this creek is a
translation of the Cree *kas-ki-te-oo asiski*.

* **Blades** (former post office)
83 A/5 - Red Deer
9-39-25-W4
52°20′N 113°32′W
Approximately 19 km east north-east of
Red Deer.

The post office, which operated here from
July 1923 through April 1934, was named
after its first postmaster, R.H. Blades. The
name was changed to Joffre. (see Joffre)

Bleak Lake (lake)
83 I/11 - Athabasca
31-65,66-23-W4
54°40′N 113°28′W
Approximately 12 km west south-west of
Athabasca.

The name for this lake has been official
since at least 1958, but its precise origin is
unknown.

Blefgen Lake (lake)
83 I/13 - Grosmont
34-67,68-26-W4
54°51′N 113°53′W
Approximately 42 km west north-west of
Athabasca.

The name for this lake was officially
approved in 1953 and commemorates T.F.
Blefgen, Director of Forestry in Alberta
from 1931 through 1948. Mr. Blefgen was
employed by the Dominion Government in
1911 in the then newly-created Rocky
Mountain Forest Reserve. He served with
the Royal Flying Corps and the Royal Air
Force during World War I. He was
supervisor of the Lesser Slave Forest
Reserve until 1927.

Bleriot Ferry Provincial Recreation Area
(recreation area)
82 P/10 - Munson
51°34′N 112°53′W

---

*denotes rescinded name or former locality.

Approximately 30 km east south-east of Three Hills.

(see Bleriot Ferry)

■ **Blindman River** (river)

83 A/5 - Red Deer
13-39-27-W4
52°22′N 113°46′W
Flows south-east into Red Deer River, approximately 9 km north north-east of Red Deer.

This is an important tributary of the Red Deer River, and joins the larger water-course a few kilometres downstream from the city. The Blindman River received its name from an incident in very early times. A party of Cree hunters suffered so severely from snow blindness that they had to camp beside the stream until their eyes were healed. The natives therefore applied the name *pas-ka-poo*, which translates "Blindman." Other sources indicate that the name is descriptive of the course of the river, as it is crooked. On the first survey map of the region the stream is named "Blindman's River."

Blindtrail Lake (lake)

83 B/15 - Buck Lake
22-44-6-W5
52°48′N 114°48′W
Approximately 48 km south south-east of Drayton Valley.

The name for this lake was made official circa May 1950, and was originally pro-posed as "Blind Trail Lake." Its precise origin is unknown.

Block Creek (creek)

83 B/10 - Carlos
25-41-5-W5
52°34′00″N 114°36′20″W

_____
*denotes rescinded name or former locality.

Flows north-east into Welch Creek, approximately 34 km north-east of Rocky Mountain House.

The Water Survey of Canada requested that this creek be named and recommended that the name of the locality closest to the location of the creek be applied, thereby proposing "Carlos Creek." Field research revealed, however, that the creek was locally known as Block Creek. It is named after Rasmus Christian Block (1886-1968) who came to the Bentley area in 1914 and purchased the south-west quarter 34-41-5-W5 in 1921 and later purchased other quarter-sections in the area. The name was officially approved 28 July 1986.

* **Blooming Prairie** (former post office)

82 P/10 - Munson
15-31-20-W4
51°40′N 112°47′W
Approximately 36 km east of Three Hills.

A post office operated here under this descriptive name from December 1910 through March 1911. Apparently, there were several blooming crocuses on a prairie setting. The name was later changed to Morrin.

Bloomsbury (locality)

83 J/1 - Barrhead
24-60-4-W5
54°13′N 114°28′W
Approximately 11 km north north-west of Barrhead.

The name for this locality, whose post office opened in September 1921, was suggested by early settlers who were former residents of the Bloomsbury school district in Manitoba. That school district may in turn have been named after the Bloomsbury district of London, England.

Bloor Lake (lake)

72 M/13 - Garden Plain
2-33,34-12-W4
51°53′N 111°35′W
Approximately 35 km north-east of Hanna.

The precise origin for the name of this feature is unknown.

Bloxham's Slough (intermittent lake)

82 O/16 - Olds
13-26-32-2-W5
51°46′N 114°11′W
Approximately 6 km south-west of Olds.

This lake was previously known as "Barrie Lake," but the name was officially changed in October 1991 to comply with current usage by local residents. Dan Bloxham married his first wife in 1910 and together with their three children farmed about five kilometres west of Olds. Bloxham's wife, Jennie, died in 1936 and Dan remarried, had five more children, and died in 1973. Dan Bloxham was a descendant of William "Buffalo Bill" Frederick Cody (1847-1917). Before the Bloxhams came to Olds, Bloxham's Slough may have been known as "Bahmes Slough," since in the 1890s a man named Bahme lived in the area.

Blue Butte (butte)

83 G/16 - Lac la Nonne
25-57-2-W5
53°58′N 114°10′W
Approximately 23 km south-east of Barrhead.

The name for this feature has been official since at least 1928, but its precise origin is unknown.

* **Blue Jay** (former post office)

83 I/15 - Grassland
16-68-17-W4
54°53′N 112°31′W

Approximately 38 km west north-west of Lac La Biche.

The descriptive name for the post office which operated here from March 1940 through July 1968 refers to the large population of Blue Jays in the district. The name was officially rescinded in 1970.

Blue Rapids (rapids)

83 G/3 - Blue Rapids
14-47-9-W5
53°03′N 115°12′W
Approximately 27 km south-west of Drayton Valley.

The name for these rapids in the North Saskatchewan River has been official since at least 1949, but its precise origin is unknown.

Blue Ridge (hamlet)

83 J/3 - Greencourt
26-59-10-W5
54°08′N 115°22′W
Approximately 20 km east of Whitecourt.

The descriptive name for this hamlet, whose post office opened December 1923, refers to the blue haze on the ridge nearby when seen from a distance.

Blueberry Creek (creek)

83 B/7 - Rocky Mountain House
4-27-39-4-W5
52°22′50″N 114°30′10″W
Flows south-east into Lasthill Creek, approximately 27 km east of Rocky Mountain House.

The locally well-established name for this creek was officially approved 7 February 1983. The Blueberry Valley School District took its name from the creek, whose name is likely descriptive.

Blueberry Hill (hill)

82 O/10 - Fallentimber Creek
6-30-5-W5
51°32′N 114°41′W
Approximately 27 km south of Sundre.

This hill has been a favourite berry-picking spot for local residents of the area for many years. There once were many blueberries growing here though the numbers have diminished over the years. The name also may be due to the fact that the top of the hill is covered with a plant which largely resembles a blueberry plant. There is some local use of the name "Big Hill."

Bluffton (hamlet)

83 B/9 - Rimbey
31-43-2-W5
52°45′N 114°17′W
Approximately 13 km north north-west of Rimbey.

The post office at this hamlet was called "Bluff Centre" from September 1906 through February 1920 and was changed to Bluffton at that time. The descriptive name refers to the bluffs of trees prevalent in the area.

* **Blumenau** (railway point)

83 A/7 - Stettler
4-39-19-W4
52°19′30″N 112°40′00″W
Approximately 74 km east of Red Deer.

The name *blumenau* means "flowering" in German. The first postmaster, Carl Stettler, came from a German-speaking area of Switzerland and chose this descriptive name to reflect the many crocuses blooming in the area during the early spring. The post office operated from February 1905 through March 1906 when the name was changed to Stettler. (see Stettler)

Boag Lake (lake)

83 H/11 - Edmonton
30-52-22-W4
53°32′N 113°14′W
Approximately 20 km east of Edmonton.

Named for Archibald Boag (1865-1922), one of the earliest settlers in the Clover Bar district. Archie Boag set out from his home near Glasgow, Scotland in 1882, coming to Alberta by Red River cart from Fort Garry and arriving here in 1883. He became a familiar figure and brought the first sheep over the Calgary Trail into the area.

Bobier Lake (lake)

83 I/11 - Athabasca
19-64-21-W4
54°33′N 113°11′W
Approximately 20 km south south-east of Athabasca.

The name for this lake has been official since at least 1958, but its precise origin is unknown.

Bodo (hamlet)

73 D/1 - Bodo
4-37-1-W4
52°09′N 110°05′W
Approximately 25 km south south-east of Provost.

This locality was originally established as a post office named "Scheck" which operated between 1928 and 1932. The post office name was changed in February of 1932 to Bodo, after Bodö, a place in northern Norway. It is not known why the change was made.

Boggy Hall (locality)

83 G/3 - Blue Rapids
34-46-9-W5
53°01′N 115°14′W
Approximately 29 km south-west of Drayton Valley.

The name for this North West Company trading post on the North Saskatchewan River is likely descriptive of the surrounding area. David Thompson visited the post in 1808.

Boggy Lake (lake)

82 O/10 - Fallentimber Creek
28-30-6-W5
51°36′N 114°47′W
Approximately 24 km south south-west of Sundre.

The name for this lake has been in use since at least 1937, and is likely descriptive of the characteristic of the lake.

* Boian (former locality)

83 H/16 - Willingdon
15-56-14-W4
53°50′N 112°01′W
Approximately 37 km north of Vegreville.

The name for the post office, which operated here from October 1913 through October 1942, is taken after a village in Bukovina, Romania. Many of the early settlers came from there. In 1888 Ikim Yurko came to this area, east of Willingdon, to look over the country and lived with the Indians for a while. He was impressed with the district and through his efforts a group of settlers arrived from Romania in 1899. They named their new settlement Boian after their village in Bukovina in their homeland.

Bolloque Creek (creek)

83 I/5 - Dapp
27-61-26-W4
54°22′N 113°49′W
Flows south into Dapp Creek, approximately 18 km north of Athabasca.

(see Bolloque Lake)

Bolloque Lake (lake)

83 I/12 - Coolidge
11-64-25-W4
54°32′N 113°41′W
Approximately 33 km south-west of Athabasca.

The name for this lake has been official since at least 1958, but its precise origin is unknown.

Bon Accord (town)

83 H/14 - Redwater
18-56-23-W4
53°50′20″N 113°24′10″W
Approximately 30 km north of Edmonton.

"Bon Accord" is the motto of the city of Aberdeen, Scotland. It is said to have been used as the password at the taking of the castle from the English by the Aberdonians. Later Robert Bruce authorized the use of the words as the motto. At the termination of a civic function, it is usual to give the toast "Bon Accord" – "Happy to meet, sorry to part, happy to meet again." One evening in 1896, a meeting was convened at the home of Alexander "Sandy" Florence. Under the terms of the Northwest Territories School Legislature, the purpose of the meeting was to set up a school district. At the suggestion of Sandy Florence (who hailed from Aberdeen), Bon Accord was accepted as the name of the new school district. Later it became the name of the post office and was retained as the name of the hamlet and ultimately the village (taken from *Over 2000 Place Names of Alberta* [3rd edition], E.J. and Patricia M. Holmgren. 1976).

Bonar (locality)

72 M/12 - Hanna
8-31-13-W4
51°38′N 111°48′W
Approximately 10 km east of Hanna.

This Canadian National Railways station is believed to have been named after Andrew Bonar Law (1858-1923). He was born at Rexton, New Brunswick and was Prime Minister of Britain in 1922-1923. He was the first British Prime Minister born outside the country.

Bondiss (summer village)

83 I/10 - Boyle
6-65-18-W4
54°36′N 112°42′W
Approximately 40 km east south-east of Athabasca.

The Alberta & Great Waterways Railway established a station here in 1914. The post office operated here from September 1916 through July 1967, but the precise origin of the name is unknown. The summer village was incorporated 1 January 1983.

Bonlea (locality)

73 D/13 - Sedgewick
32-45-14-W4
52°56′N 111°58′W
Approximately 17 km north north-west of Killam.

The name for this locality, established as a post office in January 1914, may be descriptive. The post office closed in October 1930.

* Bonnie Glen (former post office)

83 H/4 - Kavanagh
17-47-27-W4
53°03′N 113°54′W
Approximately 30 km west north-west of Wetaskiwin.

The descriptive name for the post office, which operated here from August 1905 through January 1935, refers to the surrounding of the first post office.

---

*denotes rescinded name or former locality.

■ **Bonnie Lake** (lake)

73 L/4 - Cache Lake
3-60-13-W4
54°09'N 111°52'W
Approximately 30 km east north-east of
Smoky Lake.

The name for this lake has been official
since at least 1958, but its precise origin is
unknown.

Bonnyville (town)

73 L/7 - Bonnyville
7,18-61-5-W4
54°16'10"N 110°43'30"W
Approximately 122 km north north-west of
Lloydminster.

This town was incorporated 3 February
1958 and was named after Father F.S.
Bonny who established the first Roman
Catholic church in the district in 1910 near
Moose Lake. Father Bonny had been a
missionary in Africa before coming to
Canada. Before its incorporation as a village
in 1929, Bonnyville was known as "St.
Louis de Moose Lake."

Bonnyville Main Street, 1928

Bonnyville Beach (summer village)

73 L/2 - Muriel Lake
32-60-6-W4
54°13'50"N 110°51'46"W
Approximately 10 km west south-west of
Bonnyville.

This summer village located on the east
shore of Moose Lake was incorporated 1
January 1983 and was named for its
proximity to Bonnyville. (see Bonnyville)

Bonnyville Municipal District #87

(municipal district)

73 L/2 - Muriel Lake
59 to 63-3 to 8-W4
54°15'N 110°35'W
East north-east of Edmonton.

(see Bonnyville)

Borden Lake (lake)

73 E/15 - Elk Point
20-56-4-W4
53°52'N 111°35'W
Approximately 23 km east south-east of
Elk Point.

The name for this lake has been official
since at least 1958, but its precise origin is
unknown.

* **Bordenave** (former locality)

73 L/6 - Goodridge
27-61-9-W4
54°18'N 111°17'W
Approximately 34 km west of Bonnyville.

The name for this former locality, whose
post office operated from June 1914
through May 1952, was taken after F.H.
Bordenave, the first postmaster. The name
was officially rescinded 10 November 1970.

Border Lake (lake)

73 D/10 - Hughenden
19-42-5,6-W4
52°38'N 110°44'W

Approximately 25 km south south-east of
the town of Wainwright.

The name for this lake, in use since at least
1958, is likely descriptive of its location on
the boundary of the Wainwright Regional
Training Area.

Borradaile (locality)

73 E/7 - Vermilion
29-50-5-W4
53°20'15"N 110°42'00"W
Approximately 10 km east of Vermilion.

The Canadian Northern Railway established a station here and a post office was
established in May 1910. The name commemorates Borrowdale, Cumberland (now
Cumbria), or Borrowdale, Westmorland
(also now Cumbria), England. The name of
Borrowdale, Westmorland, is said to be
from the old Norse *Borgardair*, "valley
with a fort" of the valley of borgara, i.e., "a
stream by a fort" (Ekwall).

Boscombe (locality)

73 L/3 - Vincent Lake
4-60-10-W4
54°09'N 111°27'W
Approximately 21 km north north-west of
St. Paul.

The name for this railway point, whose
post office operated from February 1931
through August 1959, has the same name as
a town in England. It was previously called
"Deaver."

Boss Hill (hill)

83 A/10 - Donalda
2-41-20-W4
52°30'N 112°46'W
Approximately 20 km north of Stettler.

The name for this hill is descriptive, as it is
the most prominent feature on the east
shore of Buffalo Lake, and the hump of a

buffalo is referred to as "the boss." The lake takes its name from this hill.

Boss Lake (lake)
83 A/10 - Donalda
11-41-20-W4
52°30′30″N 112°46′00″W
Approximately 21 km north of Stettler.

(see Boss Hill)

Boston Hill (hill)
83 A/6 - Alix
29-40-24-W4
52°28′N 113°26′W
Approximately 21 km east of Lacombe.

The locally well-established name for this hill was officially approved in 1983 and was taken after Adam and Myrtle Boston and their family who homesteaded here circa 1911.

Botha (village)
83 A/7 - Stettler
33-38-18-W4
52°18′35″N 112°31′25″W
Approximately 12 km east south-east of Stettler.

A post office opened here in January 1910 and was named after a South African general, Louis Botha (1862-1919), who became Prime Minister of the Union of South Africa.

Boucan Lake (lake)
73 L/3 - Vincent Lake
14-58-9-W4
54°01′N 111°13′W
Approximately 5 km north-east of St. Paul.

The name for this lake was officially approved 6 July 1950, but must have been locally used long before approval because it appears on a Topographical Survey Map printed in 1925. There is no record of the origin of the name either in Alberta's

Geographical Names records or in those of the Canadian Permanent Committee on Geographical Names, but it is possible that it could have been derived from Laboucan, La Boucane, or Laboucan, a free trader who brought furs to Fort Edmonton circa 1822-1825.

Bourque Lake (lake)
73 L/10 - Marguerite Lake
33-65-4-W4
54°40′45″N 110°33′10″W
Approximately 33 km north-west of Cold Lake.

The name for this lake has been official since at least 1951, and may commemorate one of the many Bourques in the district. Bourque is a common surname in the area. A Sylvestre Bourque came to Lac La Biche Mission from Montreal in the 1880s. The lake is locally known as "Green Jackfish Lake."

Boutets Lake (lake)
73 D/6 - Brownfield
35-38-9-W4
52°19′N 111°10′W
Approximately 30 km north-east of Coronation.

The name for this lake has been in use since at least 1958, but the origin is unknown.

Bowden (town)
82 O/16 - Olds
23-34-1-W5
51°55′50″N 114°02′00″W
Approximately 42 km south south-west of Red Deer.

The post office was established here in December 1892. The town was incorporated 1 September 1981. There are three explanations for the origin of the name. The first maintains that the name commemorates a place near Manchester, England. The

second states that it recalls Bowden near Melrose in Scotland. The third, and most widely accepted version, says that a surveyor named Williamson suggested that this siding on the Edmonton-Calgary Trail takes the maiden name of his wife.

Near Bowden, 1890s

Bowden Lake (lake)
82 O/16 - Olds
NW-22-34-1-W5
51°56′25″N 114°04′00″W
Approximately 16 km north of Olds.

The lake was named after the town of Bowden probably soon after it was registered in 1894. This well-established name was officially approved 16 October 1991. (see Bowden)

Boyd Creek (creek)
83 B/9 - Rimbey
30-42-2-W5
52°39′N 114°16′W
Flows south-east into Blindman River, approximately 2 km north-west of Rimbey.

The name for this creek was made official in 1950, and commemorates Flying Officer William Boyd Anderson, of Craigmyle (1920-1942). The only information regarding his death is that he and his crew were on a secret mission and sent out an SOS in January 1942, about 65 kilometres off the English coast, but nothing was ever found of his plane or crew. He and both his brothers were killed during World War II. Two other creeks in the province were named after the Andersons of Craigmyle, as was the school at C.F.B. Penhold.

Boyle (village)
83 I/10 - Boyle
4-65-19-W4
54°35'25"N 112°48'00"W
Approximately 35 km east south-east of Athabasca.

This village, whose post office was established in February 1916, was incorporated 31 December 1953 and was named for John Robert Boyle (1871-1936), Minister of Education, Alberta, 1913. He was later appointed to the Supreme Court of Alberta.

Boyne Lake (locality)
73 L/4 - Cache Lake
1-61-12-W4
54°14'N 111°40'W
Approximately 38 km north-west of St. Paul.

The name for this locality on the shore of Floatingstone Lake, whose post office operated from September 1905 through October 1972, commemorates the Battle of the Boyne. The river in Ireland from which the battle took its name was the site of William of Orange's victory over the Stuart Monarch, James II in July 1690. It was on 11 July but is marked by Orangemen on the 12th.

Braconnier Reservoir (reservoir)
82 P/11 - Three Hills
20-31-23-W4
51°40'N 113°14'W
Approximately 10 km south-west of Three Hills.

The original owner of the property upon which this reservoir is located was a Mr. L. Braconnier, but the name is pronounced "Braconner" locally. A government campground (1.7 acres) maintained by Alberta Transportation is located adjacent to this reservoir.

Braim (hamlet)
83 A/15 - Ferintosh
18-45-19-W4
52°53'00"N 112°45'15"W
Approximately 13 km south south-east of Camrose.

The origin of the name of this hamlet, established 19 September 1983, is unknown.

Bray Lake (lake)
83 H/7 - Tofield
23-50-21-W4
53°19'30"N 112°58'00"W
Approximately 42 km south-east of Edmonton.

The name of this lake appears on a Sectional Map as early as 1928. It is not clear for whom the feature is named. It may be after a Sergeant-Major W.R. Bray, originally of the North West Mounted Police and later a brand inspector at Medicine Hat and Suffield. Another source suggests that the lake is named after L.T. Bray, a Dominion Land Surveyor in the area circa 1906.

Brayet Lake (lake)
73 L/12 - Beaver Lake
15-65-13-W4
54°38'N 111°53'W

Approximately 18 km south south-east of Lac La Biche.

The name for this lake has appeared on maps since 1918, but its precise origin is unknown. It is locally known as "Wobby Lake," after Robert "Wobby" Pruden, who lived at its north end in the 1930s.

Brazeau Canal (canal)
83 B/14 - Brazeau Forks
18,27-46,45-11,10-W5
52°54'N 115°25'W
Approximately 46 km south-west of Drayton Valley.

(see Brazeau River)

Brazeau Dam (dam)
83 B/13 - Nordegg River
NE-18-46-11-W5
52°58'N 115°35'W
Approximately 50 km south-west of Drayton Valley.

This dam measures 67.8 m in height and has a storage capacity of 577,000 acre feet. (see Brazeau River)

Brazeau Dam (locality)
83 B/13 - Nordegg River
17-46-11-W5
52°58'N 115°34'W
Approximately 50 km south-west of Drayton Valley.

(see Brazeau River)

Brazeau Forks (river junction)
83 B/14 - Brazeau Forks
34-45-9-W5
52°55'N 115°14'W
Approximately 37 km south south-west of Drayton Valley.

(see Brazeau River)

Brazeau Reservoir (reservoir)
83 B/14 - Brazeau Forks
24-46-12-W5
52°58′45″N 115°36′30″W
Approximately 52 km south-west of
Drayton Valley.

(see Brazeau River)

Brazeau River (river)
83 B/13 - Nordegg River
11-46-11-W5
52°55′N 115°14′W
Flows east into North Saskatchewan River,
approximately 28 km south south-west of
Drayton Valley.

This river and the other surrounding
features are named after Joseph E. Brazeau,
a native of Missouri who entered the fur
trade in 1830. He was an employee of the
Hudson's Bay Company, serving as clerk
and postmaster at Edmonton, Jasper and
Rocky Mountain House from 1852 to 1864.
This linguist was of great help to the
Palliser Expedition and was spoken of with
highest praise.

* **Breage** (former post office)
73 E/7 - Vermilion
36-50-7-W4
53°22′N 110°51′W
Approximately 4 km east of Vermilion.

The post office operated here from April
1905 through March 1906 when the name
was changed to Vermilion. (see Vermilion)
Breage is said to be a Welsh name, but there
is a town called Breage in Cornwall,
England.

* **Breda** (former locality)
83 A/3 - Delburne
3-36-22-W4
52°04′N 113°04′W
Approximately 38 km south-west of
Stettler.

A post office operated here from June 1914
through June 1926, but the origin for the
name is unknown. Breda is a city in the
Netherlands that played a large part in the
wars between Spain and the House of
Orange-Nassau in the 16th and 17th
centuries.

Breland Lake (lake)
73 L/3 - Vincent Lake
23-58-9-W4
54°03′N 111°14′W
Approximately 6 km north-east of St. Paul.

The name for this lake has been official
since at least 1958 and may be taken after
Alfred or Zacharie Breland, who filed on a
special permit homestead in 1910.

Bremner (locality)
83 H/11 - Edmonton
7-53-22-W4
53°34′N 113°15′W
Approximately 27 km east of Edmonton.

The name for the post office, formerly
"Hortonburg" (1908-1912), which operated
here from August 1912 through January
1973, is taken after J.C.C. "Charlie"
Bremner (1864-1927). Bremner came from
Scotland, and arrived in Alberta to homestead with Archie Boag in 1882.

Brent Lake (lake)
72 M/13 - Garden Plain
26-33-12-W4
51°52′N 111°35′W
Approximately 32 km north-east of Hanna.

According to the *Cummins Rural Directory*
Map #89, published circa 1919, this lake
appeared as "Brett Lake." The reason for
the change is not clear, and the precise
origin for either name is unknown.

Brereton Lake (lake)
83 I/13 - Grosmont
24-67-26-W4
54°48′N 113°50′W

Approximately 37 km west north-west of
Athabasca.

This lake was officially named in 1953 in
honour of Private Alexander Picton
Brereton, V.C. (1893-1976). The Victoria
Cross was presented to him after his service
in World War I when he saved his platoon
which would otherwise have been annihi-
lated during an attack. He returned to
farming and eventually acquired some land
in the Elnora district. He also served in
Canada in World War II.

Breton (village)
83 G/1 - Warburg
2-48-4-W5
53°06′40″N 114°28′10″W
Approximately 36 km east south-east of
Drayton Valley.

The post office, previously called "Key-
stone," opened under the name of Breton in
March 1927. The village is named after
Douglas Corney Breton (1883-1953), the
Member of the Legislative Assembly for the
Leduc constituency from June 1926
through June 1930. He and brother
Lawrence immigrated to Canada in 1903. In
1904, they filed claim to the N1/2 20-49-2-
W5. In 1912 the Breton brothers built and
operated the Telfordville store in the
Strawberry Creek valley. Breton served in
World War I as a commissioned officer. He
moved to England with his family in 1934.

Bretona (locality)
83 H/6 - Cooking Lake
33-51-23-W4
53°27′N 113°20′W
Within the south-east city limits of Edmonton.

The Canadian Northern Railway established a station here before 1915. The origin
for the name Bretona is not known. The
post office, which served this community,
was called Hercules, mile 37.6 on the
Strathcona Branch.

_____
*denotes rescinded name or former locality.

Bretville Junction (railway point)

83 H/11 - Edmonton
17-53-23-W4
53°34′00″N 113°22′15″W
Approximately 18 km east of Edmonton.

The name for this station was officially applied in 1960. Its origin is unknown.

Brewster Creek (creek)

83 B/11 - Baptiste River
16-42-10-W5
52°38′N 115°22′W
Flows east into Grace Creek, approximately 42 km north-west of Rocky Mountain House.

The name for this creek has been official since at least 1958, but its precise origin is unknown.

Bridge Lakes (lakes)

83 I/3 - Thorhild
13-60-23,24-W4
54°12′N 113°27′W
Approximately 25 km east of Westlock.

The name for these two lakes connected by a stream has been official since at least 1958 and is likely descriptive.

Brièreville (locality)

73 L/5 - Goodfish Lake
28-63-12-W4
54°28′N 111°46′W
Approximately 35 km south south-east of Lac La Biche.

The post office operated here from February 1917 through August 1970 and was named after J.C.O. Brière, the first postmaster.

Briggs (locality)

83 A/5 - Red Deer
10-39-28-W4
52°21′N 113°57′W
Approximately 7 km north of Red Deer.

The Canadian Northern Railway established a station called "Tannis" at this point on its Brazeau Branch circa 1914. The name was changed in 1922 to Briggs; the origin of the name is unknown.

Brightbank (locality)

83 G/8 - Genessee
23-51-2-W5
53°25′N 114°11′W
Approximately 52 km west south-west of Edmonton.

The descriptive name for this locality, whose post office operated from March 1908 through August 1918 and then reopened from December 1921 through January 1956, likely refers to its location on the North Saskatchewan River.

Brightview (locality)

83 A/13 - Bearhills Lake
7-46-25-W4
52°57′N 113°37′W
Approximately 18 km west of Wetaskiwin.

The name for this locality, whose post office operated from February 1907 through July 1970, is taken after A. Goodhand's farm. Mr. Goodhand was the first postmaster, and the name is likely descriptive.

Briker Lake (lake)

73 E/1 - Paradise Valley
19-47-2-W4
53°04′N 110°16′W
Approximately 33 km south-west of Lloydminster.

The name for this lake has been official since at least 1958, but its precise origin is unknown.

Brock Lake (lake)

83 G/15 - Sangudo
4-56-6-W5
53°48′N 114°50′W
Approximately 27 km south-east of Mayerthorpe.

The name for this lake was officially applied in 1950. Corporal George W. Brock, M.I.D., of Edmonton, was killed in action during World War II. The lake is locally known as "Big Stinking Lake," as one summer the lake dried up, killed the fish and caused the area to smell.

* **Brook** (former post office)

83 A/6 - Alix
25-40-24-W4
52°28′N 113°19′W
Approximately 27 km south-west of Bashaw.

The name for this post office, which operated from May 1904 through March 1906, was taken after the maiden name of the wife of the first postmaster, James H. Bellhouse. The name was later changed to Tees. (see Tees)

* **Brooksley** (former locality)

83 A/5 - Red Deer
25-38-26-W4
52°17′N 113°35′W
Approximately 15 km west north-west of Red Deer.

A post office operated under this name from March 1908 through December 1926. The school district was originally called "Brookfield," a name suggested by Marshall Boomer (d. 1929), who came from

_____

*denotes rescinded name or former locality.

Brookfield, Nova Scotia. The name for the post office was changed to avoid duplication.

Brosseau (hamlet)

73 E/13 - Hairy Hill
35-55-12-W4
53°47′N 111°41′W
Approximately 10 km north north-east of Two Hills.

A post office was established here January 1904 and was named after Edmond Brosseau, merchant, farmer and first postmaster. Brosseau was born at Laprairie, Quebec, in 1842 and was a resident of Alberta for 33 years. He served in the Union Army in the American Civil War after which he tried gold mining in British Columbia and along the Peace River. After this he came to the St. Albert area.

Brosseau, Lac (lake)

73 E/13 - Hairy Hill
13-56-12-W4
53°50′N 111°39′W
Approximately 16 km north north-east of Two Hills.

(see Brosseau)

Brown Creek (creek)

82 O/10 - Fallentimber Creek
25-31-7-W5
51°41′N 114°59′W
Flows east into Williams Creek, approximately 26 km south-west of Sundre.

The name for this creek has been official since 1958, but its origin is unknown.

Brown Lake (lake)

73 L/12 - Beaver Lake
20-66-11-W4
54°43′N 111°38′W
Approximately 23 km east of Lac La Biche.

The name for this lake was officially adopted in 1951 and commemorates Flight Lieutenant W.W.L. Brown (1916-1944) of Edmonton. F/L Brown was killed in action 13 August 1944.

Brownfield (hamlet)

73 D/6 - Brownfield
6-39-10-W4
51°19′N 111°26′W
Approximately 26 km north of Coronation.

Originally established as a post office in March 1907, this locality was named after Charles Dee Brownfield (1880-1943), a locally well-known rancher who established the first post office and later went on to champion the movement for brand inspection. In 1922, he was made a brand inspector.

Bruce (hamlet)

83 H/1 - Holden
30-48-14-W4
53°10′N 112°02′W
Approximately 20 km north-west of Viking.

A post office was established here in March 1909 and was named after A. Bruce Smith, manager of the Grand Trunk Pacific Telegraph Company. The name was changed from "Hurry."

Bruce Lake (lake)

73 D/7 - Czar
29-39-7-W4
52°23′N 110°58′W
Approximately 40 km south-east of Hardisty.

The name for this lake has been in use since at least 1958 although the precise origin is unknown.

Bruderheim (town)

83 H/15 - Lamont
32-55-20-W4
53°48′20″N 112°56′00″W
Approximately 37 km north-east of Edmonton.

The name of this community and town was originally the name chosen by and for the congregation of the Moravian Colony at this place. The original German spelling is for most other languages an awkward one. The umlaut over the U in Bruderheim caused much distress in interpretation for government agencies at the time of naming in 1895. By leaving out the umlaut, however, the meaning was changed. Andreas Lilge and the Moravian settlers selected the name which means "brethren home" for their congregation and projected community. The Moravian church was often referred to as the "Brethren's Church." This colony was composed of migrants from Poland to Volynia, Russia who emigrated to Alberta and settled in 1894. The post office opened in September 1895.

Brule Creek (creek)

83 G/12 - Carrot Creek
17-54-11-W5
53°40′N 115°36′W
Flows north-east into Lobstick River, approximately 44 km south-west of Mayerthorpe.

The name for this creek has been official since at least 1950. Its name is taken from its proximity to Brule, which was founded as a mining town in 1912 by the Mackenzie and Mann interests of the Canadian Northern Railway. The mine was closed in 1928. The term *brule* is the French word for "burnt." It likely refers to the burnt timber along the shores of the nearby lake.

Brunos Hill (hill)

83 A/10 - Donalda
9-42-21-W4
52°36'00"N 112°58'15"W
Approximately 1 km north of Bashaw.

The well-established local name which
residents of the Bashaw area had requested
be made official was approved in January
1979. Mr. G. Stedel, a resident of the
Bashaw area since 1900, stated that the hill
to the north of Bashaw was known by this
name when he arrived in the vicinity. The
hill was named for the Bruno family, one of
the few Métis families that settled and
stayed here. Robert Bruno was nicknamed
"teapot," another was nicknamed "coffee-
pot," and Paul was the youngest. It is
rumoured that the nicknames emerged
from the brothers' crooked noses. During
World War I, the Bruno brothers left the
area.

Bryson Lake (lake)

73 E/6 - Mannville
15-50-10-W4
53°18'N 111°23'W
Approximately 34 km west of Vermilion.

The name for this lake has been official
since at least 1958, but its precise origin is
unknown.

Buck Creek (hamlet)

83 G/2   Drayton Valley
36-47-7-W5
53°06'N 114°54'W
Approximately 13 km south south-east of
Drayton Valley.

A post office was established here in June
1925, and was named for its proximity to
Buck Lake. (see Buck Lake)

Buck Lake (hamlet)

83 B/15 - Buck Lake
11-46-6-W5
52°57'N 114°47'W
Approximately 33 km south south-east of
Drayton Valley.

A post office was established here in
November 1952 and was named after the
lake upon whose shore it is situated. (see
Buck Lake) It was previously called
"Minnehik."

Buck Lake (lake)

83 B/15 - Buck Lake
23-46-6-W5
52°58'30"N 114°45'00"W
Approximately 30 km south south-east of
Drayton Valley.

The name for this lake appears as "Bull
Lake" on Arrowsmith's map of 1859. It is a
rough translation of a native name which is
likely descriptive. The Cree call the lake *ya-
pe-oo*, or "bull moose." In Father
Lacombe's Cree dictionary (see Lacombe),
he defines *ayabe* as meaning "bull."

Buck Lake House (trading post)

83 G/7 - Tomahawk
17-50-5-W5
53°20'N 114°45'W
Approximately 12 km east north-east of
Drayton Valley.

A Hudson's Bay Company trading post
was built here in 1800 above the mouth of
Bucklake Creek. (see Bucklake Creek)

Buck Lake Indian Reserve #133C

(Indian reserve)

83 B/15 - Buck Lake
17-45-5-W5
52°52'N 114°41'W
Approximately 42 km south south-east of
Drayton Valley.

(see Buck Lake)

* Buckhorn (former post office)

83 B/9 - Rimbey
NW1/4-24-43-1-W5
52°45'N 114°05'W
Approximately 18 km north-west of
Rimbey.

The post office operated here from 1
February 1908 through 31 October 1929.
The name was taken after the pair of deer
horns that adorned the post office gateway.
The first postmaster, Abraham Davidson,
was an avid hunter.

Buckinghorse Lake (lake)

83 H/4 - Kavanagh
16-48-27-W4
53°09'N 113°54'W
Approximately 27 km west south-west of
Leduc.

The name for this lake was officially
approved in 1950, but its precise origin is
unknown.

Bucklake Creek (creek)

83 G/7 - Tomahawk
17-50-5-W5
53°19'N 114°42'W
Flows north into North Saskatchewan
River, approximately 11 km east north-east
of Drayton Valley

This creek flows out of Buck Lake and is
named for this association. David
Thompson called this watercourse "Sturgeon Creek."

Buffalo Coulee (coulee)

73 E/3 - Buffalo Creek
15-49-9-W4
53°13'N 111°15'W
Approximately 30 km south-west of
Vermilion.

(see Buffalo Creek)

Buffalo Creek (creek)

73 E/2 - Grizzly Bear Creek
33-46-6-W4
53°01′N 110°49′W
Flows east into Battle River, approximately
20 km north of Wainwright.

The name for this creek was officially
adopted in 1940 and may refer to the
Buffalo Park Riders.

Buffalo Hill (hill)

73 D/11 - Hardisty
22-43-8-W4
52°42′N 111°05′W
Approximately 10 km north-east of
Hardisty.

The name for this hill has been in use since
at least 1954 and is very likely descriptive of
the early herds of buffalo that roamed the
expanses of the original Buffalo Park.

Buffalo Lake (lake)

73 D/14 - Irma
31-43-7-W4
52°45′N 111°00′W
Approximately 11 km south of the town of
Wainwright.

The name for this lake has been in use since
at least 1958 and is likely named after the
herds of buffalo that roamed the area in the
early part of the century.

Buffalo Lake (lake)

83 A/7 - Stettler
25-40-21-W4
52°27′N 112°54′W
Approximately 13 km south-east of
Bashaw.

This lake was named on the David
Thompson map of 1814 and was labelled

"Bull Lake" on Palliser's map of 1860. The
Cree name for it is rendered *mustus*. The
descriptive name was applied from the
resemblance (long ago but not now) of its
outline to a buffalo hide stretched out for
the purpose of being dressed. The small
stream, *la queue* , represented the tail of the
animal, according to Palliser's notes. It was,
apparently, a favourite buffalo hunting
ground judging by the numerous bones
found there. The name in Stoney is rendered *ta-toong-gamna*, according to
Tyrrell.

Buffalo Lake (Métis Settlement)

73 L/5 - Goodfish
63, 64-16, 17-W4
54°20′N 112°15′W
North-east of Edmonton.

Beaver River Métis Colony was created by
the 1939 Order-in-Council No. 379/39. It
is now known simply as Buffalo Lake, not
Beaver River Métis Colony or Caslan. This
was also known previously as the western
portion of Beaver River Métis Association
Area 7, along with Kikino.

* Buffalo Park (former locality)

73 D/10 - Hughenden
3-43-6-W4
52°40′N 110°45′W
A 518 sq. km park, approximately 20 km
south of the town of Wainwright.

This former locality was named after the
Buffalo Park Riders, who, in peak years
handled over 8,000 buffalo through the
corrals. The Department of National
Defence took over the area 1 July 1940.

Buffalo View (locality)

73 D/10 - Hughenden
10-42-6-W4
52°36′N 110°46′W
Approximately 26 km south of the town of
Wainwright.

The post office, which operated here from
June 1912 through November 1929, was
located at the southern boundary of the
Dominion Government's Buffalo Park, and
it is from this location that the locality
received its descriptive name.

Buford (hamlet)

83 H/4 - Kavanagh
19-49-27-W4
53°14′N 113°57′W
Approximately 25 km west of Leduc.

A post office operated here from October
1903 through May 1969 and was named
after a town in North Dakota, from where
many of the early settlers came. Glen Park
was opened on the original site of Buford.
Buford is a common name in the States
because of the number of Bufords who
were Generals in the Civil War.

Bull Creek (lake)

83 B/6 - Crimson Lake
32-38-8-W5
52°19′N 115°06′W
Flows south-east into Cow Creek, approximately 14 km south-west of Rocky
Mountain House.

The name for this creek has been official
since at least 1958, but its precise origin is
unknown.

Bull Creek (creek)

83 J/3 - Green Court
6-60-9-W5
54°09′N 115°22′W
Flows north-east into Athabasca River,
approximately 22 km east of Whitecourt.

The name for this creek has been official
since at least 1958, but its precise origin is
unknown.

Bulwark (locality)

73 D/4 - Castor
1-38-12-W4
52°14′N 111°35′W

---

*denotes rescinded name or former locality.

Approximately 20 km north north-west of Coronation.

A post office, originally called "Lindsville" when it was opened, operated at this site from February 1916 through May 1965. It is a bit north of the royal line, the one that has stations like Coronation, Consort, and Fleet, and may have been named in association with the line. A bulwark is a defense line above the water line in a warship, and at the time, the British Empire was viewed as a bulwark.

Bunder Lake (lake)

73 L/5 - Goodfish Lake
23-61-12-W4
54°16'N 111°42'W
Approximately 41 km north-west of St. Paul.

The name for this lake has been official since 4 May 1950, but its precise origin is unknown. It is locally pronounced "Bunter Lake."

Buoyant (locality)

82 P/11 - Three Hills
26-29-25-W4
51°31'N 113°25'W
Approximately 25 km south south-west of Three Hills.

A Canadian Pacific Railway station was established here in 1921. The origin for the name is unknown.

* Burbank (former locality)

83 A/5 - Red Deer
24-39-27-W4
52°22'N 113°45'W
Approximately 17 km north north-east of Red Deer.

The Canadian National Railway established a station here sometime prior to 1928, and

likely named it after Luther Burbank (1849-1926), a famous American horticulturalist. The name was rescinded in February 1970.

Burns Lake (lake)

82 P/12 - Lonepine Creek
29-31-27-W4
51°41'N 113°48'W
Approximately 23 km east south-east of Olds.

The name for this lake has been official since 1928, and was taken after Patrick Burns (1856-1937). He was once described by Alberta's Premier John Brownlee as "a grand pioneer, a true Canadian gentleman, a philanthropist and a prince of good fellows." Burns was born in Oshawa, Ontario, and eventually made his way to Calgary where he quickly became one of the best known ranchmen of the West. He built up a large meat packing business, and owned land in this vicinity. He was called to the Senate in 1931 and remained a senator until he resigned in 1936.

Burnstick Lake (lake)

82 O/15 - Sundre
35-7-W5
51°59'12"N 114°52'50"W
Approximately 27 km north-west of Sundre.

The official name was changed 27 October 1991 from "Burntstick Lake" to reflect local usage. Owners of cottages surrounding the lake initiated the request for the change of the name. The precise origin for the name is unknown.

Burnt Lake (lake)

73 L/16 - Medley River
67-3-W4
54°48'N 110°26'W
Approximately 41 km north north-west of Cold Lake.

The name for this lake was officially adopted 17 January 1951 and, like many other lakes like it in the province, refers to the fact that it was once surrounded by burnt-over forest.

* Burnt Lake (former locality)

83 B/1 - Markerville
4-38-1-W5
52°14'N 114°03'W
Approximately 19 km west of Red Deer.

The post office operated here from July 1901 through August 1916. A lake was formed nearby when a fire burnt a large area of peat moss. That lake is now dry.

Burnt Lake (lake)

83 I/9 - Hylo
4-11-66-16-W4
54°41'20"N 112°19'10"W
Approximately 25 km south south-west of Lac La Biche.

The descriptive name for this lake has been official since at least 1945, and its Cree name is *Pahkwateo Sagahegan* translating "Groundfire Lake." The name Burnt Lake has been in local use since 1914. The surrounding country has been consistently plagued by fires for many years. From 1914 to circa 1919, the Northwest Lumber Company had one thousand loggers working out of five camps around this feature, which at that time was surrounded by a vast dense forest of mature white spruce trees.

Butcher Creek (creek)

82 O/16 - Olds
32-34-3-W5
51°59'N 114°23'W
Flows north-east into Red Deer River, approximately 23 km north north-west of Olds.

The name for this creek has been in use since at least 1968, but its precise origin is unknown.

Burtonsville (locality)
83 G/7 - Tomahawk
27-50-4-W5
53°20'15"N 114°30'45"W
Approximately 33 km east north-east of
Drayton Valley.

A post office operated here from June 1909
through December 1967 and was named for
the first postmaster, Cornelius Burton, who
opened the outlet in his home.

Busby (hamlet)
83 H/13 - Morinville
24-57-27-W4
53°57'N 113°53'W
Approximately 50 km north north-west of
Edmonton.

The post office, opened here in April 1915,
may have been named after Edward Busby,
the Inspector of Customs in the Yukon
during the Klondike Gold Rush. The post
office was previously called "Independence."

Bushy Head Corner (locality)
73 D/11 - Hardisty
21-43-8-W4
52°43'N 111°06'W
Approximately 15 km east north-east of
Hardisty.

The name for this locality has been in use
since at least 1952, but its origin is unknown.

Bushy Head Hill (hill)
73 D/11 - Hardisty
21-43-8-W4
52°43'N 111°07'W
Approximately 15 km east south-east of
Hardisty.

The name for this hill has been in use since
at least 1953, but its origin is unknown.

Bushy Head Lake (lake)
73 D/15 - Wainwright
35-44,45-7-W4
52°51'N 110°55'W
Approximately 4 km south-west of the
town of Wainwright.

The name for this lake has been in use since
at least 1951, but its origin is unknown.

Buster Creek (creek)
83 B/10 - Carlos
19-41-7-W5
52°33'N 114°59'W
Flows north into North Saskatchewan
River, approximately 20 km north north-
west of Rocky Mountain House.

The precise origin for the name of this
creek is not certain; however, a local tale
purports that the Long family had a dog
named Buster. When he died, he was
washed away in this creek.

Butte (locality)
83 B/2 - Caroline
24-37-6-W5
52°11'N 114°44'W
Approximately 25 km south south-east of
Rocky Mountain House.

A post office operated here from February
1939 through March 1969 and was named
for a prominent mound in the area. Apparently, this butte is shaped like a kneeling
buffalo. The native legend attached to the
hill maintains that the Great Spirit placed it
as a promise that there would always be
buffalo.

* Butze (former locality)
73 D/9 - Chauvin
10-43-1-W4
52°42'N 110°03'W

Approximately 30 km north north-east of
Provost.

A station was established here in 1910, by
the Grand Trunk Pacific Railway, later
amalgamated into Canadian National
Railways. It was named after A. Butze,
purchasing agent for the Grand Trunk
Pacific.

Byemoor (hamlet)
82 P/16 - Farrell Lake
6-35-16-W4
51°59'N 112°17'W
Approximately 44 km north north-west of
Hanna.

The hamlet of Byemoor owes its original
existence to the coming of the railroad. It
was first known as Wilson's Siding, as it
was built on land bought from John "Jack"
Wilson, an early homesteader, by the
Canadian National Realties Company in
1924. The post office was established in
November 1925 under the name Byemoor,
a name taken from the original school
district. The name was suggested by
Leonard Browne (1884-1952), after his
home which existed by moorland in
England. He was born at Stockton-on-
Tees, also known as "By-the-Moor."
Several names were put into a hat when the
community was choosing a name for itself,
and the name Byemoor was picked by
Buster Browne, Leonard's son. At its peak,
Byemoor boasted a population of 150; that
number has diminished significantly over
the years. One local resident refers to the
area as a "hunter's paradise," as it is
abundant with lakes and prairie wildlife.

Byers Lake (lake)
73 D/12 - Lougheed
3-43-11-W4
52°40'N 111°31'W
Approximately 16 km west of Hardisty.

---

*denotes rescinded name or former locality.

The name for this lake has been in use since
at least 1950, and it is located on land once
owned by a family known as the Byers.

Byers Lake (lake)
83 G/9 - Onoway
33-53-1-W5
53°37'N 114°05'W
Approximately 40 km west north-west of
Edmonton.

The name for this lake was officially
adopted in 1950 and was taken after the
Byers family, the original owners of the
land upon which the lake sits.

C.F.B. Cold Lake (Canadian Forces Base)

73 L/9 - Marie Lake
5-62-2-W4
54°25′N 110°16′W
Approximately 9 km south-west of Cold
Lake.

(see Cold Lake)

Cabin Lake (lake)

73 E/9 - Marwayne
21-54-2-W4
53°40′N 110°14′W
Approximately 46 km north north-west of
Lloydminster.

The name for this lake was officially
adopted in 1940, but the precise origin is
unknown.

Cache Creek (creek)

73 L/4 - Cache Lake
31-59-12-W4
54°08′N 111°47′W
Flows south into Cache Lake, approximately 33 km north-west of St. Paul.

This creek was officially named 6 April
1950 for its proximity to Cache Lake. (see
Cache Lake)

* Cache Lake (former post office)

73 L/4 - Cache Lake
33-59-12-W4
54°08′N 111°43′W
Approximately 33 km west north-west of
St. Paul.

The post office operated here from February 1917 through December 1922, when the
name was changed to Spedden. (see Cache
Lake)

* Cache Lake (lake)

73 L/4 - Cache Lake
59-12-W4
54°06′N 111°47′W

*denotes rescinded name or former locality.

Approximately 33 km west north-west of
St. Paul.

The name for this lake is a translation of the
Cree name, *astachikuwin*. Early Indians
had a storehouse (cache) here for buffalo
meat, and hauled the meat to winter
quarters as required.

Cache Lake (lake)

83 I/16 - Plamondon
20-68-14-W4
54°54′N 112°06′W
Approximately 16 km north north-west of
Lac La Biche.

The descriptive name for this lake has been
official since at least 1958. It has been
referred to as "Hidden Lake" in the past
because it is "cached" in the hills, and
before the land was cleared was difficult to
find.

Cadogan (hamlet)

73 D/8 - Provost
1-39-4-W4
52°19′N 110°27′W
Approximately 12 km west south-west of
Provost.

The post office opened at this one-time
village in March 1909, and was likely named
after George Henry, the fifth Earl Cadogan
(1840-1915), Under Secretary for the
Colonies from 1878 to 1880 and Lord
Lieutenant of Ireland (1895-1902).

* Cadron (former post office)

83 I/1 - Smoky Lake
24-58-16-W4
54°02′N 112°15′W
Approximately 17 km south-east of Smoky
Lake.

The name for this post office, which
operated from July 1937 through September 1958, is taken after a district in Ukraine
from where many early settlers came.

Cairns (hamlet)

73 D/7 - Czar
8-39-4-W4
52°21′N 110°33′W
Approximately 19 km west south-west of
Provost.

A Canadian Pacific Railway station was
established here in 1909, followed by a post
office in February 1911. The precise origin
for the name is uncertain, but the Gaelic
word *cairn* means "round pile of stones,"
and the name may have been applied
descriptively.

Calahoo (hamlet)

83 H/12 - St. Albert
31-54-27-W4
53°43′N 113°58′W
Approximately 35 km north-west of
Edmonton.

A Canadian Northern Railway station was
established here in 1915 and was named for
William Calahoo, a Métis of Iroquoian
origin, who came to the west with the early
bateaux brigades. The post office opened in
May 1917.

Calder Lake (lake)

73 E/14 - St. Paul
21-57-8-W4
53°57′N 111°08′W
Approximately 13 km south-east of St.
Paul.

The name for this lake has been official
since at least 1958, but its precise origin is
unknown.

C

Calhoun Bay (bay)

83 B/15 - Buck Lake
30-46-6-W5
52°59′30″N 114°44′00″W
Approximately 90 km west south-west of Edmonton.

A Provincial Recreation Area was established by Order-in-Council in 1988, and was named for its proximity to this feature. The name is well-established in local usage, and apparently is taken after Henry Calhoun, a homesteader who came to this area from Louisiana in the 1940s. A Joe Calhoun established a second homestead in this area as well.

Calmar (town)

83 H/5 - Leduc
25-49-27-W4
53°16′N 113°49′W
Approximately 42 km south-west of Edmonton.

The post office opened here in April 1900. The town was incorporated 19 January 1954. C.G. Blomquist was the first postmaster and he suggested the name to commemorate his home town of Kalmar, Sweden.

Calthorpe (locality)

72 M/9 - Esther
13-31-2-W4
51°40′N 110°08′W
Approximately 41 km north north-east of Oyen.

This locality was named after a place in Norfolk, England of the same name.

Cameron Lake (lake)

83 A/2 - Big Valley
10-38-19-W4
52°15′N 112°37′W
Approximately 7 km south-east of Stettler.

The name for this lake has been official since at least 1958, but its precise origin is unknown.

Cameron Lakes (lakes)

83 G/9 - Onoway
2-54-1-W5
53°38′N 114°02′W
Approximately 37 km west north-west of Edmonton.

The name for this lake was officially approved in 1950 and commemorates Flight Lieutenant Thomas Henry Cameron (1919-1945), of the R.C.A.F., who earned the D.F.C. for destroying three enemy aircraft. He became one of the first to fly the Mosquito – a wooden fighter-bomber – in France. He was killed in action when his plane crashed in Holland.

Camp Bay (bay)

83 H/10 - Elk Island Park
12-14-54-20-W4
53°40′00″N 112°51′00″W
Approximately 40 km east of Edmonton, in Elk Island National Park.

This name appears to be the name used by the local wardens for this bay on the south shore of Astotin Lake. The name was officially approved 17 October 1991.

Camp Creek (creek)

83 J/8 - Shoal Creek
14-61-4-W5
54°17′N 114°28′W
Flows east into Shoal Lake, approximately 18 km north north-east of Barrhead.

The name for this creek was officially adopted in 1958 and is taken from its proximity to the locality of the same name. (see Camp Creek)

Camp Creek (locality)

83 J/7 - Fort Assiniboine
6-61-4-W5
54°15′N 114°35′W
Approximately 20 km north-west of Barrhead.

The name for this locality, whose post office opened in August 1934, is taken for its proximity to the creek of the same name, where it is said that natives often camped.

Camp Lake (lake)

73 E/4 - Viking
10-48-11-W4
53°07′N 111°31′W
Approximately 18 km east of Viking.

The name for this lake has been official since at least 1941, but its precise origin is unknown.

Camp Lake (lake)

73 E/14 - St. Paul
31-57-10-W4
53°58′N 111°29′W
Approximately 13 km west south-west of St. Paul.

The name for this lake has been official since at least 1955, but its precise origin is unknown.

Camp Lake (lake)

83 I/11 - Athabasca
10-64-21-W4
54°32′N 113°05′W
Approximately 25 km south south-east of Athabasca.

The name for this lake has been official since at least 1952, but its precise origin is unknown.

Camp Spring (spring)

73 D/11 - Hardisty
32-43-8-W4
52°44′55″N 111°07′20″W

Approximately 15 km east north-east of
Hardisty.

This spring, located in the Wainwright
Regional Training Area, was used as a
camping spot by the Buffalo Park Riders
when they repaired fences in the area. (see
Buffalo Park)

Camp Wainwright (Canadian Forces Base)
73 D/15 - Wainwright
44-6,7-W4
52°49′N 110°53′W
Immediately south-west of the town of
Wainwright.

(see Wainwright)

Campbell (locality)
83 H/12 - St. Albert
12-54-25-W4
53°38′N 113°34′W
Approximately 4 km north-east of St.
Albert.

The Edmonton, Dunvegan and British
Columbia Railway established a station
here before 1915 and named it after Alex
Campbell, one-time traffic manager for the
railway. He later left to live in Pocatello,
Idaho.

Campbell Creek (creek)
73 E/7 - Vermilion
1-52-5-W4
53°28′N 110°36′W
Flows south-east into Vermilion River,
approximately 20 km north-east of Vermilion.

This creek drains Campbell Lake. (see
Campbell Lake)

* **Campbell Hill** (former locality)
72 M/11 - Youngstown
9-32-8-W4
51°44′N 111°05′W
Approximately 58 km north-west of Oyen.

A post office operated at this site from 1913
through 1926. The site was on a hill, and
R.J. Campbell was one of the early settlers
who first applied for a post office.

Campbell Lake (lake)
73 E/7 - Vermilion
19-52-5,6-W4
53°30′N 110°44′W
Approximately 18 km north north-east of
Vermilion.

The name has been associated with this lake
since at least 1905 when the land around it
was purchased from the Canadian Pacific
Railway by a real estate man named W.A.
Campbell. Other homesteaders around the
lake included B.G. Somerset and R.M.
Somerset. The lake was also locally known
as "Somerset Lake" for a time.

Campbell Park (railway point)
83 H/12 - St. Albert
4-12-24-24-W4
53°38′30″N 113°33′50″W
Approximately 5 km north of Edmonton.

This siding was named after Keith
Campbell, the former executive vice-
president of the Canadian Pacific Railway.
The name was officially approved 12 March
1980.

Campbellton Heights (locality)
83 H/11 - Edmonton
22-53-23-W4
53°35′N 113°18′W
Approximately 15 km east north-east of
Edmonton.

This is a country residence subdivision. The
precise origin for the name is not known.

* **Campbelltown** (former hamlet)
83 H/11 - Edmonton
27-52-23-W4
53°31′N 113°19′W
Approximately 12 km east of Edmonton.

(see Sherwood Park)

Camping Lakes (lakes)
83 I/14 - Sawdy
35-67,68-21-W4
54°50′N 113°07′W
Approximately 19 km north-east of
Athabasca.

The name for these lakes has been official
since at least 1953, but its precise origin is
unknown.

Campsie (hamlet)
83 J/2 - Thunder Lake
26-59-5-W5
54°08′N 114°39′W
Approximately 16 km west of Barrhead.

A post office operated here from June 1909
through September 1969 and was named
after a town in Strathclyde, Scotland.
William Wallace was the first postmaster
and he was a Scotsman. The term
"Campsie" is from the Gaelic *cam sith*,
translating "crooked hill" or "hill-range,"
according to James B. Johnston, author of
Place Names of Scotland, 3rd edition, 1970.

Camrose (city)
83 H/2 - Camrose
2-47-20-W4
53°01′15″N 112°49′30″W
Approximately 70 km south-east of
Edmonton.

The name for this city was previously
"Sparling;" however, that name became so

frequently confused with that of Sperling in Manitoba and Stirling in Alberta that it was changed to Camrose and the post office opened with this name in May 1905. The precise derivation of the name is not known. Perhaps the most reasonable, and possibly authentic explanation of the name is that it was selected from the British postal guide in 1905, and named after Camrose in Pembrokeshire (now Dyfed), Wales. There are two versions of the origin of the name. The first version is that it appears in 1324 as *kamros*, from the Welsh, *cam rhos*, which means "crooked moor," but this in itself is a variation, so it may be that Camrose is an Anglicized form of *camrhos*, *cam* meaning "crooked," and *rhos* meaning "heather." A second possibility is that the name means "valley of roses" from the Welsh *cwm*, which means "valley" and thus Camrose.

Camrose County #22 (county)

83 A/13 - Bearhills Lake
17 to 22-41 to 49-W4
52°50′N 113°40′W
South-east of Edmonton.

(see Camrose)

Camrose Creek (creek)

83 A/15 - Ferintosh
8-46-20-W4
52°57′N 112°52′W
Flows south into Battle River, approximately 8 km south south-west of Camrose.

(see Camrose)

Canard, Lac (lake)

73 E/14 - St. Paul
36-56-10-W4
53°52′45″N 111°21′00″W
Approximately 13 km south south-west of St. Paul.

The name for this lake was officially adopted in 1941, and reflects the abundance

of wild ducks which once inhabited the area. *Canard* is the French equivalent of "duck."

Cannell (railway point)

83 H/12 - St. Albert
21-53-25-W4
53°36′N 113°37′W
Approximately 3 km south of St. Albert.

A post office operated here from December 1913 through December 1952 and was named after William Cannell (1867-1922), former president of the Acme Brick Company.

Canoe Lake (lake)

73 L/16 - Medley River
10-69-3-W4
54°58′N 110°23′W
Approximately 56 km north north-west of Cold Lake.

The name for this lake has been official since 17 January 1951, and is a rough translation of the Cree *waskwayuse sagahegan*, or "Birch Boat Lake."

Canoe Lake (lake)

83 I/11 - Athabasca
16-65-21-W4
54°37′N 113°08′W
Approximately 16 km south-east of Athabasca.

The name for this lake was officially adopted in 1945, but its precise origin is unknown.

Canyon Creek (creek)

83 B/10 - Carlos
15-8-41-7-W5
52°31′N 114°58′W
Flows north-west into the North Saskatchewan River, approximately 16 km north north-west of Rocky Mountain House.

Fred Green gave this creek its appropriately descriptive name, referring to the steep canyon through which the feature flows.

Caprona (locality)

83 A/2 - Big Valley
14-36-20-W4
52°06′N 112°44′W
Approximately 25 km south of Stettler.

Canadian National Railways established a station here in 1921, but the precise origin for the name is unknown.

Captain Eyre Lake (lake)

73 D/7 - Czar
12-30-38-5-W4
52°18′N 110°43′W
Approximately 30 km west south-west of Provost.

Milo Yearious an oldtimer had named the lake after a Captain Ayre, who homesteaded on the east side where the water runs out of the lake. Ayre was born in Ohio, had served in the United States Army, and participated in the Spanish-American War of 1898. Captain Ayre was trying to establish a horse ranch with 12 cayuse mares, but his endeavour proved unsuccessful. He lived at the lake from 1909 to 1911, and left after his wife apparently left him for an old lover. Shortly afterward, Captain Ayre left the area for parts unknown. The road beside Captain Eyre Lake used to be the original boundary line that separated Alberta from Saskatchewan between the years 1905 and 1908. This lake would have been in Saskatchewan until 1908 when the boundary line was transferred to the 4th Meridian.

Carbondale (hamlet)

83 H/12 - St. Albert
8-55-24-W4
53°45′N 113°32′W
Approximately 22 km north of Edmonton.

The name for this hamlet, whose post office operated from August 1932 through August 1955, was descriptively named for the coal mines and deposits in the area.

Cardiff (hamlet)
83 H/13 - Morinville
26-55-25-W4
53°47'N 113°36'W
Approximately 27 km north of Edmonton.

The name for this hamlet was suggested by the number of coal mines in the area which was reminiscent of those in the city of the same name in Wales. The post office operated from December 1907 through November 1960.

Cardinal Creek (creek)
73 L/5 - Goodfish Lake
4-61-12-W4
54°15'N 111°45'W
Flows north-west into Reed Lake, approximately 44 km north-west of St. Paul.

This creek was officially named 5 April 1950 for its proximity to Cardinal Lake. (see Cardinal Lake)

Cardinal Lake (lake)
73 L/3 - Vincent Lake
30-58-9-W4
54°03'N 111°20'W
Approximately 6 km north of St. Paul.

The name for this lake was officially approved 6 July 1950, its precise origin is unknown.

Cardinal Lake (lake)
73 L/12 - Beaver Lake
31-64-11-W4
54°35'N 111°40'W
Approximately 30 km south-east of Lac La Biche.

The name for this lake was officially adopted in 1951 and is likely taken after the bird.

Carey Lake (lake)
73 L/4 - Cache Lake
34-58-11-W4
54°03'N 111°33'W
Approximately 18 km west north-west of St. Paul.

The name for this lake was officially adopted 6 April 1950, but its precise origin is unknown.

Carlos (locality)
83 B/10 - Carlos
22-41-5-W5
52°33'N 114°38'W
Approximately 27 km north-east of Rocky Mountain House.

A post office operated here from June 1914 through January 1969 and was named in appreciation of Carlos Sleeper's efforts to petition for it. Sleeper was an early homesteader of the area.

Carlson Lake (lake)
73 E/6 - Mannville
16-20-51-8-W4
53°25'04"N 111°08'05"W
Approximately 22 km west north-west of Vermilion.

The locally well-established name for this lake was officially approved 22 January 1991 and derives from the Carlson family, the first family to have homesteaded the land upon which the lake is situated.

* Carlton Hill (former post office)
83 J/1 - Barrhead
26-59-4-W5
54°08'N 114°36'W
Approximately 15 km west of Barrhead.

The origin for the name of this post office, which operated from May 1917 through March 1931, is unknown.

Carnwood (locality)
83 G/2 - Drayton Valley
35-48-5-W5
53°11'N 114°38'W
Approximately 23 km east of Drayton Valley.

A post office opened here in June 1926 and was named after a parish in Devonshire, England, spelled "Cornwood." There was an error in the original spelling of the post office.

Caroline (village)
83 B/2 - Caroline
14-36-6-W5
52°05'N 114°45'W
Approximately 34 km south south-east of Rocky Mountain House.

The first Caroline post office was opened in August 1908 by Mr. and Mrs. Harvey Langley. They used the name of their only child, Caroline. When the village was organized in 1952 the name was used since the post office was already so named.

Carrier Lake (lake)
73 E/4 - Viking
28-47-11-W4
53°05'N 111°34'W
Approximately 18 km east of Viking.

The name for this lake has been official since at least 1958, but its precise origin is unknown.

Carroll Lakes (lakes)
73 L/4 - Cache Lake
23-25-59-12-W4
54°07'N 111°40'W
Approximately 29 km north-west of St. Paul.

---

*denotes rescinded name or former locality.

The name for this group of lakes was officially approved 6 April 1950, but its precise origin is unknown.

Carrot Creek (creek)

83 G/12 - Carrot Creek
35-54-14-W5
53°43'N 115°58'W
Flows north into McLeod River, approximately 34 km east north-east of Edson.

The descriptive name for this creek refers to the abundance of wild carrots here. It was known to the Overlanders of 1862 as "Root River," and to the Crees as *oskatask*, translating "carrot," a parsnip-like tuber, prized by the Indians for its medicinal qualities.

Carrot Creek (locality)

83 G/12 - Carrot Creek
28-53-13-W5
53°37'N 115°51'W
Approximately 38 km east of Edson.

The post office opened here in September 1910 and was named for its proximity to Carrot Creek. (see Carrot Creek)

Carstairs (town)

82 O/9 - Didsbury
17-30-1-W5
51°34'N 114°06'W
Approximately 82 km south south-west of Red Deer.

The Canadian Pacific Railway owned the land upon which Carstairs sits before 1893. The post office opened in September 1900 and was named after Carstairs, Lanarkshire (now Strathclyde), Scotland. Apparently, the first settlers were of Scottish descent.

Cartier Creek (creek)

82 O/10 - Fallentimber Creek
36-31-7-W5
51°42'N 114°52'W

Flows south-east into the Red Deer River, approximately 18 km south-west of Sundre.

The name for this creek has been official since 1958, but its origin is unknown.

Cartlidge Creek (creek)

82 O/10 - Fallentimber Creek
25-29-6-W5
51°31'00"N 114°42'45"W
Flows south into Silver Creek, approximately 33 km south south-west of Sundre.

This small permanent foothills stream was named after the original Cartlidge homestead through which it flows.

Carvel (hamlet)

83 G/9 - Onoway
34-52-2-W5
53°32'N 114°13'W
Approximately 14 km west of Stony Plain.

The Grand Trunk Pacific Railway, later absorbed into Canadian National Railways, established a station here in 1911, and called it "Carvel Station." A post office was opened in February 1915 and operated until May 1950 when the "Station" was dropped from the name. It is named after the novel, *Richard Carvel*, written by Winston Churchill (1871-1947), an American novelist.

Carvel Corner (locality)

83 G/9 - Onoway
4-53-2-W5
53°33'N 114°13'W
Approximately 48 km west of Edmonton.

The name for this locality was officially adopted in 1957. (see Carvel)

* Casavant (former post office)

83 H/13 - Morinville
SW-3-58-25-W4
53°58'N 113°38'W

Approximately 25 km south south-east of Westlock.

The post office operated here from July 1911 through February 1931 and was named after Emile Casavant, the first postmistress.

Caslan (hamlet)

83 I/10 - Boyle
16-65-17-W4
54°37'45"N 112°30'30"W
Approximately 38 km south-west of Lac La Biche.

The Alberta and Great Waterways Railway Company established a station here in 1914. A post office opened in March 1933. The origin for the name is unknown.

Castle Island (summer village)

83 G/9 - Onoway
35-54-3-W5
53°43'N 114°20'W
Approximately 58 km west north-west of Edmonton.

This summer village on an island in Lac Ste Anne, was incorporated 1 January 1955. Apparently, at one time the island was owned by a Frenchman, Count DeCaze, the first Indian Agent. The island was once known as "Constance Island." Count Decazes dreamed of building a castle out of stones on this island, but he died he before he was able to complete it.

Castor (town)

73 D/4 - Castor
35-37-14-W4
52°13'10"N 111°54'10"W
Approximately 140 km east of Red Deer.

The name for this town is apparently related to the fact that it is close to Beaverdam Creek. *Castor* is the Latin word for beaver, and the prevalence of beaver in the area at the time of its naming was noteworthy. The town was incorporated in

1909, and the beaver were still plentiful even by 1921.

Castor Creek (creek)

73 D/5 - Alliance
2-39-12-W4
52°20'N 111°37'W
Flows north into Battle River, approximately 22 km north-east of Castor.

(see Castor)

Cattalo Bridge (bridge)

73 D/10 - Hughenden
26-42-6-W4
52°38'50"N 110°45'50"W
Approximately 22 km south south-east of the town of Wainwright.

This bridge was built across Ribstone Creek in the 1950s by the Department of National Defence and is named after the Cattalo (buffalo-shorthorn hybrid) that were still being bred there at that time in order to take advantage of the best qualities of both the male buffalo and the domestic cow. All the bulls that were derived of this experiment, however, grew to be sterile and production was discontinued in Buffalo Park.

Cattalo Lake (lake)

73 D/10 - Hughenden
14-43-7-W4
52°42'50"N 110°56'00"W
Approximately 15 km south of the town of Wainwright.

(see Cattalo Bridge)

Cawes Lake (lake)

83 H/6 - Cooking Lake
11-51-24-W4
53°23'N 113°27'W
Approximately 22 km south-east of Edmonton.

The name for this lake has been in use since at least 1953, but its precise origin is unknown. It was, apparently, originally known as "Sandy Lake."

Central Park (hamlet)

83 A/5 - Red Deer
NE-4-39-27-W4
52°20'N 113°49'W
Approximately 5 km north of Red Deer.

The origin for the name of this hamlet, whose subdivision plan was registered in Edmonton in June 1958 but which was not officially established until 31 May 1985, is unknown.

Centurion Field (plain)

73 D/11 - Hardisty
8-43-8-W4
52°43'30"N 111°07'35"W
Approximately 22 km east north-east of Hardisty.

This field is used by the Department of National Defence for brigade-sized parades and was officially named in 1970 when the Centurion tank went out of Canadian service. At that time, a concrete and stone memorial was erected on the field commemorating the passing of the Centurion. The British Centurion tank served as Canada's main battle tank for 25 years. Canada tended to rely on armament designs of its allies, often modified to meet Canadian needs.

Chailey (locality)

73 E/11 - Myrnam
30-52-9-W4
53°32'N 111°18'W
Approximately 35 km south-east of Two Hills.

The name for this locality, whose post office operated from March 1907 through November 1956, was taken after the hometown of the first postmaster, C.H. Brown. He came from Chailey, in Sussex, England.

Chain Lakes (lakes)

82 P/16 - Farrell Lake
11-33-16-W4
51°50'N 112°09'W
Approximately 25 km north north-east of Hanna.

This feature, along with several others like it in Alberta, has a descriptive name. These groups of lakes may have been caused by glacial action.

Chain Lakes (lakes)

83 I/13 - Grosmont
18-69-23,24-W4
54°58'N 113°30'W
Approximately 32 km north north-west of Athabasca.

The name for this feature has been official since 1953 and is likely descriptive.

Chain Lakes (lake)

83 A/11 - Chain Lakes
6-41,42-24,25-W4
52°35'N 113°25'W
Approximately 16 km south-east of Ponoka.

The name for this feature has been official since 1959 and is likely descriptive.

Chambers Creek (creek)

83 B/11 - Baptiste River
2-41-10-W5
52°30'15"N 115°20'15"W
Flows north into Baptiste River, approximately 35 km north-west of Rocky Mountain House.

The name for this creek has been official since at least 1958, but its precise origin is unknown.

Chandler Lake (lake)

73 L/1 - Reita Lake
19-59-1-W4
54°07'N 110°09'W

Approximately 33 km south of Grand Centre.

The name for this lake was officially adopted in 1950 and commemorates Flying Officer A.J. Chandler, A.F.M., of Ribstone, who was killed in World War II.

Channel Spring (spring)

73 D/11 - Hardisty
29-43-8-W4
52°44'15"N 111°07'55"W
Approximately 20 km east north-east of Hardisty.

According to Lieutenant Colonel M.R. Gentles, C.D., of the Wainwright Regional Training Area, the name was first used during the Buffalo Park days after a concrete channel was constructed to protect the spring from the buffalo. (see Buffalo Park)

Chap Hill (hill)

73 D/11 - Hardisty
27-43-8-W4
52°44'N 111°05'W
Approximately 18 km south-west of the town of Wainwright.

The name for this feature has been in use since at least 1954, but the precise origin is unknown.

Chappell Lake (lake)

73 L/4 - Cache Lake
15-60-11-W4
54°11'N 111°34'W
Approximately 28 km north-west of St. Paul.

The name for this lake has been official since 6 April 1950 and may be after J. Chappell, an early settler.

---

*denotes rescinded name or former locality.

Charlotte Lake (lake)

73 L/7 - Bonnyville
4-11-61-5-W4
54°15'30"N 110°37'00"W
Approximately 7 km east of Bonnyville.

The name for this lake has been official since 2 June 1950. (see Elinor Lake)

Charlton Muskeg (muskeg)

82 O/10 - Fallentimber Creek
11-30-6-W5
51°33'30"N 114°44'00"W
Approximately 29 km south south-west of Sundre.

This waterlogged swamp with a deep accumulation of organic material became commonly known as Charlton Muskeg because of its proximity to the Charlton homestead on the edge of the muskeg. This particular feature is unusual for two reasons: first, its large size; and second, its location, which is much farther south than any similarly large muskeg areas.

* Charron (former post office)

83 I/16 - Plamondon
18-68-16-W4
54°53'N 112°26'W
Approximately 36 km west north-west of Lac La Biche.

The post office, which operated here from December 1917 through November 1968, was named after a trapper of mixed blood background who worked in the area.

Charron Lake (lake)

83 I/15 - Grassland
2-33-67-17-W4
54°50'16"N 112°31'59"W
Approximately 37 km west north-west of Lac La Biche.

(see Charron)

Chatwin Lake (lake)

73 L/7 - Bonnyville
4-61-6-W4
54°15'15"N 110°51'00"W
Approximately 7 km west south-west of Bonnyville.

The name for this lake has been official since at least 1958, but its precise origin is unknown.

Chauvin (village)

73 D/9 - Chauvin
7-43-1-W4
52°41'40"N 110°08'30"W
Approximately 38 km north of Provost.

A Grand Trunk Pacific station was established here in 1908 and followed by a post office in April 1909. The settlement was named after George von Chauvin, a director of the G.T.P.'s parent, the Grand Trunk Railway of London, England.

Chedderville (locality)

83 B/2 - Caroline
17-37-6-W5
52°10'N 114°50'W
Approximately 25 km south of Rocky Mountain House.

A post office operated here from February 1926 through August 1967. The origin for its name is not certain. One source claims that many of the first settlers were from England, and more specifically, the Smith brothers were from Cheddar. Another source maintains that the name reflects the fact that this is a cheese producing area.

Cherhill (hamlet)

83 G/15 - Sangudo
9-56-5-W5
53°49'N 114°41'W
Approximately 33 km south-east of Mayerthorpe.

The post office was established at this hamlet in March 1911, and was named after A.P. Stecher, the first postmaster, with "hill" added The original site of the post office was 4.8 km north of the present one.

Cherry Grove (hamlet)

73 L/8 - Cold Lake
9-62-1-W4
54°22′N 110°06′W
Approximately 11 km south-east of Grande Centre.

A post office was established at this site in October 1932 and was descriptively named after the number of wild cherry trees which grow in the area.

Chester Lake (lake)

73 E/16 - Frog Lake
13-55-2-W4
53°45′N 110°10′W
Approximately 52 km north north-west of Lloydminster.

The name for this lake has been official since at least 1958, but its precise origin is unknown.

* Chesterwold (former locality)

83 A/13 - Bearhills Lake
31-44-27-W4
52°50′N 113°54′W
Approximately 29 km north-west of Ponoka.

A post office operated here from November 1903 through July 1934, and was named after the home town of Peter A. Cooper, the first postmaster. He was from Chesterville, Nebraska.

Chickakoo Lake (lake)

83 G/9 - Onoway
34-53-1-W5
53°37′N 114°04′W

Approximately 38 km west north-west of Edmonton.

The name for this lake has been official since at least 1950 but appears on maps made by the first surveyors of the area. The precise origin is unknown.

Chicken Creek (creek)

83 B/7 - Rocky Mountain House
2-32-40-7-W5
52°28′50″N 114°58′00″W
Flows north-west into North Saskatchewan River, approximately 12 km north of Rocky Mountain House.

The well-established name for this creek was officially approved 19 January 1983 and is likely descriptive of the fauna in the area. A farm near the source of the creek which was owned by H.C. Titford in 1917 was locally known as the "Chicken Creek Farm." Local histories of the region mention the abundance of prairie chickens and other wild fowl in the area.

Chickenhill Lake (lake)

73 L/3 - Vincent Lake
14-59-8-W4
54°06′N 111°06′W
Approximately 19 km north-east of St. Paul.

The name for this lake has been official since 6 July 1950, but its precise origin is unknown.

Chigwell (locality)

83 A/5 - Red Deer
33-40-25-W4
52°29′N 113°32′W
Approximately 13 km east north-east of Lacombe.

The Canadian Pacific Railway established a station here in 1905 and the name was suggested by Jack Pope who came from the

suburb of London, England, with the same name. The post office operated from May 1906 through May 1924, then reopened in April 1928 through April 1970.

Chip Lake (lake)

83 G/11 - Chip Lake
10-53,54-9,10-W5
53°40′N 115°23′W
Approximately 36 km south south-west of Mayerthorpe.

The name for this lake is the shortened form for "Buffalo Chip." Buffalo manure was a source of fuel for early pioneers and explorers when wood was in short supply. The name appears on Palliser's map of 1865. Southesk labels it "Dirt Lake" on his map of 1875. It has also been referred to as "Bull Dung Lake."

Chip Lake (locality)

83 G/11 - Chip Lake
32-53-10-W5
53°37′N 115°26′W
Approximately 40 km south south-west of Mayerthorpe.

The Canadian Northern Railway established a station here in 1915. It was named for its proximity to Chip Lake. The post office operated from June 1912 through March 1914, when it was called "Leaman," and then reopened as Chip Lake from March 1929 through June 1952. (see Chip Lake)

Chipman (village)

83 H/10 - Elk Island Park
30-54-18-W4
53°41′55″N 112°38′05″W
Approximately 58 km east north-east of Edmonton.

The Canadian Northern Railway established a station here in 1905 and a post office opened here in May of that same year. It was named after C.C. Chipman, (1856-1924), chief commissioner of the Hudson's Bay Company from 1891 to 1911. This village was incorporated 21 October 1913.

Chisholm (hamlet)

83 J/16 - Chisholm
26-68-2-W5
54°55'N 114°10'W
Approximately 60 km west south-west of Athabasca.

The post office, "Chisholm Mills," was established here in July 1923 and was named after Thomas Chisholm, a tie contractor for the Edmonton, Dunvegan and B.C. Railway. Chisholm was a Klondike pioneer, having run the Aurora Saloon and Dance Hall at Dawson in the days of the gold rush. He was a huge man, standing over six feet tall, weighing over 240 pounds, and it is said that he wore a watch chain of gold nuggets across his chest that "looked almost as large as a logging chain."

Chisholm Creek (creek)

83 J/16 - Chisholm
7-6,8-1-W5
54°53'N 114°09'W
Flows north-west into Athabasca River, approximately 62 km west north-west of Athabasca.

(see Chisholm)

Chisholm Mills (post office)

83 J/16 - Chisholm
26-68-2-W5
54°55'N 114°10'W
Approximately 61 km west north-west of Athabasca.

This post office opened for the hamlet of Chisholm in July 1923. (see Chisholm)

Chota Lake (lake)

73 L/5 - Goodfish Lake
35-61-12-W4
54°18'30"N 111°42'00"W
Approximately 44 km north-north-west of St. Paul.

The name for this lake has been official since 4 May 1950 and is a term in India for "small," which may be descriptive.

Christopher Lake (lake)

73 E/16 - Frog Lake
21-55-2-W4
53°46'N 110°15'W
Approximately 46 km east south-east of Elk Point.

The name for this lake has been official since at least 1958, but its precise origin is unknown.

Church Hill (hill)

83 A/5 - Red Deer
8-28-40-25-W4
52°28'N 113°32'W
Approximately 13 km east of Lacombe.

The name for this hill refers to the fact that there used to be a Methodist church on the east side of the feature. Church Hill used to be a test for cars of earlier days, but now it is just another long grade, and the church site is a cultivated hillside.

Cipher Lake (lake)

73 D/9 - Chauvin
3-43-1-W4
52°41'N 110°06'W
Approximately 37 km north north-east of Provost.

The precise origin for the name of this feature is unknown.

Clandonald (hamlet)

73 E/10 - Clandonald
17-53-5-W4
53°34'N 110°44'W
Approximately 27 km north north-east of Vermilion.

A post office was established by the name of Clandonald in February 1927; it was previously known as Wellsdale. Clan Donald is a prominent Scottish clan.

* Clark Manor (former post office)

73 D/14 - Irma
1-46-8-W4
52°56'N 111°01'W
Approximately 15 km north-west of the town of Wainwright.

The post office, which operated here from February 1911 through April 1925, was named after its first and only postmaster, J.G. Clark.

Clarke Lake (lake)

73 E/1 - Paradise Valley
14-48-3-W4
53°08'N 110°20'W
Approximately 26 km south-west of Lloydminster.

The name for this lake has been official since at least 1958, but its precise origin is unknown.

* Clarksville (former post office)

73 L/3 - Vincent Lake
18-59-10-W4
54°07'N 111°30'W
Approximately 18 km north-west of St. Paul.

The name for the post office, which operated here from March 1907 through August 1911, commemorated the first postmaster, Lewis G. Clark. The name was later changed to Abilene. (see Abilene)

Claude Lake (lake)

73 L/13 - Lac La Biche
SW-15-67-13-W4
54°47′35″N 111°54′26″W
Approximately 5 km east of Lac La Biche.

The name Claude Lake has been associated with this feature since at least 1918; however, its origin is unknown. At first there was just one big lake, but railroad construction crews had to drain the lake to make a pass for the Alberta and Great Waterways Railway, and this led to the creation of two small lakes. This lake is known locally as either "Frog Lake One" or simply "Frog Lake." "Frog" is derived from the Cree *Ayiygis Sagahegan.* It is also sometimes called "Cadieux ('Cajou')" after a farmer on the east end of the lake.

Claysmore (hamlet)

73 E/6 - Mannville
30-50-7-W4
53°21′N 111°01′W
Approximately 12 km west of Vermilion.

There is a village in Middlesex, (now Greater London), England of the same name. Perhaps this hamlet, whose post office operated until February 1926, was named for that village.

Clear Creek (creek)

83 B/2 - Caroline
9-27-37-6-W5
From 52°12′04″N 114°44′01″W
to 52°12′45″N 114°46′01″W
Flows west into Clearwater River, approximately 20 km south-east of Rocky Mountain House.

The well-established name for this creek has been in use since the early 1900s. This tributary of the Clearwater River never freezes, and is very clear. Fish and Wildlife

stocks the creek with trout and requested that the descriptive name be made official for management purposes. The name was officially approved 29 July 1986.

Clear Lake (lake)

82 P/16 - Farrell Lake
36-32-16-W4
51°47′N 112°08′W
Approximately 16 km east north-east of Hanna.

The name for this lake has been official since 1958 and is likely descriptive.

Clear Lake (lake)

83 J/2 - Thunder Lake
35-60-6-W5
54°14′N 114°47′W
Approximately 27 km north-west of Barrhead.

The name for this lake has been official since at least 1958 and is likely descriptive.

Clearbrook (locality)

83 I/3 - Thorhild
36-60-23-W4
54°14′N 113°19′W
Approximately 37 km east north-east of Westlock.

The name for the post office, which operated here from June 1946 through December 1955, is likely descriptive.

Clearwater Creek (creek)

83 H/6 - Cooking Lake
7-50-24-W4
53°18′N 113°29′W
Flows north-east into Blackmud Creek, approximately 6 km north-east of Leduc.

The name for this creek was officially approved in 1957 and is likely descriptive.

Clearwater River (river)

83 B/7 - Rocky Mountain House
15-16-39-7-W5
52°22′N 114°57′W
Flows north-west into North Saskatchewan River, approximately 2 km south-west of Rocky Mountain House.

The descriptive name for the water of this river has been in local use since at least 1814. It was officially approved 5 July 1951. The other features nearby take their name from this river.

Clement Lake (lake)

72 M/13 - Garden Plain
34-34-13-W4
51°58′N 111°46′W
Approximately 27 km west south-west of Coronation.

The precise origin for the name of this feature is unknown.

Clive (village)

83 A/6 - Alix
31-40-24-W4
52°28′40″N 113°27′00″W
Approximately 20 km east of Lacombe.

A post office opened here in May 1909. The village was incorporated 19 January 1912 and was named after Robert Clive (1725-74), founder of British rule in India. It was known previously as "Valley City."

Clover Bar (bar)

83 H/11 - Edmonton
53-23-W4
53°34′N 113°21′W
Approximately 15 km east of Edmonton.

This bar in the North Saskatchewan River was named after Thomas H. Clover (1809-1897?), a California "forty-niner" who followed gold in California, joined the Cariboo Gold Rush, and then moved to this spot near Edmonton, which eventually became known as "Clover's Bar." It was at this bar in the early 1860s that Clover had the greatest success, and the name was later shortened to simply Clover Bar. He then moved to Fort Garry, where he delivered mail for a time, and then he apparently moved to Leroy, North Dakota.

Clover Bar, 1910

Clover Bar (hamlet)
83 H/11 - Edmonton
8-53-23-W4
53°34'N 113°20'W
Approximately 10 km east of Edmonton.

A post office operated here from June 1884 through March 1970, when it was moved to Edmonton. The name for the hamlet was taken from the bar on the North Saskatchewan River. (see Clover Bar)

Clover Lawn (locality)
83 H/3 - Bittern Lake
10-48-23-W4
53°08'00"N 113°17'30"W
Approximately 19 km north north-east of Wetaskiwin.

The precise origin for the name of this locality is unknown; however, it may be descriptive.

Clover Park (locality)
83 H/11 - Edmonton
28-54-22-W4
53°44'N 113°11'W
Approximately 24 km north-east of Edmonton.

The precise origin for the name of this country residence subdivision is unknown.

Clyde (village)
83 I/4 - Westlock
35-59-25-W4
54°08'55"N 113°38'00"W
Approximately 15 km east of Westlock.

This village, whose post office opened in September 1905, was incorporated 28 January 1914. It was named after George Clyde, an original homesteader who arrived in the area in the early 1900s. His home, stocked with many essentials, became a stopping place for the early settlers in the area.

* Clymont (former post office)
83 H/5 - Leduc
32-51-26-W4
53°27'N 113°47'W
Approximately 20 km west south-west of Edmonton.

The name for the post office, which operated from June 1914 through December 1932, was after E.B. McClymont, the first postmaster.

Coal Lake (lake)
83 H/3 - Bittern Lake
27-46,48-23-W4
53°05'N 113°17'W
Approximately 12 km north-east of Wetaskiwin.

The descriptive name for this lake has been in use since 1892 and refers to a bed of coal on its shore. Palliser has this lake named "Long Lake" on his 1859 map.

* Coalbanks (former locality)
83 A/6 - Alix
16-38-23-W4
52°16'N 113°14'W
Approximately 40 km east of Red Deer.

The post office, which operated here from April 1904 through August 1912, was named for the coal mines in the area. The name was later changed to Ardley. (see Ardley)

Coalcamp Creek (creek)
82 O/10 - Fallentimber Creek
6-32-6-W5
51°43'N 114°50'W
Flows south-east into Red Deer River, approximately 15 km south-west of Sundre.

The descriptive name for this creek, which flows into the Red Deer River, refers to its location as the site of the first coal seam found in the area in the late 1890s. The name was made official in November of 1937.

Coates Lake (lake)
72 M/16 - Grassy Island Lake
26-32-1-W4
51°46'N 110°03'W
Approximately 50 km north north-east of Oyen.

Frank Coates (?-1961), for whom this lake was named, was a veteran of the South African War, one of the earliest pioneers of the district and the first one to actually file on land in 1910. Coates built a sod house south-west of the lake and remained in the area for approximately 20 years, raising a family of seven. He then moved to Edmonton with his wife, and died in January of 1961.

Codner (locality)

83 B/7 - Rocky Mountain House
33-39-6-W5
52°23'N 114°48'W
Approximately 9 km east north-east of
Rocky Mountain House.

The Canadian Northern Railway established a station here in 1914; its precise
origin is unknown. The post office that
served the area was called "Oras."

Coghill (locality)

83 A/6 - Alix
8-39-23-W4
52°21'N 113°17'W
Approximately 38 km east north-east of
Red Deer.

The Canadian Northern Railway established a station here in 1914, but the precise
origin for the name is unknown.

Cold Creek (creek)

83 B/6 - Crimson Lake
25-38-10-W5
52°18'30"N 115°14'15"W
Flows east into North Prairie Creek,
approximately 23 km south-west of Rocky
Mountain House.

The well-established name for this creek
was officially approved 8 November 1978.
The name was applied by Don McDonald,
a local rancher, former trapper and resident
for 70 years, because of the creek's cold
clear contrast with the brownish waters of
North Prairie Creek.

Cold Lake (lake)

73 L/9 - Marie Lake
20,28-63,64-1-W4
54°33'N 110°05'W
Approximately 145 km north of
Lloydminster.

The descriptive name for this large feature
refers to the temperature of the water – it is
very cold through all seasons of the year. It
is labelled "Coldwater Lake" on Turnor's
map of 1790. The local Crees called the lake
"Cold Lake" in their own language. The
other features in the area take their names
from this lake.

Cold Lake (lake)

83 A/7 - Stettler
31-38-19-W4
52°18'N 112°41'W
Approximately 2 km south of Stettler.

The name for this locality has been official
since January 1937, but its precise origin is
unknown.

Cold Lake (town)

73 L/8 - Cold Lake
24-63-2-W4
54°27'N 110°10'W
Approximately 133 km north of
Lloydminster.

This town was incorporated 2 July 1955
and was named for its proximity to the
lake.

(see Cold Lake)

Cold Lake Church and Director's Residence, 1920

Cold Lake Indian Reserve #149

(Indian reserve)

73 L/1 - Reita Lake
61-2-W4
54°18'N 110°15'W
Approximately 16 km south south-west of
Grand Centre.

(see Cold Lake)

Cold Lake Indian Reserve #149A

(Indian reserve)

73 L/8 - Cold Lake
19-63-1-W4
54°28'N 110°09'W
Approximately 3 km east south-east of
Cold Lake, on the south shore of Cold
Lake.

(see Cold Lake)

Cold Lake Indian Reserve #149B

(Indian reserve)

73 L/9 - Marie Lake
64-2-W4
54°31'N 110°15'W
Approximately 8 km north-west of Cold
Lake.

(see Cold Lake)

Cole Lake (lake)

73 L/5 - Goodfish Lake
31-62-12-W4
54°24'N 111°48'W
Approximately 45 km south south-east of
Lac La Biche.

The name for this lake has been official
since at least 1958, but its precise origin is
unknown.

Coleman Lake (lake)

83 H/7 - Tofield
29-51-20-W4
53°26'N 112°53'W

Approximately 43 km east south-east of Edmonton.

The origin for the name of this lake is unknown.

Colinton (hamlet)

83 I/11 - Athabasca
15-65-22-W4
54°37′N 113°15′W
Approximately 13 km south of Athabasca.

The Canadian Northern Railway established a station here in 1912, and it was named by J.M. Milne, an early settler who had interests in the townsite, after his former home of Colinton, Edinburgh, Scotland. The post office, previously called "Kinnoull," opened under the name Colinton in June 1913.

Colinton Creek (creek)

83 I/11 - Athabasca
10-65-22-W4
54°37′N 113°14′W
Flows north into Little Pine Creek, approximately 13 km south of Athabasca.

The name for this creek was officially applied in 1952 for its proximity to the hamlet of Colinton. (see Colinton)

College Heights (hamlet)

83 A/5 - Red Deer
11-14-40-26-W4
52°29′N 113°44′W
Approximately 4 km north of Lacombe.

A post office was established here in July 1925, and was named after a Seventh Day Adventist school on a nearby hill.

Collette Lake (lake)

73 D/9 - Chauvin
9-43-1-W4
52°41′30″N 110°05′30″W

Approximately 36 km north north-east of Provost.

This lake was named for an early settler, Dan Collette (1892-1968), who owned the land to the north of the lake for a time. He was an elected member of the municipality for several years, was responsible for road maintenance, and was known to have participated actively in many community programs. His house was on the north shore of the lake, on the road to Chauvin. The family moved to New Brunswick in the 1920s. The lake has also been known by two other local names, "Folkin Lake" and "Pelican Lake."

Collingwood Cove (hamlet)

83 H/6 - Cooking Lake
NE/SE-34-51-21-W4
53°26′N 113°00′W
Approximately 23 km south-east of Edmonton.

The origin of the name of this hamlet on the north-east shore of Cooking Lake, which was established in April 1980, is unknown.

* Columbine (former locality)

73 L/6 - Goodridge
28-61-8-W4
54°18′N 111°07′W
Approximately 27 km west north-west of Bonnyville.

The name for this locality, whose post office operated from July 1915 through February 1944, was taken after the garden plant which has a variety of colours of flowers which when inverted, resemble a cluster of five doves (Latin *columba* dove). The "dove-plant" is the English equivalent of the genus *Aquilegia*. The name was officially rescinded 10 November 1970.

Columbine Creek (creek)

73 L/6 - Goodridge
14-16-62-8-W4
54°22′N 111°09′W
Flows north into Beaver River, approximately 30 km west north-west of Bonnyville.

The name for this creek was officially adopted 28 July 1945. (see Columbine)

Comet (locality)

72 M/13 - Garden Plain
7-33-14-W4
51°49′N 111°59′W
Approximately 20 km north of Hanna.

A post office operated at this site from September 1916 through August 1918 and the first postmaster was named D.F. Halley. There is some indication that the locality was named for Comet Halley, as a play on the name of the first postmaster. The comet was named for Edmond Halley (1656-1742), who was first to predict accurately its return and the first to plot its course precisely. Halley's last appearance was in 1985, but its course was too low for it to be seen well in North America. The return of Comet Halley is scheduled for 2061.

Community Creek (creek)

82 O/10 - Fallentimber Creek
2-32-5-W5
51°43′N 114°44′W
Flows north-east into Fallentimber Creek, approximately 6 km south south-west of Sundre.

The name for this creek was made official in November 1937, but its precise origin is unknown.

Compeer (hamlet)

72 M/16 - Grassy Island Lake
25-33-1-W4
51°52′15″N 110°00′15″W

Approximately 57 km south south-east of Provost.

This hamlet was once known as "Sleepy Hollow." Its early settlers all felt equal, and the name Compeer therefore seemed appropriate. The post office opened under this name in May 1915.

Condor (hamlet)

83 B/7 - Rocky Mountain House
5-39-4-W5
52°20'N 114°33'W
Approximately 13 km west south-west of Eckville.

The Canadian Pacific Railway established a station here in 1914 and named it after H.M.S. *Condor*, a British gunboat commanded by Captain Lord Charles Beresford during the bombardment of Alexandria on 11 July 1882. The Beresfords were big landlords in Ireland. The post office opened in July 1915.

Congresbury (locality)

83 B/2 - Caroline
32-37-7-W5
52°14'N 114°58'W
Approximately 17 km south of Rocky Mountain House.

A post office operated here from September 1937 through December 1950 and was named after a town in Somerset (now Avon), England.

Conjuring Creek (locality)

83 H/4 - Kavanagh
1-49-27-W4
53°12'N 113°49'W
Approximately 20 km west south-west of Leduc.

The post office operated here from April 1900 through June 1939 and took its name from its proximity to Conjuring Creek. (see Conjuring Creek)

Conjuring Creek (creek)

83 H/5 - Leduc
31-50-26-W4
53°22'N 113°48'W
Flows north into North Saskatchewan River, approximately 26 km south-west of Edmonton.

The well-established name for this creek was suggested by the fact that it flows out of Wizard Lake. The Cree name for the watercourse is *paw-ga-mow*, translating to "vomiting" creek. James Hector labels this creek "Ecapotte's Creek," although the origin is not known.

Conn Lake (lake)

73 L/11 - Pinehurst Lake
10,11-64-8-W4
54°31'N 111°07'W
Approximately 38 km north-west of Bonnyville.

This lake was officially named in 1951 and commemorates Leading Steward J. R. Conn, M.I.D., of Hillcrest, Alberta who was killed in World War II. This and Keith Lake are known locally as "Twin Lakes."

* Connelly (former post office)

73 E/2 - Grizzly Bear Creek
11-49-6-W4
53°12'N 110°46'W
Approximately 17 km south south-east of Vermilion.

The name for the post office, which operated here from August 1913 through December 1930, is an error for Connolly. It was supposed to be named for W.A. Connolly, who was the first postmaster.

Connor Creek (creek)

83 J/2 - Thunder Lake
15-58-6-W5
54°01'N 114°50'W
Flows south-east into Paddle River, approximately 22 km east north-east of Mayerthorpe.

The name for this creek was taken after James Connor, an early settler.

Connor Creek (locality)

83 J/3 - Green Court
15-59-8-W5
54°06'N 115°08'W
Approximately 17 km north of Mayerthorpe.

The name for this locality, whose post office operated from February 1913 through June 1965, is taken after James Connor, an early settler.

Consort (village)

73 D/2 - Neutral Hills
15-35-6-W4
52°00'35"N 110°46'50"W
Approximately 53 km south-west of Provost.

This and many other adjacent railway stations including Loyalist, Throne, Veteran, and Coronation were named in the year of the coronation of King George V and his consort Queen Mary in honour of the occasion. The post office was formerly called "Sanderville."

* Content (former post office)

83 A/6 - Alix
34-38-22-W4
52°18'N 113°04'W
Approximately 50 km east of Red Deer.

This post office operated from May 1904 through April 1913 and was named after the first postmaster, A.A. Content.

Contracosta Lake (lake)

72 M/12 - Hanna
25-31-11,12-W4
51°41'N 111°35'W

Approximately 27 km east north-east of Hanna.

The precise origin for the name of this lake is unknown, but many other local names for the feature abound. They include "Brainard Flat," "Badger Lake," "Ferguson Flat" (after Benjamin Ferguson who stated a claim on section 19-31-11 W4 on 5 May 1904), and "Richdale Flat."

Cooking Lake (hamlet)

83 H/6 - Cooking Lake
13-51-22-W4
53°25′N 113°08′W
Approximately 27 km south-east of Edmonton.

The name for this hamlet, whose post office opened in August 1908, is a translation of the Cree word *opi mi now wa sioo*. This area was, apparently, a favourite camping ground for the natives.

Cooking Lake (station)

83 H/6 - Cooking Lake
14-51-22-W4
53°28′N 112°58′W
Approximately 25 km south-east of Edmonton.

(see Cooking Lake)

Cooking Lake (lake)

83 H/6 - Cooking Lake
20-51-21-W4
53°26′N 113°02′W
Approximately 33 km east south-east of Edmonton.

(see Cooking Lake)

Cooking Lake-Blackfoot Grazing, Wildlife and Provincial Recreation Area

(provincial recreation area)

83 H/10 - Elk Island Park
52-19-21-W4
53°25′N 112°50′W
Approximately 40 km east of Edmonton.

This grazing, wildlife and provincial recreation area, whose approximate size is 16 km by 10 km, was established by Order-in-Council No. 533/87 on 7 August 1987. The name became official 23 September 1991. The name comes from the Blackfoot Indians (see Blackfoot Hills) and the nearby Cooking Lake (see Cooking Lake). Concurrence was established from the ministries of Recreation and Parks, Forestry, Lands and Wildlife and the Blackfoot Steering Committee. A request for transfer of this land was processed in February of 1987 from the Provincial Recreation Area, under the Provincial Parks Act.

Coolidge (locality)

83 I/12 - Coolidge
5-65-24-W4
54°35′N 113°35′W
Approximately 17 km south-west of Athabasca.

The post office operated here from December 1937 through February 1969 and was apparently named after Calvin Coolidge (1872–1933), president of the United States from 1923 to 1929.

Cooper Creek (creek)

73 D/3 - Coronation
12-16-37-9-W4
52°10′30″N 111°14′15″W
Flows east into Ribstone Creek, approximately 17 km north-east of Coronation.

This creek needed a name because the Water Survey of Canada built several gauging stations on creeks around the

province, and some of the creeks were not named. For reference purposes, Environment Canada suggested some names, and "Talbot Creek" was the name suggested for this feature, due to its proximity to the locality of Talbot. After some research in the field, it was discovered that there was no local name for this creek, but much support for the name Cooper Creek. Herbert E. Cooper (1882-1955) was an early homesteader in this area, originally from England. He was a carpenter by trade but enjoyed many activities such as farming, shooting and trapping, and he raised three children in the area. There was a Cooper School District established in 1922 and this creek runs through the area. The name was officially approved 17 October 1991.

Copeley Lake (lake)

82 O/16 - Olds
14,23-32-2-W5
51°45′15″N 114°11′00″W
Approximately 7 km south-west of Olds.

The name for this lake has been official since 1958. Two brothers, John and Joe Copley, were homesteaders in the area from at least 1892, and although the spelling of this lake is slightly different, it may be named for them.

* **Copeville** (former post office)

72 M/12 - Hanna
33-30-14-W4
51°38′N 111°54′W
Within the town boundary of Hanna.

The original post office was named after its first postmaster, G.R. Cope. The name for the post office has since been changed to Hanna. (see Hanna)

* **Coppice Hill** (former post office)

83 H/11 - Edmonton
17-53-21-W4
53°34′N 113°03′W
Approximately 35 km east of Edmonton.

The origin for the name of this former post office is unknown.

* **Corbetts** (former post office)

73 L/6 - Goodridge
1-63-9-W4
54°25'N 111°17'W
Approximately 36 km north-west of Bonnyville.

The post office, which operated here from July 1938 through June 1952, was named after W.E. Corbett, the first postmaster. The name was officially rescinded 10 November 1970.

Cordel (locality)

83 A/8 - Halkirk
19-40-15-W4
52°27'N 112°09'W
Approximately 32 km north north-west of Castor.

The origin for the name of this locality is unknown.

Cordwood Lake (lake)

83 I/9 - Hylo
1-65-15-W4
54°36'N 112°16'W
Approximately 22 km south south-west of Lac La Biche.

The name for this lake has been official since 1948, and may refer to the term used for a measure of firewood. Cordwood is firewood sawn into short lengths for use in wood stoves common in most homesteaders' dwellings.

* **Cork** (former post office)

73 L/4 - Cache Lake
35-58-11-W4
54°04'N 111°33'W
Approximately 17 km west north-west of St. Paul.

_____
*denotes rescinded name or former locality.

A post office operated here from May 1910 through November 1956 and was named after a county in Ireland. The name was officially rescinded 10 November 1970.

Corner Lake (lake)

73 L/10 - Marguerite Lake
31-65-6-W4
54°40'30"N 110°54'30"W
Approximately 52 km west north-west of Cold Lake.

The name for this lake has been official since at least 1951, and may be descriptive in that the surveyors who worked in this area in 1916 noticed the way the lake sits squarely on the crossroads of four townships.

Corner Lake (lake)

83 G/15 - Sangudo
30-55-4-W5
53°47'N 114°35'W
Approximately 39 km south south-west of Barrhead.

The name for this lake has been official since at least 1950, but its precise origin is unknown.

Corner Lake (lake)

83 I/10   Boyle
31-64,65-17-W4
54°35'N 112°33'W
Approximately 43 km south-west of Lac La Biche.

The name for this lake has been official since at least 1948 and may refer to its location in a "corner" of the hill immediately south of it.

Cornish Lake (lake)

82 P/10 - Munson
16-32-20-W4
51°45'N 112°46'W

Approximately 35 km east north-east of Three Hills.

The name for this lake has been official since 1958, but its origin is unknown.

Coronado (locality)

83 H/14 - Redwater
36-56-23-W4
53°53'N 113°18'W
Approximately 40 km north north-east of Edmonton.

The post office at this location operated from November 1921 through August 1978. It was named after a town in California, whose name in turn had been taken from Coronado Butte, in Arizona. This butte honoured Francisco Vásquez de Coronado (1510-1554), a Spanish explorer of the North American south-west, whose expeditions resulted in the discovery of many physical landmarks. He may have been the first European explorer to see the Grand Canyon. He was appointed governor of Nueva Galicia in 1538. The name, *coronado*, translated from the Spanish, means "crowned," or "perfectly finished."

Coronation (town)

73 D/3 - Coronation
13-36-11-W4
52°05'30"N 111°27'00"W
Approximately 160 km east of Red Deer.

This town and many adjacent stations were named by the Canadian Pacific Railway in 1911 at the time of the coronation of King George V. The post office opened in December 1911. Many of the street and avenue names in Coronation reflect the royal event and include Victoria, Windsor, Mary, Queen, King, Royal, George and Edward. Even the hotel was called the Royal Crown. This town was incorporated 29 April 1912.

Cosmo (locality)
83 G/15 - Sangudo
23-57-6-W5
53°56′N 114°48′W
Approximately 23 km east of Mayerthorpe.

The name for the post office, which operated here from March 1911 through June 1955, is the Greek word for the world or universe. Six lakes in the general area also have names connected to the Greek alphabet; however the precise references are not known. The names may have been applied by one of the original surveyors to the area, but this is unconfirmed.

* **Cossack** (former locality)
83 I/2 - Waskatenau
29-60-16-W4
54°13′N 112°30′W
Approximately 13 km north north-east of Smoky Lake.

The name for the post office, which operated from July 1935 through December 1958, is the term early Ukrainian settlers used for the people of their homeland. The name was officially rescinded 24 March 1971.

Cosway (locality)
82 P/11 - Three Hills
33-29-25-W4
51°31′N 113°28′W
Approximately 24 km south south-west of Three Hills.

The origin of the name for this station on the Canadian Pacific Railway line is unknown.

Cote, Lac (lake)
73 E/11 - Myrnam
5-54-7-W4
53°38′N 110°59′W

Approximately 28 km south south-west of Elk Point.

The name for this lake has been official since at least 1958, but its precise origin is unknown.

Cottage Lake (lake)
83 G/9 - Onoway
23-52-2-W5
53°30′45″N 114°10′15″W
Approximately 45 km west of Edmonton.

The descriptive name for this lake has been official since at least 1958 and refers to the number of cottages around it.

Cotton Creek (creek)
73 E/12 - Two Hills
23-54-13-W4
53°42′N 111°49′W
Flows north into Vermilion River, approximately 5 km south-west of Two Hills.

The name for this creek has been official since at least 1958, but its precise origin is unknown.

Cotton Lake (lake)
73 D/10 - Hughenden
19-42-5-W4
52°38′N 110°43′W
Approximately 25 km south south-east of the town of Wainwright.

The origin for the name of this feature is unknown.

Cousins (locality)
73 D/2 - Neutral Hills
33-37-5-W4
52°14′N 110°39′W
Approximately 30 km south-west of Provost.

The precise origin for the name of this locality is unknown.

Cow Creek (creek)
83 B/7 - Rocky Mountain House
16-39-8-W5
52°22′N 115°05′W
Flows north into North Saskatchewan River, approximately 12 km west of Rocky Mountain House.

The name for this creek which drains Cow Lake has been official since at least 1958, and is likely named in association with the lake. (see Volume I)

Cow Moose Lake (lake)
83 I/13 - Grosmont
20-68-25-W4
54°54′N 113°46′W
Approximately 39 km north-west of Athabasca.

The name for this lake has been official since at least 1958, but its precise origin is unknown.

Coyote Creek (creek)
83 G/15 - Sangudo
15-57-5-W5
53°56′N 114°40′W
Flows north into Pembina River, approximately 28 km south-west of Barrhead.

The name for this creek has been official since at least 1958 and is likely descriptive; however, this is unconfirmed.

Coyote Hill (hill)
73 D/14 - Irma
35-44-8-W9
52°50′N 111°04′W
Approximately 11 km west of the town of Wainwright.

The precise origin for the name of this feature is unknown; however, it may be due to the number of coyotes in the area.

---

*denotes rescinded name or former locality.

Craig Lake (lake)
72 M/13 - Garden Plain
25-34-12-W4
51°56′N 111°35′W
Approximately 18 km south-west of
Coronation.

The precise origin for the name of this
feature is unknown.

Craigend (locality)
73 L/12 - Beaver Lake
4-65-13-W4
54°35′N 111°56′W
Approximately 20 km south of Lac La
Biche.

The post office operated here from September 1925 through April 1957 and its name is
a Scottish term which translates "end of
rock."

Craigmillar (locality)
73 D/7 - Czar
35-38-7-W4
52°18′N 110°54′W
Approximately 42 km west south-west of
Provost.

The first and only postmaster at this post
office, which operated from May 1913
through November 1929, William Penman,
came from Craigmillar, Edinburgh,
Scotland. There is a castle in the same area
by this name which means "rock of the bare
height."

Craigmyle (hamlet)
82 P/9 - Craigmyle
20-31-16-W4
51°40′N 112°15′W
Approximately 23 km east of Hanna.

The first post office here was called
"Lillico" when it was established in 1910. A

discussion took place in 1912 regarding the
name for a station when one was proposed
by Canadian Northern Railway officials.
One of the settlers suggested Craigmyle
after a Scottish estate and castle with which
she had been associated. It is possible that
the name of the castle was Craigmillar (see
Craigmillar) and that Craigmyle was
adopted to avoid confusion. The term *craig*
is Gaelic for "rock."

Crammond (locality)
83 B/2 - Caroline
29-35-5-W5
52°02′N 114°40′W
Approximately 26 km north of Sundre.

The post office operated here from August
1937 through June 1968 and took its name
from the school district which was established in 1930. The precise origin for the
name is unknown.

Cranberry Creek (creek)
83 B/15 - Buck Lake
7-15-44-7-W5
52°47′25″N 114°55′40″W
Flows west into Rose Creek, approximately
46 km north of Rocky Mountain House.

The well-established name for this creek
has been official since at least 1950 and is
possibly descriptive of the local flora.

Cranberry Lake (lake)
83 B/15 - Buck Lake
21-44-6-W5
52°48′N 114°48′W
Approximately 50 km north north-east of
Rocky Mountain House.

The name for this lake has been official
since 1950 and is likely descriptive.

Crane Island (island)
83 H/10 - Elk Island Park
54-20-W4
53°40′N 112°51′W
Approximately 40 km east of Edmonton.

The name for this island was officially
approved 12 December 1939 and is likely
descriptive.

Crane Lake (lake)
73 L/10 - Marguerite Lake
64-4-W4
54°31′N 110°31′W
Approximately 23 km west north-west of
Cold Lake.

In 1989 the Advisory Council for Improvement District No. 18(S) requested that the
Municipal Affairs Office, Planning Services
Division, undertake the preparation of an
Area Structure Plan for Moore Lake.
During public workshops held to discuss
development and environmental concerns,
the local residents requested that the name
revert to the original and more commonly
known Crane Lake. The lake lot owners
and regional lake users simply do not refer
to the lake as Moore Lake, the official
name. It is known as Crane Lake because of
the abundance of sandhill cranes who nest
or feed in close proximity to the lake. The
name Moore Lake was taken after Dr.
Bromley Moore, president of the Alberta
College of Physicians and Surgeons. He
was a friend of the early government land
surveyor, Marshall Hopkins. It was felt by
all residents who were interviewed that the
name should be changed to reflect a more
distinctive characterization of the lake as
well as represent the name everyone in the
region uses. The name was officially
changed in 1993.

Crane Lake (lake)
83 J/9 - Flatbush
2-64-2-W5
54°31′N 114°13′W

Approximately 45 km north north-west of
Westlock.

The name for this lake has been official
since at least 1953, but its precise origin is
unknown.

Cranes Lake (lake)

83 G/16 - Lac la Nonne
5-58-2-W5
53°59′N 114°16′W
Approximately 17 km south south-east of
Barrhead.

The name for this lake has been official
since at least 1950, but its precise origin is
unknown.

Creekland (locality)

83 G/8 - Genesee
12-50-4-W5
53°18′N 114°26′W
Approximately 37 km east north-east of
Drayton Valley.

A post office operated here from December
1936 through April 1946, but its precise
origin is unknown.

Cremona (village)

82 O/9 - Didsbury
3-30-4-W5
51°33′N 114°29′W
Approximately 28 km west of Carstairs.

The name for this village is taken after the
city of the same name in Italy famous for its
violins. The post office opened in September 1906.

Crestomere (locality)

83 A/12 - Ponoka
6-43-27-W4
52°40′05″N 113°54′55″W
Approximately 20 km west of Ponoka.

The locality became known as Crestomere
in the early 1950s when Crestomere
Consolidated School opened. The precise
origin for the name is unknown.

Crestomere Lake (lake)

83 A/12 - Ponoka
6-27-43-W4
52°40′25″N 113°55′05″W
Approximately 23 km west of Ponoka.

The lake has been known locally by this
name since the 1950s when the consolidated
school was built nearby.

Crimson Lake (locality)

83 B/6 - Crimson Lake
24-40-8-W5
52°27′N 115°02′W
Approximately 11 km north-west of Rocky
Mountain House.

This locality was named in 1959 for its
location on the south-east shore of Crimson Lake. (see Crimson Lake)

Crimson Lake (lake)

83 B/6 - Crimson Lake
23-40-8-W5
52°27′N 115°02′W
Approximately 12 km north-west of Rocky
Mountain House.

This lake was first seen by surveyors during
a dramatically coloured sunset that was
reflected in the water. The descriptive name
has been official since at least 1958.

Crimson Lake Provincial Park

(provincial park)
83 B/6 - Crimson Lake
40-7,8-W5
52°28′N 115°04′W
Approximately 14 km north-west of Rocky
Mountain House.

This provincial park was created by Order-
in-Council No. 1437/75 and encloses
Crimson Lake. (see Crimson Lake)

Crippsdale (locality)

83 I/3 - Thorhild
19-59-21-W4
54°07′N 113°09′W
Approximately 18 km north of Redwater.

The name for this locality, whose post
office operated from March 1912 through
January 1942, was named for M.J. Cripps,
the first and only postmaster.

Crooked Creek (creek)

83 B/1 - Markerville
11-31-35-3-W5
52°03′10″N 114°25′15″W
Flows north-east into Raven River,
approximately 32 km north north-east of
Sundre.

The name for this creek describes its
winding course. The district is still locally
known as Crooked Creek, the name of the
school district which operated from 1911
through 1956.

Crooked Lake (lake)

83 B/8 - Sylvan Lake
32,33-40-2-W5
52°29′N 114°14′W
Approximately 40 km north north-west of
Red Deer.

The descriptive name for this lake has been
official since 1958.

Crooked Lake (lake)

83 I/13 - Grosmont
26-68-24-W4
54°55′N 113°33′W
Approximately 28 km north north-west of
Athabasca.

The name for this lake was officially adopted in 1953 and is likely descriptive.

Crookedheel Creek (creek)

73 E/14 - St. Paul
19-57-7-W4
53°57'N 111°02'W
Flows south-west into Dog Rump Creek, approximately 10 km north-west of Elk Point.

The name for this creek appears as early as 1958, but its precise origin is unknown.

Cross Lake (lake)

73 L/12 - Beaver Lake
11-64-12-W4
54°31'N 111°43'W
Approximately 34 km south-east of Lac La Biche.

The name for this lake has been official since at least 1958, but its precise origin is unknown.

Cross Lake Provincial Park

(provincial park)

83 I/12 - Coolidge
25-65-26-W4
54°39'N 113°48'W
Approximately 30 km west south-west of Athabasca.

This park was established by Order-in-Council No. 1389/74 and is a very popular lakeside park.

Crosscut Lake (lake)

83 I/9 - Hylo
6-66-15-W4
54°41'00"N 112°15'15"W
Approximately 22 km south-west of Lac La Biche.

The name for this lake has been official since at least 1958 and, although it is unconfirmed, may refer to a type of saw

used for cutting firewood into lengths. It may date back to the days when this locality was the focus of attention for the Northwest Lumber Company; however, the crosscut saw was a tool of the homesteader more than the logger.

Crossing Lake (lake)

73 D/15 - Wainwright
20-44-7-W4
52°48'N 110°58'W
Approximately 10 km west south-west of the town of Wainwright.

The origin for the name of this feature is unknown.

Crude Hill (hill)

73 D/11 - Hardisty
14-43-8-W4
52°41'N 111°02'W
Approximately 17 km east north-east of Hardisty.

The name for this hill has been in use since at least 1954, but its origin is unknown.

Crystal Lake (lake)

73 E/6 - Mannville
29-50-10-W4
53°21'N 111°26'W
Approximately 37 km north-east of Viking.

The name for this lake has been official since at least 1958 and may be descriptive.

Crystal Springs (summer village)

83 B/16 - Winfield
23-46-1-W5
52°59'N 114°02'W
Approximately 44 km west of Wetaskiwin.

This summer village on the south-east shore of Pigeon Lake was incorporated 1 January 1957 and has a descriptive name.

Cucumber Creek (creek)

73 E/13 - Hairy Hill
11-57-14-W4
53°55'N 111°59'W
Flows north-east into North Saskatchewan River, approximately 27 km north-west of Two Hills.

The name for this creek, which flows near Cucumber Lake, has been official since at least 1958.

Cucumber Lake (lake)

83 H/16 - Willingdon
1-57-15-W4
53°54'N 112°06'W
Approximately 55 km west south-west of St. Paul.

The name for this lake has been official since at least 1958, but its precise origin is unknown; however, its elongated shape may be likened to that of a cucumber.

* Cummings (former locality)

73 E/2 - Grizzly Bear Creek
12-48-7-W4
53°07'N 110°54'W
Approximately 25 km south of Vermilion.

The name for this former locality commemorates the Cummings brothers, early general merchants. J.T. Cummings was the first postmaster at the post office, which operated from March 1908 through May 1942. The name was officially rescinded 18 January 1974.

Curlew (locality)

82 P/14 - Trochu
2-33-25-W4
51°48'N 113°27'W
Approximately 15 km north-west of Three Hills.

The name for this locality was taken from the post office, which operated from April

1906 through January 1930. The name is taken from the bird commonly called a sandpiper, of which there is an abundance in this area.

Curly Hill (hill)
73 D/11 - Hardisty
30-43-8-W4
52°44'20"N 111°08'30"W
Approximately 13 km north-east of Hardisty.

The name apparently originated during the Buffalo Park period from the buffalo wool that accumulated on the hill. (see Buffalo Park)

Currant Island (island)
73 L/13 - Lac La Biche
5-68-13-W4
54°51'N 111°57'W
Approximately 10 km north of Lac La Biche.

The name for this island in Lac La Biche has been official since 3 May 1951, but its precise origin is unknown.

Currant Lake (lake)
72 M/16 - Grassy Island Lake
19-33-3-W4
51°51'N 110°24'W
Approximately 55 km north of Oyen.

The name may be descriptive of the berries found in the area, but the precise origin for the name of this feature is unknown.

Cushing Lake (lake)
73 L/1 - Reita Lake
31-58-3-W4
54°03'N 110°26'W
Approximately 30 km south-east of Bonnyville.

The name for this lake has been official since at least 1958, but its precise origin is unknown.

Cut Bank Lake (lake)
83 H/12 - St. Albert
20-54-24-W4
53°41'N 113°31'W
Approximately 15 km north of Edmonton.

(see Cutbank Creek)

Cut-Off Coulee (coulee)
82 P/9 - Craigmyle
8,9-16-30-17-W4
51°34'00"N 112°19'40"W
Approximately 34 km west south-west of Hanna.

This coulee was used as a short-cut by ranchers in the Hand Hills when going to Delia during the early 1900s. The name refers to the head of a nearby valley adjacent to the television tower. The name is well-established among the local residents.

Cutbank Creek (creek)
83 H/5 - Leduc
9-50-27-W4
53°18'30"N 113°53'30"W
Flows north into North Saskatchewan River, approximately 30 km south-west of Edmonton.

This name is descriptive, referring to the extensive number of cutbanks found along the channel through which this creek flows. Cutbanks are usually the steeper of the two riverbanks, located at the point where a river bends. The river is usually deeper and the current swifter along this bank, and the shoreline tends to drop off steeply. A greater amount of erosion will occur along this riverbank, often creating overhangs.

Cutbank Lake (lake)
83 A/1 - Hackett
35-35-17-W4
52°03'N 112°19'W
Approximately 34 km south-west of Castor.

This descriptive name refers to the cutbanks on the edge of the lake.

Cygnet (locality)
83 A/5 - Red Deer
16-38-28-W4
52°16'N 113°57'W
Approximately 8 km west of Red Deer.

The Alberta Central Railway, acquired by the Canadian Pacific Railway in 1912, established a station here and named it for its proximity to "Swan Lake," which was later changed to Sylvan Lake. The small lake takes its name from the same source. A cygnet is a young swan.

Cygnet Lake (lake)
83 B/8 - Sylvan Lake
25-38-1-W5
52°16'30"N 114°01'00"W
Approximately 15 km west of Red Deer.

(see Cygnet)

Cynthia (hamlet)
83 G/6 - Easyford
5-50-10-W5
53°17'N 115°25'W
Approximately 30 km west north-west of Drayton Valley.

A post office was established here in November 1964, and was named after the daughter of the first hotelkeeper of the town that was dissolved in June 1959. The Gazetteer of Canada (1958 edition) lists Cynthia as a town.

Cyr, Lac (lake)
73 E/14 - St. Paul
17-57-10-W4
53°55′N 111°28′W
Approximately 13 km south-west of St.
Paul.

This lake may be named for Sylvestre Cyr,
one of the early pioneers of the St. Paul
district, who filed on a homestead in April
1909.

Czar (village)
73 D/7 - Czar
20-40-6-W4
52°27′15″N 110°49′20″W
Approximately 40 km west north-west of
Provost.

This village was incorporated 12 November
1917; after the post office having been
established 10 October 1910. In spite of the
Russian-derived word (meaning "Caesar"
or "Emperor"), the population of the
settlement contained no Slavic element.
Most of the early settlers, in fact, were of
British and Scandinavian origin from
Eastern Canada and the United States. The
origin of this name is, therefore, quite
obscure. One theory points to a possibility
that one of the grade builders was of
Russian ancestry. This branch of the
Canadian Pacific Railway was completed in
1910, and since it was required that new
sidings be given a new non-duplicated name
for identification, the name Czar was
chosen. Another possibility for the origin
of the name suggests that it may have
reminded someone of the Anglo-Russian
Treaty signed in 1907, the basis for the
Allied forces during World War I. It further
may have referred to the boss of a railway
gang, often dubbed "Czar." Quite often,
these temporary names for settlements were
changed as the community grew, but this
one remained.

D~E

Dabbs Lake (lake)
73 L/14 - Touchwood Lake
12-4-67-10-W4
54°46′20″N 111°28′50″W
Approximately 32 km east of Lac La Biche.

The name for this lake was officially applied in 1951 and commemorates Pilot Officer H.E. Dabbs, D.F.C. (1922-1942) of Daysland, who was a casualty of World War II. Its Cree name, *Hamschigosik Sagahegan*, is descriptive and translates "Little Island Lake."

* **Dakin** (former locality)
83 I/15 - Grassland
17-67-17-W4
54°48′N 112°35′W
Approximately 48 km east of Athabasca.

The post office, which operated here from June 1925 through May 1948, was named after the first postmaster and M.L.A. for Beaver River. The name was officially rescinded in 1970. (see Dakin Lake)

Dakin Lake (lake)
83 I/15 - Grassland
15-6-67-17-W4
54°46′35″N 112°34′56″W
Approximately 40 km west of Lac La Biche.

This lake and the nearby post office were named for Henry Hansford Dakin (1870-1956). Dakin was originally from Nova Scotia and came to this area to homestead in 1919. He was the Liberal M.L.A. for the area from 1930 to 1935 but was defeated in the Social Credit sweep.

* **Dalmuir** (former locality)
83 H/15 - Lamont
8-58-20-W4
54°00′N 112°57′W

*denotes rescinded name or former locality.

Approximately 27 km south-west of Smoky Lake.

A post office operated here from January 1913 through January 1956 and was named after a town near Glasgow, Scotland. The derivation of the name is the Gaelic term for "big field."

Dancing Lake (lake)
83 I/13 - Grosmont
28-69-26-W4
55°00′N 113°55′W
Approximately 50 km north-west of Athabasca.

The name for this lake has been official since at least 1958, but its precise origin is unknown.

Danube (locality)
83 I/6 - Perryvale
22-62-21-W4
54°22′N 113°04′W
Approximately 41 km south south-east of Athabasca.

The post office operated here from November 1930 through March 1942 and was named after the river in Europe.

Dapp (hamlet)
83 I/5 - Dapp
12-62-27-W4
54°22′N 113°55′W
Approximately 21 km north of Westlock.

A post office opened here in October 1917 and was named after David A. Pennicuick, an accountant with the Edmonton, Dunvegan and British Columbia Railway. It was previously known as "Eunice."

Dapp Creek (creek)
83 I/5 - Dapp
9-62-27-W4
54°21′N 113°59′W

Flows west into Pembina River, approximately 24 km north north-west of Westlock.

(see Dapp)

Dapp Lake (lake)
83 I/5 - Dapp
12-62-25-W4
54°20′N 113°36′W
Approximately 28 km north-east of Westlock.

(see Dapp)

* **Darling** (former locality)
83 I/7 - Newbrook
30-61-19-W4
54°18′N 112°50′W
Approximately 33 km north-west of Smoky Lake.

The name for this locality, whose post office operated from September 1927 through June 1952, was officially rescinded 30 July 1970. Its precise origin is unknown.

Darwell (hamlet)
83 G/10 - Isle Lake
13-54-5-W5
53°40′N 114°35′W
Approximately 42 km west north-west of Stony Plain.

The Canadian Northern Railway established a station here in 1915, and originally chose the name of a biblical character, Darwall. The "a" was changed to an "e," but it is not clear why. The post office opened in June 1916.

Davey Lake (lake)

82 P/13 - Torrington
21-34-27-W4
51°56'00"N 113°45'15"W
Approximately 15 km south-east of
Innisfail.

This lake was named in 1892 after an early
settler.

David Lake (lake)

73 D/10 - Hughenden
2-42-5-W4
52°35'N 110°37'W
Approximately 32 km south-east of the
town of Wainwright.

The precise origin for the name of this
feature is unknown.

Dawson's Hill (hill)

82 O/16 - Olds
4-9-33-1-W5
51°48'50"N 114°05'40"W
Approximately 1 km north of Olds.

John Dawson and his family lived on top of
this hill (a drumlin formed by the glaciers)
as early as the 1910s and remained there
until at least the 1930s (no later than the
1940s). The hill was a very popular spot for
tobogganing and skiing. There is still
evidence of the foundation of Dawson's
house on this hill. The locally well-
established name was officially approved 16
October 1991.

Day Lake (lake)

73 L/1 - Reita Lake
4-60-1-W4
54°09'N 110°05'W
Approximately 29 km south south-east of
Grand Centre.

The name for this lake has been official
since at least 1958, but its precise origin is
unknown.

Daysland (town)

83 A/16 - Daysland
9-45-16-W4
52°52'40"N 112°15'25"W
Approximately 40 km east south-east of
Camrose.

The Canadian Pacific Railway established a
station here in 1905 and named it after
Egerton W. Day (1863-?), the first settler
and a local landowner, who arrived in the
area in 1888. He returned to Ontario
shortly after, but came back to this area in
1904, and formed the Central Alberta Land
Corporation. The post office opened in
September 1906, and it was incorporated as
a town 2 April 1907, with E.W. Day as the
first mayor.

Dead Bull Lake (lake)

82 P/16 - Farrell Lake
34-12-34-17-W4
51°53'50"N 112°17'20"W
Approximately 36 km north-east of Hanna.

This lake received its name after an incident
involving a fight between several bulls
during the late 1800s or early 1900s. The
bulls apparently died in the lake after
becoming mired in the mud since the lake
often covers 300 acres during high water.

Deadman Lake (lake)

83 G/16 - Lac la Nonne
25-56-1-W5
53°52'N 114°01'W
Approximately 38 km south-east of
Barrhead.

The name for this lake is a rough translation
of a native name, *hahpeukaketachtch*, or
"man-who-got-stabbed." According to
Major-General Sir Sam Steele, of the Royal
North-West Mounted Police, legend has it
that a Cree was stabbed here in a drunken
row. The lake was also previously known
as "Berland Lake," after a fur trader.

Deadman's Lake (lake)

73 D/2 - Neutral Hills
15-4-38-4-W4
52°14'30"N 110°30'50"W
Approximately 22 km south-west of
Provost.

This lake takes its name from an incident
that occurred in 1896 when Charlie
Lennox, an ex-North-West Mounted Police
officer, was found dead beside the lake. The
name is well established in local use and
was officially adopted 22 January 1992.

Deadrick Coulee (coulee)

82 P/12 - Lonepine Creek
11-30-29-W4
51°34'N 113°59'W
Approximately 12 km east of Didsbury.

Charles Deadrick (pronounced Deed' rik)
bought a half-section of Canadian Pacific
Railway land along this coulee halfway
between Olds and Didsbury in 1901. Of his
five sons, three remained farming in the
area, his son John on the original farm until
at least 1969. The name is well known
locally, but the name "Baker Coulee" is
also locally used.

Deadrick Creek (creek)

82 O/9 - Didsbury
33-31-1-W5
51°43'30"N 114°05'00"W
Approximately 6 km east of Didsbury.

(see Deadrick Coulee)

Death River (river)

73 E/15 - Elk Point
15-56-7-W4
53°49'N 110°58'W
Flows north-west into North Saskatchewan
River, approximately 8 km south south-
west of Elk Point.

The name for this river has been official since at least 1958, but its precise origin is unknown.

* Deaver (former post office)

73 L/3 - Vincent Lake
9-60-10-W4
54°09′N 111°27′W
Approximately 21 km north north-west of St. Paul.

The name for the post office, which operated here from August 1916 through February 1931, was taken after G.C. Deaver, the first postmaster. The name was later changed to Boscombe.

* Debney (former railway point)

83 I/5 - Dapp
5-61-26-W4
54°16′N 113°52′W
Approximately 11 km north of Westlock.

This railway point now located in the hamlet of Pibroch was named after Philip Debney, an engineer. (see Pibroch)

Dechaine Lake (lake)

83 G/16 - Lac la Nonne
17-56-1-W5
53°50′N 114°06′W
Approximately 36 km south south-east of Barrhead.

The name for this lake has been official since at least 1958, but its precise origin is unknown.

Deep Creek (creek)

83 G/11 - Chip Lake
1-13-54-9-W5
53°39′32″N 115°11′03″W
Flows south into Lobstick River, approximately 32 km south of Mayerthorpe.

The well-established name for this creek was officially adopted 24 September 1991 and is likely descriptive.

Deep Lake (lake)

83 J/9 - Flatbush
6-65,66-2-W5
54°41′N 114°17′W
Approximately 61 km north of Barrhead.

The name for this lake is likely descriptive. It was officially changed from "Athabina Lake" 6 September 1951 to reflect local usage. "Athabina" was the name formed when "Athabasca" and "Pembina" were combined.

Deer Creek (creek)

73 E/8 - Lloydminster
14-52-4-W4
53°29′N 110°29′W
Flows south into Vermilion River, approximately 30 km north-east of Vermilion.

The name for this creek has been official since at least 1958 and is likely descriptive.

* Deerland (former locality)

83 H/15 - Lamont
2-57-20-W4
53°54′N 112°52′W
Approximately 17 km north-east of Lamont.

A post office operated here from November 1947 through October 1953 and was named for the large population of deer found in this region.

* Deermound (former locality)

83 H/6 - Cooking Lake
18-52-22-W4
53°29′N 113°14′W
Approximately 33 km east of Edmonton.

A post office operated here from September 1911 through August 1926 and was named for the large population of deer that once inhabited the region.

Delburne (village)

83 A/3 - Delburne
21-37-23-W4
52°11′50″N 113°13′50″W
Approximately 40 km east south-east of Red Deer.

The origin of this name is uncertain, but there are said to be two possible sources. The first is that before the Grand Trunk Pacific Railway arrived in 1911, the original post office was known as Gaetz Valley Post Office and was five kilometres east of the present village. When the railway came the post office was moved to the townsite and the station is said to have been named Delburne from Della Mewburn, sister of Dr. (later Colonel) F.H. Mewburn (1858-1929), a pioneer medical practitioner.

The second possible origin of the name is that when the G.T.P. reached the location of the present village the railway officials gave a list of names to the owners of the land acquired for the townsite – M.J. Manning and W.C. Clendening – who discussed names with other settlers. Delburne (sometimes in the past spelled "Delbourne") proved the most popular and so was chosen.

Delburne Lakes (lake)

83 A/3 - Delburne
27-37-23-W4
52°12′N 113°13′W
Approximately 41 km east south-east of Red Deer.

(see Delburne)

Delia (village)
82 P/9 - Craigmyle
5-31-17-W4
51°37'45"N 112°22'20"W
Approximately 30 km west of Hanna.

A post office opened here in August 1909, and was named after the wife of the local shopkeeper, A.L. Davis. Mr. Davis also had a stopping house called "Delia's Stopping House." The stopping house was very important in the early days of the development of the West. As the country north of Calgary opened up to settlement and the stage coaches began regular journeys between Calgary and Edmonton carrying mail, freight and passengers, a string of stopping houses, usually approximately 32 km apart, appeared along the trail. They would provide a place of safety and relative comfort for oxen, horses, and people, to rest and eat before journeying on the next day. The coming of the railroad in 1891 spelled the end of the stopping house. Freight and mail were sent on the rails, but for several years the stopping houses still served settlers arriving with their wagons pulled by oxen and horses. In 1913 the Canadian Northern Railway purchased land for a townsite called "Highland" as it was the highest point between Saskatoon and Drumheller on the Saskatoon-Calgary line. With the village called Highland and the post office named Delia, there was considerable confusion among local people, so the government and the railway changed the name of the village to Delia. This village was incorporated 20 July 1914.

* Delnorte (former post office)
73 E/5 - Innisfree
10-51-11-W4
53°22'N 111°32'W
Approximately 36 km east south-east of Vegreville.

---

*denotes rescinded name or former locality.

The name for this post office, which operated from May 1905 through July 1909, was a rendering of the name of Del Norte, a town in Missouri. It was then changed to Innisfree. (see Innisfree)

Delorme, Lac (lake)
73 E/14 - St. Paul
5-57-8-W4
53°54'N 111°10'W
Approximately 14 km south south-east of St. Paul.

The name for this lake has been official since at least 1958, but its precise origin is unknown.

Delph (locality)
83 I/2 - Waskatenau
18-58-18-W4
54°00'N 112°40'W
Approximately 22 km east north-east of Redwater.

The name for this locality, whose post office operated from January 1913 through January 1965, is a variation of Delft, a type of glazed earthenware from the Dutch city of that name.

Delta Lake (lake)
83 G/12 - Carrot Creek
1-55-11-W5
53°43'00"N 115°30'15"W
Approximately 53 km east north-east of Edson.

The name for this lake has been official since at least 1958. *Delta* is the fourth letter of the Greek alphabet; however, its connection to this lake is not clear.

Delusion Lakes (lake)
73 D/14 - Irma
15-44-9-W4
52°47'N 111°13'W
Approximately 13 km north north-east of Hardisty.

The precise origin for the name of this feature is unknown.

Demay (locality)
83 H/2 - Camrose
8-48-19-W4
53°07'N 112°44'W
Approximately 15 km north north-east of Camrose.

(see Demay Lake)

Demay Lake (lake)
83 H/2 - Camrose
10-48-19-W4
53°08'N 112°42'W
Approximately 15 km north north-east of Camrose.

The name for this lake was after a settler in 1893. It was formerly "Flat Lake" which is a translation of the Cree *ka-ta-ta-kwa-cha-o-ka-mak* (Tyrrell).

Denning Lake (lake)
73 L/3 - Vincent Lake
28-60-10-W4
54°13'N 111°27'W
Approximately 27 km north north-west of St. Paul.

The name for this feature was officially approved 6 July 1950 and was named after F. Denning who owned the north-east quarter-section near the lake.

Dent Lake (lake)
72 M/14 - Kirkpatrick Lake
12-34-11-W4
51°54'N 111°26'W
Approximately 21 km south of Coronation.

The precise origin for the name of this feature is unknown.

Denwood (post office)

73 D/15 - Wainwright
25-44-7-W4
52°49′N 110°53′W
Approximately 3 km south-west of the
town of Wainwright.

The origin is not known for this post office,
which is located in the Wainwright Regional Training Area in the built-up area
known as Camp Wainwright.

Deroches, Lac (lake)

73 E/4 - Viking
15-47-11-W4
53°03′N 111°32′W
Approximately 18 km east south-east of
Viking.

The name for this lake was officially
adopted 11 September 1941, but its precise
origin is unknown.

Derwent (village)

73 E/10 - Clandonald
9-54-7-W4
53°39′15″N 110°58′00″W
Approximately 27 km south of Elk Point.

The name for this village, whose post office
opened in August 1928, is taken after
Derwentwater, England, and was applied
by Canadian Pacific Railway men. This
name appears as long ago as circa 730 when
Bede wrote of *Deruuentionist fluuii*
(Derwent River). The name appears in
several counties for different features in
England. *Derwentwater* is roughly translated "river where oaks were common."
This village was incorporated 25 June 1930.

Deserters Creek (creek)

83 B/11 - Baptiste River
31-42-8-W5
52°40′N 115°08′W

Flows south-east into Baptiste River,
approximately 25 km north north-west of
Rocky Mountain House.

The name for this creek has been official
since 1959, but its precise origin is unknown.

* Desjarlais (former locality)

83 H/16 - Willingdon
9-57-14-W4
53°54′N 112°02′W
Approximately 30 km north-west of Two
Hills.

A post office operated here from December
1903 through January 1958 and was named
after David Desjarlais, the first postmaster.

Desmaw Lake (lake)

73 L/12 - Beaver Lake
1-64-14-W4
54°30′15″N 111°59′00″W
Approximately 29 km south of Lac La
Biche.

The name for this lake has been official
since at least 1958, but its precise origin is
unknown. The local name for the feature is
"Matthew's Lake," after Matthew Houle
who was a trapper circa 1930.

Deville (locality)

83 H/7 - Tofield
32-51-20-W4
53°27′N 112°55′W
Approximately 50 km east south-east of
Edmonton.

A Canadian Pacific Railway station opened
here in 1909. The post office operated here
from September 1910 through October
1985 and was named after Dr. Edouard-
Gaston Deville (1849-1924), the Surveyor-
General of Canada. Deville, as one of the
first Honorary Members of the Alpine
Club of Canada, introduced photo -

topographic surveying into this country,
and Arthur Oliver Wheeler pioneered its
application to the mapping of the Rocky
Mountains in 1895. Dr. Deville remained in
charge of surveys until his death.

Devon (town)

83 H/5 - Leduc
34-50-26-W4
53°21′40″N 113°43′10″W
Approximately 30 km south-west of
Edmonton.

Before 1947, the site where Devon now
stands was an open grain field. After the oil
discovery by Imperial Oil Ltd. in 1947,
from the Leduc #1 oil site, it was decided to
create a model town on the banks of the
North Saskatchewan River to serve the
surrounding oil fields. This company town
was named after the geological formation
(i.e., of the Devonian system) in which the
oil had been found. A Mr. Johnson of the
Imperial Oil Company of Toronto,
submitted the name for the community,
whose post office opened in September
1948. This town was incorporated 24
February 1950.

Devonia Lake (lake)

73 E/1 - Paradise Valley
19-49-1-W4
53°14′N 110°08′W
Approximately 10 km west south-west of
Lloydminster.

The name for this lake has been official
since at least 1958, but its precise origin is
unknown.

* Dewar (former locality)

83 I/9 - Hylo
SW-3-66-15-W4
54°41′N 112°10′W
Approximately 17 km south-west of Lac La
Biche.

This was an Alberta & Great Waterways Railway station before 1928. The precise origin for the name is unknown.

Dewberry (village)
73 E/10 - Clandonald
21-53-4-W4
53°35′15″N 110°31′25″W
Approximately 43 km south-east of Elk Point.

The name for this village, whose post office opened in June 1907, was suggested by a pioneer woman who happened into the local store with a bucket of dewberries. The dewberry *(Rubus pubescens)* is commonly called the trailing raspberry and is common in the parklands of Alberta in damp woods and thickets. This village was incorporated 1 January 1957.

Dewdrop Lake (lake)
82 P/16 - Farrell Lake
28-32-17-W4
51°46′N 112°21′W
Approximately 33 km north-west of Hanna.

The name for this lake has been official since 1958, but its precise origin is unknown.

* Diana (former post office)
83 A/14 - Wetaskiwin
24-46-23-W4
52°59′N 113°11′W
Approximately 11 km east north-east of Wetaskiwin.

The post office, which operated here from July 1902 through March 1906, was named after the daughter of the first postmaster, Thomas Rodberg. The name was later changed to Gwynne. (see Gwynne)

---

*denotes rescinded name or former locality.

Dick Lake (lake)
83 B/16 - Winfield
9-44-1-W5
52°46′N 114°05′W
Approximately 12 km north-east of Rimbey.

The name for this lake has been official since 1960, but its precise origin is unknown.

Dickson (hamlet)
83 B/1 - Markerville
1-36-3-W5
52°03′N 114°19′W
Approximately 24 km west of Innisfail.

This hamlet was first settled in 1903 by a group of Danish settlers from Omaha, Nebraska. The Dickson School District was organized 12 January 1906; the school was located at 1-36-3-W5. A post office operated here from February 1906 through February 1970, when it was moved to Spruceview. It was named after Dickson Creek. (see Dickson Creek)

Dickson Creek (creek)
83 B/1 - Markerville
24-36-2-W5
52°06′N 114°09′W
Flows north-east into Medicine River, approximately 15 km west north-west of Innisfail.

This creek takes its name from an early settler who came from Norway, a Mr. Benedickson.

Didsbury (town)
82 O/9 - Didsbury
18-31-1-W5
51°39′40″N 114°08′00″W
Approximately 70 km south south-west of Red Deer.

The Canadian Pacific Railway established a station here in 1892 or 1893 and named it after Didsbury, Manchester, England. The name is of ancient origin, derived from *Dedibiry* (Assize Rolls, 1246) and *Didsbiru* (Assize Rolls, 1267) and *Dyddi's brug* (Ekwall). The post office was established in January 1895. Although the name is of English origin, the original settlement was Mennonite. This town was incorporated 27 September 1906.

Dillberry Lake (lake)
73 D/9 - Chauvin
36-41-1-W4
52°35′N 110°00′W
Approximately 33 km north-east of Provost.

The name for this lake was likely derived from its location within the park of the same name.

Dillberry Lake Provincial Park
(provincial park)
73 D/9 - Chauvin
41,42-1-W4
52°35′N 110°01′W
Approximately 30 km north-east of Provost.

The origin of the name for this provincial park, established by Order-in-Council No. 810/78, is unknown.

Dina (locality)
73 D/16 - McLaughlin
33-45-1-W4
52°56′N 110°05′W
Approximately 40 km south south-west of Lloydminster.

When the post office first opened in March 1908, a name was required. It was decided by local residents to name the tiny locality after the only little girl living in the district whose name was Dina (Dee' na) Sand. The post office remained in operation using this name until April 1937.

Dinant (locality)

83 H/2 - Camrose
12-48-20-W4
53°08′N 112°49′W
Approximately 12 km north of Camrose.

The original post office at this site was called "Pretty Hill," but the name was changed in May 1913 to Dinant by one of the earliest settlers, François Adam. His home town was Dinant, Belgium. The post office closed in June 1959.

Dinosaur (railway point)

82 P/10 - Munson
14-30-20-W4
51°34′N 112°43′W
Approximately 42 km east south-east of Three Hills.

The name for this railway point is likely due to the feature's proximity to Drumheller and Dinosaur Provincial Park. The provincial park encloses one of the most extensive and productive sources of Cretaceous dinosaur fossils in the world. Over seventy million years ago, this area provided a fertile habitat for dinosaurs.

* Dinwoodie (former post office)

73 E/5 - Innisfree
4-52-13-W4
53°27′N 111°52′W
Approximately 13 km east south-east of Vegreville.

The post office operated here from October 1903 through July 1909 and was named after R. Dinwoodie, the postmaster. The name was then changed to Lavoy. (see Lavoy)

_____
*denotes rescinded name or former locality.

Dion Lake (lake)

73 E/15 - Elk Point
1-58-5-W4
56°59′N 110°37′W
Approximately 22 km north-east of Elk Point.

The name for this lake has been official since at least 1958, but its precise origin is unknown.

* Dirleton (former post office)

73 L/7 - Bonnyville
16-61-4-W4
54°16′N 110°32′W
Approximately 13 km east of Bonnyville.

A post office operated here from February 1933 through April 1960 and was named after a town in East Lothian (now Lothian), Scotland. The name was officially rescinded 3 December 1970.

Dismal Creek (creek)

83 G/4 - Zeta Lake
29-47-11-W5
53°05′N 115°34′W
Flows east into Pembina River, approximately 40 km west south-west of Drayton Valley.

The name for this creek has been official since at least 1958, but its precise origin is unknown.

Dixon Lake (lake)

73 D/10 - Hughenden
2-42-6-W4
52°35′30″N 110°45′30″W
Approximately 27 km south south-east of the town of Wainwright.

The name for this lake has been in use since at least 1958, but its precise origin is unknown.

Doan (locality)

82 O/16 - Olds
3-35-34-1-W5
51°58′N 114°03′W
Approximately 10 km south-west of Innisfail.

A Canadian Pacific Railway station was established here in 1961 and this name was suggested by the C.P.R. officials. C.L. Doan was the Reeve of the Municipal District of Red Deer No. 55, Red Deer, and had, at that time, lived in the Municipality for over fifty years and was a member of the Municipal Council for seventeen years. Mr. Doan's father was one of the earliest settlers in the district, arriving in 1894.

* Dobson (former station)

72 M/6 - Plover Lake
20-29-8-W4
51°30′N 111°06′W
Approximately 44 km west north-west of Oyen.

This former Canadian Northern Railway station was established in 1914, but the precise origin for its name is unknown. The shelter was moved to Richdale.

Dodds (locality)

83 H/2 - Camrose
15-49-18-W4
53°14′N 112°33′W
Approximately 29 km north-east of Camrose.

A post office operated here from October 1913 through May 1918 then reopened from May 1927 through March 1970. (see Dodds Lake)

Dodds Lake (lake)

83 A/4 - Innisfail
28,29-354-28-W4
52°02′00″N 113°57′20″W
Immediately north-west of Innisfail.

The lake was named for John Dodd, one of the earliest settlers in the area. He homesteaded a quarter-section on the north-east side of the lake in 1886 or 1887. The old John Dodd house still stands on the north-east shore of the lake and the Dodd family still owns the property beside the lake; a grandson and great-grandson are farming it at present.

Dodgson Lake (lake)

83 J/2 - Thunder Lake
7-59-5-W5
54°05′05″N 114°44′00″W
Approximately 22 km west of Barrhead.

This lake was named for Tom Dodgson who, in 1914, homesteaded on the north-west side of the feature. Mr. Dodgson enlisted in the Canadian Army during World War I and was subsequently killed at Vimy Ridge. The lake has been locally well known as Dodgson Lake since that time. The name was officially approved 21 July 1982.

Dog Rump Creek (creek)

73 E/15 - Elk Point
4-25-56-7-W4
53°51′53″N 110°54′55″W
Flows south into North Saskatchewan River, approximately 4 km south of Elk Point.

This feature was previously named "Atimoswe Creek," the native name for "Dog Rump Creek." It first appeared on Palliser's map of 1859 as Dog Rump Creek. The name was changed 24 September 1991 to reflect local usage.

Dogpound Creek (creek)

82 O/16 - Olds
21-32-3-W5
51°45′15″N 114°21′45″W

Flows north into Little Red Deer River, approximately 18 km west of Olds.

This name was first used in 1883 by a surveyor named Fawcett. The Cree name, *mizekampehpoocahan* means, "wolf caught in Buffalo Pound." Joseph Burr Tyrrell, a geologist and historian on the staff of the Geological Survey of Canada from 1881 until 1898, suggested the Cree name *ko-ma-tas-ta-moin*, meaning "stolen horse (or dog)" creek as another interpretation. The Stoney Indian name *so-mun-ib-wapta*, which translates as "Edge Creek," is yet another possibility. The Palliser Expedition map of 1865 shows this particular feature as "Edge Creek."
   Of these several versions of this name's origin, perhaps the most likely is its derivation from the translation given by the Cree. It refers to the dogs pounding on the creek as the Indian braves return to winter camp after hunting food. During the winter, it is said that some tribes settled along the banks of the creek, as it provided a natural roadway to the game area.

Dolberg Lake (lake)

83 J/3 - Green Court
1-60-7,8-W5
54°10′N 115°03′W
Approximately 42 km west of Barrhead.

The name for this lake has been official since at least 1958, but its precise origin is unknown.

Dolcy Lake (lake)

73 D/9 - Chauvin
26-42-4-W4
52°39′N 110°27′W
Approximately 33 km south-east of the town of Wainwright.

The name for this feature has been in use since at least 1958, but its origin is unknown.

Dolo Lake (lake)

73 E/14 - St. Paul
21,28-57-8-W4
53°57′N 111°10′W
Approximately 13 km south-east of St. Paul.

The name for this lake has been official since at least 1958, but its precise origin is unknown.

Donalda (village)

83 A/10 - Donalda
6-42-18-W4
52°35′00″N 112°34′25″W
Approximately 28 km east of Bashaw.

The Canadian Northern Railway established a station here in 1911. The name for the post office, which opened in August 1911, was changed from "Harker" (November 1907 through May 1911) and also from "Eidswold" (May 1911 through August 1911) before it took the name of a niece of Sir Donald Mann (1853-1934), Donalda Crossway. Mann was vice-president of the Canadian Northern. at the time. This village was incorporated 30 December 1912.

Donatville (hamlet)

83 I/10 - Boyle
33-66-19-W4
54°45′N 112°48′W
Approximately 30 km east north-east of Athabasca.

The name for this hamlet, whose post office operated from September 1914 through March 1980, was taken after Donat Gingras, an early settler who originated from Joliette, Quebec, and arrived in the area when he was eighteen years old.

* Dongray (former post office)

83 I/2 - Waskatenau
36-59-18-W4
54°08′N 112°34′W
Approximately 7 km west north-west of
Smoky Lake.

The post office, which operated here from
September 1920 through October 1925, was
named after John H. Gray, the first
postmaster.

Doré Lake (lake)

73 L/12 - Beaver Lake
29-66-13-W4
54°44′N 111°56′W
Approximately 4 km south-east of Lac La
Biche.

The name for this lake dates back to 1918
when it appeared on maps. The term *doré* is
French Canadian for "walleye," and
literally translates to "gilded." It is also
known locally as "School Lake."

Dorenlee (locality)

83 A/10 - Donalda
14-43-21-W4
52°42′N 112°57′W
Approximately 12 km north of Bashaw.

The name for this locality, whose post
office operated from December 1903
through July 1964, is taken after its first
postmaster, W.O. Dore, and his partner, a
Mr. Lee. The Grand Trunk Pacific opened a
railway station here in 1912.

Doris Island (island)

73 L/10 - Marguerite Lake
10-64-4-W4
54°32′N 110°31′W
Approximately 22 km west north-west of
Cold Lake, in Moore Lake.

The name for this island has been official
since at least 1958, but its precise origin is
unknown.

Douglas Lake (lake)

72 M/9 - Esther
2-32-2-W4
51°43′N 110°12′W
Approximately 45 km north north-east of
Oyen.

The precise origin for the name of this
feature is unknown.

Dovercourt (locality)

83 B/2 - Caroline
12-38-6-W5
52°14′N 114°52′W
Approximately 17 km south south-east of
Rocky Mountain House.

A post office operated here from October
1912 through April 1968 and was named by
H. Lee, the first postmaster, after
Dovercourt in England. Dovercourt, in
modern times a seaside resort adjoining
Harwich, Essex, was the name of a manor
of the Vere family, Normans who held the
area from about 1086 A.D. The manor took
in what is now Harwich. The Veres were
Earls of Oxford from 1142 to the death of
the 20th Earl in 1703.

Dowling (railway point)

72 M/13 - Garden Plain
25-32-15-W4
51°47′N 112°00′W
Approximately 8 km north-west of Hanna.

Named for its proximity to Dowling Lake.
(see Dowling Lake)

Dowling Lake (locality)

82 P/16 - Farrell Lake
34-32-16-W4
51°47′N 112°11′W

Approximately 17 km north-west of
Hanna.

(see Dowling Lake)

Dowling Lake (lake)

72 M/12 - Hanna
32-14-W4
51°44′N 112°00′W
Approximately 12 km north north-west of
Hanna.

This lake was named by J.B. Tyrrell in 1886
after Dr. Donaldson Bogart Dowling
(1858-1925), a civil engineer and geologist
who became one of the leading figures in
the Geological Survey of Canada. The other
features in the area take their names from
this feature.

* Downing (former post office)

83 I/1 - Smoky Lake
17-58-14-W4
54°02′N 112°02′W
Approximately 30 km east south-east of
Smoky Lake.

The post office operated here from August
1911 through April 1967, but the precise
origin for the name is unknown. The name
was officially rescinded in 1971.

Drader (station)

83 B/16 - Winfield
6-46-3-W5
52°56′N 114°25′W
Approximately 35 km north north-west of
Rimbey.

The Lacombe & North Western Railway,
later part of the Canadian Pacific Railway,
established a station here in 1926 and
named it after A.E. Drader, the owner of a
local sawmill.

---

*denotes rescinded name or former locality.

Dragon Lake (lake)
72 M/9 - Esther
31-1-W4
51°42′N 110°05′W
Approximately 47 km north-east of Oyen.

The precise origin for the name of this
feature is unknown.

Drayton Valley (town)
83 G/2 - Drayton Valley
8-49-7-W5
53°13′20″N 114°58′30″W
Approximately 105 km west south-west of
Edmonton.

The post office, previously called "Power-
house," opened under this name in May
1920. The name is taken after a village in
Hampshire, England, from which the wife
of the first postmaster, W.J. Drake, came.
The name Drayton is a common term from
either the Old English *draeg* or the Old
Scandinavian *drag* which means either "a
portage" or "a steep hill where more effort
was required." Drayton Valley was
incorporated as a village 30 December 1955,
a new town 1 June 1956 and as a town 1
February 1957.

Driedmeat (railway point)
83 A/15 - Ferintosh
27-45-20-W4
52°55′N 112°50′W
Approximately 19 km south south-east of
Camrose.

(see Driedmeat Hill)

Driedmeat Creek (creek)
83 A/15 - Ferintosh
6-45-19-W4
52°52′N 112°44′W
Flows south-west into Driedmeat Lake,
approximately 20 km south south-east of
Camrose.

(see Driedmeat Hill)

Driedmeat Hill (hill)
83 A/15 - Ferintosh
17-45-19-W4
52°52′N 112°44′W
Approximately 18 km south south-east of
Camrose.

The name for this hill is found on
Pinkerton's map of 1814, and Harmon's
map of 1820, and is labelled "Kihumoo
Lake." It is a translation of the Cree *ka-ke-
wuk*. Apparently, the Indians covered the
hill with buffalo meat to dry it in the sun.
In addition to this rendition of the origin,
an Indian legend accompanies the naming
of the hill, and it was told to the first
settlers. The animosity between the Cree
Indians and the Blackfoot tribe led to a law
forbidding intermarriage. However, a
young Cree brave and a Blackfoot maiden
fell in love and married secretly. They took
shelter in a cave in a hill overlooking a lake,
and in fear of being discovered, they hunted
only when necessary, drying their meat on
the hill to preserve it. A Cree happened to
pass one day, saw the meat drying in the
sun, and the young couple was discovered.
They were duly punished and it was from
this incident the hill, lake and creek
received their names.

Driedmeat Lake (lake)
83 A/15 - Ferintosh
13-44,45-19-W4
52°52′N 112°45′W
Approximately 20 km south of Camrose.

(see Driedmeat Hill)

Drink Lake (lake)
73 L/5 - Goodfish Lake
6-63-12-W4
54°25′N 111°48′W
Approximately 40 km south south-east of
Lac La Biche.

The name for this lake has been official
since 4 May 1950, but its precise origin is

unknown. The local name for the feature is
"Mud Lake."

Dry Island Buffalo Jump Provincial Park
(provincial park)
82 P/14 - Trochu
24,29-34-21,22-W4
51°57′N 51°57′W
Approximately 35 km north-east of Three
Hills.

This 997.1 hectare (2463.8 acre) provincial
park was created by Order-in-Council No.
939/75. The name incorporates two notable
features within the park: the first is a bison
jump and related archaeological sites which
are found along the west wall of the river
valley; the second is a large mesa or butte
bordered by a dry river channel on one side
and the Red Deer River on the other, which
is traditionally known as the "dry island."

Drygrass Lake (lake)
83 H/10 - Elk Island Park
21-53-19-W4
53°35′00″N 112°44′45″W
Approximately 47 km east of Edmonton.

Although it is unconfirmed, the origin for
the name of this lake is likely descriptive of
the surrounding terrain.

Drysdale Lake (lake)
73 L/3 - Vincent Lake
27-58-9-W4
54°03′00″N 111°15′15″W
Approximately 7 km north north-west of
St. Paul.

The name for this lake has been official
since at least 1958, but its precise origin is
unknown.

Duagh (locality)
83 H/11 - Edmonton
5-55-23-W4
53°43'N 113°23'W
Approximately 18 km north of Edmonton.

A post office operated here from April 1900 through March 1918 and was named after Duagh, County Kerry, in Ireland. An early settler, John Hall, suggested the name after his home in Ireland. The name was changed to "Sunny Glyde" (until it was restored again to Duagh) from March 1923 through August 1931. The derivation of the name is from *Dubh-ath* (pronounced Dooah), or "black ford," from a ford on the river Feale (Joyce).

Duck Creek (creek)
83 I/12 - Coolidge
25-65-27-W4
54°37'N 113°56'W
Flows south into French Creek, approximately 43 km west south-west of Athabasca.

(see Duck Lake)

Duck Lake (lake)
83 I/12 - Coolidge
25-65-27-W4
54°39'N 113°56'W
Approximately 44 km west south-west of Athabasca.

The name for this lake has been official since at least 1958 and is likely descriptive.

Duffield (hamlet)
83 G/9 - Onoway
26-52-3-W5
53°32'N 114°21'W
Approximately 23 km west of Stony Plain.

The Canadian Northern Railway established a station here in 1911 and named it after George Duffield Hall of Boston,

Massachusetts. The post office at this hamlet opened March 1913.

Dufrance, Lac (lake)
73 E/16 - Frog Lake
22-55-1-W4
53°46'25"N 110°04'45"W
Approximately 54 km north of Lloydminster.

The name for this lake has been official since at least 1958, but its precise origin is unknown.

Dufresne, Lac (lake)
73 E/15 - Elk Point
5-57-6-W4
53°53'N 110°52'W
Approximately 3 km east of Elk Point.

The origin for the name of this lake is unknown.

Duggans Lake (lake)
83 I/3 - Thorhild
30-60-23-W4
54°13'N 113°27'W
Approximately 28 km east north-east of Westlock.

The name for this lake was officially adopted in 1952 and was taken after William Duggan, an early homesteader who lived near the feature.

Duhamel (hamlet)
83 A/15 - Ferintosh
27-45-21-W4
52°55'N 112°58'W
Approximately 14 km south-west of Camrose.

This hamlet, whose post office operated from November 1893 through December 1958, was named after the Most Reverend Joseph Thomas Duhamel (1841-1909),

Roman Catholic Archbishop of Ottawa who presented a bell to the community while it was under the leadership of Father Hippolyte Beillevaire, a priest from France who spent more than five decades among the Métis in Alberta. It was a trading post in the 1870s known to the Indians as "*notikiwin sipi*," translating "Battle River." It became later known as "Battle River Crossing," because it was one place where the river could be forded with little difficulty. In 1880 when the five Laboucan brothers were there it was known as "Laboucan Settlement."

Duhamel Lake (lake)
83 G/10 - Isle Lake
15-54-6-W5
53°39'N 114°47'W
Approximately 39 km east south-east of Mayerthorpe.

The name for this lake has been official since at least 1958, but its precise origin is unknown. (see Duhamel)

Dunbar (railway point)
83 H/11 - Edmonton
14-53-23-W4
53°34'45"N 113°17'05"W
Approximately 6 km north of Sherwood Park.

This railway point was officially named 21 July 1982 for George E. Dunbar (d. 1974), a former superintendent in the Western Region, Canadian National Railways.

Dunstable (locality)
83 G/16 - Lac la Nonne
26-57-2-W5
53°57'N 114°12'W
Approximately 24 km south south-east of Barrhead.

A post office operated here from March 1908 through May 1969 and was named by postal authorities after a town of the same name in Bedfordshire, England.

* **Dunvegan Yards** (former railway point)
83 H/12 - St. Albert
23-53-25-W4
53°36′N 113°33′W
Within the city limits of Edmonton.

The Edmonton, Dunvegan and British Columbia Railway established a station here in 1911. As it is a terminal for the E.D. & B.C.R., its name is taken after Dunvegan, a castle in the Isle of Skye, Scotland and ancestral estate of the Chief of Clan MacLeod.

Durlingville (locality)
73 L/7 - Bonnyville
14-61-5-W4
54°17′N 110°39′W
Approximately 7 km east of Bonnyville.

The name for this locality, whose post office operated from August 1908 through December 1948, is a combination of the names of two early settlers, F. Durand and A. Islin.

Dussault Lake (lake)
83 G/10 - Isle Lake
4-54-6-W5
53°38′N 114°49′W
Approximately 41 km south south-east of Mayerthorpe.

The name for this lake has been official since at least 1958, but its precise origin is unknown.

* **Dusseldorf** (former locality)
83 J/1 - Barrhead
2-60-2-W5
54°09′N 114°13′W

Approximately 15 km east north-east of Barrhead.

The post office operated under this name from June 1910 through January 1919 and commemorated a city in Germany. The name was changed to Freedom. (see Freedom)

Dusty Lake (lake)
83 H/1 - Holden
7-48-17-W4
53°07′N 112°29′W
Approximately 28 km north-east of Camrose.

The name for this lake is a translation of the Cree *ko-pwa-o-wa-gas-takh*.

Dutch Flats (flats)
83 A/11 - Chain Lakes
28-43-22-W4
52°44′N 113°08′W
Approximately 20 km north-west of Bashaw.

The precise origin for the well-established name of this feature is unknown.

Duvernay (hamlet)
73 E/13 - Hairy Hill
26-55-12-W4
53°47′N 111°41′W
Approximately 10 km north north-east of Two Hills.

A post office operated here from September 1908 through August 1970. It was named after Ludger Duvernay (1799-1852), founder of the Société St. Jean-Baptiste in 1834. It was previously called "South Bend."

* **Duxbury** (former post office)
83 A/9 - Forestburg
27-41-15-W4
52°35′N 112°04′W

Approximately 40 km north north-west of Castor.

This village was originally established as a post office in January 1910 and the name apparently came from the local legend that there were many ducks in the area. When a post office was established in Forestburg in 1915 some three kilometres away, the post office in Duxbury was closed. (see Forestburg)

Dyke Lake (lake)
73 E/16 - Frog Lake
19-55-2-W4
53°46′N 110°17′W
Approximately 43 km east south-east of Elk Point.

The name for this lake has been official since at least 1958, but its precise origin is unknown.

Dymott Lake (lake)
73 D/15 - Wainwright
22-44-4-W4
52°48′N 110°30′W
Approximately 25 km east of the town of Wainwright.

The name for this lake has been in use since at least 1958, but its origin is unknown.

Eagle Creek (creek)
82 O/16 - Olds
5-35-3-W5
51°59′N 114°24′W
Flows north into Red Deer River, approximately 30 km west of Innisfail.

The name for this creek has been official since at least 1958, but its precise origin is unknown.

Eagle Creek (creek)
83 B/1 - Markerville
13-18-35-1-W5
52°01′N 114°08′W

Flows north-west into Little Red Deer River, approximately 12 km west of Innisfail.

The name for this creek was officially changed from "Bowden Creek" 16 October 1991. According to field research done in the area, local residents maintain that it had been known as Eagle Creek since at least 1896, when the Eagle Creek School District was formed. Local residents were not at all familiar with the previous name "Bowden Creek."

Eagle Hill (hill)
82 O/16 - Olds
33-3-W5
51°49′N 114°22′W
Approximately 20 km west of Olds.

The name Eagle Hill has been in use since 1904 when the post office and school of that name were established. The hill itself may have been known as Eagle Hill by the native Indians long before that. The name is thought to have originated from an eagle nesting on the tree-covered hill. (Some sources say more than one eagle, while others say someone probably saw an eagle fly over the hill.)

Eagle Hill (hamlet)
82 O/16 - Olds
SW1/4-6-34-3-W5
51°33′00″N 114° 25′30″W
Approximately 25 km south-west of Olds.

Initially established as a post office in June 1903, this hamlet was named for the eagle and a nearby hill. The post office was closed in August 1963 and the locality became a hamlet in 1991. (see Eagle Hill)

_____

*denotes rescinded name or former locality.

* Earlie (former locality)
73 E/1 - Paradise Valley
34-48-3-W4
53°11′N 110°22′W
Approximately 25 km west south-west of Lloydminster.

The name for this former locality, whose post office operated from December 1909 through September 1947, is an error for "Airlie." It was inspired by the song "The Bonnie House of Airlie," but when the name was submitted to the Post Office Department, it was misspelled. The name was officially rescinded 7 November 1969.

Earlie Lake (lake)
73 E/1 - Paradise Valley
31-48-3-W4
53°10′30″N 110°25′00″W
Approximately 30 km west south-west of Lloydminster.

This lake was named for its proximity to Earlie. (see Earlie)

* Earlville (former locality)
83 A/11 - Chain Lakes
12-42-24-W4
52°35′N 113°20′W
Approximately 20 km east south-east of Ponoka.

The name for the post office, which operated here from February 1904 through March 1932, was taken after Earl F. Heath, the first postmaster.

* East Edmonton (former railway point)
83 H/11 - Edmonton
6-53-23-W4
53°33′N 113°22′W
Within the city limits of Edmonton.

The descriptive name for this former station refers to its location, on the east side of Edmonton. (see Edmonton)

East Lake (lake)
73 E/6 - Mannville
31-49-7-W4
53°16′20″N 110°59′43″W
Approximately 67 km west of Lloydminster.

This lake is called East Lake because it is east of Bauer's Lake. The descriptive name was officially approved 22 January 1992.

East Lobstick Creek (creek)
83 B/7 - Rocky Mountain House
2-41-6-W5
52°29′N 114°44′W
Flows south into Lobstick Creek, approximately 18 km north-east of Rocky Mountain House.

This creek was officially named in 1958 for its proximity as a tributary of Lobstick Creek. (see Lobstick Creek)

Eastburg (locality)
83 J/1 - Barrhead
16-59-1-W5
54°06′N 114°04′W
Approximately 17 km west south-west of Westlock.

This locality, whose post office operated from September 1908 through February 1946, was named after A.E. East, the first postmaster.

* Eastervale (former post office)
73 D/6 - Brownfield
34-39-8-W4
52°25′N 111°05′W
Approximately 37 km south south-east of Hardisty.

The post office here operated from December 1922 through September 1926 and was named to commemorate the date upon which the first settlers arrived in the area, which was Easter Sunday.

* Eastgate (former locality)

83 H/14 - Redwater
15-57-22-W4
53°56′N 113°12′W
Approximately 48 km north north-east of
Edmonton.

A post office operated here from May 1909
through July 1954 and was named after
Eastgate, Rochester, England, the former
home of C.J. Woodward, the first postmaster.

Easyford (locality)

83 G/6 - Easyford
6-50-8-W5
53°17′N 115°09′W
Approximately 15 km north-west of
Drayton Valley.

The descriptive name for this locality,
whose post office operated from April 1935
through July 1966, refers to the fact that
there is an "easy ford" on the Pembina
River.

* Echohill (former post office)

83 I/4 - Westlock
6-58-26-W4
53°59′N 113°51′W
Approximately 18 km south of Westlock.

The post office, which operated here from
July 1914 through February 1931, was
descriptively named after the first farm
which was on a hill.

Eckville (town)

83 B/8 - Sylvan Lake
16-39-3-W5
52°21′45″N 114°22′00″W
Approximately 40 km west north-west of
Red Deer.

The post office for this town opened in
December 1905. The town was named after
Andy E. Eckford one of the first settlers to
the area. Apparently, a contest was held for
naming the townsite and Hattie Mitzner
(later Mrs. Stephens) came up with the
name Eckville and won. This town was
incorporated 1 July 1966.

Edberg (village)

83 A/15 - Ferintosh
14-44-20-W4
52°47′15″N 112°47′10″W
Approximately 25 km south of Camrose.

Johan A. Edstrom (1850-1910) was a local
store owner and the first postmaster of
Edberg. He combined his last name with
the term, *berg*, meaning "hill" in Swedish,
to develop a name for the post office, which
opened in April 1902. This village was
incorporated 4 February 1930.

Eddy Lake (lake)

83 H/10 - Elk Island Park
N-33-53-20-W4
53°37′30″N 112°53′35″W
Approximately 40 km east of Edmonton, in
Elk Island National Park.

The name for this lake enjoys the local
usage of the warden staff, although its
precise origin is unknown. It was officially
approved 17 October 1991.

Eden Lake (lake)

83 G/9 - Onoway
13-53-2-W5
53°35′N 114°09′W
Approximately 44 km west of Edmonton.

This lake was named by the man who
owned the quarter-section of land upon
which the lake sits and who had a fur farm
called Lake Eden Fur Farm.

* Edensville (former locality)

83 A/10 - Donalda
10-43-20-W4
52°41′N 112°44′W
Approximately 17 km north-east of
Bashaw.

The precise origin for the name of the
locality, whose post office operated from
December 1903 through February 1912,
when it was changed to Meeting Creek, is
unknown.

Edgerton (village)

73 D/16 - McLaughlin
1-44-4-W4
52°45′35″N 110°27′00″W
Approximately 29 km east south-east of the
town of Wainwright.

The name for this village, incorporated 11
September 1917, is taken after a Grand
Trunk Pacific Railway engineer, H.H.
Edgerton. The post office and station were
established in 1908.

* Edison (former post office)

83 I/4 - Westlock
5-60-26-W4
54°09′N 113°52′W
Approximately 65 km north north-west of
Edmonton.

The post office operated here under this
name from July 1904 through November
1913, when it was closed and moved to
Westlock. (see Westlock)

Edmonton (city)

83 H/11 - Edmonton
53-24-W4
53°33′N 113°28′W
Approximately 297 km north of Calgary.

The city of Edmonton takes its name from
Edmonton House, which was built by

George Sutherland of the Hudson's Bay Company in 1795. The first Edmonton House was built approximately 32 km farther down the North Saskatchewan River. Sutherland probably named his "fort" Edmonton as a compliment to his clerk, John Peter Pruden, who was a native of the original Edmonton, near London, England. The site of this first Edmonton House was on the north bank of the river about 2.5 km above the mouth of the Sturgeon River. Beside Edmonton House stood Fort Augustus, a fort built by the North West Company circa 1793. Both of these popular trading posts were destroyed by the Indians and were subsequently abandoned in 1807. New forts, or trading houses, were built by both the Hudson's Bay Company and the North West Company in 1808 on the top of the high bank within the present city of Edmonton. The actual name "Edmonton" is derived from the Anglo-Saxon Christian name *Eadhelm* and *Tun* or *ton*, which means a "field" or "enclosure."

Edmonton, Rossdale, c. 1904

Edmonton Beach (summer village)

83 G/9 - Onoway
30-52-1-W5
53°31'N 114°07'W
Approximately 40 km west of Edmonton.

A post office operated here from May 1926 through August 1941 and was named for the fact that Edmontonians retreated to this beach west of the city for holidays. This summer village was incorporated 1 January 1959. (see Edmonton)

* **Edouardville** (former station)

73 E/14 - St. Paul
27-57-8-W4
53°57'N 111°06'W
Approximately 12 km south-east of St. Paul.

The precise origin for the name of this former Canadian Northern Railway station is unknown. It is, however, located near the hamlet of St. Edouard.

Edson (town)

83 F/9 - Edson
16-53-17-W5
53°35'00"N 116°26'50"W
Approximately 192 km west of Edmonton.

This town, whose post office was previously called "Heatherwood," takes its name after Edson J. Chamberlain (1852-1924), vice-president and general manager of the Grand Trunk Pacific Railway. He became president of the parent company, the Grand Trunk Railway, after the death of Charles M. Hays. The town was officially incorporated 21 September 1911.

Edson, n.d.

Edson River (river)

83 F/9 - Edson
19-54-16-W5
53°41'30"N 116°29'00"W
Flows south-east into McLeod River, approximately 12 km north-east of Edson.

(see Edson)

Edwand (hamlet)

83 I/1 - Smoky Lake
36-59-16-W4
54°09'N 112°17'W
Approximately 12 km east north-east of Smoky Lake.

The name for this hamlet is taken after the first postmaster, Edward Anderson. It is a combination of the first three letters of his first name and the first three letters of his last name. The post office operated from June 1904 through August 1970.

Edwand Creek (creek)

83 I/1 - Smoky Lake
22-59-16-W4
54°08'N 112°18'W
Flows south into White Earth Creek, approximately 10 km east of Smoky Lake.

(see Edwand)

---

*denotes rescinded name or former locality.

Edward Lake (lake)
73 L/7 - Bonnyville
16,17-63-4-W4
54°27′N 110°34′W
Approximately 25 km west of Cold Lake.

The name for this lake has been official since at least 1958, but its precise origin is unknown. It is locally named "Rat Lake."

Egg Creek (creek)
83 H/16 - Willingdon
12-58-17-W4
54°00′N 112°24′W
Flows north into North Saskatchewan River, approximately 13 km south south-east of Smoky Lake.

The name for this creek has been in use since at least 1958, but its precise origin is unknown.

* Egg Lake (former post office)
83 I/16 - Plamondon
5-67-15-W4
54°46′N 112°15′W
Approximately 18 km west of Lac La Biche.

The post office operated here from March 1924 through January 1969 and was named for its proximity to Missawawi Lake. (see Missawawi Lake) It was previously called "Bouvier," after X. Bouvier, the first postmaster. The name was officially rescinded in 1970.

Egremont (hamlet)
83 I/3 - Thorhild
25-58-22-W4
54°02′N 113°08′W
Approximately 10 km north of Redwater.

A post office opened here in May 1908, and was named after a town in Cumberland

(now Cumbria), England, that was the former home of the wife of the first postmaster, R.C. Armstrong. The hamlet was officially established 7 August 1979.

* Eidswold (former post office)
83 A/10 - Donalda
6-42-18-W4
52°35′N 112°34′W
Approximately 27 km east of Bashaw.

The origin for the name of the post office, which operated here from May 1911 through August 1911, is unknown. The name was changed to Donalda.

Eighteen, Lake (lake)
83 J/2 - Thunder Lake
18-59-5-W5
54°05′50″N 114°43′20″W
Approximately 22 km west of Barrhead.

The descriptive name for this lake was officially approved 21 July 1982 and refers to its location in section 18.

Elbridge (locality)
83 I/3 - Thorhild
22-60-22-W4
54°13′N 113°14′W
Approximately 43 km east of Westlock.

The name for this locality, whose post office operated from October 1916 through September 1928, reopening from May 1935 through January 1947, was taken after Elbridge Duval. Duval was supposed to become the first postmaster, but died suddenly.

Elder Creek (creek)
82 O/15 - Sundre
7-4-33-7-W5
51°48′00″N 114°55′40″W
Flows north-east into Walton Creek, approximately 20 km west of Sundre.

This creek was named for the three Elder brothers who came from Scotland. Fred homesteaded in 1908, his twin brother Jim in 1909, and their older brother, Bill, in 1922. The creek ran through part of Fred's land and runs north from Stafne Ridge into Walton Creek. The name was made official 3 November 1991.

Eldorena (locality)
83 H/15 - Lamont
35-57-20-W4
53°58′N 112°52′W
Approximately 32 km south-west of Smoky Lake.

A post office operated here from February 1914 through August 1958, but its precise origin is unknown.

Election Lake (lake)
73 L/12 - Beaver Lake
26,35-64-13-W4
54°34′30″N 111°52′00″W
Approximately 23 km south south-east of Lac La Biche.

The name for this lake evolved during the course of the 1926 federal election. The Liberal candidate, C.W. Cross, was pitted against the United Farmers of Alberta candidate, D.F. Kellner. The contest included charges that some returning officers had allowed one man to vote seven times, created voters' lists from local graveyards, and created entire polling stations. One group of election officials near the shores of this lake completed a supply of unmarked balloting paper while consuming a bottle of spirits. The name arose from this incident. Mr. Cross (1872-1928), Alberta's first Attorney-General in 1905, had won the federal seat in 1925 but lost it in 1926 to Mr. Kellner (1879-1935), who was defeated by a Liberal in 1930.

---

*denotes rescinded name or former locality.

Elinor Lake (lake)
73 L/12 - Beaver Lake
6-31-65-11-W4
54°40'07"N 111°39'31"W
Approximately 24 km south-east of Lac La Biche.

A charming theory is attached to the name of this and several other lakes in the district. It is rumoured that Elinor was a girl who figured early but not very prominently in the love-life of a French-Canadian voyageur making his way up the Beaver River in the 1800s. Along the way it is said he also named lakes after Hilda, Ernestina, Reita, Charlotte, Muriel, Jessie, Liza, Barbara, Marguerite, Minnie and Helena.

Eliza, Lake (lake)
73 E/14 - St. Paul
6-56-8,9-W4
53°48'N 111°11'W
Approximately 22 km south-west of Elk Point.

The name for this lake has been official since at least 1958 and is taken for its proximity to the Lake Eliza post office. (see Lake Eliza).

Elizabeth (Métis Settlement)
73 L/1 - Reita Lake
57-2-W4
54°00'N 110°10'W
North of Lloydminster.

Elizabeth Métis Colony was created by the 1970 Order-in-Council No. 32124/70. It is now known simply as Elizabeth, not Elizabeth Metis Colony or Elizabeth Metis Settlement #9. It is named after Elizabeth Dion, the wife of Métis leader and reformer, Joseph Francis Dion (1888-1960). Joe Dion was the first president of the Métis Association of Alberta (1932-1958) and the Indian Association of Alberta, and left his wife for long periods to help the

Métis groups establish settlements. He spent one year in Elizabeth serving as supervisor and school teacher.

Elk Butte (butte)
73 D/11 - Hardisty
19-43-7-W4
52°43'N 111°01'W
Approximately 20 km south-west of the town of Wainwright.

The name for this hill has been in use since at least 1958, but the precise origin is unknown.

Elk Butte Lake (lake)
73 D/10 - Hughenden
21-43-7-W4
52°42'N 110°58'W
Approximately 15 km south south-west of the town of Wainwright.

The name for this lake is likely taken from its proximity to Elk Butte. The lake and the butte were named at approximately the same time.

Elk Island (island)
83 H/10 - Elk Island Park
9-15-54-20-W4
53°40'N 112°51'W
Approximately 46 km east north-east of Edmonton.

The descriptive name for this island in Astotin lake refers to the many elk found on the island and in the surrounding area.

Elk Island (locality)
83 H/15 - Lamont
25-55-21-W4
53°47'N 112°59'W
Approximately 43 km north-east of Edmonton.

(see Elk Island)

Elk Island National Park (national park)
83 H/9 - Mundare
21-27-18-W4
53°36'N 112°53'W
Approximately 45 km east north-east of Edmonton.

This area once boasted a large population of wildlife, including elk, moose, bear and deer. The Canadian Government set this area aside as a reserve. The former name, the "Cooking Lake Forest Reserve," has been incorporated into a provincial recreation area, and this park became Elk Island National Park.

Elk Island Park, 1940

Elk Point (town)
73 E/15 - Elk Point
1-57-7-W4
53°54'N 110°54'W
Approximately 90 km north north-west of Lloydminster.

The town of Elk Point was incorporated 1 January 1962. The following is taken from the local history of Elk Point and District called *Reflections*: "Mr. Higby was an American from Elk Point, South Dakota, who became a bartender in Vegreville about 1905. Having such a close association with the "sauce," he found himself becoming an alcoholic. Determined to cure himself he loaded supplies on a raft and floated down the North Saskatchewan River, putting ashore where our bridge is now located. Here he dug a cave in the bank, making it snug with a door and a window so he could have a view of the river, and settled down. He found it difficult to develop a taste for the river water. It hadn't the kick he was used to. But he got his kicks from other things. The country was beautiful. He became a trapper and roamed far and wide. Mr. Higby returned to Vegreville in the spring of 1906. He told newcomers of his hideaway, praising its country and bounteous river, and many chose to homestead at his Elk Point."

Elk River (river)

83 B/13 - Nordegg River
8-46-12-W5
52°57′N 115°39′W
Flows east into Brazeau Reservoir, approximately 58 km south-west of Drayton Valley.

The name for this river has been official since at least 1958 and likely reflects the number of elk formerly in the area.

Elkton (locality)

82 O/10 - Fallentimber Creek
17-31-4-W5
51°39′N 114°32′W
Approximately 17 km south south-east of Sundre.

The post office here operated from June 1907 through March 1969, and was named for its proximity to the Red Deer River. The early fur traders mistakenly referred to the elk as red deer.

Elkton Creek (creek)

82 O/10 - Fallentimber Creek
17-31-4-W5
51°39′N 114°32′W

Flows north-east into Little Red Deer River, approximately 16 km south south-east of Sundre.

(see Elkton)

Ellerslie (railway point)

83 H/6 - Cooking Lake
29-51-24-W4
53°25′40″N 113°29′30″W
Within the southern city limits of Edmonton.

The city of Edmonton usually attempts to retain, whenever possible, any names of historical significance. There are two possibilities for the origin of the name. One is that it is taken after the one of the Scottish manors of Sir William Wallace, and another is that it is taken after a favourite character in a novel by Sir Walter Scott. The name is derived from *Alder Lea*, or "Alder Meadow."

Ellscott (hamlet)

83 I/10 - Boyle
1-64-20-W4
54°30′15″N 112°54′00″W
Approximately 34 km south-east of Athabasca.

The name for this hamlet was taken after L. Scott, an agent with the Alberta & Great Waterways Railway. The post office opened December 1916.

Elnora (village)

82 P/14 - Trochu
10-35-23-W4
51°59′35″N 113°12′00″W
Approximately 32 km north of Three Hills.

The post office opened here under this name in September 1908. At that time, settlers had asked for the settlement to be named "Stewartville," but the name was turned down by the Post Office Depart-

ment to avoid duplication with another place in Canada that already bore that name. The people then met at the house of Alex Hogg, and it was decided that the community should be called Elnora by combining the first names of Elinor Hogg and Nora Edwards, wives of the first postmasters. Alex Hogg arrived in 1906 and William Edwards in 1908. This village was incorporated 22 July 1929.

Elspeth (locality)

83 B/8 - Sylvan Lake
33-38-2-W5
52°19′N 114°13′W
Approximately 12 km south-east of Eckville.

The Canadian Northern Railway established a station here in 1914, but the origin for the name is unknown.

Embarras (locality)

83 F/7 - Erith
8-50-20-W5
53°18′N 116°53′W
Approximately 44 km south-west of Edson.

(see Embarras River)

Embarras River (river)

83 F/7 - Erith
5-52-18-W5
53°27′N 116°37′W
Flows north-east into McLeod River, approximately 19 km south-west of Edson.

The locally well-established name for this river was approved in 1927 and is probably associated with the French word for an obstruction because the river is obstructed by driftwood.

Emerald Lake (lake)

83 H/10 - Elk Island Park
4-54-19-W4
53°38′00″N 112°44′45″W

Approximately 50 km east north-east of Edmonton.

The name was made official 28 February 1980 because Merrill Taylor, an Edmonton contractor, used it for his small holding company, Emerald Lake Estates.

Emilien, Lac (lake)

73 E/11 - Myrnam
4-53-8-W4
53°32′N 111°07′W
Approximately 28 km north-west of Vermilion.

This lake appears as "Lake Emilien" in the *Cummins Rural Directory* circa 1920; however, the precise origin for the name is unknown.

Emslie Lake (lake)

83 J/9 - Flatbush
23-64-2-W5
54°33′N 114°12′W
Approximately 48 km north north-west of Westlock.

The name for this lake has been official since at least 1948 when it appears on a field map of the area, but its precise origin is unknown.

End Lake (lake)

73 E/9 - Marwayne
33-54-2-W4
53°42′N 110°14′W
Approximately 48 km south-east of Elk Point.

The name for this lake has been official since at least 1958, but its precise origin is unknown.

Endiang (hamlet)

82 P/16 - Farrell Lake
26-34-16-W4
51°57′N 112°10′W

Approximately 38 km north north-east of Hanna.

The name for this place is the Chippewa term for "my home," and was suggested by the first postmaster, W.H. Foreman. The post office opened January 1910.

English Bay (bay)

73 L/9 - Marie Lake
21-64-2-W4
54°33′N 110°13′W
Approximately 6 km north of Cold Lake.

The name for this bay on Cold Lake has been official since 17 January 1951, but its precise origin is unknown.

English Creek (creek)

82 O/16 - Olds
11-21-32-3-W5
51°45′40″N 114°22′00″W
Flows north-west into Dogpound Creek, approximately 19 km west south-west of Olds.

The locally well-established name for this creek has been in use since 1910 when a number of families from England settled along this creek. There was a flood in 1932 which destroyed some of the original beauty of the small creek.

Ensleigh (locality)

72 M/14 - Kirkpatrick Lake
6-34-8-W4
51°53′N 111°08′W
Approximately 33 km south-east of Coronation.

The precise origin for the name of this feature is unknown. The post office operated here from April 1910 through August 1936.

Entwistle (village)

83 G/10 - Isle Lake
20-53-7-W5
53°35′35″N 115°00′03″W
Approximately 42 km south south-east of Mayerthorpe.

The post office opened here in June 1908 and was named after James G. Entwistle, an early settler of the Magnolia district. He was a locomotive engineer on the Grand Trunk Railway in Ontario and moved west from Winnipeg circa 1904-05. He was the first postmaster. This village was incorporated 1 January 1955.

Equity (locality)

82 P/14 - Trochu
31-32-23-W4
51°47′N 113°14′W
Approximately 9 km north of Three Hills.

This Canadian Northern Railway station was previously known as Ghost Pine, but the name was changed after 1916 (see Ghost Pine). The reason and origin for the change of name is unknown but may have occurred to avoid duplication with another station of the same name.

Eric Lake (lake)

73 D/16 - McLaughlin
3-44-3-W4
52°45′30″N 110°21′30″W
Approximately 37 km east south-east of the town of Wainwright.

The name for this lake has been in use since at least 1958, but its precise origin is unknown.

Ernest Lake (lake)

73 E/2 - Grizzly Bear Creek
27-47-6-W4
53°05′N 110°48′W
Approximately 56 km south-west of Lloydminster.

The name for this lake has been official since at least 1958, but its precise origin is unknown.

Ernestina Lake (lake)

73 L/1 - Reita Lake
6-61-3-W4
54°14′N 110°27′W
Approximately 20 km east of Bonnyville.

(see Elinor Lake)

Ernie, Lake (lake)

83 B/7 - Rocky Mountain House
NE-19,24-39-6-W5
52°22′20″N 115°51′35″W
Approximately 4 km east of Rocky Mountain House.

The name Lake Ernie is well-established in local usage, but its precise origin is unknown. The request for official naming came from Tony Nette of the Fish and Wildlife office at Rocky Mountain House. The name was officially approved 16 October 1991.

Erskine (hamlet)

83 A/7 - Stettler
6-39-20-W4
52°20′N 112°53′W
Approximately 12 km west of Stettler.

There is speculation that the origin of the name is linked to the landholdings in Alberta of the fourth Duke of Sutherland (1851-1913), whose wife was Lady Millicent Fanny St. Clair-Erskine (1867-1955), eldest daughter of the fourth Earl of Rosslyn. The post office was formerly called "Liberal."

Erskine Lake (lake)

83 A/7 - Stettler
35-38-21-W4
52°18′N 112°53′W

Approximately 13 km west south-west of Stettler.

(see Erskine)

Ervick (locality)

83 H/2 - Camrose
1-47-21-W4
53°01′N 112°57′W
Approximately 8 km west of Camrose.

This locality was named after the roadmaster in charge of the subdivision.

Esther (hamlet)

72 M/9 - Esther
29-31-2-W4
51°42′N 110°16′W
Approximately 40 km north north-east of Oyen.

A post office was established here in June 1914 and was named after Anna Esther Landreth, daughter of the first postmaster, Y.B. Olsen.

Estridge Lake (lake)

73 D/16 - McLaughlin
6-45-3-W4
52°50′N 110°25′W
Approximately 30 km east of the town of Wainwright.

The name for this lake has been in use since at least 1958, but its precise origin is unknown.

Eta Lake (lake)

83 G/5 - Eta Lake
12-51-12-W5
53°23′30″N 115°38′00″W
Approximately 49 km west north-west of Drayton Valley.

The name for this lake has been official since at least 1958. *Eta* is the fifth letter of the Greek alphabet; however, its connection to this lake is not clear.

Ethel Lake (lake)

83 G/15 - Sangudo
30-55-6-W5
53°47′N 114°52′W
Approximately 25 km south-east of Mayerthorpe.

The name for this lake has been official since at least 1958, but its precise origin is unknown.

Ethel Lake (lake)

73 L/9 - Marie Lake
14-64-3-W4
54°32′N 110°21′W
Approximately 12 km north-west of Cold Lake.

(see Elinor Lake)

Ethel Lake (locality)

73 L/8 - Cold Lake
35-63-3-W4
54°29′N 110°22′W
Approximately 13 km west north-west of Cold Lake.

A post office operated here from February 1935 through November 1943 and takes its name from its location on Ethel Lake. (see Ethel Lake)

* Ethelwyn (former post office)

73 E/10 - Clandonald
15-54-5-W4
53°39′N 110°39′W
Approximately 31 km south south-east of Elk Point.

The name for the post office, which operated here from April 1910 through May 1939, commemorated Ethel MacDonald, the wife of an early settler, H. MacDonald. The name was officially rescinded 14 January 1970.

* Eunice (former post office)

83 I/5 - Dapp
12-62-27-W4
54°22'N 113°55'W
Approximately 21 km north north-west of
Westlock.

The post office operated under this name
from May 1913 through October 1917 and
was named after Eunice Duduit, daughter
of a local landowner. The name was
changed to Dapp. (see Dapp)

Evansburg (village)

83 G/11 - Chip Lake
30-53-7-W5
53°36'05"N 115°01'35"W
Approximately 39 km south of
Mayerthorpe.

The post office opened in February 1914
and was named for Henry Marshall Erskine
Evans (1876-1973), former Mayor of
Edmonton and advisor to the Alberta
Government. Originally from Toronto, Mr.
Evans moved to Winnipeg in 1900, where
he became business manager of the *Winnipeg Tribune*. He came to Edmonton in 1904
on his way to prospect for coal seams along
the Pembina River. He became president of
the Edmonton Board of Trade in 1914. In
1946 he was made an officer of the Order of
the British Empire for meritorious service
in war work. The village was incorporated
31 December 1953.

Evarts (locality)

83 B/8 - Sylvan Lake
7-38-2-W5
52°16'N 114°16'W
Approximately 13 km south south-east of
Eckville.

A post office operated here from July 1907
through June 1969 and was named after
Louis P. Evarts, an early settler.

Evarts, 1902

Evergreen (locality)

83 B/2 - Caroline
5-38-4-W5
52°14'N 114°32'W
Approximately 50 km west of Red Deer.

The descriptive name for this locality refers
to the numerous spruce trees in the area.
The post office here operated from October
1910 through July 1969.

* Ewing (former locality)

83 A/2 - Big Valley
23-36-21-W4
52°07'N 112°53'W
Approximately 24 km south of Stettler.

The post office operated here from August
1903 through March 1926 and was named
after John Ewing, an Ontarian who moved
to the area and settled near the lake in 1898.
He was the first postmaster.

Ewing Lake (lake)

83 A/2 - Big Valley
12-37-20,21-W4
52°10'N 112°52'W
Approximately 20 km south south-west of
Stettler.

(see Ewing Lake)

Excelsior (locality)

83 H/14 - Redwater
28-55-24-W4
53°47'N 113°30'W
Approximately 26 km north of Edmonton.

Northern Alberta Railways established a
station here in 1905. The post office
operated here from January 1905 through
June 1931, but the precise origin of the
name is unknown.

Eyehill Creek (creek)

73 D/1 - Bodo
1-38-1-W4
52°14'N 110°00'W
Approximately 25 km south-east of
Provost, on the Saskatchewan-Alberta
boundary.

The name for this creek which flows into
Saskatchewan has been in use since 1958,
but its precise origin is unknown.

Fabyan (hamlet)

73 D/15 - Wainwright
18-45-7-W4
52°53'N 110°59'W
Approximately 10 km north-west of the
town of Wainwright.

A Grand Trunk Pacific Railway station was
established here in 1909, and was named
after the summer resort of Fabyan in New
Hampshire. The post office operated from
May 1917 through October 1979. The
American community may have been
named after Robert Fabyan, an English
chronicler and onetime Sheriff of London,
who wrote a history of England from the
arrival of Brutus to 1400 A.D.

Fair Creek (creek)

82 O/10 - Fallentimber Creek
5-31-5-W5
51°38'N 114°39'W
Flows east into Fallentimber Creek,
approximately 12 km south of Sundre.

The name for this creek has been official
since November 1937, but its precise origin
is unknown.

Fairydell (locality)

83 I/4 - Westlock
8-58-24-W4
54°01'N 113°33'W
Approximately 24 km south-east of
Westlock.

The name for this locality, whose post
office operated from September 1910
through November 1939, is likely descriptive.

Fairydell Creek (creek)

83 I/3 - Thorhild
14-59-24-W4
54°06'N 113°29'W

Flows north into Redwater River, approximately 26 km east south-east of Westlock.

(see Fairydell)

Fallentimber Creek (creek)

82 O/15 - Fallentimber Creek
9-32-5-W5
51°45'N 114°39'W
Flows north into Red Deer River, approximately 9 km south of Sundre.

The name for this creek has been in use
since at least 1892 when A.P. Coleman
(1852-1939), a charter member of the
Alpine Club of Canada, wrote in his
journal that he and his party camped here.
The descriptive name is a translation of the
Cree word, *kow-ikh-ti-kow*. The Stoney
equivalent is *o-ta-ha-wap-ta*.

Fallis (hamlet)

83 G/10 - Isle Lake
22-53-5-W5
53°35'N 114°38'W
Approximately 43 km west north-west of
Stony Plain.

The Grand Trunk Pacific Railway established a station here in 1910. The post office
opened in March of that same year and was
named after W.S. Fallis, an executive of
Sherwin-Williams Company of Canada,
Montreal-based paint manufacturers. Mr.
Fallis later became president of Sherwin-
Williams and of the Canadian Manufacturers' Association.

Falun (hamlet)

83 A/13 - Bearhills Lake
10-46-27-W4
52°57'N 113°50'W
Approximately 30 km west of Wetaskiwin.

This hamlet was named for a mining town
in Sweden noted for its copper mines.
Many of the early settlers, including the
man who proposed the name, John Strom,

came from there. The post office opened in
December 1904.

Falun Creek (creek)

83 H/4 - Kavanagh
30-46-26-W4
53°00'15"N 113°45'43"W
Flows north into Bigstone Creek, approximately 32 km west north-west of
Wetaskiwin.

(see Falun)

Farming Island (island)

83 G/10 - Isle Lake
3-55-4-W5
53°43'00"N 114°29'55"W
Approximately 50 km south-east of
Mayerthorpe, in Lac Ste Anne.

The name for this island appears on a
Surveys map of 1953, and has been official
since at least 1958, but its precise origin is
unknown.

Farrant (locality)

83 A/5 - Red Deer
31-39-26-W4
52°24'N 113°44'W
Approximately 7 km south of Lacombe.

The Canadian Northern Railway established a station here in 1914, but the precise
origin for the name is unknown.

Farrell Creek (creek)

82 P/16 - Farrell Creek
35-33-18-W4
51°53'N 112°27'W
Flows north-east into Farrell Lake, approximately 43 km north-west of Hanna.

(see Farrell Lake)

---

*denotes rescinded name or former locality.

Farrell Lake (lake)
82 P/16 - Farrell Lake
34-33-17-W4
51°52′N 112°20′W
Approximately 35 km north-west of
Hanna.

This lake was named in 1907 after Lionel
Farrell, an early rancher and the first settler
in the area. Farrell, a native of Wyoming,
arrived in the area with his wife in 1903.
Farrell Lake was previously known as
"Long Lake," a name descriptive of the
length of the lake. The creek takes its name
from this lake.

Fawcett (hamlet)
83 J/9 - Flatbush
16-64-1-W5
54°32′N 114°05′W
Approximately 46 km north north-west of
Westlock.

The Edmonton, Dunvegan and British
Columbia Railway established a station
here and named it after the resident
engineer during the construction of the
railway. The settlement was previously
known as "French Creek." The post office
opened in March 1915.

Fawn Lake (locality)
83 J/1 - Barrhead
23-58-1-W5
54°02′N 114°02′W
Approximately 25 km east south-east of
Barrhead.

This locality, whose post office operated
here from February 1911 through August
1947, is named for its proximity to a former
small lake of the same name. It is likely the
lake had a legend attached to it concerning a
young deer.

Federal (locality)
73 D/4 - Castor
19-36-11-W4
52°06′30″N 111°34′00″W
Approximately 7 km west of Coronation.

A Canadian Pacific Railway station was
established here in 1910 and took its name
from concept of the Federal Government.
The post office operated from August 1912
through July 1962.

Fedorah (locality)
83 H/14 - Redwater
10-57-23-W4
53°55′N 113°20′W
Approximately 40 km north north-east of
Edmonton.

This locality was named in 1908 after the
play *Fédora* written by the French playwright Victorien Sardou (1831-1908).
Sardou, in the manner common to the time,
wrote several plays in order to feature a
particular performer and *Fédora* was
written for Sarah Bernhardt who played the
title role of Princess Fédora. While the
locality was named for the play, the "h"
was apparently added later by postal
officials when the post office was established in the area, although it is not known
why. Albert Leroy, an immigrant from
Belgium, was the first postmaster, and he
recommended the name for the post office.

Felix Lake (lake)
73 L/3 - Vincent Lake
11-58-9-W4
54°00′15″N 111°14′00″W
Approximately 5 km east north-east of St.
Paul.

The name for this lake has been official
since at least 1958, but its precise origin is
unknown.

Fenn (locality)
83 A/2 - Big Valley
1-37-20-W4
52°08′N 112°44′W
Approximately 21 km south of Stettler.

The Canadian Northern Railway established a station here in 1911. The name for
the post office, which opened in April 1917,
originated by way of three possible
theories: one, that the village was named for
the Fen Country in England (because of the
marshy resemblance); two, that it was
named for a young boy who worked for the
railroad crew by bringing the men water;
and three, that it takes the name of one of
the railway officials.

* **Fenner** (former locality)
72 M/14 - Kirkpatrick Lake
4-33-10-W4
51°50′N 111°22′W
Approximately 35 km north-east of Hanna.

This former locality takes its name from
George Fenner, a settler in the area who
was also the first postmaster. The post
office operated from August 1912 through
April 1937.

* **Ferguson Flats** (former locality)
73 E/15 - Elk Point
2-58-5-W4
53°58′N 110°37′W
Approximately 20 km north-east of Elk
Point.

The name for the post office, which
operated here from September 1912
through August 1945, was taken after W.R.
Ferguson, the first postmaster. The name
was officially rescinded in 1970.

Ferintosh (village)
83 A/15 - Ferintosh
3-44-21-W4

52°46'00"N 112°58'05"W
Approximately 29 km south south-west of
Camrose.

The post office was established here in May
1910, and the name was proposed by a local
resident, Dr. J.R. McLeod, a member of the
first Legislature of Alberta, 1905. The name
is taken after the village of Ferintosh, in
Ross and Cromarty (now Highland),
Scotland. Ferintosh was also the name of a
whisky from a privileged distillery in the
lairdship of Ferintosh belonging to Forbes
of Culloden. This village was incorporated
9 January 1911.

Ferlow Junction (locality)

83 A/15 - Ferintosh
5-46-20-W4
52°57'N 112°53'W
Approximately 10 km south south-west of
Camrose.

The name for this locality has been official
since 1960, but its origin is unknown.

Fern Creek (locality)

83 G/1 - Warburg
32-47-2-W5
53°06'N 114°15'W
Approximately 52 km west north-west of
Wetaskiwin.

A post office operated here from May 1913
through May 1955, and was named for its
proximity to a creek upon whose shores
many ferns grew.

Fernand Lake (lake)

83 I/4 - Westlock
27-59-27-W4
54°07'N 113°58'W
Approximately 7 km south-west of
Westlock.

The name for this lake has been official
since at least 1958, but its precise origin is
unknown.

Ferry Point (river crossing)

83 A/10 - Donalda
8-32-43-18-W4
52°44'50"N 112°34'00"W
Approximately 40 km south-east of
Camrose.

This was formerly a ferry crossing on the
Battle River. There was once a small trading
post on the north bank. Mr. Olsen and his
brothers hauled lumber from Wetaskiwin
in 1905 and built the Ferry Point Church.
At that time there was only a small ferry
that served the early settlers. The crossing is
now a modern bridge on secondary
highway 850.

* Ferrybank (former locality)

83 A/13 - Bearhills Lake
36-43-27-W4
52°45'N 113°47'W
Approximately 17 km north-west of
Ponoka.

A post office operated here from December
1905 through February 1927. There was a
ferry in operation nearby on the Battle
River. It was known previously as "Fairy
Bank," from the odd shape of the ravine.

* Fertility (former locality)

72 M/13 - Garden Plain
22-33-13-W4
51°51'N 111°47'W
Approximately 25 km north north-east of
Hanna.

The descriptive name for this former post
office refers to the land upon which it was
situated.

Field Lake (lake)

73 L/12 - Beaver Lake
11-24-66-14-W4
54°43'48"N 111°59'23"W
Approximately 5 km south of Lac La Biche.

The name for this lake has been official
since at least 1958 and commemorates R.
Field, a druggist from Lac La Biche. A
common local name for the feature is
"Long Lake." It has also been recorded by
Ross Cox as "Le Petit Lac de Biche" from
1817. Field Lake was part of a major fur
trade route for 25 years, until 1824.

Fifteen Lake (lake)

83 G/1 - Warburg
15-48-4-W5
53°08'N 114°29'W
Approximately 34 km east south-east of
Drayton Valley.

The name for this lake was suggested by a
Topographical Survey Engineer whose
name is not known, prior to 1950. It is
likely descriptive of its location in Section
15-Tp 48-R4-W5M.

Figure Lake (lake)

83 I/7 - Newbrook
11-63-18-W4
54°26'N 112°36'W
Approximately 54 km south-east of
Athabasca.

The name for this lake has been official
since at least 1958, but its precise origin is
unknown.

Fish Lake (lake)

73 D/11 - Hardisty
2-43-10-W4
52°41'N 111°21'W
Approximately 5 km west of Hardisty.

---

*denotes rescinded name or former locality.

The name for this lake was approved in 1960, and is likely descriptive of the plethora of fish to be found in it.

Fisher Creek (creek)

73 L/11 - Pinehurst Lake
36-66-8-W4
54°44'N 111°05'W
Flows south-west into Wolf River, approximately 42 km east of Lac La Biche.

The name for this creek has been official since at least 1958, but its precise origin is unknown.

Fisher Home (locality)

83 G/1 - Warburg
14-47-2-W5
53°03'N 114°10'W
Approximately 55 km west north-west of Wetaskiwin.

A post office operated here from March 1907 through September 1969 and the name reflected the fact that the first postmaster was an ardent fisherman.

Fishing Lake (lake)

73 E/16 - Frog Lake
3-57-2-W4
53°54'N 110°13'W
Approximately 44 km east of Elk Point.

The name for this lake has been official since at least 1958 and probably refers to the plentiful fish in the lake.

Fishing Lake (Métis Settlement)

73 L/1 - Reita Lake
57-2-W4
54°00'N 110°10'W
North of Lloydminster.

A Métis Colony was created by Order-in-Council No. 2125/70 and took its name from the lake. (see Fishing Lake) Its name has been changed from Fishing Lake Métis Colony and Fishing Lake Métis Settlement #10.

Fitzallen (locality)

83 H/9 - Mundare
6-53-14-W4
53°33'N 112°03'W
Approximately 6 km north of Vegreville.

The Canadian Pacific Railway established a station here in 1931 and named it after Mr. Fitzallen, a one-time secretary of the town of Vegreville.

Fitzgerald Lake (lake)

72 M/14 - Kirkpatrick Lake
3-33-8-W4
51°48'N 111°04'W
Approximately 40 km south-east of Coronation.

The precise origin for the name of this feature is unknown.

Five Kill Hill (hill)

73 E/1 - Paradise Valley
1,12-49-4-W4
53°12'17"N 110°27'12"W
Approximately 31 km west south-west of Lloydminster.

The name for this hill was officially approved 22 January 1991 and is believed to be from the Cree *neeanan-kahnipahate*, "the place where five were killed." There is a competing local legend that at one time five North West Mounted Police were killed on or near the site and the name was used to identify the place.

Five Mile Island (island)

83 J/3 - Green Court
23-60-8-W5
54°11'N 115°07'W
Approximately 38 km east of Whitecourt.

The name for this island in the Athabasca River has been official since at least 1958 and likely describes its length.

Flag Hill (hill)

82 P/16 - Farrell Lake
12-33-17-W4
51°49'20"N 112°16'30"W
Approximately 32 km north-west of Hanna.

The name is derived from the ranching period when a cowboy, Bob Cooney, tied a gunny sack to a tree in order to mark the location of a sick cow. The sack on this small hill later became a landmark for residents in the area.

Flag Lake (lake)

73 D/11 - Hardisty
27-11-W4
52°34'N 111°29'W
Approximately 18 km south-west of Hardisty.

The name for this lake has been in use since at least 1958, but its precise origin is unknown.

* Flagstaff (former post office)

73 D/11 - Hardisty
4-41-12-W4
52°28'N 111°32'W
Approximately 32 km south-west of Hardisty.

(see Flagstaff Hill)

Flagstaff County #29 (county)
73 D/12 - Lougheed
39 to 46-10 to 17-W4
52°40'N 111°50'W
South-east of Camrose.

This county is named after Flagstaff Hill.
(see Flagstaff Hill)

Flagstaff Hill (hill)
73 D/12 - Lougheed
16-41-11-W4
52°32'N 111°34'W
Approximately 40 km south-west of
Hardisty.

This hill gives the former post office and
the county their names. The name is a
rough translation from the Cree *his-ki-wa-
or-nis ka-hko-hta-ke*, or "flag-hanging
hill." The hill was apparently a gathering
place for the Sarcee.

Flammand, Lac (lake)
73 E/14 - St. Paul
11-57-8-W4
53°54'N 111°05'W
Approximately 13 km west of Elk Point.

This lake may commemorate Joseph
Flammand, an early homesteader who filed
on a special permit circa 1909.

Flat Creek (creek)
83 I/10 - Boyle
13-18-66-19-W4
From 54°45'00"N 112°52'24"W
to 54°42'34"N 112°52'23"W
Flows north into Pine Creek, approximately 28 km east north-east of Athabasca.

The name for this creek, which drains Flat
Lake, has been official since at least 1928.

Flat Lake (lake)
73 L/3 - Vincent Lake
7-59-8-W4
54°05'N 111°12'W
Approximately 14 km north north-east of
St. Paul.

(see Flat Lake)

Flat Lake (lake)
83 I/10 - Boyle
12-25-65,66-19,20-W4
54°39'17"N 112°53'57"W
Approximately 28 km east south-east of
Athabasca.

The descriptive name for this lake has been
official since at least 1928. It is a translation
from the French "Le Lac Plat."

Flat Lake (locality)
73 L/3 - Vincent Lake
28-59-8-W4
54°08'N 111°09'W
Approximately 19 km north north-east of
St. Paul.

The descriptive name for this locality,
whose post office operated from March
1909 through September 1970, refers to the
surrounding terrain which is very flat, and
the nearby lake which is shallow.

Flatbush (hamlet)
83 J/9 - Flatbush
1-66-2-W5
54°42'N 114°09'W
Approximately 55 km west of Athabasca.

The descriptive name for this hamlet
reflects the countryside, flat and full of
trees. The post office opened in January
1916, closed in April 1917, and reopened in
April 1923.

Flatbush Creek (creek)
83 J/9 - Flatbush
10-66-2-W5
54°42'N 114°13'W
Flows west into Pembina River, approximately 58 km west of Athabasca.

(see Flatbush)

Fleeinghorse Lake (lake)
73 D/8 - Provost
10-39-2-W4
52°20'N 110°13'W
Approximately 6 km east of Provost.

The name for this lake has been in use since
at least 1958, but its precise origin is
unknown.

Fleet (hamlet)
73 D/4 - Castor
1-37-13-W4
52°09'N 111°44'W
Approximately 15 km south-east of Castor.

There are two different explanations for the
origin of this name. The first states that the
name was changed from "The Hub" in the
coronation year of King George V in
honour of the British Fleet. The second
maintains that the Canadian Pacific
Railway station, established in 1910, was
named for the company's fleet of ships. The
post office operated from August 1912
through January 1973 under this name.

Fleming Slough (marsh)
83 A/4 - Innisfail
35-36-28-W4
52°08'N 113°53'W
Approximately 15 km south south-west of
Red Deer.

Named after the Fleming family who
owned the land next to this feature.

* Floating Stone (former locality)

73 L/5 - Goodfish Lake
5-61-11-W4
54°16′N 111°36′W
Approximately 35 km north-west of St. Paul.

This former locality, whose post office operated from August 1930 through September 1947, has a descriptive name taken for its proximity to Floatingstone Lake. (see Floatingstone Lake) The name was officially rescinded 10 November 1970.

■ **Floatingstone Lake** (lake)

73 L/4 - Cache Lake
31,32-60-11-W4
54°13′N 111°38′W
Approximately 33 km north-west of St. Paul.

The descriptive name for this lake has been official since circa 1911 and is a translation of the Cree name, *assinkagama*. A solitary stone stands up 3.6-4.5 metres (12-15 ft) out of the lake, giving it the illusion that it is "floating" on the water.

Flyingcamp Lake (lake)

83 I/16 - Plamondon
8-67-15-W4
54°47′00″N 112°15′30″W
Approximately 19 km west of Lac La Biche.

The name for this lake appeared on a township map dated 1922 and was officially approved in January 1948. Its precise origin is not clear, but it may have been near a fishing or survey camp base. It has also been known locally as "Patenaud Lake" and "Lebeuf Lake."

Flyingshot Lake (lake)

83 H/10 - Elk Island Park
2-53-20-W4
53°32′N 112°51′W
Approximately 49 km east of Edmonton.

The name for this lake has been official since at least 1958, but its precise origin is unknown.

Foisy (locality)

73 E/13 - Hairy Hill
4-57-11-W4
53°53′N 111°35′W
Approximately 22 km south-west of St. Paul.

The name for this locality, whose post office opened in September 1919, is named after Aladin Foisy, the first postmaster.

* Foreman (former locality)

83 A/8 - Halkirk
21-40-16-W4
52°27′N 112°13′W
Approximately 35 km east north-east of Stettler.

The post office, which operated here from September 1905 through March 1946, was named after E.R. (Dick) Foreman, the first postmaster and early settler. In 1891 William Foreman and his wife, along with his son, Dick, and his wife, Mary (nee Ennis) left the Muskoka area of Ontario for Red Deer, Alberta. The family left to live in B.C. permanently in 1916.

Forestburg (village)

83 A/9 - Forestburg
2-42-15-W4
52°35′00″N 112°03′50″W
Approximately 27 km south south-west of Killam.

The post office opened here in January 1915. There are two possible origins of the name. One maintains that it was named for Forestburg, South Dakota, the former home of an early resident. Another is that it was taken after Forestburg, Ontario, as some of the settlers came from that province. When the Canadian Northern Railway was built here in 1915 the post office was known as "Duxbury" and was approximately four kilometres south of the present village, incorporated 21 August 1919.

Fork Creek (creek)

73 L/6 - Goodridge
6-63-10-W4
54°25′N 111°29′W
Flows south-east into Beaver River, approximately 50 km south-east of Lac La Biche.

(see Fork Lake)

Fork Lake (lake)

73 L/5 - Goodfish Lake
8-21-63-11-W4
54°27′46″N 111°35′40″W
Approximately 41 km south south-east of Lac La Biche.

The descriptive name for this lake has been official since 16 January 1911 and refers to its shape like the prongs of a fork.

Fork Lake (locality)

73 L/5 - Goodfish Lake
20-63-11-W4
54°28′N 111°37′W
Approximately 44 km south-east of Lac La Biche.

The post office operated here from October 1917 through July 1970 and was named for its location on Fork Lake. (see Fork Lake)

Forshee (railway point)

83 B/9 - Rimbey
25-41-2-W5
52°33′N 114°09′W

_____
*denotes rescinded name or former locality.

Approximately 12 km south-east of Rimbey.

The Lacombe and North Western Railway established a station here in 1919 and named it after a place of the same name in Virginia. The post office operated here from November 1911 through January 1914, then reopened from April 1936 through May 1968.

Forsyth Lake (lake)

73 L/7 - Bonnyville
6-62-6-W4
54°20′N 110°54′W
Approximately 12 km north-west of Bonnyville.

The name for this lake has been official since at least 1958, but the precise origin is unknown.

Fort Island (island)

73 E/14 - St. Paul
17-55-8-W4
53°45′N 111°10′W
Approximately 23 km south-west of Elk Point, in the North Saskatchewan River.

The name for this island likely refers to a fur trading fort nearby, but its precise origin is unknown.

Fort Kent (hamlet)

73 L/7 - Bonnyville
25-61-5-W4
54°19′N 110°37′W
Approximately 12 km north-east of Bonnyville.

The post office was established here in July 1922. The name was suggested by a former resident of a town of the same name in Maine.

Fort Saskatchewan (city)

83 H/11 - Edmonton
33-54-22-W4
53°42′54″N 113°11′42″W
Approximately 35 km north-east of Edmonton.

Fort Saskatchewan was established in 1875 by Inspector W.O. Jarvis as the first North West Mounted Police post in the region. In Cree *simaganis arilamik* means "soldier house," and *saskatchewan* is the equivalent of "swift current." The citizens of Edmonton complained that the post was not built nearer Edmonton, but surveys for a railroad through the Yellowhead Pass crossed the river at that point and the site was considered suitable for transport purposes. The Canadian Pacific Railway was not built through the Yellowhead Pass, but the post remained. The town was incorporated 1 July 1904. The city was incorporated 1 July 1985.

Fort Saskatchewan, 1898

Forth (locality)

83 A/4 - Innisfail
8-38-27-W4
52°15′N 113°49′W
Immediately south of Red Deer.

The station was named in 1920 by Canadian Pacific Railway officials after the river in Scotland over whose estuary, the Firth of Forth, the Forth Railway Bridge was built. Opened in 1889 the huge cantilever bridge was one of the great engineering achievements of the nineteenth century.

Fox Lake (lake)

72 M/12 - Hanna
18-31-14-W4
51°39′30″N 111°59′00″W
Part of the St. Louis Lakes, approximately 4 km west of Hanna.

This lake was named for James Fox, an early settler in the vicinity of the lake, originally from Ontario. While biographical details of Mr. Fox are sketchy, the name is well-established within the area.

Foxall Lakes (lakes)

83 A/2 - Big Valley
28-37-21-W4
52°12′N 112°58′W
Approximately 21 km south-west of Stettler.

This group of three lakes, originally simply "Foxall Lake," were named in honour of Benjamin Foxall, an early homesteader who lived around the lake circa 1904.

* Frains (former post office)

83 I/15 - Grassland
35-66-18-W4
54°45′N 112°35′W
Approximately 42 km west of Lac La Biche.

The origin for the name of the post office, which operated here from March 1934 through April 1969, is unknown. The name was officially rescinded 28 April 1970.

Franchere (locality)

73 L/6 - Goodridge
8-61-7-W4
54°16′N 111°02′W
Approximately 18 km west of Bonnyville.

This locality, whose post office operated from December 1929 through November 1977, was named after Gabriel Franchère, the author of *Relation d'un voyage à la côte du Nord-Ouest de l'Amerique Septentrionale* (1820). This was the first published description of a journey through the Rockies by way of the Athabasca River. Franchère (1786-1863) travelled east from the Columbia River via Moose Lake in 1814.

Francis Lake (lake)

73 L/13 - Lac La Biche
11-11-69-11-W4
54°57'38"N 111°34'20"W
Approximately 34 km north-east of Lac La Biche.

The name for this lake was officially adopted 3 May 1951 and commemorates a native named Philip Francis.

Francis Lake (lake)

83 I/12 - Coolidge
18-66-25-W4
54°42'00"N 113°47'00"W
Approximately 33 km west of Athabasca.

The name for this lake has been official since at least 1958, but its precise origin is unknown.

Frank Lake (lake)

83 I/11 - Athabasca
20-64-21-W4
54°33'N 113°08'W
Approximately 22 km south-east of Athabasca.

The name for this lake has been official since at least 1958, but its precise origin is unknown.

Fraspur (locality)

83 G/2- Easyford
10-47-4-W5
53°02'N 114°30'W
Approximately 39 km south-east of Drayton Valley.

A lumber mill belonging to the D.R. Fraser & Co. Ltd. was moved here in 1927. The lumber company began in Edmonton in 1881. This locality may take its name from the company.

* Freda (former locality)

72 M/15 - Monitor
7-33-7-W4
51°48'N 110°58'W
Approximately 45 km south-east of Coronation.

The origin of the name for this former locality, at which a post office operated from 1924 through 1931, is unknown.

Freedom (locality)

83 J/1 - Barrhead
4-60-2-W5
54°09'N 114°14'W
Approximately 11 km east north-east of Barrhead.

This locality was renamed in January 1919 with the change of name for the post office, commemorating the Allied victory over the Central powers in World War I. But the community situated west of Westlock in the Barrhead district predated this name by nearly a decade. The school district was established on 11 March 1912 to be followed in 1913 with the building of the school. The original homesteaders in the area were Germans or were of German origin, and named the post office Dusseldorf. The Great War had a considerable impact on the German heritage of Alberta. Several names of German origin were changed during and after the war, and this was no exception. The change was made official 5 March 1921.

French Creek (creek)

83 J/9 - Flatbush
3-64-1-W5
54°30'N 114°05'W
Flows south-west into Pembina River, approximately 56 km south-west of Athabasca.

(see French Creek)

* French Creek (former hamlet)

83 J/9 - Flatbush
16-64-1-W5
54°32'N 114°05'W
Approximately 56 km west south-west of Athabasca.

The origin for the name of this former hamlet is unknown. The name was changed to Fawcett in March 1915. (see Fawcett)

Frenchman Lake (lake)

73 L/11 - Pinehurst Lake
14-16-64-10-W4
54°32'30"N 111°27'26"W
Approximately 42 km south-east of Lac La Biche.

The name for this lake has been in use since at least 1928, and may refer to a Métis trapper family.

Frenchman's Creek (creek)

73 D/5 - Alliance
10-1-39-12-W4
52°19'40"N 111°35'50"W
Flows north into Battle River, approximately 26 km north-east of Castor.

This creek became known by this name when the area around the creek was settled by francophones.

Freshwater Lake (lake)

73 D/9 - Chauvin
12-42-1-W4
52°36'N 110°00'W

Approximately 35 km north-east of Provost, on the Alberta-Saskatchewan boundary.

The name for this lake has been in use since at least 1958 and is likely descriptive.

Fresnoy (locality)

73 L/2 - Muriel Lake
35-60-6-W4
54°14'N 110°48'W
Approximately 5 km south-west of Bonnyville.

The name for the post office, which operated here from August 1918 through June 1929, commemorated the town in Aisne, France, north-east of St. Quentin captured by Canadian troops 13 April 1917.

* **Fribourg** (former locality)

73 E/11 - Myrnam
18-55-9-W4
53°44'N 111°16'W
Approximately 29 km east north-east of Two Hills.

The name for the post office, which operated here from September 1911 through May 1932, was taken after a town in Switzerland, the former home of the first postmaster, M. Carrel.

Frog Creek (creek)

73 E/16 - Frog Lake
18-55-3-W4
53°45'N 110°26'W
Flows south into North Saskatchewan River, approximately 33 km south-east of Elk Point.

(see Frog Lake)

Frog Lake (locality)

73 E/16 - Frog Lake
17-56-3-W4
53°50'N 110°25'W
Approximately 34 km east south-east of Elk Point.

The post office opened here in April 1911 and was named for its proximity to Frog Lake. (see Frog Lake)

Frog Lake Settlement, 1885

Frog Lake (lake)

73 E/16 - Frog Lake
12-56,57-2,3-W4
53°55'N 110°20'W
Approximately 39 km east of Elk Point.

(see Frog Lake)

Frog Lake (lake)

83 G/2 - Drayton Valley
28-48-4-W5
53°11'N 114°32'W
Approximately 30 km east of Drayton Valley.

The name for this lake appears as early as 1859 and is labelled on Palliser's map. It is a translation of a Cree name, *ah-yik-sa-kha-higan*. Frog Lake was the scene of the massacre of nine people by a band of Big

Bear's Indians at the outbreak of the Riel Rebellion in 1885. Included in the individuals were two Oblate missionaries, Father Léon Fofard, and Father Félix Marchand.

Fulton Creek (creek)

83 H/11 - Edmonton
11-53-24-W4
53°33'N 113°25'W
Flows north-west into a steel plant immediately south-east of Edmonton.

This creek was named for Daniel S. Fulton, one of the earliest homesteaders in the Clover Bar district, who arrived from Nova Scotia in 1884. He operated a coal mine which began running in 1902. Fulton Place is a subdivision in Edmonton, and is also named for him.

Fyten Reservoir (reservoir)

82 P/11 - Three Hills
4,9-30-24-W4
51°33'N 113°20'W
Approximately 18 km south of Three Hills.

The name for this reservoir was supplied by a field topographer in 1975. The name has been used on record with a licence supplied by the Municipal District of Kneehill No. 48, since 1964. The property was originally owned by George Fyten and the reservoir is named after him.

Gadois Lake (lake)

73 E/15 - Elk Point
19-57-4-W4
53°56'N 110°35'W
Approximately 21 km east north-east of Elk Point.

The name for this lake has been official since at least 1958, but its precise origin is unknown.

Gadsby (village)
83 A/8 - Halkirk
27-38-17-W4
52°17'50"N 112°21'20"W
Approximately 25 km east of Stettler.

The name for this village, whose post office opened in November 1909, was taken after M.F. Gadsby, of Ottawa. This village was incorporated 6 May 1910.

Gadsby Lake (lake)
83 A/11 - Chain Lakes
22-41-23-W4
52°32'30"N 113°14'00"W
Approximately 19 km west south-west of Bashaw.

The name for this lake was taken after James Gadsby, an early settler. Gadsby (?-1932) originally hailed from St. Catharines, Ontario. After spending much of his life in the United States and in other parts of Alberta, he ultimately came to this district where he remained until his death. The village was incorporated 6 May 1910.

Gaetz Creek (creek)
83 A/3 - Delburne
2-38-24-W4
52°15'N 113°19'W
Flows north into Red Deer River, approximately 40 km east of Red Deer.

(see Gaetz Valley)

Gaetz Lakes (lake)
83 A/5 - Red Deer
22-38-27-W4
52°17'N 113°45'W
Approximately 2 km north north-east of Red Deer.

(see Gaetz Valley)

* **Gaetz Valley** (former post office)
83 A/3 - Delburne
21-37-23-W4
51°12'N 113°14'W
Approximately 42 km east south-east of Red Deer.

The post office operated here from August 1907 through August 1911 and was named after Rev. Leonard Gaetz (1841 - 1907), early homesteader and Methodist minister.

Gainer (railway point)
83 H/6 - Cooking Lake
16-52-24-W4
53°29'N 113°29'W
Immediately east of Edmonton.

The origin for the name of this railway point along the Canadian Pacific Railway is unknown.

Gainford (hamlet)
83 G/10 - Isle Lake
14-53-6-W5
53°35'N 114°47'W
Approximately 43 km north north-east of Drayton Valley.

A post office opened here in October 1910. It was previously called "Seba." The name Gainford is taken after a town in Durham, England. It is a combination from the Old English *gegn*, meaning "direct" and "ford."

Galahad (village)
73 D/12 - Lougheed
10-41-14-W4
52°30'55"N 111°56'00"W
Approximately 33 km north of Castor.

The post office opened here under the name Galahad in May 1907, but the area had previously been known as "Galahad," likely after the famous knight of the Round Table. This village was incorporated 5 March 1918.

Galloway (locality)
83 F/10 - Bickerdike
34-52-20-W5
53°32'N 116°53'W
Approximately 31 km west south-west of Edson.

The Grand Trunk Pacific Railway established a station here in 1911 and named it after David Ernest Galloway, one-time assistant to the president of the Grand Trunk Pacific and later assistant vice-president of the Canadian National Railways. Mr. Galloway started with the Grand Trunk Railway in Hamilton in 1901 and was later in Montreal and Toronto.

Gambling Lake (lake)
83 H/7 - Tofield
20-50-20-W4
53°20'N 112°54'W
Approximately 33 km north north-west of Camrose.

The name for this lake has been official since at least 1958, but its precise origin is unknown.

Gamma Lake (lake)
83 G/12 - Carrot Creek
15-55-11-W5
53°44'50"N 115°33'00"W
Approximately 34 km south-west of Mayerthorpe.

The name for this lake has been official since at least 1958. *Gamma* is the third letter of the Greek alphabet; however, its connection to this lake is unknown.

Garden Plain (locality)
72 M/13 - Garden Plain
32-33-13-W4
51°52'N 111°47'W
Approximately 26 km north north-east of Hanna.

The name for this locality, whose post office operated from January 1910 through October 1927, is likely descriptive of the fertility of the soil.

Gardenview (locality)

83 G/15 - Sangudo
32-57-4-W5
53°59′N 114°33′W
Approximately 19 km south-west of Barrhead.

The post office, which operated here from February 1938 through April 1957, had a descriptive name.

Garfield (locality)

82 O/9 - Didsbury
20-30-3-W5
51°35′N 114°23′W
Approximately 20 km west of Carstairs.

The post office, which operated here from June 1926 through June 1956, was named after James A. Garfield (1831-81), President of the United States from 4 March to 19 September 1881. It is not known who named the small locality after the President, who was shot on 2 July 1881 in a Washington Railway station by Charles J. Guiteau, a lawyer and disappointed office seeker. He died 11 weeks later. Vice-President Chester A. Arthur was sworn in on 20 September to succeed him.

■ **Garner Lake** (lake)

73 L/4 - Cache Lake
21-60-12-W4
54°12′N 111°44′W
Approximately 36 km north-west of St. Paul.

The name for this lake has been official since 28 July 1945 and is taken after G. Garner who owned the north-west quarter, Sec 24, Tp 60, Rg 12, W4M in 1904.

*denotes rescinded name or former locality.

Garner Lake Provincial Park

(provincial park)

73 L/4 - Cache Lake
16-60-12-W4
54°11′N 111°44′W
Approximately 35 km north-west of St. Paul.

This 73.68 hectare (182.08 acre) park was created by Order-in-Council No. 977/69 and was named for its position on Garner Lake. (see Garner Lake)

Garnier Lakes (lakes)

73 E/15 - Elk Point
8-58-4-W4
54°00′30″N 110°34′40″W
Approximately 24 km north-east of Elk Point.

These two lakes were officially named for Gus Garnier on 4 September 1981. He homesteaded a quarter-section at the south end of the south lake circa 1912, and his name has been associated with the lakes since then. The two lakes are distinguished locally as "Big Garnier Lake" (formerly Bluet Lake) and "Little Garnier Lake."

Garrington (locality)

82 O/16 - Olds
24-34-4-W5
51°56′N 114°26′W
Approximately 20 km north-east of Sundre.

The name for the post office, which operated here from May 1908 through September 1949, was taken after the son of the first postmaster, H.C. Monday.

Garson Lake (lake)

73 E/9 - Marwayne
3-55-1-W4
53°43′N 110°04′W
Approximately 50 km north of Lloydminster.

The name for this lake has been official since at least 1958, but its precise origin is unknown.

* **Garth** (former post office)

73 L/10 - Marguerite Lake
16-64-7-W4
54°33′N 110°59′W
Approximately 34 km north-west of Bonnyville.

The post office operated here from January 1939 through September 1964 and has the same name as the Old English term for "garden." The name was officially rescinded 10 November 1970.

Garth (locality)

83 B/6 - Crimson Lake
12-39-8-W5
52°21′N 115°01′W
Approximately 7 km south-west of Rocky Mountain House.

A post office operated here from August 1913 through April 1917 and was named after a railway official.

Gartly (locality)

82 P/10 - Munson
11-30-19-W4
51°34′N 112°35′W
Approximately 45 km west south-west of Hanna.

A Canadian Northern Railway station was established here in 1914 and its name is that of a parish in Aberdeenshire (now Grampian), Scotland.

Gat Lake (lake)

73 D/10 - Hughenden
3-43-6-W4
52°41′N 110°47′W
Approximately 19 km south of the town of Wainwright.

The name for this lake has been in use since at least 1958, but its origin is unknown.

Geall Lake (lake)
83 I/5 - Grassland
16-62-27-W4
54°22'N 114°00'W
Approximately 28 km north north-west of Westlock.

The name for this lake has been official since at least 1958, but its precise origin is unknown.

Gedeon Lake (lake)
73 E/15 - Elk Point
4-56-7-W4
53°48'N 110°58'W
Approximately 11 km south south-west of Elk Point.

The name for this lake has been official since at least 1958, but its precise origin is unknown.

Genesee (locality)
83 G/8 - Genesee
27-50-3-W5
53°21'N 114°20'W
Approximately 63 km west south-west of Edmonton.

A post office operated here from March 1916 through April 1969. The name was suggested by Bert White who came from Genesee, Idaho, and his suggestion was adopted by a meeting of settlers of the area. Genesee, Idaho takes its name from the town of Geneseo, in the Genesee Valley of western New York state. The name is said to come from an Iroquoian word meaning "valley beautiful."

Genesee Lake (reservoir)
83 G/8 - Genesee
26&27-50-3-W5
53°21'N 114°20'W

Approximately 50 km west south-west of Edmonton.

Edmonton Power's Genesee Project created a cooling/recreational reservoir at this location commencing July 1984. (see Genesee)

Genest Lake (lake)
73 D/6 - Brownfield
2-39-9-W4
52°19'N 111°13'W
Approximately 30 km north-east of Coronation.

The name for this lake has been in use since at least 1958, but its origin is unknown.

Geneva Lake (lake)
73 E/6 - Mannville
13-52-9-W4
53°29'N 111°12'W
Approximately 29 km north-west of Vermilion.

This lake and the nearby post office were named simultaneously. (see Lake Geneva)

Geoffrey Lake (lake)
83 G/16 - Lac la Nonne
32-56-1-W5
53°53'N 114°06'W
Approximately 33 km south south-east of Barrhead.

The name for this lake has been official since at least 1958, but the origin is unknown.

George Lake (lake)
83 A/9 - Forestburg
21-41-15-W4
52°32'N 112°06'W
Approximately 50 km north-east of Stettler.

The name for this lake has been official since at least 1958, but its precise origin is unknown.

George Lake (lake)
83 G/16 - Lac la Nonne
28-57-1-W5
53°57'N 114°05'W
Approximately 27 km south-east of Barrhead.

The name for this lake appears on a township plan of 1911. The origin is unknown; however, it was once called "Trap Lake," after an early native's unpleasant adventure here with a trap.

George Lake (lake)
83 I/11 - Athabasca
18-64-23-W4
54°32'N 113°28'W
Approximately 23 km south south-west of Athabasca.

The name for this lake has been official since at least 1958, but its precise origin is unknown.

Gerharts Lake (lake)
83 G/9 - Onoway
22-53-1-W5
53°36'N 114°03'W
Approximately 39 km west of Edmonton.

The name for this lake has been official since at least 1950 and was named after the early homesteaders who owned the land upon which the lake sits.

Ghost Lake (lake)
83 I/13 - Grosmont
16-68-24-W4
54°53'N 113°37'W
Approximately 28 km north-west of Athabasca.

The name for this lake has been official since at least 1958, but its precise origin is unknown.

* Ghost Pine (former railway point)

82 P/14 - Trochu
31-32-23-W4
51°47′N 113°14′W
Approximately 9 km north of Three Hills.

This railway point is now called Equity. (see Ghost Pine Creek and Equity)

Ghost Pine Creek (locality)

82 P/11 - Three Hills
5-32-22-W4
51°43′N 113°04′W
Approximately 14 km east of Three Hills.

A post office operated here from March 1907 through February 1970 and was named for its proximity to Ghostpine Creek. (see Ghostpine Creek)

Ghostpine Creek (creek)

82 P/10 - Fallentimber Creek
14-30-22-W4
51°34′N 112°59′W
Flows south-east into Red Deer River, approximately 25 km south-east of Three Hills.

Indian legend has it that about 1830, on the shores of Pine Lake, the Blackfoot Indians raided a sleeping camp of Cree and murdered every man, woman and child in the band. Only one Cree warrior survived since he had been away from the camp on a hunting expedition. When he returned and found all his family and friends murdered, the Cree painted his face black in mourning and set out on the trail of the Blackfoot. The lone Cree managed to kill and scalp many of his rival tribesmen, stealthily raiding their camps at night or else ambush-

ing any brave who became separated from the main group. For years afterwards, Cree Indians avoided Pine Lake. They thought the region was haunted by ghosts of the murdered people and it contained a weird-looking pine tree; the lake became known as Ghostpine. Ghostpine Creek flows from here and forms a junction with the Red Deer River, shortly after joining Three Hills Creek.

Gibbons (town)

83 H/14 - Redwater
10-56-23-W4
53°49′40″N 113°19′50″W
Approximately 30 km north of Edmonton.

The name for this town has undergone many changes. It was originally known as "Astleyville," then "Battenburg," before it was changed in September 1920 to honour William Reynolds Gibbons, who left Orillia, Ontario, with his family in April of 1892. This town was incorporated 1 April 1977.

* Gibbons Station (former post office)

83 H/14 - Redwater
10-56-23-W4
53°50′N 113°20′W
Approximately 28 km north north-east of Edmonton.

(see Gibbons)

Gibbs Lake (lake)

73 E/6 - Mannville
12-51-11-W4
53°22′50″N 111°29′45″W
Approximately 39 km east south-east of Vegreville.

The well-established name for this lake was officially approved 11 August 1978. It was named after the original homesteader of the land, Gibb Roy, a well-liked homesteader who lived on the south-west quarter of Section 12 from 1904 until his death in 1975.

Gilbert Lake (lake)

83 I/11 - Athabasca
6-64-21-W4
54°30′15″N 113°09′00″W
Approximately 24 km south south-east of Athabasca.

The name for this lake appeared on a Sectional Map dated 1948, but its precise origin is unknown.

Gilby (locality)

83 B/8 - Sylvan Lake
20-40-3-W5
52°28′N 114°23′W
Approximately 12 km north of Eckville.

A post office operated here from July 1909 through January 1930 and was likely named after its first postmaster, O. Gilbertson.

Gillespie Lake (lake)

73 D/8 - Provost
11-39,40-2-W4
52°25′N 110°11′W
Approximately 10 km north-east of Provost.

The name for this lake has been in use since at least 1958, but its origin is unknown.

Gilpatrick Creek (creek)

83 B/8 - Sylvan Lake
5-39-2-W5
52°19′50″N 114°15′00″W
Flows south-east into Medicine River, approximately 8 km south-east of Eckville.

The locally well-established name for this creek was officially approved 22 January 1992. It is taken after George Gilpatrick, a homesteader who came to the area from Anita, Iowa circa 1922, and owned the south-east quarter of Sec 1-Tp39-R3-W5.

---

*denotes rescinded name or former locality.

Gilt Edge (locality)
73 D/15 - Wainwright
17-46-5-W4
52°57′N 110°43′W
Approximately 20 km north-east of the
town of Wainwright.

An early settler, Edward Monaghan, when
looking over the area, exclaimed he thought
the area to be rich with promise or "gilt-
edged," and the name was used for the post
office, which opened in June 1908.

Gladu Lake (lake)
83 H/12 - St. Albert
9-54-27-W4
53°39′N 113°54′W
Approximately 31 km west north-west of
Edmonton.

The name for this lake is taken after the
Métis family whose name is sometimes
spelled Gladue. They were early settlers
who came to the area from Minnesota
through Winnipeg circa 1855.

Glen Park (locality)
83 H/4 - Kavanagh
5-49-27-W4
53°12′N 113°55′W
Approximately 25 km west south-west of
Leduc.

The post office here took over when
Buford moved six and a half kilometres
north to the railway, and operated from
December 1939 through February 1969. It
was named after the Glen Park Cheese
Company.

Glendon (village)
73 L/6 - Goodridge
8-61-8-W4
54°15′15″N 111°09′15″W
Approximately 28 km west of Bonnyville.

This village was incorporated 1 January
1956. Its post office opened in September
1912 and was named after the maiden name
of the mother of the first postmaster, J.P.
Spencer.

Glenevis (hamlet)
83 G/15 - Sangudo
34-55-4-W5
53°48′N 114°31′W
Approximately 37 km south south-west of
Barrhead.

The name for this hamlet was suggested by
the first postmaster, John A. McLeod, after
his wife's hometown in Glennevis, Cape
Breton Island, N.S. The post office opened
in May 1913. One of the "n"s was omitted
in the original spelling.

Glenford (locality)
83 G/16 - Lac la Nonne
1-56-2-W5
53°48′N 114°12′W
Approximately 53 km north-west of
Edmonton.

The name for this locality, whose post
office operated from March 1909 through
August 1960, is a combination of "glen"
and the last syllable of the name of the first
postmaster, Thomas Rutherford.

* Glenhewitt (former locality)
83 A/12 - Ponoka
33-42-28-W4
52°40′N 113°58′W
Approximately 18 km east of Rimbey.

A post office operated here from November 1911 through April 1930 and was
named after the first postmaster, J.J.
Hewitt.

* Gleniffer (former locality)
83 B/1 - Markerville
35-35-2-W5
52°03′N 114°10′W

Approximately 36 km south-west of Red
Deer.

(see Gleniffer Lake)

Gleniffer Lake (reservoir)
83 B/1 - Markerville
24-35-2,3-W5
52°01′30″N 114°17′00″W
On the Red Deer River behind Dickson
Dam, approximately 40 km south-west of
Red Deer.

The name for this reservoir was officially
approved 28 June 1984, and was taken after
the former post office of Gleniffer, which
operated from October 1913 through April
1918. This was the nearest named point to
the site of the dam. William Robertson was
the postmaster at Gleniffer, and with his
wife and seven children emigrated from
Paisley, Scotland, to homestead circa 1902.
The name Gleniffer was likely derived from
the Gleniffer Braes (hills) south-west of
Paisley.

Glenister (locality)
83 J/2 - Thunder Lake
20-58-6-W5
54°02′N 114°51′W
Approximately 32 km west south-west of
Barrhead.

The name for this locality, whose post
office operated from February 1910
through November 1964, is a substitute for
Glenroy, the name originally requested by
the settlers.

* Glenshaw (former post office)
83 I/10 - Boyle
1-64-20-W4
54°30′N 112°54′W
Approximately 35 km south-east of
Athabasca.

The post office operated here under this
name from August 1915 through December

1916. It was likely named for L.C. Shaw, the first postmaster. The name was later changed to Ellscott. (see Ellscott)

Glory Lake (lake)

83 G/9 - Onoway
22-53-1-W5
53°35′N 114°04′W
Approximately 38 km west of Edmonton.

The name for this lake has been official since at least 1958, but its precise origin is unknown.

Godfrey Lake (lake)

73 D/4 - Castor
24-35-13-W4
52°01′N 111°43′W
Approximately 30 km west south-west of Coronation.

The name for this lake has been in use since at least 1923 when it appeared on a Wainwright sectional map, but the origin is unknown.

Godson Lake (lake)

73 E/3 - Buffalo Creek
10-49-10-W4
53°12′N 111°23′W
Approximately 30 km north-east of Viking.

The name for this lake has been official since at least 1958, but its precise origin is unknown.

Gold River (river)

83 I/16 - Plamondon
19-69-15-W4
54°58′N 112°14′W
Flows south into La Biche River, approximately 30 km north north-west of Lac La Biche.

The name for this river has been official since at least 1958, but its precise origin is unknown.

Golden Days (summer village)

83 G/1 - Warburg
15-47-1-W5
53°03′N 114°03′W
Approximately 43 km west north-west of Wetaskiwin.

The name for this summer village, incorporated 1 January 1965, reflects the "golden days of summer."

Golden Spike (locality)

83 H/5 - Leduc
21-51-27-W4
53°25′N 113°55′W
Approximately 28 km west south-west of Edmonton.

A post office operated here from March 1907 through February 1962. It may have been named for the spike driven by Donald Smith (see Strathcona Heights) when the Canadian Pacific Railway was completed in 1885.

* Good Hope (former locality)

83 H/10 - Elk Island Park
18-54-20-W4
53°39′N 112°57′W
Approximately 37 km east north-east of Edmonton.

The name for the post office, which operated here from March 1907 through November 1945, reflected the optimism of the early settlers for the future.

Goodfish Lake (lake)

73 L/5 - Goodfish Lake
5-24-61-13-W4
54°17′15″N 111°49′14″W
Approximately 48 km north-west of St. Paul.

The descriptive name for this feature refers to the multitude of birds and game animals in the vicinity, and the number of fish that were found in the lake in 1855 when the Reverend H.B. Steinhauer first visited it. Certain members of his party had set a net in the water before retiring for the night, and when they arose the next morning they found that they had caught more whitefish than could possibly be eaten fresh, so they remained to dry their catch before journeying to Whitefish Lake. The French equivalent for the lake has been recorded as "Lac Bon Poisson."

Goodfish Lake (locality)

73 L/5 - Goodfish Lake
24-61-13-W4
54°18′N 111°50′W
Approximately 47 km north-west of St. Paul.

The post office here was previously called "Whitefish Lake" and opened in April 1918. It took its name from the nearby lake. (see Goodfish Lake)

Goodridge (locality)

73 L/6 - Goodridge
30-62-9-W4
54°23′N 111°21′W
Approximately 43 km west north-west of Bonnyville.

This locality, whose post office opened in December 1932, was named after the Good brothers. Joseph H. Good (1888-1957) was the first postmaster. He and his brother, Richard, moved to the area from County Cork, Ireland, in 1929. There is no ridge in the vicinity.

Goodridge Lake (lake)

83 J/8 - Shoal Creek
9-63-2-W5
54°26′N 114°14′W
Approximately 35 km north north-east of Barrhead.

The name for this lake has been official since at least 1958, but its precise origin is unknown.

Goodwin Lake (lake)

83 J/4 - Whitecourt
8-59-13-W5
54°05′N 115°54′W
Approximately 16 km south-west of Whitecourt.

The name for this lake has been official since at least 1958, but its precise origin is unknown.

Goose Lake (hamlet)

73 L/12 - Beaver Lake
33-64-11-W4
54°34′N 111°36′W
Approximately 31 km south-east of Lac La Biche.

This hamlet, whose post office operated from August 1932 through July 1963, is named after the bird.

Goose Lake (lake)

72 M/11 - Youngstown
34-31-10-W4
51°41′N 111°20′W
Approximately 42 km east of Hanna.

The precise origin for the name of this feature is unknown.

Goose Lake (lake)

83 H/10 - Elk Island Park
12-53-20-W4
53°34′N 112°48′W
Approximately 55 km east of Edmonton.

The precise origin for the name of this lake is unknown.

---

*denotes rescinded name or former locality.

Gooseberry Lake (lake)

73 D/2 - Neutral Hills
26-36-6-W4
52°07′15″N 111°45′30″W
Approximately 41 km south-west of Provost.

The name for this lake, which is likely descriptive, has been in use since at least 1884, when mention was made of it in some notes by an early settler, F.W. Wilken. He noted that the water was quite saline, but made no mention of the origin of the name.

Gooseberry Lake Provincial Park

(provincial park)

73 D/2 - Neutral Hills
26-36-6-W4
52°07′N 110°44′W
Approximately 42 km south-west of Provost.

This 51.79 hectare (128.00 acre) park was created by Order-in-Council No. 529/66. The origin of the name of the lake from which the name of this park is taken is unclear; it was, however, named before 1886, and probably is descriptive of a local food resource. (see Gooseberry Lake)

Goosequill Lake (lake)

83 A/3 - Delburne
1-36-23-W4
52°03′N 113°09′W
Approximately 26 km north of Trochu.

The name for this lake is an approximate translation of the Cree word *manikwanan*.

* Gopher Head (former locality)

82 P/15 - Rumsey
6-35-18-W4
51°59′N 112°36′W
Approximately 37 km south south-east of Stettler.

The name for the post office, which operated here from December 1908 through January 1930, is taken from the nearby hill. (see Gopher Head)

Gopher Head (hill)

82 P/15 - Rumsey
32-33-18-W4
51°53′N 112°31′W
Approximately 50 km south south-east of Stettler.

This feature is locally well established and is prominent for miles. The shape of the hill is likened to that of a gopher's head and it is probable the appellation derives from this characteristic.

Gopher Lake (lake)

72 M/11 - Youngstown
3-32-10-W4
51°43′N 111°21′W
Approximately 40 km east north-east of Hanna.

The name for this lake is likely due to the large population of gophers to be found in the area.

Gosling Lake (lake)

83 B/15 - Buck Lak
23-44-6-W5
52°48′N 114°46′W
Approximately 39 km west north-west of Rimbey.

The name for this lake has been official since at least 1958, but its precise origin is unknown.

Gough Lake (lake)

83 A/2 - Big Valley
21-35-18-W4
52°02′N 112°31′W
Approximately 34 km south south-east of Stettler.

This lake was named by J.B. Tyrrell after a member of the Geological Survey party of 1884-1887.

* Gourin (former post office)
83 I/16 - Plamondon
23-67-17-W4
54°49′N 112°28′W
Approximately 35 km east of Lac La Biche.

The post office, which operated here from August 1923 through July 1967, was named after the capital of the French cantons from which the first postmaster, Joseph Ulliac, came in 1914 accompanied by his family of 17 members. The name was officially rescinded in 1970.

Grace Creek (creek)
83 B/11 - Baptiste River
5-41-9-W5
52°30′15″N 115°15′15″W
Flows north-west into Baptiste River, approximately 35 km north-west of Rocky Mountain House.

The name for this creek has been official since at least 1958, but its precise origin is unknown.

Graham Creek (creek)
82 O/10 - Fallentimber Creek
19-30-5-W5
51°34′N 114°41′W
Flows south-east into Big Prairie Creek, approximately 27 km south of Sundre.

This creek was named after the Graham School in the vicinity.

* Graminia (former locality)
83 H/5 - Leduc
1-51-27-W4
53°23′N 113°50′W
Approximately 27 km south-west of Edmonton.

A post office operated here from June 1908 through April 1946 and its descriptive name is taken from the Latin term *gramen*, meaning "grass."

Granada (locality)
83 G/11 - Chip Lake
25-53-10-W5
53°37′N 115°21′W
Approximately 41 km south south-west of Mayerthorpe.

The post office operated by this name from October 1927 through May 1933. The name for the post office was changed to Northville, but Granada remained for the settlement. It may be named after the Moorish kingdom of southern Spain that was captured by the troops of Ferdinand and Isabella in 1492.

Grand Centre (town)
73 L/8 - Cold Lake
35-62-2-W4
54°24′30″N 110°12′20″W
Approximately 128 km north of Lloydminster.

The name for this town, which was incorporated 1 April 1958, expressed the hopes of early settlers for prosperity. The post office opened in May 1937.

Grandeur Lake (lake)
73 L/12 - Beaver Lake
5-64-12-W4
54°31′N 111°47′W
Approximately 31 km south south-east of Lac La Biche.

The well-established name for this lake has been official since at least 1958, but its precise origin is unknown.

* Grandin (former post office)
73 L/12 - Beaver Lake
27-64-13-W4
54°34′N 111°52′W
Approximately 23 km south south-east of Lac La Biche.

The post office operated here from March 1911 through May 1967 and was named after Msgr. Vital-Julien Grandin, O.M.I. (1829-1902), who entered the Oblates on 28 December 1851 and was the first Bishop of St. Albert. The name was officially rescinded 27 October 1970.

Grandview (summer village)
83 B/16 - Winfield
27-46-1-W5
52°59′N 114°04′W
Approximately 45 km west of Wetaskiwin.

The name for this summer village, which was incorporated 1 January 1967, is taken after the district of Grandview which received its name from the superb view one received while gazing across Watelet Lake.

Grant Lake (lake)
73 D/7 - Czar
21-39-7-W4
52°22′N 110°57′W
Approximately 37 km west of Provost.

The name for this lake has been in use since at least 1958, but its precise origin is unknown.

Grass Lake (lake)
73 D/11 - Hardisty
12-42-11-W4
52°36′N 111°27′W
Approximately 12 km south-west of Hardisty.

The name for this lake which has been in use since at least 1958, is likely descriptive.

---

*denotes rescinded name or former locality.

Grass Lake (lake)

83 I/11 - Athabasca
1-64-24-W4
54°30′215″N 113°29′45″W
Approximately 32 km south-west of
Athabasca.

The name for this lake has been official
since at least 1958 and is likely descriptive.

Grassland (hamlet)

83 I/15 - Grassland
28-67-18-W4
54°49′N 112°41′W
Approximately 40 km east north-east of
Athabasca.

The descriptive name for this hamlet,
whose post office opened in December
1927, refers to the grassy terrain of the area.

Grassy Island Lake (lake)

72 M/16 - Grassy Island Lake
15-33-3-W4
51°50′N 110°20′W
Approximately 55 km north of Oyen.

The name for this lake is descriptive.

Grassy Island Lake (lake)

73 L/3 - Vincent Lake
1-61-10-W4
54°14′N 111°23′W
Approximately 28 km north of St. Paul.

The name for this lake has been official
since 6 July 1950 and is a translation of the
Cree *kamschigwaskasik sagahegan*, which
is likely descriptive.

Grassy Lake (lake)

73 D/14 - Irma
12-44-8-W4
52°46′45″N 111°02′30″W

_____

*denotes rescinded name or former locality.

Approximately 19 km south-west of the
town of Wainwright.

According to Lieutenant-Colonel M.R.
Gentles, C.D., of the Wainwright Regional
Training Area, the name for this small
permanent lake is descriptive. The lake is
surrounded by a large seasonally flooded
grassy area and was the site of the first
military airfield at what was then known as
Camp Wainwright. The field is known as
the Grassy Lake Landing Field and was
built in 1943.

Grattan Creek (creek)

73 D/14 - Irma
11-45-8-W4
52°52′N 111°03′W
Flows east into Battle River, approximately
14 km west north-west of the town of
Wainwright.

The name for this creek has been in use
since at least 1958, but its origin is unknown.

* Gratz (former post office)

73 E/15 - Elk Point
15-56-6-W4
53°50′N 110°48′W
Approximately 9 km south south-east of
Elk Point.

The name for the post office, which
operated here from October 1913 through
July 1958, was taken after a place in
Germany where J. Vogel, the first postmaster, was born. The name was officially
rescinded 22 April 1970.

Gray, Lake (lake)

83 I/13 - Grosmont
31-67-26-W4
54°50′N 113°57′W
Approximately 45 km west north-west of
Athabasca.

The name for this lake was officially
adopted in 1952 and commemorates
Lieutenant Robert Hampton "Hammy"
Gray, V.C., D.S.C., M.I.D., a naval pilot
serving with the aircraft carrier *Formidable*,
who was killed on 9 August 1945, the day
the atomic bomb was dropped on Naga-
saki, the second and final A-bomb of the
war. Lt. Gray was born in Trail B.C., and
grew up in nearby Nelson.

Grays Lake (lake)

72 M/15 - Monitor
28-32-7-W4
51°47′N 110°56′W
Approximately 57 km north north-west of
Oyen.

The name for this lake was officially
approved 1 February 1967, but its precise
origin is not known.

Greasy Lake (lake)

73 D/10 - Hughenden
9-45-4-W4
52°51′30″N 110°32′00″W
Approximately 23 km east of the town of
Wainwright.

The name for this feature has been in use
since at least 1958, but its origin is unknown.

Green Court (hamlet)

83 J/3 - Green Court
14-58-9-W5
54°01′N 115°14′W
Approximately 10 km north-west of
Mayerthorpe.

A post office operated here from July 1908
through January 1982. It was named by
Hamilton Baly, the first postmaster, who
taught at the King's School in Canterbury,
Kent, England, and who originally named it
Greencourt (changed to two words in 1950)
after the court outside this cathedral school.

Green Glade (locality)

73 D/8 - Provost
6-41-1-W4
52°29'N 110°09'W
Approximately 20 km north north-west of
Provost.

The descriptive name for this locality was
applied 13 July 1908, and the post office
operated until 2 October 1951.

* Greenlawn (former locality)

73 E/10 - Clandonald
36-54-5-W4
53°42'N 110°35'W
Approximately 28 km south-east of Elk
Point.

The descriptive name for this former
locality, whose post office operated from
April 1908 through March 1945, referred to
the fact that the original post office was
built on a grassy slope. The name was
officially rescinded 14 January 1970.

Greenshields (hamlet)

73 D/15 - Wainwright
14-44-6-W4
52°47'N 110°46'W
Approximately 8 km south-east of the town
of Wainwright.

The post office here opened in August
1909, and was named after a director of the
Grand Trunk Pacific Railway, E.B.
Greenshields, president of the Montreal
Drygoods wholesale firm of Greenshields
Ltd. The post office was previously known
as "Holmstead."

Greenstreet Lake (lake)

73 L/4 - Cache Lake
14-60-11-W4
54°12'N 111°33'W

_____
*denotes rescinded name or former locality.

Approximately 27 km north-west of St.
Paul.

The name for this lake has been official
since 6 November 1950. The place was
named after the Greenstreets, early land-
owners of the area, including L.M.
Greenstreet, W. Greenstreet and Mrs. C.
Greenstreet.

Gregory Lake (lake)

83 I/2 - Waskatenau
33-60-18-W4
54°13'20"N 112°38'00"W
Approximately 16 km north-west of
Smoky Lake.

The name for this lake was officially
adopted 21 December 1979 and commemorates Gregory Purich (1884-1967), the
original homesteader of the land around the
feature. Mr. Purich came to Canada in 1907
and worked for several years in Ontario
and Calgary, eventually filing on a homestead north-west of Smoky Lake in 1917.
With his wife and four children he lived on
this homestead until 1948 when he retired
to Smoky Lake. He was very well known
and well liked by the community and is
remembered for his carpentry work,
especially in the construction of the church
at Barich.

Grenier Lake (lake)

83 I/15 - Grassland
15-67-17-W4
54°48'N 112°31'W
Approximately 36 km west of Lac La
Biche.

The name for this lake has been official
since at least 1958, but its precise origin is
unknown.

Griesbach (locality)

83 H/11 - Edmonton
9-54-22-W4
53°39'N 113°11'W

Within the north-east city limits of Edmonton.

A post office operated here from July 1955
through May 1959 and was an army base. It
was named for William Antrobus
Griesbach, C.B., C.M.G., D.S.O.,
V.D.(Volunteer Officer's Decoration), K.C.
(1878-1945), who served in the Boer War,
was called to the Bar in 1901 and served as
alderman and Mayor of Edmonton, 1905-
06 and 1907, respectively. In World War I,
Griesbach served as a Major, second in
command of the divisional cavalry squadron attached to the 1st Canadian Division,
was promoted to Lieutenant-Colonel of the
49th Battalion (Infantry) of the Canadian
Expeditionary Force in France, and later to
Brigadier-General of the 1st Canadian
Infantry Brigade. He was made a senator in
September 1921 and was promoted to
Major-General in November of that same
year. He was Inspector General for
Western Canada in 1940 and retired from
that position 31 March 1943.

Griesbach Island (island)

83 H/10 - Elk Island Park
3-23-54-20-W4
53°40'25"N 112°50'30"W
Approximately 40 km east of Edmonton, in
Elk Island National Park.

The name for this island in Astotin Lake
was officially approved 17 October 1991.
(see Griesbach)

Grim Lake (lake)

83 B/9 - Rimbey
11-42-2-W5
52°36'N 114°11'W
Approximately 8 km south-east of Rimbey.

The name for this lake has been official
since at least 1958, but its precise origin is
unknown.

Grizzly Bear Creek (creek)
73 E/2 - Grizzly Bear Creek
25-47-5-W4
53°05′N 110°36′W
Flows south-east into Battle River, approximately 33 km north north-east of the town of Wainwright.

The name for this creek is a translation from the Cree *mist-a-ya*, and is likely descriptive.

Groat Creek (creek)
83 J/4 - Whitecourt
22-58-13-W5
54°02′N 115°50′W
Flows west into McLeod River, approximately 16 km south-west of Whitecourt.

The name for this creek has been official since at least 1958, and appeared on a sectional field map dated 1948, but its precise origin is unknown.

Grose Lake (lake)
83 A/7 - Stettler
3-39-21-W4
52°20′N 112°56′W
Approximately 15 km west of Stettler.

The name for this lake has been official since at least 1958, but its precise origin is unknown.

Grosmont (locality)
83 I/13 - Grosmont
10-68-24-W4
54°51′N 113°33′W
Approximately 25 km north-west of Athabasca.

The descriptive name for this locality, whose post office operated from September 1912 through January 1970, refers to the large hill located to the north. The name is French for "big mountain."

Grosvenor Park (locality)
83 H/11 - Edmonton
19-52-23-W4
53°30′N 113°22′W
Within the city limits of Edmonton.

This is an industrial subdivision of Edmonton, established after 1958. It is likely named after one of the private companies of the Grosvenor family. Gerald Grosvenor, 6th Duke of Westminster, was probably the largest holder of commercial real estate in the U.K.

Grygus Lake (lake)
83 I/15 - Grassland
NW-8-68-17-W4
54°52′N 112°34′W
Approximately 50 km north-east of Athabasca.

The request to name this lake was submitted by Katherine Lewicki for her father, who owned the land on which the lake is situated. Michael Grygus (1902-1959) came to Canada with his family from Poland in 1938 and homesteaded the area around the lake. He died in a farming accident. The name is well-established in local usage and was officially approved 5 May 1987.

Gull Creek (creek)
73 L/13 - Lac La Biche
3-69-12-W4
54°56′00″N 111°45′15″W
Flows north-west into Piche River, approximately 24 km north-west of Lac La Biche.

The name for this creek was officially adopted in May 1951 and is likely descriptive.

Gull Lake (summer village)
83 A/5 - Red Deer
22-40-28-W4
52°27′47″N 113°56′20″W

Approximately 12 km west south-west of Lacombe.

This summer village was incorporated 25 March 1913. (see Gull Lake)

■ **Gull Lake** (lake)
83 A/12 - Ponoka
40-28-W4
52°34′N 114°00′W
Approximately 17 km south-east of Rimbey.

The Cree name for this lake is *kiaskus*. The Stoney equivalent is rendered *pi-cha-tto-amna*. The name "Gull" for this lake first appears on Arrowsmith's map of 1859. It is labelled "Long Lake" on David Thompson's map of 1814.

Gull Point (point)
83 H/10 - Elk Island Park
1-27-54-20-W4
53°41′20″N 112°51′15″W
Approximately 40 km east of Edmonton, in Elk Island National Park.

The well-established local name for this point in Astotin Lake was officially approved 17 October 1991.

Gumbo Lake (lake)
72 M/11 - Youngstown
36-31-8-W4
51°42′N 111°02′W
Approximately 53 km north-west of Oyen.

The precise origin for the name of this feature is unknown.

Gun Hill (hill)
73 D/11 - Hardisty
28-43-8-W4
52°43′N 111°06′W
Approximately 20 km south-west of the town of Wainwright.

The precise origin for the name of this feature in the Wainwright Regional Training Area is unknown.

Gunn (hamlet)

83 G/9 - Onoway
2-55-3-W5
53°44'N 114°20'W
Approximately 32 km north-west of Stony Plain.

The name for this hamlet, whose post office opened in July 1915, is taken after Peter Gunn (1864-1927), a Member of the Legislative Assembly from 1909 to 1917; he was with the Hudson's Bay Company for 27 years.

Gunner Hill (hill)

73 D/10 - Hughenden
31-42-5-W4
52°39'N 110°42'W
Approximately 14 km south south-east of the town of Wainwright.

The precise origin for the name of this feature is unknown.

Gurneyville (locality)

73 L/2 - Muriel Lake
31-59-5-W4
54°08'N 110°45'W
Approximately 14 km south of Bonnyville.

The name for this locality, whose post office opened in October 1910, was taken after the maiden name of the wife of Alex Hall, the first postmaster.

Guy Lake (lake)

83 G/16 - Lac la Nonne
28-56-1-W5
53°52'N 114°05'W
Approximately 35 km south south-east of Barrhead.

The name for this lake has been official since at least 1958, but its precise origin is unknown.

Gwynne (hamlet)

83 A/14 - Wetaskiwin
24-46-23-W4
52°59'N 113°11'W
Approximately 11 km east north-east of Wetaskiwin.

The name for this hamlet, whose post office was known as "Diana" before March 1906, is taken after Julia Maude Gwynne, the second wife of Sir Collingwood Schreiber (1831-1918). Schreiber worked for several railways before becoming chief engineer of government railways in 1873. In 1880, he succeeded Sir Sandford Fleming as chief engineer of the Canadian Pacific Railway, and in 1892 became federal Deputy Minister of Railways and Canals. He played a major part in the building of the National Transcontinental Railway, the eastern extension of the Grand Trunk Pacific Railway from Winnipeg to Quebec and on to Moncton, N.B. Schreiber, a Canadian Pacific divisional point in Ontario north of Lake Superior, was also named after him.

Hackett (locality)
83 A/1 - Hackett
36-36-18-W4
52°08′N 112°27′W
Approximately 28 km south-east of Stettler.

There are two possibilities for the origin of the name of this locality, whose post office operated from July 1926 through March 1956. One notes that the name, as a surname, is an Anglo-Norman diminutive of "hake," a kind of fish, and second, that the name is derived from an early verbal expression, "hack it." The stories about this incident vary on the precise details, but most of them tell of a fencing foreman ordering his crew to tear down an illegal fence, or to "hack it" down.

Haddock (locality)
83 G/13 - Hattonford
2-56-14-W5
53°49′N 115°59′W
Approximately 39 km north-east of Edson.

The first post office, which opened March 1915, was named after Maude Haddock, a pioneer resident of the area and the first postmistress. Mrs. Haddock and her husband, John, arrived in Canada from Wichita, Kansas, in 1910 and came to Alberta in 1913 where they homesteaded north of Peers. Mrs. Haddock was active in community affairs and became a charter member of the Women's Institute. She died in Edson in 1971. The post office closed in June 1969.

Haight (locality)
83 H/8 - Riley
30-50-16-W4
53°21′N 112°19′W
Approximately 25 km south-west of Vegreville.

The Canadian Northern Railway established a station here in 1911. It was named for Captain Haight, a transport officer of the Hudson's Bay Company on the Athabasca River. The post office operated from November 1921 through October 1967.

Hail Lake (lake)
72 M/14 - Kirkpatrick Lake
32-32-10-W4
51°47′N 111°22′W
Approximately 42 km north-east of Hanna.

The precise origin for the name of this feature is unknown.

■ **Hairy Hill** (village)
73 E/13 - Hairy Hill
23-55-14-W4
53°45′40″N 111°58′25″W
Approximately 18 km north-west of Two Hills.

The post office opened here in February 1907. The name was derived from the fact that the nearby hill was covered with mats of hair. According to George Chrapka, a native of Hairy Hill, "The first settlers, on moving into this district some threescore years ago, chose the site for their new homes on a large flat hill. This hill, however, was somewhat different from any other they had seen. Everywhere they looked they saw large mats of hair covering the ground. Naturally, they were puzzled, but with the coming of spring also came the answer. One bright morning they saw a hundred or more buffalo roaming lazily along the slopes of the hill. On going to the spot they found fresh mats of hair. This solved the 'hairy mystery' and also suggested a name for this locality." Like most mammals, buffalo get very thick coats in winter to protect themselves from the cold. When spring arrives, however, the buffalo rub themselves on the ground or in nearby shrubbery to loose themselves of these heavy coats. This village was incorporated 16 March 1946.

Halach (locality)
83 I/5 - Dapp
20-61-25-W4
54°18′N 113°43′W
Approximately 19 km north north-east of Westlock.

The post office operated here from March 1946 through April 1968 and was named after a district in Ukraine.

Halcreek (locality)
83 I/5 - Dapp
4-62-25-W4
54°20′N 113°40′W
Approximately 22 km north-east of Westlock.

The origin for the name of this locality is unknown.

Haley Lake (lake)
83 I/4 - Westlock
29-59-25-W4
54°08′N 113°42′W
Approximately 10 km east of Westlock.

The name for this lake has been official since at least 1958, but its precise origin is unknown.

Half-Breed Ford (bridge)
73 D/10 - Hughenden
13-8-43-5-W4
52°41′50″N 110°42′10″W
Approximately 20 km south-east of the town of Wainwright.

According to Lieutenant-Colonel M. R. Gentles, C.D., Wainwright Regional Training Area, the ford was on the natural line of travel between three Métis settlements south-east of Wainwright. The name has been in use since at least the 1880s.

Half Moon Bay (summer village)

83 B/8 - Sylvan Lake
11-39-2-W5
52°20′45″N 114°10′00″W
Approximately 26 km west north-west of Red Deer.

The summer village of Half Moon Bay was formed 25 October 1977 by Order-in-Council No. 1131/77, effective 1 January 1978. The name describes its placement west of a bay shaped like a semi-circle, on Sylvan Lake.

Half Moon Lake (hamlet)

83 H/6 - Cooking Lake
11,12-6-52-21-W4
53°27′N 113°05′W
Approximately 28 km east of Edmonton.

This hamlet was officially established 5 November 1987 and is situated on a lake shaped like a half-moon.

Halfway Lake (lake)

83 I/4 - Westlock
3-60-24-W4
54°09′N 113°32′W
Approximately 24 km east of Westlock.

The name for this lake is descriptive of its position between Athabasca Landing and the city of Edmonton. It has been in use since at least 1906 and is a translation of the Cree name *abitau*.

Halfway Lake (locality)

83 I/3 - Thorhild
25-59-24-W4
54°08′N 113°27′W
Approximately 23 km east of Westlock.

The name for the post office, which operated here from September 1906 through October 1958, is taken for its proximity to the lake of the same name. (see Halfway Lake)

Halkirk (village)

83 A/8 - Halkirk
24-38-16-W4
52°17′15″N 112°09′10″W
Approximately 19 km north-west of Castor.

The Canadian Pacific Railway built a station here in 1910. It was named after Halkirk, Caithnes, (now Highland) Scotland. The village was incorporated 12 February 1912.

* Hamilton Lake (former post office)

73 D/3 - Coronation
31-35-9-W4
52°03′N 111°17′W
Approximately 12 km east south-east of Coronation.

The post office, which operated here from March 1910 through June 1912, was named after the now dry lake located nearby (see Hamilton Lake). The name was changed to Throne. (see Throne)

Hamilton Lake (lake)

72 M/14 - Kirkpatrick Lake
12-35-9,10-W4
51°59′N 111°19′W
North of Kirkpatrick Lake, approximately 25 km east south-east of Coronation.

This lake was named after E.H. Hamilton, a member of the Geological Survey of Canada party of 1885. The lake dried up around 1928, but the name was reinstated 6 November 1971.

Hamilton Lake (lake)

73 L/4 - Cache Lake
1-59-14-W4
54°04′N 111°57′W
Approximately 33 km east of Smoky Lake.

The name for this lake has been official since 6 April 1950, but its precise origin is unknown.

Hamlin (locality)

73 E/13 - Hairy Hill
5-58-13-W4
53°58′N 111°54′W
Approximately 32 km north north-west of Two Hills.

The name for this locality, whose post office operated from October 1913 through October 1981, is taken after Hamelin, England. The mother of the first postmaster, R.H. Perley, came from there. The "e" was dropped on the suggestion of the Post Office authorities.

Hamlin Lake (lake)

73 L/12 - Beaver Lake
10-13-65-12-W4
54°37′33″N 111°40′30″W
Approximately 25 km south-east of Lac La Biche.

(see Hamlin)

Handhills Creek (creek)

82 P/9 - Craigmyle
35-29-16-W4
51°31′N 112°09′W
Flows south-east into Handhills Lake, approximately 20 km south-west of Hanna.

This creek was named for its proximity to the Hand Hills. The name for the hills, one of the more prominent features of south-eastern Alberta, is a translation of a native name; however, the origin attached to the name has more than a single focus. Tyrrell, the noted geologist, reported: "They [the hills] are called by the Crees *michichi ispatinan* or 'hand hills' on account of their resemblance to the outstretched fingers of the hand, the top of the table land not being flat but composed of five ridges which radiate from a centre lying to the south-east." Tyrrell mentions them as being called *o-chun-um-bin* in Stoney. Another version is that the name means "little hand." A Blackfoot chief who was killed on one of these hills had one small hand, according to Peter Erasmus and John Leech. This chief was born crippled, his hand resembling the claw of an animal, and the other children in his band, while he was growing up, threw stones at him, and called him "Little Hand." He grew up compensating for his disability and became a great warrior.

Hanmore Lake (lake)

83 I/7 - Newbrook
30-61-17,18-W4
54°17'N 112°31'W
Approximately 21 km north of Smoky Lake.

The name for this lake has been official since at least 1958 and apparently commemorates a survey party or parties unknown in the Lac La Biche district. Until 1969, when the county map was issued, this lake was locally called "Little Whitefish Lake," in acknowledgement of both its excellent jumbo whites and its proximity to "Big" Whitefish Lake.

Hanna (town)

72 M/12 - Hanna
9-31-14-W4
51°38'30"N 111°56'00"W
Approximately 145 km east south-east of Red Deer.

This town was named after David Blythe Hanna (1858-1938), who was born in Scotland and came to Canada in 1882. He was associated with the Grand Trunk, New

York West Shore and Buffalo Railway, as well as the Manitoba and Northwestern Railway and the Lake Manitoba Railway and Canal Co. In 1902 he was third vice-president of Canadian Northern and in charge of its operation upon its incorporation. During his term of office Canadian Northern built its line from Saskatoon to Calgary and the community became one of the most important divisional points along the line. When the Canadian Government took over the Canadian Northern Railway in 1918, he resigned. He was then appointed president of Canadian National Railways, the new company into which the government-owned lines were assembled In 1922, he retired from railway service. He was then appointed first chairman of the Liquor Control Board of Ontario and retired from that in 1928. The town was incorporated 14 April 1914.

Hanna Townsite, 1912

Hansen Lake (lake)

73 L/16 - Medley River
27,34-68-2-W4
54°56'N 110°13'W
Approximately 52 km north of Cold Lake.

This lake was named in 1951 and commemorates Pilot Officer L.L.H. Hansen, M.I.D. (1920-1944) of Lethbridge, who was killed in World War II.

Hansman Lake (lake)

73 D/8 - Provost
32-39,40-3-W4
52°24'N 110°23'W
Approximately 9 km north-west of Provost.

The name for this lake has been in use since at least 1958, but its origin is unknown.

Hanson Ford (river crossing)

73 D/14 - Irma
5-44-8-W4
52°46'N 111°08'W
Approximately 19 km south-west of the town of Wainwright.

The name for this river crossing has been official since 1958, but its origin is unknown.

Happy Hollow (locality)

73 L/10 - Marguerite Lake
4-64-4-W4
54°30'N 110°33'W
Approximately 25 km east of Cold Lake.

A post office operated here from July 1939 through April 1953 and its name expressed the hopes of early settlers.

Hardisty (town)

73 D/11 - Hardisty
6-43-9-W4
52°40'N 111°18'W
Approximately 110 km east south-east of Camrose.

This town, incorporated 16 January 1911, was named after Senator Richard Hardisty (1831-1889), who was born in Ontario at a trading post on Lake Nipissing. He entered the service of the Hudson's Bay Company in 1849 and became a Chief Factor like his father and grandfather before him. He was the last Chief Factor at Fort Edmonton. In

1865 he married Eliza Victoria McDougall, daughter of the Reverend George McDougall. In 1888 he was appointed to the Senate of Canada; he died a year later.

Hare Island (island)
83 I/9 - Hylo
23-66-15-W4
54°44'N 112°09'W
Approximately 13 km west south-west of Lac La Biche.

The name for this island in Missawawi Lake is likely descriptive.

Hargwen (railway point)
83 F/11 - Dalehurst
36-52-22-W5
53°32'N 117°06'W
Approximately 43 km west of Edson.

The Grand Trunk Pacific Railway established a station here in 1911 and named it after a friend of the chief clerk of the railway. The post office operated from February 1913 through August 1916.

* Harker (former post office)
83 A/10 - Donalda
6-42-18-W4
52°35'N 112°34'W
Approximately 27 km east of Bashaw.

The post office, which operated here from November 1907 through May 1911, was named after the first postmaster, D.C. Harker. The name was changed to "Eidswold" and then to Donalda.

Harmattan (hamlet)
82 O/16 - Olds
24-32-4-W5
51°46'N 114°25'W

Approximately 14 km east south-east of Sundre.

A post office operated here from May 1900 through August 1966 and was named by the department after a dry hot wind that blows on the Atlantic coast of Africa from the interior during December, January and February.

* Harmon (former locality)
73 D/3 - Coronation
15-36-11-W4
52°06'N 111°30'W
Approximately 4 km west of Coronation.

The origin for the name of this former locality is unknown.

Harold Lake (lake)
73 L/7 - Bonnyville
29-63-4-W4
54°28'N 110°35'W
Approximately 27 km west of Cold Lake.

The name for this alkali lake has been official since at least 1958, but its precise origin is unknown. It is locally referred to as "Whitewood Lake."

Harold Lakes (lakes)
73 E/1 - Paradise Valley
22-47-2-W4
53°04'N 110°12'W
Approximately 28 km south south-west of Lloydminster.

The name for these two lakes was officially changed from "Harold Lake" to "Harold Lakes" 7 November 1969, but the precise origin is unknown.

* Harrison (former railway point)
83 A/5 - Red Deer
10-39-27-W4
52°20'N 113°48'W
Approximately 5 km north of Red Deer.

The origin for the name for this Canadian Pacific Railway station is unknown. The name was changed to Labuma. (see Labuma)

Hart Hill (hill)
73 D/14 - Irma
26-44-8-W4
52°49'N 111°04'W
Approximately 12 km west of the town of Wainwright.

The name for this hill has been in use since at least 1958, but the origin is unknown.

Hart Lake (lake)
73 D/14 - Irma
13-44-8-W4
52°47'N 111°02'W
Approximately 12 km west south-west of the town of Wainwright.

The origin for the name of this lake is unknown.

Hartshorn (locality)
82 P/16 - Farrell Lake
22-34-17-W4
51°56'N 112°20'W
Approximately 43 km south-west of Castor.

The post office, which operated here from July 1910 through January 1929, was named after its first postmaster, D.H. Hartshorn.

Hasse Lake (lake)
83 G/8 - Genesee
12,13-52-2-W5
53°29'N 114°10'W
Approximately 45 km west of Edmonton.

The well-established name for this lake was requested for official approval by R.J. Paterson, senior manager and biologist with Land and Forests (1968), Charles B. Lane, regional fish biologist, Edson (1969), and

---

*denotes rescinded name or former locality.

C.W. Scott, Fish and Wildlife (1975). It was named for Frederick Hasse who registered land in 1936. The name was officially approved 30 October 1975.

Hasse Lake Provincial Park

(provincial park)
83 G/8 - Genesee
14-52-2-W5
53°29′30″N 114°10′45″W
Approximately 44 km west of Edmonton.

This provincial park was established by Order-in-Council No. 1125/70 and is named because it is adjacent to Hasse Lake. (see Hasse Lake)

Hastings Coulee (coulee)

83 A/9 - Red Deer
9-41-16-W4
52°30′30″N 112°15′15″W
Runs south into Battle River, approximately 38 km north-east of Stettler.

The name for this coulee has been official since at least 1958, but its precise origin is unknown.

Hastings Creek (creek)

83 H/7 - Tofield
18-51-18-W4
53°25′N 112°39′W
Flows east into Beaverhill Lake, approximately 5 km north-east of Tofield.

This creek, a ridge in southern Alberta and the nearby lake were all named by J. B. Tyrrell after Tom Hastings, a member of the 1884 Geological Survey Party. The Cree name for the creek is *kak-si-chi-wukh* or "swift current."

Hastings Lake (lake)

83 H/7 - Tofield
20-51-20-W4
53°25′N 112°55′W
Approximately 17 km west north-west of Tofield.

The Cree name for this lake is *a-ka-ka-kwa-tikh*, which translates, "the lake that does not freeze." (see Hastings Creek)

Hatfield Lake (lake)

83 A/11 - Chain Lakes
36-41-22-W4
52°34′45″N 113°01′15″W
Approximately 4 km west of Bashaw.

The well-established name for this lake was officially approved in January 1979. It was proposed by Arlen Adams, the Reeve for the County of Camrose at that time, along with other residents. The J.S. Hatfield family homesteaded on the north side of the lake circa 1910.

Hattie Lake (lake)

73 D/13 - Sedgewick
18-46-11-W4
52°58′N 111°34′W
Approximately 20 km south-east of Viking.

The precise origin for the name of this lake is unknown.

Hattonford (locality)

83 G/13 - Hattonford
27-55-12-W5
53°46′N 115°42′W
Approximately 48 km east north-east of Edson.

A post office operated here from April 1917 through August 1970, but the precise origin for the name is unknown.

Haunted Lakes (lake)

83 A/6 - Alix
31-39,40-22-W4
52°24′N 113°09′W
Approximately 31 km west north-west of Stettler.

The name for this lake was approved 17 January 1951. Most of the versions of the origin of the name involve a group (of undetermined numbers) of Indians who saw a deer or elk in the frozen lake, attempted to kill it, and were drowned. Another legend attached to this feature deals with the separation of the Beaver and Sarcee Indian tribes. A giant elk, upset because his antlers had been mistaken for wood, rose and split the ice of the frozen lake, thereby separating into two segments the once unified tribe.

The owner of Haunted Lake Ranch told the tale in a slightly different manner. According to him, two young braves had observed an elk's head and antlers in what appeared to be the middle of the lake and decided to get them from an Indian camp on the south side. Before they could reach their destination, however, the antlers began to move mysteriously, and before the braves could control their astonishment, the ice broke, and the young natives disappeared. Indian folklore claims that the lake has been haunted by these braves since that time.

* Hawkins (former station)

73 D/14 - Irma
9-45-8-W4
52°52′N 111°08′W
Approximately 17 km west of the town of Wainwright.

A Grand Trunk Pacific Railway station was established here in 1909 and was named after an accountant in the office of the vice-president of the railway.

---

*denotes rescinded name or former locality.

Hay Lakes (village)
83 H/3 - Bittern Lake
6-49-21-W4
53°13′50″N 113°03′20″W
Approximately 45 km south-east of
Edmonton.

A post office opened here in August 1913
and was named for its proximity to a
nearby lake whose name is a translation of
the Cree term *a pi chi koo ohi was*, meaning
little swamp. This village was incorporated
17 April 1928.

Hay Marsh (marsh)
73 D/10 - Hughenden
1,2-43-6-W4
52°40′N 110°45′W
Approximately 19 km south south-east of
the town of Wainwright.

The precise origin for the name of this
feature is unknown.

Haynes (railway point)
83 A/6 - Alix
4-39-24-W4
52°19′N 113°24′W
Approximately 30 km east of Red Deer.

The name for this locality, whose post
office operated from October 1900 through
June 1964, is taken after Isaac Haynes
(1852-?), an early homesteader who settled
in the area in 1889. Haynes and his family
lived on the banks of the creek and were the
first settlers.

Haynes Creek (creek)
83 A/6 - Alix
32-38-23-W4
52°19′N 113°15′W
Flows south-east into Red Deer River,
approximately 37 km west of Stettler.

(see Haynes)

Hayter (hamlet)
73 D/8 - Provost
17-39-1-W4
52°22′N 110°07′W
Approximately 10 km east of Provost.

A post office opened at this one-time
village in August 1909, and was named after
Hayter Reed, manager of the Canadian
Pacific Railway hotels system. He was
appointed assistant Indian Commissioner
for Manitoba and the Northwest Territories in 1884 and in 1893 became deputy
superintendent-general for Indian Affairs.
He left the public service in 1897. He was
named to the railway post in 1903.

Hazeldine (hamlet)
73 E/9 - Marwayne
18-53-3-W4
53°35′N 110°27′W
Approximately 37 km north-east of
Vermilion.

The name for this hamlet was taken after
Hazeldean, Sussex, England. From the Old
English *denu*, "a valley"; the first part of
the name probably alludes to the
hazelwood tree. The post office operated
from December 1927 through January
1975.

Hazelwood Lake (lake)
83 A/4 - Innisfail
N1/2-29-35-28-W4
52°02′20″N 113°58′01″W
1 km north-west of Innisfail on the north
side of Hwy 54, on the golf course site.

The proposal to have the official name for
this lake changed was made by Charles
Dallas of Innisfail in September 1988.
Apparently, in the 1920s there had been an
unsuccessful attempt to change the name
"Mud Lake" to "Hazelwood Lake." There
is a grove of hazelwood trees beside the
lake (Mr. Dallas included a sample of the

nuts picked from the trees around the lake)
and there was a farm nearby called
"Hazelwood Farm" (this farm no longer
exists). There was a great deal of support by
many local residents for the name change
for its aesthetic appeal, and it was officially
approved 17 October 1991.

Heart Lake (locality)
82 P/16 - Farrell Lake
18-34-16-W4
51°55′N 112°15′W
Approximately 35 km north-west of
Hanna.

The name for the post office, which
operated here from March 1901 through
August 1928, was due to its proximity to
the nearby lake that is shaped like a heart.

Heart Lake (lake)
82 P/16 - Farrell Lake
1-1-34-17-W4
51°53′00″N 112°16′15″W
Approximately 38 km north-west of
Hanna.

The name for this lake is descriptive of its
shape.

Heatburg (locality)
83 A/6 - Alix
3-39-23-W4
52°19′N 113°14′W
Approximately 35 km west of Stettler.

The Grand Trunk Pacific Railway established a station here in 1911 on its Calgary
branch which ran south from Tofield, and
named it "Bullocksville." The name was
changed in 1922, but the origin is unknown.

Heath (locality)
73 D/15 - Wainwright
15 NE 13-44-5-W4
52°48′N 110°36′W

Approximately 20 km east south-east of the town of Wainwright.

The Grand Trunk Pacific Railway established a station here in 1908. It was named after a chief official of the Grand Trunk Pacific Water Department. The post office was established 1 January 1911.

Heatherdown (locality)

83 G/9 - Onoway
1-54-2-W5
53°39′N 114°09′W
Approximately 45 km west north-west of Edmonton.

The post office operated here from November 1903 through December 1965 and underwent several name changes before this name was chosen. The first name suggested was "Willowdale," but was abandoned when it was learned there was such a place elsewhere in what was then the Northwest Territories. The next selection was appropriately descriptive, "Pine Ridge," because of a pine-covered ridge winding through a portion of the region, but this name was also duplicated in the province. The current name was ultimately settled upon, and is also descriptive.

* Heatherwood (former post office)

83 F/9 - Edson
15-53-17-W5
53°35′N 116°26′W
Within the town limits of Edson.

The post office, which operated here from August 1910 through September 1911, was called Heatherwood, despite the fact that local residents and the Grand Trunk Pacific Railway proposed the name Edson. Apparently, postal officials were concerned that Edson may be confused with another locality in Alberta called "Edison." This

*denotes rescinded name or former locality.

issue was later dismissed, and the name became Edson, after Edson J. Chamberlain, vice-president and general manager of the railway. The origin for the name Heatherwood is unknown. (see Edson)

Hebert Lake (lake)

83 A/2 - Big Valley
19-37-18-W4
52°11′45″N 112°34′00″W
Approximately 13 km south of Stettler.

The precise origin for the name for this lake is unknown; however, local residents seem to concur that it may be named for an early surveyor.

* Hector (former locality)

73 E/7 - Vermilion
10-52-7-W4
53°28′N 110°58′W
Approximately 17 km north north-west of Vermilion.

The name for this former locality, whose post office operated from September 1923 through September 1927, commemorates Hector Eckford, a casualty at Vimy Ridge in World War I.

Hedin Creek (creek)

83 J/4 - Whitecourt
18-59-11-W5
54°06′05″N 115°38′35″W
Flows north-east into Whitecourt Creek, approximately 5 km south-east of Whitecourt.

The name for this creek was officially adopted 6 March 1986 and commemorates Erik Hedin, a homesteader who arrived in the area in 1917. He farmed the land until his death in 1951.

Heinsburg (hamlet)

73 E/15 - Elk Point
22-55-4-W4
53°46′N 110°31′W

Approximately 28 km south-east of Elk Point.

The post office, which opened here in November 1913, was named after its first postmaster, John Heins.

Heisler (village)

83 A/9 - Edmonton
2-43-16-W4
52°40′15″N 112°13′03″W
Approximately 51 km north-east of Stettler.

This village was incorporated 1 January 1961. It was named after Martin Heisler, the landowner from whom the townsite was purchased. The post office opened 18 October 1915.

Heldar (locality)

83 J/1 - Barrhead
22-58-7-W5
54°01′N 114°57′W
Approximately 16 km north-east of Mayerthorpe.

The name for this locality, whose post office operated from August 1914 through October 1967, was taken from the name of Dick Heldar, the hero in *The Light That Failed*, a novel by Rudyard Kipling (1865-1936).

Helena Lake (lake)

73 L/12 - Beaver Lake
7-4-66-11-W4
54°40′52″N 111°36′57″W
Approximately 25 km south-east of Lac La Biche.

The local name for this feature is "Big Ghost Lake." (see Elinor Lake)

Helina (locality)

73 L/6 - Goodridge
32-63-10-W4
54°29′N 111°29′W

Approximately 44 km south-east of Lac La Biche.

A post office operated here from June 1947 through August 1970, but the precise origin for its name is unknown.

Helliwell Lake (lake)
83 I/4 - Westlock
1-61-25-W4
54°14′N 113°37′W
Approximately 18 km north-east of Westlock.

The name for this lake has been official since at least 1958, but its precise origin is unknown.

Helmer Creek (creek)
82 O/10 - Fallentimber Creek
29-31-7-W5
51°41′N 114°57′W
Flows north-east into Red Deer River, approximately 25 km south-west of Sundre.

This creek takes its name from Mount Helmer which was named after Brigadier-General Richard Alexis Helmer, C.M.G. (1864-1920). Helmer was a musketry expert and chemist whose life interest was in the Canadian Militia. He was an alderman for ten years and mayor twice in the City of Hull. He was a marksman and a member of Canadian rifle teams in international competition. His only son, Alexis, an artillery officer, was killed in World War I.

Hemaruka (hamlet)
72 M/14 - Kirkpatrick Lake
33-32-8-W4
51°47′N 111°06′W
Approximately 62 km east north-east of Hanna.

The name for this hamlet, previously known as "Zetland," was changed in 1927.

*denotes rescinded name or former locality.

It is a combination of the first two letters of the names of the four daughters of A.E. Warren, general manager, Central Region, Canadian National Railways. The names of the four girls were Helen, Margaret, Ruth and Kathleen. Mr. Warren had been a senior executive of both the Canadian Northern Railway and the Grand Trunk Pacific Railway and, after the Canadian National Railways absorbed both, held various posts with the C.N.R.

Henday (locality)
82 O/16 - Olds
25,36-34-1-W5
51°57′N 114°01′W
Approximately 10 km south-west of Innisfail.

For tariff purposes, it was necessary to give a name to the end of this trackage and it was suggested by Canadian Pacific Railway officials that this name be used. It was in honour of Anthony Henday of the Hudson's Bay Company, the first white man to record his presence in Alberta. Henday arrived in October, 1754, and is supposed to be the first man to sight the mountains from Antler Hill, north-east of Innisfail, and to leave a record of doing so.

* **Hercules** (former post office)
83 H/6 - Cooking Lake
33-51-23-W4
53°27′N 113°20′W
Approximately 12 km south-east of Edmonton.

The post office, which operated here from February 1913 through February 1969, was the outlet for Bretona. (see Bretona) It was named after E. Hercules Murphy, the first postmaster.

Heron Island (island)
83 H/10 - Elk Island Park
10-15-54-20-W4
53°39′55″N 112°51′45″W

Approximately 40 km east of Edmonton, in Elk Island National Park.

This name was requested by the Canadian Parks Service for navigational purposes within the park. There is little settlement around the park and all local usage appears to ensue from the wardens who use the names on their own maps. The request was forwarded by the Canadian Permanent Committee on Geographical Names in order that the names would appear on the new NTS map sheets being produced for the area. The name was officially approved 17 October 1991.

Hespero (locality)
83 B/8 - Sylvan Lake
1-39-4-W5
52°19′N 114°27′W
Approximately 7 km south-west of Eckville.

The Canadian Pacific Railway established a station here in 1914 and named it after Hesper, the evening star of Greek mythology. The post office, which operated by this name from June 1916 through September 1960, was previously called "Pitcox."

Hicklon Lake (lake)
82 O/9 - Didsbury
29-30-2-W5
51°36′00″N 114°14′30″W
Approximately 11 km south-west of Didsbury.

The precise origin for the name of this lake is unknown. It is also known as "Tuggle Slough."

Hidden Lake (lake)
73 E/7 - Vermilion
34-50-5-W4
53°21′N 110°38′W
Approximately 14 km east of Vermilion.

The name for this lake has been official since at least 1958 and is likely descriptive.

High Island (island)

83 H/10 - Elk Island Park
23-4-20-W4
53°41′N 112°50′W
Approximately 40 km east of Edmonton, in Elk Island National Park.

The precise origin for the name of this island in Astotin Lake is unknown.

Highland Creek (creek)

82 O/10 - Fallentimber Creek
28-31-5-W5
51°41′N 114°39′W
Flows east into Fallentimber Creek, approximately 12 km south of Sundre.

The name for this creek may be due to its proximity to Highland Ridge and has been official since November 1937. (see Highland Ridge)

Highland Park Hill (hill)

83 A/14 - Wetaskiwin
29-44-21-W4
52°49′20″N 113°00′30″W
Approximately 26 km south south-west of Camrose.

The name for this hill was very well-established locally, and was officially approved 20 October 1983. The precise origin for the name is unknown.

Highland Ranch (locality)

82 P/14 - Trochu
28-33-24-W4
51°52′N 113°21′W
Approximately 23 km north north-west of Three Hills.

The name for this locality is derived from the concept that the area was rich for ranching and the fact that many of the early settlers were from Scotland. The post office operated here from September 1908 through July 1920.

Highland Ridge (ridge)

82 O/10 - Fallentimber Creek
23-31-6-W5
51°40′N 114°44′W
Approximately 15 km south of Sundre.

The name for this ridge has been official since November 1937 and is likely descriptive.

Highridge (locality)

83 J/1 - Barrhead
30-58-1-W5
54°03′N 114°08′W
Approximately 20 km south-east of Barrhead.

The name for this locality, whose post office operated from April 1929 through May 1969, was applied by a pioneer couple named Mr. and Mrs. High who noted the ridge near where the post office was located. It was a former Northern Alberta Railways station.

Highvale (locality)

83 G/7 - Tomahawk
34-51-4-W5
53°27′N 114°30′W
Approximately 43 km north-west of Drayton Valley.

A.C. Brooks, the first postmaster, suggested the name for this locality to commemorate his former home, Highgate, in Ontario. The post office operated from August 1909 through August 1970.

Highway (hamlet)

83 G/14 - Mayerthorpe
31-56-10-W5
53°53′N 115°29′W
Approximately 25 km west south-west of Mayerthorpe.

The name for this hamlet is descriptive of its location near Highway 43, off secondary road 647. The post office operated here from April 1926 through July 1966.

Hilda Lake (lake)

73 L/9 - Marie Lake
8-64-3-W4
54°31′N 110°26′W
Approximately 18 km west north-west of Cold Lake.

(see Elinor Lake)

Hill Twelve (hill)

82 O/15 - Sundre
10-12-33-7-W5
51°49′00″N 110°51′30″W
Approximately 15 km west of Sundre.

The name for this hill is descriptive of its location, on Sec12, Tp 33, R7, W5M. The name has become locally well-established, and has been in use since the early 1920s. The first surveyors came to the area in 1893, so the name may have originated as early as that. The homesteaders' trail to Bearberry went over Hill Twelve in the early days. The hill has always been used for grazing. The name was officially approved 23 September 1991.

* Hillend (former locality)

83 A/4 - Innisfail
31-35-27-W4
52°03′N 113°44′W
Approximately 20 km south of Red Deer.

The descriptive name for this former locality, whose post office operated from July 1902 through March 1928, refers to the

---

*denotes rescinded name or former locality.

placement of the settlement at the end of a range of hills.

Hilliard (hamlet)
83 H/9 - Mundare
5-54-17-W4
53°39′N 112°29′W
Approximately 10 km north-west of Mundare.

This hamlet was named after Hilliard McConkey, an early settler. The post office was established in September 1918.

Hillsdown (locality)
83 A/4 - Innisfail
6-38-25-W4
52°14′N 113°33′W
Approximately 17 km east of Red Deer.

This descriptive name refers to the fact that the land sloped downward from here to the Red Deer River. The post office operated from June 1902 through August 1967.

Hind Lake (lake)
73 E/2 - Grizzly Bear Creek
11-49-5-W4
53°13′N 110°37′W
Approximately 22 km south-east of Vermilion.

(see Hindville)

* Hindville (former locality)
73 E/2 - Grizzly Bear Creek
36-48-5-W4
53°12′N 110°36′W
Approximately 25 km south-east of Vermilion.

This former locality, whose post office operated from March 1909 through March

_____
*denotes rescinded name or former locality.

1966, was named for its first postmaster, Thomas Hind. The name was officially rescinded 18 January 1974.

Hivon, Lac (lake)
73 E/11 - Myrnam
27-53-8-W4
53°36′N 111°05′W
Approximately 34 km north north-west of Vermilion.

The name for this lake has been official since 9 November 1941, but its precise origin is unknown.

Hobden Lake (lake)
73 E/15 - Elk Point
17-57-7-W4
53°55′N 110°59′W
Approximately 5 km north-west of Elk Point.

This lake is likely named for the Hobden family, headed by John (1865-1950) and Katherine, originally from Sussex, England. They arrived in the Elk Point district in 1911 and took up a homestead near this feature.

Holborn (locality)
83 G/8 - Genesee
NE-33-51-1-W5
53°27′N 114°05′W
Approximately 35 km west of Edmonton.

On 14 August 1903 the Holborn School District No. 881 was established. The school was built during the winter of 1905 and opened in the spring of 1906. The post office followed in March 1913 and was named after Charlie Holborn, the first settler in the area to file on a homestead in 1901. The post office closed in July 1944. The school was permanently closed in 1965 due to declining enrolment.

Holden (village)
83 H/1 - Holden
14-49-16-W4
53°14′00″N 112°14′05″W
Approximately 45 km north-east of Camrose.

The post office here was originally called "Vermilion Valley," but the name was changed to Holden in May 1907. It is taken after James Bismark Holden (1876-1956) who was born in Singhampton, Ontario, and went to Manitoba in 1894 where he got a job as an elevator agent for a Winnipeg grain firm. In 1898 he moved to Strathcona where he became a Homestead Inspector. Two years later he took up a homestead near the present town of Vegreville and entered into a real estate partnership with his brother-in-law. He was elected to the Alberta Legislature in a 1906 by-election, as a Liberal for the constituency of Vermilion. He was re-elected in 1909 and was a member until 1913. The following year he became Mayor of Vegreville. After a few years of inactivity, he served as Mayor of Vegreville again from 1921 through 1945, a record.

Hollow Lake (lake)
83 I/7 - Newbrook
10,2-61-19-W4
54°15′15″N 112°45′15″W
Approximately 26 km north-west of Smoky Lake.

The descriptive name for this lake has been in use since at least 1935 and refers to its location in a hollow.

Hollow Lake (locality)
83 I/2 - Waskatenau
4-61-19-W4
54°14′N 112°46′W
Approximately 26 km north-west of Smoky Lake.

The post office operated here from July 1935 through April 1970 and took its name from the nearby lake. (see Hollow Lake)

Holmes Crossing (locality)

83 J/7 - Fort Assiniboine
31-61-5-W5
54°19'N 114°44'W
Approximately 32 km north-west of Barrhead.

This locality was named after William "Billy" Holmes, an early homesteader who arrived here circa 1905. A ferry was established on this point on the Athabasca River in 1906, but was unmanned. The ferry was therefore consistently on the wrong side of the river when needed. Mr. Holmes became the ferryman as a result, and remained in that capacity until 1913. When the post office was opened in August 1908, Mr. Holmes became the first post-master and the site was named for him. It remained open through December 1917. It then reopened from June 1938 through March 1957.

* **Holmstead** (former post office)

73 D/15 - Wainwright
14-44-6-W4
52°47'N 110°46'W
Approximately 8 km south-east of the town of Wainwright.

The origin of the name of this post office, which operated from August 1907 through May 1909, is unknown. The name was changed to Greenshields. (see Greenshields)

* **Holmstown** (former post office)

73 D/12 - Lougheed
33-43-11-W4
52°44'N 111°33'W
Approximately 10 km south-east of Sedgewick.

_____
*denotes rescinded name or former locality.

The origin of the name of this post office, which operated from May 1905 through May 1908, is unknown. It was later changed to Lougheed. (see Lougheed)

Holyoke (locality)

73 L/2 - Muriel Lake
36-59-5-W4
54°08'N 110°37'W
Approximately 16 km south south-east of Bonnyville.

A post office, originally called "Holy Oak," operated here from April 1931 through August 1958. There is a city in Massachusetts and a town in Colorado of the same name, and the "Holy Oak" was a tree worshipped by the Druids.

Homeglen (railway point)

83 B/16 - Winfield
22-44-1-W5
52°48'N 114°05'W
Approximately 15 km north north-east of Rimbey.

The descriptive name for the post office, which operated here from March 1909 through May 1951, was suggested by James Burns, the first settler to the area.

Hondo (locality)

83 O/1 - Smith
23-70-1-W5
55°04'N 114°02'W
Approximately 63 km north-west of Athabasca.

The Edmonton, Dunvegan & British Columbia Railway established a station here in 1914 and named it after a town of the same name in Texas. The post office opened in November 1930. The descriptive name may refer to the definition of the word used to describe a broad, low-lying gully in the U.S. Southwest.

Honey Lake (lake)

73 L/12 - Beaver Lake
S-W-28-65-12-W4
54°38'40"N 111°46'01"W
Approximately 18 km south south-east of Lac La Biche.

The name for this lake was officially applied in 1951 and commemorates Lance Sergeant Hedley Arthur Honey, M.I.D., of Edmonton, who was killed during World War II. The local name for this feature is "Sandy Lake," a descriptive name.

Hook Lake (lake)

73 E/14 - St. Paul
5-57-7-W4
53°54'00"N 111°00'30"W
Approximately 8 km west of Elk Point.

The name for this lake has been official since 9 November 1941, but its precise origin is unknown.

Hoople Lake (lake)

83 G/10 - Isle Lake
28-52-7-W5
53°31'30"N 114°58'00"W
Approximately 33 km north of Drayton Valley.

The name for this lake has been official since at least 1958, but its precise origin is unknown.

Hope Lake (lake)

83 G/15 - Sangudo
35-56-6-W5
53°53'N 114°47'W
Approximately 26 km east south-east of Mayerthorpe.

The name for this lake has been official since at least 1958, but its precise origin is unknown.

Hope Lake (lake)
83 I/10 - Boyle
14-28-65-18-W4
54°39′22″N 112°39′00″W
Approximately 40 km east of Athabasca.

This lake may have been named for Jimmy
Hope, a Métis who was mentioned a
number of times in records of the Lac La
Biche Mission throughout 1853.

Hope Valley (locality)
73 D/15 - Wainwright
19-46-4-W4
52°58′N 110°35′W
Approximately 25 km north-east of the
town of Wainwright.

A post office operated here from August
1911 through January 1948 and expressed
the optimism of the early settlers and the
position of the post office in a valley.

Horburg (locality)
83 B/6 - Crimson Lake
6-40-9-W5
52°25′N 115°17′W
Approximately 25 km west north-west of
Rocky Mountain House.

The Canadian Northern Railway established a station here in 1914, but the precise
origin of the name is unknown.

Horen (locality)
83 G/7 - Tomahawk
7-52-5-W5
53°29′N 114°44′W
Approximately 33 km north north-east of
Drayton Valley.

The post office operated here from April
1939 through June 1970, but the origin for
the name is unknown.

Hornbeck (hamlet)
83 F/10 - Bickerdike
2-53-19-W5
53°33′N 116°41′W
Approximately 18 km west south-west of
Edson.

The name for this hamlet may commemorate an early settler. Local legend maintains
that this man arrived in the Big Eddy area
in 1906 with one travel companion and a
herd of horses. They were on their way to
Prairie Creek, but inclement weather cut
the journey short. The horses died of
starvation, and Hornbeck went mad.
Apparently, he shot up the local store,
decimating the winter's food supply. Four
other men were in the store. One left to
find the police in Lac Ste Anne while the
other three stayed behind in an attempt to
constrain Hornbeck. They ended up
shooting Hornbeck in self-defence.

Horne Lake (lake)
73 L/12 - Beaver Lake
6-23-65-11-W4
54°38′10″N 111°33′40″W
Approximately 30 km south-east of Lac La
Biche.

The name for this lake was officially
applied in 1951 and commemorates
Warrant Officer A.M. Horne, D.F.C.,
(1909-1943) of Edmonton, who was killed
in World War II. The feature is known
locally as "Ghost Lake," which may be a
translation from the Cree.

Horne Lake (lake)
83 J/4 - Whitecourt
35-58-13-W5
54°04′N 115°50′W
Approximately 13 km south-west of
Whitecourt.

The name for this lake has been official
since at least 1958, but its precise origin is
unknown.

Hornpile Lake (lake)
73 L/3 - Vincent Lake
15-59-8-W4
54°06′N 111°07′W
Approximately 17 km north-east of St.
Paul.

The name for this lake has been official
since 6 July 1950, but its precise origin is
unknown.

* Horse Hill (former locality)
83 H/11 - Edmonton
9-54-23-W4
53°39′20″N 113°20′00″W
Within the city limits of Edmonton.

This locality is now contained within the
boundaries of the City of Edmonton. The
post office operated separately from April
1896 through August 1919 and was named
after the nearby Horse Hills where the
horseguard or wintering ranch of the
Hudson's Bay Company in Edmonton, was
formerly situated.

Horse Island (island)
83 G/10 - Isle Lake
28-54-4-W5
53°42′N 114°32′W
Approximately 48 km south-east of
Mayerthorpe.

Many pioneers and travellers swam their
packhorses across this narrow portion of
Lac Ste Anne surrounding the island, rather
than cross it via the ferry. This is how the
island received its name.

Horse Lake (lake)
83 G/16 - Lac la Nonne
13-55-4-W5
53°45′15″N 114°28′00″W
Approximately 43 km south-east of
Mayerthorpe.

The name for this lake has been official since at least 1958, but its precise origin is unknown.

Horse Lake (lake)

83 I/16 - Plamondon
10-10-68-16-W4
54°52′15″N 112°21′05″W
Approximately 25 km west north-west of Lac La Biche.

The name for this lake has been official since at least 1958, but its precise origin is unknown.

Horseguard Creek (creek)

83 B/8 - Sylvan Lake
16-10-39-3-W5
52°20′42″N 114°21′18″W
Flows east into Medicine River, approximately 5 km south of Eckville.

This creek was previously called "Lasthill Creek," although the origin is unknown. The post office nearby was established as Horseguards in November 1913, but its name was changed in January 1916 to Alhambra. The geographical name was changed to Horseguard Creek 24 September 1991 to reflect current local usage.

* Horseguards (former post office)

83 B/7 - Rocky Mountain House
1-39-6-W5
52°20′N 114°40′W
Approximately 14 km east south-east of Rocky Mountain House.

The post office operated here from November 1913 through January 1916 when the name was changed to Alhambra.

Horsehills Creek (creek)

83 H/11 - Edmonton
4-54-23-W4
53°41′N 113°24′W
Flows south-east into North Saskatchewan River, approximately 14 km east of Edmonton.

(see Horse Hill)

Horseshoe Bay (summer village)

73 L/3 - Vincent Lake
25-59-10-W4
54°07′35″N 111°21′56″W
Approximately 16 km north north-west of St. Paul.

This summer village, which was incorporated 1 January 1985, has a descriptive name referring to the shape of the bay on the western shore of Vincent Lake.

Horseshoe Hill (hill)

73 D/11 - Hardisty
35-43-8-W4
52°44′N 111°03′W
Approximately 16 km east north-east of Hardisty.

The precise origin for the name of this feature is unknown; however, it is likely descriptive of its shape.

Horseshoe Lake (lake)

83 H/12 - St. Albert
18,19-53-25-W4
53°35′N 113°40′W
Approximately 5 km south south-west of St. Albert.

The descriptive name for this lake has been in use since at least 1963.

Horseshoe Lake (lake)

83 I/5 - Dapp
36-63-26-W4
54°29′30″N 113°47′00″W

Approximately 42 km south-west of Athabasca.

The name for this lake has been official since at least 1958 and is descriptive of its shape.

Horseshoe Lake (lake)

83 J/9 - Flatbush
9-65-2-W5
54°37′00″N 114°15′30″W
Approximately 62 km west south-west of Athabasca.

The name for this lake has been official since at least 1958 and is descriptive of its shape.

Horseshoe Lake (locality)

82 P/13 - Torrington
20-34-27-W4
51°56′N 113°47′W
Approximately 17 km south-east of Innisfail.

The name for this locality is taken from its proximity to a lake, named due to its shape which resembles a horseshoe. The post office operated from August 1913 through January 1927.

* Hortonburg (former post office)

83 H/11 - Edmonton
7-53-22-W4
53°34′N 113°15′W
Approximately 27 km east of Edmonton.

A post office operated here under this name from March 1908 through August 1912. It was named after Mary Horton, the first postmistress. The name was later changed to Bremner. (see Bremner)

Hoselaw (locality)

73 L/2 - Muriel Lake
18-60-6-W4
54°11′N 110°54′W

Approximately 15 km south-west of Bonnyville.

This locality, whose post office opened in December 1912, is named after a loch in Roxburghshire (now Borders), Scotland.

Hoselaw Lake (lake)

73 L/2 - Muriel Lake
23-59-7-W4
54°07′N 110°56′W
Approximately 22 km south-west of Bonnyville.

(see Hoselaw)

House Mountain (hill)

83 J/4 - Whitecourt
21-58-12-W5
54°02′00″N 115°43′00″W
Approximately 10 km south of Whitecourt.

The name is descriptive of the hill's shape, particularly when viewed from the south-east, as the 1143 m (3750 ft) hill resembles a house and there were at one time two trees at the top which were the "chimney pipes." The hill is on the old Tête Jaune Trail and it was well known to travellers along that route. The hill is also locally known as "Whitecourt Mountain" because of another House Mountain at the north end of the Swan Hills and because Alberta Forest Service has a lookout on the hill which is called "Whitecourt Lookout." The name House Mountain was officially adopted 22 October 1982.

Howie Lake (lake)

83 I/14 - Sawdy
32-68,69-23-W4
54°56′N 113°29′W
Approximately 26 km north north-west of Athabasca.

The name for this lake has been official since at least 1958, but its precise origin is unknown.

Huard Lake (lake)

83 H/3 - Bittern Lake
31-46-23-W4
53°01′N 113°19′W
Approximately 5 km north north-east of Wetaskiwin.

The origin for the name of this lake is unknown.

Hubbles Lake (lake)

83 G/9 - Onoway
9-53-1-W5
53°34′N 114°05′W
Approximately 38 km west of Edmonton.

The name for this lake was officially approved in 1950 and was named for Mr. Wesley James "Wes" Hubble, an entrepreneur who started a summer resort and beach on the lake.

Hubert Lake (lake)

83 J/9 - Flatbush
14-64-2-W5
54°32′N 114°12′W
Approximately 49 km north north-east of Barrhead.

The name for this lake appears on the Fort Assiniboine Sectional Sheet No. 364 dated 1948, but its precise origin is unknown.

Huggett (locality)

83 G/8 - Genesee
18-50-1-W5
53°19′N 114°08′W
Approximately 48 km west south-west of Edmonton.

A post office operated here from August 1910 through December 1915 and then reopened from November 1924 through March 1958. It was named after J. Huggett, the first postmaster.

Hughenden (village)

73 D/15 - Wainwright
8-41-7-W4
52°32′N 111°01′W
Approximately 30 km south-east of Hardisty.

The Canadian Pacific Railway established a station here in 1909. It was named by Charles E. Stockdill, an official of the C.P.R., after Hughendon, Buckingham-shire, the estate in England of Benjamin Disraeli, Lord Beaconsfield (1804-1881). This village was incorporated 27 December 1917.

Hughenden Lake (lake)

73 D/15 - Wainwright
7-41-7-W4
52°32′N 111°01′W
Approximately 29 km south-east of Hardisty.

(see Hughenden)

Hulbert Crescent (locality)

83 H/11 - Edmonton
21-52-23-W4
53°30′N 113°20′W
Approximately 11 km east of Edmonton.

The precise origin for the name of this country residence subdivision is unknown.

Hummock Lake (lake)

83 A/3 - Delburne
35-35,36-23-W4
52°03′N 113°10′W
Approximately 25 km north of Trochu.

The name for this lake has been in use since at least 1893, and is likely descriptive of the surrounding area. According to the *Oxford Concise Dictionary* (1982), a hummock is defined as "hillock, knoll, rising ground, especially in marsh; hump or ridge in icefield, [16th c., of unknown origin]."

* Hunka (former locality)

83 H/16 - Willingdon
30-57-16-W4
53°57'N 112°22'W
Approximately 20 km south south-east of Smoky Lake.

The post office operated under this name from July 1902 through July 1909 and was named after Wasyl Hunka, a pioneer settler. The name was later changed to Sniatyn. (see Sniatyn)

Hunt Lake (lake)

82 P/16 - Farrell Lake
27-34-15-W4
51°56'N 112°03'W
Approximately 35 km north north-west of Hanna.

The name for this lake has been in official use since at least 1958 and is taken after the Hunt brothers, early settlers in the area who operated a ranch near it. The three Hunt brothers had settled near Content at the turn of the century. In 1905, Harold persuaded his brothers, Jack and Alf, to move to this area close to what later became known as Hunt Lake. These three men had what was perhaps the only log house in the area, when Jack and Alf brought the logs from their former home at Content.

Huppie Lake (lake)

73 L/12 - Beaver lake
9-24-64-13-W4
54°33'09"N 111°49'21"W
Approximately 17 km south of Lac La Biche.

This lake may be named for Thomas Huppie, a Red River man associated with the fur trade in the North who later ran the post office and a general store at Grandin. There was also a Forest Officer, J.M.

Huppie, at Lac La Biche circa 1950. The lake was once locally known as "Duck Lake" as wild ducks used to cover it.

Hurdy (railway point)

83 K/1 - Windfall Creek
19,30-60-14-W5
54°12'N 116°05'W
Approximately 28 km west north-west of Whitecourt.

The name for this station was officially approved 18 September 1970 and honours a World War II hero from the district, Private John Hurdy (1922-1944) of the Canadian Scottish Regiment. The original proposal from Canadian National Railways was "North Windfall"; however, at that time, qualifying terms such as North, South, etc. were discouraged.

* Hurry (former post office)

83 H/1 - Holden
30-48-14-W4
53°10'N 112°02'W
Approximately 21 km north-west of Viking.

A post office operated here under this name from December 1905 through March 1909. Its precise origin is unknown. The name was later changed to Bruce. (see Bruce)

Hurstwood Park (locality)

83 H/11 - Edmonton
20-52-23-W4
53°30'N 113°22'W
Approximately 10 km east of Edmonton.

The origin for the name of this country residence subdivision is unknown.

Huxley (hamlet)

82 P/14 - Trochu
17-34-23-W4
51°56'N 113°14'W
Approximately 11 km north of Trochu.

This town was named in 1907, apparently after Thomas Henry Huxley (1825-1895), a noted British biologist whose speculations on philosophy and religion led him to the powerful advocacy of the principle of agnosticism. He was a friend of Charles Darwin, author of *The Origin of Species*. Huxley found in Darwin's theory an intelligible hypothesis on which to base a study of evolution.

Hylo (hamlet)

83 I/9 - Hylo
4-66-15-W4
54°41'N 112°13'W
Approximately 20 km south-west of Lac La Biche.

Hylo was originally the name of a village on the Alberta and Great Waterways Railway. During the construction of this railway, the workers indulged in a card game known as faro, using counters, shuffling boxes, and the like. One of the oldest of all gambling games played with cards, faro was one of the favourite pastimes of highborn gambling Europeans of the eighteenth and nineteenth centuries. Faro was introduced to North America with the flood of European immigrants. With news of gold in the north, the settlers, along with their games, moved toward the towns of the gold rush. Faro was one of their amusements, but gradually fell out of favour, due to dishonest practices. Hylo is a strategic term used in this game, and it is likely from this that the locality received its name. Faro got its name from the Egyptian king, or Pharaoh, pictured in a card of the French pack (Faro originated in France). The post office opened at this site in December 1921.

Ice Lake (lake)

83 G/15 - Sangudo
26-56-5-W5
53°52'N 114°37'W

---

*denotes rescinded name or former locality.

Approximately 35 km east south-east of Mayerthorpe.

The name for this lake has been official since at least 1958, but its precise origin is unknown.

Idamay (locality)

72 M/15 - Monitor
22-33-7-W4
51°51'N 110°54'W
Approximately 62 km north north-west of Oyen.

The post office operated here from August 1929 through October 1959, and was named after Ida May Gerig, the daughter of its first postmaster, Jacob Gerig.

Ille Lake (lake)

83 B/15 - Buck Lake
10,11-32-44-5-W5
52°50'20"N 114°41'20"W
Approximately 37 km north-west of Rimbey.

This lake was officially named 7 February 1983 after John Ille, an early homesteader, trapper and millhand. Mr. Ille was an American by birth. He became a recluse after developing a disfiguring disease (a cancer or ulcer) on his face.

Imperial Mills (hamlet)

73 L/13 - Lac La Biche
27-69-12-W4
55°00'15"N 111°44'00"W
Approximately 30 km north-east of Lac La Biche.

The post office, which operated here under this name from May 1949 through December 1959, was previously called "Blefgen." Imperial Mills commemorated the Imperial Lumber Company which had a sawmill nearby.

---

* Independence (former post office)

83 H/13 - Morinville
24-57-27-W4
53°57'N 113°53'W
Approximately 50 km north north-west of Edmonton.

A post office operated here under this name from April 1903 through January 1919, but its precise origin is unknown. The name was later changed to Busby. (see Busby)

Indian Lake (lake)

73 E/7 - Vermilion
8-51-7-W4
53°23'30"N 110°59'00"W
Approximately 63 km west north-west of Vermilion.

Originally called "Swimming Pond," the name for this feature was changed 22 January 1992 to reflect local usage of the more commonly used name. The precise origin for the name is, however, not known.

Infantry Hill (hill)

73 D/10 - Wainwright
28-42-6-W4
52°38'N 110°47'W
Approximately 23 km south of the town of Wainwright.

The precise origin for the name of this hill is unknown, but it is likely a name inspired by the proximity of the Wainwright Regional Training Area.

Inland (locality)

83 H/8 - Ryley
20-51-15-W4
53°25'N 112°11'W
Approximately 10 km south-west of Vegreville.

The descriptive name for the station on the Canadian Northern Railway's Battle River branch was established here in 1911 and the post office, which operated from April 1923 through February 1969, refers to the locality's distance from the sea.

Innis Lake (lake)

82 O/16 - Olds
27-32-2-W5
51°46'N 114°12'W
Approximately 7 km west south-west of Olds.

The name for this lake has been in use since at least 1906, and was named after the Innis brothers, early homesteaders. It is said that during the dry years of the late nineteenth century they dug a hole in the middle of the lake in order to get water for their cattle, but in the wet years that followed, Innis Lake became large enough for boating and many picnics were held here.

Innisfail (town)

83 A/4 - Innisfail
21-35-28-W4
52°01'20"N 113°57'30"W
Approximately 30 km south south-west of Red Deer.

This town, whose post office opened in April 1892, has an Irish origin. Some speculate that the name was proposed by Mrs. Estella Scarlett, after the Irish homeland of her grandmother. Others maintain that the name was suggested by an Irish official of the Canadian Pacific Railway. There is, apparently, no place on record in Ireland with the name Innisfail. The name *Innis Vail* is a Gaelic term referring to the country of Ireland and means "Isle of Destiny." The settlement was originally named "Poplar Grove." This town was incorporated 20 November 1903.

Innisfail, early 1900s

Innisfree (village)
73 E/5 - Innisfree
3-51-11-W4
53°22'50"N 111°31'50"W
Approximately 37 km south-east of Vegreville.

This village was once called Delnorte. According to Maude Nodwell (nee Puckette), whose father was an early resident and whose homestead was a favourite stopping place, the change of name was suggested by Sir Edmund Walker, president of the Canadian Bank of Commerce from 1907 to 1924. The surrounding area reminded him of his residence, Innisfree, beside Lake Simcoe, north of Toronto, and he suggested that he would build a bank here if the early residents changed the name to Innisfree. The name means "healthy island." The post office opened with this name in September 1909 and the village was incorporated 11 March 1911.

* Iquelon Beach (former locality)
83 H/2 - Camrose
2-49-20-W4
53°12'N 112°49'W
Approximately 21 km north of Camrose.

*denotes rescinded name or former locality.

The origin for the name of this former locality is unknown.

Ireton (locality)
83 H/5 - Leduc
30-49-25-W4
53°16'N 113°39'W
Approximately 7 km west of Leduc.

This locality was named after Henry Ireton (1611-1651), a general in the army of the parliamentary forces under Oliver Cromwell during the Civil War in England. He was also Cromwell's son-in-law. He was in the process of subduing Ireland when he died of fever after the capture of Limerick.

Irish Creek (creek)
73 E/9 - Marwayne
32-53-3-W4
53°38'N 110°25'W
Flows south-east into Vermilion River, approximately 44 km south-east of Elk Point.

The name for this creek has been official since at least 1958, but its precise origin is unknown.

Irma (village)
73 D/14 - Irma
27-45-9-W4
52°54'40"N 111°14'00"W
Approximately 26 km west north-west of the town of Wainwright.

The village is named after a daughter of William Wainwright, second vice-president of the Grand Trunk Pacific Railway. The post office opened in May 1909. The village was incorporated 30 May 1912. (see Wainwright)

Iron Creek (creek)
73 D/11 - Hardisty
22-43-9-W4
52°43'N 111°14'W

Flows east into Battle River, approximately 7 km north-east of Hardisty.

The precise origin for the name of this creek is unknown.

Iron River (locality)
73 L/7 - Bonnyville
18-63-6-W4
54°27'N 110°55'W
Approximately 23 km north north-west of Bonnyville.

A post office opened here in August 1925 and was named for the iron ore deposits on the banks of the nearby river.

Ironwood Lake (lake)
73 L/12 - Beaver Lake
6-12-65-10,11-W4
54°36'30"N 111°32'00"W
Approximately 35 km south-east of Lac La Biche.

The name for this lake has been official since 7 February 1951, but its precise origin is unknown. The Cree have two names for this feature: *kamistigwapskasik sagahegan,* or "Little Stony Island Lake;" and *chipay sagahegan,* or "Skeleton Lake."

Irvine Creek (creek)
83 H/5 - Leduc
31-50-25-W4
53°22'N 113°31'W
Flows west into Blackmud Creek, immediately south of Edmonton.

The precise origin for the name of this creek is unknown.

* Irwinville (former locality)
73 E/9 - Marwayne
30-52-3-W4
53°31'N 110°26'W
Approximately 33 km north-east of Vermilion.

The name for the post office, which operated here from July 1908 through December 1927, was named after J. Sam Irwin, the first settler in the area. He later became the postmaster.

Island Creek (creek)

83 I/14 - Sawdy
31-67-23-W4
54°51'N 113°29'W
Flows south-east into Athabasca River, approximately 16 km north-west of Athabasca.

The name for this creek which flows out of Island Lake has been official since at least 1958. (see Island Lake)

Island Lake (lake)

83 I/13 - Grosmont
36-67,68-24-W4
54°50'N 113°32'W
Approximately 22 km north-west of Athabasca.

The name for this lake has been official since at least 1958 and refers to the number of islands in it. The other surrounding features take their names from this lake.

Island Lake (summer village)

83 I/13 - Grosmont
26-67-24-W4
54°49'56"N 113°32'55"W
Approximately 23 km north-west of Athabasca, on the west shore of Island Lake.

This summer village, incorporated 1 January 1958, takes its name from the nearby lake. (see Island Lake)

Island Lake South (summer village)

83 I/13 - Grosmont
25-67-24-W4
54°49'30"N 113°31'51"W

Southwestern shore of Island Lake, approximately 22 km north-west of Athabasca.

The name for this summer village, incorporated 1 January 1983, is descriptive of its location on Island Lake. (see Island Lake)

Islay (hamlet)

73 E/7 - Vermilion
9-51-4-W4
53°24'N 110°33'W
Approximately 22 km east north-east of Vermilion.

The first settlers were the Gilchrist family, who moved to the area from Victoria county in Ontario. They originally came from Islay, Scotland. A Canadian Northern Railway station was established here in 1905. The post office opened in January 1907.

Isle Lake (lake)

83 G/10 - Isle Lake
31-53-5-W5
53°37'N 114°43'W
Approximately 45 km south-east of Mayerthorpe.

The descriptive name for this lake appears on the Palliser map of 1865. Other names for the lake, according to historical maps, include "Lac des Isles" or "Lac des Islets," from the many islands in the lake. On 4 March 1859, Hector noted in his journal: "ten miles after crossing the Pembina River, having passed over a ridge of land that forms the watershed of the Saskatchewan, and which is within a few miles of the Pembina River, we reached a series of large lakes, on the ice of which we travelled very fast. The largest of these, Lac des Isles, is 13 miles long from east to west."

Islet Lake (lake)

83 H/7 - Tofield
2-52-20-W4
53°27'30"N 112°50'00"W
Approximately 45 km east of Edmonton.

The name for this lake has been official since at least 1958 and is likely descriptive.

Ispas (locality)

73 E/13 - Hairy Hill
35-56-13-W4
53°53'N 111°48'W
Approximately 20 km north of Two Hills.

The name for this locality, whose post office operated from October 1911 through August 1970, is the Ukrainian word for "God the Saviour." It commemorates the birthplace in Bukovina, at the time a largely Slavic territory of the Austro-Hungarian Empire, of N. Pawlink, the first postmaster.

Itaska Beach (summer village)

83 G/1 - Warburg
28-47-1-W5
53°04'30"N 114°05'00"W
Approximately 48 km west north-west of Wetaskiwin.

The name for this summer village, which was incorporated 30 June 1953, is descriptive and is from the Cree *itaskweyaw*, roughly translating to "edge of the woods."

J~K

Jack Fish Lake (lake)

73 E/11 - Myrnam
20-53-9-W4
53°36'N 111°17'W
Approximately 40 km north-west of Vermilion.

The descriptive name for this lake was officially approved 24 September 1991.

Jack Fish Lake (lake)

83 G/8 - Genesee
16-52-2-W5
53°29'N 114°14'W
Approximately 50 km west of Edmonton.

The name for this lake has been official since at least 1958 and is likely descriptive.

Jackfish Creek (creek)

73 L/7 - Bonnyville
34-63-5-W4
54°29'N 110°40'W
Flows south-east into Beaver River, approximately 18 km north north-east of Bonnyville.

The name for this creek has been official since at least 1958 and is likely descriptive.

Jackfish Lake (lake)

83 I/14 - Sawdy
23-67-21-W4
54°49'N 113°06'W
Approximately 16 km north-east of Athabasca.

The descriptive name for this lake has been official since at least 1958 and likely refers to the number of jackfish in it.

Jackpine Creek (creek)

83 F/15 - Nosehill Creek
14-57-20-W5
53°56'N 116°52'W
Flows north into Athabasca River, approximately 53 km north north-west of Edson.

The name for this creek has been official since at least 1958 and is likely descriptive.

* Jackson Coulee (former post office)

73 D/14 - Irma
4-46-10-W4
52°57'N 111°24'W
Approximately 38 km west north-west of the town of Wainwright.

The post office operated here from July 1908 through September 1909 and was named after its first and only postmaster, Edwin Jackson. The name was later changed to Jarrow. (see Jarrow)

Jackson Creek (creek)

82 O/15 - Sundre
36-33-5-W5
51°52'N 114°44'W
Flows north-east into Red Deer River, approximately 10 km north north-east of Sundre.

The name for this creek has been official since 1958, and may be named for Alan and Ruby Jackson, who moved to the Eagle Valley District in 1954, living on the NE1/4 30-33-4-5, later moving to SW1/4 1-33-5-5.

Jackville (locality)

82 O/9 - Didsbury
36-29-3-W5
51°32'N 114°18'W
Approximately 14 km west south-west of Carstairs.

The origin is unknown for the name of this post office, which operated from May 1904 through December 1917.

Jalna (locality)

83 G/14 - Mayerthorpe
36-55-8-W5
53°48'N 115°03'W
Approximately 20 km south south-east of Mayerthorpe.

The name for this locality is likely taken after the School District #4545, established 13 April 1931. The name may have been taken from Mazo de la Roche's 1927 novel *Jalna*, the first of 15 novels in the *Jalna* series. Miss de la Roche (1885-1961) was a bestseller. Her Jalna novels have had total sales of over nine million copies.

James Lake (lake)

73 D/16 - McLaughlin
1-44-1-W4
52°46'N 110°01'W
Approximately 58 km east of the town of Wainwright, on the Alberta-Saskatchewan boundary.

The precise origin for the name of this lake is unknown.

James River (river)

82 O/15 - Sundre
13-34-5-W5
51°54'N 115°34'W
Flows south-east into Red Deer River, approximately 15 km north-east of Sundre.

The name for this river, officially approved 2 December 1941, is taken after James Dickson, a celebrated Stoney Chief who was one of the councillors who signed Indian Treaty No. 7 in 1877. His name was "Ji-mis" in Cree.

---

*denotes rescinded name or former locality.

James River Bridge (locality)

82 O/15 - Sundre
27-34-5-W5
51°56′N 114°38′W
Approximately 17 km north of Sundre.

The name for this locality, whose post office opened in July 1916, was taken after the James River. (see James River)

Jamieson Lake (lake)

73 D/15 - Wainwright
3-44-7-W4
52°45′30″N 110°56′00″W
Approximately 10 km south of the town of Wainwright.

The name of this lake, in the Wainwright Regional Training Area, has been in use since at least 1916, when it appeared on old sectional maps of the Department of the Interior. It is named after Colonel Frederick Charles Jamieson (1875-1966) who came to Alberta from Ontario to homestead in 1895. His interests lay in law, however, and he began its study in 1896. In 1899 he was admitted to the Bar of the Northwest Territories and later was associated with A.C. Rutherford, first Premier of Alberta. Colonel Jamieson served in the South African War and in World War I in various command capacities. In 1918 he commanded the 250th Canadian Rifles which he took to Siberia. From 1931 to 1935 he was a Member of the Legislature of Alberta, but most of his interests consistently remained with military affairs.

January Creek (creek)

83 F/9 - Edson
16-54-14-W5
53°40′15″N 116°00′15″W
Flows north into McLeod River, approximately 30 km north-east of Edson.

The name for this creek has been official since at least 1958, but its precise origin is unknown.

Jarrow (hamlet)

73 D/14 - Irma
4-46-10-W4
52°57′N 111°24′W
Approximately 38 km west north-west of the town of Wainwright.

The name for this hamlet is taken after a town in Durham (now in Tyne and Wear), England. The post office experienced two name changes during its early years. Before 1909, it was called "Jackson Coulee," after its first postmaster, Edwin Jackson. It was also known as "Junkins" from April 1910 through October 1929. The Grand Trunk Pacific Railway had a series of stations in alphabetical order, and Jarrow was one of them. Others included Hawkins, Irma, Kinsella, etc.

Jarvie (hamlet)

83 I/5 - Dapp
15-63-27-W4
54°27′N 113°59′W
Approximately 35 km north north-west of Westlock.

This post office, which opened in February 1920, was known originally as "Jarvis" after a man who may have been a surveyor/engineer on the Edmonton, Dunvegan and British Columbia Railway. The name was changed in 1914 by the Post Office ostensibly to avoid duplication with another place of the same name. This was a typical practice of officials of the Post Office and many names in Alberta were later changed. This has since been discontinued.

Jarvis Bay (bay)

83 A/10 - Donalda
20,29-41-21-W4
52°33′00″N 112°59′30″W
Approximately 3 km south of Bashaw.

This bay is named for the Jarvis family who homesteaded on its north side. The well-established name was officially approved 20 October 1983. Dave Jarvis was the first of this family to venture forth in 1903 or 1904; his father, John, followed a year later. John Jarvis homesteaded south-west of Buffalo Lake on the "leg of the lake." The summer saw the building of their home while they lived with John's uncle Henry, after whom Jarvis Bay was named.

Jarvis Bay Provincial Park

(provincial park)

83 B/8 - Sylvan Lake
9-39-1-W5
52°21′N 114°05′W
Approximately 20 km west north-west of Red Deer.

The Jarvis family was among the first to locate a summer campsite along Sylvan Lake in 1905. (see Jarvis Bay)

* Jasper Place (former locality)

83 H/11 - Edmonton
13-52-25-W4
53°33′N 113°34′W
Within the city limits of Edmonton.

This former town was amalgamated into the city of Edmonton in 1964 and is now a suburb.

Jeffrey (locality)

83 I/4 - Westlock
18-59-24-W4
54°07′N 113°34′W
Approximately 19 km east south-east of Westlock.

The post office, which operated at this locality from May 1906 through April 1961, was named for Jeffrey Garon, the first postmaster.

---

*denotes rescinded name or former locality.

Jenkins Hill (hill)
83 A/11 - Chain Lakes
32-42-23-W4
52°40′00″N 113°17′30″W
Approximately 119 km east of Ponoka.

The well-established name for this hill was
officially approved 20 October 1983 and
was taken after Reuben Jenkins who lived
on top of the hill at the turn of the century.

Jessie Lake (lake)
73 L/7 - Bonnyville
7-61-5-W4
54°15′15″N 110°44′00″W
Approximately 2 km south of Bonnyville.

(see Elinor Lake)

Joffre (hamlet)
83 A/5 - Red Deer
9-39-25-W4
52°20′N 113°32′W
Approximately 19 km east of Red Deer.

A post office operated here from July 1923
through October 1962 and was named for
Marshal Joseph Jacques Césaire Joffre
(1852-1931), who was appointed Commander-in-Chief of all French armies from
2 December 1915 until December 1916. He
was created a Marshal of France – the first
since 1870 – that month was made a
member of the French Academy in December 1918. The post office was previously
known as "Blades."

John Lake (lake)
73 E/9 - Marwayne
11-55-1-W4
53°44′N 110°02′W
Approximately 51 km north of
Lloydminster.

The name for this lake has been official
since at least 1958, but its precise origin is
unknown.

Johnnys Lake (lake)
83 G/9 - Onoway
31-52-2-W5
53°32′N 114°17′W
Approximately 51 km west of Edmonton.

The name for this lake has been established
since at least 1950, and the Geographic
Board of Alberta files maintain that it was
named after some of the workers on the
railway named Johnny.

Jones Creek (creek)
83 A/3 - Delburne
11-38-25-W4
52°14′45″N 113°27′30″W
Flows south into Red Deer River, approximately 30 km east of Red Deer.

This creek was officially named 3 October
1991 after Tom Jones, who settled near
where the creek empties into the Red Deer
River.

Jordan Lake (lake)
83 H/10 - Elk Island Park
2-54-20 W4
53°38′05″N 112°50′20″W
Approximately 40 km east of Edmonton, in
Elk Island National Park.

The well-established name for this lake was
officially approved 17 October 1991. It was
requested by the Canadian Permanent
Committee on Geographical Names as the
updated map sheet for this area was being
prepared. It was named for Daniel Jordan, a
squatter who lived in the park at the turn of
the century. When squatter's rights were
abolished in 1909, he was given $900 and
left the park.

Joseph Lake (lake)
83 H/6 - Cooking Lake
6-50-21-W4
53°17′N 113°04′W

Approximately 38 km south-east of
Edmonton.

The name for this lake has been official
since at least 1958, but its precise origin is
unknown.

Josephburg (hamlet)
83 H/11 - Edmonton
32-54-21-W4
53°43′N 113°05′W
Approximately 30 km north-east of
Edmonton.

This hamlet was named for a town in
Galicia, formerly part of the old Austro-
Hungarian Empire. The first settlers hailed
from two villages, Brigidau and Josefsberg,
thirteen kilometres apart. From 1888 to
1890 many families left for Canada and
took up homesteads near Medicine Hat,
naming their settlement Josefsburg. After
two successive crop failures owing to
drought they sought new land near Edmonton, arriving in 1891. One group took up
land eight kilometres east of Fort Saskatchewan and named the new settlement
Josefsberg. In December 1893, Josefsberg
Public School District #296 was established
and Gus Doze, the first secretary-treasurer,
began to spell the name of the district
"Josephburg," which has been used ever
since.

June (railway point)
83 A/5 - Red Deer
36-40-26-W4
52°29′N 113°36′W
Approximately 9 km east north-east of
Lacombe.

This Canadian Pacific Railway point was
named after the only daughter of George
Walker, who later (1948-1955) was chairman of the railway. Other sources speculate
it may be named after the month in which
the siding was built.

* Junkins (former post office)

73 D/14 - Irma
24-49-11-W4
52°57′N 111°24′W
Approximately 35 km north north-west of
Hardisty.

This former post office, which operated
from September 1909 through April 1910,
was named after the vice president of a
finance company. The name was later
changed to Jarrow. (see Jarrow)

Kahwin (locality)

83 I/1 - Smoky Lake
9-58-16-W4
54°00′15″N 112°20′00″W
Approximately 17 km south-east of Smoky
Lake.

The post office operated here from March
1912 through February 1969 and its name
reflected the opposition by local residents
to the original name proposed "Ostasik," a
Russian word. *Kahwin* is the Sioux Indian
term for "no."

Kakina Lake (lake)

83 G/16 - Lac la Nonne
24-56-2-W5
53°51′N 114°10′W
Approximately 33 km south south-east of
Barrhead.

The name for this lake has been official
since at least 1958, but its precise origin is
unknown.

Kaleland (locality)

73 E/12 - Two Hills
10-55-13-W4
53°44′N 111°51′W
Approximately 9 km west north-west of
Two Hills.

The name for this locality, whose post
office operated from August 1914 through
November 1957, was likely suggested by
early Scottish settlers. "Kale" or "Kail" is
the name the Scots apply to a hardy type of
cabbage, resistant to the severe winter
temperatures in Scotland. *Kailyard* is the
common Scottish name for cabbage patch.

* Kanata (former locality)

83 A/7 - Stettler
17-40-20-W4
52°25′N 112°51′W
Approximately 14 km north north-west of
Stettler.

The name for the post office, which
operated from March 1908 through March
1926, is the same as that for Canada. The
Huron Indian term means a collection of
huts, or a village. It refers to the dwellings
of a father, three sons and a son-in-law who
squatted here.

* Kansas (former post office)

82 O/9 - Didsbury
35-30-3-W5
51°37′N 114°19′W
Approximately 15 km west south-west of
Didsbury.

The post office, which was named after the
American state, operated here from June
1903 through July 1908 when its name was
changed to Westcott. (see Westcott)

Kapasiwin (summer village)

83 G/9 - Onoway
1-53-4-W5
53°33′N 114°27′W
Approximately 55 km west of Edmonton.

The name for this summer village, incorporated 28 August 1918, is a translation of the
Cree Indian word for "camp." It is the
oldest summer village in Alberta, and was
previously known as "Wabamun Beach."

The post office operated from August 1930
through June 1950.

Kasha (locality)

83 A/5 - Red Deer
16-40-27-W4
52°27′N 113°50′W
Approximately 7 km west south-west of
Lacombe.

The Lacombe & North Western Railway
established a station here in 1924 and
named it for J. Kasha, the original owner of
the land upon which the locality is situated.

Katchemut Creek (creek)

83 H/7 - Tofield
3-51-18-W4
53°23′N 112°44′W
Flows north-east into Beaverhill Lake,
approximately 13 km north of Tofield.

This creek was named for Chief
Katchemut, a Cree chief who came from
Fort Pitt in the 1850s with 400 braves to
battle the Blackfoot for this hunting
ground. The Chief continued to live near
the present town of Tofield and was
ultimately buried on the bank of this creek.

Kathleen Lake (lake)

83 F/16 - Shiningbank Lake
23-56-15-W5
53°51′N 116°07′W
Approximately 36 km north-east of Edson.

The name for this lake has been official
since at least 1958, but its precise origin is
unknown.

Kavanagh (hamlet)

83 H/4 - Kavanagh
36-48-25-W4
53°11′N 113°31′W
Approximately 10 km south of Leduc.

This hamlet was named in 1911 after Charles Edmund Kavanagh, then superintendent of Railway Mail Service, stationed in Winnipeg. The post office operated from March 1925 through February 1980.

Keephills (hamlet)

83 G/8 - Genesee
34-51-3-W5
53°24'00"N 114°25'00"W
On Wabamun Creek, approximately 45 km west of Edmonton.

The name for this hamlet was suggested by George H. Collins, the first postmaster, after a town in Buckinghamshire, England. The post office operated from February 1909 through March 1967. The small community was moved in 1983 by TransAlta Utilities from 17-51-3-W5M because it was in the path of an open-pit coal mining excavation. The coal was being mined for a TransAlta electric generating station.

Kehiwin Creek (creek)

73 L/2 - Muriel Lake
11-59-7-W4
54°05'30"N 111°57'00"W
Flows north-west into Bangs Lake, approximately 27 km north-east of St. Paul.

(see Kehiwin Indian Reserve #123)

Kehiwin Indian Reserve #123

(Indian reserve)
73 L/2 - Muriel Lake
28-59-6-W4
54°08'N 110°50'W
Approximately 19 km south south-west of Bonnyville.

This Cree Indian Reserve and the nearby creek and lake were named after Chief Keheewin who signed the treaty of 1876. Chief Keheewin was named after the eagle (*kehew* in Cree). As a young man he distinguished himself by his bravery in many fights with the Blackfoot and became a chief early in life. Later, he joined the Roman Catholic Church and was known as a good Christian. He was also well looked upon by the Hudson's Bay Company factors. He died in 1887 at Onion Lake, Saskatchewan.

■ Kehiwin Lake (lake)

73 L/2 - Muriel Lake
36-58-7-W4
54°04'N 110°54'W
Approximately 29 km east north-east of St. Paul.

(see Kehiwin Indian Reserve #123)

Keith Lake (lake)

73 L/11 - Pinehurst Lake
15-64-8-W4
54°32'N 111°08'W
Approximately 41 km north-west of Bonnyville.

The name for this lake was officially applied in 1951, and commemorates Flying Officer G.N. Keith, D.F.C., of Taber, Alberta.

Keiver's Lake (lake)

82 P/12 - Lonepine Creek
25-31-26-W4
51°41'15"N 113°33'20"W
Approximately 20 km west of Three Hills.

This lake was named after George Edward Keiver (1879-1958) who settled on the land around the lake in 1902. His son Alvin took over the family farm and the land on the south shore has been a public place for many years. In 1929 a community hall was built there. Later, land was donated for the purpose of building a United Church camp and pavilion. More recently, this has been the site of the Alberta Motor Association's annual summer camp for its school patrol program.

Kelly Creek (creek)

82 O/15 - Sundre
24-33-8-W5
51°51'20"N 114°59'35"W
Flows south-east into Bearberry Creek, approximately 20 km west north-west of Sundre.

This locally well-established name is taken after Robert Kelly and his family who came to Bearberry in the 1920s or 1930s and lived on the homestead of Ed Weston. They were originally from Northern Ireland and had lived in Calgary when they first came to Canada. They remained in Bearberry until the 1950s. The name was officially approved 3 October 1991.

Kelly Lake (lake)

83 G/15 - Sangudo
34-56-6-W5
53°53'N 114°49'W
Approximately 24 km east south-east of Mayerthorpe.

The name for this lake has been official since at least 1958, but its precise origin is unknown.

Kelsey (hamlet)

83 A/15 - Ferintosh
4-45-18-W4
52°51'N 112°33'W
Approximately 27 km south-east of Camrose.

The Canadian Northern Railway established a station here in 1916 and named it after Moses S. Kelsey, an early settler who was originally from Millbank, South Dakota. He arrived in the area in 1901 and homesteaded on the quarter-section on which the station was located later. The post office opened in February 1917.

Kenilworth Lake (lake)
73 E/7 - Vermilion
21-50-4-W4
53°19′N 110°32′W
Approximately 33 km east of Vermilion.

The name for this lake appears on the Vermilion Sheet No. 316, and was officially approved 3 October 1911. The precise origin of the name, however, is unknown.

Kennedy Creek (creek)
83 I/3 - Thorhild
4-61-22-W4
54°14′N 113°14′W
Flows south-east into North Saskatchewan River, approximately 20 km east north-east of Redwater.

The name for this creek has appeared on maps since at least 1951; it is sometimes referred to as "Little Sucker Creek." The precise origin of the name is unknown.

Kenning Slough (slough)
83 A/4 - Innisfail
27-36-28-W4
52°07′N 113°55′W
Approximately 20 km south-west of Red Deer.

This feature was likely named after an early family in the region, the Kennings.

Kerensky (locality)
83 I/3 - Thorhild
13-58-22-W4
54°01′N 113°08′W
Approximately 7 km north of Redwater.

The Canadian Northern Railway established a station here in 1920 and named it after Aleksandr Fyodorovich Kerensky (1881-1970), head of the provisional

government of Russia after the fall of Czar Nicholas and before the outbreak of the Bolshevik Revolution, who ruled from July to November 1917.

Kern's Lake (lake)
73 E/6 - Mannville
14-50-8-W4
53°18′47″N 111°04′21″W
Located approximately 73 km west of Lloydminster.

The locally well-established name for this lake apparently derives from the family said to have settled on the land near the lake. The name was officially approved 22 January 1991.

Kerr Lake (lake)
83 I/9 - Hylo
11-9-64-14-W4
54°31′20″N 112°04′55″W
Approximately 29 km south of Lac La Biche.

The name for this lake was officially approved 8 December 1945, but its precise origin is unknown. It is locally known as "Shit Lake."

* Kessler (former post office)
73 D/6 - Brownfield
26-38-8-W4
52°17′N 111°02′W
Approximately 36 km north-west of Coronation.

The name for this post office, which operated from November 1911 through February 1966, was taken after a community of the same name in Montana. The name was officially rescinded 3 March 1971.

Kettle Lake (lake)
83 G/9 - Onoway
34-53-1-W5
53°37′N 114°03′W

Approximately 38 km west north-west of Edmonton.

The name for this lake has been official since 1950 and is named after the early homesteaders from Aylesbury, Buckinghamshire, England, who owned the land upon which the lake sits.

Kevisville (locality)
83 B/1 - Markerville
25-35-4-W5
52°01′45″N 114°25′30″W
Approximately 52 km south-west of Red Deer.

A post office operated here from May 1910 through June 1962 and was named after the first postmaster, Charles W. Kevis.

* Keystone (former post office)
83 G/1 - Warburg
19-48-3-W5
53°09′N 114°26′W
Approximately 38 km east of Drayton Valley.

A post office operated here from December 1912 through April 1927, but the precise origin of the name is unknown. The name was later changed to Breton.

Kikino (hamlet)
83 I/8 - Victor Lake
18-63-14-W4
54°27′N 112°08′W
Approximately 37 km south south-west of Lac La Biche.

The origin for the name of this hamlet, whose post office opened in November 1944, is Cree for "our home."

Kikino (Métis Settlement)
83 I/8 - Victor Lake
19-63-15-W4
54°27′N 112°16′W
South of Lac La Biche.

With the passage of Order-in-Council No. 379/39, Goodfish Lake Colony No. 7 was created by the Alberta Government on 29 March 1939. This Métis Settlement was also known previously as Beaver River Métis Settlement Association Area 7, and encompassed what is now known as Kikino and Buffalo Lake. The name was changed by the residents to Kikino in 1941.

Kilini Creek (creek)
83 G/9 - Onoway
31-53-1-W5
53°38'N 114°09'W
Flows north into Matchayaw Lake, approximately 45 km west north-west of Edmonton.

The name for this creek has been official since at least 1958 , its precise origin is unknown.

Killam (town)
73 D/13 - Sedgewick
17-44-13-W4
52°47'25"N 111°51'20"W
Approximately 70 km east south-east of Camrose.

This town was set up by the Canadian Pacific Railway in 1906 when it was incorporated as a village. The establishment of the post office followed in March 1907. It was incorporated as a town 1 May 1965. The town takes its name from the Honourable A.C. Killam, (1849-1908), the first chief commissioner of the Board of Railway Commissioners. There were five streets, namely: Stanley, Minto, Dufferin, Monck, and Aberdeen; and three avenues, namely: Lansdowne, Lorne, and Lisgar. All were named in honour of the first eight Governors General of Canada from 1867 through 1904.

Killarney Lake (lake)
73 D/9 - Chauvin
4-42-1-W4
52°35'N 110°06'W
Approximately 29 km north-east of Provost.

This lake is likely named after the famous lakes in Kerry, Ireland.

Killarney Lake (locality)
73 D/9 - Chauvin
34-41-1-W4
52°34'N 110°04'W
Approximately 27 km north north-east of Provost.

The name for this locality is taken from the nearby lake. The post office operated here from December 1912 through March 1932. (see Killarney Lake)

Kilsyth (locality)
83 J/9 - Flatbush
1-65-2-W5
54°36'N 114°09'W
Approximately 53 km north north-west of Westlock.

The Edmonton, Dunvegan & British Columbia Railway established a station here in 1914 and likely named it after Kilsyth, Stirlingshire (now Strathclyde), Scotland. The name is said to be from the Gaelic *ceall* (church) or *coill* (wood), "church of the arrows or arrow wood." (Johnston)

Kilsyth Creek (creek)
83 J/9 - Flatbush
18-65-1-W5
54°38'N 114°09'W
Flows north-west into Pembina River, approximately 57 km west of Athabasca.

(see Kilsyth)

Kilsyth Lake (lake)
83 J/9 Flatbush
8-65-1-W5
54°36'N 114°07'W
Approximately 55 km west south-west of Athabasca.

The name for this lake was officially approved 7 May 1953 and is taken from the feature's proximity to Kilsyth. (see Kilsyth)

Kimura Lake (lake)
83 H/14 - Redwater
29-57-22-W4
From 53°57'00"N 113°14'00"W
to 53°57'50"N 113°15'00"W
Between Redwater and Sturgeon valleys, approximately 45 km north of Edmonton.

This lake was officially named 9 December 1984 in commemoration of Mr. and Mrs. Toyomatsu Kimura, who homesteaded around the lake in the Redwater area in 1912. A small number of other Japanese families also settled in the area at that time. Mr. Kimura farmed until his eightieth year before retiring. He died in 1975 at the age of 91.

King Lake (lake)
83 J/9 - Flatbush
26-64-2-W5
54°33'N 114°11'W
Approximately 50 km north north-east of Barrhead.

The name for this lake appears on the Fort Assiniboine Sectional Sheet No. 364 dated 1948, but its precise origin is unknown.

Kingman (hamlet)
83 H/2 - Camrose
8-49-19-W4
53°13'N 112°44'W
Approximately 23 km north-east of Camrose.

This hamlet was named after F.W. Kingsbury, the first postmaster at this outlet. Early Norwegian settlers requested a post office for a rather large area, and one was granted in 1897, named "Northern." As more settlers arrived, the need to separate post offices into smaller and more manageable areas became necessary; hence this post office came into operation in May 1907. It was intended to call the settlement Kingsbury, but there was already a town by that name so Kingman was selected as a compromise.

Kinikinik (locality)

83 I/11 - Athabasca
1-65-21-W4
54°35'N 113°00'W
Approximately 17 km south-east of Athabasca.

The post office, which operated here from December 1917 through March 1939, carries the Indian name for the common bearberry *Arctostaphylos uvauris.* The Indians used the berries of this tough trailing shrub to make a kind of pemmican and the dried leaves to smoke in their pipes.

Kinikinik Lake (lake)

83 I/11 - Athabasca
31-64-20-W4
54°35'N 113°01'W
Approximately 23 km south-east of Athabasca.

(see Kinikinik)

Kinnaird Lake (lake)

73 L/13 - Lac La Biche
6-67-10-W4
54°46'38"N 111°31'13"W
Approximately 30 km east of Lac La Biche.

The name for this lake has been official since 1921 and is taken after D.G. Kinnaird, an early homesteader.

Kinokamau Lake (lake)

83 H/12 - St. Albert
16-53-25-W4
53°35'N 113°38'W
Approximately 14 km north-west of Edmonton.

The name for this lake has been official since at least 1958, but its precise origin is unknown.

Kinosiu Lake (lake)

83 I/9 - Hylo
17-66-16-W4
54°43'52"N 112°14'50"W
Approximately 24 km south south-west of Lac La Biche.

The descriptive name for this lake is a translation from the Cree, and may be translated either as "a fish," which is *kinoseo* or "long," which is *kinosiu.* The local residents sometimes refer to the feature as "Long Lake."

* **Kinoull** (former post office)

83 I/11 - Athabasca
15-65-22-W4
54°37'N 113°15'W
Approximately 12 km south south-east of Athabasca.

The post office operated here under this name from August 1911 through June 1913 and was then changed to Colinton, but its origin is unknown. (see Colinton)

Kinsella (hamlet)

73 D/13 - Sedgewick
27-46-11-W4
52°59'N 111°32'W
Approximately 32 km south-east of Viking.

The name for this hamlet commemorates the private secretary to the vice-president of the Grand Trunk Pacific Railway. The post office opened here January 1910.

Kipp Lake (lake)

83 J/1 - Barrhead
35-59-4-W5
54°09'20"N 114°29'10"W
Approximately 6 km north-west of Barrhead.

The name was proposed for this feature by the Barrhead Historical Society. Gustav Kipp and family homesteaded land adjoining this lake circa 1914. The name was officially approved 6 March 1986.

Kirk Lake (lake)

83 H/12 - St. Albert
17-53-25-W4
53°35'N 113°40'W
Approximately 17 km north-west of Edmonton.

The name for this lake was officially approved in 1963. Its precise origin is unknown.

Kirkpatrick Lake (lake)

72 M/14 - Kirkpatrick Lake
35-33-10-W4
51°52'N 111°18'W
Approximately 50 km north-east of Hanna.

The precise origin for the name of this feature is unknown.

Kiron (locality)

83 A/15 - Ferintosh
33-45-19-W4
52°57'N 112°42'W
Approximately 13 km south-east of Camrose.

The Canadian Northern Railway established a station here in 1916 and named it after a place of the same name in Iowa.

Kirriemuir (hamlet)

72 M/16 - Grassy Island Lake
13-34-3-W4
51°56′N 110°18′W
Approximately 47 km south of Provost.

A post office opened here in April of 1915 and took the name of a town in Forfarshire (later Angus, now Tayside), Scotland. The town in Scotland was situated in a fertile agricultural area, and apparently, the person who named this place was reminded of the other. The name is from the Gaelic *ceathramh* (pronounced cerrou) *mor*, meaning "big quarter or division," according to Johnston. Kirriemuir was the birthplace of Sir James Barrie (1860-1937), novelist and playwright, author of *Peter Pan*, who called the town "Thrums" in the stories.

Kitscoty (village)

73 E/8 - Lloydminster
26-50-3-W4
53°20′30″N 110°20′00″W
Approximately 23 km west north-west of Lloydminster.

The name for this village, whose post office opened in March 1907, is taken after the town of the same name in Kent, England. The place in England is derived from Kit's Coty House, a cromlech north of Aylesford in Kent. It is a relic of an unknown past, set on a close-cut green in the midst of a cornfield, and consists of four large, irregular slabs of stone, three upright and the fourth and largest balanced on them.

Kitto Lake (lake)

83 G/7 - Tomahawk
29-50-5-W5
53°20′N 114°42′W
Approximately 24 km north-east of Drayton Valley.

The name for this lake has been official since at least 1958. There is a possibility that the lake may commemorate Franklin Hugo Kitto (b. 1880) who was with the Department of the Interior as a surveyor. He wrote a number of studies on Alberta, Saskatchewan and Manitoba.

Kitty Lake (lake)

73 E/7 - Vermilion
9 50-6-W4
53°18′N 110°49′W
Approximately 7 km south south-east of Vermilion.

The name for this lake has been official since at least 1958, but its precise origin is unknown.

Knee Hill Valley (locality)

82 P/13 - Torrington
6-35-26-W4
51°58′N 113°42′W
Approximately 35 km south south-east of Red Deer.

The post office, which operated here from July 1894 through September 1969, was named for its proximity to the Knee Hills. (see Knee Hills)

Knee Hills (hills)

82 P/13 - Torrington
19-32-25-W4
51°45′N 113°32′W
Approximately 40 km south south-east of Red Deer.

The descriptive name for these hills is due to their shape. The name in Cree is *mi-chig-wun* and in Stoney *che-swun-de-ba-ha*. Both translate roughly to Knee Hills.

Kneehill Municipal District #48

(municipal district)

82 P/11 - Three Hills
28 to 34-22 to 26-W4
51°40′N 113°15′W
South-east of Red Deer.

(see Knee Hills)

Knight (railway point)

83 K/2 - Marsh Head Creek
1-60-18-W5
54°09′N 116°33′W
Approximately 58 km west of Whitecourt.

The name for this station on the Sangudo subdivision of Canadian National Railways was officially approved 18 January 1974. Canadian Northern Railway built the first part of this line, eventually to Whitecourt. The portion past there, to Kaybob and Grizzly was likely added by C.N.R. Its precise origin is unknown.

Knob Hill (locality)

83 B/16 - Winfield
22-46-3-W5
52°59′N 114°21′W
Approximately 39 km north of Rimbey.

The descriptive name for this locality, whose post office operated from April 1914 through November 1953, refers to the number of knobs and hills in the area.

* Koknee (former locality)

73 E/2 - Grizzly Bear Creek
27-49-5-W4
53°15′N 110°38′W
Approximately 17 km south-east of Vermilion.

The name for the post office, which operated here from September 1936 through June 1960, was originally the name of School District #2066, established 26

---

*denotes rescinded name or former locality.

November 1909. The name was chosen and submitted to the Department of Education by Tom Elliott, and is a misinterpretation of *kokanee*, a Kootenay Indian word translating "red fish." The stern wheeler *Kokanee* plied the waters of Kootenay Lake, B.C., from 1896 to 1923 when it was dismantled. The name was officially rescinded 18 January 1974.

Konah Lake (lake)

73 L/12 - Beaver Lake
11-65-13-W4
54°36′N 111°51′W
Approximately 20 km south south-east of Lac La Biche.

The name for this lake has appeared on maps since at least 1918, but its precise origin is unknown.

Koney Island (island)

83 H/6 - Cooking Lake
30-51-21-W4
53°26′N 113°06′W
Approximately 30 km east south-east of Edmonton.

The name for this island has been official since at least 1958, but its precise origin is unknown.

Krakow (locality)

83 H/9 - Mundare
15-55-17-W4
53°44′40″N 112°26′20″W
Approximately 42 km south of Smoky Lake.

A post office operated here from February 1904 through December 1943 and was named after a city in Galicia (then part of the Austro-Hungarian Empire) from which many of the early inhabitants came. The name was chosen by a group of the earliest Austrian settlers. Krakow, or Cracow, was the capital of Poland from 1320 to 1609.

The region had a chequered history. In the carving up of Poland in 1795 it went to Austria. After many changes in the nineteenth century, it became part of the revived Poland in 1919.

Kurth Lake (lake)

82 P/15 - Rumsey
32-32-20-W4
51°47′N 112°48′W
Approximately 30 km east south-east of Trochu.

The name for this lake was officially approved in December 1968 and appeared on a sectional map of the area in 1922. Its origin is unknown.

Kuusamo (railway point)

83 B/8 - Sylvan Lake
5-26-38-2-W5
52°17′N 114°11′W
Approximately 6 km south-west of Sylvan Lake.

Kuusamo is a Finnish word meaning "green trees" or "spruce trees". This area was settled originally by Finns. The first school in the area was called the Kuusamo School (S.D. #755, est. 1902) and was near the present site of the United Grain Growers elevator, in 35-38-2-W5M. The Kuusamo School District still exists. The Kuusamo cemetery is close by.

La Corey (hamlet)

73 L/7 - Bonnyville
13-63-6-W4
54°27′N 110°46′W
Approximately 19 km north of Bonnyville.

The post office opened here in December 1917, but the origin for the name is unknown.

Labuma (locality)

83 A/5 - Red Deer
10-39-27-W4
52°20′N 113°48′W
Approximately 6 km north of Red Deer.

The precise origin for the name of this Canadian Pacific Railway station is unknown. It was known previously as "Harrison."

Labyrinth Lake (lake)

83 H/3 - Bittern Lake
5-48-22-W4
53°07′N 113°12′W
Approximately 18 km north north-east of Wetaskiwin.

The descriptive name for this lake has been in use since at least 1892 and refers to its shape.

Lac Bellevue (locality)

73 E/14 - St. Paul
7-56-9-W4
53°49′N 111°20′W
Approximately 18 km south of St. Paul, on the north shore of Lac Bellevue.

The name for this locality, whose post office operated from August 1915 through September 1955, is taken from the view of the nearby lake. (see Lac Bellevue)

* **Lac Canard** (former locality)

73 E/14 - St. Paul
5-57-9-W4
53°52′N 111°18′W
Approximately 9 km south of St. Paul.

A post office operated here from December 1917 through July 1932 and its name was likely taken after the lake. The name was officially rescinded 12 August 1970. (see Canard, Lac)

Lac La Biche (town)

73 L/13 - Lac La Biche
6-67-13-W4
54°46′N 111°58′W
Approximately 84 km east of Athabasca.

Lac La Biche was incorporated as a village on 24 July 1919 and became a town on 31 December 1950. The name has been in use since at least 1790. (see Lac La Biche) Lac La Biche marked a stop on a once important trading route. From Fort George, explorers were able to come in over a height of land down the Beaver River to Lac La Biche, en route to the Athabasca River and north. David Thompson, an early explorer and geographer, who apprenticed to the Hudson's Bay Company in 1784, but transferred to and became a partner of the North West Company in 1797, was the man who built the first trading post in the Lac La Biche area in 1798. He used this post as his headquarters during the following winter. As Thompson was a North West Company man, it came as no surprise in that era of intense rivalry that Peter Fidler set up Greenwich House for the Hudson's Bay Company just eleven months later. In 1914, the railway reached Lac La Biche bringing many settlers, the majority of whom were Catholic French Canadians.

Lac La Biche, old mission, 1890

Lac La Biche Mission (locality)

83 I/16 - Plamondon
68-15-W4
54°52′N 112°16′W
Along the south-west shore of Lac La Biche, immediately north-west of the town of Lac La Biche.

(see Lac La Biche)

Lac La Biche Settlement (settlement)

83 I/16 - Plamondon
1-67,68-14,15-W4
54°49′N 112°10′W
Along the south-west shore of Lac La Biche, immediately north-west of the town of Lac La Biche.

(see Lac La Biche)

Lac la Nonne (locality)

83 G/16 - Lac la Nonne
12-57-3-W5
53°55′N 114°18′W

Approximately 25 km south south-east of Barrhead.

The post office operated here from March 1908 through May 1968 and was named for its proximity to Lac la Nonne. (see Lac la Nonne)

Lac Ste Anne (locality)

83 G/9 - Onoway
30-54-3-W5
53°41'N 114°26'W
Approximately 67 km west north-west of Edmonton.

The post office operated here from May 1903 through December 1963 and was named for its location on Lac Ste Anne. (see Lac Ste Anne)

Lac Ste Anne, n.d.

Lac Ste Anne (settlement)

83 G/9 - Onoway
19-54-4,5-W5
53°41'N 114°26'W
Approximately 68 km west north-west of Edmonton.

(see Lac Ste Anne)

Lac Ste Anne County #28 (county)

83 G/1 - Wabamun Lake
54-59-1-9-W5
53°45'N 114°30'W
West north-west of Edmonton.

(see Lac Ste Anne)

Lacombe (town)

83 A/5 - Red Deer
30-40-26-W4
52°28'00"N 113°43'40"W
Approximately 22 km north north-east of Red Deer.

This town, whose post office opened in December 1891, was named after Father Albert Lacombe, of the Oblates of Mary Immaculate (1827-1916). He was born in Lower Canada to humble parents, helped with the farm work but became an altar boy and went on to the Collège de l'assomption, and to be a secretary at the Bishop's Palace in Quebec. In 1849 Father Lacombe was ordained and left for the mission field on loan to the Bishop of Dubuque, Iowa, to join Father Georges Antoine Belcourt at Pembina. He succeeded Father Jean-Baptiste Thibault at Lac Ste Anne, where his work was largely among the Métis, though, when Dr. James Hector arrived, Father Lacombe had been on a tour among the Blackfoot with a view to starting a mission for them. Later he set up a mission at St. Albert and gained influence among the Blackfoot. The native name for this community is *kamaymatooskak* in Cree, translated "place of balm of Gilead trees," and is descriptive. The post office was known previously as "Barnett." This town was incorporated 10 May 1902.

Lacombe County #14 (county)

83 A/12 - Ponoka
39 to 41-23 to 4-W4 & 5
52°30'N 113°45'W
North of Red Deer.

(see Lacombe)

Lacombe Lake (lake)

83 A/5 - Red Deer
10-40-27-W4
52°26'N 113°48'W
Approximately 6 km south-west of Lacombe.

(see Lacombe)

Lacroix, Lac (lake)

73 L/12 - Beaver Lake
26-65-13-W4
54°39'N 111°51'W
Approximately 17 km south-east of Lac La Biche.

The name for this lake was officially approved 4 October 1910 and is the French translation of the Cree *ayamihewattik sakahegan*, or "Cross Lake." A cross was erected near the lake by natives. It is now referred to locally as "Cross Lake."

Lafond (hamlet)

73 E/14 - St. Paul
6-57-10-W4
53°53'N 111°29'W
Approximately 16 km south-west of St. Paul.

The post office opened here in July 1907 and was named after its first postmaster, C.B. Lafond. Lafond was a homesteader who arrived in the area from Quebec at the turn of the century.

Lake Eliza (locality)

73 E/14 - St. Paul
5-56-8-W4
53°48'N 111°10'W
Approximately 19 km south-west of Elk Point.

The post office operated here from December 1914 through June 1968 and was named by Oscar Johnson (1891-1963), a homesteader who arrived in the area from Sweden in 1910.

* Lake Geneva (former locality)

73 E/11 - Myrnam
28-52-8-W4
53°30′N 111°10′W
Approximately 27 km north-west of
Vermilion.

The post office operated here from April
1910 through July 1937 and was likely
named after Geneva, Switzerland. Two
early settlers, A. Golish and Gus
Christenson, suggested this name ("after a
famous lake") to settle a disagreement at a
meeting to find a name for the school
district. The name was officially rescinded
14 January 1970.

Lake Isle (locality)

83 G/10 - Isle Lake
8-54-5-W5
53°39′N 114°43′W
Approximately 44 km south-east of
Mayerthorpe.

The name for this locality, whose post
office opened in June 1915, is taken from its
position on Isle Lake. (see Isle Lake) It was
previously called "Shearwater."

Lake Majeau (locality)

83 G/16 - Lac la Nonne
19-56-3-W5
53°52′N 114°26′W
Approximately 30 km south of Barrhead.

The post office operated here from October
1923 through November 1967 and was
named for its proximity to Majeau Lake.
(see Majeau Lake)

* Lake Thomas (former post office)

73 E/4 - Viking
12-47-12-W4
53°03′N 111°38′W
Approximately 13 km south-east of Viking.

The post office operated here under this
name from November 1907 through
February 1910 commemorating one of the
earliest residents. The name was then
changed to Philips. (see Philips)

Lakedell (locality)

83 B/16 - Winfield
22-46-1-W5
52°58′N 114°04′W
Approximately 46 km west of Wetaskiwin.

A summer post office operated here from
June 1953 through August 1972. The
descriptive name refers to the locality's
position on Pigeon Lake.

Lakesend (locality)

73 D/6 - Brownfield
21-38-8-W4
52°17′N 111°04′W
Approximately 32 km north-east of
Coronation.

The descriptive name for this former post
office was due to the fact that it was
situated on the end of a small lake. The post
office operated from November 1912
through September 1931. The name was
later changed to Airways. (see Airways)

Lakeview (summer village)

83 G/9 Onoway
12-53-4-W5
53°34′N 114°27′W
Approximately 51 km north-east of
Drayton Valley.

The name for this summer village, which
was incorporated as a village 25 October
1913, is descriptive.

Lakeview Lake (lake)

83 A/3 - Delburne
10-15-35-24-W4
52°01′00″N 113°20′30″W
Approximately 40 km south-east of Red
Deer.

This lake was named before 1928 after the
Lakeview community which has a descriptive name.

Lakeview Lake (lake)

83 I/5 - Dapp
29-63-26-W4
54°29′N 113°54′W
Approximately 35 km north of Westlock.

The name for this lake has been official
since at least 1958 and is likely descriptive.

Lambert Creek (creek)

83 F/7 - Erith
2-51-21-W5
53°23′N 116°59′W
Flows south-east into Embarras River,
approximately 38 km south-west of Edson.

The name for this creek has been official
since at least 1958, and is likely named after
an early owner of the land nearby. Lambert
was a local timber operator in the area for
many years.

* Lambert Park (former locality)

83 H/11 - Edmonton
25-52-24-W4
53°31′N 113°25′W
Within the city limits of Edmonton.

This name commemorates Lambton
County, Ontario, the home town of W.C.
Hands, the first reeve. It is now a subdivi-
sion of the city of Edmonton.

Lambert Pond (lake)

83 F/9 - Edson
12-8-53-17-W5
53°34′00″N 116°28′50″W
Approximately 3 km south-west of Edson
immediately north of the C.N.R. track.

This lake is stocked by Fish and Wildlife
primarily for young people, and the name

---

*denotes rescinded name or former locality.

was officially approved 20 October 1983. Historically, this small lake provided water for the railway steam engines. The lake was also known as "Laurence's Lake" and "Keeler's Pond." (see Lambert Creek)

Lamerton (locality)

83 A/6 - Alix
3-41-22-W4
52°30′N 113°05′W
Approximately 9 km south-west of Bashaw.

A post office operated here from August 1893 through November 1913 and was named after a town in Devonshire, England. The Canadian Northern Railway established a station here in 1914.

Lamont (town)

83 H/15 - Lamont
20-55-19-W4
53°45′35″N 112°46′50″W
Approximately 50 km north-east of Edmonton.

Lamont was named in 1906 in honour of Mr. Justice John Henderson Lamont (1865-1936), a native of Ontario who received his early education and university training there. He was called to the Ontario Bar in 1895 and practiced law in Toronto until 1899, when he moved to Prince Albert. In 1904 he was elected to the House of Commons as member for Saskatchewan, N.W.T., but resigned the following year and was elected to the Legislative Assembly of Saskatchewan as member for Prince Albert. From 1905 through 1907 he served as the first Attorney-General of the new province and in the latter year was appointed a judge of the Supreme Court of Saskatchewan. In 1927 he was appointed to the Supreme Court of Canada. This town was incorporated 31 May 1968.

Lamont Creek (creek)

83 H/15 - Lamont
16-55-19-W4
53°45′15″N 112°45′15″W
Flows north into Beaverhill Creek, approximately 54 km north-east of Edmonton.

(see Lamont)

Lamont Island (island)

83 H/10 - Elk Island Park
22-54-20-W4
53°41′N 112°51′W
Approximately 43 km east north-east of Edmonton.

(see Lamont)

* **Lamoral** (former locality)

83 B/6 - Crimson Lake
2-40-11-W5
52°25′N 115°28′W
Approximately 43 km north-west of Rocky Mountain House.

The Canadian Northern Railway established a station here in 1914. The precise origin for the name is unknown, but the station may have borne the given name of a Belgian aristocrat involved in the financing of Martin Nordegg's Brazeau Collieries Ltd., to which this rail line headed.

Lancaster Park (Canadian Forces Base)

83 H/11 - Edmonton
21-54-24-W4
53°40′N 113°29′W
Within the city limits of Edmonton.

This Canadian Forces Base was named after the Lancaster bomber used in World War II. The post office opened in November 1951.

* **Landonville** (former post office)

73 E/10 - Clandonald
2-55-6-W4
53°43′N 110°47′W

Approximately 25 km south-east of Elk Point.

The name for the post office, which operated here from March 1908 through May 1968, was taken after J.H. Landon, early settler and first postmaster. The name was officially rescinded 14 January 1970.

Landry Lake (lake)

73 L/2 - Muriel Lake
25-60-5-W4
54°13′N 110°38′W
Approximately 10 km south-east of Bonnyville.

The name for this lake has been official since 2 May 1957, but its precise origin is unknown.

Lane Lake (lake)

73 L/10 - Marguerite Lake
18-66-6-W4
54°43′N 110°55′W
Approximately 53 km north-west of Cold Lake.

The name for this lake was officially applied 17 January 1951 and commemorates Brigadier John Lane, D.S.O., of Edmonton, who was killed in November 1944 in the Netherlands. He commanded the divisional artillery of the 4th Canadian Armoured Division.

Lanes Lake (lake)

73 D/4 - Castor
30-37-14-W4
52°12′N 111°59′W
Approximately 6 km west of Castor.

This lake was named after John Lane, a well-known rancher who operated his horse ranch near it.

*denotes rescinded name or former locality.

Lang Lake (lake)

73 E/6 - Mannville
29-50-10-W4
53°20′N 111°25′W
Approximately 37 km north-east of Viking.

The name for this lake has been official since at least 1958, but its precise origin is unknown.

Langford Park (locality)

83 G/10 - Isle Lake
16-53-4-W5
53°35′N 114°32′W
Approximately 50 km north-east of Drayton Valley.

The post office operated here from August 1938 through June 1970 and was likely named after the first postmaster, E.W. Langford.

* **Lanuke** (former locality)

73 E/9 - Marwayne
20 54-12-W4
53°40′N 111°45′W
Approximately 6 km north of Two Hills.

The post office, which operated here from January 1908 through March 1928, was named after a local farmer.

Larkspur (summer village)

83 I/5 - Dapp
7-63-25-W4
54°26′20″N 113°45′53″W
Approximately 30 km north north-east of Westlock.

The post office, which operated from November 1908 through November 1909, was named after the wildflower, the larkspur, abundantly found throughout the foothills and forested regions during June and July. The flowers have an irregular shape with a long spur. A summer village was established here 1 January 1985, and took the same name.

Larry Lake (lake)

83 H/7 - Tofield
2-50-21-W4
53°17′30″N 112°57′00″W
Approximately 21 km west south-west of Tofield.

The name for this lake has been in use since at least 1958, but its precise origin is unknown.

Lauretta Island (island)

73 L/11 - Pinehurst Lake
16-64-10-W4
54°32′N 111°27′W
Approximately 43 km south-east of Lac La Biche.

The well-established name for this island in Frenchman Lake appeared on a map dated 1918 and was officially adopted 7 February 1951. Its precise origin is unknown.

Laurier Lake (lake)

73 E/15 - Elk Point
22-56-4-W4
53°51′N 110°31′W
Approximately 25 km east south-east of Elk Point.

The name for this lake has been official since at least 1958, but its precise origin is unknown.

Lavesta (locality)

83 B/9 - Rimbey
21-43-3-W5
52°43′N 114°23′W
Approximately 13 km north-west of Rimbey.

A post office operated here from June 1911 through August 1937 and was named after Vesta McGee, the daughter of the first postmaster, R.F. McGee.

Lavoy (village)

73 E/5 - Innisfree
4-52-13-W4
53°27′30″N 111°51′40″W
Approximately 14 km east south-east of Vegreville.

This village, whose post office was known as Dinwoodie before July 1906, was named after Joseph Lavoy, an early settler.

Lawrence Lake (lake)

83 I/13 - Grosmont
23-69-25-W4
54°59′N 113°42′W
Approximately 43 km north-west of Athabasca.

The name for this lake has appeared on the Geological Survey Map of Alberta, 16 mi. to 1 in., dated 1937. Its precise origin, however, is unknown.

Lawson Lake (lake)

73 E/7 - Vermilion
13-50-6-W4
53°19′N 110°46′W
Approximately 8 km south-east of Vermilion.

The name for this lake has been official since at least 1958, but its precise origin is unknown.

Lawton (locality)

83 J/1 - Barrhead
27-58-4-W5
54°02′N 114°29′W
Approximately 16 km south-west of Barrhead.

---

*denotes rescinded name or former locality.

The origin for the name of this locality, whose post office operated from March 1908 through May 1965, is unknown.

* **Le Goff** (former post office)

73 L/8 - Cold Lake
17-62-2-W4
54°22′N 110°16′W
Approximately 7 km south south-west of Grand Centre.

The post office operated here from April 1913 through May 1968 and was named after Father Laurent Le Goff, a Roman Catholic missionary. He was stationed here at the time of the Northwest Rebellion of 1885. Le Goff was the post office for Beaver River. (see Beaver River)

Lea Park (locality)

73 E/9 - Marwayne
14-54-3-W4
53°40′N 110°20′W
Approximately 44 km south-east of Elk Point.

The descriptive name for this locality, whose post office operated from November 1911 through January 1955, refers to its location on a flat plain near the North Saskatchewan River.

Lea Park Provincial Recreation Area

(recreation area)

73 E/9 - Marwayne
3-14-54-3-W4
53°39′N 110°20′W
Approximately 45 km north-west of Lloydminster.

(see Lea Park)

Leahurst (locality)

83 A/7 - Stettler
26-39-19-W4
52°23′N 112°38′W
Approximately 10 km north north-east of Stettler.

The Canadian Northern Railway established a station here in 1911. The precise origin for the name is unknown.

Leaman (locality)

83 G/11 - Chip Lake
36-53-11-W5
53°37′N 115°29′W
Approximately 44 km south south-west of Mayerthorpe.

The Grand Trunk Pacific Railway established a station here in 1911 and named it after a cousin of Henry Philips, secretary of the company. The name was changed back and forth to Chip Lake. The post office operated as Leaman from March 1914 through March 1929, and then reopened in June 1952 and operated through December 1959.

Leane Lake (lake)

73 D/9 - Chauvin
27-41-1-W4
52°33′N 110°04′W
Approximately 28 km north north-east of Provost.

The precise origin of the name of this lake is unknown.

* **Leasowe** (former locality)

83 H/5 - Leduc
3-51-26-W4
53°23′N 114°44′W
Approximately 22 km south-west of Edmonton.

A post office operated here from April 1914 through November 1928 and was named after a village near Chester, England. It was originally known as "Middleton," and the school district retained that name.

Lebeaus Lake (lake)

83 I/4 - Westlock
6-61-25-W4
54°14′30″N 113°44′00″W
Approximately 13 km north north-east of Westlock.

This lake was officially named in 1952 after Mr. Lebeau, an early homesteader who later became Reeve of the Municipality of Pibroch.

Leduc (city)

83 H/5 - Leduc
26-49-25-W4
53°15′50″N 113°32′32″W
Approximately 30 km south of Edmonton.

Lieutenant-Governor Edgar Dewdney established a telegraph station here as part of Dominion Telegraph circa 1890. He gave it the name Leduc in commemoration of Father Hippolyte Leduc (1842-1918), of the Oblates of Mary Immaculate. Father Leduc was ordained priest in the Oblate order in 1864, came west in 1865 to Pembina and in 1867 to St. Albert and Edmonton. His other ministries brought him to Calgary and Lac Brochet. Leduc was incorporated as a village in 1899 , a town 15 December 1906 and a city 1 September 1983. Its claim to fame occurred in 1947 when Imperial Leduc No. 1 oil well came into production, setting off the Alberta oil boom.

Leduc, AM Anderson General Store, 1900

Lee Lake (lake)

82 P/15 - Rumsey
7-35-18-W4
51°59′N 112°34′W
Approximately 50 km east north-east of Trochu.

The name for this lake has been official since 1958, but its origin is unknown.

Lee Lake (lake)

83 I/11 - Athabasca
6-64-21-W4
54°30′15″N 113°11′00″W
Approximately 24 km south south-east of Athabasca.

The name for this lake has been official since at least 1958, but its precise origin is unknown.

Leech Lake (lake)

83 J/3 - Green Court
23-59-9-W5
54°06′30″N 115°14′30″W
Approximately 29 km east of Whitecourt.

*denotes rescinded name or former locality.

The name for this lake has been official since at least 1958 and is likely descriptive.

Leedale (locality)

83 B/9 - Rimbey
2-42-4-W5
52°35′N 114°29′W
Approximately 17 km south-west of Rimbey.

A post office operated by this name from December 1917 through January 1970 and was named after William H. Lee, one of the first postmasters. It was previously known as "Wittenberg."

Leeshore (locality)

83 I/2 - Waskatenau
13-58-20-W4
54°01′N 112°49′W
Approximately 20 km east north-east of Redwater.

The precise origin for the name of this locality, whose post office operated from May 1908 through July 1958, is unknown.

Legal (village)

83 H/13 - Morinville
24-57-25-W4
53°56′50″N 113°35′45″W
Approximately 28 km south south-west of Westlock.

This French-Canadian settlement was founded in 1898 and was named after Emile Joseph Légal (1849-1920), who became Bishop of St. Albert in 1902 and the first Roman Catholic Archbishop of Edmonton in 1912. He came to what is now Alberta in 1881 and spent many years in missionary work. He was the author of *Short Sketches of the History of the Catholic Churches and Missions in Central Alberta.* Archbishop Légal, an Oblate, was born near Nantes, France, and came to Canada in 1880. The

post office opened in May 1900. This town was incorporated 20 February 1914.

Leicester Lake (lake)

73 L/13 - Lac La Biche
11-67-13-W4
54°46′N 111°52′W
Approximately 7 km east of Lac La Biche.

The name for this lake has been official since 3 May 1951, but appeared on a map dated 1918. Its precise origin is unknown.

* **Leighton** (former post office)

73 E/9 - Marwayne
15-53-1-W4
53°34′N 110°05′W
Approximately 33 km north of Lloydminster.

The name for the post office, which operated from May 1911 through January 1960, was suggested by J.V. Armstrong, the first postmaster, after one of several villages in England with the same name. The name was officially rescinded 14 January 1970.

Leithead Lake (lake)

83 A/1 - Hackett
29-35-15-W4
52°02′N 112°07′W
Approximately 24 km south-west of Castor.

The lake was named after William Leithead, who lived by the lake (NW-19-35-15-W4) in the early homesteading days.

Leming Lake (lake)

73 L/9 - Marie Lake
2-65-4-W4
54°35′N 110°29′W
Approximately 25 km north-west of Cold Lake.

The name for this lake has been official since 17 September 1951, but its precise origin is unknown. The feature was previously called "Island Lake."

Lemp Lake (lake)

73 D/15 - Wainwright
33-44-5-W4
52°50′N 110°40′W
Approximately 13 km east of the town of Wainwright.

The precise origin of the name of this lake is unknown.

Leo (locality)

83 A/1 - Hackett
34-35-17-W4
52°03′N 112°22′W
Approximately 36 km west south-west of Castor.

One of the first elevators of the Alberta Wheat Pool was built here in 1924. The post office operated from June 1908 through July 1957 and was named after Leo Fuson, a grandson of the first postmaster, O.L. Longshore, who came from Oklahoma in 1906.

Leslieville (hamlet)

83 B/7 - Rocky Mountain House
26-39-5-W5
52°23′N 114°36′W
Approximately 17 km west of Eckville.

The post office was established at this hamlet in January 1907 and was named after Leslie Reilly, whose family settled here in 1903.

Lessard (locality)

73 L/7 - Bonnyville
12-63-5-W4
54°26′N 110°38′W
Approximately 20 km north north-east of Bonnyville.

The post office operated here from May 1921 through February 1962 and was named after Senator Prosper Edmond Lessard (1873-1931), who was elected to the Alberta Legislature as a Liberal for Pakan in 1909, and in 1913 and 1917 for St. Paul. He was called to the Senate in 1925.

Lessard Lake (lake)

83 G/15 - Sangudo
27-55-5-W5
53°47′N 114°39′W
Approximately 37 km south-east of Mayerthorpe.

The precise origin for the name of this lake which has been official since at least 1958 is unknown. It is known locally as "Jackfish Lake."

Letendre, Lac (lake)

73 E/4 - Viking
29-47-11-W4
53°05′N 111°34′W
Approximately 14 km east of Viking.

The name for this lake has been official since September 1941, but its precise origin is unknown.

Letour Lake (lake)

83 G/7 - Tomahawk
20-50-5-W5
53°20′N 114°41′W
Approximately 23 km north-east of Drayton Valley.

The name for this lake has been official since at least 1958, but its precise origin is unknown.

Levering Lake (lake)

83 H/3 - Bittern Lake
16-49-22-W4
53°14′N 113°09′W
Approximately 25 km east of Leduc.

This lake is named after Bishop J. Mortimer Levering of the Moravian Church, who was here on official business in 1904.

* Liberal (former post office)

83 A/7 - Stettler
6-39-20-W4
52°20′N 112°53′W
Approximately 12 km west of Stettler.

The precise origin of the name for the post office, which operated from August 1903 through July 1906, is unknown. The name was later changed to Erskine.

Lick Creek (creek)

83 B/6 - Crimson Lake
11-38-9-W5
52°15′15″N 115°18′45″W
Flows south into Prairie Creek, approximately 20 km south-west of Rocky Mountain House.

The precise origin for the name of this creek is unknown.

Lily Lake (lake)

83 G/10 - Isle Lake
34-54-5-W5
53°42′N 114°39′W
Approximately 42 km south-east of Mayerthorpe.

The name for this lake was likely applied by surveyors, as it appears on a map produced by the Surveys and Mapping Branch dated 1953. Its precise origin is unknown.

---

*denotes rescinded name or former locality.

Lily Lake (lake)

83 H/14 - Lamont
20-57-23-W4
53°57′N 113°23′W
Approximately 38 km north of Edmonton.

This somewhat marshy-looking sheet of water was named by Charles Mair circa 1908 and is a translation of the Cree term *ascutamo sakaigon*.

Limestone Creek (creek)

83 H/16 - Willingdon
4-57-16-W4
53°54′N 112°28′W
Flows east into Egg Creek, approximately 22 km south of Smoky Lake.

The name for this creek has been official since at least 1958, its precise origin is unknown.

Limestone Lake (lake)

83 H/15 - Lamont
31-56-17-W4
53°53′00″N 112°30′30″W
Approximately 17 km south of Smoky Lake.

This lake feeds Limestone Creek, but the precise origin of its name is unknown.

Linaria (locality)

83 J/8 - Shoal Creek
24-61-2-W5
54°18′N 114°08′W
Approximately 26 km north north-east of Barrhead.

The name for this locality, whose post office operated from January 1918 through September 1969, is taken from the flaxseed, also known as linaria.

---

*denotes rescinded name or former locality.

Lincoln (locality)

83 I/12 - Coolidge
36-65-24-W4
54°40′N 113°30′W
Approximately 15 km west south-west of Athabasca.

The post office operated here from February 1933 through January 1966 and the settlement was named in the early 1900s by early black settlers in commemoration of Abraham Lincoln (1809-1865), the six-teenth President of the United States. Lincoln abolished slavery in the United States during his term in office.

Lindale (locality)

83 G/7 - Tomahawk
21-49-5-W5
53°15′N 114°39′W
Approximately 21 km east of Drayton Valley.

The post office opened here in July 1914, and was named after Charles Lindell, the first settler and the first postmaster. He arrived in the area from Kalmar, Sweden, in 1905 to homestead and later established a logging camp. The original name suggested for the post office was "Lindell Valley," however, the name Lindale was the one chosen by postal authorities.

Lindale (locality)

83 H/11 - Edmonton
11-53-22-W4
53°34′N 113°08′W
Approximately 27 km east of Edmonton.

The precise origin for this country residence subdivision is unknown.

Lindbergh (hamlet)

73 E/15 - Elk Point
34-56-5-W4
53°53′N 110°40′W
Approximately 15 km east of Elk Point.

This hamlet, whose post office opened in January 1929, was named by Sir Henry Thornton, president of Canadian National Railways, after Charles Lindbergh (1902-1974), the American pilot who in 1927 was the first to fly solo from west to east across the Atlantic Ocean. For this he won the Raymond Orteig prize.

Lindbrook (locality)

83 H/7 - Tofield
12-51-20-W4
53°24′N 112°48′W
Approximately 8 km north-west of Tofield.

A post office operated here from May 1937 through October 1969 and took the name of the school district established in 1909-1910. Two of the first trustees were E. Lindberg and F.L.L. Sherbrook, and by combining the first part of the first name and the second part of the second name the result was Lindbrook.

* Lindsville (former post office)

73 D/4 - Castor
1-38-12-W4
52°15′N 111°35′W
Approximately 20 km north north-west of Coronation.

The name for this post office, which operated from December 1908 through February 1916, was taken after its first postmaster, T. Lind. The name was later changed to Bulwark. (see Bulwark)

Line Island (island)

83 H/10 - Elk Island Park
16-15-54-20-W4
53°40′10″N 112°50′25″W
Approximately 40 km east of Edmonton, in Elk Island National Park.

The name for this island enjoys the local usage of the warden staff, and is likely descriptive of its shape. It was officially approved 17 October 1991.

* **Linfield** (former locality)
83 J/2 - Thunder Lake
36-59-5-W5
54°09′N 114°36′W
Approximately 15 km west of Barrhead.

The name for this former locality, whose post office operated from July 1914 through August 1934, was taken after C. Linfield, the first postmaster. The name was officially rescinded in 1958.

Link Lake (lake)
82 P/16 - Farrell Lake
34-32-17-W4
51°47 N 112°20′W
Approximately 32 km north-west of Hanna.

The name for this lake has been in use since at least 1958, but its precise origin is unknown.

Linn Valley (hamlet)
83 A/5 - Red Deer
SE-6-39-27-W4
52°19′N 113°52′W
Approximately 6 km north of Red Deer.

The subdivision plan for this hamlet was registered at the Land Titles Office in Edmonton in July 1960 and was at that time known as Valleyview. In 1979 the county wished to take advantage of a Hamlet Street Assistance Grant provided by Alberta Transportation and Utilities. In order to do that, the subdivision, known as "Valleyview," had to be designated a hamlet under the Municipal Government Act, which the county applied for, as

approved by County Council. However, because there was already a town in Alberta with the name Valleyview, the county was required to change the name, in case some time in the future this hamlet became a village or a town. The residents of the subdivision were informed of this and asked to submit suggestions for a new name. The residents finally agreed on the name Linn Valley; Linn came from the surname of the owners of this quarter-section many years ago. In 1980 the new Linn Valley was designated a hamlet.

Lisburn (hamlet)
83 G/15 - Sangudo
23-56-6-W5
53°51′N 114°46′W
Approximately 26 km south-east of Mayerthorpe.

The Canadian Northern Railway established a station here in 1915, and presumably named it after a town of the same name near Belfast in Antrim, Ireland (now Northern Ireland). The post office operated from May 1916 through April 1975. It was previously known as "Merebeck."

Little Bear Lake (lake)
73 L/9 - Cold Lake
19-64-2-W4
54°33′N 110°18′W
Approximately 1 km west of Cold Lake.

The name for this lake was officially adopted 9 May 1978. It is also referred to locally as "Hasse Lake," but this name was chosen to avoid confusion with a lake of the same name west of Edmonton. It is the only lake in the area stocked with rainbow trout and has become a very popular fishing spot for local fishermen since 1964 when it was first stocked. This small lake is just east of a larger lake locally known as "Bear Lake," officially Ethel Lake.

Little Beaver Creek (creek)
83 B/10 - Carlos
19-41-7-W5
52°33′N 114°59′W
Flows west into North Saskatchewan River, approximately 20 km north of Rocky Mountain House.

The name for this creek has been official since at least 1958 and is a contrast to Big Beaver Creek.

Little Beaver Lake (lake)
83 A/15 - Ferintosh
9-44-21-W4
52°46′20″N 112°58′50″W
Immediately west of Ferintosh.

The precise origin for the well-established name for this long narrow lake is unknown.

Little Beaver Lake (lake)
83 I/9 - Hylo
2-65-16-W4
54°36′N 112°19′W
Approximately 30 km south-west of Lac La Biche.

The name for this lake has been official since at least 1958. It is drained by the Amisk River. (see Amisk River) There is a Beaver Lake approximately 30 km to the north-east.

Little Brule Creek (creek)
83 G/12 - Carrot Creek
35-53-11-W5
53°38′00″N 115°30′15″W
Flows north into Lobstick River, approximately 43 km south south-west of Mayerthorpe.

Brûlé is French for "burnt." The name for the creek has been official since at least 1958, but its precise origin is unknown.

Little Egg Creek (creek)

83 H/12 - St. Albert
12-55-24-W4
53°44′N 113°31′W
Flows south-east into Sturgeon River, approximately 23 km north of Edmonton.

The name for this creek has been official since at least 1958, but its precise origin is unknown.

Little Elk Buttes (hill)

73 D/10 - Hughenden
20-43-7-W4
52°43′N 110°58′W
Approximately 15 km south south-west of the town of Wainwright.

The name for this hill has been in use since at least 1958, but its origin is unknown.

Little Flag Lake (lake)

73 D/12 - Lougheed
18-41-11-W4
52°32′N 111°35′W
Approximately 25 km south-west of Hardisty.

The name for this lake has been in use since at least 1958, but its origin is unknown. There is, however, a Flag Lake within a few kilometres, and the name for this lake may be due to its proximity and relative size to Flag Lake.

Little Garner Lake (lake)

73 L/4 - Cache Lake
34-60-12-W4
54°14′N 111°42′W
Approximately 38 km north-west of St. Paul.

(see Garner Lake)

Little Gem (locality)

72 M/10 - Sedalia
18-32-7-W4
51°44′N 110°58′W
Approximately 55 km north north-west of Oyen.

The name for this locality, whose post office operated from October 1927 through October 1956, describes the feelings its early settlers had about the area, since they felt it to be a good place to settle.

Little Hay Lake (lake)

83 H/3 - Bittern Lake
5-49-21-W4
53°12′N 113°02′W
Approximately 24 km north-west of Camrose.

This lake is likely named for its proximity to the village of Hay Lakes. (see Hay Lakes)

* Little Hay Lakes (former village)

83 H/6 - Cooking Lake
34-49-22-W4
53°16′N 113°08′W
Approximately 36 km north north-west of Camrose.

This village is now known as New Sarepta. (see New Sarepta)

Little Island Lake (lake)

83 G/10 - Isle Lake
7-55-5-W5
53°44′N 114°43′W
Approximately 37 km south-east of Mayerthorpe.

The name for this lake has been official since at least 1958 and is descriptive of the two islands contained in it.

Little Johnson Lake (lake)

83 I/10 - Boyle
10-19-65-17-W4
54°38′25″N 112°33′10″W
Approximately 41 km west south-west of Lac La Biche.

(see Big Johnson Lake)

Little Paddle River (river)

83 G/15 - Sangudo
20-57-7-W5
53°56′30″N 114°59′00″W
Flows east into Paddle River, approximately 13 km east of Mayerthorpe.

This feature was descriptively named for its proximity as a tributary to Paddle River. (see Paddle River)

Little Pine Creek (creek)

83 I/11 - Athabasca
13-11-65-22-W4
From 54°37′27″N 113°15′26″W
to 54°34′5″N 113°09′33″W
Flows north-west into Tawatinaw River, approximately 10 km south of Athabasca.

The name for this creek has been official since at least 1958 and is likely descriptive.

Little Red Deer River (river)

83 B/1 - Markerville
16-35-1-W5
52°00′15″N 114°14′00″W
Flows north-east into Red Deer River, approximately 32 km south-west of Red Deer.

The name for this river is a translation of a native name, and has been in use since at least 1859. The Cree equivalent is *was-ke-sis-si-pi-sis*, while the Blackfoot call it *asino-ka-sis-ughty*. The Stoney term is rendered *pachidi waptan*. (see Red Deer River)

---

*denotes rescinded name or former locality.

Little Rock Island Lake (lake)

73 L/1 - Reita Lake
33-58-2-W4
54°03′00″N 110°15′30″W
Approximately 17 km south of Grand
Centre.

The name for this lake has been official
since 1950 and was named by early Métis
settlers from the numerous small rocks
found on the island in the lake.

Little Strawberry Creek (creek)

83 G/1 - Warburg
11-48-3-W5
53°08′N 114°24′W
Flows north-east into Strawberry Creek,
approximately 43 km east of Drayton
Valley.

The name for this creek has been official
since at least 1958 and was likely named for
its proximity as a tributary to Strawberry
Creek.

Little Sundance Creek (creek)

83 F/10 - Bickerdike
31-53-18-W5
53°37′N 116°37′W
Flows south-east into Sundance Creek,
approximately 11 km west south-west of
Edson.

This creek is likely named for its proximity
to Sundance Lake. The name has been
official since at least 1958.

Little Sundance Lake (lake)

83 F/11 - Dalehurst
11-55-21-W5
53°44′N 117°01′W
Approximately 43 km west north-west of
Edson.

The name for this lake has been official
since at least 1959, and was likely named for
its proximity to Little Sundance Creek.

Little Tawayik Lake (lake)

83 H/10 - Elk Island Park
16-53-20-W4
53°34′N 112°53′W
Approximately 42 km east of Edmonton, in
Elk Island National Park.

(see Tawayik Lake)

Liza Lake (lake)

73 L/7 - Bonnyville
23-61-6-W4
54°17′N 110°48′W
Approximately 4 km west of Bonnyville.

(see Elinor Lake)

Lloyd Creek (creek)

83 B/9 - Rimbey
31-43-2-W5
52°44′N 114°08′W
Flows south-west into Blindman River,
approximately 2 km north-east of Rimbey.

This creek was named in 1950 after Flight
Lieutenant Lloyd George Anderson (1917–
1944), one of three brothers from
Craigmyle, who was killed in World War
II. (see Boyd Creek)

Lloydminster (city)

73 E/8 - Lloydminster
1-50-1-W4
53°16′47″N 110°01′36″W
Approximately 235 km east of Edmonton.

Lloydminster is nicknamed "The Border
City" because it is astride the Alberta-
Saskatchewan border. It takes its name
from George Exton Lloyd (1865-1940),
chaplain to the All British Colony, familiarly known as the Barr Colony after its
first leader, the Rev. I.M. Barr (1849-1937).

George E. Lloyd ultimately became Bishop
of Saskatchewan. The name literally means
"Lloyd's monastery." Minster was the Old
English word for "monastery." This city
was incorporated 1 January 1958.

Lloyds Hill (locality)

73 D/2 - Neutral Hills
22-37-6-W4
52°12′N 110°47′W
Approximately 38 km south-west of
Provost.

The post office, which operated here from
June 1915 through December 1962, was
named after its first postmistress, Mrs. G.L.
Lloyd.

Lobstick (locality)

83 G/11 - Chip Lake
30-53-8-W5
53°36′N 115°10′W
Approximately 40 km south of
Mayerthorpe.

The name for this former station is taken
after its proximity to the Lobstick River.
(see Lobstick River)

Lobstick Creek (creek)

83 B/7 - Rocky Mountain House
24-39-5-W5
52°22′N 114°35′W
Flows south-east into Horseguard Creek,
approximately 24 km east of Rocky
Mountain House.

The precise origin for the name of this
creek is unknown; however, it may be near
a lobstick. (see Lobstick River)

Lobstick River (river)

83 G/11 - Chip Lake
33-53-9-W5
53°37′N 115°17′W
Flows east into Chip Lake, approximately
42 km south south-west of Mayerthorpe.

A lobstick is a jackpine or lodgepole pine with the lower branches cut off, causing the upper ones to bush out, resulting in a distinctive appearance that was a common landmark in fur trade days. This feature appeared as "Lobstick Creek" on Palliser's map of 1865, descriptively named after a tall lobstick on its bank that marked the point at which the trail struck the creek. In 1862 the river was known to the Overlanders as "Buffalo-Dung River." The Overlanders were a group of men who travelled from eastern Canada to the Cariboo Gold Rush in 1862. The name Lobstick River was submitted for approval to the Canadian Geographic Board by A.O. Wheeler on 1 February 1911. This tributary to the Pembina River is known to the Cree as *misticipikwam-akesot*.

Lobstick Settlement (settlement)
83 I/2 - Waskatenau
15-58-18-W4
54°01′N 112°36′W
Approximately 15 km south-west of Smoky Lake.

(see Lobstick River)

Lochearn (locality)
83 B/7 - Rocky Mountain House
21-39-7-W5
52°22′N 114°58′W
Approximately 4 km west of Rocky Mountain House.

Both the Canadian Pacific Railway and the Canadian Northern Railway established a station here in 1914 and named it after the nearby "Loch Ernie."

Lockhart (locality)
83 B/9 - Rimbey
18-41-2-W5
52°32′N 114°16′W
Approximately 13 km south of Rimbey.

A post office operated here from September 1906 through December 1925 and was named after James Lockhart, the first postmaster.

Lochinvar (locality)
83 A/12 - Ponoka
15-41-26-W4
52°32′N 113°40′W
Approximately 20 km west of Ponoka.

The post office operated here from May 1907 through May 1920 and was likely named after Lochinvar, a loch in Kirkcudbrightshire (now Dumfries and Galloway), Scotland. The Canadian Pacific Railway station took the name of the post office when it was established later. The name may also commemorate Lochinvar, the hero of a ballad in Scott's *Marmion*:: "O, young Lochinvar has come out of the west / Through all the wide Border his steed was the best...." The name means "Loch on a height."

Lodge Lake (lake)
83 I/9 - Hylo
13-66-17-W4
54°43′30″N 112°27′10″W
Approximately 32 km west of Lac La Biche.

The name for this lake has been official since at least 1958 and likely refers to beaverlodges on the lake at one time. There is an old lodge mouldering on the north-east shore of the lake. Two local names for the lake are "Bobtail Lake," another descriptive name, and "Pearson Lake," after Tom Pearson who was the earliest settler on the shores of the lake, living there from 1920 to 1928.

Lodgepole (hamlet)
83 G/3 - Blue Rapids
31-47-9-W5
53°06′N 115°19′W

Approximately 27 km south-west of Drayton Valley.

The name for this former town, whose post office opened in August 1956, was taken after the lodgepole pine tree which is plentiful in the area.

Lofty Lake (lake)
83 I/9 - Hylo
8-22-66-17-W4
54°43′30″N 112°28′55″W
Approximately 35 km west of Lac La Biche.

The name for this lake was officially adopted 1 June 1948; however, its precise origin is unknown. Some speculation maintains that the name may be descriptive. It is sometimes referred to by local residents as "Line Lake."

Lombell (locality)
83 J/3 - Green Court
5-59-9-W5
54°05′N 115°18′W
Approximately 7 km north-west of Mayerthorpe.

A railway station was established here in 1921, but the origin for the name is unknown.

Lone Pine Lake (lake)
83 I/8 - Victor Lake
4-9-63-14-W4
54°25′30″N 112°03′00″W
Approximately 39 km south of Lac La Biche.

The name for this lake appears on the Alberta sectional map No. 365 dated 1915. It may be a translation from the Cree, and Pastor Erasmus refers to the lake by this name in describing the roundabout trek of the dissident Cree and Métis from Goodfish to Fort Victoria in 1885. There is some evidence that there was an island once in the lake which had on it a white spruce, sometimes referred to as "pine."

Lonepine Creek (creek)

82 P/12 - Lonepine Creek
4-31-26-W4
51°37'N 113°36'W
Flows south-east into Kneehills Creek, approximately 22 km south-west of Three Hills.

The name for this creek has been official since at least 1958, but its precise origin is unknown.

Lonepine Lake (lake)

83 A/2 - Big Valley
6-38-18,19-W4
52°14'N 112°34'W
Approximately 13 km south-east of Stettler.

According to local residents, the lake was named after a large, single spruce tree that used to grow on the lake's north-east shore. Although the tree was a spruce, the name became Lonepine and the tree served as a familiar landmark in the district.

Long Island (island)

83 H/10 - Elk Island Park
54-20-W4
53°40'N 112°51'W
Approximately 40 km east of Edmonton, in Elk Island National Park.

The name for this island in Astotin Lake has been in use since at least 1958 and is likely descriptive.

Long Island (island)

73 L/13 - Lac La Biche
29-67-13-W4
54°49'N 111°57'W
Approximately 6 km north of Lac La Biche.

The descriptive name for this island in Lac La Biche has been official since 3 May 1951.

Long Island Lake (lake)

83 I/5 - Dapp
24-63-26-W4
54°27'N 113°47'W
Approximately 33 km north of Westlock.

The name for this lake has been official since at least 1958 and is descriptive.

Long Island Point (point)

83 H/10 - Elk Island Park
3-22-54-20-W4
53°40'30"N 112°52'10"W
Approximately 40 km east of Edmonton, in Elk Island National Park.

The name for this point in Astotin Lake was officially approved 17 October 1991. (see Long Island)

Long Lake (hamlet)

83 I/7 - Newbrook
25-63-19-W4
54°27'N 112°45'W
Approximately 45 km south-east of Athabasca.

This hamlet was named for its proximity to Long Lake and Long Lake Provincial Park. (see Long Lake)

Long Lake (lake)

83 H/4 - Kavanagh
14-47-27-W4
53°03'N 113°52'W
Approximately 33 km west north-west of Wetaskiwin.

The name for this lake has been in use since at least 1958 and is likely descriptive.

Long Lake (lake)

83 I/11 - Athabasca
20-65-22-W4
54°38'N 113°18'W
Approximately 9 km south of Athabasca.

The name for this lake has been official since at least 1958 and is descriptive of its shape.

Long Lake (near Clover Bar), c. 1910

Long Lake (lake)

83 I/12 - Coolidge
36-64-25-W4
54°35'N 113°39'W
Approximately 27 km south-west of Athabasca.

The descriptive name for this lake has been official since at least 1958.

Long Lake (lake)

73 E/16 - Frog Lake
30-56-1-W4
53°52'N 110°09'W
Approximately 49 km east of Elk Point.

The name for this lake has been official since at least 1958 and is likely descriptive.

Long Lake Provincial Park

(provincial park)

83 I/7 - Newbrook

14-63-19-W4

54°27′N 112°45′W

Approximately 47 km south-east of
Athabasca.

The name for this 763.83 hectare (1887.47
acre) provincial park, created by Order-in-
Council No. 1074/71 is directly related to
the physical description of the lake on
which it is situated. The long, narrow shape
is characteristic of many glacially formed
lakes.

Longhurst Lake (lake)

83 G/8 - Genesee

36-51-1-W5

53°27′00″N 114°00′30″W

Approximately 33 km west south-west of
Edmonton.

This feature was named in 1950 after Major
Willmot George Longhurst, M.I.D. (1913-
1944), of Edmonton. He was killed in
World War II. The local name for the lake
is "Dog Lake."

Lonira (locality)

83 J/3 - Green Court

4-59-10-W5

54°05′N 115°26′W

Approximately 17 km south-east of
Whitecourt.

A railway station was established here in
1921. The name is a combination of the
former homes of Mr. Bowman, the postmaster, and his wife, that is London and
Iroquois, Ontario. The post office operated
here from February 1913 through February
1956.

Looking Back Lake (lake)

83 H/6 - Cooking Lake

15-50-22-W4

53°19′N 113°08′W

Approximately 32 km south-east of
Edmonton.

The name for this lake has been in use since
at least 1958, but its precise origin is
unknown.

Looma (locality)

83 H/6 - Cooking Lake

35-50-23-W4

53°21′45″N 113°14′50″W

Approximately 25 km south-east of
Edmonton.

This post office, which operated from May
1920 through February 1981, was previously known as "Looma Vista," which may
have been a descriptive name – "loom"
refers to a vague first appearance of land
when one is at sea, and "vista" is an
indication a long narrow view as between
trees. It is not known why the name was
shortened.

* Looma Vista (former locality)

83 H/6 - Cooking Lake

35-50-23-W4

53°22′N 113°15′W

Approximately 25 km south-east of
Edmonton.

A post office operated under this name
from May 1908 through August 1913 until
it was changed to Looma. (see Looma)

Loon Lake (lake)

73 D/16 - McLaughlin

10-44-4-W4

52°47′N 110°29′W

Approximately 25 km east south-east of the
town of Wainwright.

The name for this lake has been in use since
at least 1958, but the precise origin is
unknown.

Loranger, Lac (lake)

73 E/4 - Viking

14-48-11-W4

53°08′N 111°31′W

Approximately 20 km east north-east of
Viking.

The name for this lake was officially
approved 11 September 1941, but its precise
origin is unknown.

Lorraine (locality)

73 D/5 - Alliance

12-39-12-W4

52°20′N 111°35′W

Approximately 12 km north-east of Castor.

The post office, which operated here from
March 1907 through June 1920, was named
after the daughter of its first postmaster, Ed
Wimmer.

Loseman Lake (lake)

73 L/16 - Medley River

20-68-3-W4

54°54′N 110°26′W

Approximately 50 km north north-west of
Cold Lake.

The name for this lake has been official
since 17 January 1951 and is pronounced
"Lossman." Its precise origin is unknown.

Lost Creek (creek)

83 G/12 - Carrot Creek

14-55-14-W5

53°44′50″N 115°57′45″W

Flows south-east into McLeod River,
approximately 34 km east north-east of
Edson.

The name for this creek has been established since 1933, but its precise origin is
unknown.

---

*denotes rescinded name or former locality.

Lostpoint Lake (lake)
83 H/14 - Redwater
36-56-23-W4
53°53'N 113°17'W
Approximately 37 km north north-east of Edmonton.

The name for this lake has been official since at least 1958, but its precise origin is unknown.

Lottie Lake (lake)
73 L/4 - Cache Lake
NE-33-58-11-W4
54°03'N 111°34'W
Approximately 15 km west of St. Paul.

The origin for the name of this lake is unknown.

Lottie Lake (hamlet)
73 L/4 - Cache Lake
33-58-11-W4
54°04'N 111°35'W
Approximately 20 km west north-west of St. Paul.

This hamlet, established 16 July 1985, takes its name from the lake upon whose eastern shore it sits. (see Lottie Lake)

Lougheed (village)
73 D/12 - Lougheed
33-43-11-W4
52°44'40"N 111°32'30"W
Approximately 10 km south-east of Sedgewick.

This village, previously known as "Holmstown," was named after Sir James Alexander Lougheed, K.C.M.G. (1854-1925), a lawyer who moved to Calgary in 1882 from Toronto. He was called to the Canadian Senate in 1889 and from 1914 to 1918, was chairman of the Military Hospitals Commission. In 1920, he became federal Minister of the Interior, Super-

intendent-General of Indian Affairs and Minister of Mines, which he held until the election of the Mackenzie King Government the following year. Peter Lougheed (b. 1928), former Premier of Alberta, is a grandson. This village was incorporated 7 November 1911.

Louis Lake (lake)
73 E/10 - Clandonald
3,4-55-6-W4
53°43'18"N 110°48'40"W
Approximately 20 km south of Elk Point.

Previously known as "Landon Lake," this feature was named for the family who homesteaded the land upon which the feature is situated. The school district was named Louis School District, however, and the lake eventually became known as Louis Lake. The name was officially changed 24 September 1991 to reflect the current local usage.

Louis Lake (lake)
83 H/3 - Bittern Lake
25-48-22-W4
53°11'30"N 113°05'30"W
Approximately 24 km north-west of Camrose.

The name for this lake has been official since at least 1958, but its precise origin is unknown.

Louis Lake (lake)
83 B/6 - Crimson Lake
5-40-8-W5
52°24'30"N 115°07'00"W
Approximately 15 km west north-west of Rocky Mountain House.

The name for this lake has been in use since at least 1958, but its precise origin is unknown.

Lousana (hamlet)
83 A/3 - Delburne
14-23-36-23-W4
52°07'N 113°10'W
Approximately 10 km south-east of Red Deer.

The name for this hamlet, whose post office opened in December 1912, was named after the home town of William H. Biggs, known as Judge Biggs. Around the turn of the century, after retiring, Mr. Biggs moved from St. Louis and settled in Alberta to engage in ranching. He became associated with other farmers in promoting a new town and post office, donated ground for the townsite, and suggested that the new place and post office be named in honour of his former home, Louisiana, Missouri. This was unacceptable to postal authorities, and the name was therefore shortened to Lousana.

Low Water Lake (lake)
83 H/13 - Morinville
4-56-27-W4
53°48'N 113°57'W
Approximately 42 km north-west of Edmonton.

The name for this lake may be descriptive, referring to its level compared to Isle Lake, Lake Wabamun and Chip Lake. Apparently, this group of lakes was part of one large body during glacial times.

Lowden Lake (lake)
83 A/2 - Big Valley
5-37-19-W4
52°09'N 112°42'W
Approximately 21 km south of Stettler.

The lake was named for a family who settled near the lake and started a ranch in the late 1890s.

■ **Lower Mann Lake** (lake)

73 L/3 - Vincent Lake
6-60-10-W4
54°10′N 111°29′W
Approximately 25 km north-west of St.
Paul.

The name for this lake was officially
approved 28 July 1945 and refers to its
location downstream from Upper Mann
Lake.

Lower Stony Creek (creek)

82 O/15 - Sundre
12-35-7-W5
51°59′45″N 114°50′10″W
Flows south-east into James River, approximately 18 km north north-west of Sundre.

The locally well-established names for
Lower Stony Creek and Upper Stony
Creek have been in use since the early
1920s. They were previously known
respectively as "East Stony Creek" and
"West Stony Creek." The name changes
were officially approved 3 October 1991.
The precise origin for either name is
unknown, although it is likely descriptive
of their location with respect to each other.

Lower Therien Lake (lake)

73 E/14 - St. Paul
NW-14-19-57-9-W4
53°57′N 111°20′W
Approximately 7 km south south-west of
St. Paul.

The Therien lakes are named after Rev. J.A.
Therien, O.M.I. (1862-1936), first director
of the colony of St. Paul des Métis. (see
Therien) This lake was locally known as
"Three Mile Lake."

Loyalist (hamlet)

72 M/15 - Monitor
9-35-7-W4
51°58′N 110°57′W
Approximately 36 km east south-east of
Coronation.

This and many other adjacent settlements
along the Canadian Pacific Railway line,
including Consort, Veteran, Throne, and
Coronation, were named in the Coronation
year of King George V, in deference to the
Crown. The post office operated from
January 1913 through August 1962. The
line runs from Kerrobert, Saskatchewan, to
Lacombe.

Loyalist Creek (creek)

72 M/15 - Monitor
6-36-7-W4
51°58′N 110°59′W
Flows east into Monitor Creek, approximately 50 km south south-west of Provost.

This creek was named for its proximity to
the hamlet of Loyalist. (see Loyalist)

Loyalist Creek Reservoir (reservoir)

72 M/15 - Kirkpatrick Lake
6-35-7-W4
51°58′N 110°59′W
Approximately 35 km east south-east of
Coronation.

(see Loyalist)

Lucia Lake (lake)

73 D/16 - McLaughlin
27-45-4-W4
52°54′N 110°29′W
Approximately 26 km east north-east of the
town of Wainwright.

The name for this lake has been in use since
at least 1958, but its precise origin is
unknown.

Lucky Lake (lake)

83 I/7 - Newbrook
10-62-18-W4
54°21′N 112°37′W
Approximately 28 km north north-west of
Smoky Lake.

The name for this lake has appeared on
maps since 1915, but its precise origin is
unknown. It is sometimes locally referred
to as "South Twin Lake," a descriptive
name.

Lumba Lake (lake)

73 L/5 - Goodfish Lake
26-63-12-W4
54°28′30″N 111°42′00″W
Approximately 36 km south south-east of
Lac La Biche.

The name for this lake has been official
since 5 April 1950. Its precise origin is
unknown. It is locally called "Birch Lake,"
and this name has been associated with the
feature since 1913.

Lumni Hill (hill)

82 P/11 - Three Hills
4-2-32-22-W4
51°42′35″N 113°01′25″W
Approximately 17 km east of Three Hills.

The hill became known by this name after
the establishment of the Lumni School
District on 10 December 1912. The name
was proposed by C.V. Rogers, the first
secretary-treasurer, who noted that the
name means "enlightenment." Following
the construction of the school on the south
side of the hill, it became known as Lumni
Hill.

* **Lundemo** (former locality)

83 H/2 - Camrose
30-48-20-W4
53°10′N 112°55′W
Approximately 19 km north north-west of
Camrose.

_____

*denotes rescinded name or former locality.

A post office operated here from June 1908 through May 1949 and was named after a place in Norway which was the former home of the first postmaster, John Waldum.

Lunnford (locality)

83 J/1 - Barrhead
1-59-3-W5
54°04′N 114°19′W
Approximately 8 km south-east of Barrhead.

The name for this locality, whose post office operated from October 1910 through October 1967, was taken after E.L. Lunn, the first postmaster. Mr. Lunn also worked the ferry that crossed the Pembina River and became known as "Lunn's ford." He was originally from England and secured his homestead patent in 1911.

Lure (locality)

73 D/4 - Castor
9-37-11-W4
52°10′N 111°30′W
Approximately 10 km north-west of Coronation.

Apparently, the name for this locality was chosen to entice settlers to the West.

* **Luzan** (former locality)

83 H/16 - Willingdon
36-55-16-W4
53°48′N 112°15′W
Approximately 38 km south of Smoky Lake.

A post office operated here from May 1913 through January 1939 and was named after Luzan, Romania. The name was suggested by the first postmaster, Simon Ewaniuk.

Lynn Lake (lake)

83 A/10 - Donalda
13-41-20-W4
52°31′30″N 112°45′30″W
Approximately 16 km east south-east of Bashaw.

The name for this lake has been official since at least 1958, but its origin is unknown.

Lynx Lake (lake)

73 L/13 - Lac La Biche
34-68-13-W4
54°56′N 111°54′W
Approximately 20 km north of Lac La Biche.

The name for this lake has been official since 3 May 1951, and is likely descriptive.

---

*denotes rescinded name or former locality.

Ma-Me-O Beach (summer village)

83 A/13 - Bearhills Lake
14-46-28-W4
52°58'09"N 113°57'52"W
On the south shore of Pigeon Lake, approximately 40 km west of Wetaskiwin.

The name for this summer village, whose post office opened in June 1932, is a corruption of the Cree word *mee-mee-o*, translating "place of lots of shorebirds." Another source suggests that the term *ma-me-o* is the Cree term for "white pigeon." Its location on the southern shore of Pigeon Lake gives the settlement its descriptive name. This summer village was incorporated 31 December 1948.

Ma-Me-O Beach Provincial Park (provincial park)

83 A/13 - Bearhills Lake
15-46-28-W4
52°59'N 113°57'W
Approximately 40 km west of Wetaskiwin.

(see Ma-Me-O Beach)

Mac Lake (lake)

83 H/7 - Tofield
9-50-20-W4
53°18'N 112°53'W
Approximately 33 km north of Camrose.

The name for this lake has been official since at least 1958, but its precise origin is unknown.

MacBeth Lake (lake)

73 L/1 - Reita Lake
34-58-1-W4
54°03'N 110°04'W
Approximately 40 km south of Grand Centre.

The name for this lake has been official since at least 1958, but its precise origin is unknown.

MacDonald Creek (creek)

83 J/1 - Barrhead
11-58-3-W5
54°00'15"N 114°20'00"W
Flows west into Pembina River, approximately 15 km south south-east of Barrhead.

The name for this creek has been official since at least 1958, but its precise origin is unknown.

* MacDonald Crossing (former locality)

83 G/16 - Lac la Nonne
10-58-3-W5
54°00'N 114°21'W
Approximately 15 km south of Barrhead.

(see Belvedere)

Macdonald Lake (lake)

73 E/6 - Mannville
17-52-9-W4
53°29'13"N 111°16'50"W
Approximately 95 km west north-west of Lloydminster.

The locally well-established name for this lake was officially approved 22 January 1991 and derives from the name of the family who reside on the land upon which the lake is located.

MacKay (hamlet)

83 G/12 - Carrot Creek
8-54-11-W5
53°39'N 115°35'W
Approximately 45 km south-west of Mayerthorpe.

The Canadian Northern Railway established a station here in 1911 and named it after one of the contractors, J.C. MacKay.

M~N~O

The post office operated from January 1928 through July 1981.

Magee Lake (lake)

83 A/11 - Chain Lakes
27-41-24-W4
52°33'30"N 113°23'00"W
Approximately 15 km south-east of Ponoka.

The name for this lake is apparently taken after an early homesteader.

Magnolia (locality)

83 G/10 - Isle Lake
30-53-6-W5
53°37'N 114°52'W
Approximately 43 km south south-east of Mayerthorpe.

The name for this locality, whose post office operated from June 1908 through September 1970, may have been taken after any of 25 places in the United States of the same name. The magnolia tree, cultivated for its foliage and flowers, was named after Pierre Magnol (1638-1715), a professor of botany at Montpellier, France.

Magnolia Bridge (hamlet)

83 G/10 - Isle Lake
19-53-6-W5
53°35'N 114°52'W
Approximately 45 km south south-east of Mayerthorpe.

Some of the settlers had lived near Magnolia Bluffs, in Washington, and because they saw a resemblance between the two places, gave the new settlement this name. (see Magnolia)

Mahaska (locality)

83 G/13 - Hattonford
6-57-13-W5
53°53′N 115°56′W
Approximately 30 km south south-west of Whitecourt.

A post office operated here from February 1913 through December 1949 and was named after a county in the state of Iowa. That county was named after an Indian chief.

Majeau Lake (lake)

83 G/16 - Lac la Nonne
7-57-3-W5
53°54′N 114°25′W
Approximately 24 km south of Barrhead.

This lake was named for Eli Majeau and family, early homesteaders from Montreal and the first white settlers in the district. They were known for their hospitality, and their home was a stopping place for many locals.

Majors Lake (lake)

83 I/13 - Grosmont
28-67-24-W4
54°50′N 113°36′W
Approximately 25 km north-west of Athabasca.

The name for this lake has been official since at least 1958, but its precise origin is unknown.

Makaoo Indian Reserve #120

(Indian reserve)

73 E/9 - Marwayne
23-54-1-W4
53°41′N 110°02′W
Approximately 45 km north of Lloydminster.

_____
*denotes rescinded name or former locality.

This Cree Indian reserve was formed in 1879 and was named after a chief of that name.

Mallaig (hamlet)

73 L/3 - Vincent Lake
25-60-10-W4
54°13′N 111°22′W
Approximately 25 km north north-west of St. Paul.

The name for this hamlet, whose post office opened in October 1928, was taken after a town in Inverness-shire (now Highland) Scotland.

Malmo (locality)

83 A/14 - Wetaskiwin
14-44-23-W4
52°47′N 113°13′W
Approximately 22 km south south-east of Wetaskiwin.

A post office operated here from September 1911 through July 1933 and was named by the early settlers who came from Malmo, Nebraska. The place in Nebraska takes its name from Malmö, Sweden.

Maloney Lake (lake)

73 L/8 - Cold Lake
29-63-3-W4
54°29′N 110°25′W
Approximately 13 km north-west of Cold Lake.

The name for this lake has been official since 6 July 1950 and honours an early homesteader.

* Maloy (former post office)

73 L/6 - Goodridge
18-62-8-W4
54°21′N 111°11′W
Approximately 30 km west north-west of Bonnyville.

A post office operated here from July 1915 through October 1966 and was named after a town in Iowa, which in turn was likely named after Målöy in western Norway. The name was officially rescinded 19 November 1970.

Manatokan Creek (creek)

73 L/7 - Bonnyville
34-62-7-W4
54°24′N 110°57′W
Flows south into Beaver River, approximately 21 km north-west of Bonnyville.

(see Manatokan Lake)

Manatokan Lake (lake)

73 L/7 - Bonnyville
12-23-63-7-W4
54°28′00″N 110°57′47″W
Approximately 27 km north north-west of Bonnyville.

The name for this lake has been official since 2 June 1950, but its precise origin is unknown. It is known locally both as "Jackfish Lake" and "Bonanza Lake."

Manawan Lake (lake)

83 H/13 - Morinville
5-57-25-W4
53°54′N 113°41′W
Approximately 30 km north of Edmonton.

The name for this lake is the Cree equivalent of "egg-gathering place," and it is at the "Lac des Oeufs" that early fur-traders would gather duck eggs. The name is found on a list submitted for approval by the Geographic Board of Canada dated 26 June 1911.

Mandy Lake (lake)

83 H/7 - Tofield
10-50-21-W4
53°18′N 112°58′W

Approximately 39 km south-east of Edmonton.

The name for this lake has been official since at least 1958, but its precise origin is unknown.

Manly (locality)
83 G/9 - Onoway
27-53-2-W5
53°36′N 114°12′W
Approximately 51 km west north-west of Edmonton.

A post office operated here from March 1908 through February 1920 and was named after Manley, in England, former home of some of the early settlers.

Manly Corner (locality)
83 G/9 - Onoway
16-53-2-W5
53°34′N 114°13′W
Approximately 50 km west north-west of Edmonton.

This locality was named in 1956 and this corner is the centre of the Manly district and is the junction of Highways 16 and 43. In 1907, when pioneers arrived there, the corner was ncar the site of the Manly School, General Store and post office. (see Manly)

Mannville (village)
73 E/6 - Mannville
25-50-9-W4
53°20′25″N 111°11′00″W
Approximately 22 km west of Vermilion.

The name for this village, incorporated 29 December 1906, was chosen by Davidson and McRae, land agents for the Canadian Northern Railway in Winnipeg, to com-

memorate Sir Donald Mann (1853-1934), one of the partners in the firm of Mackenzie and Mann who held the contacts for the grading. William Mackenzie and Donald Mann, both knighted in January 1911, were the founding fathers of the Canadian Northern Railway, Mackenzie as president and Mann as vice-president.

Manola (hamlet)
83 J/1 - Barrhead
16-59-2-W5
54°06′N 114°14′W
Approximately 11 km east south-east of Barrhead.

The post office for this hamlet operated from December 1907 through December 1923 and then reopened from June 1927 through June 1970. The name Manola was one of three names, including Eureka and Orlando, suggested by Mrs. J. A. McPhee, an early settler who was from California. Mr. and Mrs. McPhee also named their second daughter Manola.

* **Maple Ridge** (former locality)
83 H/6 - Cooking Lake
20-52-33-W4
53°29′50″N 113°22′00″W
Immediately east of Edmonton.

The precise origin for the name of this former locality is unknown.

Mapova (locality)
83 I/6 - Perryvale
25-61-22-W4
54°18′N 113°09′W
Approximately 50 km west north-west of Smoky Lake.

The name for the post office, which operated here from November 1930 through May 1968, is a combination of letters of the names of the first three

settlers: "M" for Musklak, "A" for Alho, and "P" for Papowich. The name is pronounced Ma pov a.

Marguerite Lake (lake)
73 L/10 - Marguerite Lake
18-65-5-W4
54°38′00″N 110°44′30″W
Approximately 40 km west north-west of Cold Lake.

(see Elinor Lake)

Marie Creek (creek)
73 L/8 - Cold Lake
11-1-63-3-W4
54°25′N 110°19′W
Flows south-west into Beaver River, approximately 7 km west of Grand Centre.

(see Marie Lake)

Marie Lake (lake)
73 L/9 - Marie Lake
16-65-2-W4
54°37′N 110°18′W
Approximately 20 km north north-west of Cold Lake.

The name for this lake has been official since at least 1928 and is a corruption of the Cree name *methai*, pronounced "merai," which is a fish.

Marion Lake (lake)
83 A/1 - Hackett
24-37-18-W4
52°13′N 112°26′W
Approximately 24 km south-east of Stettler.

According to local residents, this lake was likely named before pioneer settlement (pre 1900), although it was not officially recognized until after 1928, and thus was possibly named by an early survey party; however, its precise origin is unknown.

---

*denotes rescinded name or former locality.

Markerville (hamlet)

83 B/1 - Markerville
26-36-2-W5
52°08′N 114°10′W
Approximately 19 km north-west of Innisfail.

The story of the settlement of the country west of Innisfail begins in 1888. On 27 June of that year, 12 families came from Pembina County, Dakota Territory, to settle in this district. These fifty people struggled together to build a workable community. The first post office was named "Tindastoll," after a mountain in Iceland. In 1889 several more families arrived in the area, including the now famous Icelandic poet, Stephán G. Stephansson. In 1894 the first cheese factory was opened in the district, but it was not a great success for its owner, Mr. Powell. Markerville takes its name from C.P. Marker, a one-time dairy commissioner of first the Northwest Territories and then after 1905, Alberta. It was made official in 1902 with the opening of the post office.

Markerville (original town), n.d.

---

*denotes rescinded name or former locality.

Marlboro (hamlet)

83 F/10 - Bickerdike
6-53-19-W5
53°33′N 116°47′W
Approximately 25 km west south-west of Edson.

The post office, which operated at this hamlet from September 1912 through April 1976, was named after the marl deposits in the area. This substance was used in making cement. A cement plant was built here in 1912.

Martineau River (river)

73 L/9 - Marie Lake
14-65-1-W4
54°38′N 110°03′W
Flows between Primrose Lake and Cold Lake, approximately 20 km north north-east of Cold Lake.

This river was named in 1909 and commemorates A. Martineau, a former Hudson's Bay Company manager at Cold Lake.

Marwayne (village)

73 E/9 - Marwayne
26-52-3-W4
53°31′N 110°20′W
Approximately 33 km north-west of Lloydminster.

Settlement in this district began circa 1903 and among the pioneers were the Marfleet family. The post office opened in January 1906 and its name was a combination of the first syllable in the Marfleet family name and the first syllable of the town from which they came, Wainfleet, Lincolnshire, England. The village was incorporated 31 December 1952.

Marwayne Creek (creek)

73 E/9 - Marwayne
21-52-3-W4
53°31′N 110°24′W

Flows west into Vermilion River, approximately 36 km north-west of Lloydminster.

(see Marwayne)

* **Mary Lake** (former locality)

73 E/10 - Clandonald
25-53-7-W4
53°37′N 110°56′W
Approximately 30 km north of Vermilion.

The name for the post office, which operated here from July 1912 through August 1932, was taken after a nearby lake unofficially named by Charles Hogoban after his wife, Mary.

Maskawau Creek (creek)

83 H/7 - Tofield
10-26-51-19-W4
53°27′N 112°43′W
Flows east into Wakinagan Creek, approximately 53 km east south-east of Edmonton.

The name for this creek has been official since at least 1958, but its precise origin is unknown.

Maskwa Creek (creek)

83 A/13 - Bearhills Lake
27-46-25-W4
52°59′N 113°33′W
Flows north into Bigstone Creek, approximately 13 km west north-west of Wetaskiwin.

The name for this creek has been official since at least 1958, but its precise origin is unknown.

Mastin Lake (lake)

83 I/11 - Athabasca
7-64-21-W4
54°31′N 113°09′W
Approximately 24 km south south-east of Athabasca.

The name for this lake has been official since at least 1958, but its precise origin is unknown.

Matchayaw Lake (lake)
83 G/9 - Onoway
33-54-1-W5
53°42 N 114°06′W
Approximately 44 km north-west of Edmonton.

The name for this lake is the Cree word for "bad spirit." It was labelled "Little Manito" on Palliser's map of 1865.

Mather Reservoir (reservoir)
73 D/4 - Castor
36-37-13-W4
52°13′15″N 111°44′00″W
Approximately 10 km east of Castor.

This feature was named after the Mather family, early settlers of the land on which the reservoir is situated.

Matthews Crossing (locality)
83 G/10 - Isle Lake
24-54-7-W5
53°41′N 114°54′W
Approximately 35 km south-south-east of Mayerthorpe.

A post office operated at this ferry crossing of the Pembina River from May 1913 through March 1923 and was named after the first postmaster, M.H. Matthews.

Matthews Lake (lake)
73 L/12 - Beaver Lake
2-28-66-12-W4
54°44′00″N 111°45′15″W
Approximately 15 km east of Lac La Biche.

The name for this lake was officially applied in 1951 and commemorates Flying Officer L.W. Matthews, D.F.M. (1920-1944), of Calgary, who was killed during World War II.

Matts Creek (creek)
83 B/2 - Caroline
30-36-7-W5
52°08′N 114°59′W
Flows north-west into Swan Creek, approximately 24 km south of Rocky Mountain House.

This creek was named in 1956 after the late Matthew Bredshaw, long-time resident of the Rocky Mountain House district who had a cabin beside the feature and stocked the stream with beaver.

* Maughan (former post office)
73 E/10 - Clandonald
34-52-7-W4
53°33′N 110°58′W
Approximately 21 km north north-west of Vermilion.

A post office operated here from December 1907 through June 1958 and was named after Keith Maughan, an early homesteader and the first postmaster. The name was officially rescinded in 1970.

* Maunders (former locality)
72 M/13 - Garden Plain
27-32-12-W4
51°50′N 111°35′W
Approximately 28 km north-east of Hanna.

A post office operated here from May 1914 through 1 January 1933 under this name, the maiden name of the wife of the first postmaster, C.S. Finbeiner. The name was then changed to Spondin.

Maurice Lake (lake)
73 L/12 - Beaver Lake
22,23-65-13-W4
54°38′N 111°52′W
Approximately 16 km south south-east of Lac La Biche.

The name for this lake appeared on a topographical map dated 1918, and has been official since at least 1958, but its precise origin is unknown.

Maxwell Lake (lake)
83 J/2 - Thunder Lake
22-59-4-W5
54°06′50″N 114°30′20″W
Approximately 6 km west south-west of Barrhead.

This name was proposed by the Barrhead and District Historical Society to commemorate an early settler in the district. John Maxwell was the one of the first (if not the first) to homestead land adjoining the lake. It immediately became known as "Maxwell Lake" and has carried the name ever since. Mr. Maxwell came from Nova Scotia circa 1908. The name was officially approved 6 March 1986.

May Lake (lake)
73 L/9 - Marie Lake
16-66-3-W4
54°42′N 110°23′W
Approximately 30 km north north-west of Cold Lake.

The name for this lake appeared on a topographical map dated 1918, and was officially adopted 17 January 1951, but its precise origin is unknown.

Mayatan Lake (lake)
83 G/8 - Genesee
13-52-3-W5
53°29′N 114°18′W
Approximately 54 km west of Edmonton.

___

*denotes rescinded name or former locality.

The name for this lake has been official since at least 1958, but its precise origin is unknown.

Mayerthorpe (town)

83 G/14 - Mayerthorpe
28-57-8-W5
53°57'00"N 115°08'10"W
Approximately 116 km west north-west of Edmonton.

The name for this town, whose post office opened in July 1910, is a combination of the name of the first postmaster, R.I. Mayer, and an early teacher (Thorpe). This town was incorporated 20 March 1961.

Mayton (locality)

82 P/13 - Torrington
14-33-27-W4
51°50'N 113°44'W
Approximately 22 km south-east of Innisfail.

The first settlers to this district hailed from May City, Iowa, and it was in remembrance of their original home that this name was chosen for the post office, which operated from March 1902 through October 1932.

Mazy Lake (lake)

83 A/10 - Donalda
12-42-20-W4
52°36'N 112°44'W
Approximately 18 km east north-east of Bashaw.

The origin of the name of this lake is unknown.

McBernie Lake (lake)

83 I/9 - Hylo
2-66-14-W4
54°41'00"N 112°00'30"W

Approximately 10 km south of Lac La Biche.

The name for this lake, officially approved 1 June 1948, has been in use since 1922 and commemorates S. McBernie, an early citizen of Lac La Biche. It is locally known as "Latik's Lake," after a Polish settler who lived nearby.

McCafferty Lake (lake)

73 D/10 - Hughenden
33-42-4-W4
52°39'N 110°32'W
Approximately 30 km south-east of the town of Wainwright.

The name for this lake was officially approved in October 1971, but its precise origin is unknown.

McCarthy Lake (lake)

83 I/9 - Hylo
22-66-14-W4
54°44'N 112°02'W
Approximately 6 km south south-west of Lac La Biche.

The name for this lake was officially approved 1 June 1948, has been in use since 1922 and commemorates H. McCarthy, a policeman from Lac La Biche.

McCullough Lake (lake)

73 L/4 - Cache Lake
20-60-11-W4
54°12'N 111°36'W
Approximately 31 km north-west of St. Paul.

The name for this lake was officially approved 6 April 1950, but its precise origin is unknown.

McDonald Ford (river crossing)

73 D/11 - Hardisty
36-43-9-W4
52°44'15"N 111°10'15"W

Approximately 12 km north-east of Hardisty.

The name for this crossing on the Battle River has been in use since at least 1958, but its precise origin is unknown.

* McDonaldville (former locality)

73 E/1 - Paradise Valley
36-47-3-W4
53°06'N 110°18'W
Approximately 30 km south-west of Lloydminster.

The post office operated here from December 1908 through June 1942 and was named after Adam McDonald, an early settler. The name was officially rescinded in November 1969.

McDougall Flats (flats)

82 O/15 - Sundre
7-31-32-5-W5
51°47'N 114°42'W
Approximately 4 km south-west of Sundre.

In the early 1890s, the McDougalls obtained a very large parcel of land on the flats of the Red Deer River. The McDougall Ranch was run by Dave McDougall and his son, Dave Jr., until about 1907, when a hard winter killed about half their stock. Soon after this, they sold out. Dave's father George and brother John were both missionaries to the Indians. The flats to the west of the Red Deer River at Sundre have since been known by this name. The west portion of the flats is sometimes referred to as the "Bearberry Prairie" on maps, but the majority of residents are unfamiliar with the name: it may have come about before the McDougalls. The flats are also sometimes referred to as the "Sundre Flats." The name McDougall Flats was officially approved for this feature 23 September 1991.

McDougall Lake (lake)
73 L/9 - Marie Lake
1-65-4-W4
54°35'25"N 110°28'27"W
Approximately 25 km north-west of Cold
Lake.

The locally well-established name for this
lake was officially approved 3 June 1986. It
is from Sam McDougall, a trapper who
lived on the north shore of the lake.

McFadden Lake (lake)
83 H/6 - Cooking Lake
15-51-22-W4
53°25'N 113°09'W
Approximately 35 km east south-east of
Edmonton.

The name for this lake commemorates John
McFadden, an early settler who arrived
from Montana circa 1892.

McGuffin Lake (lake)
73 L/13 - Lac La Biche
16-3-67-11-W4
54°46'35"N 111°35'13"W
Approximately 25 km east of Lac La Biche.

This lake was officially named 3 May 1951,
and commemorates Squadron Leader W.C.
McGuffin, D.F.C. (1915-1944) of London,
Ontario and then Calgary, Alberta, who
was killed in World War II. The local name
for the feature is "Island Lake," referring to
the many islands in the lake. The Cree
equivalent is rendered *kamshtigowa
sagahegan.*

McIntyre Lake (lake)
73 D/16 - McLaughlin
16-44-1-W4
52°47'N 110°06'W
Approximately 50 km north north-east of
Provost.

The name for this lake has been in use since
at least 1958, but its precise origin is
unknown.

McKay Lake (lake)
73 D/12 - Lougheed
5-43-11-W4
52°40'N 111°32'W
Approximately 16 km west of Hardisty.

The name for this lake has been in use since
at least 1958, but its origin is unknown.

McKee Lake (lake)
82 P/15 - Rumsey
31-32-19-W4
51°47'N 112°40'W
Approximately 38 km east south-east of
Trochu.

The name has been official since 1958, and
may be after an early homesteader, H.L.
McKee, who owned a half-section of land
on the west shore.

McLaughlin (hamlet)
73 D/16 - McLaughlin
25-46-2-W4
52°59'N 110°10'W
Approximately 33 km south south-west of
Lloydminster.

John M. and Thomas McLaughlin were
early settlers in the area and it is after them
that the post office was named in June 1908.

McLeod River (river)
83 J/4 - Whitecourt
35-59-12-W5
54°09'N 115°42'W
Flows north-east into Athabasca River at
Whitecourt.

The name has been in use since at least
1814, when it was marked "McLeods
River" on David Thompson's map. It may
be named after Archibald Norman McLeod

(c.1796-1837), a North West Company fur
trader who became a partner before 1799,
and went to the Athabasca country in 1802.

McLeod Valley (locality)
83 G/12 - Carrot Creek
2-55-14-W5
53°43'N 115°59'W
Approximately 23 km east north-east of
Edson.

A post office operated here from February
1913 through October 1967 and was named
after the McLeod River. (see McLeod
River)

McRae (locality)
73 L/5 - Goodfish Lake
10-62-12-W4
54°21'N 111°43'W
Approximately 49 km south south-east of
Lac La Biche.

The name for this locality, whose post
office opened in October 1924, is taken
after William M. McRae, the first postmaster.

Meadowbrook (locality)
83 I/5 - Dapp
35-63-25-W4
54°29'N 113°38'W
Approximately 36 km south-west of
Athabasca.

The name for this locality, whose post
office operated from November 1915
through October 1951, is descriptive of the
countryside.

Meadowview (locality)
83 G/15 - Sangudo
33-57-5-W5
53°58'N 114°40'W
Approximately 30 km east of Mayerthorpe.

A post office operated here from March 1913 through March 1983 and the name, suggested by Colin Campbell, describes the view of a nearby meadow.

Meanook (hamlet)

83 I/11 - Athabasca
31-64-22-W4
54°34′N 113°20′W
Approximately 16 km south of Athabasca.

The Canadian Northern Railway established a station here in 1912. The name for this hamlet, whose post office operated from January 1914 through July 1975, is the Cree word meaning "good camping place."

Mearns (hamlet)

83 H/13 - Morinville
28-56-26-W4
53°52′N 113°48′W
Approximately 14 km north-west of Morinville.

This was a station for the Edmonton, Dunvegan and British Columbia Railway in 1912. The post office operated from June 1928 through July 1961. The name may be taken after a village near Glasgow in Scotland.

Medicine Flats (flat)

83 B/1 - Markerville
7-36-1-W5
52°04′00″N 114°07′30″W
Approximately 31 km south-west of Red Deer.

The locally well-established name for these flats was officially approved 7 February 1983. (see Medicine River)

* **Medicine Hat Junction**

(former railway point)

72 M/12 - Hanna
8-31-13-W4
51°38′N 111°49′W
Approximately 9 km east of Hanna.

(see Batter Junction)

Medicine Lake (lake)

83 B/15 - Buck Lake
36-43,44-6-W5
52°45′N 114°45′W
Approximately 43 km north north-east of Rocky Mountain House.

(see Medicine River)

Medicine Lodge Hills (hill)

83 B/8 - Sylvan Lake
40-2,3-W5
52°28′N 114°17′W
Approximately 36 km north-west of Red Deer.

The name for these hills has been in use since at least 1928 and is taken from the fact that this was a favourite site for native spring festivals.

Medicine River (river)

83 B/1 - Markerville
5-36-1-W5
52°04′N 114°06′W
Flows south-east into Red Deer River, approximately 31 km south south-west of Red Deer.

The name for this river has been in use since 1859 when it was labelled on Arrowsmith's map. It is a translation of a native name. The Cree term is *muskiki and nipagwasimow sipi*, or "Sundance River." The Stoney name is *to-go-wap-ta*, or "Mussel River."

Log drive on Medicine River, 1904

Medley (post office)

73 L/8 - Cold Lake
5-63-2-W4
54°25′N 110°16′W
Approximately 5 km west of Grand Centre.

This post office serves the nearby Canadian Forces Base and was established in October 1957. (see Medley River)

Medley River (river)

73 L/9 - Marie Lake
11-65-2-W4
54°36′N 110°11′W
Flows south into Cold Lake, approximately 16 km north of the town of Cold Lake.

This river was named before 1928 and commemorates Corporal C. Medley of Calgary, who was killed in World War I.

Meeting Creek (creek)

83 A/9 - Forestburg
25-41-17-W4
52°33′N 112°20′W
Flows east into Battle River, approximately 38 km north-east of Stettler.

The Cree name for this creek is *nukh-kwa-ta-to*, according to Tyrrell. The Northern

Cree and the Blackfoot of the south frequently met at this creek during their buffalo hunts. The hamlet takes its name from this watercourse.

Meeting Creek (hamlet)
83 A/10 - Donalda
5-43-19-W4
52°41′N 112°44′W
Approximately 20 km north-east of Bashaw.

The post office here operated from June 1905 through October 1911 and was named for its proximity to Meeting Creek. The post office opened again in February 1912. In the interim, the locality was known as "Edenville." (see Meeting Creek)

Mellowdale (locality)
83 J/1 - Barrhead
21-60-3-W5
54°13′N 114°22′W
Approximately 9 km north of Barrhead.

The name for this locality, whose post office operated from August 1909 through February 1969, was originally proposed as "Melrose." This was changed to its present name by the Post Office Department in Ottawa. The precise origin for either name is unknown.

Mellstrom Lake (lake)
73 L/12 - Beaver Lake
10-64-13-W4
54°31′N 111°53′W
Approximately 28 km south of Lac La Biche.

The name for this lake was officially applied in 1951 and commemorates Flight Lieutenant M.L. Mellstrom, D.F.C. (1914-1945), of Calgary, who was killed in World War II. It is locally referred to as "Woycenko's Lake," after a nearby farmer.

*denotes rescinded name or former locality.

Menaik (locality)
83 A/13 - Bearhills Lake
35-43-25-W4
52°45′15″N 113°31′15″W
Approximately 10 km north north-east of Ponoka.

The Canadian Pacific Railway established a station here between 1908 and 1910. The post office operated from June 1928 through June 1980. The name is the Cree equivalent of "tamarack." A variation, *minahik*, is the word for "pine."

Mere Lake (lake)
83 G/9 - Onoway
32-53-1-W5
53°38′N 114°06′W
Approximately 47 km west north-west of Edmonton.

The name for this lake has been official since at least 1950 but appears on maps made by the first surveyors of the area. "Mere" is an old name for "lake."

* **Merebeck** (former post office)
83 G/15 - Sangudo
23-56-6-W5
53°51′N 114°46′W
Approximately 26 km east south-east of Mayerthorpe.

The post office operated here by this name from August 1914 through May 1916 when the name was changed to Lisburn. The origin of the name "Merebeck" is not known.

Meridian Lake (lake)
73 E/16 - Mannville
36-55-1-W4
53°47′N 110°01′W
Approximately 56 km north of Lloydminster, on the Alberta-Saskatchewan boundary.

The name for this lake has been official since at least 1958 and is likely descriptive of its location on the Fourth Meridian.

Metiskow (hamlet)
73 D/7 - Czar
3-40-5-W4
52°24′N 110°38′W
Approximately 27 km west north-west of Provost.

The name for this hamlet is a rough transliteration of the Cree term *metosi skaw*, which translates as "many trees." The name was likely descriptive of the area when the post office was established in September 1910.

Mewassin (locality)
83 G/8 - Genesee
31-51-2-W5
53°27′N 114°17′W
Approximately 53 km west south-west of Edmonton.

A post office operated here from May 1903 through March 1917 and then reopened from February 1924 through May 1928. Its descriptive name is a native word for "good."

Mewatha Beach (summer village)
83 I/10 - Boyle
12-65-19-W4
54°36′47″N 112°44′50″W
Approximately 37 km east south-east of Athabasca.

The precise origin for the name of this summer village incorporated 8 November 1977 is unknown.

Meyer Lake (lake)
83 I/13 - Grosmont
15-69-24-W4
54°58′N 113°34′W
Approximately 35 km north-west of Athabasca.

The name for this lake has been official since at least 1958, but its precise origin is unknown.

Michaud Lake (lake)

83 G/15 - Sangudo
25-55-7-W5
53°47'N 114°54'W
Approximately 25 km south-east of Mayerthorpe.

The lake is known locally as "Honk Lake," probably due to the number of geese that use the lake. The precise origin for the name Michaud, official since at least 1958, is unknown.

Michel Lake (lake)

73 L/2 - Muriel Lake
33-58-5-W4
54°03'N 110°41'W
Approximately 23 km north north-east of Elk Point.

The name for this lake has been official since 2 May 1957, but its precise origin is unknown.

Michichi (hamlet)

82 P/10 - Munson
19-30-18-W4
51°35'N 112°32'W
Approximately 43 km west south-west of Hanna.

The name for this hamlet, whose post office operated from April 1921 through October 1971, is taken for its proximity to Michichi Creek and was previously called "Mecheche." The creek has five branches, which may correspond to the five fingers of a hand. The name *Michichi* is the Cree word for "hand" or "little hand."

Michigan Centre (locality)

83 H/4 - Kavanagh
35-48-26-W4
53°11'30"N 113°41'00"W
Approximately 13 km south of Leduc.

Although it is not verified, the name for this locality is likely taken after the state of Michigan.

Mickel Lake (lake)

83 I/11 - Athabasca
15-64-21-W4
54°32'N 113°05'W
Approximately 24 km south south-east of Athabasca.

The name for this lake has been official since at least 1958, but its precise origin is unknown.

Middle Creek (creek)

73 E/15 - Elk Point
13-56-5-W4
53°50'N 110°36'W
Flows south-west into North Saskatchewan River, approximately 20 km east south-east of Elk Point.

The descriptive name for this creek appears on the Arrowsmith map of 1859. The nearby locality takes its name from this creek.

Middle Creek (locality)

73 E/15 - Elk Point
7-56-4-W4
53°49'N 110°34'W
Approximately 22 km east south-east of Elk Point.

This was a station on the Canadian Northern Railway. (see Middle Creek)

Mikwan Lake (lake)

83 A/3 - Delburne
14-36-23-W4
52°06'N 113°11'W
Approximately 30 km north of Trochu.

The name for this lake has been official since at least 1958, but its precise origin is unknown. *Mikkwa* is the Cree term for "red."

Miles Lake (lake)

83 I/11 - Athabasca
24-64-24-W4
54°33'N 113°29'W
Approximately 23 km south-west of Athabasca.

The name for this lake has been official since at least 1958, but its precise origin is unknown.

Military Point (point)

83 H/7 - Tofield
3-12-52-21-W4
53°28'N 112°58'W
Approximately 46 km east of Edmonton.

The name for this point has been official since at least 1958, but its precise origin is unknown.

Mill Creek (creek)

83 H/11 - Edmonton
33-52-24-W4
53°33'N 113°29'W
Flows into North Saskatchewan River within the city limits of Edmonton.

This creek was named for a water mill operated by William Bird from 1871 to 1874, although the limited flow of water inhibited the operation of the mill.

Mill Lake (lake)

73 L/13 - Lac La Biche
16-35-68-13-W4
54°56'10"N 111°51'43"W
Approximately 20 km north north-east of
Lac La Biche.

The name for this lake was officially
adopted 3 May 1951, but its precise origin
is unknown.

Millard Lake (lake)

73 D/16 - McLaughlin
25-45-4-W4
52°54'N 110°27'W
Approximately 29 km east north-east of the
town of Wainwright.

The name for this lake has been official
since at least 1958, but its origin is unknown.

Millers Lake (lake)

83 F/10 - Bickerdike
8-53-19-W5
53°33'N 116°46'W
Approximately 24 km west of Edson.

The name for this lake was locally well-
established and used by Fish and Wildlife
on their stocking maps for many years. It
was officially approved in 1976, but its
precise origin is unknown.

Millet (town)

83 H/3 - Bittern Lake
29,32-47-24-W4
53°05'35"N 113°28'00"W
Approximately 15 km north north-west of
Wetaskiwin.

One version of the origin for the name of
this town, incorporated 15 September 1983,
is that it derives from the famous French

painter, Jean François Millet (1815-1875).
The chairman of the Canadian Pacific
Railway at the time of the naming, Sir
William Cornelius Van Horne, was an
ardent admirer of Millet's paintings and
owned a number of them.

A second version of the origin of the
name, and one derived from old timers, is
that it was named for a fur buyer, August
(or John) Millet. He was an independent fur
trader who devoted some time to the
Hudson's Bay Company, and occasionally
contracted to the North-West Mounted
Police at Fort Saskatchewan. Millet also
worked for Father Lacombe as a canoeman
on long river trips. When the railway
sidings were to be named, Sir William asked
Father Lacombe to name stations from
Lacombe north on the Calgary-Edmonton
line, and the priest suggested the name for
this place to commemorate his travelling
companion. Apparently, Millet was
drowned in the Red Deer River while
attempting to cross it, and he is believed to
have been buried in the vicinity.

Milnerton (locality)

82 P/13 - Torrington
11-35-26-W4
51°59'N 113°36'W
Approximately 25 km south south-east of
Red Deer.

The origin is unknown for the name of the
post office, which operated here from
November 1903 through March 1921.

Minaret (locality)

82 O/9 - Didsbury
18-32-1-W5
51°44'N 114°08'W
Approximately 8 km north of Didsbury.

A Canadian Pacific Railway station was
established here in 1902. In 1912 it was
called "Rosebud." The origin of the name
Minaret is unknown.

Minburn (village)

73 E/6 - Mannville
14-50-10-W4
53°18'55"N 111°22'00"W
Approximately 34 km west of Vermilion.

The Canadian Northern Railway established a station here in 1905. The post office
opened in October 1906 and the village was
incorporated 24 June 1919. It is named after
Mina Burns, a writer of western articles for
magazines, who lived in Ottawa.

Minburn County #27 (county)

73 E/6 - Mannville
53 to 56-7 to 15-W4
53°19'N 111°30'W
North-east of Camrose.

(see Minburn)

* **Ministik Lake** (former locality)

83 H/6 - Cooking Lake
10-51-21-W4
53°23'N 113°00'W
Approximately 39 km east south-east of
Edmonton.

A post office operated here from January
1908 through December 1927 and was
named for its proximity to Ministik Lake.
(see Ministik Lake)

Ministik Lake (lake)

83 H/7 - Tofield
34-50-21-W4
53°21'N 113°01'W
Approximately 37 km east south-east of
Edmonton.

The descriptive name for this lake, which
contains many islands, is taken from the
Cree *ministik*, "island."

Mink Creek (creek)

83 B/15 - Buck Lake
3-46-6-W5
52°56'N 114°46'W

Flows north and east into Buck Lake, approximately 35 km south south-east of Drayton Valley.

The name for this creek has been official since at least 1958, but its precise origin is unknown.

Mink Creek (creek)

83 G/9 - Onoway
27-52-3-W5
53°31'N 114°22'W
Flows west into Wabamun Creek, approximately 56 km west of Edmonton.

The name for this creek has been official since at least 1958, but its precise origin is unknown.

Mink Creek (creek)

83 J/3 - Green Court
32-59-10-W5
54°09'N 115°27'W
Flows north-east into Athabasca River, approximately 15 km east of Whitecourt.

The name for this creek has been official since at least 1958, but its precise origin is unknown.

Mink Island (island)

83 H/10 - Elk Island Park
22-54-20-W4
53°40'30"N 112°52'00"W
Approximately 40 km east of Edmonton, in Elk Island National Park.

The name for this island in Astotin Lake was requested by the Canadian Parks Service for navigational purposes within the park. There is little settlement around the park and all local usage appears to ensue from the wardens who use the names on their own maps. The request was forwarded by the Canadian Permanent Committee on Geographical Names in order that the names would appear on the NTS map

sheets being produced for the area. The name was officially approved 17 October 1991.

Mink Lake (lake)

83 G/9 - Onoway
28-52-2-W5
53°31'N 114°14'W
Approximately 48 km west of Edmonton.

This lake was named when the railway went through and perhaps a mink was seen on the lake and the name was applied.

Minnie Lake (lake)

73 L/6 - Goodridge
23-61-8-W4
54°17'N 111°06'W
Approximately 34 km west of Bonnyville.

(see Elinor Lake)

Minnow Lake (lake)

83 F/8 - Moose Creek
31-50-14-W5
53°21'30"N 116°02'00"W
Approximately 36 km south-east of Edson.

The well-established name for this lake was officially adopted 16 January 1976 and is likely descriptive.

Mintlaw (locality)

83 A/4 - Innisfail
34-37-28-W4
52°13'N 113°54'W
Approximately 7 km west south-west of Red Deer.

The Canadian Pacific Railway established a station here in 1914 and named it after a village in Aberdeenshire (now Grampian), Scotland.

Miquelon Lake Provincial Park

(provincial park)

83 H/2 - Camrose
20-49-20-W4
53°15'N 112°53'W
Approximately 67 km east south-east of Edmonton.

(see Miquelon Lakes)

Miquelon Lakes (lakes)

83 H/7 - Tofield
30-49-20-W4
53°15'15"N 112°55'00"W
Approximately 63 km south-east of Edmonton.

These lakes may have been named for P.A. Miquelon (1834-1899) in 1895. This land surveyor came west from Quebec in 1883 and was the first to survey the lake. Another source suggests that the person after whom the lakes were named was a close friend of the chief surveyor. A French island off the south coast of Newfoundland also bears the name Miquelon. The precise origin of the name Miquelon is not certain; it is spelled variously on old maps – Michelon and Miquelon.

Mirror (village)

83 A/6 - Alix
28-40-22-W4
52°28'00"N 113°06'35"W
Approximately 17 km south south-west of Bashaw.

A post office opened here in October 1911 and the settlement was hailed as a divisional point on the Calgary branch of the Grand Trunk Pacific Railway. The *Daily Mirror* was a newspaper in London, England, and this village took its name from it.

Mirror Bay (bay)

83 A/6 - Alix
23-40-22-W4
52°27'30"N 113°04'00"W

Approximately 19 km south south-west of Bashaw.

The precise origin of the name of this shallow bay on the west shore of Buffalo Lake is not known, but it may be due to its proximity to the village of Mirror. (see Mirror)

Mirror Lake (lake)

83 H/2 - Camrose
3-47-20-W4
53°01′N 112°50′W
Within the city limits of Camrose.

The name for this lake, which was once a reservoir, was officially approved in 1962. It is within a park area in the city of Camrose, and its name is likely descriptive.

* **Mirror Landing** (former post office)

83 O/1 - Smith
23-71-1-W5
55°10′N 114°02′W
Approximately 70 km north-west of Athabasca.

The post office operated under this name from October 1913 through April 1957. The origin for the name is not known, and the name was later changed to Smith. (see Smith)

Mishow Creek (creek)

83 G/7 - Tomahawk
21-50-6-W5
53°20′N 114°48′W
Flows south-east into North Saskatchewan River, approximately 17 km north-east of Drayton Valley.

The name for this creek has been official since at least 1958, but its precise origin is unknown.

_____
*denotes rescinded name or former locality.

Missawawi Lake (lake)

83 I/9 - Hylo
14-21-66-15-W4
54°43′55″N 112°12′50″W
Approximately 15 km west south-west of Lac La Biche.

The name for this lake has been official since 4 October 1910 and is the native term that translates "Big Egg Lake." The French called it "Grand Lac des Oeufs."

Missing Lake (lake)

83 H/3 - Bittern Lake
14-48-22-W4
53°09′N 113°06′W
Approximately 24 km north-west of Camrose.

The name for this lake has been official since at least 1958, but its precise origin is unknown.

Mission Beach (hamlet)

83 G/1 - Warburg
30-47-1-W5
53°05′N 114°07′W
Approximately 53 km west north-west of Wetaskiwin.

The name for this hamlet which was established in July 1990 is taken after its proximity to the Rundle Mission, established in 1848. The Rev. Robert Terrill Rundle (1811-1896) was a Methodist missionary and circuit clergyman who arrived at Fort Edmonton in 1840. He became a master of the Cree language. The establishment of permanent missions was not his strength, and the mission at Pigeon Lake was started by his follower, Benjamin Sinclair.

Mistatim Lakes (lakes)

83 H/12 - St. Albert
22-53-25-W4
53°36′N 113°36′W
Approximately 18 km north of Edmonton.

The name for these lakes is the Cree word for "horse." When horses first appeared on the western plains of Canada, circa 1750, the natives were unsure of their species. A story told to David Thompson in 1787 by an older native related that these large animals reminded the Indians of a stag without horns, but as they were domesticated like the dog they were called "Big Dog."

Misty Lake (lake)

72 M/16 - Grassy Island Lake
16-33-3-W4
51°49′N 110°23′W
Approximately 53 km north of Oyen.

The precise origin for the name of this feature is unknown.

Mitchell Lake (lake)

73 E/15 - Elk Point
3-57-5-W4
53°54′N 110°39′W
Approximately 17 km east of Elk Point.

The name for this lake has been official since at least 1958, but its precise origin is unknown.

Modeste Creek (creek)

83 G/7 - Tomahawk
29-49-5-W5
53°15′15″N 114°42′30″W
Flows north into North Saskatchewan River, approximately 37 km south-east of Drayton Valley.

The name for this creek, although wrongfully applied to Poplar Creek until 1977, has been in official use since at least 1958, but its origin is unknown.

* **Molstad** (former post office)

83 A/16 - Daysland
31-45-17-W4
52°55′N 112°28′W
Approximately 26 km east south-east of Camrose.

The post office, which operated here from April 1904 through May 1907, was named after the first and only postmaster, O. Molstad. The name was changed to Bawlf. (see Bawlf)

Monitor (hamlet)

72 M/15 - Monitor
6-35-4-W4
51°58′N 110°34′W
Approximately 46 km south south-west of Provost.

The post office was originally established as "Sounding Lake" until it was changed on 1 December 1913. The name was apparently suggested by an early settler, Jack Deadmarsh, after a village in England.

Monitor Creek (creek)

72 M/14 - Kirkpatrick Lake
14-35-4-W4
52°00′N 111°28′W
Flows east into Sounding Creek, approximately 42 km south south-west of Provost.

(see Monitor)

* Monkman (former post office)

73 E/10 - Clandonald
10-54-7-W4
53°39′N 110°58′W
Approximately 28 km south of Elk Point.

The post office, which operated here from May 1920 through August 1928, took the name of Albert P.J. Monkman, the postmaster. It was previously called "Peguis" (after the Manitoba Indian name) and is now known as Derwent. (see Derwent)

Mons Lake (lake)

83 I/1 - Smoky Lake
17-60-16-W4
54°11′30″N 112°22′00″W

---
*denotes rescinded name or former locality.

Approximately 11 km north-east of Smoky Lake.

The name for this lake, locally known as "Bear Lake" likely commemorates Mons, the Belgian city captured by Canadian troops only hours before the armistice of 11 November 1918.

Montagnais Lake (lake)

73 L/3 - Vincent Lake
19-58-9-W4
54°02′N 111°20′W
Approximately 5 km north north-west of St. Paul.

The name for this lake has been official since 6 July 1950, but its precise origin is unknown.

Montambeault Lake (lake)

73 D/6 - Brownfield
7,8-39-9-W4
52°20′N 111°16′W
Approximately 30 km north of Coronation.

The name for this lake has been in use since at least 1958, but its origin is unknown.

Montana Indian Reserve #139

(Indian reserve)

83 A/11 - Chain Lakes
28-43-24-W4
52°44′N 113°26′W
Approximately 12 km north-east of Ponoka.

This Indian reserve was named for the Montana Band. Their chief, Keeskayo, also known as Bobtail, was a famous Cree chieftain. The name has been in use since 1885.

* Monvel (former locality)

83 A/7 - Stettler
6-41-19-W4
52°30′N 112°44′W

Approximately 19 km east south-east of Bashaw.

The origin for the name of the post office, which operated from December 1906 through July 1928, is not known. It was originally spelled "Monval."

Moon Lake (locality)

83 G/7 - Tomahawk
33-51-7-W5
53°27′N 114°57′W
Approximately 25 km north of Drayton Valley.

A post office operated here from August 1926 through September 1971 and was named after a nearby lake. The lake has a legend attached to it that an early settler witnessed a sunset over the lake and thought it was a lovely sight. The name is also a translation of a native name.

Moonshine Lake (lake)

73 L/1 - Reita Lake
17-58-1-W4
54°01′N 110°07′W
Approximately 44 km south of Grand Centre.

The name for this lake was officially adopted in 1950. An early Métis settler named Marcel Cardinal manufactured home brew here before being apprehended by the R.C.M.P. circa 1920.

Moore's Hill (hill)

82 O/16 - Olds
4-27-32-3-W5
51°46′00″N 114°21′00″W
Approximately 18 km west south-west of Olds.

The name for this hill is locally well established and is taken after an early homesteader. William Howard Moore and his six children (Mrs. Moore died in 1911) bought the house on the hill in 1916 from Hugh Noble, when the hill was known as "Noble Hill." The Moores had come to the area two years earlier from Michigan. The house on Moore's Hill was owned by the family from 1916 through 1963. Mr. Moore died in 1953. The name was officially approved 3 October 1991.

Moose Creek (creek)

83 F/9 - Edson
1-53-17-W5
53°33′N 116°22′W
Flows north into McLeod River, approximately 5 km south south-east of Edson.

The name for this creek has been official since at least 1958 and is likely descriptive, as there is a large population of moose in the area.

Moose Creek (creek)

83 B/3 - Tay River
7-19-35-8-W5
From 51°55′00″N 115°11′48″W
to 52°01′05″N 115°07′35″W
Flows north-east into Clearwater River, approximately 41 km south south-west of Rocky Mountain House.

The name for this feature was originally proposed in 1941 by J.A. MacDonald of the Dominion Land Survey. He noted at that time that it was a well-established local name, due to the number of moose found in the area. The name "Moose Creek," was not approved because it was said to be too common. Since that time, because of the fact that the name was so popular, Fish & Wildlife proposed that the name Moose Creek be made official as the stream was widely known as such by the residents. Further, the documentation of Fish &

Wildlife record this stream as Moose Creek. For management purposes, the name Moose Creek was also desired. The problem with the name was that there was another creek within 20 kilometres whose official name was also Moose Creek. Fish & Wildlife called that creek "Moosewallow Creek" in their documents and publications. The name Moose Creek was made official 7 February 1983.

■ Moose Hills (hills)

73 E/15 - Elk Point
57-7-W4
53°57′N 111°00′W
Approximately 10 km north-west of Elk Point.

The name for these hills appears on Palliser's map of 1859 and is a translation of the Cree *mooswachi*.

■ Moose Lake (lake)

73 L/7 - Bonnyville
4-18-61-6-W4
54°16′11″N 110°54′00″W
Approximately 15 km west of Bonnyville.

This feature originally appeared as "Moon Lake" on Harmon's Map of 1820. The lake was called "Lac d'Orignal" by fur traders such as Angus Shaw, who established the first North West Company post in 1789. The traders reached the lake via the Beaver River and Mooselake River, an incredibly tedious 15-kilometre stretch of water that took about nine days to cover.

Moose Lake Provincial Park

(provincial park)
73 L/7 - Bonnyville
14-61-7-W4
54°15′N 110°56′W
Approximately 13 km west of Bonnyville.

(see Moose Lake) This 735.72 hectare (1818.02 acre) park was created by Order-in-Council No. 782/72 and is on a large

lake with nice sand beaches and good fishing. It is a short drive from Bonnyville and is surrounded by other good fishing spots.

Moose Mountain (hill)

82 O/16 - Olds
13-9-35-3-W5
51°59′35″N 114°22′35″W
Approximately 23 km west south-west of Innisfail.

The name for this feature is well established in local usage, and has been in use since the early 1920s. The precise origin of the name is not clear, although Jimmy Wotherspoon (1902-1967) and the Moose Mountain Hall appear to be very well known. Jimmy came to Canada about 1920 with an uncle named Grundy and ran a post office in the Moose Mountain area. Jimmy was a remittance man (remittance men were often "black sheep" of the family sent off to the colonies where they regularly received money from home) and was well off. In the 1930s he built on this land the Moose Mountain Hall, where many dances were held. The name Moose Mountain was officially approved for this 1051 m hill 3 October 1991.

* Moose Ridge (former locality)

82 O/16 - Olds
6-35-3-W5
51°58′N 114°20′W
Approximately 26 km north-east of Sundre.

A post office operated here from March 1925 through June 1934 and was named for the abundance of moose in the area. It was previously known as "Mountain House."

Moose Wallow (locality)

83 J/2 - Thunder Lake
23-60-7-W5
54°12′N 114°57′W
Approximately 36 km west north-west of Barrhead.

---

*denotes rescinded name or former locality.

The descriptive name for this locality, whose post office operated from November 1911 through September 1969, refers to the number of moose in the area at its inception. Many wallows could be found along a nearby creek. A wallow is a muddy place in which some animals, including moose and bison, roll to rid themselves of flies, etc. School District #4554, established in June 1931, also took its name from this locality.

Moosehills Creek (creek)

73 E/15 - Elk Point
23-56-5-W4
53°52′N 110°38′W
Flows south-east into North Saskatchewan River, approximately 18 km east south-east of Elk Point.

(see Moose Hills)

■ **Moosehills Lake** (lake)

73 E/15 - Elk Point
22-57-6-W4
53°56′N 110°48′W
Approximately 7 km north-east of Elk Point.

(see Moose Hills)

Mooselake River (river)

73 L/7 - Bonnyville
16-4-62-7-W4
From 54°21′27″N 111°00′00″W
to 54°16′08″N 110°57′07″W
Flows north-west into Beaver River, approximately 25 km north-west of Bonnyville.

(see Moose Lake)

Moosewallow Creek (creek)

83 B/3 - Tay River
29-37-8-W5
52°12′15″N 115°06′30″W

Flows north-east into Vetch Creek, approximately 20 km south-west of Rocky Mountain House.

Originally, this creek was called "Moose Creek," but Fish & Wildlife renamed it Moosewallow Creek to avoid confusion with another Moose Creek located within 20 kilometres of this creek. The name was officially approved 3 October 1991. (see Moose Creek)

* **Mooswa** (former locality)

73 E/15 - Elk Point
26-56-5-W4
53°53′N 110°39′W
Approximately 18 km east south-east of Elk Point.

The name for this former locality, whose post office operated from November 1912 through January 1929, is the Cree word for "moose." The post office was previously called "Tyrol." It is now called Lindbergh. (see Lindbergh)

Mooswa Creek (creek)

73 E/15 - Elk Point
26-56-5-W4
53°53′N 110°37′W
Flows west into Moosehills Creek, approximately 17 km east of Elk Point.

(see Mooswa)

Morecambe (hamlet)

73 E/11 - Myrnam
18-54-10-W4
53°40′N 111°28′W
Approximately 18 km east south-east of Two Hills.

The name for this hamlet, whose post office operated from March 1929 through March 1984, is taken after Morecambe Bay in Lancashire, England. A similar-sounding name roughly means "curve of the sea."

Morinville (town)

83 H/13 - Morinville
34-55-25-W4
53°47′45″N 113°38′40″W
Approximately 32 km north north-west of Edmonton.

This predominantly French-speaking community, whose post office opened in January 1893, was founded in the spring of 1891 by Abbé Jean-Baptiste Morin (1852-1911). Abbé Morin was born at St. Paul-de Joliette, Quebec, and studied at Rigaud and Montreal, where he was ordained in 1884. In 1894 he published a pamphlet, "Le Nord-ouest Canadien et ses Resources Agricoles." He founded several other French-speaking settlements in Alberta. This town was incorporated 18 April 1911.

Morinville, 1908

Morning Lake (lake)

73 D/16 - McLaughlin
8-44-3-W4
52°46′N 110°24′W
Approximately 33 km east of the town of Wainwright.

The name for this lake has been official since 1958, but its origin is unknown.

Morningside (hamlet)

83 A/12 - Ponoka
35-41-26-W4
52°35'N 113°38'W
Approximately 12 km south south-west of
Ponoka.

The Canadian Pacific Railway established a
station here circa 1892 and named it after a
suburb of Edinburgh, Scotland. The post
office operated from January 1901 through
January 1982. It was officially recognized as
a hamlet 13 August 1979.

Morrin (village)

82 P/10 - Munson
15-31-20-W4
51°39'35"N 112°45'50"W
Approximately 36 km east of Three Hills.

The origin of the name of this village,
incorporated 16 April 1920 and previously
known as "Blooming Prairie," is not clear.
Although there is a folk tale that maintains
that the descriptive label was changed to the
prosaic name of Morrin to appease the
bloomin' English, the accepted version is
that Morrin was so named in honour of the
engineer who brought in the first train over
the newly laid steel. Canadian National
Railways records state that this village may
have been named after Joseph Morrin
(1792-1861), the first president of the
Medical Board of Lower Canada. Dr.
Morrin was born in Scotland and came to
Canada at an early age. He was educated in
Quebec and London and practised in
Quebec City.

Mortimer Lake (lake)

82 P/15 - Rumsey
28-32-20-W4
51°46'N 112°46'W
Approximately 35 km east of Three Hills.

The name for this lake has been official
since 1968, but its precise origin is unknown.

Moss Lake (lake)

73 L/5 - Goodfish Lake
28-62-13-W4
54°23'N 111°53'W
Approximately 41 km south of Lac La
Biche.

The name for this lake was officially
approved 4 May 1960 and is likely descriptive, referring to the sphagnum moss of
muskeg or soft algae prone to this type of
shallow lake.

Mosside (locality)

83 J/2 - Thunder Lake
32-58-4-W5
54°04'N 114°34'W
Approximately 12 km south-west of
Barrhead.

A post office operated here from March
1908 through March 1966 and was named
after a Moss Side, a suburb of Manchester,
England.

Mother Mountain (hill)

82 P/9 - Craigmyle
4-33-29-17-W4
51°31'30"N 112°20'30"W
Approximately 32 km west south-west of
Hanna.

Mother Mountain is the well-established
name among local residents for the highest
of the hills that comprise the Hand Hills.
The name is considered to be descriptive, as
the "mother" of the other hills. The name
has also been recorded as "Mothers'" or
"Mother's" Mountain. An additional
interpretation of the origin of the name is
that Indian mothers used the hill as a
lookout to spot returning hunting or war
parties. This is, however, unconfirmed.

Mott Lake (lake)

73 D/15 - Wainwright
26-44-7-W4
52°48'N 110°54'W
Approximately 4 km south-west of the
town of Wainwright.

The name for this feature was changed in
1916 from "Horse Lake" to honour a war
casualty. Private Frank E. Mott of the 49th
Battalion was killed in World War I. Before
the war, he and his brother Herman
operated a meat market in Wainwright.

Mound (locality)

82 O/16 - Olds
32-33-4-W5
51°51'N 114°31'W
Approximately 12 km north-east of Sundre.

A post office operated at this locality from
March 1905 through September 1958 and
was descriptively named for its proximity
to a hillock. The name was suggested by the
first postmaster, P.J. Neary.

* Mountain House (former locality)

82 O/16 - Olds
6-35-3-W5
51°58'N 114°20'W
Approximately 27 km north-east of Sundre.

The descriptive name for this trading post,
from which the post office took its name,
refers to its proximity to the mountains.
The post office operated under the name
Mountain House from December 1905
through March 1925, at which time the
name was changed to Moose Ridge.

Mountain View County #17 (county)

82 O/9 - Didsbury
29 to 33-27 & 28-W4
and 29 to 33-1 to 6-W5
51°36'N 114°20'W
South south-west of Red Deer.

---

*denotes rescinded name or former locality.

The name for this county is descriptive of the area's view of the Rocky Mountains.

Mouse Creek (creek)

82 O/10 - Fallentimber Creek
8-20-30-7-W5
51°36′N 114°56′W
Flows north into Fallentimber Creek, approximately 33 km south-west of Sundre.

The name for this creek has been official since November 1937, but its precise origin is unknown.

* Moyerton (former locality)

73 E/1 - Paradise Valley
30-47-3-W4
53°05′N 110°25′W
Approximately 35 km south-west of Lloydminster.

The name for the post office, which operated out of the home of Harry Warren from December 1909 through September 1940, was chosen by the Postal Department. Its precise origin is unknown, and the name was officially rescinded in November 1969.

Mud Creek (creek)

83 B/2 - Caroline
3-37-6-W5
From 52°09′18″N 114°51′30″W
to 52°10′10″N 114°46′00″W
Flows east into Clearwater River, approximately 26 km south south-east of Rocky Mountain House.

In the early 1900s the stream was known as "Muskeg Creek" as it drained a large muskeg area nearby. For 50 or 60 years, local residents called the stream Mud Creek. The name became established among the residents of Chedderville.

_____
*denotes rescinded name or former locality.

Alberta Fish & Wildlife stock the creek yearly and requested that this name be made official. It was officially approved 28 July 1986.

Mud Lake (lake)

83 H/10 - Elk Island Park
23-53-20-W4
53°36′N 112°51′W
Approximately 40 km east of Edmonton.

The name for this lake has been official since at least 1958 and is likely descriptive.

Mud Lake (lake)

83 I/14 - Sawdy
19-68-23-W4
54°54′N 113°29′W
Approximately 25 km north-west of Athabasca.

The name for this lake has been official since at least 1958 and is likely descriptive.

Mud Lake (lake)

83 J/3 - Green Court
36-59-8-W5
54°09′N 115°03′W
Approximately 41 km east of Whitecourt.

The name for this lake has been official since at least 1958 and is likely descriptive.

Mudhen Lake (lake)

73 D/9 - Chauvin
24-41-1-W4
52°32′00″N 110°00′15″W
Approximately 28 km north-east of Provost on the Alberta-Saskatchewan boundary.

The name for this lake has been official since at least 1958, but its precise origin is unknown.

Mudspring Lake (lake)

82 P/15 - Rumsey
16-33-20-W4
51°50′N 112°46′W
Approximately 31 km east of Trochu.

The name for this lake has been in official since 1958, but its precise origin is unknown.

Muir Lake (lake)

83 H/12 - St. Albert
32-53-27-W4
53°37′N 113°57′W
Approximately 32 km west north-west of Edmonton.

The name for this lake was officially approved in 1973, but its precise origin is unknown.

* Mulga (former locality)

73 E/3 - Buffalo Creek
13-49-8-W4
53°13′N 111°04′W
Approximately 18 km south south-west of Vermilion.

The post office, which operated here from August 1911 through July 1936, was named after the mulga tree, a widely distributed shrubby acacia (*Acacia aneura*) native to Australia. The postmaster, Perry Fielding, lived in Australia for a while.

Mulhurst Bay (hamlet)

83 H/4 - Kavanagh
14-47-28-W4
53°04′30″N 114°00′00″W
Approximately 43 km east north-east of Wetaskiwin.

The Pigeon Lake Chamber of Commerce, in association with the County of Wetaskiwin No. 10, made an application to have the name of the hamlet of Mulhurst changed to Mulhurst Bay. Located in a bay along the shores of the picturesque Pigeon Lake, Mulhurst residents felt that the name should portray the location. The name change was made official 30 October 1992.

Mundare (town)

83 H/9 - Mundare
19-53-16-W4
53°35′30″N 112°20′20″W
Approximately 77 km east of Edmonton.

The town of Mundare was incorporated 4 January 1951 and is centred in an unusually fertile farming area. Most of the Mundare pioneers came from Halchyná, an area in the steppes of Ukraine where similar soil type and climatic conditions prevailed. In 1903, the spelling was Mundaire. The *Encyclopedia Canadiana* of 1963 states the community "was named after a French missionary, Father Mundaire;" however, according to *Memories of Mundare*, the local history of the settlement of this area, and *Post Offices of Alberta*, the settlement was named after William Mundare, one of the earliest station agents of the area in 1906. Many people in the area say that Mundare is a corruption of the Ukrainian word for "monastery." The post office opened in October 1916.

Munro Lake (lake)

73 L/12 - Beaver Lake
18-64-11-W4
54°33′N 111°39′W
Approximately 33 km south-east of Lac La Biche.

The name for this lake was officially applied in 1951 and commemorates Lieutenant Campbell Stuart Munro, M.I.D., of Calgary, who was killed in World War II.

Munson (village)

82 P/10 - Munson
15-30-20-W4
51°33′40″N 112°44′05″W
Approximately 40 km east south-east of Three Hills.

The post office opened here in March 1911, and the resulting village, which was incorporated 5 May 1911, was likely named by the Canadian Northern Railway after J.A. Munson, K.C., of Munson, Allan, Laird & Davis, a Winnipeg law firm. The firm may have been retained by the Canadian Northern.

Munyass Lake (lake)

83 I/5 - Dapp
2-63,64-24-W4
54°30′10″N 113°32′00″W
Approximately 29 km south south-west of Athabasca.

The name for this lake has been official since at least 1958, but its precise origin is unknown.

Muriel (locality)

73 E/15 - Elk Point
10-57-6-W4
53°54′N 110°49′W
Approximately 7 km east north-east of Elk Point.

The precise origin for the name of this locality is unknown.

Muriel Creek (creek)

73 L/8 - Cold Lake
19-62-2-W4
54°23′N 110°19′W
Flows north-east into Beaver River, approximately 6 km south-west of Grand Centre.

(see Muriel Lake)

Muriel Lake (lake)

73 L/2 - Muriel Lake
33-59,60-5-W4
54°09′N 110°40′W
Approximately 15 km south of Bonnyville.

(see Elinor Lake)

Muriel Lake (locality)

73 L/2 - Muriel Lake
25-60-4,5 W4
54°13′N 110°37′W
Approximately 11 km south-east of Bonnyville.

A post office operated here from February 1930 through January 1951 and was named after Muriel Gurney, mother-in-law of the first postmaster at Gurneyville. (see Elinor Lake)

Murray Island (island)

73 L/9 - Marie Lake
13-65-1-W4
54°37′N 110°00′W
Approximately 22 km north north-east of Cold Lake, on the Alberta-Saskatchewan boundary.

The name for this island in Cold Lake commemorates Bert Murray, a member of an early survey party.

Murray Valley (valley)

82 O/16 - Olds
3-32-33-2-W5
51°52′50″N 114°15′30″W
Approximately 10 km north-west of Olds.

The locally well-established name for this valley is taken from the Murray family. Mr. and Mrs. James Murray and their seven children (five sons and two daughters) arrived in 1889 and by squatters' rights established a home and ranch in what then became known as Murray Valley. This name was known as early as 1899. The

Murrays came to Canada from Northumberland, England, in 1885 and settled in Hamilton, Ontario, moving to south-west Calgary the next year. Mrs. Murray died in 1908 and Mr. Murray in 1915. One son, the late Archie, was on the farm 55 years. The name was officially approved 3 October 1991.

* Murray Valley (former locality)
82 O/16 - Olds
28-33-2-W5
51°51′N 114°14′W
Approximately 12 km north-west of Olds.

A post office operated here from June 1903 through February 1927 and was named for the Murray family, the earliest settlers to the area. (see Murray Valley)

Mushroom Lake (lake)
73 D/16 - McLaughlin
10,15-45-4-W4
52°52′45″N 110°29′30″W
Approximately 25 km east north-east of the town of Wainwright.

The name for this lake has been official since at least 1958, but its precise origin is unknown.

Musidora (hamlet)
73 E/12 - Two Hills
29-54-11-W4
53°42′N 111°35′W
Approximately 12 km east of Two Hills.

A post office was established here in May 1909 and, apparently, was named by Edvert Robarge (?-1928) who was a mail carrier whose route extended between Beauvallon and Duvernay. Although it cannot be confirmed, it seems Mr. Robarge named this place after his former home in France.

Muskeg Creek (creek)
83 A/13 - Bearhills Lake
11-45-28-W4
52°52′N 113°57′W
Flows east into Battle River, approximately 33 km north-west of Ponoka.

The name for this creek has been official since at least 1959 and is likely descriptive.

Muskeg Creek (creek)
83 I/11 - Athabasca
16-65-23-W4
54°38′N 113°26′W
Flows north-east into Athabasca River immediately north of Athabasca.

The name for this creek has been official since at least 1958 and is likely descriptive.

Muskeg Lake (lake)
83 G/9 - Onoway
25-53-3-W5
53°37′N 114°18′W
Approximately 55 km west of Edmonton.

The descriptive name for this lake has been official since at least 1958.

Muskeg Lake (lake)
83 I/5 - Dapp
17-62-25-W4
54°22′N 113°43′W
Approximately 47 km south south-west of Athabasca.

The name for this lake has been official since at least 1958 and is likely descriptive.

Muskrat Creek (creek)
83 B/15 - Buck Lake
22-45-5-W5
52°54′N 114°39 W
Flows north-west into Buck Lake, approximately 26 km south-east of Drayton Valley.

The name for this creek is likely descriptive, and is a translation of the Cree name *wachask*. The Stoney equivalent is *hthumptodab wapta*.

Mynarski Park (post office)
83 A/4 - Innisfail
14-37-28-W4
52°11′N 113°54′W
Approximately 20 km south south-west of Red Deer.

The post office opened here in April 1954 and was named for Pilot Officer Andrew Charles Mynarski (1916-1944), a Winnipeg native who was posthumously awarded the Victoria Cross in World War II. The name was chosen by Royal Canadian Air Force personnel as a tribute to the memory of the heroic fighter pilot of a Lancaster bomber who died of burns after trying to free the trapped R.C.A.F. Gunner of the doomed aircraft. The R.C.A.F. gunner survived.

Myr Lake (lake)
73 E/14 - St. Paul
5-56-9-W4
53°48′20″N 111°18′30″W
Approximately 21 km south of St. Paul.

The name for this lake was officially approved 21 December 1979 and is the Ukrainian word for "peace." A cottage development was in process by Lac Bellevue Properties at the time of the original naming proposal by Ms. Loretta Foley.

Myriad Lake (lake)
83 H/3 - Bittern Lake
31-47-23-W4
53°09′40″N 113°13′30″W
Approximately 18 km north-east of Wetaskiwin.

The name for this lake has been official since at least 1958, but its precise origin is unknown.

Myrnam (village)
73 E/11 - Myrnam
14-54-9-W4
53°39′40″N 111°13′45″W
Approximately 35 km east south-east of
Two Hills.

The name for this village, whose post office
opened in August 1908, is the Russian word
for "peace to us." Many of the settlers were
of Ukrainian origin. The village was
incorporated on 22 August 1930.

Mystery Lake (locality)
83 J/2 - Thunder Lake
1-60-7-W5
54°09′N 114°55′W
Approximately 34 km west of Barrhead.

The name for this locality, whose post
office operated from December 1930
through August 1970, was taken after a
nearby lake that has since dried up. Apparently, F.W. Harris found the lake near his
homestead, but when he told his friend of
the feature, it was not easy to find the
second time, and they thereby concluded
that its location was a mystery.

Naco (locality)
72 M/10 - Sedalia
33-31-6-W4
51°42′N 110°48′W
Approximately 45 km north north-west of
Oyen.

The name for this locality is taken after a
town in Arizona. The post office operated
from April 1926 through April 1968.

Nadeau Lake (lake)
73 L/12 - Beaver Lake
12-32-64-12-W4
54°35′54″N 111°47′26″W
Approximately 15 km south south-east of
Lac La Biche.

The name for this lake is well established
and commemorates an old Canadian hunter
who lived near the lake. His daughter was
married to a young native Indian who had
just killed a buffalo. The freeman (likely a
retired voyageur), named Nadeau, was
hungry also, but shared half this buffalo
with Gabriel Franchère in 1814.

Nakamun (locality)
83 G/16 - Lac la Nonne
21-56-2-W5
53°51′30″N 114°14′00″W
Approximately 33 km south south-east of
Barrhead.

The post office operated here from February 1911 through November 1960 and was
named for its proximity to Nakamun Lake.
(see Nakamun Lake)

Nakamun Lake (lake)
83 G/16 - Lac la Nonne
34-56-2 W5
53°53′N 114°13′W
Approximately 30 km south south-east of
Barrhead.

The name for this lake has been official
since at least 1928 and is the Cree word for
"song of praise."

Nakamun Park (summer village)
83 G/16 - Lac la Nonne
34-56-2-W5
53°53′N 114°12′W
Approximately 32 km south south-east of
Barrhead.

The name for this summer village, incorporated 1 January 1966, is taken after its
location on Nakamun Lake. (see Nakamun
Lake)

Namao (hamlet)
83 H/11 - Edmonton
33-54-24-W4
53°43′N 113°29′W
Approximately 17 km north of Edmonton.

The post office opened here in May 1892
and its name is the Cree word for sturgeon.
The hamlet is close to the Sturgeon River.

Namao, 1907

Namepi Creek (creek)
83 I/2 - Waskatenau
19-59-20-W4
54°07′N 112°59′W
Flows south-east into North Saskatchewan
River, approximately 20 km east north-east
of Redwater.

The name for this creek has been shown on
maps since at least 1911, and was labelled
"Carp Brook" on David Thompson's map
of 1814. Its precise origin is unknown.

Naples (locality)
83 J/1 - Barrhead
20-60-2-W5
54°12′N 114°16′W
Approximately 12 km north-east of
Barrhead.

The name for this locality, whose post office operated from December 1923 through September 1969, is taken after the Italian city as many Italians settled here.

Napoleon Lake (lake)

83 A/4 - Innisfail
SW-29-35-28-W4
52°01′46″N 113°58′22″W
Approximately 30 km south south-west of Red Deer.

The name for this lake originated in the 1880s when Napoléon Remillard journeyed from Montana to Alberta and settled immediately south of Innisfail (then called "Poplar Grove") near the lake. He operated the first stopping house in the area: the cabin-stopping house that he built on his homestead in 1890 has been preserved as a private museum by an Innisfail oldtimer. Napoléon Remillard lived in the area for 15 or 20 years before moving on to British Columbia.

Narrow Lake (lake)

83 I/12 - Coolidge
17-65-24-W4
54°38′N 113°36′W
Approximately 25 km south-west of Athabasca.

The name for this lake has been official since at least 1958 and is likely descriptive.

The Narrows (narrows)

83 H/10 - Elk Island Park
2-21-53-20-W4
53°35′15″N 112°53′00″W
Approximately 40 km east of Edmonton, in Elk Island National Park.

The name for this constricted section of water between Tawayik Lake and Little Tawayik Lake is descriptive. The name was officially approved 17 October 1991.

Narrows, The (narrows)

83 A/10 - Donalda
9-16-41-20-W4
52°31′50″N 112°49′00″W
Approximately 13 km east south-east of Bashaw.

The name for these narrows on Buffalo Lake is descriptive. The feature was also known locally as "Salmon Narrows."

* Naughton Glen (former locality)

73 E/6 - Mannville
32-53-10-W4
53°36′N 111°25′W
Approximately 23 km south-east of Two Hills.

The origin for the name of the post office, which operated here from September 1909 through June 1931, is unknown.

Navarre (locality)

83 A/14 - Wetaskiwin
22-45-24-W4
52°54′N 113°25′W
Approximately 10 km south of Wetaskiwin.

The Canadian Pacific Railway established a station here between 1912 and 1914 and named it after the Spanish province. The derivation of the name is Spanish, *Nava* and *erri*. The descriptive name refers to the region of hills and valleys.

Neapolis (locality)

82 P/12 - Lonepine Creek
11-31-28-W4
51°39′N 113°52′W
Approximately 18 km east of Didsbury.

A post office operated here from March 1903 through February 1914, but the origin of the name is unknown.

Neerlandia (hamlet)

83 J/8 - Shoal Creek
34-61-3-W5
54°20′N 114°22′W
Approximately 23 km north of Barrhead.

The first settlers and homesteaders who came into the district in 1913 were from the Netherlands and called their settlement Neerlandia after their homeland. The first post office was established in April 1913 in the home of Mr. A. Mast, one of the first four settlers. The name, Nederland, means "low land."

Nelson Creek (creek)

73 D/6 - Brownfield
27-39-11-W4
52°23′N 111°29′W
Flows north into Battle River, approximately 32 km north of Coronation.

This creek was named for Mr. Nelson, an early cattleman of the area, but biographical details about him are not available.

Nelson Lake (lake)

73 D/6 - Brownfield
8-38-9-W4
52°15′30″N 111°14′30″W
Approximately 24 km north north-east of Coronation.

(see Nelson Creek)

Nelson Lake (lake)

83 A/11 - Chain Lakes
2-43-24-W4
52°40′N 113°22′W
Approximately 14 km east of Ponoka.

This lake was named in 1955 after V.D. Nelson, an early homesteader who owned land in the area for over fifty years.

---

*denotes rescinded name or former locality.

Nelson Lake (lake)

83 J/9 - Flatbush
8-64-2-W5
54°31′00″N 114°15′30″W
Approximately 46 km north of Barrhead.

The origin for the name of this lake is unknown.

* **Nestor** (former post office)

73 E/4 - Viking
14-48-14-W4
53°08′N 111°55′W
Approximately 11 km north-west of Viking.

The post office operated by this name from March 1908 through December 1916. It was then changed to Torlea. (see Torlea)

Nestow (hamlet)

83 I/4 - Westlock
31-60-24-W4
54°14′N 113°36′W
Approximately 19 km north-east of Westlock.

The name for this hamlet, whose post office operated from March 1908 through December 1916, is the Cree word for "brother-in-law." The significance of this choice of name is not known.

Netook (locality)

82 O/16 - Olds
34-33-1-W5
51°53′N 114°03′W
Approximately 12 km north-east of Olds.

The Canadian Pacific Railway established a station here between 1913 and 1916. The name is taken from the Blackfoot *nee-tuck-kis*, translating "lone pine tree," and has

been recorded as early as 1792, when Peter Fidler mentioned in his journal that he and his party were approximately 20 kilometres away from a point of woods containing a large single pine tree called nee-tuck-kis. According to David Thompson, the Indians made offerings there. A post office operated here from March 1928 through April 1958.

Neutral Hills (locality)

73 D/2 - Neutral Hills
33-37-7-W4
52°14′N 110°57′W
Approximately 35 km north of Coronation.

The post office operated in this area from May 1913 through April 1965 and was named for its location in the Neutral Hills. (see Neutral Hills)

Neutral Hills (hills)

73 D/2 - Neutral Hills
18-37-6-W4
52°11′N 110°52′W
Approximately 45 km north-east of Coronation.

There are two Indian legends about the Neutral Hills. According to the first, taken from a local history entitled *In the Shadows of the Neutrals* (1967), there were no hills in the area and the Blackfoot and Cree roamed far and wide. This was a land of food, water and fuel. Constant warfare was waged between the two tribes with no one appearing to win. But the omnipotent Great Spirit caused the great barrier of the Neutral Hills to rise between the rival tribes one night. In the morning the amazed warriors beheld the hills. They followed the line of hills until they came to a gap where they met, smoked the peace pipe, and agreed to fight each other no more. That the area was frequented by Indians at one time is evidenced by the finds of Indian remains. The second legend is that the Blackfoot and Cree fought long over the

right to hunt and fish here. Finally they decided that there was enough for all and they declared peace. They erected an eighteen-foot-high statue of an Indian maiden, near the western end of the hills, and proclaimed that as long as the Sun Goddess reigned, there would be no more war. One day two braves, rivals for the hand of the chief's daughter, fought a duel to the death in which both died. That night a great thunderstorm raged. When the Indian maid visited the scene of the storm next day she found that the lightning had split off a large piece of rock from the statue, which now lay flat beside it. On this she laid branches and flowers and declared that forever more this should be a place for feasting. And according to this legend, that was how the Neutral Hills were named.

Neutral Valley (locality)

73 D/2 - Neutral Hills
32-36-6-W4
52°08′N 110°48′W
Approximately 43 km north-east of Coronation.

The post office operated here from May 1913 through June 1932 and was named for its location in the Neutral Hills. (see Neutral Hills)

Neville Lake (lake)

83 J/1 - Barrhead
2-60-3-W5
54°10′N 114°20′W
Approximately 6 km north-east of Barrhead.

The name for this lake appears on a sectional sheet for Fort Assiniboine dated 1948, but its precise origin is unknown.

Nevis (hamlet)

83 A/6 - Alix
1-39-22-W4
52°20′N 113°01′W
Approximately 23 km west of Stettler.

---

*denotes rescinded name or former locality.

The post office opened in April 1911 and was named after the Ben Nevis coal mine near the village. Its possible derivative is that of Ben Nevis in Scotland. The name Ben Nevis suggests "mountain in the clouds."

Nevis Junction (railway point)

83 A/6 - Alix
31-38-21-W4
52°18'N 113°01'W
Approximately 22 km west of Stettler.

(see Nevis)

New Brigden (hamlet)

72 M/9 - Esther
35-31-4-W4
51°42'N 110°29'W
Approximately 40 km north of Oyen.

The name for this hamlet, whose post office opened 15 July 1912, was taken after Brigden, Ontario, whence some of the first settlers had come.

* New Hill (former locality)

83 B/1 - Markerville
17-37-3-W5
52°10'N 114°25'W
Approximately 43 km west south-west of Red Deer.

A post office operated here from August 1908 through December 1930 and its name is descriptive of the many hills around the district.

* New Kiew (former locality)

73 E/12 - Two Hills
20-53-13-W4
53°36'N 111°52'W
Approximately 16 km north-east of Vegreville.

This predominantly Ukrainian settlement was originally named Kiev after the city in Ukraine. The post office was named New Kiew and operated from August 1932 through January 1954.

* New Lindsay (former locality)

73 E/1 - Paradise Valley
31-47-1-W4
53°05'N 110°08'W
Approximately 20 km south south-west of Lloydminster.

The first postmaster here was John Lindsay. The post office, which operated from April 1911 through September 1938, took the name "New Lindsay" to avoid duplication with Lindsay, the county town of Victoria County in Ontario.

* New Lunnon (former locality)

83 H/14 - Redwater
27-55-23-W4
53°47'N 113°20'W
Approximately 26 km north north-east of Edmonton.

A post office operated here from August 1893 through May 1927 and was named for the vernacular of some Londoners for the English capital.

New Norway (village)

83 A/15 - Ferintosh
11-45-21-W4
52°52'10"N 112°57'10"W
Approximately 18 km south south-west of Camrose.

The name for this village is reminiscent of the homeland of many of the early settlers, who were from Norway. The post office opened in June 1903. This village was incorporated 6 May 1910.

New Sarepta (village)

83 H/6 - Cooking Lake
33-49-22-W4
53°16'25"N 113°08'45"W
Approximately 40 km south-east of Edmonton.

A post office opened here in June 1905, but the origin for the name is not clear. One account maintains that it was named after the city near Sidon, the modern village of Sarafand (St. Luke 4:26); however, the connection to this village is not known. It was formerly called "Little Hay Lakes." It was one of the Phoenician towns between Tyre and Sidon, mentioned in I Kings xvii as the place where the prophet Elijah performed a miracle. A second account, written by Mrs. Bertha McLean, notes that many of the early settlers in the area had been born in Vohlynia, Russia, and that they had come to make their homes in this part of Canada at the suggestion of Bishop Clement Hoyler of the Moravian Church. At the time of the immigration to Canada and the search for new homes in a strange land the leases on their farms in Vohlynia, held by the Czarina of Russia, were about to expire and they feared for the terms that would have to be signed for renewal. The name is also regarded by those in the district to be in remembrance of a Russian settlement, Sarepta, and selected by Bishop Clement Hoyler. The word "new" was added to distinguish this community from a settlement in Ontario of the same name. This village was incorporated 1 January 1960.

Newbrook (hamlet)

83 I/7 - Newbrook
5-62-20-W4
54°19'N 112°57'W
Approximately 40 km north-west of Smoky Lake.

The post office opened here in June 1917, and its first location was apparently close to a creek.

Newton Creek (creek)
83 J/1 - Barrhead
11-58-3-W5
54°00′15″N 114°12′00″W
Flows west into Pembina River, approximately 10 km south-east of Barrhead.

The name for this feature appears on a Surveys and Mapping Branch map of 1953. H.F. Cruickshank made the official proposal to have the creek named after the Newtons, early settlers who built a house on its bank. Mr. and Mrs. Henry Newton arrived in the area in 1904 as the first settlers, and were well respected among the community and friends to all newcomers.

Newton Lake (lake)
83 G/16 - Lac la Nonne
11-58-2-W5
53°59′45″N 114°11′00″W
Approximately 20 km south-east of Barrhead.

The name for this lake has been official since at least 1958, but its precise origin is unknown.

Nicot Lake (lake)
83 I/16 - Plamondon
29-68-14-W4
54°55′N 112°07′W
Approximately 19 km north north-west of Lac La Biche.

The name for this lake has been official since at least 1958; its precise origin is unknown. It was locally known as "School Junction Lake" until the school section was sold.

Nilrem (locality)
73 D/11 - Hardisty
1-41-9-W4
52°30′N 111°10′W
Approximately 20 km south-east of Hardisty.

The post office, which operated here from November 1911 through January 1921, was named after Merlin, the half-legendary magician of the sixth century. A town in Ontario was also named Merlin, and in order to avoid the duplication of the name, the letters were reversed and the new name applied to this locality.

Niobe (locality)
83 A/4 - Innisfail
3-36-28-W4
52°03′N 113°54′W
Approximately 27 km south of Red Deer.

A Canadian Pacific Railway station was established here and was named after the cruiser, H.M.C.S. *Niobe*, one of two warships Canada bought from Britain when the Royal Canadian Navy was established. The massive four-funnelled *Niobe* arrived in Halifax on 21 October 1910, the 105th anniversary of the Battle of Trafalgar. The other warship, H.M.C.S. *Rainbow*, a light cruiser assigned to the West Coast, arrived in Esquimalt on 7 November 1910.

Nisbet (locality)
82 P/13 - Torrington
14-34-28-W4
51°55′N 113°53′W
Approximately 15 km south south-east of Innisfail.

An early homesteader, H.M. Nisbet was the oldest settler in the area, and it was after him that the post office, which operated from June 1912 through June 1943, was named.

Nisku (hamlet)
83 H/5 - Leduc
26-50-25-W4
53°20′N 113°32′W
Approximately 8 km north of Leduc.

The post office opened here in June 1925, and the name may be the Cree word for "goose."

Nitchi Creek (creek)
82 O/10 - Fallentimber Creek
13-31-7-W5
51°39′N 114°51′W
Flows north into Red Deer River, approximately 13 km west south-west of Sundre.

The name for this creek has been official since November 1937, but its origin is unknown.

Niton (hamlet)
83 G/12 - Carrot Creek
18-54-12-W5
53°39′N 115°45′W
Approximately 45 km east of Edson.

The Grand Trunk Pacific Railway established a station here in 1911. The post office operated from October 1908 through May 1970. The name is "not in" reversed. It may suggest that the station agent was often absent. Another theory suggests that the name may be that of one of the railway construction contractors.

Niton Junction (hamlet)
83 G/12 - Carrot Creek
31-53-12-W5
53°37′N 115°46′W
Approximately 43 km east of Edson.

The well-established name for this hamlet was officially approved in October 1955. The post office opened in March 1956. (see Niton)

No Name Creek (creek)
83 B/11 - Baptiste River
20-42-8-W5
52°38′N 115°08′W
Flows north-east into Baptiste River, approximately 34 km north north-west of Rocky Mountain House.

The name for this creek has been official since at least 1958, but its precise origin is unknown.

No Outlet Lake (lake)
83 G/16 - Lac la Nonne
33-55-3-W5
53°47′N 114°22′W
Approximately 38 km south of Barrhead.

The name for this lake has been official since at least 1958 and likely describes the fact that there are no streams that drain the feature.

Nojack (locality)
83 G/12 - Carrot Creek
29-53-11-W5
53°36′30″N 115°34′15″W
Approximately 55 km east of Edson.

A hotel and service station were constructed on Highway #16 approximately four kilometres south of MacKay, with a large amount of credit. The name which is a colloquial term meaning "no money" was chosen and has been perpetuated by local business establishments. The name was officially approved in 1974.

Nonne, Lac la (lake)
83 G/16 - Lac la Nonne
24-57-3-W5
53°56′N 114°19′W
Approximately 21 km south south-east of Barrhead.

The name for this lake has been recorded since at least May 1827 when it appeared as "Lac La Nane" in Edward Ermatinger's journal. The Cree name is rendered *mi-ka-sioo*, "eagle." There is some controversy concerning the precise origin of the name Lac la Nonne. One explanation is that it is for a duck, the whitewinged scoter (*Melanitta deglandi*) which is common on

the lake and whose white bars and white head spots suggests a black-robed nun. A duck of similar colouring found in England is colloquially known as "the nun." A second suggestion is that it was named for the nuns of the nearby Lac Ste Anne Mission, although the latter was not founded until 1844.

Noral (hamlet)
83 I/9 - Hylo
28-65-16-W4
54°39′N 112°22′W
Approximately 27 km south-west of Lac La Biche.

The Alberta and Great Waterways Railway established a station here in 1914 en route to Fort McMurray. The name may be a contraction of Northern Alberta. The post office operated from October 1921 through January 1969.

Norberg Lake (lake)
73 L/5 - Goodfish Lake
16-61-11-W4
54°17′N 111°35′W
Approximately 37 km north-west of St. Paul.

The name for this lake was officially adopted 4 May 1950 and was taken after B. Norberg, J.C. Norberg and O.M. Norberg, who owned land in the area.

Norbuck (locality)
83 G/1 - Warburg
35-46-4-W5
53°01′N 114°29′W
Approximately 42 km south-east of Drayton Valley.

The Lacombe and North Western Railway established a station here in 1926. It was on the north trail to Buck Lake, and the name

Norbuck was a combination of "north" and "buck." The post office operated from October 1929 through June 1969.

Nordegg River (river)
83 B/14 - Brazeau Forks
13-45-10-W5
52°53′N 115°18′W
Flows north into Brazeau River, approximately 43 km south south-west of Drayton Valley.

This river was named after Martin Nordegg (1868-1948), general manager of Brazeau Collieries Ltd. Little is known about Martin Nordegg's life before 1906. He was born in Silesia, Germany. His family name was Cohen or Cohn, and became Nordegg only after his arrival in Canada. He studied photochemistry and engineering at the Technical College in Charlottenburg and served for a time in the German army. Nordegg established a coal mine, a railway and a townsite within ten years. His memoirs, edited by T.D. Regehr, are entitled *The Possibilities of Canada Are Truly Great*.

Norglenwold (summer village)
83 B/8 - Sylvan Lake
6-39-1-W5
52°19′30″N 114°07′30″W
Approximately 20 km west north-west of Red Deer.

This summer village was formed 1 January 1965. Its name is a composite of the names of the many subdivisions that came to form the summer village, namely, Northey's Point, Glen Innes and Whitewold. Lyle's Landing came in later.

Norma (locality)
83 H/9 - Mundare
31-54-14-W4
53°43′N 112°03′W

Approximately 95 km west north-west of Edmonton.

The name for the post office, previously called "Spring Creek," which operated here from May 1950 through August 1966, was taken after the municipal district that was established in 1918. A prize was offered for the best name of not more than five letters. This name honours Norma V. Richardson, an early settler.

Norman Lake (lake)

83 J/9 - Flatbush
23-64-2-W5
54°33′N 114°11′W
Approximately 59 km west south-west of Athabasca.

The name for this lake has been official since at least 1958, but its precise origin is unknown.

Normandeau (locality)

73 L/12 - Beaver Lake
34-64-12-W4
54°35′N 111°44′W
Approximately 27 km south-east of Lac La Biche.

A post office operated here from December 1914 through June 1931 and commemorates Abbé Joseph-Aldéric Normandeau, an early Roman Catholic missionary with a parish at Legal.

Normandeau Lake (lake)

73 L/12 - Beaver Lake
25-64-12-W4
54°34′28″N 111°41′14″W
Approximately 28 km south south-east of Lac La Biche.

This feature was once known to the Métis as "Cardinal Lake," after a family of that name who lived beside it. (see Normandeau)

Normandin Lake (lake)

73 D/10 - Hughenden
30-43-5-W4
52°44′N 110°44′W
Approximately 14 km south-east of the town of Wainwright.

The name for this lake has been in use since at least 1928, and is taken after an early homesteader who lived on its shores.

Norris Beach (summer village)

83 B/16 - Winfield
W-13-46-1-W5
52°58′N 114°02′W
Approximately 44 km west of Wetaskiwin.

The summer village of Norris Beach was established by Order-in-Council No. 224/89 effective 31 December 1989. The land upon which the summer village is located was once owned by Paul Norris, one-time City of Edmonton alderman, who registered the subdivision subsequently known as Norris Beach.

Norris Creek (creek)

83 H/10 - Elk Island Park
16-53-19-W4
53°37′N 112°44′W
Flows south-east into Beaverhill Lake, approximately 33 km west of Vegreville.

The name for this creek was taken after an Edmonton old-timer, John "Jack" Norris (1829-1916), who came to Canada from Scotland in 1849 as an employee of the Hudson's Bay Company He lived in Bow Valley, but later came to Edmonton where he became a trader and was in partnership with Robert Logan from 1864 to 1874 near Beaverhill Lake. Later he opened a hardware and grocery store in Edmonton in partnership with Ed Carey. Norris and Carey's store became known both as a business establishment and as a meeting place.

North Buck Lake (lake)

83 I/10 - Boyle
6-66-17-W4
54°41′42″N 112°33′57″W
Approximately 39 km west south-west of Lac La Biche.

The name for this lake has been official since at least 1958 and although the local residents descriptively refer to it as simply "Buck Lake," the "North" was likely added to avoid duplication with the Buck Lake 240 kilometres to the south-west.

North Cooking Lake (hamlet)

83 H/7 - Tofield
6-52-20-W4
53°28′N 112°57′W
Approximately 40 km east south-east of Edmonton.

A post office opened here in October 1912 and was descriptively named for its location on the north shore of Cooking Lake. (see Cooking Lake)

North Edmonton (locality)

83 H/11 - Edmonton
23-53-20-W4
53°35′N 113°26′W
Within the city limits of Edmonton.

A post office operated here from November 1909 through January 1962. (see Edmonton)

North Island (island)

83 H/10 - Elk Island Park
13-23-54-20-W4
53°41′15″N 112°50′55″W
Approximately 40 km east of Edmonton, in Elk Island National Park.

The name of this island was officially approved 17 October 1991 and is likely descriptive of the feature's location in Astotin Lake.

* North Junction (former railway station)

83 A/5 - Red Deer
11-39-27-W4
52°20′30″N 113°47′45″W
Approximately 13 km south of Red Deer Junction, within the city of Red Deer.

The name for this railway junction was rescinded in February 1970. Its precise origin is likely descriptive.

* North Kotzman (former post office)

83 I/1 - Smoky Lake
12-60-17-W4
54°10′N 112°23′W
Approximately 8 km north north-east of Smoky Lake.

The origin of the name of the post office, which operated here from October 1936 through January 1962, is unknown. The name was officially rescinded in 1971.

North Prairie Creek (creek)

83 B/6 - Crimson Lake
32-38-9-W5
52°19′N 115°14′W
Flows south-east into Prairie Creek, approximately 18 km south-west of Rocky Mountain House.

The name for this creek has been official since at least 1958, and is taken from its proximity as a northern tributary to Prairie Creek.

North Raven River (river)

83 B/2 - Caroline
30-36-4-W5
52°07′N 114°33′W
Flows south-east into Raven River, approximately 43 km south-east of Rocky Mountain House.

_____

This river was named for its proximity as a northern tributary of the Raven River. It was once known as "Stauffer's Creek"

■ North Saskatchewan River (river)

73 E/9 - Marwayne
34-53-1-W4
53°37′15″N 110°05′00″W
Flows into Saskatchewan to Hudson Bay, approximately 37 km north of Lloydminster.

This is one of the Canadian Prairies' great rivers. It is fed by the Saskatchewan Glacier, an outlet of the Columbia Icefield. The water of this river furnishes the drinking water for several settlements along its course, measuring some 1,223 kilometres in length from the Columbia Icefield to Hudson Bay. The descriptive name is taken from the Cree Indian term *kis-is-ska-tche-wan* meaning "swift current."

North Saskatchewan River, n.d.

Northbank (locality)

83 I/2 - Waskatenau
25-58-18-W4
54°03′N 112°33′W
Approximately 11 km south south-west of Smoky Lake.

The descriptive name for this locality, whose post office operated from August 1907 through March 1952, refers to its position near the north bank of the North Saskatchewan River.

* Northern (former post office)

83 H/7 - Tofield
10-50-19-W4
53°18′N 112°41′W
Approximately 8 km south of Tofield.

The name for this post office, which operated from March 1898 through December 1904, was changed to Bardo. (see Bardo)

Northern Valley (locality)

73 E/15 - Elk Point
33-55-6-W4
53°48′N 110°50′W
Approximately 13 km south-west of Elk Point.

A post office was established here in 1910 and had a descriptive name. The outlet has since been closed.

Northleigh (locality)

83 G/7 - Tomahawk
34-50-6-W5
53°22′N 114°48′W
Approximately 20 km north-east of Drayton Valley.

The name for the post office, which operated at this locality from February 1915 through July 1956, was suggested by its first postmaster, H.G. Foye, who was a casualty of World War I. The name is taken after a place of the same name in Devonshire, England.

* Northville (former post office)

83 G/11 - Chip Lake
25-53-10-W5
53°37′N 115°21′W

Approximately 41 km south south-west of Mayerthorpe.

The precise origin for the name of this post office, which operated for the community of Granada from March 1933 through March 1978, is unknown.

* Norway Valley (former locality)

73 E/16 - Frog Lake
16-55-3-W4
53°46′N 110°23′W
Approximately 38 km east south-east of Elk Point.

The name for the post office, which operated here from February 1923 through June 1959, was taken after School District #3916, established in March 1920. There were a number of Norwegian settlers in this valley.

Nose Hill (hill)

73 D/3 - Coronation
12-37-9-W4
52°10′N 111°10′W
Approximately 32 km east north-east of Coronation.

The name for this hill is a rough translation of the Cree word *os-ke-wu-na-chio*.

Nosehill Creek (creek)

83 F/15 - Nosehill Creek
35-55-20-W5
53°47′N 116°52′W
Flows north into Athabasca River, approximately 54 km north-west of Edson.

The name for this creek has been official since at least 1958, but its precise origin is unknown.

Noyes Crossing (locality)

83 G/9 - Onoway
8-55-1-W5
53°44′N 114°06′W
Approximately 47 km north-west of Edmonton.

Daniel E. Noyes (1828-1910), after whom this place was named, was born in Vermont and took part in the California gold rush and then came to the Cariboo in 1859. He was a goldseeker, a packer, and a businessman who opened a stopping place here at the ferry crossing on the Sturgeon River. He became the first postmaster for the post office, which operated from September 1906 through June 1956.

Nugent (locality)

83 B/16 - Winfield
11-44-3-W5
52°48′N 114°18′W
Approximately 16 km north north-west of Rimbey.

A post office operated here for a short time, from April 1911 through May 1928, and was named by the only postmaster, M. Donovan, after his wife's maiden name.

Nuorison Creek (creek)

83 B/8 - Sylvan Lake
10-39-3-W5
52°20′45″N 114°20′50″W
Flows south-west into Medicine River, approximately 35 km west of Red Deer.

The name for this creek was officially approved 29 July 1986. It was requested by the couple who live on the land through which the creek runs. The name is a Finnish word which means "young people's." The creek is fed by a spring next to which a youth hall was erected in 1906 and called Nuorison Sali (*sali* is the Finnish word for hall). The Young People's Hall was owned by the Loyal Finns of Canada. Until 1914,

most Finnish settlers went to the United States, although a small minority came directly to Canada, particularly when the economy of Canada was attractive. Many worked on the Canadian Pacific Railway, and later in the lumber and manufacturing industries. In 1908 a community hall was built and the name Nuorison was again applied. Neither of the structures existed at the time of the naming application, and most of the early residents of the area were of Finnish descent It was therefore felt that if the creek carried this name, the history of the area would be aptly commemorated.

Oakley Lake (lake)

83 I/15 - Grassland
18-67-18-W4
54°47′00″N 112°44′45″W
Approximately 36 km east north-east of Athabasca.

The name for this lake has been official since at least 1958, but its precise origin is unknown.

Obed Lake (lake)

83 F/11 - Dalehurst
11-53-22-W5
53°34′N 117°08′W
Approximately 48 km east of Edson.

This lake was officially named in 1967 and takes its name from its proximity to Obed. The locality was named after Lieutenant-Colonel John Obed Smith (1864-1937), a Briton who came to Canada as a young man. He served the Manitoba Government until 1901 when he began his career serving on various commissions for emigration.

Oberlin (locality)

83 A/7 - Stettler
23-38-21-W4
52°17′N 112°54′W
Approximately 12 km south-west of Stettler.

_____
*denotes rescinded name or former locality.

A Canadian Northern Railway station was established here in 1914 and was likely named after Oberlin, a community in Ohio noted for Oberlin College, the first coeducational college in the United States.

Observation Hill (hill)

73 D/10 - Hughenden
32-42-6-W4
52°39′N 110°50′W
Approximately 20 km south of the town of Wainwright.

The name for this hill has been in use since at least 1958 and is likely descriptive.

Octopus Lake (lake)

83 F/10 - Bickerdike
36-52-19-W5
53°32′N 116°40′W
Approximately 19 km west south-west of Edson.

The name for this lake has been official since at least 1958, and is likely descriptive of its shape, as the feature has many bays and outlets.

Ohaton (hamlet)

83 A/15 - Ferintosh
14-46-19-W4
52°59′N 112°40′W
Approximately 13 km east south-east of Camrose.

The name for this hamlet, whose post office opened in September 1906, is a combination of the names Osler, Hammond & Nanton of a prominent Winnipeg financial firm.

Okanes Lake (lake)

73 E/2 - Grizzly Bear Creek
33-48-6-W4
53°11′N 110°49′W
Approximately 19 km south of Vermilion.

The name for this lake has been official since at least 1958, but its precise origin is unknown.

Okwanim Creek (creek)

73 D/5 - Alliance
20-39-14-W4
52°22′N 111°59′W
Flows north-east into Paintearth Creek, approximately 49 km north-west of Coronation.

The name for this creek has been in use since at least 1958, but its origin is unknown.

Old Canoe Island (island)

73 L/12 - Beaver Lake
23-66-13-W4
54°44′N 111°51′W
Approximately 9 km south-east of Lac La Biche.

The name for this island in Beaver Lake has been official since at least 1958, but its precise origin is unknown.

Oldman Creek (creek)

83 H/11 - Edmonton
13-53-23-W4
53°34′15″N 113°15′15″W
Flows north into North Saskatchewan River, approximately 21 km north north-east of Edmonton.

The name for this creek may possibly have reference to a local name, "Old Man's Knoll," over which passed the trail from Edmonton to Fort Garry. This trail runs on the south side of the North Saskatchewan River.

Oldman Lake (lake)

72 M/11 - Youngstown
32-31-10-W4
51°42′N 111°23′W
Approximately 41 km east north-east of Hanna.

The precise origin for the name of this feature is unknown.

Olds (town)

82 O/16 - Olds
32-32-1-W5
51°47′35″N 114°07′00″W
Approximately 58 km south south-west of Red Deer.

This town, whose post office opened in April 1892, has experienced a number of name changes in considering an official name. Early names reflected various stages of development and area history. First it was known as "Lone Pine" because of the Lone Pine stopping place on the Edmonton trail just north-east of the present town. It was then called "Sixth Siding," reflecting the period of railroad construction, and the next name, "Hay City," gave a clue to the new and important trade in feed and cattle when Pat Burns discovered the good grazing lands to the east and south-east for his first ranching operations. David Shannon declined to accept the honour of having the town named "Shannon," and those responsible for finding a name finally settled on another Canadian Pacific Railway official, George Olds, and at last, the place had a name. This town was incorporated 1 July 1905.

Olds Creek (creek)

82 O/16 - Olds
34-33-2-W5
51°53′N 114°12′W
Flows north into Little Red Deer River, approximately 23 km north north-west of Olds.

(see Olds)

Oliva Lake (lake)

73 E/4 - Viking
30-47-11-W4
53°04′N 111°36′W
Approximately 13 km east of Viking.

The name for this lake has been official since at least 1958, but its precise origin is unknown.

Oliver (railway point)

83 H/11 - Edmonton
5-54-23-W4
53°38′N 113°22′W
Approximately 14 km north-east of Edmonton.

This locality is now a subdivision of Edmonton and was named in 1905 after the Honourable Frank Oliver (1853-1933), Commissioner of the Board of Railway Commissioners from 1923 to 1928. He was Minister of the Interior in the Laurier Cabinet from 1905 through 1911. Oliver was elected to the Northwest Territories Legislature in 1888 and after serving eight years in that assembly, was elected to the House of Commons. He was the publisher of the *Edmonton Bulletin* from 1880 to 1923.

Oliver Lake (lake)

83 H/6 - Cooking Lake
9-50-21-W4
53°18′N 113°01′W
Approximately 41 km south-east of Edmonton.

The origin for the name of this lake is unknown.

Olson Ridge (ridge)

82 O/10 - Fallentimber Creek
32-29-7-W5
51°32′N 114°54′W
Approximately 40 km south-west of Sundre.

This ridge takes its name from one of the early settlers to the area. Mr. Olson was a highly respected oldtimer in the Water Valley region. He lived in a small cabin beside the Little Red Deer River and entertained hundreds of people yearly with his stories of hunting, fishing, trapping and prospecting. His sawmills provided much of the lumber for the buildings in the area.

Olympic Lake (lake)

73 L/12 - Beaver Lake
12-64-14-W4
54°31′N 111°59′W
Approximately 27 km south of Lac La Biche.

The name for this lake has been official since at least 1958, but its precise origin is unknown. It is locally referred to as "Island Lake."

Onion Lake (lake)

73 E/16 - Frog Lake
19-55-1-W4
53°46′N 110°09′W
Approximately 52 km east south-east of Elk Point.

The name for this lake has been official since at least 1958, but its precise origin is unknown.

Onoway (village)

83 G/9 - Onoway
35-54-2-W5
53°42′20″N 114°11′10″W
Approximately 50 km west north-west of Edmonton.

The post office opened here in May 1904 with W.P. Beaupre as the first postmaster. The post office was originally to be called "Beaupre," but this name was a duplicate. *Beaupre* is roughly translated as "good, rich, sweet or lush meadow." The name *Onoway* is a native Chipewyan term for "fair field," and was therefore adopted. A second version of the origin of the name is that it was taken from the poem "Hiawatha" in which the Indian singer began the lines of a canto with the exclamation "Onaway," which in English means "awake." The original spelling was changed to Onoway, probably in error. This village was incorporated 25 June 1923.

Opal (hamlet)

83 H/14 - Redwater
9-58-22-W4
53°59′N 113°14′W
Approximately 50 km north north-east of Edmonton.

It is not clear how this hamlet received its name, but apparently it was a selected name. The post office opened in November 1912.

Open Creek (creek)

83 B/10 - Carlos
31-42-6-W5
52°37′N 114°44′W
Flows north into Medicine River, approximately 21 km west of Rimbey.

The name for this creek has been official since at least 1958, but its precise origin is unknown.

* Orbindale (former locality)

73 E/3 - Buffalo Creek
16-47-8-W4
53°03′N 111°08′W
Approximately 29 km north-west of Wainwright.

The name for this former locality, whose post office operated from December 1907 through June 1938, is a combination of the names of the first two white babies born in the district, Orbin and Dale.

---

*denotes rescinded name or former locality.

Ord Lake (lake)

83 H/3 - Bittern Lake
23-49-24-W4
53°14′N 113°23′W
Approximately 11 km east south-east of
Leduc.

The name for this lake has been official
since at least 1958, but its precise origin is
unknown.

Orkney Hill (hill)

82 P/10 - Munson
4-30-21-W4
51°32′15″N 112°53′45″W
Approximately 30 km south-east of Three
Hills.

This hill is named after the Orkney District
which is named after the Orkney School
District established in June 1912. The use of
the name Orkney reflects the Scottish
homeland of eight of the original settlers
who took up homesteads in the area around
1903. The name Orkney Hill has been in
local usage since the establishment of the
original school district.

Osborne Creek (creek)

73 L/7 - Bonnyville
35-63-7-W4
54°29′N 110°57′W
Flows south into Manatoken Lake, approximately 27 km north-west of
Bonnyville.

The name for this creek was officially
approved 2 June 1950, but its precise origin
is unknown.

Osborne Lake (lake)

73 L/7 - Bonnyville
5-64-6-W4
54°30′30″N 110°53′00″W
Approximately 28 km north north-west of
Bonnyville.

The name for this lake was officially
approved 17 January 1951, but its precise
origin is unknown.

Oster Lake (lake)

83 H/10 - Elk Island Park
32-53-20-W4
53°38′N 112°54′W
Approximately 42 km east north-east of
Edmonton.

The name for this lake has been official
since at least 1958. It was named after the
Osters, a Swedish family who homesteaded
on its shores. They were remembered by all
as being a lot of fun. When the park was
bought by the government, the Osters were
not willing to leave their land, and were
eventually given the responsibility of
tending the entrance gate.

Otway (locality)

83 B/7 - Rocky Mountain House
15-39-7-W5
52°22′N 114°55′W
Immediately south-east of Rocky Mountain
House.

This former station was named after
Thomas Otway (1652-1685), an English
dramatist.

Outlet Lake (lake)

73 L/12 - Beaver Lake
21-66-13-W4
54°43′N 111°55′W
Approximately 7 km south-east of Lac La
Biche.

The descriptive name for this lake has
appeared on maps since at least 1918 and
refers to its location at the outlet of Beaver
Lake.

Outline Lake (lake)

73 L/12 - Beaver Lake
31-65-12-W4
54°40′N 111°48′W
Approximately 14 km south-east of Lac La
Biche.

The name for this lake has been official
since at least 1958, but its precise origin is
unknown.

Owen Lake (lake)

83 H/7 - Tofield
29-50-20-W4
53°20′N 112°53′W
Approximately 16 km west south-west of
Tofield.

The name for this lake has been official
since at least 1958, but its precise origin is
unknown.

Owl River (locality)

73 L/13 - Lac La Biche
14-68-13-W4
54°53′N 111°53′W
Approximately 17 km north north-east of
Lac La Biche.

A post office operated here from July 1935
through December 1943 and was named for
its proximity to Owl River. (see Owl River)

Owl River (river)

73 L/13 - Lac La Biche
19-68-13-W4
From 55°00′00″N 111°52′03″W
to 55°13′04″N 111°30′00″W
Flows south into Lac La Biche, approximately 16 km north of Lac La Biche.

The name for this river is a translation from
the Cree *oohoo seepee*, and is likely descriptive. The French equivalent is "la Rivière au
Hibou."

Owlseye (locality)

73 L/3 - Vincent Lake
4-59-10-W4
54°04′N 111°26′W
Approximately 12 km north-west of St.
Paul.

Previously known as "Owlseye Lake," the
name for this locality was shortened to
Owlseye 6 July 1950. (see Owlseye Lake)

* **Owlseye Lake** (former post office)

73 L/3 - Vincent Lake
4-59-10-W4
54°04′N 111°26′W
Approximately 12 km north-west of St.
Paul.

A post office operated here from May 1913
through November 1971 and took its name
from the nearby lake. The name for the
locality was later shortened to Owlseye.
(see Owlseye Lake)

Owlseye Lake (lake)

73 L/3 - Vincent Lake
35-58-10-W4
54°03′N 111°22′W
Approximately 9 km north-west of St. Paul.

The legend attached to this lake maintains
that its name commemorates a hunter so
nicknamed who was killed by Indians here.

Oxbow Lake (lake)

83 H/10 - Elk Island Park
30-53-20-W4
53°36′N 112°57′W
Approximately 41 km east of Edmonton.

The name for this lake has been official
since at least 1958, but its precise origin is
unknown.

Oxville (locality)

73 D/16 - McLaughlin
10-46-2-W4
52°57′N 110°13′W
Approximately 38 km south south-west of
Lloydminster.

The post office here operated here from
May 1907 through July 1931 and was
named in commemoration of the early
settlers who arrived by ox-drawn wagons.

Oxyoke Lake (lake)

83 A/2 - Big Valley
3,4-37-20-W4
52°09′N 112°48′W
West of Marion Lake, approximately 55 km
east south-east of Red Deer.

The name for this lake which has been
official since at least 1958 is possibly
descriptive of its shape.

---

*denotes rescinded name or former locality.

P~Q~R

■ **Paddle River** (river)

83 J/1 - Barrhead
16-59-2-W5
54°05′00″N 114°14′45″W
Flows east into Pembina River, approximately 11 km east of Barrhead.

This river is mentioned in Edward Ermatinger's York Factory Express Journal of 1827. An entry by James Hector, dated 15 January 1859, mentions the river on his way from Edmonton to Jasper. It is a translation of the Cree name *aby sipi*, possibly applied because a canoe could be propelled on it upstream by use of the paddle alone, in comparison to the swifter Pembina River where recourse had to be made to the pole and track line.

Paddle River Dam (dam)

83 G/14 - Mayerthorpe
18-1-57-8-W5
53°53′30″N 115°04′00″W
Approximately 8 km south-east of Mayerthorpe.

The name for this dam was officially approved 23 June 1981 and is taken for its location on the Paddle River. (see Paddle River)

Paddy Creek (creek)

83 G/3 - Blue Rapids
19-49-10-W5
53°08′N 115°22′W
Flows south-east into Pembina River, approximately 17 km south-west of Drayton Valley.

The name for this creek has been official since at least 1958, but its precise origin is unknown.

Padstow (locality)

83 G/14 - Mayerthorpe
14-56-8-W5
53°50′N 115°05′W

Approximately 14 km south-east of Mayerthorpe.

The name for this locality, whose post office operated from October 1911 through May 1951, is taken after a town of the same name in Cornwall, England.

Paintearth County #18 (county)

73 D/4 - Castor
35 to 39-9 to 16-W4
52°10′N 111°35′W
East of Red Deer.

(see Paintearth Creek)

Paintearth Creek (creek)

73 D/5 - Alliance
25-39-14-W4
52°24′N 111°49′W
Flows east into Battle River, approximately 43 km north-west of Coronation.

The fact that this creek is actually historically Paintearth Creek is in dispute. It is referred to as Vermilion Creek by James Hector. The Paintearth Creek that was mentioned by him is now known as Castor Creek. The name Paintearth is derived from the red ochre abundant in the area and used by natives to paint their faces. The name has been in use since at least 1965. The county takes its name from this creek.

Pakan (locality)

83 I/1 - Smoky Lake
12-58-17-W4
54°01′N 112°24′W
Approximately 13 km south of Smoky Lake.

This locality commemorates a Cree Indian chief at Whitefish Reserve, known as James Seenum in the Indian Department records. Pakan is his native name, and translates as "the nut" in English. The post office operated from June 1887 through September 1960 and was previously called "Victoria," after Queen Victoria, suggested by the Rev. George McDougall, who chose the place as the site of a Methodist mission in 1862. The name was changed to Pakan to avoid duplication.

Pakan Creek (creek)

73 E/13 - Hairy Hill
2-58-11-W4
53°59′N 111°32′W
Flows west into Saddlelake Creek, approximately 23 km west of St. Paul.

(see Pakan)

Pakan Lake (lake)

73 E/13 - Hairy Hill
23-57-11-W4
53°56′N 111°32′W
Approximately 15 km west south-west of St. Paul.

(see Pakan)

Pakkwaw Lake (lake)

83 A/4 - Innisfail
15-36-27-W4
52°06′N 113°47′W
Approximately 13 km north-east of Innisfail.

The lake was named by the Cree Indians. The word *pakkwaw* is the Cree equivalent for "dry" or "shallow" which describes the lake's dry, sloughy appearance.

Papineau Hill (hill)

83 A/6 - Alix
18-40-23-W4
52°26′30″N 113°18′30″W

Approximately 27 km south-west of Bashaw.

This hill was named after the William Papineau family, who in settled near the hill circa 1918.

Park Court (locality)

83 G/10 - Isle Lake
3-55-7-W5
53°43′N 114°58′W
Approximately 31 km south south-east of Mayerthorpe.

An early resident, Mrs. N. Bigland, was reminded of an English park when she looked at the surrounding countryside, and suggested the name for the post office, which operated here from October 1910 through June 1955.

Parkland Beach (summer village)

83 B/9 - Rimbey
NE-10-42-1-W5
52°36′30″N 114°03′30″W
Approximately 13 km east south-east of Rimbey.

This collection of subdivisions was formed into the Summer Village of Parkland Beach effective 1 January 1984, under the Municipal Government Act, Order-in-Council No. 687/83. The name is likely descriptive of its location on the north-west shore of Gull Lake.

Parkland County #31 (county)

83 G/8 - Genesee
51-53-1-10-W5
53°25′N 114°30′W
West of Edmonton.

The name for this county is descriptive of the surrounding landscape.

Parlby Creek (creek)

83 A/6 - Alix
16-40-23-W4
52°27′N 113°14′W
Flows east into Mirror Bay, approximately 15 km south south-west of Bashaw.

The names for the creek and lake appear as early as 1894 where they are found on the Red Deer Sectional Map No. 215, 2nd edition, and on the plan of the township 18 May 1894. There was some discussion as to whether the lake and creek were named for Irene (Marryat) Parlby (1868-1965), the first woman cabinet minister in Alberta; however, she did not arrive in the area until 1897. The names Walter C.H. Parlby and Edward M.H. Parlby are indicated on a plan of Township 40, Range 23, 18 May 1894, 1st edition, south of Parlby Lake and Parlby Creek. According to notes by an early surveyor, John McAree, in 1893, they were named after an early settler. Another one of the general cards housed within the Geographical Names Programme notes that the creek and lake were named after Messrs. Parlby of Lamerton.

Parlby Lake (lake)

83 A/6 - Alix
15-40-23-W4
52°26′N 113°13′W
Approximately 25 km south-west of Bashaw.

(see Parlby Creek)

Parsons Lake (lake)

73 D/15 - Wainwright
35-43-6-W4
52°45′15″N 110°46′15″W
Approximately 17 km south-east of the town of Wainwright.

The name for this lake has been in use since at least 1958, but its precise origin is unknown.

Parting Lake (lake)

83 J/2 - Thunder Lake
22-58-6-W5
54°02′N 114°49′W
Approximately 24 km east north-east of Mayerthorpe.

The name for this lake was officially approved 16 January 1958, but its precise origin is unknown.

Partridge Lake (lake)

83 J/8 - Shoal Creek
3-63-2-W5
54°25′N 114°13′W
Approximately 37 km north north-east of Barrhead.

The name for this lake has been official since at least 1958, but its precise origin is unknown.

* Partridge Hill (former locality)

83 H/11 - Edmonton
7-54-21-W4
53°40′N 113°06′W
Approximately 28 km east north-east of Edmonton.

A post office operated here from October 1904 through December 1912. The name was taken after the school district which was founded in 1894, but it is not clear who proposed it. One account maintains that it was named by C.E. Flintoff, an early settler who was standing on a low hill with some friends when a flock of partridges flew up. Another account states that it was named by Albert Peebles, one of the first homesteaders in the area.

Pasatchaw Lakes (lake)

73 E/9 - Marwayne
29-52-1-W4
53°31′N 110°07′W
Approximately 27 km north north-west of Lloydminster.

The name for this lake was officially approved 26 June 1911, but its precise origin is unknown.

Patenaude, Lac (lake)

73 E/9 - Elkwater Lake
16-55-1-W4
53°44′N 110°05′W
Approximately 57 km east south-east of Elk Point.

The name for this lake has been official since at least 1958, but its precise origin is unknown.

Paterson Lake (lake)

73 E/16 - Frog Lake
30-55-3-W4
53°47′N 110°27′W
Approximately 33 km south-east of Elk Point.

The name for this lake was officially approved 21 May 1942, but its precise origin is unknown.

Pathfinder (locality)

73 E/11 - Myrnam
10-53-8-W4
53°33′N 111°07′W
Approximately 30 km north-west of Vermilion.

The name for this former locality, whose post office operated from October 1914 through December 1947, is descriptive of the function of early settlers. The name was officially rescinded 14 January 1970.

* Patience (former locality)

83 H/4 - Kavanagh
17-47-26-W4
53°03′N 113°45′W
Approximately 29 km west north-west of Wetaskiwin.

*denotes rescinded name or former locality.

A post office operated here from November 1903 through December 1952. The name was established in 1902 because it required patience of the early settlers to open and close twenty-three gates along the rough road in the vicinity. The first postmaster and storekeeper was A.L. Dickens, and he named the settlement.

Patricia Hill (hill)

73 D/10 - Hughenden
19-42-5-W4
52°38′N 110°41′W
Approximately 26 km south south-east of the town of Wainwright.

The name for this hill has been in use since at least 1958, but its precise origin is unknown.

Paul Lake (lake)

83 H/10 - Elk Island Park
4-54-20-W4
53°38′N 112°54′W
Approximately 39 km east of Edmonton.

The name for this lake has been official since at least 1958. It was named for John Paul, an early homesteader who arrived in the area circa 1906.

Paxson (locality)

83 I/11 - Athabasca
6-66-20-W4
54°41′00″N 113°00′15″W
Approximately 18 km east of Athabasca.

The name for this locality, whose post office operated from May 1913 through April 1969, commemorates a former employee of G. Schaffer, the first postmaster.

Peace Hills (hills)

83 A/14 - Wetaskiwin
28-46-24-W4
52°59′N 113°26′W

Approximately 3 km north-west of Wetaskiwin.

The name for these hills is a translation of the Cree Indian name *wi-ta-ski-oocha-ka-tin-ow*. The Cree and Blackfoot made peace here circa 1867, and the event was commemorated by a monument which was erected in 1927. Alexander Henry the younger, fur trader and explorer, on his map dated 1 October 1810, labelled the hills "Grosses Buttes."

Peanut Lake (lake)

83 J/1 - Barrhead
15-58-3-W5
54°01′N 114°21′W
Approximately 12 km south of Barrhead.

The well-established name for this lake was officially approved 16 January 1976 and is descriptive of the feature's shape.

Pear Lake (lake)

83 I/11 - Athabasca
36-65-22-W4
54°40′N 113°12′W
Approximately 8 km south-east of Athabasca.

The name for this lake has been official since at least 1958 and is likely descriptive of its shape.

Pearl Lake (lake)

82 P/16 - Farrell Lake
29-32-15-W4
51°46′N 112°06′W
Approximately 18 km north-west of Hanna.

The name for this lake has been official since 1958, but its precise origin is unknown.

Pearson Lake (lake)
73 E/6 - Mannville
16-50-10-W4
53°19′N 111°24′W
Approximately 36 km north-east of Viking.

The name for this lake has been official since at least 1958, but its precise origin is unknown.

* Peat (former locality)
73 E/15 - Elk Point
34-55-7-W4
53°48′N 110°57′W
Approximately 12 km south south-west of Elk Point.

The name for this former locality, whose post office operated from December 1915 through November 1955, is an error for Peet. John Peet was the first postmaster, and the original intention was to name the post office after him. The name was officially rescinded in April 1970.

Peavey (locality)
83 H/13 - Morinville
34-56-25-W4
53°53′N 113°38′W
Approximately 38 km north of Edmonton.

The origin of the name of this locality is unknown.

Peavine (locality)
83 J/2 - Thunder Lake
1-59-7-W5
54°05′N 114°55′W
Approximately 21 km north-east of Mayerthorpe.

The post office operated here from June 1908 through October 1967 and was named

for the number of peavines that grew in the area. The Purple Wild Vine, a native legume, is a perennial wildflower common throughout the wooded areas of Alberta, and noticeable particularly in July.

Peers (hamlet)
83 G/12 - Carrot Creek
16-54-14-W5
53°40′N 115°59′W
Approximately 30 km east of Edson.

The Grand Trunk Pacific Railway established a station here in 1911. The name for this hamlet, whose post office opened in December 1912, is taken after the family name of Marion Peers, mother of Sir Charles Peers Davidson (1841-1929), Chief Justice of the Superior Court of Quebec from 1912 to 1915. He was the author of *Statutes Relating to Banks and Banking*, published in 1876.

Pekse Creek (creek)
82 O/15 - Sundre
23-34-6-W5
51°56′N 114°45′W
Flows south-east into James River, approximately 18 km north north-west of Sundre.

This creek may be named for Fred Pekse or Karl Pekse, early homesteaders originally from Latvia, who owned land through which this creek flows. Both men and their families arrived in the James River area in 1910.

Peleck Lakes (lakes)
73 L/4 - Cache Lake
20-58-13-W4
54°01′N 111°54′W
Approximately 37 km north north-west of Two Hills.

The name for these lakes was officially approved 6 April 1950, but its precise origin is unknown.

Pelican Island (island)
73 L/13 - Lac La Biche
36-67-14-W4
54°51′N 111°59′W
Approximately 10 km north of Lac La Biche.

The name for this island in Lac La Biche, as are other features around the province with the same name, is taken after the white pelican (*Pelecanus erythrorhynchos*). Although this bird was once very common, its numbers have diminished significantly since Alexander Mackenzie passed through the area in 1789, and made mention of the species.

Pelican Lake (lake)
73 D/16 - McLaughlin
20-45-3-W4
52°53′N 110°24′W
Approximately 30 km east north-east of the town of Wainwright.

The name for this lake has been in use since at least 1958, but its precise origin is unknown.

Pelican Point (point)
83 A/10 - Donalda
16-41-20-W4
52°31′25″N 112°49′30″W
Approximately 12 km south-east of Bashaw.

The well-established name for this point was officially approved 19 February 1979. Arlen Adams, the Reeve for the County of Camrose, along with other local residents of the Bashaw area, requested that the name be officially recognized. G. Stedel, a resident of the Bashaw area since 1900, said that this name had been in use for the feature since at least the 1930s. He stated that the descriptive name refers to the pelicans frequently seen in the shallow water off this point.

Pembina (locality)

83 G/3 - Blue Rapids
18-48-8-W5
53°08′N 115°09′W
Approximately 15 km south south-west of
Drayton Valley.

The post office operated here from July
1934 through May 1954 and was named for
its proximity to the Pembina River. (see
Pembina River)

* **Pembina Crossing** (former locality)

83 G/16 - Lac la Nonne
10-58-3-W5
53°59′N 114°21′W
Approximately 15 km south of Barrhead.

The name for this locality was changed to
Belvedere in 1905. (see Belvedere)

Pembina Heights (locality)

83 J/1 - Barrhead
24-60-2-W5
54°12′30″N 114°09′00″W
Approximately 18 km north-east of
Barrhead.

A post office operated here, on the banks of
the Pembina River, from March 1961
through October 1967. (see Pembina River)

■ **Pembina River** (river)

83 J/9 - Flatbush
29-66-2-W5
54°44′45″N 114°17′00″W
Flows west into Athabasca River, approximately 64 km west of Athabasca.

The name for this river dates back to at
least 1810 when David Thompson noted:
"We went ten miles in this distance...we
crossed the Pembinaw (Pembina) River of

forty yards in width and shoal...." The term
is a corruption of the Cree name
neepinmenan, roughly "summer berry."
The other features take their names from
this river.

Pembina River (near Edson), n.d.

Pembina River Provincial Park

(provincial park)

83 G/10 - Isle Lake
29-53-7-W5
53°36′N 114°59′W
Approximately 40 km south of
Mayerthorpe.

This 165.41 hectare (408.76 acre) park was
created by Order-in-Council No. 1712/72
and was named for its location on the
Pembina River. (see Pembina River)

Pembridge (locality)

83 G/15 - Sangudo
10-57-5-W5
53°54′N 114°40′W
Approximately 32 km south-east of
Mayerthorpe.

The name for the post office, which
operated here from February 1939 through
September 1970, is a combination of the
terms Pembina (from the river) and bridge.

Pemburton Hill (locality)

83 G/8 - Genesee
20-50-2-W5
53°20′N 114°15′W
Approximately 57 km south-west of
Edmonton.

The name for this locality, whose post
office operated from June 1913 through
March 1937, commemorates its postmaster,
C. Burton. The prefix "Pem" was added to
distinguish this post office from
Burtonsville.

Pemukan (locality)

72 M/16 - Grassy Island Lake
1-35-4-W4
51°58′N 110°27′W
Approximately 43 km south of Provost.

The name for this former Canadian Pacific
Railway station is the Cree word for
"across the water."

Penhold, 1904

Penhold (town)

83 A/4 - Innisfail
36-36-28-W4
52°08′10″N 113°52′50″W
Approximately 15 km south of Red Deer.

The name for this town, originally proposed as "Essexville," was chosen when the Calgary-Edmonton rail line was built. One of the railway officials accidentally dropped his pen, and the nib stuck in a map. The name for the town, incorporated 1 September 1980, became Penhold.

Peninsula, The (peninsula)

83 A/10 - Donalda
15,22-41-20-W4
52°32'30"N 112°48'00"W
Approximately 13 km south-east of Bashaw.

The name for this feature in Buffalo Lake has been in use since at least 1905 and is descriptive.

Peninsula Lake (lake)

73 D/14 - Irma
11-45-11-W4
52°51'N 111°29'W
Approximately 17 km north-east of Sedgewick.

The name for this lake has been in use since at least 1958, but its precise origin is unknown. It is also known locally as "Pendleton's Lake," after a homesteader, Henry Fay Pendleton.

Pennington Lake (lake)

83 A/4 - Innisfail
34-36-28-W4
52°08'N 113°55'W
Approximately 18 km south south-west of Red Deer.

This lake was named in 1919 after the Pennington family who lived beside it for many years and who were pioneers in the Penhold area.

* **Peno** (former locality)

83 H/15 - Lamont
13-57-18-W4
53°55'N 112°41'W
Approximately 25 km south south-west of Smoky Lake.

A post office operated here from September 1909 through April 1961, but the origin for the name is unknown.

Peno Creek (creek)

83 H/15 - Lamont
13-57-19-W4
53°56'N 112°41'W
Flows north-east into North Saskatchewan River, approximately 16 km south south-west of Smoky Lake.

The name for this creek was officially approved in 1958. (see Peno)

Peno Lake (lake)

83 H/15 - Lamont
24-57-19-W4
53°56'N 112°43'W
Approximately 24 km south south-west of Smoky Lake.

The name for this lake was officially approved in 1958. (see Peno)

Perbeck (locality)

82 P/14 - Trochu
5-34-22-W4
51°58'N 113°06'W
Approximately 17 km north-east of Trochu.

The post office, which operated here from May 1908 through November 1944, was named by the first postmaster, George Hibbs, after his birthplace, the Isle of Purbeck, Dorset, England. The Post Office Department changed the spelling.

Percy Lake (lake)

73 E/3 - Buffalo Creek
4-49-10-W4
53°12'N 111°24'W
Approximately 29 km east north-east of Viking.

The precise origin of the name of this feature is unknown.

Percy Lake (lake)

72 M/16 - Grassy Island Lake
18-34-3-W4
51°55'N 110°26'W
Approximately 48 km south south-west of Provost.

The precise origin for the name of this feature is unknown.

Perryvale (hamlet)

83 I/6 - Perryvale
22-63-23-W4
54°28'N 113°23'W
Approximately 30 km south-west of Athabasca.

The name for this hamlet, whose post office opened in August 1913, is a combination the name of one of the first postmasters (Perry) and the fact that it was in a valley (vale). It was once locally known as "Lewiston" after T. Lewis, the first postmaster.

Peterson Lake (lake)

73 D/10 - Hughenden
34-42-6-W4
52°39'N 110°46'W
Approximately 21 km south south-east of the town of Wainwright.

The name for this lake has been in use since at least 1958, but its origin is unknown.

Peterson Pond (pond)
73 D/15 - Wainwright
1-14-44-7-W4
52°47'N 110°54'W
Approximately 6 km south-west of
Wainwright.

The name for this water feature has been
official since at least 1958, but its precise
origin is unknown.

Philips (locality)
73 E/4 - Viking
12-47-12-W4
53°03'N 111°38'W
Approximately 14 km south-east of Viking.

The Grand Trunk Pacific Railway established a station here in 1909 and named it
after Henry Philips, secretary of the
railway. The post office, previously known
as "Lake Thomas," operated here from
February 1910 through January 1944.

* Phoenix (former locality)
83 B/6 - Crimson Lake
30-39-10-W5
52°23'N 115°25'W
Approximately 35 km west of Rocky
Mountain House.

The post office here operated from November 1923 through April 1933, closing
because of "limited usefulness." The name
is taken from the city in Arizona. Phoenix
was a station on the Canadian Northern
Railway's Brazeau branch, which served
Brazeau Collieries Ltd. at Nordegg. These
coal mines were closed in 1956.

Phyllis Lake (lake)
83 B/2 - Caroline
17-36-7-W5
52°06'N 114°58'W

Approximately 32 km south of Rocky
Mountain House.

The lake was officially named 30 March
1977, after Phyllis Vincey, the daughter of
George R. Vincey who came to the district
in 1911. Mr. Vincey operated a general
store at Ricinus for a short time, then
homesteaded in the area. Phyllis was the
first white child to visit the lake.

Pibroch (hamlet)
83 I/5 - Dapp
5-61-26-W4
54°16'N 113°52'W
Approximately 12 km west of Westlock.

This hamlet was established as a village in
1910 and a municipal district in 1912 and is
apparently named after a Scottish settlement which in turn was named for bagpipe
music. The post office operated from May
1910 through December 1981. The railway
station was formerly known as "Debney"
after Philip Debney, one of the engineers.

Pickardville (hamlet)
83 I/4 - Westlock
36-58-27-W4
54°03'N 113°53'W
Approximately 10 km south of Westlock.

The name for this hamlet, whose post office
opened in October 1907, is taken after its
first postmaster, William Pickard. The
spelling was originally "Picardville."
However, it was officially changed to its
present name 27 December 1966.

Pigeon Hills (hills)
83 G/1 - Warburg
23-47-1-W5
53°04'N 114°04'W
Approximately 44 km west north-west of
Wetaskiwin.

These hills, formerly known as "Woodpecker Hills," are named for their proximity to Pigeon Lake. The Cree name is *hmi-
hmoo*, and in Stoney the name is rendered
ka-ka-gamma. The Blackfoot call the hills
nommo, according to the Report of the
Geological Survey for 1882-4. (see Pigeon
Lake)

Pigeon Lake (lake)
83 G/1 - Warburg
4-47-1-W5
53°01'N 114°02'W
Approximately 45 km west of Wetaskiwin.

The name for this lake has been in use since
1858 when Hector recorded it in his
journal. It was known previously as
"Woodpecker Lake," a translation from the
Cree *hmi-hmoo sa-kha-higan*. The Stoney
equivalent is *ke-gemni-wap-ta*. The nearby
hills were also known as "Woodpecker
Hills." All the other features take their
names from this lake.

Pigeon Lake Creek (creek)
83 A/13 - Bearhills Lake
15-46-28-W4
52°53'N 113°55'W
Flows south into Battle River, approximately 32 km north-east of Rimbey.

The Stoney Indians had their own name for
this creek and Pigeon Lake, *ke-gemni-wap-
ta*; the Cree name, *hmihmoo sa-kha-higan
sipisis* roughly translated to "Woodpecker
Lake Creek" according to Tyrrell.

Pigeon Lake Indian Reserve #138A
(Indian reserve)
83 A/13 - Bearhills Lake
23-46-28-W4
52°59'N 113°57'W
Approximately 39 km west of Wetaskiwin.

(see Pigeon Lake)

---

*denotes rescinded name or former locality.

Pigeon Lake Provincial Park
(provincial park)
83 G/1 - Warburg
6-47-1-W5
53°01′N 114°08′W
Approximately 34 km south south-west of
Calmar.

The name for this 249 hectare (615.30 acre)
park, created by Order-in-Council No.
849/76, is taken after its location on Pigeon
Lake. (see Pigeon Lake)

Pikes Lake (lake)
73 D/4 - Castor
27-35-12-W4
52°02′N 111°37′W
Approximately 15 km south-west of
Coronation.

The name for this lake has been in use since
at least 1958, but its origin is unknown.

Pilot Bluff (hill)
83 A/7 - Stettler
29-40-19-W4
52°28′N 112°43′W
Approximately 12 km north of Stettler.

The name for this feature has been in use
since at least 1893 when it was described as
a navigational point. Because of the thick
crown of poplar on its crest, it could be
seen for a distance of approximately 24
kilometres from the south-east and about
nine to eleven kilometres in other direc-
tions. It is locally known as "Pilot Knob."

Pine Creek (creek)
83 K/2 - Marsh Head Creek
14-25-59-18-W5
54°08′N 116°35′W
Flows north into Athabasca River, approximately 57 km west of Whitecourt.

The name for this creek has been official
since at least 1958 and is likely descriptive.

Pine Creek (creek)
83 I/15 - Grassland
3-69-17-W4
From 54°45′00″N 112°53′40″W
to 54°56′39″N 112°30′42″W
Flows east into La Biche River, approximately 40 km north-west of Lac La Biche.

The name for this creek has been official
since at least 1958 and is likely descriptive.

Pine Island (island)
83 H/10 - Elk Island Park
2-23-54-20-W4
53°40′15″N 112°50′15″W
Approximately 40 km east of Edmonton, in
Elk Island National Park.

The name for this island in Astotin Lake
was officially approved 17 October 1991
and is likely descriptive.

Pine Lake (lake)
83 A/3 - Delburne
13-36-25-W4
52°06′N 113°27′W
Approximately 30 km south-east of Red
Deer.

The name for this feature is a shortened
form for Ghostpine Lake. The story goes
that an Indian battle took place there and
since then the natives believe the lake and
area to be haunted by the ghosts of the
fallen Indians. At night their souls howl
through the pine trees like the wind. The
creek still bears the original name. (see
Ghostpine Creek)

Pine Lake (hamlet)
83 A/3 - Delburne
22-36-25-W4
52°07′N 113°29′W

Approximately 28 km south-east of Red
Deer.

The post office opened at this hamlet in
December 1895, and was named for its
location on Pine Lake. (see Pine Lake) It
was originally on Ghost Pine Lake. (see
Ghost Pine Lake)

Pine Lake (lake)
83 I/11 - Athabasca
27-64-21-W4
54°34′N 113°05′W
Approximately 15 km south-east of
Athabasca.

The name for this lake, official since 1958, is
likely descriptive.

Pinedale (hamlet)
83 F/9 - Edson
22-53-15-W5
53°36′N 116°36′W
Approximately 22 km east of Edson.

A post office operated here from March
1931 through December 1943. Its precise
origin is unknown.

Pinehurst Lake (lake)
73 L/11 - Pinehurst Lake
27-65-10-W4
54°39′N 111°25′W
Approximately 38 km east south-east of
Lac La Biche.

The name for this lake has been established
since at least 1915 and may refer to the
great pressure-ridge which runs all the way
along the northwest shore of the lake and
may be the highest and longest such ridge
in the district. The Cree refer to the lake as
pusakan sagahegan: puskan means "punk"
which was needed in starting a fire with
flint and steel and might consist of either
poplar wood or birch. It is drained by Punk
Creek.

Pioneer (locality)

83 F/16 - Shiningbank Lake
23-55-15-W5
53°46′N 116°08′W
Approximately 28 km north-east of Edson.

A post office operated here from March 1925 through June 1969 and the name was descriptive of the people. It was previously known as "Mussel."

Piper Creek (creek)

83 A/5 - Red Deer
9-38-27-W4
52°15′15″N 113°48′15″W
Flows north-west into Waskasoo Creek, within the city limits of Red Deer.

This creek is named after Frank Elvin Piper (1873-1963), who lived in the area for many years. He came to Red Deer in 1891, settled there and opened a brick plant, which operated from 1892 to 1914. After World War I work began in the plant again; it was not successful and ended in the 1920s. Mr. Piper worked in the northern part of Alberta for a time but returned in 1950 to Red Deer, where he lived for the rest of his life.

Pipestone (hamlet)

83 H/4 - Kavanagh
18-47-26-W4
53°03′N 113°47′W
Approximately 30 km west north-west of Wetaskiwin.

The precise origin of the name of this hamlet is unknown.

Pipestone Creek (creek)

83 A/14 - Wetaskiwin
25-46-23-W4
52°59′N 113°13′W

Flows south-east into Battle River, approximately 14 km east of Wetaskiwin.

The precise origin for the name of this feature is unknown.

* Plain Lake (former post office)

73 E/12 - Two Hills
15-53-12-W4
53°34′N 111°42′W
Approximately 14 km south south-east of Two Hills.

The post office operated here from June 1910 through November 1958. The name was officially rescinded 14 January 1970. (see Plain Lake)

Plain Lake (lake)

73 E/12 - Two Hills
27-53-12-W4
53°36′N 111°42′W
Approximately 12 km south south-east of Two Hills.

The descriptive name for this lake refers to its position between two plains. The former post office took its name from its proximity to this lake.

Plamondon (village)

83 I/16 - Plamondon
35-67-16-W4
54°50′55″N 112°20′20″W
Approximately 25 km west north-west of Lac La Biche.

The name for this village, incorporated 1 January 1965, was taken after Joseph Plamondon (1861-1923), the first postmaster. The first Plamondons came to Canada from France in 1671 and settled in Quebec. Joseph arrived in this area to homestead in 1908. The settlement was originally called "Plamondonville" but was later shortened to Plamondon when the post office opened in May 1909.

Plamondon Creek (creek)

83 I/16 - Plamondon
1-19-67-16-W4
From 54°52′33″N 112°17′56″W
to 54°46′07″N 112°17′56″W
Flows east into Lac La Biche, approximately 25 km north-west of Lac La Biche.

(see Plamondon)

Plante Lake (lake)

83 I/11 - Athabasca
2-64-21-W4
54°30′10″N 113°04′00″W
Approximately 27 km south south-east of Athabasca.

The name for this lake has been official since at least 1958, but its precise origin is unknown.

Plover Lake (lake)

73 E/8 - Lloydminster
35-49-3-W4
53°16′N 110°19′W
Approximately 28 km west south-west of Lloydminster.

The name for this lake has been official since 21 May 1940, but its precise origin is unknown.

Plum Lake (lake)

83 I/11 - Athabasca
25-64,65-21-W4
54°34′30″N 113°03′00″W
Approximately 23 km south-east of Athabasca.

The name for this lake has been official since at least 1958, but its precise origin is unknown.

Plunger Lake (lake)

83 J/2 - Thunder Lake
28-60-6-W5
54°13′N 114°50′W

Approximately 30 km west north-west of Barrhead.

The name for this lake was officially adopted 16 January 1958, but its precise origin is unknown.

Poe (locality)
83 H/8 - Ryley
30-49-16-W4
53°16'N 112°20'W
Approximately 27 km south-east of Tofield.

The Grand Trunk Pacific Railway established a station here in 1909 and named it after Edgar Allan Poe (1809-1849), the American writer, literary critic, and essayist. The post office operated at this site from February 1912 through February 1964.

Point Alison (summer village)
83 G/9 - Onoway
2-53-4-W5
53°33'N 114°29'W
Approximately 63 km west of Edmonton.

The precise origin for the name of this summer village, incorporated 31 December 1950, is unknown.

Point Thirteen (point)
83 A/10 - Donalda
12-41-21-W4
52°31'00"N 112°53'35"W
Approximately 8 km south south-east of Bashaw.

The well-established name for this point has been in use since at least 1920 and was officially approved. The point of land extending into Buffalo Lake has been locally known as Point Thirteen since 1920, when extensive cottage development occurred here. The name originated from

the fact that the point extends into the lake from Section 13.

Pointe-aux-Pins Creek (creek)
83 H/11 - Edmonton
36-53-23-W4
53°38'00"N 113°15'15"W
Flows north-west into North Saskatchewan River, approximately 20 km north north-east of Edmonton.

The name for this creek is the French for the abundance of pine trees in the area.

Poison Creek (creek)
83 G/11 - Chip Lake
36-54-11-W5
53°43'N 115°29'W
Flows south-east into Chip Lake, approximately 36 km south south-west of Mayerthorpe.

The name for this creek has been in use since at least 1910 when A.P. Coleman noted: "Even Poison Creek, in its lovely and peaceful surroundings, we drank from without harm, if without enthusiasm...." The name likely describes its muddy appearance.

Poitras, Lac (lake)
73 E/13 - Hairy Hill
24-56-11-W4
53°51'00"N 111°30'30"W
Approximately 20 km south-west of St. Paul.

The name for this lake has been official since at least 1958, but its precise origin is unknown. According to the *Cummins Rural Directory*, circa 1920, there was a J. Poitras who owned the land near the lake.

Polly Lake (lake)
72 M/9 - Esther
7-31-1-W4
51°38'N 110°08'W

Approximately 40 km north north-east of Oyen.

The precise origin for the name of this feature is unknown.

Ponoka (town)
83 A/12 - Ponoka
4-43-25-W4
52°40'35"N 113°35'00"W
Approximately 37 km south south-west of Wetaskiwin.

Originally this railway siding was known as "Siding 14" when the railway extended to it in 1891. Apparently several of the early settlers wanted it named "Yescabba," but the name finally chosen was Ponoka, a corruption of *Ponokaii*, the Blackfoot word for elk. The town was incorporated on 15 October 1904. A post office opened in May 1897.

Ponoka County #3 (county)
83 A/12 - Ponoka
42-44-22-5-W4&5
52°40'N 113°50'W
West south-west of Wetaskiwin.

(see Ponoka)

Poplar Bay (summer village)
83 G/1 - Warburg
32-46-1-W5
53°00'05"N 114°06'00"W
Approximately 50 km west of Wetaskiwin.

This summer village was incorporated 1 January 1967. The request for a name for this community was made by J.G. Trudel in 1965 on behalf of the local residents. The submission included three preferences – "West Cove," "West Bay" and "Poplar Bay."

Poplar Creek (creek)
83 G/1 - Warburg
25-46-3-W5
53°00'15"N 114°17'30"W

Flows north-west into Bucklake Creek, approximately 19 km east of Drayton Valley.

The name for this creek, although wrongfully applied to Modeste Creek until 1977, has been in official use since at least 1958, and is descriptive of the many poplar trees in the area.

Porter Lake (lake)

73 D/16 - McLaughlin
13-44-3-W4
52°47'N 110°18'W
Approximately 38 km east of Wainwright.

The name for this lake has been in use since at least 1958, but its origin is unknown.

Porters Butte (hill)

82 P/11 - Three Hills
3-30-23-W4
51°32'30"N 113°10'30"W
Approximately 20 km south south-east of Three Hills.

This butte received its name from the original homesteaders on whose property it stands. The Porter family originally came from Quebec and moved onto the land in 1910. The two Porter brothers, Thomas and Robert, homesteaded on adjacent sections.

Posthill Lake (lake)

83 A/2 - Big Valley
35-37-21-W4
52°13'N 112°53'W
Approximately 60 km east of Red Deer.

The lake was named for Bill Posthill and his family who established a haying camp by the lake in the 1890s.

Potter Creek (creek)

83 B/9 - Rimbey
23-42-3-W5
52°38'45"N 114°17'30"W

Flows north-east into Boyd Creek, approximately 2 km west of Rimbey.

This creek was officially named 7 February 1983 after Dr. Potter who settled by the creek circa 1904. Potter Creek School District was also named after Dr. Potter. The school was 6.5 kilometres west and 1.6 kilometres south of Rimbey. Dr. Potter remained in the area for only a few years.

POW Hill (hill)

73 D/15 - Wainwright
1-25-44-7-W4
52°48'55"N 110°52'30"W
Approximately 5 km south-west of the town of Wainwright.

During World War I, 17,000 German soldiers were held as prisoners of war at what was then called Camp Wainwright. This hill overlooks the site of the former POW camp.

Powder Lake (lake)

83 I/16 - Plamondon
9-35-66-17-W4
54°45'15"N 112°27'00"W
Approximately 32 km west of Lac La Biche.

The name for this lake has been official since at least 1958 and commemorates a family of Métis living in the meadow on its north-east shore in the 1930s. The Powders were originally a branch of the Decouin family, nicknamed "Kaskites." This was translated into the French "Le Poudre," and in time into the English "Powder." The lake is sometimes referred to as "Island Lake." J. C. Rudman, the original owner of the land around the lake, refused to allow the lake to be named after himself, so the name Powder Lake was made official. Many local people still refer to the feature as "Rudman Lake."

Prairie Creek (creek)

83 B/7 - Rocky Mountain House
9-38-7-W5
52°15'15"N 114°57'15"W
Flows north into Clearwater River, approximately 5 km south of Rocky Mountain House.

The name for this creek was labelled "Prairie River" on Arrowsmith's map of 1859. The Cree name for the watercourse is *maskuta*. The Stoney call it *tin-dow-wap-ta*.

Prairie Lake (lake)

73 E/16 - Frog Lake
11-56-1-W4
53°50'N 110°02'W
Approximately 60 km east of Elk Point.

The name for this lake has been official since at least 1958 and is likely descriptive of the surrounding area.

Prefontaine Lake (lake)

83 G/15 - Sangudo
32-55-6-W5
53°48'N 114°51'W
Approximately 26 km south-east of Mayerthorpe.

This name appears on a township map dated 1907, but its origin is unknown. There is a notation that says the local name is "Berry Island Lake." The descriptive name refers to the two small islands in the lake where berries were found.

Prentice Creek (creek)

83 B/7 - Rocky Mountain House
18-40-7-W5
52°26'30"N 114°59'30"W
Flows north-east into North Saskatchewan River, approximately 10 km north north-west of Rocky Mountain House.

The name for this creek dates from 1865 when it appears on the Palliser map of the expedition of 1857-60. Its precise origin is unknown.

Prentiss (locality)

83 A/5 - Red Deer
24-39-26-W4
52°22′N 113°38′W
Approximately 17 km north-west of Red Deer.

The Canadian Northern Railway established a station here in 1914. The precise origin is unknown; however, there is a place near Jackson, Mississippi, which has the same name.

Pretty Hill (hill)

83 H/2 - Camrose
32-47-20-W4
53°05′N 112°54′W
Approximately 10 km north north-west of Camrose.

The descriptive name for this hill is a rough translation of the Cree name *ka-mi-wa-sit-is-pa-tin-ow.*

Prevo (locality)

83 B/8 - Sylvan Lake
1-39-1-W4
52°20′N 114°01′W
Approximately 13 km west of Red Deer.

The Canadian Northern Railway established a station here about 1914 and called it "Norma." The name was changed to Prevo some time before 1928. According to Canadian National Railways records, "Prevo" might have been the phonetic spelling of the French surname Prevost, but its origin is unclear.

Price Creek (creek)

83 I/11 - Athabasca
16-65-23-W4
54°38′N 113°26′W
Flows north-west into Muskeg Creek, approximately 13 km south-west of Athabasca.

This creek drains Price Lake, and its name has been official since at least 1958. (see Price Lake)

Price Lake (lake)

83 I/11 - Athabasca
17-64-23-W4
54°32′N 113°26′W
Approximately 22 km south south-west of Athabasca.

The name for this lake has been official since at least 1958, but its precise origin is unknown.

* Primrose (former post office)

73 E/15 - Elk Point
10-57-4-W4
53°56′N 110°32′W
Approximately 24 km east of Elk Point.

The name for the post office, which operated here from August 1930 through March 1965, was taken after the flower. The primrose, or "first rose" bears pale yellowish flowers in early spring and grows wild in woods, in hedges and on banks. The name was officially rescinded 22 April 1970.

Primrose Lake (lake)

73 L/16 - Medley River
13-67-1-W4
54°48′N 110°01′W
Approximately 40 km north north-east of Cold Lake, mostly in Saskatchewan.

This lake on the Alberta-Saskatchewan boundary was surveyed on 19 April 1909,

Primrose Day, the anniversary of the death of Benjamin Disraeli, Earl of Beaconsfield (1804-1881), Prime Minister of Great Britain in 1865 and again from 1874 to 1880. The name was officially adopted 17 January 1951.

* Primula (former locality)

73 E/15 - Elk Point
4-56-5-W4
53°48′N 110°40′W
Approximately 17 km south-east of Elk Point.

The post office, which operated here from December 1913 through March 1965, was likely named after the flower of the same name, more familiarly known as the "field daisy." The name was officially rescinded 22 April 1970.

Prospect Hill (hill)

83 A/6 - Alix
13-40-23-W4
52°26′30″N 113°10′30″W
Approximately 22 km south-west of Bashaw.

The well-established name was officially approved 5 May 1983. It was originally named by James Gadsby, who applied the descriptive name for the fine view of Buffalo Lake from its summit.

Prospect Valley (locality)

73 D/16 - McLaughlin
6-45-2-W4
52°51′N 110°17′W
Approximately 40 km east of the town of Wainwright.

The name for the post office, which operated here from June 1910 through April 1930, reflected the thoughts and hopes of its early settlers for prosperity.

* **Prosperity** (former locality)

83 I/15 - Grassland
30,19-67-19-W4
54°49'N 112°53'W
Approximately 29 km east north-east of
Athabasca.

A post office operated here from October
1930 through April 1969 and was named by
the early settlers to express their high hopes
for the future wealth of the community.
The name was officially rescinded in 1970.

Provost (town)

73 D/8 - Provost
17-39-2-W4
52°21'20"N 110°16'00"W
Approximately 105 km south south-west of
Lloydminster.

The Canadian Pacific Railway established a
station here in the fall of 1907, and the post
office followed in March 1908. The term
Provost is the title applied to the Chief
Magistrate of a Scottish town and is the
equivalent of Mayor in Canada. Many of
the streets in the town are named after
Scottish urban centres. Apparently, the site
was initially called "Lakeview" because
Fleeing Horse Lake was within sight. The
name Provost was applied by the C.P.R.
Land Department in the fall of 1907. This
town was incorporated 29 December 1952.

Provost Municipal District #52

(municipal district)

73 D/7 - Czar
36 to 42-1 to 9-W4
52°25'N 110°40'W
South south-west of Lloydminster.

(see Provost)

Pruden Lake (lake)

73 L/12 - Beaver Lake
13-16-65-13-W4
54°38'42"N 111°55'03"W
Approximately 16 km south of Lac La
Biche.

The name for this lake dates from at least
1918 and likely commemorates an early fur
trader, Pat Pruden, a Métis who was
involved in the 1885 Rebellion. Mr.
Pruden's trading post was on section 31-65-
13-W4.

Pullar Lake (lake)

73 L/11 - Pinehurst Lake
18-66-9-W4
54°43'N 111°22'W
Approximately 40 km east of Lac La Biche.

The name for this lake was officially
applied in 1951 and commemorates Flight
Lieutenant W.S. Pullar, D.F.C. (1918-1944),
of Delia, who was killed in World War II.
The local name for the feature is "Crooked
Lake."

Punk Creek (creek)

73 L/11 - Pinehurst Lake
23-64-9-W4
54°33'N 111°14'W
Flows south-east into Sand River, approximately 43 km north-west of Bonnyville.

The name for this creek, which flows out of
Pinehurst Lake, has been official since 17
February 1951. (see Touchwood Lake)

Puskiakiwenin Indian Reserve #122

(Indian reserve)

73 E/15 - Elk Point
27-57-4-W4
53°57'N 110°31'W
Approximately 33 km east of Elk Point.

This Indian reserve was named after a chief
notorious for his love of gambling.

* **Quarrel** (former locality)

83 A/16 - Daysland
22-46-16-W4
52°59'N 112°15'W
Approximately 13 km north of Daysland.

The name for the post office, which
operated here from May 1905 through
April 1928, was taken from its proximity to
a lake which is now dry. The lake was a
camping place for early natives where there
were many quarrels among hunting parties.
The Cree name is *kekatomoki
chewonepekah*, which translates as "quarrel
spring lake."

Queenie Creek (creek)

73 E/10 - Clandonald
14-53-7-W4
53°34'N 110°55'W
Flows north-west into Slawa Creek,
approximately 30 km south of Elk Point.

The name for this creek has been official
since at least 1958, but its precise origin is
unknown.

Queensdale Place (locality)

83 H/11 - Edmonton
15-53-22-W4
53°35'N 113°10'W
Approximately 25 km north-east of
Edmonton.

The precise origin for the name of this
country residence subdivision is unknown.

Qui Barre, Rivière (river)

83 H/12 - St. Albert
36-54-27-W4
53°44'N 113°53'W
Flows south into Sturgeon River, approximately 28 km north-west of Edmonton.

The name for this river has been in use
since at least 1880. The Cree name for it is
ma-ta-hi-to-si-pi-sis. The French name is

descriptive and was given by lumbermen who could not use the river for driving logs.

Radford's Hill (hill)

82 O/9 - Didsbury
15-32-2-W5
51°44′50″N 114°12′00″W
Approximately 7 km south-west of Olds.

This hill is named after the Radford family, early homesteaders of the area. Charles Radford came to the Didsbury area from Nebraska in 1900 and his family soon followed. His son Preston, one of seven children, later bought a half-section north-west of his father's (E1/2-16-32-2-W5). By 1970, Preston and a sister, Margaret, were the only children still living. Preston's son, Boyd, now runs his father's farm, but the Radfords no longer own the original homestead.

Radial Lake (lake)

83 B/6 - Crimson Lake
21-40-9-W5
52°28′N 115°13′W
Approximately 22 km west north-west of Rocky Mountain House.

The name for this lake has been official since at least 1958, but its precise origin is unknown.

Radway (village)

83 I/2 - Waskatenau
32-58-20-W4
54°03′35″N 112°56′55″W
Approximately 15 km north north-east of Redwater.

The name for this village, whose post office opened in June 1910, commemorates Orland S. Radway, the first postmaster and storekeeper in the district, who arrived in 1909. His father settled here in 1897. The name "Radway Centre" was the original

proposal, but the shortened form was ultimately adopted. This village was incorporated 7 July 1943.

Raft Lake (lake)

73 E/10 - Clandonald
5-54-5-W4
53°38′N 110°43′W
Approximately 33 km south south-east of Elk Point.

The name for this lake has been official since at least 1958, but its precise origin is unknown.

Rainy Creek (creek)

83 B/8 - Sylvan Lake
33-40-2-W5
52°29′N 114°14′W
Flows south-east into Blindman River, approximately 22 km north-west of Red Deer.

The name for this creek has been official since at least 1958, but its precise origin is unknown.

Rainy Lake (lake)

73 D/15 - Wainwright
4-44-6-W4
52°45′N 110°48′W
Approximately 10 km south south-east of the town of Wainwright.

The name for this lake has been in use since at least 1958, but its precise origin is unknown.

Ranch (locality)

83 P/4 - Pelican
27-70-26-W4
55°05′N 113°53′W
Approximately 55 km north-west of Athabasca.

A post office operated here from July 1935 through April 1956 and has a descriptive

name. Orval Hayes owned a large herd of cattle; as he was the only postmaster, the locality was named to reflect his herd.

Ranfurly (hamlet)

73 E/5 - Innisfree
15-51-12-W4
53°25′N 111°41′W
Approximately 27 km east south-east of Vegreville.

The Canadian Northern Railway established a station here in 1905 and named it after Sir Uchter John Mark Knox (1856-1933), 5th Earl of Ranfurly, Governor of New Zealand from 1897 to 1904. The post office opened in September 1906.

Rangeton (locality)

83 G/14 - Mayerthorpe
13-55-8-W5
53°45′N 115°03′W
Approximately 23 km south-east of Mayerthorpe.

A post office operated here from December 1930 through September 1967 and its name describes the surrounding cattle country.

Raspberry Island (island)

83 H/10 - Elk Island Park
10-23-54-20-W4
53°40′55″N 112°50′10″W
Approximately 40 km east of Edmonton, in Elk Island National Park.

The name for this island in Astotin Lake was officially approved 17 October 1991. It was requested by the Canadian Parks Service for navigational purposes within the park. There is little settlement around the park and all local usage appears to ensue from the wardens who use the names on their own maps. The request was forwarded by the Canadian Permanent Committee on Geographical Names in order that the names would appear on the new NTS map sheets being produced for the area.

Raspberry Lake (lake)

72 M/11 - Youngstown
16-32-10-W6
51°44'N 111°23'W
Approximately 40 km east north-east of
Hanna.

The precise origin for the name of this
feature is unknown, but it may be descriptive due to a proliferation of raspberry
bushes in the area.

* **Rat Lake** (former post office)

73 L/7 - Bonnyville
14-63-4-W4
54°27'N 110°30'W
Approximately 20 km west of Cold Lake.

A post office operated here from December
1926 through September 1958 and was
named after the muskrat. The name was
officially rescinded in 1971.

Raven (locality)

83 B/1 - Markerville
15-36-4-W5
52°05'15"N 114°29'00"W
Approximately 44 km south-east of Rocky
Mountain House.

A post office operated here from February
1905 through August 1970 and took its
name from the fact that the North and
South branches of the Raven River traverse
the municipal district and join here. (see
Raven River)

Raven River (river)

83 B/1 - Markerville
15-346-4-W5
52°06'N 114°29'W
Flows south-east into Red Deer River,
approximately 47 km south-west of Red
Deer.

---

*denotes rescinded name or former locality.

The name for this river has been in use
since at least 1916 and is a translation of the
Cree name *ka-ka-koo*. The Stoney term is
rendered *kai-him-bu-wap-ta*.

Ravine (locality)

83 G/11 - Chip Lake
19-54-9-W5
53°41'N 115°20'W
Approximately 34 km south south-west of
Mayerthorpe.

The name for this locality, whose post
office operated from September 1911
through March 1932 and then reopened
from March 1935 through November 1952,
is descriptive. The original site for the post
office was in a ravine.

Ravine Lake (lake)

73 E/1 - Paradise Valley
3-49-3-W4
53°12'N 110°20'W
Approximately 25 km west south-west of
Lloydminster.

The name for this lake has been official
since at least 1958 and is likely descriptive.

Red Deer (city)

83 A/5 - Red Deer
21-38-27-W4
52°16'15"N 113°48'17"W
Approximately 135 km south of Edmonton.

The city of Red Deer takes its name from
the Red Deer River, which flows through
it. The name is a translation of the Indian
name, *was-ka-sioo* in Cree, meaning "Elk
River," and *pa-chi-ci* in Stoney (Tyrrell).
The river received its name due to the
numerous elk in the area in early days,
mistaken by the Scottish factors for the red
deer of their homeland. For a number of

years the Calgary-Edmonton trail crossed
the river at a point known as Red Deer
Crossing and, with the coming of the
Canadian Pacific Railway to Calgary, traffic
over the trail increased and a trading post
and stopping place were established. The
present city owes its location to a combination of circumstances whereby Rev.
Leonard Gaetz (1841-1907) gave some
1,240 acres of land to the Canadian Pacific's
Calgary and Edmonton Railway for a
townsite. With the coming of the railway
the former Red Deer Crossing came to an
end. This city was incorporated 25 March
1913.

Red Deer, 54th St., looking west, 1913

Red Deer County #23 (county)

83 A/4 - Penhold
34 to 39-21 to 28-W4
and 34 to 39-1 to 4-W5
52°05'N 113°50'W
South of Red Deer.

(see Red Deer)

Red Deer Junction (locality)

83 A/5 - Red Deer
15-39-27-W4
52°21'N 113°46'W
Approximately 8 km north of Red Deer.

(see Red Deer)

Red Deer Lake (lake)

83 A/10 - Bashaw
4-43-21-W4
52°40′N 112°59′W
Approximately 34 km south-east of
Wetaskiwin.

(see Red Deer)

Red Fox Island (island)

73 L/13 - Lac La Biche
17-68-13-W4
54°54′N 111°56′W
Approximately 13 km north of Lac La
Biche.

The name for this island in Lac La Biche
was officially adopted 5 March 1951 and is
likely taken after the animal.

Red Lake (lake)

73 E/9 - Marwayne
32-54-1-W4
53°43′N 110°07′W
Approximately 48 km north north-west of
Lloydminster.

The name for this lake has been official
since at least 1958, but its precise origin is
unknown.

* Red Lodge (former locality)

82 O/16 - Olds
2-34-2-W5
51°57′N 114°13′W
Approximately 12 km north north-west of
Olds.

A post office operated here from April 1896
through August 1933 and took its name
from the name of the ranch of the second
postmaster, Colin Thompson. The name
for his ranch was due to its proximity to the
Red Deer River.

Red Lodge Provincial Park

(provincial park)

82 O/16 - Olds
29-34-2-W5
51°56′30″N 114°14′45″W
Approximately 23 km south-west of
Innisfail.

The park is on land once owned by Thomas
Critchley, who arrived in the area from
England with his wife in 1894. He had been
a captain in the British Army. With the help
of neighbours he built an imposing sixteen-
room log house named Red Deer Lodge. It
is said that the front was painted red. In
1896, a post office was opened by Mr.
Critchley. Later, the Critchleys sold the
property and left the district. Shortly after
this the house was destroyed by fire;
however, the post office had already been
moved and was named Red Lodge. There is
another story that attributes the name to a
ranch in the area called the Red Lodge
Ranch. (see Red Lodge)

Red Willow (hamlet)

83 A/7 - Stettler
19-40-18-W4
52°27′N 112°34′W
Approximately 17 km north-east of Stettler.

The original placement of this hamlet was
approximately 6 kilometres east of its
present site; it was moved to the current
location when the Canadian Northern
Railway's Battle River branch was established. It is thought, by a former resident of
the hamlet, that it was named in 1902 or
1903 for the red willows growing in the
area. The post office was established in
August 1903, operated until July 1912, and
reopened under the name Red Willow in
March 1915. Between these dates the post
office was called "Coralynn."

Red Willow Creek (creek)

83 A/9 - Forestburg
25-41-18-W4
52°33′N 112°28′W
Flows north-east into Meeting Creek,
approximately 35 km east of Bashaw.

(see Red Willow)

Redclay Creek (creek)

83 I/1 - Smoky Lake
29-58-14-W4
54°02′N 112°03′W
Flows east into North Saskatchewan River,
approximately 21 km east south-east of
Smoky Lake.

The name for this creek has been official
since at least 1958 and is likely descriptive.

Redspring Creek (creek)

73 L/1 - Reita Lake
22-59-1-W4
54°06′N 110°04′W
Flows north-east out of Redspring Lake
into Saskatchewan, approximately 24 km
south-east of Grand Centre.

The name for this creek has been official
since at least 1958. (see Redspring Lake)

Redspring Lake (lake)

73 L/1 - Reita Lake
16-59-1-W4
54°06′N 110°05′W
Approximately 34 km south south-east of
Grand Centre.

The name for this lake has been official
since at least 1958 and may be descriptive.

Redwater (town)

83 H/14 - Redwater
30-57-21-W4
53°57′00″N 113°06′50″W
Approximately 45 km north north-east of
Edmonton.

---

*denotes rescinded name or former locality.

This town was named for its proximity to the Redwater River, a tributary of the North Saskatchewan River. Originally this river appeared as "Vermilion River" on David Thompson's map of 1814, but the change was made to avoid duplication. The beds of ochre near the riverbed give the water a distinctive colour. The post office opened in December 1909. This town was incorporated 31 December 1950.

Redwater River (river)

83 H/15 - Lamont
1-57-21-W4
53°54'N 112°59'W
Flows south-east into North Saskatchewan River, approximately 52 km north-east of Edmonton.

(see Redwater)

Reed Lake (lake)

73 L/4 - Cache Lake
4-61-12-W4
54°14'N 111°44'W
Approximately 42 km north-west of St. Paul.

The descriptive name for this lake was officially adopted 28 July 1945 and refers to the large number of reeds and reedbeds detached from the mainland and submerged in the lake.

Reflex Lakes (lakes)

73 D/9 - Chauvin
36-42-1-W4
52°40'N 110°01'W
Approximately 40 km north north-east of Provost, on the Alberta-Saskatchewan boundary.

The name was suggested by F.D. Henderson in January 1918 because one part of the lake mirrored the other. Since there are now two lakes, it was recommended by Mr. A.I. Bereskin, in January 1965, that the plural name for two lakes be approved, and it was officially adopted February 1965.

Reid Lake (lake)

83 J/9 - Flatbush
34-64-2-W5
54°34'N 114°13'W
Approximately 51 km north north-east of Barrhead.

This name appears on Sectional Map No. 364 published in 1948. The precise origin for the name is unknown.

Reilly Lake (lake)

73 E/8 - Lloydminster
12-24-52-1-W4
53°29'00"N 110°00'15"W
Approximately 22 km north of Lloydminster, on the Alberta-Saskatchewan boundary.

The name for this lake appeared on Sectional Map No. 316 published in 1928, but no origin information was provided.

Reita Creek (creek)

73 L/8 - Cold Lake
4-62-2-W4
52°19'15"N 110°14'00"W
Flows north-east into Beaver River, approximately 6 km south of Grand Centre.

(see Reita Lake)

Reita Lake (lake)

73 L/1 - Reita Lake
32-59-3-W4
54°08'N 110°25'W
Approximately 25 km south-east of Bonnyville.

(see Elinor Lake)

* Ribstone (former post office)

73 D/9 - Chauvin
24-43-3-W4
52°43'N 110°20'W
Approximately 34 km east south-east of the town of Wainwright.

The post office was named Ribstone in May 1907, but was changed in 1914 to Dunn. (see Dunn)

Ribstone (hamlet)

73 D/9 - Chauvin
17-43-2-W4
52°42'00"N 110°15'30"W
Approximately 44 km south-west of the town of Wainwright.

The name for this hamlet is likely due to its proximity to Ribstone Creek. A post office opened here in April 1914. (see Ribstone Creek)

Ribstone Creek (creek)

73 D/16 - McLaughlin
33-43-2-W4
52°45'15"N 110°14'00"W
Flows north-east into Battle River, approximately 46 km south of Lloydminster.

The name for this stream has been in use since 1865, when it appeared on Captain Palliser's map (see Beaverdam Creek). According to Tyrrell, it is a rough translation of the Cree *as-sin-i-kos-pike-gan-it*. A large stone nearby bears marks resembling a man's ribs.

Ribstone Lake (lake)

73 D/15 - Wainwright
3-44-5-W4
52°46'N 110°39'W
Approximately 18 km east south-east of the town of Wainwright.

(see Ribstone Creek)

---

*denotes rescinded name or former locality.

Rice's Coulee (coulee)
82 O/16 - Olds
13-31-32-2-W5
51°47'35"N 114°17'00"W
Approximately 11 km west of Olds.

This feature was named for the William Rice family who moved to the hill overlooking the coulee from the north (Rice's Hill) in 1908. There were seven children in the family: Henry, George, Milton, Tillie, Alta, Phoebe and Lilly. Another daughter and son died very young. The name was officially adopted 16 October 1991.

Rice's Hill (hill)
82 O/16 - Olds
13-35-32-3-W5
51°47'00"N 114°17'30"W
Approximately 11 km west of Olds.

The name for this hill was officially approved 16 October 1991. (see Rice's Coulee)

Rich Lake (locality)
73 L/12 - Beaver Lake
5-64-11-W4
54°30'N 111°37'W
Approximately 37 km south-east of Lac La Biche.

A post office operated here from December 1932 through September 1982 and was named for its proximity to Rich Lake. (see Rich Lake)

Rich Lake (lake)
73 L/12 - Beaver Lake
8-14-64-11-W4
54°32'10"N 111°32'46"W
Approximately 38 km south-east of Lac La Biche.

The descriptive name for this lake refers to the number of muskrats in it. It is a translation from the Cree *sonyaw*.

Rich Valley (hamlet)
83 G/16 - Lac la Nonne
22-56-3-W5
53°51'N 114°21'W
Approximately 30 km south of Barrhead.

The post office at this hamlet, operated from June 1907 through April 1968, was previously known as "Onion Prairie." The name Rich Valley was drawn from a hat and was suggested by the daughter of the first postmaster, E. Carlin. The name describes the quality of the crops in the area.

Richdale (hamlet)
72 M/12 - Hanna
34-30-12-W4
51°37'N 111°36'W
Approximately 23 km east of Hanna.

The descriptive name for this hamlet refers to the quality of the soil at the time of its naming in 1910. The post office operated until July 1973.

Richmond Lake (lake)
83 J/2 - Thunder Lake
31-58-4-W5
54°03'30"N 114°35'00"W
Approximately 15 km south-west of Barrhead.

The name for this lake was proposed by the Barrhead and District Historical Society in honour of Thomas Richmond and family, early settlers from England, who homesteaded the land adjoining the lake circa 1908. The name was officially approved 6 March 1986.

Ricinus (locality)
83 B/2 - Caroline
9-36-7-W5
52°05'N 114°57'W
Approximately 33 km south of Rocky Mountain House.

A post office operated here from August 1913 through October 1968 and has the name of the Latin term for the castor-oil plant.

Ridgeclough (locality)
73 D/16 - McLaughlin
2-46-1-W4
52°56'N 110°02'W
Approximately 32 km south of Lloydminster.

The first postmaster, W.B. Gordon, came from a farm in Ontario with the same name. The post office operated from April 1912 through November 1931. There is a place in Scotland of the same name.

Riel (hamlet)
73 E/15 - Elk Point
4-56-4-W4
53°49'00"N 110°31'30"W
Approximately 25 km east south-east of Elk Point.

This hamlet was named after Louis Riel, the Métis leader hanged at Regina in 1885 for treason for his part in the rebellion that year.

Rife (locality)
73 L/3 - Vincent Lake
17-60-7-W4
54°10'N 111°00'W
Approximately 20 km south-west of Bonnyville.

The name for this locality, whose post office operated from April 1910 through February 1969, was supplied by the Post Office Department. Rife is also the name of a district in England.

Rifles Ridge (ridge)
73 D/10 - Hughenden
22-42-6-W4
52°38'N 110°46'W

Approximately 23 km south of the town of Wainwright.

The name for this ridge was submitted by Major B.M. Lilley in 1954. The name was changed to Rifles Ridge in 1981, as it was named after a regiment, The Queen's Own Rifles of Canada. The ridge is in the Wainwright Regional Training Area.

Rimbey (town)
83 B/9 - Rimbey
28-42-2-W5
52°40'55"N 114°14'00"W
Approximately 48 km north-east of Red Deer.

This town, incorporated 13 December 1948, was named after three brothers, Sam, Ben, and Jim Rimbey, who were settlers. Jim was the first postmaster. Before 1903, the settlement was known as "Kansas Ridge," as many of the first homesteaders hailed from Kansas.

Ring Lake (lake)
83 I/11 - Athabasca
30-64-23-W4
54°34'N 113°29'W
Approximately 20 km south south east of Athabasca.

The name for this lake has been official since at least 1958, but its precise origin is unknown.

Rishaug Lake (lake)
82 P/10 - Munson
10-32-20-W4
51°43'00"N 112°45'30"W
Approximately 35 km east of Three Hills.

The name for this lake has been official since 1958, but its origin is unknown.

----
*denotes rescinded name or former locality.

Riverbend (railway point)
83 H/11 - Edmonton
15-54-23-W4
53°40'N 113°18'W
Approximately 28 km north north-east of Edmonton.

The Canadian Northern Railway established a station here in 1912 and gave it its descriptive name, which refers to the bend in the North Saskatchewan River nearby.

Rivercourse (hamlet)
73 E/1 - Paradise Valley
34-46-1-W4
53°01'N 110°03'W
Approximately 29 km south of Lloydminster.

The name for this hamlet, whose post office opened in June 1907, is descriptive of its proximity to the Blackfoot Coulee.

* Riverton (former locality)
73 E/9 - Marwayne
17-54-3-W4
53°39'N 110°25'W
Approximately 41 km south-east of Elk Point.

The name for the post office, which operated here from February 1914 through May 1939, was taken after School District #2128, established 24 February 1910. The Department of Education chose the name Riverton for the School District for its proximity to the Vermilion River.

Riverview (hamlet)
73 E/15 - Elk Point
23-56-5-W4
53°52'N 110°39'W
Approximately 20 km east south-east of Elk Point.

The name of this hamlet is for the view of the North Saskatchewan River.

Rivière Qui Barre (hamlet)
83 H/13 - Morinville
30-55-26-W4
53°47'N 113°52'W
Approximately 12 km west south west of Morinville.

The name for this hamlet, whose post office opened in August 1895, is taken from its proximity to the river, which was descriptively named by lumbermen. The water level in the river was very shallow, and it was therefore impossible for the lumbermen to drive their logs on it.

Robb Lake (lake)
72 M/14 - Kirkpatrick Lake
34-34-10-W4
51°58'N 111°21'W
Approximately 17 km south south-east of Coronation.

The precise origin for the name of this feature is unknown.

Robinson (locality)
83 G/15 - Sangudo
34-56-7-W5
53°53'N 114°58'W
Approximately 15 km south-east of Mayerthorpe.

The name for this Canadian Northern Railway station was officially approved 13 March 1947, but its precise origin is unknown.

Rochester (hamlet)
83 I/6 - Perryvale
24-62-24-W4
54°22'N 113°27'W
Approximately 30 km north north-east of Westlock.

The name for this hamlet, whose post office opened in September 1913, was taken after Herbert Rochester, secretary to Malcolm

H. MacLeod, general manager and chief engineer of the Canadian Northern Railway. In 1912 the Canadian Northern built a railway to Athabasca Landing from Edmonton and a townsite was laid out to which the name "Ideal Flat" was applied. This was unacceptable to the residents, and the name was then changed to Rochester.

Rochfort Bridge (hamlet)

83 G/14 - Mayerthorpe
7-57-7-W5
53°55′N 115°02′W
Approximately 10 km south-east of Mayerthorpe.

The name for this hamlet, whose post office was previously called "Wanekville," is taken after Cooper Rochfort who came to the area in 1905. He, with his partner Percy Michaelson, hoped to hold large tracts of land for ranching. They also had an interest in some mining ventures. The bridge spanning the Paddle River is 800 metres east of the hamlet.

Rochon Sands (summer village)

83 A/7 - Stettler
19-40-20-W4
52°27′14″N 112°52′49″W
Approximately 17 km north-west of Stettler.

This summer village and the nearby provincial park were named for the Daniel Rochon family, early homesteaders in the area. Mr. Rochon operated a livery barn where the settlement is located. According to one source, the place was at one time known as "New Switzerland." This summer village was incorporated 17 May 1929.

Rochon Sands Provincial Park

(provincial park)

83 A/7 - Stettler
24-40-21-W4
52°27′30″N 112°53′15″W

Approximately 20 km north-west of Stettler.

This 116.08 hectare (286.85 acre) provincial park was established by Order-in-Council No. 573/79, and was named for its proximity to Rochon Sands. (see Rochon Sands)

Rock Island Lake (lake)

73 E/16 - Frog Lake
18-56-1-W4
53°50′N 110°07′W
Approximately 52 km east of Elk Point.

The name for this lake was officially approved 21 May 1942 and is likely descriptive.

Rockeling Bay (bay)

83 A/10 - Donalda
27-41-20-W4
52°33′00″N 112°48′00″W
Approximately 15 km east of Bashaw.

This feature was originally known as "Rocketing Bay," according to longtime residents, because of the huge flocks of ducks that could be seen "rocketing" into the bay in the fall. The name has undergone several spelling changes since that time. The name Rockeling Bay was applied to a school built in SE29-41-20-W4 in 1905 (this may be when the first spelling change occurred) and is still in use as a district name.

Rocky Children's Pond (pond)

83 B/7 - Rocky Mountain House
33-39-7-W5
52°24′N 114°56′W
Approximately 10 km north-west of Rocky Mountain House.

The name of this small pond refers to the fact that it is close to Rocky Mountain House and is stocked with fish for the express use of children and older people. (see Rocky Mountain House)

Rocky Ford (locality)

73 D/14 - Irma
9-44-8-W4
52°46′55″N 111°06′55″W
Approximately 16 km south-west of the town of Wainwright.

This is the name of the former Park Warden's cabin at the West Park Gate. The name is taken from the village of Rockyford, 42 km south-west of Drumheller, the former home of Bud Cotton, a Buffalo Park warden from 1909 until 1940. (see Buffalo Park)

Ferry Crossing, Rocky Mountain House, 1890s

Rocky Mountain House (town)

83 B/7 - Rocky Mountain House
22-39-7-W5
52°22′20″N 114°55′00″W
Approximately 75 km west of Red Deer.

The North West Company established a fort here in 1799. It was named for its proximity to the Rocky Mountains. The Hudson's Bay Company built Acton House nearby under the direction of James Bird, but this fort was eventually abandoned in 1821 when the two companies merged and chose Rocky Mountain House as the post. From 1828 to 1861, Rocky Mountain House was open only in the winter months for trade. It was abandoned in 1861, rebuilt in 1864, but finally closed permanently in 1875 in favour of a post at Calgary. The post was known in Blackfoot as *a-pastan* (Nelson), in Stoney as *ti-shi-a* and in Cree as *kai-ashas-sin-wati was-ka-higan* (Tyrrell). The post office opened in August 1912. This town was incorporated 31 August 1939.

Rocky Rapids (hamlet)

83 G/7 - Tomahawk
4-50-7-W5
53°17'N 114°57'W
Approximately 9 km north of Drayton Valley.

The descriptive name for this hamlet, whose post office opened in March 1909, refers to the rapids in the North Saskatchewan River near it. The name was chosen by W. Jeffrey, the first postmaster; he and his brother were early homesteaders in the area.

* Rodef (former locality)

83 H/15 - Lamont
6-57-17-W4
53°53'N 112°32'W
Approximately 24 km south of Smoky Lake.

The origin of the name of this locality is unknown.

* Rodino (former locality)

73 E/3 - Vermilion
20-48-10-W4
53°08'N 111°26'W
Approximately 26 km east north-east of Viking.

The name of this post office, which operated from May 1911 through March

_____
*denotes rescinded name or former locality.

1939, was chosen by the Post Office Department, but its precise origin is unknown.

Rolly View (hamlet)

83 H/6 - Cooking Lake
29-49-23-W4
53°15'15"N 113°20'00"W
Approximately 13 km east of Leduc.

The name for this hamlet, whose post office opened in January 1939, is descriptive of the view of the countryside. The hamlet was officially recognized 5 January 1980.

Rom Hill (hill)

73 D/11 - Hardisty
29-43-8-W4
52°44'N 111°07'W
Approximately 14 km east north-east of Hardisty.

The name for this hill has been in use since at least 1958, but its origin is unknown.

Romeo Creek (creek)

83 J/2 - Thunder Lake
28-59-7-W5
54°07'N 114°59'W
Flows south into Connor Creek, approximately 20 km east north-east of Mayerthorpe.

This creek drains Romeo Lake. (see Romeo Lake)

Romeo Lake (lake)

83 J/2 - Thunder Lake
31-58-6-W5
54°03'N 114°53'W
Approximately 20 km north-east of Mayerthorpe.

This lake was named after J.R. Romeo (1854-1948), an early settler from the southern United States who, with his family, was the first to arrive in the Peavine

district in 1907 by covered wagon. When they came to this lake they filed on six quarter-sections and Mr. Romeo built his log house on high land west of this lake. The house later became a well-known stopping place for settlers in the area.

Ronan (locality)

83 G/14 - Mayerthorpe
15-56-9-W5
53°50'N 115°16'W
Approximately 15 km south south-west of Mayerthorpe.

The name for this locality, whose post office operated from April 1912 through August 1958, is taken after a town of the same name in Montana.

Roros (locality)

73 D/16 - McLaughlin
10-45-2-W4
52°52'N 110°12'W
Approximately 44 km east of the town of Wainwright.

A post office was established here in November 1914 and operated until June 1931. Many of the early settlers were of Norwegian descent, and the post office was named after the Roros copper mine in Norway. The name was originally applied to School District #2193 which was established in May 1910.

Rosalind (village)

83 A/16 - Daysland
17-44-17-W4
52°47'10"N 112°26'40"W
Approximately 15 km south-west of Daysland.

The name for this village, whose post office opened in June 1905, is a combination of the names of two surrounding school districts; Montrose and East Lynne. Montrose may have been named after a town in Angus (now Tayside), Scotland, and the name East Lynne was suggested by an early settler after he read a book of the same name. This village was incorporated 1 January 1966.

Roseland Lake (lake)

73 L/12 - Beaver Lake
12-21-66-12-W4
54°43'30"N 111°44'30"W
Approximately 15 km south-east of Lac La Biche.

The name for this lake was officially applied in 1951 and commemorates Flight Lieutenant A.W. Roseland, US Air Medal (1915-1944), of Youngstown, Alberta, who was killed in World War II.

Roselea (locality)

83 J/2 - Thunder Lake
1-59-6-W5
54°05'N 114°45'W
Approximately 23 km south-west of Barrhead.

The name for this locality, whose post office operated from August 1913 through October 1967, was suggested by the first postmaster, Harry Howard. Roselea was the name of his mother's cottage in England.

Rosenheim (locality)

73 D/1 - Bodo
14-37-2-W4
52°10'N 110°10'W
Approximately 20 km south of Provost.

Many early settlers were from Bavaria, and when this post office was established in March 1909 it was named after a town in Bavaria. It closed in July 1946.

Rosenroll (railway point)

83 H/3 - Bittern Lake
36-46-22-W4
53°01'N 113°03'W
Approximately 13 km east south-east of Wetaskiwin.

The post office operated here from February 1903 through July 1910 and was named after A.S. Rosenroll, member of the Legislative Assembly for Wetaskiwin. The name was changed to Bittern Lake. The post office then reopened as Rosenroll from August 1912 through July 1918.

Rosevear (locality)

83 F/9 - Edson
16-54-15-W5
53°40'N 116°09'W
Approximately 20 km north-east of Edson.

The Grand Trunk Pacific Railway established a station here in 1911. The post office operated from December 1914 through June 1969. The locality was named after J.M. Rosevear, chief clerk of the railway's audit department.

Rosinan Lake (lake)

73 E/14 - St. Paul
8-57-8-W4
53°54'N 111°09'W
Approximately 18 km west of Elk Point.

The name of this lake has been official since at least 1958, but its precise origin is unknown.

Ross Creek (creek)

83 H/11 - Edmonton
34-53-21-W4
53°38'N 113°01'W
Flows north-west into North Saskatchewan River, approximately 32 km north-east of Edmonton.

Walter Gordon Ross (1854-1940), for whom this creek was officially named 13 March 1947, was one of the original members of the North West Mounted Police, having participated in the march west in 1874. He was also a member of the detachment that established Fort Saskatchewan two years later. In 1885 he was a dispatch rider during the North West Rebellion. When he left the force he turned his hand to farming, trapping and fur trading. This led him to open a store and for a number of years he was also postmaster and telegrapher. Later he opened another store at Edna, now called Star. Among his other interests were real estate and insurance.

Ross Haven (summer village)

83 G/9 - Onoway
8-55-3-W5
53°44'N 114°24'W
Approximately 33 km south of Barrhead.

The precise origin of the name of this summer village, incorporated 1 January 1962, is unknown.

Ross Lake (lake)

73 E/16 - Frog Lake
11-56-4-W4
53°49'N 110°29'W
Approximately 29 km east south-east of Elk Point.

The name for this lake has been official since at least 1958, but its precise origin is unknown.

Rosse Lake (lake)

73 D/6 - Brownfield
18-38-9-W4
52°16'N 111°17'W
Approximately 25 km north north-east of Coronation.

The name for this lake has been in use since at least 1958, but its origin is unknown.

Rossington (locality)

83 J/1 - Barrhead
4-60-1-W5
54°10'N 114°05'W
Approximately 18 km west of Westlock.

The name for this locality, whose post office operated from June 1910 through February 1969, is likely taken after Rossington Moulton, an early settler and the first postmaster.

Rosyth (hamlet)

73 D/11 - Hardisty
22-42-9-W4
52°38'N 111°13'W
Approximately 7 km south-east of Hardisty.

The name for this hamlet was taken after the famous naval base in Scotland on the Firth of Forth north-west of Edinburgh. The post office operated from January 1911 through August 1960.

Rough Creek (creek)

83 B/6 - Crimson Lake
27-39-11-W5
52°24'N 115°29'W
Flows north-east into North Saskatchewan River, approximately 38 km west of Rocky Mountain House.

The name of this creek has been official since at least 1958 and is likely descriptive.

Rough Lake (lake)

73 D/10 - Hughenden
27-43-6-W4
52°44'N 110°47'W
Approximately 12 km south south-east of the town of Wainwright.

The name of this lake has been in use since at least 1958, but its origin is unknown. It is also known locally as "Wilcox Lake."

Round Hill (hamlet)

83 H/2 - Camrose
30-48-18-W4
53°10'N 112°38'W
Approximately 22 km north-east of Camrose.

The descriptive name for this hamlet, whose post office opened in September 1904, refers to the round-shaped hill three kilometres to the west.

Round Lake (lake)

73 D/2 - Neutral Hills
12-36-6-W4
52°04'13"N 110°43'30"W
Approximately 44 km south-east of Provost.

The name of this lake has been in use since at least 1905 when it first appeared on a Department of the Interior Township Map. It was officially approved 22 January 1992. The descriptive name refers to the round shape of the feature.

Round Lake (lake)

83 A/2 - Big Valley
11-30-36-19-W4
52°08'23"N 112°42'30"W
Approximately 22 km south of Stettler.

The descriptive name for this lake is well established in local usage and was officially approved 3 October 1991.

Round Lake (lake)

83 G/10 - Isle Lake
36-53-7-W5
53°37'N 114°53'W
Approximately 40 km south south-east of Mayerthorpe.

The descriptive name for this lake has been established since at least 1865, when it appeared on Palliser's map, and refers to its shape.

Round Valley (locality)

83 G/7 - Tomahawk
28-50-7-W5
53°21'N 114°57'W
Approximately 11 km north of Drayton Valley.

The descriptive name for this locality, whose post office operated from July 1934 through May 1966, refers to the surrounding countryside.

Rourke Creek (creek)

83 O/1 - Smith
27-69-1-W5
55°00'N 114°04'W
Flows north into Athabasca River, approximately 65 km north-west of Athabasca.

The name has been official since at least 1958, but its precise origin is unknown.

Rowley (hamlet)

82 P/15 - Rumsey
21-32-20-W4
51°46'N 112°47'W
Approximately 35 km east north-east of Three Hills.

A Canadian Northern Railway station was established here in 1911 and was named after Charles Walsh Rowley, Canadian Bank of Commerce manager in Calgary (1902-11) and Winnipeg (1911-20), who became an assistant general manager in Toronto in 1925. The Commerce provided financial backing for the building of the Canadian Northern. A post office opened in June 1912.

Royal Park (locality)

83 H/9 - Mundare
31-52-15-W4
53°32'N 112°13'W
Approximately 12 km north-west of Vegreville.

In response to an earlier article on the origin of Royal Park and its basis on a royal visit, the following is an excerpt from the *Edmonton Journal* of 19 October 1978: "Alex Wynchuck, a retired farmer from Royal Park, who now lives in Vegreville, said Raith was just a whistle stop along the CNR line. In 1919, he explained, a Steve Jeremy (he couldn't remember how to spell the last name) began building a general store which was opened in 1920. After the store opened, he said, Mr. Jeremy circulated a petition to re-name Raith to Jeremy. The petition was sent to Ottawa to see if Postal Authorities would agree, Mr. Wynchuck said. It came back that they wouldn't agree but they asked if the local people would be in favour of Royal Park." The name "Raith" was never officially adopted because of duplication with another Raith in Ontario near Thunder Bay. The post office operated as Royal Park from July 1921 through April 1970, and its name is likely descriptive of the surrounding park lands.

Roydale (locality)

83 G/15 - Sangudo
3-58-7-W5
53°59'N 114°58'W
Approximately 13 km east north-east of Mayerthorpe.

The origin of the name of this locality, whose post office operated from March 1908 through July 1925, is unknown.

Rumsey (village)

82 P/15 - Rumsey
24-33-21-W4
51°50'30"N 112°50'25"W
Approximately 26 km east of Trochu.

The post office at this village, which takes its name from a banker, Reginald Arthur Rumsey (1875-1919), was established in April 1911. Mr. Rumsey was chief inspector

(1911-1919) of the Canadian Bank of Commerce and later an assistant general manager with C.W. Rowley (see Rowley). Mr. Rumsey's early time with the Commerce included a stint at Dawson, Yukon in the Gold Rush days.

Rushmere Lake (lake)

72 M/14 - Kirkpatrick Lake
18-33-8-W4
51°49'N 111°07'W
Approximately 36 km south-east of Coronation.

The precise origin of the name of this feature is unknown.

Rusylvia (locality)

73 E/10 - Clandonald
28-53-6-W4
53°37'N 110°50'W
Approximately 29 km north of Vermilion.

The name for the post office, which operated here from February 1912 through October 1968, is a combination of Latin words reflecting "wooded country."

Ruttan Lake (lake)

83 J/9 - Flatbush
9-65-2-W5
54°37'N 114°15'W
Approximately 54 km north north-east of Barrhead.

The name for this lake was officially approved 4 May 1948 and commemorates Private Wilmot Ruttan of Flatbush, Alberta, who was killed in World War II. His homestead adjoined the section in which the lake is situated.

Ryley (village)

83 H/8 - Ryley
4-50-17-W4
53°17'30"N 112°25'40"W
Approximately 19 km south-east of Tofield.

A post office opened here in November 1908 and was named for George Urquhart Ryley, land commissioner for the Grand Trunk Pacific Railway, which established a station here in 1909. Mr Ryley was a Dominion land surveyor who worked for the Department of the Interior for 23 years before joining the railway as land commissioner in 1905. This village was incorporated 2 April 1910.

S

Sabine (locality)

83 A/2 - Big Valley
26-37-19-W4
52°12'N 112°36'W
Approximately 14 km south-east of Stettler.

The origin for the name of this locality is unknown.

* **Sacred Heart** (former locality)

73 E/7 - Vermilion
26-57-13-W4
53°56'N 111°49'W
Approximately 34 km west south-west of St. Paul.

A post office operated here from June 1903 through December 1931 and all the postmasters were missionaries.

Saddle Lake (hamlet)

73 E/13 - Hairy Hill
34-57-12-W4
53°58'N 111°41'W
Approximately 26 km west of St. Paul, on Indian Reserve #125.

The post office operated here from July 1893 through January 1955 and then reopened in December 1974. (see Saddle Lake)

Saddle Lake (lake)

73 L/4 - Cache Lake
13-58-12-W4
54°01'N 111°39'W
Approximately 23 km west of St. Paul.

The name for this lake has been official since at least 1911, but its precise origin is not clear. Apparently, there was a shortage of buffalo at one time and the natives were forced to ice-fish on the lake. The Cree call the lake *unechekekeskwapewin*, roughly translating "dark objects sitting on the ice."

Saddle Lake Indian Reserve #125

(Indian reserve)

73 L/4 - Cache Lake
26-58-12-W4
54°02'N 111°41'W
Approximately 130 km north-east of Edmonton.

(see Saddle Lake)

Saddlelake Creek (creek)

73 E/13 - Hairy Hill
10-58-12-W4
53°59'N 111°42'W
Flows south-west into North Saskatchewan River, approximately 23 km north of Two Hills.

(see Saddle Lake)

St. Albert (city)

83 H/12 - St. Albert
9-54-25-W4
53°38'42"N 113°37'08"W
Immediately north-west of Edmonton.

This area was known among the Métis as the "Big Lake Settlement." It was named by Bishop Alexandre Taché on 14 January 1861 after the patron saint of Father Albert Lacombe, O.M.I. (see Lacombe). The two

St. Albert, 1907

were travelling from Fort Edmonton to Lac Ste Anne in search of a location for a new mission. This was the chosen site. The city, which was incorporated in 1976, grew gradually around the mission.

St. Albert Settlement (settlement)

83 H/12 - St. Albert
4-54-25-W4
53°38'N 113°37'W
Immediately north-west of Edmonton.

(see St. Albert)

St. Brides (locality)

73 E/13 - Hairy Hill
3-58-11-W4
53°59'N 111°33'W
Approximately 16 km west of St. Paul.

The post office opened here in February 1928, but the precise origin for the name is unknown.

St. Edouard (hamlet)

73 E/14 - St. Paul
4-58-8-W4
53°59'N 111°08'W
Approximately 12 km east of St. Paul.

The name for this hamlet, whose post office operated from March 1909 through September 1969, is taken after the first two settlers in the area, Edouard Côté and Edouard Labrie. Before the post office opened, the name of the church was also St. Edouard.

---

*denotes rescinded name or former locality.

St. Francis (locality)

83 G/8 - Genesee
2-50-3-W5
53°17'N 114°20'W
Approximately 50 km east of Drayton
Valley.

The post office, which operated here from
October 1936 through April 1969, was
named after the local church of St. Francis
d'Assisi.

St. Ives Lake (lake)

73 E/8 - Lloydminster
4-52-2-W4
53°27'N 110°14'W
Approximately 26 km north-west of
Lloydminster.

The name for this lake has been official
since at least 1958, but its precise origin is
unknown.

St. Lawrence Lake (lake)

73 D/8 - Provost
11-39-1-W4
52°21'N 110°01'W
Approximately 17 km east of Provost, on
the Alberta-Saskatchewan boundary.

The name for this lake has been official
since 1958, but its origin is unknown.

St. Lina (hamlet)

73 L/6 - Goodridge
20-61-10-W4
54°18'N 111°27'W
Approximately 35 km north north-west of
St. Paul.

The post office opened here in September
1912 and was named after Alina Mageau,
wife of one of the first postmasters, L.
Mageau.

St. Lina Creek (creek)

73 L/6 - Goodridge
20-62-10-W4
54°23'N 111°28'W
Flows north-west into Beaver River,
approximately 48 km north north-west of
St. Paul.

(see St. Lina)

St. Louis Lakes (lake)

72 M/12 - Hanna
17-31-14-W4
51°39'N 111°58'W
Approximately 4 km west of Hanna.

Previously known as "Hanalta Lake," a
combination of Hanna and Alberta, the
name for this lake was renamed St. Louis
Lakes, but the precise origin is not known.

St. Michael (hamlet)

83 H/15 - Lamont
9-56-18-W4
53°50'N 112°38'W
Approximately 13 km north-east of
Lamont.

The name for this hamlet, whose post office
opened in August 1923, is taken from the
name of the local church. St. Michael was
one of the seven archangels of Christian
legend.

St. Patrick Lakes (lake)

73 D/15 - Wainwright
13-44-5-W4
52°47'N 110°36'W
Approximately 18 km east of the town of
Wainwright.

The name for these lakes has been official
since 1958, but its origin is unknown.

St. Paul (town)

73 E/14 - St. Paul
4-58-9-W4
53°59'25"N 111°17'30"W
Approximately 115 km east north-east of
Edmonton.

The year 1866 was the year that saw the
first attempt at settlement in this area. The
mission of St. Paul des Cris was established,
but was not welcomed and was eventually
abandoned after an epidemic of smallpox in
1874. For approximately the next twenty
years, various legal difficulties and obstacles
related to land grants were met and dealt
with through Ottawa until, in January
1896, the colony of St. Paul des Métis was
declared officially open by Father Albert
Lacombe (see Lacombe). Father Adéodat
Therien (see Therien) was appointed to take
charge. He arrived in July of 1896, and his
first responsibility was setting up a mission
house. He completed this building on
Christmas Eve of that year, in time for
Midnight Mass. The post office of St. Paul
des Métis was opened 1 August 1899. By
1909, the missionary intent was abandoned
and the settlement was opened to all. The
colony ultimately grew into a village which
became incorporated in 1912. Its name was
shortened to St. Paul in 1929. This town
was incorporated 15 December 1936.

Old sawmill at St. Paul, 1920s

St. Paul County #19 (county)

73 E/14 - St. Paul
55 to 62-4 to 13-W4
53°55′N 111°10′W
North-west of Lloydminster.

(see St. Paul)

St. Paul Junction (railway point)

83 H/11 - Edmonton
31-53-23-W4
53°37′N 113°23′W
Approximately 12 km north-east of
Edmonton.

The precise origin for the name of this
urban community on the Canadian
Northern Railway line is unknown.

St. Pierre Lake (lake)

73 L/2 - Muriel Lake
31-58-5-W4
54°04′N 110°43′W
Approximately 21 km north-east of Elk
Point.

The name for this lake has been official
since 2 May 1957, but its precise origin is
unknown.

St. Thomas Lake (lake)

83 G/16 - Lac la Nonne
20-55-3-W5
53°46′N 114°24′W
Approximately 39 km south of Barrhead.

The name for this lake has been official
since at least 1958, but its precise origin is
unknown.

St. Vincent (hamlet)

73 L/3 - Vincent Lake
3-60-9-W4
54°09′N 111°16′W
Approximately 18 km north of St. Paul.

This hamlet, whose post office opened in
July 1918, was named for its proximity to
Vincent Lake. (see Vincent Lake) It was
previously called "Denisville." St. Denis is
the patron saint of France. Early trappers
called this settlement "La Croupe au
Chien" or "Dog's Rump."

■ **Ste Anne, Lac** (lake)

83 G/9 - Onoway
32-54-3-W5
53°42′N 114°24′W
Approximately 61 km west north-west of
Edmonton.

This lake, known to natives as "Devil's
Lake," "Manitou" and "Divine Lake," is
the "Manito Lake" of David Thompson
and appears as "Lac St. Ann" on the Palliser
map. The present name dates from 1844
when Father Jean-Baptiste Thibault
founded one of the first Catholic missions
on the western prairies here. Ste Anne was
the mother of the Blessed Virgin Mary,
whose feast date is July 26. Many Christian
Natives annually go on a pilgrimage to Lac
Ste Anne towards the end of July. It was a
place of pilgrimage before the coming of
the Europeans, as, apparently, the waters of
this lake have healing properties.

Saint Cyr, Lac (lake)

73 E/14 - St. Paul
1-57-9-W4
53°54′N 111°12′W
Approximately 13 km south-east of St.
Paul.

The name for this lake has been official
since 11 September 1941, but its precise
origin is unknown.

Sakayo Lake (lake)

83 I/16 - Plamondon
17-67-15-W4
54°48′00″N 112°14′45″W

Approximately 20 km west north-west of
Lac La Biche.

This lake is known locally as "Blackbird
Lake." Two sources state that the name is a
native word for blackbird; however, the
Geographical Names Program has not been
able to confirm its meaning.

Salisbury Corner (locality)

83 H/11 - Edmonton
20-52-23-W4
53°31′N 113°21′W
Approximately 12 km east of Edmonton.

The origin for the name of this country
residence subdivision is unknown.

Salt Lake (lake)

72 M/9 - Esther
5-31-2-W4
51°38′00″N 110°15′30″W
Approximately 35 km north north-east of
Oyen.

The precise origin for the name of this
feature is unknown.

Salter's Lake (lake)

83 G/9 - Onoway
26-54-2-W5
53°41′25″N 114°11′25″W
Approximately 49 km north-west of
Edmonton.

This lake is named after Arnold "Jack"
Salter (1901-?) who came to the area from
his native Wales in April 1923. His well-
known sheep were entered in many local
fairs and stock shows.

Samson Indian Reserve #137
(Indian reserve)

83 A/11 - Chain Lakes
32-43-23-W4
52°44′N 113°19′W
Approximately 23 km south of Wetaskiwin.

These Cree reserves were named after Chief Samson. (see Samson Lake)

Samson Indian Reserve #137A

(Indian reserve)

83 A/11 - Chain Lakes
4-44-24-W4
52°45'N 113°26'W
Approximately 25 km south south-west of Wetaskiwin.

(see Samson Lake)

Samson Lake (lake)

83 A/11 - Chain Lakes
27-43-23-W4
52°44'00"N 113°15'30"W
Approximately 27 km south south-east of Wetaskiwin.

This lake and the surrounding features were all named after Chief Samson. The name for this lake was changed from "Battle River Lake" to avoid duplication with another Battle Lake in Alberta.

Samuel Lake (lake)

83 J/9 - Flatbush
33-64-2-W5
54°35'N 114°13'W
Approximately 55 km north north-east of Barrhead.

The name for this lake has been official since at least 1958, but its precise origin is unknown.

Sand Creek (creek)

83 B/14 - Brazeau Forks
33-45-9-W5
52°56'N 115°14'W
Flows east into North Saskatchewan River, approximately 36 km south south-west of Drayton Valley.

The name for this creek has been official since at least 1958 and is likely descriptive.

Sand River (river)

73 L/11 - Pinehurst Lake
15-29-64-8-W4
From 54°30'00"N 111°11'02"W
to 54°45'00"N 111°08'30"W
Flows south-east into Beaver River, approximately 23 km north-west of Bonnyville.

The descriptive name for this river has been official since January 1911.

Sandhill Lake (lake)

83 I/15 - Grassland
3-67-17-W4
54°46'54"N 112°31'44"W
Approximately 37 km west of Lac La Biche.

The name for this lake has been official since at least 1958, but its precise origin is unknown.

* **Sandholm Beach** (former hamlet)

83 G/1 - Warburg
22-47-1-W5
53°03'N 114°03'W
Approximately 27 km south-west of Calmar.

This former hamlet is now included in the summer village of Golden Days. The descriptive name, officially rescinded 26 January 1965, referred to the proximity of the settlement to the sandy beach. (see Golden Days)

Sandy Beach (summer village)

83 G/16 - Lac la Nonne
35-55-1-W5
53°48'N 114°02'W
Approximately 46 km north-west of Edmonton.

The name for this summer village, which was incorporated 1 January 1956, is taken from its location on Sandy Lake. (see Sandy Lake)

* **Sandy Beach** (former locality)

83 H/10 - Elk Island Park
24-54-20-W4
53°41'N 112°50'W
Approximately 47 km east north-east of Edmonton.

The precise origin for the name of this locality is not known; however, it may be descriptive.

Sandy Lake (lake)

83 G/16 - Lac la Nonne
26-55-1-W5
53°47'N 114°02'W
Approximately 44 km north-west of Edmonton.

The name for this lake is descriptive. The name goes as far back as 19 May 1827, when Edward Ermatinger in his York Factory Express Journal noted that when en route from Fort Assiniboine to Edmonton "...3 men set off to make a wear (weir) at Berlands Lake to supply fish on our

Sandy Lake, 1901

arrival...." It is speculation that he may have been referring to this Sandy Lake, as the trader Berland was active in the area at the time. Sandy Lake appears on the Palliser map of 1865 (see Beaverdam Creek), and Hector, in 1859, refers to "Sandy Lakes" as forming part of the route from Fort Edmonton to Fort Assiniboine.

Sandy Lake (lake)

73 D/15 - Wainwright
19-44-7-W4
52°49′N 110°59′W
Approximately 10 km west south-west of the town of Wainwright.

The name for this lake has been in use since at least 1958 and is likely descriptive.

* Sandy Rapids (former post office)

73 L/6 - Goodridge
5-24-63-8-W4
54°28′N 111°04′W
Approximately 32 km north-west of Bonnyville.

The post office, which operated here from January 1934 through March 1960, was named after the nearby Sand River. The name was officially rescinded 10 November 1970. (see Sand River)

Sandybeach Lake (lake)

73 E/8 - Lloydminster
1-52-1-W4
53°28′00″N 110°00′15″W
Approximately 22 km north of Lloydminster on the Alberta-Saskatchewan boundary.

The name for this lake has been official since at least 1958 and is likely descriptive.

_____
*denotes rescinded name or former locality.

Sang Lake (lake)

83 F/9 - Edson
9-53-15-W5
53°34′N 116°09′W
Approximately 20 km east of Edson.

This lake was named in 1951 after Tom Sang, a pioneer settler whose original homestead was near the shore of the lake.

Sangudo (village)

83 G/15 - Sangudo
36-56-7-W5
53°53′25″N 114°54′00″W
Approximately 18 km east south-east of Mayerthorpe.

The first name suggested for the settlement here was "Deep Creek." However, this was a duplication. The early settlers were interested in finding an original name, and they therefore "created" one by using the initial letters of some of their names, including: S for Sutton or sides; A for Alberta; N for Nanton where Mrs. Albers originally lived; G for Gaskell; U for their being united in that name; D for Deep Creek, their previous proposal; and O for Orangeville, their school district, which was organized before there was a post office. Another suggestion for the origin of the name Sangudo maintains that it is a combination of the names of Santa and Guso (or Guda), American towns. The post office opened in April 1912, and the village was incorporated 12 April 1937.

Sapper Hill (hill)

73 D/11 - Hardisty
36-43-8-W4
52°44′30″N 111°01′40″W
Approximately 16 km south-west of the town of Wainwright.

Sapper is the traditional name given to army engineers, taken from the medieval

term meaning to sap or undermine. The name for this hill in the Wainwright Regional Training Area has been in use for at least 30 years.

Sara Lake (lake)

83 J/9 - Flatbush
15-65-2-W5
54°38′N 114°13′W
Approximately 56 km north north-east of Barrhead.

Sara Hughes was the first woman to live on the banks of this lake. The Hughes family have homesteaded and/or leased all land adjoining this lake since the early 1900s. The name was submitted to the Geographic Board of Alberta for official approval in commemoration of Mrs. Hughes by John M. Hughes on 30 January 1933.

Sarcee Butte (butte)

82 P/10 - Munson
11-31-22-W4
51°38′N 113°00′W
Approximately 20 km east south-east of Three Hills.

This name has enjoyed local usage since at least the late nineteenth century. The name was also applied to the first school built in 1908, called Sarcee Butte School. The site locality received its name from a prehistoric Indian campsite (believed to be Sarcee) on the summit that gives a commanding view of the surrounding area.

* Sarrail (former post office)

83 I/15 - Grassland
32-66-18-W4
54°45′N 112°41′W
Approximately 39 km east of Athabasca.

The name for the post office, which operated here from November 1916 through April 1969, commemorates

General Maurice Paul Emmanuel Sarrail (1856-1929), a commander of the French 3rd Army in World War I. After the war, he devoted himself to politics and stood, unsuccessfully, as Radical deputy for Paris. He was French High Commissioner in Syria in 1924-25, his final appointment. The name was officially rescinded in 1970.

Saturday Lake (lake)

83 I/7 - Newbrook
29-62-18-W4
54°24′N 112°41′W
Approximately 33 km north north-west of Smoky Lake.

The name for this lake has been official since at least 1958, but its origin is unknown. It is locally referred to as "Hay Lake," as hay was cut here and this is where horses were pastured.

Sauer Lake (lake)

83 G/9 - Onoway
33-53-1-W5
53°36′45″N 114°04′30″W
Approximately 38 km west of Edmonton.

The name for this lake was first submitted for official approval by R.J. Paterson of the Department of Lands and Forests in November 1968. George Sauer's homestead was adjacent to the lake, and the well-established name for the lake became Sauer Lake. The name was officially approved 21 March 1978.

Saunders Lake (lake)

83 H/6 - Cooking Lake
32-49-24-W4
53°16′N 113°28′W
Approximately 8 km east of Leduc.

The name for this lake has been official since at least 1958, but its precise origin is unknown.

Saville Farm (locality)

73 D/14 - Irma
6-44-8-W4
52°45′45″N 111°09′40″W
Approximately 20 km south-west of the town of Wainwright.

The name for this locality is taken after the original settler family, the Savilles.

Saville Ford (river crossing)

73 D/14 - Irma
6-44-8-W4
52°45′31″N 111°09′00″W
Approximately 21 km south-west of the town of Wainwright.

The name for this river crossing has been official since at least 1958. (see Saville Farm)

Savouye Lake (lake)

73 L/13 - Lac La Biche
16-68-13-W4
54°53′N 111°55′W
Approximately 13 km north north-east of Lac La Biche.

The name for this lake appears on a map dated 1918, but its precise origin is unknown.

Sawmill Hill (hill)

82 O/15 - Sundre
5-32-32-6-W5
51°47′15″N 114°49′25″W
Approximately 11 km west of Sundre.

There were at least two or three sawmills on this hill. In the late 1930s, a fire went through here, destroying some of them. Some people consider Sawmill Hill the part of the hill where the road goes up before the bend in the road. The name is well-established in local usage, and was officially approved 3 October 1991.

Scapa (hamlet)

72 M/13 - Garden Plain
31-33-14-W4
51°52′N 111°59′W
Approximately 25 km north of Hanna.

The name for this locality is taken after a British naval base of both World War I and World War II in the Orkney Islands, Scotland, where the Germans surrendered and scuttled their fleet on 21 June 1919. The name *Scapa Flow* means "boat isthmus." A post office operated from December 1925 through November 1985.

Schneider Lake (lake)

73 D/12 - Lougheed
12-41-13-W4
52°31′00″N 111°45′15″W
Approximately 33 km west south-west of Hardisty.

The name for this lake has been official since at least 1958, but its precise origin is unknown.

Schott's Lake (lake)

82 O/15 - Sundre
14-1-33-7-W5
51°48′30″N 114°52′00″W
Approximately 16 km west of Sundre.

The name for this lake was officially approved 3 October 1991 and is taken after the Schott family who once owned the land on which it is situated.

Schrader Creek (creek)

82 O/16 - Olds
6-34-34-4-W5
51°58′N 114°29′W
Flows east into Red Deer River, approximately 24 km north-east of Sundre.

(see Schrader's Hill)

Schrader's Hill (hill)

82 O/16 - Olds
4-5-33-3-W5
51°47'45"N 114°24'00"W
Approximately 20 km west of Olds.

Mr. and Mrs. J.C. Schrader and their five children came to the area from Iowa in 1901. After a year in the Westerdale area, they decided to return to Iowa, but this was not possible so they homesteaded 19 kilometres west of Olds. They soon had a house, barn and other buildings erected on their land on the top of the hill, which became locally known as Schrader's Hill. The Schraders' home was a popular stopping house for travellers, as it was halfway between Olds and Sundre. Schrader Creek, running into the Red Deer River, is also named for the J.C. Schrader family who later bought a ranch here. The name has been used for this feature since circa 1903 and a quarter-section on the hill is still owned by R.C. Schrader.

Schultz Lake (lake)

83 H/6 - Cooking Lake
30-49-23-W4
53°16'N 113°21'W
Approximately 30 km south of Edmonton.

The origin of the name of this feature is unknown.

Schultz Lake (lake)

73 D/5 - Alliance
3-41-12-W4
52°29'N 111°39'W
Approximately 30 km south-west of Hardistry.

The name for this lake has been official since at least 1958, but its precise origin is unknown.

Scollard (locality)

82 P/15 - Rumsey
19-34-20-W4
51°56'N 112°50'W
Approximately 30 km east north-east of Trochu.

The origin of the name of the post office, which operated from May 1911 through August 1969, is unclear. It may be taken after Clinton Scollard (1860-1932), an American poet and author. Other sources suggest that it was named after a railroad official or after David Joseph Scollard (1862-1934), Roman Catholic Bishop of Sault Ste Marie, Ontario.

Scotfield (hamlet)

72 M/11 - Youngstown
10-30-10-W4
51°33'N 111°20'W
Approximately 42 km east of Hanna.

A post office operated at this site from March 1914 through November 1969, and was called Scotfield because it was on land owned by William John Scott.

Scotford (locality)

83 H/14 - Redwater
20-55-21-W4
53°46'N 113°05'W
Approximately 35 km north-east of Edmonton.

A Canadian Northern Railway station was opened here in 1905 and its name is a combination of the first premiers of Saskatchewan and Alberta – Walter Scott (1867-1938) and Alexander Cameron Rutherford (1858-1941). Mr. Scott was the publisher of the *Regina Leader* for many years. He was a Liberal member of Parliament for the Northwest Territories beginning in 1900 until he became Saskatchewan's first Premier. Mr. Rutherford was a lawyer in Strathcona when he was

elected to the Northwest Territories Legislature in 1902. Three years later Prime Minister Laurier called on him to form the first Alberta Government.

Scott Lake (lake)

73 D/7 - Czar
2-21-38-4-W4
52°16'35"N 110°30'56"W
Approximately 19 km south-west of Provost.

The locally well-established name for this lake was officially approved 22 January 1992 and is derived from the name of the first family to homestead on the land. In 1919, this section was noted to have been homesteaded by T.J. Scott.

Scott Lake (lake)

83 G/10 - Isle Lake
7-55-5-W5
53°44'N 114°44'W
Approximately 36 km south-east of Mayerthorpe.

Mr. and Mrs. William Scott came to the Onoway district from Michigan in 1904. They were early homesteaders who owned land near this lake.

Scovil Lake (lake)

73 E/3 - Buffalo Creek
36-46-9-W4
53°01'N 111°11'W
Approximately 29 km north-west of Wainwright.

The name for this lake has been official since at least 1958, but its precise origin is unknown.

* Seba (former post office)

83 G/10 - Isle Lake
14-53-6-W5
53°35'N 114°47'W
Approximately 41 km north north-east of Drayton Valley.

---

*denotes rescinded name or former locality.

A post office operated by this biblical name (see Seba Beach) from November 1913 through March 1926. It was then changed to Gainford. (see Gainford)

Seba Beach (summer village)

83 G/10 - Isle Lake
6-53-5-W5
53°33'N 114°44'W
Approximately 40 km north north-east of Drayton Valley.

The name for this summer village, which was incorporated 2 August 1920, was apparently chosen by postal authorities. The post office opened in July 1915, and the name may have been taken after Seba, one of the sons of Cush from Genesis 10:7 in the Bible. The connection is not clear. The name also appears in Psalm 72.

Sedalia (hamlet)

72 M/10 - Sedalia
21-31-5-W4
51°41'N 110°40'W
Approximately 38 km north north-west of Oyen.

The name for this hamlet, whose post office opened July 1911, is taken after Sedalia, Missouri, the former home of some of the early residents.

Sedgewick (town)

73 D/13 - Sedgewick
9-44-12-W4
52°46'40"N 111°41'50"W
Approximately 80 km east south-east of Camrose.

The post office in this town opened March 1907 and was named after Robert Sedgewick (1848-1906). Born in Aberdeen, Scotland, he came to Nova Scotia at an early age. He earned his Bachelor of Arts

degree from Dalhousie College in 1867, after which he studied law and was called to the Ontario Bar in 1872, and that of Nova Scotia the following year. He practised law in Halifax and was made Queen's Counsel in 1880. In 1888 he became Deputy Minister of Justice and five years later a judge of the Supreme Court of Canada. This town was incorporated 1 May 1966.

Seibert Lake (lake)

73 L/11 - Pinehurst Lake
4-21-66-9-W4
54°43'04"N 111°18'00"W
Approximately 42 km east of Lac La Biche.

The name of this lake has been official since 1918 and commemorates Frederick Victor Seibert (1885-1966), Dominion Land Surveyor, who surveyed this area and a large parcel of country stretching all the way to the Saskatchewan border circa 1916. Fred Seibert later became industrial commissioner for Canadian National Railways. Seibert won the Julian C. Smith Medal of the Engineering Institute of Canada, a top award for an engineer, in 1952. The local name for the feature is "Worm Lake," a translation from the Cree *mohteo sagahegan* or *munghoos sagahegan*.

September Lake (lake)

83 I/13 - Grosmont
16-67-25-W4
54°48'00"N 113°45'30"W
Approximately 33 km west north-west of Athabasca.

The name for this lake has been official since at least 1958, but its precise origin is unknown.

* Shalka (former post office)

73 E/13 - Hairy Hill
13-56-14-W4
53°52'N 111°56'W
Approximately 22 km north-west of Two Hills.

The name for the post office, which operated here from September 1911 through May 1928 and reopened from December 1931 through January 1970, was taken after Matt Shalka, the first postmaster. The name was officially rescinded 12 August 1970.

Shalka Lake (lake)

73 E/13 - Hairy Hill
14-56-14-W4
53°50'N 111°58'W
Approximately 21 km north-west of Two Hills.

(see Shalka)

* Shandro (former locality)

83 H/16 - Willingdon
27-57-15-W4
53°57'N 112°10'W
Approximately 28 km south-east of Smoky Lake.

A post office operated here from January 1905 through May 1922, and then reopened September 1923 and operated until October 1953. It was named for Andrew Shandro (1886-1942), a native of Bukovina, who came to Canada in 1898. He was homestead inspector from 1907 to 1910 and in 1913 he was elected Liberal M.L.A. for Whitford and remained in this seat until 1921. Other interests included real estate and the machinery business. From 1936 until his death he was farmers' agent at the Board of Review hearings.

Shantz (locality)

82 O/9 - Didsbury
27-31-4-W5
51°41'N 114°29'W
Approximately 17 km south-east of Sundre.

Jacob Y. Shantz (1822-1909), a Mennonite layman from Ontario, arrived in the Didsbury area as immigrant agent in 1892

---

*denotes rescinded name or former locality.

and was the government representative in charge of locating settlers in the area. Although he did not remain around Didsbury very long, some of his relatives followed. He has been credited with establishing the town of Didsbury at its present location. It had been the normal practice on the part of railway companies, where possible, to honour an individual in recommending station names.

Shaver River (river)

73 L/16 - Medley River
26-69-1-W4
54°59'N 110°11'W
Flows south-east into Saskatchewan, approximately 55 km north north-east of Cold Lake.

The name for this river was officially adopted 28 July 1945 and commemorates P.A. Shaver (1869-1960), Dominion Land Surveyor, who was engaged in railway construction and irrigation projects near Calgary and Red Deer River and surveyed in the Peace River country.

Shaw Lake (lake)

73 L/13 - Lac La Biche
5-5-67-11-W4
54°46'59"N 111°39'20"W
Approximately 21 km east of Lac La Biche.

The name for this lake was officially adopted 28 July 1945, but its precise origin is unknown. There is some speculation that it may be named after P.J. Shaw, a commercial fisherman who figured in the minutes of the Lac La Biche Board of Trade circa 1930. It was formerly called "Desjarlais Lake," after early settlers who lived nearby.

* **Shearwater** (former post office)

83 G/10 - Isle Lake
8-54-5-W5
53°39'N 114°43'W
Approximately 44 km south-east of Mayerthorpe.

The post office operated here by this name from October 1914 through June 1915, when it was changed to Lake Isle. (see Lake Isle)

Sheep Coulee (coulee)

82 P/12 - Lonepine Creek
35-29-29-W4
51°32'N 113°59'W
Runs east into Rosebud River, approximately 13 km east south-east of Carstairs.

The name for this coulee has been official since 1958, but its precise origin is unknown.

* **Shepenge** (former locality)

73 E/13 - Hairy Hill
6-56-12-W4
53°49'N 111°47'W
Approximately 9 km north north-west of Two Hills.

The name for this former locality, whose post office operated from November 1911 through March 1953, is a derivation of the Ukrainian *Shypnci*, a town in the Russian Empire. The name was officially rescinded 12 August 1970.

Sherlock Lake (lake)

73 D/16 - McLaughlin
12-44-1-W4
52°47'N 110°00'W
Approximately 49 km north north-east of Provost, on the Alberta-Saskatchewan boundary.

The name for this lake has been official since at least 1958, but its origin is unknown.

Sherring Lake (lake)

83 I/9 - Hylo
4-14-64-14-W4
54°32'30"N 112°01'50"W
Approximately 26 km south of Lac La Biche.

The name for this lake has been official since at least 1958 and is apparently named after a local resident; however, no details are known about this person.

Sherritt Lake (lake)

73 L/4 - Cache Lake
4-59-13-W4
54°04'N 111°53'W
Approximately 37 km east of Smoky Lake.

The name for this lake has been official since at least 1958, but its precise origin is unknown.

Sherwood Park (hamlet)

83 H/11 - Edmonton
27-52-23-W4
53°31'N 113°19'W
Immediately east of Edmonton.

The precise origin of the name is not known, but the choice may have been a promotional idea to induce people to live in this planned subdivision amid rural surroundings. The population has exceeded 31,000 for this, one of the largest hamlets in the world. The associations with Sherwood Forest, England, are complemented by the name of the school, Robin Hood. The original name was to have been "Campbelltown." The post office opened here in May 1957.

Shining Bank (locality)

83 G/13 - Hattonford
35-56-14-W5
53°53'N 115°59'W
Approximately 34 km south south-west of Whitecourt.

The post office operated here from April 1911 through June 1969 and was named for its proximity to Shiningbank Lake. (see Shiningbank Lake)

Shiningbank Lake (lake)

83 F/16 - Shiningbank Lake
29-56-14-W5
53°53′N 116°02′W
Approximately 37 km south south-west of Whitecourt.

The descriptive name for this lake has been in use since at least 1928 and refers to the yellow clay bank of the hills from which dirt and stones keep falling. These deposits shine like gold in the sun and are visible for miles.

Shirley Lake (lake)

83 H/10 - Elk Island Park
5-54-20-W4
53°38′N 112°55′W
Approximately 41 km east north-east of Edmonton.

The name for this lake has been official since at least 1958 and was named after Superintendent B.I. Love's daughter. Dr. Love managed Elk Island National Park from 1936 through 1959.

Shoal Creek (creek)

83 J/8 - Shoal Creek
23-62-1-W5
54°23′N 114°02′W
Flows east into Pembina River, approximately 38 km north-east of Barrhead.

(see Shoal Lake Creek)

Shoal Creek (locality)

83 J/8 - Shoal Creek
28-61-2-W5
54°18′N 114°14′W

Approximately 29 km north-east of Barrhead.

The name for this locality, whose post office operated from August 1915 through September 1969, is taken for its proximity to Shoal Creek. (see Shoal Lake Creek)

Shoal Lake (lake)

83 J/8 - Shoal Creek
7-61-3-W5
54°15′30″N 114°27′30″W
Approximately 16 km north of Barrhead.

The name for this lake has been official since at least 1958. (see Shoal Lake Creek)

Shoal Lake Creek (creek)

83 G/7 - Tomahawk
6-51-4-W5
53°22′N 114°34′W
Flows south-east into North Saskatchewan River, approximately 33 km east north-east of Drayton Valley.

The term "shoal" is equivalent to "shallow." The name may possibly be descriptive of a shallow lake from which this creek drained. The name has been in use since at least 1958.

Shonts (locality)

83 H/7 - Tofield
21-50-18-W4
53°20′N 112°35′W
Approximately 9 km south-east of Tofield.

The Grand Trunk Pacific Railway established a station here in 1909 and named it after Theodore Perry Shonts, (1856-1919), president of several U.S. railroads, who was chairman of the Isthmian Canal Commission (1905-07), set up to study potential construction of the Panama Canal.

Shooting Lake (lake)

83 A/1 - Hackett
15-37-17-W4
52°12′N 112°21′W
Approximately 30 km east south-east of Stettler.

The precise origin of the name of this lake is unclear. Many local people feel it was named because of the abundance of hunters in the area in the fall. Another theory shared by the oldest residents in the area maintains that it is a descriptive name referring to the various inlets of the lake that seem to "shoot" outward.

Shorncliffe Creek (creek)

73 D/7 - Czar
6-40-7-W4
52°25′N 110°59′W
Flows north-east into Shorncliffe Lake, approximately 43 km west north-west of Provost.

This creek and the nearby lake were named before 1928 in commemoration of the military camp at Shorncliffe, Kent, England, during World War I. According to Ekwall, the name means "a steep projecting rocky cliff."

Shorncliffe Lake (lake)

73 D/7 - Czar
25-40-7-W4
52°28′N 110°52′W
Approximately 43 km west north-west of Provost.

Originally, this lake was known as "Czar Lake." (see Shorncliffe Creek)

Shuckburgh Slough (lake)

83 A/7 - Stettler
2-39-20-W4
52°19′00″N 112°45′30″W
Immediately west of Stettler.

The locally well-established name for this lake was officially approved 5 May 1983. It is named after the Shuckburgh family, early settlers. The sons still farm near the lake.

Sidcup (locality)

73 D/16 - McLaughlin
30-46-3-W4
52°59′N 110°25′W
Approximately 34 km north-east of Wainwright.

The post office, which operated here from October 1913 through March 1932, has the same name as a place in Kent, England, which, according to Ekwall, is said to mean "set camp."

* Sideview (former locality)

73 L/5 - Goodfish Lake
26-61-11-W4
54°18′N 111°33′W
Approximately 39 km north north-west of St. Paul.

A post office operated here from July 1913 through September 1950, but the precise origin for the name is unknown. The name was officially rescinded 10 November 1970.

Siegner Lake (lake)

73 D/16 - McLaughlin
30-44-1-W4
52°49′N 110°07′W
Approximately 48 km south of Lloydminster.

The name for this lake has been official since 1958, but its origin is unknown.

Siewert Flat (flat)

82 P/13 - Torrington
23-32-26-W4
51°46′30″N 113°35′25″W

_____
*denotes rescinded name or former locality.

Approximately 23 km north-west of Three Hills.

Dan Siewert was the former owner of the land. The lake dried up circa 1950-60, so the owner planted hay there and put in a drainage ditch. There is water here only during the spring.

Signal Hill (hill)

73 D/10 - Hughenden
20-42-5-W4
52°38′N 110°41′W
Approximately 26 km south-east of the town of Wainwright.

The name for this hill in the Wainwright Regional Training Area has been official since 1958, but its precise origin is unknown.

Siler Creek (creek)

73 E/14 - St. Paul
24-56-8-W4
53°51′N 111°04′W
Flows south-east into North Saskatchewan River, approximately 13 km south south-west of Elk Point.

The name for this creek has been official since at least 1958, but its precise origin is unknown. It drains Stony Lake, known as "Siler Lake" until 1979.

Silver Beach (summer village)

83 H/4 - Kavanagh
11-47-28-W4
53°02′19″N 113°59′19″W
Approximately 40 km west north-west of Wetaskiwin.

The name for this village, incorporated 31 December 1953, is descriptive.

Silver Creek (creek)

82 O/10 - Fallentimber Creek
35-29-6-W5
51°32′N 114°44′W

Flows south-east into Little Red Deer River, approximately 32 km south of Sundre.

The name for this creek has been in use since at least 1958, but its precise origin is unknown.

Silver Creek (railway point)

83 K/1 - Windfall Creek
29-60-16-W5
54°13′N 116°21′W
Approximately 43 km west north-west of Whitecourt.

The name for this point on Canadian National Railways' Sangudo subdivision was officially approved 18 January 1974; however, its precise origin is unknown.

Silver Heights (locality)

73 D/6 - Brownfield
3-39-9-W4
52°19′N 111°14′W
Approximately 30 km north-east of Coronation.

The name for this post office, which operated from May 1923 through September 1966, is taken after Lord Strathcona's residence, near Winnipeg. (see Strathcona)

Silver Sands (summer village)

83 G/10 - Isle Lake
3-54-5-W5
53°38′N 114°39′W
Approximately 47 km south-east of Mayerthorpe.

The name for this summer village, incorporated 1 January 1969, is likely descriptive.

Simmo Lake (lake)

73 E/15 - Elk Point
6-57-5-W4
53°53′N 110°43′W
Approximately 12 km east of Elk Point.

The name for this lake was officially adopted 21 May 1942 in place of "Simmie Lake" and "Simmons Lake." Its precise origin is unknown.

* **Simmons** (former station)

83 H/11 - Edmonton
23-54-22-W4
53°41′N 113°06′W
Approximately 30 km north-east of Edmonton.

The origin of the name of this former station is unknown.

Sinclair Lake (lake)

73 L/10 - Marguerite Lake
23-66-5-W4
54°44′N 110°39′W
Approximately 42 km north-west of Cold Lake.

The name for this lake was officially applied in 1951 and commemorates Wing Commander F. Willard Sinclair, D.F.C., Croix de Guerre (1898-1946), of Calgary, who served in World War II. The local name for the feature is "Spring Lake," and refers to the number of mineral springs in the nearby hills.

Sinkhole Lake (lake)

83 G/6 - Easyford
20-50-9-W5
53°20′N 115°16′W
Approximately 23 km north-west of Drayton Valley.

The name for this lake has been official since at least 1958 and may be descriptive, as a sinkhole is defined as a "cavity in limestone, etc., into which water disappears."

Sinking Lake (lake)

73 L/2 - Muriel Lake
4-60-6-W4
54°09′N 110°50′W
Approximately 15 km south south-west of Bonnyville.

The name for this lake has been official since 1911, but its precise origin is unknown.

Sion (locality)

83 G/16 - Lac la Nonne
36-56-2-W5
53°53′N 114°09′W
Approximately 31 km south south-east of Barrhead.

A post office operated here from May 1904 through May 1968. The name is a biblical one, spelled "Zion," and symbolizes many things, including Jerusalem, the Promised Land, and Heaven. The original settlers had high hopes for their community.

Sir Winston Churchill Provincial Park

(provincial park)

73 L/13 - Lac La Biche
30-67-13-W4
54°50′N 111°59′W
Approximately 6 km north of Lac La Biche.

This 239.33 hectare (591.40 acre) provincial park was created by Order-in-Council No. 888/65 and was named after Sir Winston Leonard Spencer Churchill, K.G., P.C., O.M., C.H. (1874-1965). This English statesman and writer was a correspondent for the *Morning Post* of London during the Boer War, and wrote about his several adventures while in South Africa. He returned to England to be elected to Parliament, during which he made a dramatic move by switching parties. He continued to become a forceful speaker, and maintained that the only way to keep peace was to prepare for war. During World War I, Churchill was sent to France. He devoted much attention to the control and development of the air force and to both military and civilian aircraft experimentation and development. He returned to the Conservative Party in 1924. Churchill was awarded the Nobel Prize for Literature in 1953. Besides many foreign decorations and honorary degrees, he was the recipient of several medals, prizes and other tributes. He was made a Knight of the Garter in 1953.

Sisib Lake (lake)

83 H/7 - Tofield
13-51-21-W4
53°25′N 112°58′W
Approximately 38 km east south-east of Edmonton.

The name for this lake has been official since at least 1958, but its origin is unknown.

Sittingstone Lake (lake)

83 A/10 - Donalda
35-41-21-W4
52°34′N 112°55′W
Approximately 11 km north north-east of Bashaw.

The name for this lake has been in use since at least 1928 and may be a translation of a native name.

Skaro (locality)

83 H/15 - Lamont
16-57-19-W4
53°55′N 112°47′W
Approximately 29 km south-west of Smoky Lake.

The name for the post office, which operated from July 1904 through April 1964, was taken after K.H. Skaro, the first postmaster, an early settler from Norway.

---

*denotes rescinded name or former locality.

Skaro Lake (lake)
83 H/15 - Lamont
24-57-19-W4
53°56'N 112°43'W
Approximately 27 km south-west of
Smoky Lake.

(see Skaro)

Skeleton Lake (lake)
83 I/10 - Boyle
19-65-18-W4
54°38'50"N 112°43'44"W
Approximately 53 km south-west of Lac La
Biche.

The Indian name is said to mean "place of
the skeletons" – there is an Indian burial
ground nearby. In Cree, the name is
rendered *cheply sakahigan.*

Skukum Lake (lake)
83 I/16 - Plamondon
33-68-14-W4
54°55'N 112°05'W
Approximately 20 km north north-west of
Lac La Biche.

The name for this lake dates back to 1930
and was officially adopted 3 June 1954. It
may derive from an English expression
which may well come from the Chinook
jargon "skookum," meaning big, grand,
okay, etc., or "that's good."

Skunk Creek (creek)
83 B/6 - Crimson Lake
13-38-11-W5
52°16'40"N 115°27'35"W
Approximately 28 km south-west of Rocky
Mountain House.

Don McDonald, rancher, former trapper
and resident of the Strachan area for 70
years, states that during the 1920s he

trapped along this creek and caught skunks
in his traps here during a time when skunks
were very rare in the area. Ever since then
the creek has been referred to by this name
by the local residents.

Slawa (railway point)
73 E/11 - Myrnam
34-53-7-W4
53°37'N 111°57'W
Approximately 43 km east of Two Hills.

The post office operated here from March
1912 through May 1950 and its name is the
Russian word for "praise."

Slawa Creek (creek)
73 E/11 - Myrnam
17-55-8-W4
53°45'N 111°10'W
Flows north-west into North Saskatchewan
River, approximately 24 km south-west of
Elk Point.

(see Slawa)

* **Sleepy Hollow** (former post office)
72 M/16 - Grassy Island Lake
25-33-1-W4
51°52'N 110°00'W
Approximately 57 km south south-east of
Provost.

(see Compeer)

Slough Creek (creek)
83 A/8 - Halkirk
28-40-16-W4
52°28'15"N 112°14'45"W
Flows south-east into Paintearth Creek,
approximately 30 km north north-west of
Castor.

The name for this creek has been official
since at least 1958 and may be descriptive.

Slow Lake (lake)
73 D/10 - Hughenden
5-43-5-W4
52°41'N 110°41'W
Approximately 22 km south south-east of
the town of Wainwright.

The name for this lake has been official
since 1958, but its precise origin is unknown.

Smith (hamlet)
83 O/1 - Smith
23-71-1-W5
55°10'N 114°02'W
Approximately 70 km north-west of
Athabasca.

The name for this hamlet, whose post office
opened in April 1957, is taken after W.
Rathbone Smith, former general manager of
the Edmonton, Dunvegan and British
Columbia Railway. The post office was
previously known as "Mirror Landing."

Smith Creek (creek)
82 O/15 - Sundre
19-32-7-W5
51°49'N 114°53'W
Flows north into Bearberry Creek, approximately 17 km west of Sundre.

This creek was named after one of the men
employed in staking coal claims in this
vicinity. It has been in use since at least
1906. According to the *Cummins Rural
Directory*, an N. Smith and F. Smith were
owners of quarter-sections of land through
which the creek flows.

* **Smith Lake** (former locality)
73 L/8 - Cold Lake
7-61-3-W4
54°16'N 110°26'W
Approximately 20 km east of Bonnyville.

A post office operated here from May 1940 through May 1956, but its precise origin is unknown. The name was officially rescinded in 1971.

Smith Lake (lake)

73 L/4 - Cache Lake
2-59-11-W4
54°04′N 111°33′W
Approximately 18 km west north-west of St. Paul.

The name for this lake has been official since 6 April 1950, but its precise origin is unknown.

Smithfield (locality)

83 G/9 - Onoway
10-53-3-W5
53°34′N 114°20′W
Approximately 56 km west of Edmonton.

The name for this locality has been official since at least 1958, but its precise origin is unknown.

Smoky Creek (creek)

83 I/1 - Smoky Lake
4-59-17-W4
54°05′N 112°29′W
Flows south-east into North Saskatchewan River, approximately 12 km south south-west of Smoky Lake.

(see Smoky Lake)

Smoky Lake (lake)

83 I/2 - Waskatenau
23-59-18-W4
54°07′N 112°37′W
Approximately 10 km west of Smoky Lake.

The name for this lake is a translation of the Cree name *kaskapatau sakahigan*. According to legend, Smoky Lake was named by the Indians for a smoke-like vapour which rose from the lake, obscuring the opposite shore. Alexander Henry the younger, in his journal dated 10 July 1810, mentions this feature as "Lac qui Fume," or "the lake who smokes."

Smoky Lake (town)

83 I/1 - Smoky Lake
22-59-17-W4
54°06′50″N 112°28′00″W
Approximately 88 km north-east of Edmonton.

This town, incorporated 1 February 1962, takes its name from the nearby lake. (see Smoky Lake.) The post office was opened May 1909, and the Canadian Northern Railway established a station here in 1919.

* Smoky Lake Centre (former post office)

83 I/2 - Waskatenau
10-59-18-W4
54°06′N 112°37′W
Approximately 10 km west of Smoky Lake.

The post office operated under this name from July 1914 through September 1916, when it was changed to Warspite. (see Warspite)

Smoky Lake County #13 (county)

83 I/1 - Smoky Lake
62 to 69-17 to 24-W4
54°09′N 112°20′W
North-east of Edmonton.

(see Smoky Lake)

Snail Lake (lake)

73 L/3 - Vincent Lake
12-59-10-W4
54°05′N 111°21′W
Approximately 11 km north north-west of St. Paul.

The name for this lake has been official since 6 July 1950, but its precise origin is unknown.

Snake Hills (hills)

73 E/13 - Hairy Hill
24-57-13-W4
53°57′N 111°47′W
Approximately 28 km north of Two Hills.

The name for these hills goes back to 1859 when it appears on Arrowsmith's map. It is a translation of the Cree name *kinapikuchachltenau* and refers to an Indian tradition regarding the feature.

Snake Lake (lake)

82 P/15 - Rumsey
27-34-20-W4
51°57′00″N 112°45′30″W
Approximately 35 km north-east of Trochu.

The name for this lake is a translation of the Cree name *kinapik* and in Stoney *mnohemna*, according to Tyrrell. The name is likely descriptive.

Snakes Head, The (hill)

82 O/15 - Sundre
9-33-5-W5
51°49′N 114°40′W
Approximately 1 km north of Sundre.

The name for this hill has been official since at least 1958 and is descriptive of its shape.

* Sniatyn (former locality)

83 H/16 - Willingdon
30-57-16-W4
53°57′N 112°22′W
Approximately 19 km south south-east of Smoky Lake.

The name for the post office, which operated from July 1909 through April 1920 and then again from June 1936

---

*denotes rescinded name or former locality.

through April 1949, was taken after a town in Galicia from which settlers came. The post office was known as "Hunka" between these dates.

Snipe Hills (hills)
73 E/13 - Hairy Hill
34-56-13-W4
53°53′N 111°50′W
Approximately 21 km north of Two Hills.

The name for these hills has been official since at least 1928 and may take its name from a small snipe-like bird that used to live in the area. Apparently these birds make a sound "paa-paa" before it is going to rain.

Snug Cove (locality)
73 L/11 - Pinehurst Lake
19-65-9-W4
54°38′N 111°21′W
Approximately 43 km east south-east of Lac La Biche.

The descriptive name for this locality, whose post office operated from April 1948 through September 1951, refers to its position in a small cove on Pinehurst Lake.

Soars Lake (lake)
73 L/1 - Reita Lake
31-59-1-W4
54°09′N 110°09′W
Approximately 30 km south of Grand Centre.

The name for this lake has been official since at least 1958, but its precise origin is unknown.

Soda Lake (lake)
83 H/16 - Willingdon
19-55-14-W4
53°46′N 112°05′W

Approximately 23 km west north-west of Two Hills.

The name for this lake has been in use since at least 1893 when it was described as being a shallow lake having a large deposit of alkaline sediment on its shore.

* Soda Lake (former station)
83 H/16 - Willingdon
24-55-14-W4
53°47′N 112°04′W
Approximately 15 km west north-west of Two Hills.

A post office operated here from February 1907 through January 1939 and was named after the nearby Soda Lake. (see Soda Lake)

Soft Creek (creek)
73 E/2 - Grizzly Bear Creek
21-49-5-W4
53°14′N 110°40′W
Flows south-west into Grizzly Bear Creek, approximately 17 km south-east of Vermilion.

The name for this creek has been official since at least 1958, but its precise origin is unknown.

Soldan Lake (lake)
83 G/9 - Onoway
19-53-1-W5
53°35′N 114°08′W
Approximately 38 km west north-west of Edmonton.

This lake was officially named in 1950, after Bill Soldan and his family, early homesteaders who arrived in the area from Ukraine in 1911 and received title to the land upon which the lake sits, in 1916.

Sonia Lake (lake)
83 I/16 - Plamondon
34-66-15-W4
54°46′N 112°10′W

Approximately 13 km west of Lac La Biche.

The name for this lake has been official since at least 1958, but its precise origin is unknown.

Sorenson Lake (lake)
72 M/14 - Kirkpatrick Lake
26-32-11-W4
51°46′N 111°27′W
Approximately 36 km north-east of Hanna.

The precise origin for the name of this feature is unknown.

Sounding Creek (creek)
73 D/1 - Bodo
14-35-4-W4
52°00′15″N 110°28′00″W
Flows north into Sounding Lake, approximately 30 km south-west of Provost.

The creek gets its name from its association with Sounding Lake. (see Sounding Lake)

* Sounding Creek (former locality)
72 M/14 - Kirkpatrick Lake
25-34-11-W4
51°57′N 111°27′W
Approximately 16 km south of Coronation.

A post office operated here from June 1909 through October 1914, and takes its name from the nearby creek. (see Sounding Creek)

Sounding Creek Reservoir (reservoir)
72 M/10 - Sedalia
13-30-6-W4
51°34′N 110°43′W
Approximately 30 km north-west of Oyen.

(see Sounding Creek)

---

*denotes rescinded name or former locality.

Sounding Lake (lake)

73 D/2 - Neutral Hills
5-37-4-W4
52°09′N 110°32′W
Approximately 24 km south-west of
Provost.

The Blackfoot term for this feature is
oghta-kway (Nelson), and in Cree it is
called *ni-pi-kap-hit-i-kwek*, both roughly
translating as "sounding water" (Tyrrell).
There is an Indian legend attached to the
lake that states that an eagle with a snake in
its claws flew out of the lake causing a
rumbling noise like thunder. Another
legend maintains that the buffalo were born
from the depths of the water, and their
births caused the mysterious rumbling
sounds.

* Sounding Lake (former post office)

72 M/15 - Monitor
10-35-4-W4
51°58′N 110°34′W
Approximately 44 km south-west of
Provost.

This post office was named for its proximity to the lake of the same name. The name
was later changed to Monitor. (see Sounding Lake)

Sounding Lake (locality)

73 D/2 - Neutral Hills
21-36-4-W4
52°06′N 110°30′W
Approximately 50 km south south-west of
Provost.

The name for this post office, which
operated from June 1915 through September 1952, is the approximate translation of
the Cree word *ni pi kat hit i kewk*, or
"sounding water."

---

*denotes rescinded name or former locality.

South Baptiste (summer village)

83 I/12 - Buchanan Lake
21-66-24-W4
54°43′22″N 113°33′51″W
Southern shore of Baptiste Lake, approximately 18 km west of Athabasca.

The descriptive name for this summer
village, incorporated 1 January 1983, refers
to its location on Baptiste Lake. (see
Baptiste Lake)

South Bay (bay)

83 H/10 - Elk Island Park
14-14-54-20-W4
53°40′10″N 112°51′35″W
Approximately 40 km east of Edmonton, in
Elk Island National Park.

The name for this bay on the south shore of
Astotin Lake was officially approved 17
October 1991.

* South Bend (former hamlet)

73 E/13 - Hairy Hill
26-55-12-W4
53°47′N 111°41′W
Approximately 8 km north north-east of
Two Hills.

The post office here operated from September 1907 through September 1908 when the
name was changed to Duvernay. (See
Duvernay)

South Carrot Creek (creek)

83 G/12 - Carrot Creek
19-52-13-W5
53°30′15″N 115°54′15″W
Flows north into Carrot Creek, approximately 34 km east of Edson.

The name for this creek has been official
since at least 1958 and is likely descriptive
for its proximity as a tributary to Carrot
Creek. (see Carrot Creek)

South Cooking Lake (hamlet)

83 H/6 - Cooking Lake
13-51-22-W4
53°25′N 113°08′W
Approximately 29 km west of Edmonton.

The name for this hamlet is descriptive of
its location: south of Cooking Lake. (see
Cooking Lake)

South Cooking Lake, 1885

* South Ferriby (former locality)

73 E/9 - Marwayne
2-54-2-W4
53°38′N 110°11′W
Approximately 43 km north north-west of
Lloydminster.

The post office operated here from March
1913 through September 1944 and was
named after the home in Lincolnshire,
England, of the first postmaster's wife. The
name was officially rescinded 14 January
1970. North Ferriby and South Ferriby in
England are on opposite sides of the
Humber, the tidal estuary of the rivers
Ouse and Trent. North Ferriby was in
Yorkshire and South Ferriby in Lincolnshire, but both are now part of Humber-
side.

South Junction (railway junction)
83 A/5 - Red Deer
17-38-27-W4
52°16′N 113°49′W
Within the city of Red Deer.

The name for this railway junction is
descriptive.

South View (summer village)
83 G/10 - Isle Lake
9-54-5-W5
53°39′N 114°40′W
Approximately 44 km south-east of
Mayerthorpe.

This summer village was incorporated 1
January 1970 and, because of its location on
the north shore of Isle Lake, likely has a
descriptive name.

Spankie Lake (lake)
73 L/12 - Beaver Lake
15-66-12-W4
54°43′N 111°43′W
Approximately 17 km east south-east of
Lac La Biche.

The name for this lake was officially
applied in 1951 and commemorates Flight
Lieutenant Edward Spankie, D.F.C., (1915-
1945) of Bowden, Alberta, who was killed
during World War II.

Spear Lake (lake)
83 I/11 - Athabasca
30-66-21-W4
54°44′N 113°10′W
Approximately 9 km east of Athabasca.

The name for this lake has been official
since at least 1958, but its precise origin is
unknown.

Spedden (hamlet)
73 L/4 - Cache Lake
34-59-12-W4
54°08′N 111°43′W

Approximately 33 km west north-west of
St. Paul.

The post office here was previously called
"Cache Lake," and opened under this name
in December 1922. There is some confusion
over the origin of the name. One source
states that there was a Canadian Northern
Railway station erected here in 1920, and it
was named for R. Shedden (1819?-1849), an
English sailor who took his yacht, the
schooner *Nancy Dawson*, to the Arctic in
1849 in search of Sir John Franklin (1786-
1847). Another source maintains that the
station here was first called "Ashmont,"
and the first post office was called "Cache
Lake." According to this source, one of the
workmen in the surveying party, a Mr.
Speddin, died during construction and the
hamlet was subsequently named in his
honour.

Spencer Lake (lake)
73 L/14 - Touchwood Lake
14-67-9-W4
54°48′25″N 111°16′15″W
Approximately 45 km east of Lac La Biche.

The name for this lake was officially
adopted in 1945 and commemorates James
Spencer, the Hudson's Bay post manager at
Lac La Biche from 1900 through 1919. The
Cree name for this feature is rendered
sakemes sagahegan, translating "Mosquito
Lake." The local residents also refer to this
feature as "Mosquito Lake."

Spider Lake (lake)
83 H/3 - Bittern Lake
14-48-22-W4
53°08′N 113°07′W
Approximately 23 km north-west of
Camrose.

The name for this lake has been official
since at least 1958, but its precise origin is
unknown.

Spondin (locality)
72 M/13 - Garden Plain
27-33-12-W4
51°52′N 111°36′W
Approximately 28 km north-east of Hanna.

The precise origin of the name of this
feature, previously known as "Maunders,"
is unknown. The post office operated under
this name from January 1933 through
March 1969.

Spotted Creek (creek)
83 A/6 - Alix
22-42-23-W4
52°37′N 113°14′W
Flows south-east into Spotted Lake,
approximately 15 km south south-west of
Bashaw.

(see Spotted Lake)

Spotted Horse Lake (lake)
83 I/13 - Grosmont
27-68-26-W4
54°55′N 113°52′W
Approximately 44 km north-west of
Athabasca.

The name for this lake has been official
since at least 1958, but its precise origin is
unknown.

Spotted Lake (lake)
83 A/6 - Alix
32-40-22-W4
52°29′N 113°08′W
Approximately 16 km south south-west of
Bashaw.

The descriptive name for this lake is a
translation from the Cree word *mahsenasou
sakahigan*, derived from the "spots" of
open water and rushes seen on the lake. The
creek takes its name from this feature.

* Spring Lake (former locality)

83 A/16 - Daysland
1-44-16-W4
52°45′N 112°12′W
Approximately 12 km south south-east of
Daysland.

The name for the post office, which
operated here from March 1904 through
January 1928, was taken after its proximity
to a small lake fed by springs, formerly
known as "Never-Go-Dry Lake."

Spring Lake (lake)

83 G/9 - Onoway
30-52-1-W5
53°31′N 114°08′W
Approximately 41 km west of Edmonton.

The descriptive name for this lake has been
official since at least 1950 and refers to the
fact that it was fed by springs and has
outlets that appear to run like springs.

Springdale (locality)

83 B/16 - Winfield
34-44-2-W5
52°49′30″N 114°12′00″W
Approximately 22 km north of Rimbey.

A post office operated here from January
1906 through December 1948 and was
named after the large number of springs
found in the area.

* Springpark (former locality)

73 E/15 - Elk Point
18-57-6-W4
53°56′N 110°46′W
Approximately 5 km north north-east of
Elk Point.

The descriptive name for this former
locality, whose post office operated from

May 1913 through November 1951, refers
to the springs that ran throughout the
settlement. The name was officially
rescinded 22 April 1970.

Spruce Coulee (coulee)

83 A/9 - Forestburg
8-42-17-W4
52°36′40″N 112°25′40″W
Approximately 30 km south of Daysland.

The well-established name for this coulee is
taken after the tall, straight spruce that grew
in the Battle River Valley and in here. They
were felled by hand, limbed, and hauled to
the building sites.

Spruce Creek (creek)

82 P/12 - Lonepine Creek
6-16-32-26-W4
51°44′N 113°38′W
Flows east into Kneehills Creek, approximately 25 km west of Three Hills.

The name for this creek has been official
since 1958, but its precise origin is unknown.

Spruce Grove (city)

83 H/12 - St. Albert
4-53-27-W4
53°32′50″N 113°54′50″W
Approximately 27 km west of Edmonton.

The descriptive name for this city refers to
the fact that there were large groves of
trees, mostly spruce, before the influx of
settlers to the area. The post office was
established in July 1894 and was on John A.
McPherson's farm, whose house was near a
particularly fine grove of spruce. When the
Grand Trunk Pacific Railway station was
built through here in 1910, the original post
office was moved slightly west.

Spruce Grove, n.d.

Spruce Island (island)

83 H/10 - Elk Island Park
10-15-54-20-W4
53°40′05″N 112°51′30″W
Approximately 40 km east of Edmonton, in
Elk Island National Park.

The descriptive name for this island was
officially approved 17 October 1991.

Spruce Island Lake (lake)

83 H/10 - Elk Island Park
4-54-20-W4
53°38′N 112°53′W
Approximately 38 km east of Edmonton.

The name for this lake has been official
since at least 1958 and is likely descriptive.

Spruce Island Lake (lake)

83 I/12 - Coolidge
1-64-26-W4
54°30′10″N 113°47′00″W
Approximately 40 km south-west of
Athabasca.

The name for this lake has been official
since at least 1958, and may be descriptive
as there are two islands in the feature.

* Spruce Valley (former post office)

83 I/15 - Grassland
2-68-19-W4
54°51′N 112°48′W
Approximately 37 km east north-east of
Athabasca.

The descriptive name for the post office,
which operated here from March 1935
through April 1938, and reopened from
November 1951 through April 1969, refers
to the number of spruce trees in the area.
The name was officially rescinded in 1970.

Sprucefield (locality)

83 I/2 - Waskatenau
8-60-19-W4
54°11′N 112°49′W
Approximately 23 km north-west of
Smoky Lake.

The descriptive name for this locality,
whose post office operated from August
1913 through August 1929 and reopened
from September 1939 through April 1970,
refers to the number of spruce trees in the
area.

Spruceview (hamlet)

83 B/1 - Markerville
11-36-3-W5
52°05′N 114°19′W
Approximately 25 km west north-west of
Innisfail.

The School District of Spruce View #2744,
was established on 25 May 1912 replacing
the earlier Petersen School District for
which there is no date. Spruce View was
also the name of the homestead of a
neighbouring settler, Knud Knudson, and is
likely descriptive. The site was called the
"Dickson Corner" and businesses were
known by names such as "The Corner

Store." A proper survey was conducted in
1957 and in 1958 the first hamlet committee
was elected. The post office opened in
February 1970.

Sputinow (hamlet)

73 E/16 - Frog Lake
17-57-2-W4
53°55′N 110°16′W
Approximately 42 km east of Elk Point.

The descriptive name for this hamlet is the
Cree word for "high hill." The post office
opened in December 1946.

Square Lake (lake)

73 L/13 - Lac La Biche
9-25-68-13-W4
54°54′68″N 111°50′53″W
Approximately 17 km north north-east of
Lac La Biche.

The descriptive name for this lake has been
official since 5 March 1951 and refers to its
shape. Its shores are parallel to each other
and the length of each shore is approximately the same measurement. The Cree
call this feature is *asawesis sagahegan*, or
"Perch Lake."

Square Lake (lake)

73 L/1 - Reita Lake
35-58-3-W4
54°03′N 110°21′W
Approximately 40 km south south-west of
Grand Centre.

The descriptive name for this lake was
officially approved 3 May 1951.

Stafne Ridge (ridge)

82 O/15 - Sundre
29-32-7-W5
51°47′N 114°57′W
Approximately 22 km west of Sundre.

The name for this ridge has been in use
since at least 1958, but its origin is unknown.

Standish Lake (lake)

73 L/14 - Touchwood Lake
18-68-7-W4
54°53′N 111°04′W
Approximately 59 km east north-east of
Lac La Biche.

The name for this lake was officially
applied in 1951 and commemorates Sapper
William Henry Francis Standish, M.I.D., of
Calgary, who was killed in World War II.
Trappers refer to this feature as "Eagle
Lake."

Stanger (locality)

83 G/15 - Sangudo
22-55-6-W5
53°46′30″N 114°49′00″W
Approximately 30 km south-east of
Mayerthorpe.

A post office operated here from June 1911
through June 1974. The origin for the name
is not clear. It may be named after the
former home of A.J. Butler, the first
postmaster, from England. Another source
states that the name is taken after a village
in South Africa as two of the first settlers,
A.J. Butler and a Mr. Cawes, were Boer
War veterans.

Stanley Lake (lake)

83 I/11 - Athabasca
14-64-21-W4
54°32′N 113°03′W
Approximately 25 km south south-east of
Athabasca.

The name for this lake has been official
since at least 1958, but its precise origin is
unknown.

Stanmore (hamlet)

72 M/12 - Hanna
20-30-11-W4
51°35′N 111°30′W
Approximately 29 km south-east of Hanna.

The name is taken from a village in Middlesex (now Greater London), England. A post office operated here from October 1913 through July 1970. The name means "stony mere" or rocky lake.

Staplehurst (locality)

73 E/8 - Lloydminster
33-50-1-W4
53°21′N 110°05′W
Approximately 10 km north-west of Lloydminster.

The name for this locality, whose post office operated from April 1910 through December 1927, commemorates the home town in Kent, England, of the first postmaster, R.C. Rawle.

Star (hamlet)

83 H/15 - Lamont
9-56-19-W4
53°49′N 112°46′W
Approximately 7 km north of Lamont.

The name for this hamlet, whose post office operated from November 1899 through February 1985, was previously "Edna," after the daughter of the first postmaster, Ed Knowlton. Before that it was known as "Beaver Creek." The hamlet received its present name in 1899 at the suggestion of the Rev. Arthur Whiteside, a resident minister, 1896-97. Its precise origin is uncertain, but it may have been a promotional name.

Star Lake (lake)

83 G/9 - Onoway
20-52-2-W5
53°30′45″N 114°16′20″W
Approximately 51 km west of Edmonton.

The name for this lake was submitted to the former Geographic Board of Alberta for approval by R.J. Paterson, senior management biologist of Fish & Wildlife, in November 1968. The locally well-established name was officially approved 3 October 1978, but its precise origin is unknown.

Starland Municipal District #47

(municipal district)

82 P/10 - Munson
29 to 34-17 to 22-W4
51°40′N 112°30′W
South south-east of Red Deer.

The municipal district was established in 1912, but the origin for the name is unknown.

Starvation Butte (butte)

72 M/9 - Esther
SE-4-31-2-W4
51°37′31″N 110°13′10″W
Approximately 37 km north-east of Oyen.

There is an Indian grave on top of this butte, and it is believed by some that the name is a translation of a native name that reflected a year in which buffalo were scarce.

Stauffer (locality)

83 B/2 - Caroline
14-37-5-W5
52°10′N 114°36′W
Approximately 31 km south-east of Rocky Mountain House.

Joseph Emmet Stauffer, from whom this locality took its name, was born in 1874 near Manassas, Virginia, the son of Benjamin and Mary (Betzner) Stauffer, and grew up in Berlin (later Kitchener), Ontario. He arrived at Didsbury in 1902 and was principal of the public school for a year. He was variously a forest ranger,

homestead inspector, president of the Didsbury Board of Trade, and Liberal M.L.A for Didsbury, becoming deputy speaker of the House. Mr. Stauffer was involved in business, farming and real estate, and operated a sawmill at Sundre. He became chairman of the local improvement district later named in his honour when it became a municipality. The post office opened here in May 1907.

Stebbing Lake (lake)

73 L/6 - Goodridge
5-63-7-W4
54°25′N 111°01′W
Approximately 25 km north-west of Bonnyville.

The name for this lake has been official since 4 May 1950, but its precise origin is unknown.

Steele Lake (lake)

83 I/12 - Coolidge
29-65-25-W4
54°39′N 113°44′W
Approximately 33 km west south-west of Athabasca.

The name for this lake was officially adopted in 1906 and commemorates Ira John Steele, Dominion Land Surveyor.

Steep Hill (hill)

73 D/11 - Hardisty
25-43-8-W4
52°44′N 111°02′W
Approximately 17 km south-west of the town of Wainwright.

The name for this hill has been in use since at least 1958, but its origin is unknown. It is believed by some, however, that the name should correctly be "Jeep Hill."

Stettin (locality)

83 G/16 - Lac la Nonne
10-56-1-W5
53°49'N 114°04'W
Approximately 52 km north-west of
Edmonton.

A post office operated here from April 1913
through April 1932 and was named after
Stettin, formerly in Germany but since
World War II in Poland. The first postmaster, J. Libke, came from there.

Stettler (town)

83 A/7 - Stettler
5-39-19-W4
52°19'25"N 112°42'40"W
Approximately 74 km east of Red Deer.

This town is named after Carl Stettler
(1861-1919), a native of Berne, Switzerland.
He arrived in Alberta in 1903 from the
United States, and homesteaded three
kilometres west of here. His homestead
became the centre of a German-Swiss
colony and a post office was opened on his
land in February 1905. It was known as
"Blumenau." The hamlet of Stettler came
into being in 1905 with the coming of the
Canadian Pacific Railway branch from
Kerrobert to Lacombe. The post office was
moved to the site of the present town in
March 1906 and the hamlet named in
honour of Carl Stettler. He became the first
postmaster and the C.P.R. land agent.
When the hamlet became a village in 1906
he was one of the first councillors. This
town was incorporated 23 November 1906.

Stettler County #6 (county)

83 A/2 - Big Valley
33 to 40-16 to 22-W4
52°10'N 112°45'W
East of Red Deer.

(see Stettler)

Stewart Lake (lake)

82 P/12 - Lonepine Creek
1-32-27-W4
51°43'N 113°42'W
Approximately 25 km east south-east of
Olds.

The name for this lake has been official
since 1958, but its origin is unknown. The
early homesteaders who lived near the lake
included C.N. Stuart, J.N. Stuart and C.
Stuart. The spelling may have been altered
over the years.

Stewartfield (locality)

83 J/2 - Thunder Lake
19-58-4-W5
54°02'N 114°34'W
Approximately 15 km south-west of
Barrhead.

The name of this locality, whose post office
operated from April 1919 through October
1967, commemorates the birthplace of Earl
Haig's mother, a daughter of Hugh Veitch
of Stewartfield, Aberdeenshire (now
Grampian), Scotland. Field Marshal Haig
(1861-1928) was commander-in-chief of the
British Expedition Force in France and
Flanders from December 1915 to 1919.

Still Lake (lake)

73 E/2 - Grizzly Bear Creek
24-49-5-W4
53°14'N 110°36'W
Approximately 20 km south-east of
Vermilion.

The name for this lake has been official
since at least 1958, but its precise origin is
unknown.

Stirlingville (locality)

82 P/12 - Lonepine Creek
14-30-27-W4
51°34'N 113°42'W
Approximately 27 km east of Carstairs.

The origin for the name of this locality has
been official since 1958, but its origin is
unknown.

Stonelaw (locality)

82 P/16 - Farrell Lake
33-33-18-W4
51°52'N 112°29'W
Approximately 46 km north-west of
Hanna.

The post office, which operated here from
August 1913 through March 1931, was
named by John Watts after his former
home, Stonelaw, Scotland.

Stony Creek (creek)

73 L/4 - Cache Lake
29-58-12-W4
54°02'30"N 111°44'00"W
Flows south-east into Saddle Lake, approximately 26 km west of St. Paul.

The name for this creek has been official
since at least 1958 and is likely descriptive.

Stony Creek (creek)

82 O/10 - Fallentimber Creek
26-29-5-W5
51°30'15"N 114°35'00"W
Flows north into Little Red Deer River,
approximately 28 km south of Sundre.

The name for this creek has been official
since 1958, but its precise origin is unknown.

Stony Creek (creek)

83 J/4 - Whitecourt
30-59-13-W5
54°08'N 115°56'W
Flows north into Athabasca River, approximately 17 km west north-west of
Whitecourt.

The name for this creek has been official
since at least 1958 and is possibly descriptive.

* Stony Lake (former locality)

73 E/14 - St. Paul
34-56-8-W4
53°53′N 111°08′W
Approximately 18 km south-east of St. Paul.

The post office operated here from April 1932 through September 1944 and the name was taken after the nearby lake. The name was officially rescinded 12 August 1970. (see Stony Lake)

Stony Lake (lake)

73 E/14 - St. Paul
26-56-8-W4
53°51′N 111°05′W
Approximately 20 km south-east of St. Paul.

The name for this lake is a translation of the Cree word *ka as sinis kak* and is likely descriptive.

Stony Plain (town)

83 G/9 - Onoway
36-52-1-W5
53°31′50″N 114°01′25″W
Approximately 30 km west of Edmonton.

The origin of the name is generally attributed to the region having been the former camping grounds of the Stoney Indians, but geologist and geographer Dr. James Hector of the Palliser expedition, under the date of 10 January 1885, states that the plain "well deserves the name from being covered with boulders which are rather rare in general in this district or country." This town was incorporated 10 December 1908.

Stony Plain Indian Reserve #135

(Indian reserve)

83 H/5 - Leduc
15-52-26-W4
53°29′N 113°45′W

Approximately 15 km west south-west of Edmonton.

(see Stony Plain)

Stormy Creek (creek)

82 O/10 - Fallentimber Creek
3-31-7-W5
51°37′N 114°55′W
Flows south-east into Fallentimber Creek, approximately 25 km south-west of Sundre.

The name for this creek has been official since November 1937, but its precise origin is unknown.

Stouffers Lake (lake)

73 L/16 - Medley River
5-67-1-W4
54°47′N 110°07′W
Approximately 36 km north of Cold Lake.

The name for this lake has been official since 17 January 1951 and is taken after "Old Man" Stouffer, an early fox rancher and fisherman of the district.

Stove Lake (lake)

83 H/7 - Tofield
19-50-20-W4
53°20′N 112°55′W
Approximately 44 km east south-east of Edmonton.

The name for this lake has been official since at least 1958, but its precise origin is unknown.

Strachan (locality)

83 B/6 - Crimson Lake
7-38-8-W5
52°16′N 115°08′W
Approximately 28 km south-west of Rocky Mountain House.

The post office was called "Vetchland," because of the abundance of wild vetch,

until 1917, when it was renamed after David Gordon Strachan, killed in World War I. It operated from April 1917 through January 1968.

Strathcona County #20 (county)

83 H/11 - Edmonton
50-55-21-26-W4
53°29′N 113°11′W
East of Edmonton.

(see Strathcona Heights)

Strathcona Heights (locality)

83 H/14 - Redwater
11-57-23-W4
53°55′N 113°17′W
Approximately 41 km north north-east of Edmonton.

This country residence subdivision and the former village that is now annexed to the city of Edmonton were named after Donald Alexander Smith, 1st Baron Strathcona and Mount Royal (1820-1914). Smith joined the Hudson's Bay Company in 1838 and worked his way through the ranks from apprentice clerk to chief commissioner in 1871. He was a director and principal shareholder of the company by 1883. In 1889 he was chosen Governor. He was an enthusiastic supporter of the Canadian Pacific Railway and it was with his financial backing that the progress of the railway was possible. He was invited to drive in the last spike in 1885 when the railway was completed. In 1896 he founded Royal Victoria College for Women at McGill University in Montreal.

Strawberry Creek (creek)

83 G/8 - Genesee
12-48-3-W5
53°16′N 114°14′W
Flows north-east into North Saskatchewan River, approximately 43 km west south-west of Edmonton.

---

*denotes rescinded name or former locality.

The name for this creek is a translation of the Cree name *a-te-min,* and is likely descriptive.

Strawberry Hills (hill)

83 B/15 - Buck Lake
12-44-7-W5
52°46′30″N 114°52′30″W
Approximately 43 km north of Rocky Mountain House.

The name for this hill was officially named in February 1983 after John Strawberry, who lived for some years near Medicine Hat. He died in 1961 on the Sunchild Reserve at the age of 111.

Streamstown (hamlet)

73 E/8 - Lloydminster
26-51-2-W4
53°26′N 110°11′W
Approximately 20 km north-west of Lloydminster.

The name for this hamlet, whose post office opened in September 1906, is taken after a town in Westmeath, Ireland. It was named by the Rev. R. Smith.

Stretton Creek (creek)

73 E/8 - Lloydminster
5-51-2-W4
53°23′N 110°16′W
Flows north into Vermilion River, approximately 34 km north-west of Lloydminster.

This creek was previously called "Stretton Brook," and the generic was officially changed in June 1961. The name commemorates Stretton, Cheshire, England, from which many of the earliest settlers came.

*denotes rescinded name or former locality.

Strome (village)

83 A/16 - Daysland
23-44-15-W4
52°48′55″N 112°04′05″W
Approximately 15 km east south-east of Daysland.

The name for this village, whose post office opened in July 1906 is taken after a place in Scotland called Stromeferry, in Ross and Cromarty (now Highland). It was previously called "Knollton," after the first postmaster, Mac Knoll. Another source maintains that it is named after a pioneer Swedish family. This village was incorporated 3 February 1910.

Stronach Lake (lake)

83 I/10 - Boyle
23-64-19-W4
54°33′00″N 112°45′15″W
Approximately 38 km south-east of Athabasca.

The name for this lake has been official since at least 1958, but its precise origin is unknown.

Stry (locality)

73 L/4 - Cache Lake
27-58-13-W4
54°03′N 111°52′W
Approximately 37 km west of St. Paul.

The name for this locality, whose post office operated from May 1910 through May 1968, was named after a town in Poland, the former home of some of the first settlers.

* Stubno (former locality)

73 E/11 - Myrnam
6-53-10-W4
53°33′N 111°28′W
Approximately 27 km south-east of Two Hills.

The post office, which operated here from September 1921 through June 1958, was named after Stubno, Poland, the former home of M. Stepanick, the first postmaster. The name was officially rescinded 14 January 1970.

Sturgeon (railway point)

83 H/14 - Redwater
19-55-22-W4
53°46′15″N 113°15′10″W
Approximately 29 km north north-east of Edmonton.

The name for this railway point was requested by Canadian National Railways officials, as a name was required for tariff and operating purposes only. It was officially approved 15 February 1978. (see Sturgeon River)

Sturgeon Municipal District #90

(municipal district)
83 H/14 - Redwater
54 to 57-20 to 27-W4
53°50′N 113°35′W
North of Edmonton.

(see Sturgeon River)

Sturgeon River (river)

83 H/14 - Redwater
32-55-22-W4
53°48′N 113°14′W
Flows south-east into North Saskatchewan River, approximately 33 km north north-east of Edmonton.

The name for this river dates from David Thompson's map of 1814, where it is labelled "Sturgeon Rivulet." It refers to the abundant number of sturgeon caught in the watercourse. The Cree name for the river is *mi-koo-oo-pow,* or "Red Willow." The other features in the area take their names from this river.

Sturgeon Valley (hamlet)

83 H/12 - St. Albert
24-54-25-W4
53°41'N 113°33'W
Approximately 18 km north of Edmonton.

This hamlet was established in 1985 and was named for its location on the Sturgeon River. (see Sturgeon River)

Sturgeon Valley, 1907

Sturgis Lake (lake)

73 E/6 - Mannville
18-50-9-W4
53°19'N 111°18'W
Approximately 31 km west of Vermilion.

The name for this lake has been official since at least 1958, but its precise origin is unknown.

Styal (locality)

83 G/11 - Chip Lake
28-53-8-W5
53°36'N 115°05'W
Approximately 39 km south of Mayerthorpe.

---

*denotes rescinded name or former locality.

The post office operated here from January 1919 through May 1964. The name is likely taken after a village in Cheshire, England, spelled Styhale circa 1200. It was previously called "Imrie."

Sucker Lake (lake)

83 F/10 - Bickerdike
18-53-20-W5
53°34'30"N 116°56'30"W
Approximately 33 km west of Edson.

This shallow lake surrounded by muskeg is descriptively named, referring to the number of sucker fish inhabiting it. The name, which was officially approved 21 March 1978, has been used in Fishery and Forestry records since the late 1960s.

Sugden (locality)

73 L/5 - Goodfish Lake
15-62-11-W4
54°21'N 111°33'W
Approximately 44 km north north-west of St. Paul.

The name for this locality, whose post office operated from July 1916 through September 1969, was taken after D.S. Sugden, the first postmaster.

Sullivan Lake (lake)

73 D/4 - Castor
21-35-14-W4
52°01'N 111°57'W
Approximately 35 km west south-west of Coronation.

John W. Sullivan was astronomer and secretary to the Palliser expedition (see Beaverdam Creek). This lake and the nearby locality were named for him. The Cree name for this feature is *ka ki no ka mak*, which translates to "Long Lake."

Sullivan Lake (lake)

73 E/7 - Vermilion
11-50-6-W4
53°18'N 110°46'W
Approximately 50 km west of Lloydminster.

The name for this lake has been official since 1958, but its precise origin is unknown.

Sullivan Lake (locality)

73 D/4 - Castor
21-35-14-W4
52°01'N 111°57'W
Approximately 28 km west south-west of Coronation.

The post office, which operated here from April 1909 through February 1958, was named for its proximity to Sullivan Lake. (see Sullivan Lake)

* Sulphur Springs (former post office)

73 D/9 - Chauvin
7-41-2-W4
52°31'N 110°16'W
Approximately 19 km north of Provost.

The name for this post office, which operated from December 1913 through October 1927, is descriptive.

Sun Creek (creek)

83 B/15 - Buck Lake
10-45-6-W5
52°52'N 114°47'W
Flows north-east into Mink Creek, approximately 36 km south south-east of Drayton Valley.

The name for this creek has been official since at least 1958, but its precise origin is unknown.

Sundance (locality)

83 G/10 - Isle Lake
36-52-5-W5
53°32′N 114°36′W
Approximately 43 km north north-east of
Drayton Valley.

The post office name was changed from
"Little Volga" in July 1923, and operated
until November 1967. The origin for the
present name is not precise but was thought
at the time to be more or less in keeping
with some of the other native names
throughout the vicinity. Sundance Thermal
Plant was erected in the area in 1970.

Sundance Beach (summer village)

83 G/1 - Warburg
29-47-1-W5
53°05′N 114°06′W
Approximately 51 km west north-west of
Wetaskiwin.

The name for this summer village on the
north shore of Pigeon Lake reflects the
native influence in the area. The Natives, in
days gone by, at certain times of the year,
used to hold "sun dances," at which the
young braves were initiated into the tribe.
This summer village was incorporated 1
January 1970.

Sundance Creek (creek)

83 F/10 - Bickerdike
9-53-19-W5
53°34′10″N 116°44′30″W
Flows east into McLeod River, approximately 12 km west south-west of Edson.

The name was officially approved 2
December 1980, but the name has been
locally established since 1916 when it
appeared on the Sectional Map Sheet No.
313 of that year. Its precise origin is
unknown.

Sundance Lake (lake)

83 F/10 - Bickerdike
6-55-20-W5
53°44′N 116°58′W
Approximately 43 km north north-west of
Edson.

The name for this lake has been official
since at least 1958, but its precise origin is
unknown.

Sundre (town)

82 O/15 - Sundre
4-33-5-W5
51°47′50″N 114°38′40″W
Approximately 77 km south-west of Red
Deer.

The town takes its name from Sundre,
Norway, the home of N.T. Hagen, the first
settler and postmaster, who arrived in 1906.
As a young man he first went to the United
States and later came to Canada. When he
arrived in the Sundre area he purchased
land and the store from David McDougall.
The name Sundre (*Söndre*) means "south."
The post office opened in January 1909.
This town was incorporated 1 January
1956.

Sunken Lake (lake)

73 D/7 - Czar
22-39-5-W4
52°22′N 110°39′W
Approximately 26 km west of Provost.

The likely descriptive name for this lake has
been official since 1958, but its precise
origin is unknown.

* Sunland (former locality)

83 H/16 - Willingdon
1-58-16-W4
53°38′N 112°15′W
Approximately 21 km south south-east of
Smoky Lake.

The post office, which operated here from
April 1910 through January 1959, has a
descriptive name.

Sunny Lake (lake)

73 E/7 - Vermilion
29-49-5-W4
53°15′30″N 110°42′00″W
Approximately 14 km south-east of
Vermilion.

The name for this lake has been official
since at least 1958, but its precise origin is
unknown.

Sunnybrook (hamlet)

83 G/1 - Warburg
3-49-2-W5
53°12′N 114°13′W
Approximately 27 km west south-west of
Calmar.

The name for this hamlet, whose post office
opened in December 1912, is descriptive. It
is on the banks of a creek. It was previously
known as "Stones Corner."

Sunnybrook Creek (creek)

83 G/8 - Genesee
28-49-2-W5
53°15′15″N 114°13′45″W
Flows north into Strawberry Creek,
approximately 57 km west south-west of
Edmonton.

(see Sunnybrook)

* Sunnyside (former locality)

83 B/8 - Sylvan Lake
17-39-1-W5
52°22′N 114°07′W
Approximately 23 km north-west of Red
Deer.

_____

*denotes rescinded name or former locality.

The precise origin for the name of this locality, which became part of the summer village of Birchcliff in 1971, is unknown, but is likely descriptive. The name was officially rescinded 18 January 1974.

Sunnyslope (hamlet)
82 P/12 - Lonepine Creek
13-31-26-W4
51°39′N 113°33′W
Approximately 20 km west south-west of Three Hills.

The hamlet of Sunnyslope, nestled in the valley of the Knee Hills, had its beginnings at the turn of the century. The first post office was established in December 1903. Peter Giesbrecht, the first postmaster, was asked to choose a suitable name for the post office. He was of German descent and as he enjoyed the vista of the surrounding hills in the sunlight, he said "Sonniges Thale," in German, meaning Sunny Valley. From this suggestion came the descriptive name Sunnyslope. The post office closed in August 1966.

Sunrise Beach (summer village)
83 G/16 - Lac la Nonne
35-55-1-W5
53°47′30″N 114°03′00″W
Approximately 46 km north-west of Edmonton.

This summer village was established by Order-in-Council No. 769/88 effective 31 December 1988. The original owner of the land, Adolf Hastman, subdivided the land and the area became known as Sunrise Beach. The resort cottages are on the west side of Sandy Lake and the view of sunrises is particularly spectacular, according to local residents.

Sunset Beach (summer village)
83 I/12 - Coolidge
26-66-24-W4
54°44′35″N 113°31′56″W

Approximately 16 km west of Athabasca, on the east shore of Baptiste Lake.

The name for this summer village, incorporated 1 May 1977, is likely descriptive.

Sunset Hill (hill)
83 B/8 - Sylvan Lake
21-40-2-W5
52°27′50″N 114°13′40″W
Approximately 27 km north-west of Red Deer.

The well-established name for this hill was officially approved 7 February 1983. Its precise origin is unknown. The feature is associated with an Indian legend involving Maskepetoon, the great peace chief of the Crees, who underwent a six-day fast on this hill which ultimately led to a vision that earned him his name.

Sunset Lake (lake)
73 E/11 - Myrnam
15-54-8-W4
53°40′N 111°05′W
Approximately 28 km south south-west of Elk Point.

The well-established name for this lake was officially approved 24 September 1991, and is likely descriptive.

Sunset Lake (lake)
83 G/12 - Carrot Creek
9-55-12-W5
53°45′N 115°43′W
Approximately 50 km east north-east of Edson.

The name for this lake has been in use since at least 1933 where it appears on a Sectional map sheet, and is likely descriptive.

Sunset Point (summer village)
83 G/9 - Onoway
26-54-3-W5
53°42′N 114°21′W

Approximately 58 km west north-west of Edmonton.

This summer village on the north-east shore of Lac Ste Anne was incorporated 1 January 1959 and has a descriptive name.

Surprise Hill (hill)
82 P/9 - Craigmyle
28-31-17-W4
51°41′N 112°23′W
Approximately 32 km west north-west of Hanna.

The name for this hill has been official since 1958, but its origin is unknown.

Survey Hill (hill)
73 D/11 - Hardisty
23-43-8-W4
52°43′N 111°04′W
Approximately 18 km south-west of the town of Wainwright.

The name for this hill, located in the Wainwright Regional Training Area, may be descriptive.

Swalwell (hamlet)
82 P/11 - Three Hills
9-30-24-W4
51°34′N 113°19′W
Approximately 16 km south of Three Hills.

The post office, which opened here in November 1911 was named after a local auditor with the Grand Trunk Pacific Railway. The name was changed from "Rawdonville."

Swartz Creek (creek)
83 F/9 - Edson
6-31-52-17-W5
From 53°15′20″N 116°20′55″W
to 53°32′05″N 116°29′40″W
Flows east into McLeod River, approximately 7 km south south-west of Edson.

This creek was officially named 17 October 1991 after Maurice Swartz, an early and long-time merchant of Edson, who, like many other merchants and railroaders, took homesteads in the area surrounding Edson. Mr. Swartz's homestead was south across the McLeod River on this creek. The creek is well known to local residents, hunters and fishermen.

Swift Lake (lake)

73 D/10 - Hughenden
33-42-6-W4
52°39′N 110°47′W
Approximately 20 km south of the town of Wainwright.

The name for this lake has been official since 1958, but its precise origin is unknown.

Sylvan Creek (creek)

83 A/5 - Red Deer
19-38-28-W4
52°16′30″N 113°59′45″W
Flows east into Red Deer River, approximately 5 km west of Red Deer.

(see Sylvan Lake)

Sylvan Glen (locality)

83 I/12 - Coolidge
30-64-26-W4
54°33′N 113°55′W
Approximately 44 km south-west of Athabasca.

The origin of the name of this locality, whose post office operated from January 1930 through September 1951, is unknown.

■ Sylvan Lake (lake)

83 B/8 - Sylvan Lake
27-39-2-W5
52°23′N 114°13′W
Approximately 24 km west north-west of Red Deer.

The name for this lake has undergone many changes over the years. It was called "Snake Lake" by the early natives. The Cree term for it is known as *wa-pi-sioo,* and in Stoney it is rendered *ko-gamna.* David Thompson labelled it "Methy Lake" on his 1814 map. Palliser called it "Swan Lake" in 1859. "Sylvan" is from the Latin *silvanus.* As a noun it is defined as "one who inhabits a wood or forest; a being of the woods. The adjective is close to this definition: "belonging to, related to, situated in, or characteristic of a wood or woods."

Sylvan Lake (town)

83 B/8 - Sylvan Lake
33-38-1-W5
52°18′40″N 114°04′50″W
Approximately 20 km west of Red Deer.

The post office opened in May 1907 and was named for its position on Sylvan Lake. This resort town, incorporated 20 May 1946, has grown significantly since that time. (see Sylvan Lake)

Sylvester Creek (creek)

83 B/13 - Nordegg River
36-43-12-W5
52°45′15″N 115°36′15″W
Flows north-west into Nordegg River, approximately 67 km north-west of Rocky Mountain House.

The name for this creek has been official since at least 1958, but its precise origin is unknown.

Syson Lake (lake)

73 D/4 - Castor
25-35-13-W4
52°02′N 111°43′W
Approximately 5 km south of Coronation.

This lake was named after Richard M. Syson, who originally came to Canada as a Barr Colonist in 1903. He homesteaded 10 kilometres north of Stettler and died in February of 1958. He was given the opportunity to name the lake following a survey party custom that called for each man to name a lake.

Tail Creek (creek)

83 A/6 - Alix
23-39-22-W4
52°22′N 113°04′W
Flows south into Red Deer River, approximately 25 km west of Stettler.

This creek drains Buffalo Lake and resembles the tail of a stretched skin. The Stoney name is *sin-doo*; the French name is *La Que*; in Cree, it is called *o-sooi*. There was a settlement close by of the same name, used each season in the 1870s by the Métis for the buffalo hunt.

Tailor Lake (lake)

83 I/11 - Athabasca
6-64-22-W4
54°31′N 113°19′W
Approximately 24 km south of Athabasca.

The name for this lake has been official since at least 1958, but its precise origin is unknown.

Tait Lake (lake)

83 A/11 - Chain Lakes
11-20-41-23-W4
52°32′20″N 113°17′00″W
Approximately 21 km west south-west of Bashaw.

The name for this lake goes back to at least 1894 when the lake received the name of Thomas Tait, an early settler of mixed-blood background.

Talbot (locality)

73 D/3 - Coronation
6-38-9-W4
52°14′N 111°16′W
Approximately 20 km north north-east of Coronation.

A post office opened here in March 1907 and closed in April 1970. This locality was named after Peter Talbot (1854-1919), a member of the Senate of Canada from 1906 to his death in 1919. A farmer in the Lacombe district, he declined an offer by Prime Minister Laurier to be the first premier of the newly created province of Alberta.

Tamarack Lake (lake)

83 G/16 - Lac la Nonne
30-56-2-W5
53°53′N 114°16′W
Approximately 30 km south south-east of Barrhead.

The name for this lake has been official since at least 1958 and is likely descriptive. The tamarack is one of the three native larches in Canada.

Tanglefoot Lake (lake)

83 A/6 - Alix
13-40-23-W4
52°27′N 113°11′W
Approximately 20 km south-west of Bashaw.

The descriptive name for this lake was suggested by a Mrs. Westhead, and refers to its thickly wooded banks. The name has been associated with this feature since at least 1905, but was not officially approved until 17 January 1955.

* Tannis (former railway point)

83 A/5 - Red Deer
10-39-28-W4
52°21′N 113°57′W
Approximately 7 km north of Red Deer.

The origin for the name of this former railway point is unknown. The name was changed to Briggs. (see Briggs)

T~U~V

Taplow (locality)

72 M/12 - Hanna
15 30 13-W4
51°34′N 111°44′W
Approximately 16 km south-east of Hanna.

This Canadian Northern Railway point was established in 1920, and was probably named after Taplow, a village in Buckinghamshire, England. According to K. Cameron, author of *English Place Names* (1969), the British place-name appears as *Tappelawe* in 1196, meaning, "Taeppa's burial mound."

Tattum Lake (lake)

83 J/9 - Flatbush
35-64-2-W5
54°35′N 114°12′W
Approximately 52 km north north-east of Barrhead.

The name for this lake has been official since at least 1958, but its precise origin is unknown.

Tawakwato Lake (lake)

83 I/9 - Hylo
3-66-15-W4
54°41′22″N 112°12′47″W
Approximately 20 km south-west of Lac La Biche.

The name for this lake has evolved from an Indian legend, and is Cree for "gap-toothed." It is locally known as "Hylo Lake" for its proximity to the hamlet and railway siding of the same name.

Tawatinaw (hamlet)
83 I/6 - Perryvale
26-61-24-W4
54°18′N 113°29′W
Approximately 29 km north-west of
Westlock.

This hamlet, whose post office operated
from October 1911 through September
1986, was named for its proximity to the
Tawatinaw River. (see Tawatinaw River)

Tawatinaw Lake (lake)
83 I/6 - Perryvale
12-62-24-W4
54°20′N 113°28′W
Approximately 30 km north-east of
Westlock.

(see Tawatinaw River)

Tawatinaw River (river)
83 I/11 - Athabasca
12-31-64-22-W4
From 54°30′00″N 113°21′35″W
to 54°43′14″N 113°16′40″W
Flows north into Athabasca River at
Athabasca.

The name for this feature is derived from a
Cree word, descriptively meaning "river
which divides the hills" or "valley river."

Tawayik Lake (lake)
83 H/10 - Elk Island Park
21-53-20-W4
53°36′N 112°53′W
Approximately 42 km east of Edmonton, in
Elk Island National Park.

The name for this lake is a Cree term
translating, "in the middle of" or, literally,
"middle lake." No other information about
the origin of the name is known.

Taylor (station)
83 A/14 - Wetaskiwin
23-46-24-W4
52°59′N 113°22′W
Within the city limits of Wetaskiwin.

The precise origin of the name of this
railway station is unknown.

Taylor Lake (lake)
83 I/3 - Thorhild
20-59-23-W4
54°07′N 113°25′W
Approximately 30 km east of Westlock.

The name for this lake has been official
since at least 1958, but its precise origin is
unknown.

Teepee Lake (lake)
73 E/1 - Paradise Valley
22-49-3-W4
53°13′44″N 110°21′18″W
Approximately 30 km west south-west of
Lloydminster.

The locally well-established name for this
lake has been in widespread use since at
least 1904, when it appears on a Department of the Interior Township Map. Its
precise origin, however, is unknown. The
name was officially adopted 22 January
1991.

Tees (hamlet)
83 A/6 - Alix
25-40-24-W4
52°28′N 113°19′W
Approximately 27 km south-west of
Bashaw.

The Canadian Pacific Railway established a
station here in 1905 and named it after W.E.
Tees, original owner of the townsite. The
post office was known as "Brook" until
March 1906 when it opened under the name
Tees.

Telegraph Creek (creek)
73 E/15 - Elk Point
15-55-5-W4
53°45′08″N 110°39′56″W
Flows north into North Saskatchewan
River, approximately 16 km east of Elk
Point.

The name may trace back to the time of the
Riel Rebellion when the government
attempted to build a telegraph line on the
south side of the North Saskatchewan
River, at the mouth of this creek. The
attempt was abandoned when the builders
were not able to cross the river with the
line. For many years afterwards, there were
telegraph poles to be seen at the mouth of
this feature.

Telford Lake (lake)
83 H/5 - Leduc
36-49-25-W4
53°16′N 113°31′W
Immediately north-east of Leduc.

Robert T. Telford (1860-1932) was the first
settler on this lake, which bears his name.
He arrived in the area in 1889 having served
the North-West Mounted Police for four
years previously. His land consisted of the
entire townsite of what is now Leduc, and
he was its first businessman, mayor and
became the first M.L.A. for the riding of
Leduc in 1905, representing it for ten years
as a Liberal.

Telfordville (hamlet)
83 G/8 - Genesee
36-49-2-W5
53°16′N 114°10′W
Approximately 52 km south-west of
Edmonton.

A post office operated here from December
1904 through March 1969 and was named
after R.T. Telford. (see Telford Lake)

Temple Creek (creek)

82 O/15 - Sundre
13-33-7-W5
51°50′30″N 114°59′00″W
Flows east into Bearberry Creek, approximately 21 km west north-west of Sundre.

This creek was named after Phil Temple and his family. The name is well established in local usage, and was officially approved 3 October 1991. Phil Temple came to Canada from England in 1924 with his parents and one sister (another sister was born in Bearberry). They moved to Bearberry circa 1927 and soon after bought the quarter-section of land homesteaded by George Lunt. The Temples also bought some land along the James River. Since the 1960s, Phil Temple has lived in the Yukon. Before the Temples came to the area, the creek was known as "Pearce Creek," after George Pearce and his family, who lived there previously.

Ten Mile Creek (creek)

82 P/12 - Lonepine Creek
36-31-29-W4
51°42′N 113°59′W
Flows east into Lonepine Creek, approximately 20 km east south-east of Olds.

The name for this creek has been official since 1958, but its precise origin is unknown.

Tent Lake (lake)

73 L/12 - Beaver Lake
2-65-13-W4
54°36′N 111°52′W
Approximately 20 km south south-east of Lac La Biche.

The name for this lake dates from 1918, but its precise origin is unknown. There is some

speculation that the name originated from the Cree, but this is unconfirmed.

Tepee Lake (lake)

73 L/13 - Lac La Biche
34-68-13-W4
54°55′N 111°54′W
Approximately 18 km north north-east of Lac La Biche.

The name has been official since 3 May 1951, but its precise origin is unknown. The spelling for this name is the British variant of "teepee."

* The Hub (former post office)

73 D/4 - Castor
30-36-12-W4
52°09′N 111°44′W
Approximately 15 km south-east of Castor.

The precise origin of the name of this post office, which operated from January 1911 through August 1912, is unknown. The name was later changed to Fleet. (see Fleet)

Therien (hamlet)

73 L/3 - Vincent Lake
34-60-9-W4
54°14′N 111°16′W
Approximately 28 km north of St. Paul.

The name for this hamlet, whose post office operated from December 1909 through October 1984, is taken after the Rev. J. Adéodat Therien (1862-1936) of the Oblates of Mary Immaculate. Father Therien was the first director of the colony of St. Paul des Métis.

Thin Lake (lake)

73 L/3 - Vincent Lake
19-60-7-W4
54°13′N 111°02′W
Approximately 21 km west south-west of Bonnyville.

The name has been official since 6 July 1950 and is likely descriptive.

Thinlake River (river)

73 L/6 - Goodridge
9-8-61-7-W4
54°16′00″N 111°00′15″W
Flows east into Moose Lake, approximately 17 km west of Bonnyville.

(see Thin Lake)

Thomas Lake (lake)

73 E/4 - Viking
4-48-12-W4
53°07′N 111°42′W
Approximately 6 km east north-east of Viking.

The name has been official since at least 1958, but its precise origin is unknown.

Thompson Lake (lake)

73 D/6 - Brownfield
25-40-11-W4
52°28′N 111°26′W
Approximately 25 km south south-west of Hardisty.

The name has been official since 1958, but its origin is unknown.

Thompson Lakes (lake)

73 L/1 - Reita Lake
3-60-2-W4
54°09′N 110°14′W
Approximately 36 km east south-east of Bonnyville.

The name was changed in 1952 from Thompson Lake to Thompson Lakes. The precise origin is unknown.

Thorhild (village)

83 I/3 - Thorhild
6-60-21-W4
54°00′20″N 113°07′35″W
Approximately 24 km north of Redwater.

---

*denotes rescinded name or former locality.

The name for this village, whose post office opened in March 1914, has a Scandinavian flavour. According to Dave Yachimec, the secretary-treasurer of the village in 1972, the original site of the post office was on a hill and during thunderstorms there were frequent lightning strikes nearby. Local tradition maintains that M.G. Jardy, the first postmaster, named the nearby hill "Thor's Hill" after the Norse god of thunder, and the village took its name from the hill. This village was incorporated 31 December 1949.

Thorhild County #7 (county)

83 I/3 - Thorhild
58to 63-21 to 23-W4
54°08'N 113°05'W
North north-east of Edmonton.

(see Thorhild)

Thorsby (village)

83 G/1 - Warburg
14-49-1-W5
53°13'35"N 114°02'55"W
Approximately 49 km south-west of Edmonton.

Many of the original homesteaders in this district were Scandinavians and the community was named after *Thor*, the god of thunder in Norse mythology. *By* is the Norse term for "village." The village was incorporated 31 December 1949.

Three Hills (hills)

82 P/11 - Three Hills
18-32-23-W4
51°44'N 113°15'W
Approximately 5 km north-east of Three Hills.

These three hills were mentioned in a geological report of 1886. They run from north-west to south-east, and the highest measures approximately 60 metres. The old

buffalo trail crosses the creek and is one of the oldest trails in Alberta, used long before the Edmonton and Calgary trail. The Cree name for the hills is *nis-to*; it is rendered *pa-ha-amni* in Stoney. The name is descriptive, and the nearby town and creek take their names from these hills.

Three Hills (town)

82 P/11 - Three Hills
36-31-24-W4
51°42'05"N 113°16'10"W
Approximately 75 km south south-east of Red Deer.

A post office was established in December 1904, and it takes its name from the nearby hills. (see Three Hills). This town was incorporated 1 January 1929.

Threehills Creek (creek)

82 P/10 - Munson
3-30-21-W4
51°32'N 112°53'W
Flows south-east into Red Deer River, approximately 32 km south-east of Three Hills.

(see Three Hills)

Throne (locality)

73 D/3 - Coronation
31-35-9-W4
52°03'N 111°17'W
Approximately 12 km south-east of Coronation.

This post office was known as "Hamilton Lake" until June 1912. Its name was changed to align with adjacent stations along the Canadian Pacific Railway's Kerrobert-Lacombe line such as Consort, Loyalist, Veteran and Coronation. The new names commemorated the coronation year of King George V in 1911.

Thunder Lake (hamlet)

83 J/2 - Thunder Lake
29-59-5-W5
54°08'N 114°43'W
Approximately 21 km west of Barrhead.

This hamlet was established 8 July 1982 and is likely named for its proximity to Thunder Lake. (see Thunder Lake)

Thunder Lake (lake)

83 J/2 - Thunder Lake
30-59-5-W5
54°08'00"N 114°44'30"W
Approximately 25 km west of Barrhead.

According to local Indian tradition, the name of this shallow lake is a translation of an Indian word. The cracking of the ice in winter can be heard for miles around the shore and resembles the sound of thunder.

Thunder Lake Provincial Park

(provincial park)
83 J/2 - Thunder Lake
29-59-5-W5
54°08'N 114°44'W
Approximately 23 km west of Barrhead.

This 207.87 hectare (513.67 acre) provincial park was created by Order-in-Council No. 1204/67 and is named from the lake. (see Thunder Lake)

Tieland (locality)

83 J/16 - Chisholm
14-67-2-W5
54°48'N 114°11'W
Approximately 58 km west of Athabasca.

At one time Northern Alberta Railways took a number of ties and timber from this area. The locality takes its descriptive name from this fact.

Tiger Lily (locality)
83 J/2 - Thunder Lake
13-60-6-W5
54°11′N 114°46′W
Approximately 25 km north-west of
Barrhead.

The name for this locality, whose post
office opened in December 1934, is taken
after the flower. The tiger lily is the western
wood lily (*Lilium philadelphicum var.
andinum*), which was growing abundantly
at the time of this area's settlement.

Tiger Lily Lake (lake)
83 J/2 - Thunder Lake
31-59-5-W5
54°08′40″N 114°44′20″W
Approximately 23 km west of Barrhead.

The name for this lake was officially
approved 9 July 1980 and is taken for its
proximity to the locality of Tiger Lily. At
the time that this lake was being named, a
subdivision and cottage development
project was underway. (see Tiger Lily)

Tinchebray (locality)
73 D/5 - Alliance
11-40-14-W4
52°26′N 111°56′W
Approximately 40 km south south-west of
Sedgewick.

A post office was established here in
October 1907, and was named after
Tinchebrai in France, where the Roman
Catholic Pères de Ste Marie-de-Tinchebrai
have a college. Five or six members of the
order settled here in the summer of 1904.
The post office closed in February 1932.

* **Tindastoll** (former post office)
83 B/1 - Markerville
20-36-1-W5
52°06′N 114°06′W
Approximately 31 km south-west of Red
Deer.

The name for the post office, which
operated here from June 1892 through
December 1912, is taken after a mountain in
Iceland, the land from where many of the
first settlers originated.

Tindastoll Creek (creek)
83 B/1 - Markerville
29-36-1-W5
52°07′N 114°07′W
Flows west into Medicine River, approximately 30 km south-west of Red Deer.

The name for this creek has been official
since at least 1958. (see Tindastoll)

Tipper Lake (lake)
82 P/15 - Rumsey
25-32-20-W4
51°46′N 112°42′W
Approximately 30 km east north-east of
Three Hills.

The name for this lake has been official
since December 1968, but its origin is
unknown.

Tit Willow Lake (lake)
73 D/10 - Hughenden
2 43 6 W4
52°40′N 110°47′W
Within the Wainwright Regional Training
Area, approximately 18 km south south-
east of the town of Wainwright.

The name for this lake is likely descriptive
of the bird.

Toad Creek (creek)
83 G/9 - Onoway
17-55-1-W5
53°44′N 114°06′W
Flows south into Sturgeon River, approximately 45 km west north-west of Edmonton.

The name for this creek which drains Toad
Lake has been official since at least 1958,
and likely takes its name from the lake.

Toad Lake (lake)
83 G/16 - Lac la Nonne
28-55-2-W5
53°47′N 114°13′W
Approximately 40 km south south-east of
Barrhead.

The name for this lake has been official
since at least 1958 and is likely descriptive.

Todd Lake (intermittent lake)
82 O/15 - Sundre
5-36-32-7-W5
51°47′13″N 114°52′12″W
Approximately 15 km west south-west of
Sundre.

The well-established name for this lake was
officially approved 3 October 1991. The
Todd family lived by the lake at one time;
however, they were not the original
homesteaders of this quarter-section. Ernie
Green lived there until at least the mid-
1940s. By 1959, Rex Logan owned the
quarter-section.

Tofield (town)
83 H/7 - Tofield
1-51-19-W4
53°22′45″N 112°40′00″W
Approximately 57 km east south-east of
Edmonton.

This town was named after Dr. J.H.
Tofield, an early settler in the district. He

was born in Yorkshire and educated at Oxford. He later took degrees in Engineering and Medicine, and served in India as an army doctor. It may be that his ancestors originated from Stewkley in Buckinghamshire, England, which was seen as the "home of the Tofields." Dr. Tofield arrived in Edmonton in 1882 and served as an army medical officer in the Riel Rebellion. He died in 1918. The name Tofield was first applied to the school district and in March 1898 to the post office, which was formerly known as "Logan." This town was incorporated 10 September 1909.

Tolland (locality)

73 E/2 - Grizzly Bear Creek
22-48-5-W4
53°08'N 110°40'W
Approximately 44 km west south-west of Lloydminster.

The post office operated here from April 1913 through September 1970 and was named after Tolland, Massachusetts, the former home of O.H. Webber, the first postmaster.

Tolman (locality)

82 P/14 - Trochu
23-33-22-W4
51°50'N 113°01'W
Approximately 12 km north-east of Trochu.

The post office, which operated here from August 1908 through December 1918, was named after the J.A. Tolman family who homesteaded in the area. Mr. Tolman was the first postmaster.

Tomahawk (hamlet)

83 G/7 - Tomahawk
12-51-6-W5
53°24'N 114°46'W
Approximately 24 km north north-east of Drayton Valley.

This hamlet was named by the first settler after Tomahawk, Wisconsin. Lewis Shaw (1869-1950) originally came from Ontario and worked in lumber camps in Minnesota and Wisconsin before heading west. This name was chosen from among others submitted. The post office opened in April 1907.

Tomahawk Creek (creek)

83 G/7 - Tomahawk
5-51-5-W5
53°22'N 114°42'W
Flows south-east into North Saskatchewan River, approximately 16 km north-east of Drayton Valley.

(see Tomahawk)

Tompkins Lake (lake)

73 L/5 - Goodfish Lake
18-62-12-W4
54°22'N 111°48'W
Approximately 46 km south south-east of Lac La Biche.

The name for this lake has been official since 4 May 1950, but its precise origin is unknown.

Toodles Lake (lake)

73 L/13 - Lac La Biche
1-67-13-W4
54°46'N 111°51'W
Approximately 8 km east of Lac La Biche.

The name for this lake has appeared on maps since 1918, but the origin is unknown.

Torlea (locality)

73 E/4 - Viking
13-48-14-W4
53°08'30"N 111°55'00"W
Approximately 10 km north-west of Viking.

The name for this locality, whose post office operated from December 1916

through September 1953, may have a descriptive name. "Tor" is a term for hill and "lea" means "a tract of open grassland." It was previously called "Nestor."

Torrington (village)

82 P/13 - Torrington
34-32-26-W4
51°47'25"N 113°36'25"W
Approximately 26 km west north-west of Three Hills.

This village was named by the Canadian Pacific Railway, possibly after Torrington in Devon, England. The name apparently means "hill pasture homestead." The first post office was established in July 1930. This village was incorporated 1 January 1964.

Touchwood Lake (lake)

73 L/14 - Touchwood Lake
2-24-67-10-W4
54°49'20"N 111°24'20"W
Approximately 37 km east of Lac La Biche.

The name for this lake has been official since at least 1928, and likely refers to birch punk, used to start fires with flint and steel, nicknamed "touchwood." The feature is known locally as "Trout Lake."

Tower Hill (hill)

73 D/14 - Irma
11-44-8-W4
52°46'N 111°04'W
Approximately 11 km south-west of the town of Wainwright.

This hill was locally called "Observation Butte," but its descriptive name, Tower Hill, was made official in 1971.

Tower Hill (hill)

83 H/10 - Elk Island Park
12-15-54-20-W4
53°40'00"N 112°52'30"W

Approximately 40 km east of Edmonton, in Elk Island National Park.

The name for this 708 m (2360 ft.) hill was officially approved 17 October 1991. The name was requested by the Canadian Permanent Committee on Geographical Names.

Town Lake (lake)
83 B/16 - Winfield
32-45-3-W5
52°56′N 114°24′W
Approximately 33 km north north-west of Rimbey.

This lake may be descriptively named for its position on the township line dividing Tp 45 and Tp 46. It may have been previously called "Township Lake," as the origin for the locality on its northwestern shore reads "after Township Lake" in the 1928 publication *Place Names of Alberta*.

Town Lake (locality)
83 B/16 - Winfield
32-45-3-W5
52°56′N 114°25′W
Approximately 33 km north north-west of Rimbey.

The Lacombe and North Western Railway established a station here in 1926 and named it for its position on Town Lake. (see Town Lake)

Trail Creek (creek)
82 O/16 - Olds
33-33-2-W5
51°53′00″N 114°15′15″W
Flows north-west into Little Red Deer River, approximately 18 km north north-west of Olds.

The precise origin of the name of this feature is unknown.

Trail Lake (lake)
73 L/12 - Beaver Lake
17-65-13-W4
54°37′N 111°56′W
Approximately 17 km south of Lac La Biche.

The name for this lake appears on a map dated 1918 and likely refers to a trail between Craigend and Christy Creek.

Trap Lake (lake)
73 L/12 - Beaver Lake
25-66-13-W4
54°44′45″N 111°50′00″W
Approximately 8 km east of Lac La Biche.

The name has been official since at least 1958 and may possibly be descriptive.

Trapeze Lake (lake)
83 I/9 - Hylo
22-65-16-W4
54°38′N 112°19′W
Approximately 29 km south-west of Lac La Biche.

The name for this lake has been official since at least 1958, but its precise origin is unknown.

Trappers Lake (lake)
83 H/10 - Elk Island Park
36-53-21-W4
53°37′N 112°58′W
Approximately 37 km east of Edmonton.

The name for this lake has been official since at least 1958, but its precise origin is unknown.

Trappers Lake (lake)
83 J/2 - Thunder Lake
13-58-6-W5
54°01′N 114°46′W
Approximately 26 km south-west of Barrhead.

The name for this lake has been official since at least 1958, but its precise origin is unknown.

Tremblay Lake (lake)
83 I/16 - Plamondon
SE-3-67-15-W4
54°46′49″N 112°12′04″W
Approximately 16 km west of Lac La Biche.

This lake was named after Duncan Tremblay, a Métis in the area whose was mentioned in the notes of the Oblate priests. Mr. Tremblay was well known in the area circa 1870-1915, and his grandson still farms on the shore of the lake.

Tremble, Lac (lake)
73 E/10 - Clandonald
30-52-4-W4
53°31′N 110°35′W
Approximately 26 km north-east of Vermilion.

The name for this lake has been official since at least 1958, but its precise origin is unknown.

* Trenville (former locality)
83 A/3 - Delburne
32-36-22-W4
52°08′N 113°06′W
Approximately 35 km south-west of Stettler.

The post office operated here from April 1905 through January 1927 and was named after three Trenaman families who homesteaded and built the Trenville Store and Stopping House in the area. The school and store also derived their names from this family.

Trevithick (locality)
83 H/6 - Cooking Lake
34-51-23-W4
53°27′N 113°18′W
Approximately 15 km east south-east of Edmonton.

The precise origin for the name of this country residence subdivision is unknown.

* **Tring** (former locality)
73 E/9 - Marwayne
14-53-3-W4
53°35′N 110°18′W
Approximately 39 km north north-west of Lloydminster.

The post office, which operated here from June 1908 through May 1931, was named after a town in Hertfordshire, England.

Tristram (locality)
83 A/11 - Chain Lakes
16-42-23-W4
52°36′N 113°15′W
Approximately 17 km west of Bashaw.

A post office operated here from March 1907 through July 1929 and was named after Tristram W. Fry, the first postmaster.

Trochu (town)
82 P/14 - Trochu
17-33-23-W4
51°49′35″N 113°13′40″W
Approximately 62 km south south-east of Red Deer.

Colonel Armand Trochu (1857-1930) led a group of army officers from France in 1905

to establish the St. Ann Ranch Trading Company. The resulting community became known as "Trochu Valley," shortened to Trochu in 1911. When World War I broke out, many of the officers returned to their homeland. They had originally left the army and France in protest against the government's anti-Catholic stand with regard to education. Many of them died in the war. This town was incorporated 1 August 1962.

Trout Creek (creek)
83 B/6 - Crimson Lake
3-40-11-W5
52°23′N 115°29′W
Flows east into North Saskatchewan River, approximately 38 km west of Rocky Mountain House.

The name for this creek has been official since at least 1958 and is likely descriptive.

Trowel Lake (lake)
83 H/3 - Bittern Lake
24-48-22-W4
53°10′N 113°06′W
Approximately 24 km north-west of Camrose.

The shape of this lake is likened to that of a trowel and the name has been official since at least 1958.

Truman (locality)
73 L/6 - Goodridge
19-63-8-W4
54°27′N 111°12′W
Approximately 54 km north of St. Paul.

The name for this locality, whose post office operated from July 1948 through September 1963, commemorates Harry S. Truman (1884-1972) who was the 33rd President of the United States at the time. The school district was named at the same time.

Tucker Lake (lake)
73 L/10 - Marguerite Lake
2-18-64-4-W4
54°32′50″N 110°37′10″W
Approximately 28 km west north-west of Cold Lake.

The name for this lake has been official since at least 1958, but its precise origin is unknown. It is referred to locally as "Little Jackfish Lake."

Tulabi Lake (lake)
73 E/16 - Frog Lake
14-55-2-W4
53°45′15″N 110°12′00″W
Approximately 50 km south-east of Elk Point.

The name for this lake has been official since at least 1958, but its precise origin is unknown.

Tulliby Lake (hamlet)
73 E/9 - Marwayne
2-55-2-W4
53°43′N 110°11′W
Approximately 52 km east south-east of Elk Point.

A post office was established here in February 1935 and was named after the tullibee or cisco fish. This lake herring is a small cousin of the whitefish, and inhabits many of Alberta's northern lakes. Its habits closely resemble those of the whitefish, and at first glance it presents a similar appearance.

Tuttle (locality)
83 A/4 - Innisfail
30-37-27-W4
52°13′N 113°50′W
Approximately 5 km south of Red Deer.

The Canadian Pacific Railway established a siding here in 1892-93 and named it after W.W. Tuttle, a local rancher.

Tweedie (locality)

73 L/13 - Lac La Biche
17-68-12-W4
54°53′N 111°47′W
Approximately 18 km north-east of Lac La Biche.

The Alberta and Great Waterways Railway established a station here in 1917 and named it after Thomas Mitchell March Tweedie (1871-1944), a prominent Conservative politician in Alberta. Mr. Tweedie was Member of the Legislative Assembly for Calgary Centre from 1911 to 1917 and Member of Parliament for Calgary West from 1917 to 1921. He did not run for the Commons again that year and was named a judge of the Supreme Court of Alberta. He became Chief Justice in August 1944 and died in October of that year.

Twin Island Lake (lake)

83 H/6 - Cooking Lake
10-52-22-W4
53°28′N 113°09′W
Approximately 23 km east of Edmonton.

There are two islands in the middle of this lake. The descriptive name has been official since at least 1958.

Twin Lake (lake)

73 E/8 - Lloydminster
35-50-4-W4
53°21′N 110°29′W
Approximately 35 km west north-west of Lloydminster.

The name for this lake has been official since at least 1958 and is likely descriptive.

Twin Lakes (lakes)

73 D/7 - Czar
21-39-4-W4
52°22′30″N 110°31′59″W
Approximately 19 km west of Provost.

The well-established local name for these two small water features was officially approved 22 January 1992 and is descriptive.

Twin Lakes (lakes)

83 B/7 - Rocky Mountain House
6-40-7-W5
52°24′50″N 114°59′50″W
Approximately 6 km north-west of Rocky Mountain House.

The name for these lakes was made official 29 July 1986. The name is descriptive; however, one of the lakes is drying up. Local residents used the lakes as a popular camping spot for 30 or 40 years. Parks and Recreation developed the lake as a provincial park camping spot in 1983.

Twin Lakes (lakes)

83 J/2 - Thunder Lake
35-58-6-W5
54°04′N 114°47′W
Approximately 26 km west south-west of Barrhead.

The name for these two lakes, connected by a small stream, has been official since at least 1958 and is descriptive.

Twining (locality)

82 P/11 - Three Hills
2-31-24-W4
51°38′N 113°17′W
Approximately 8 km south of Three Hills.

The post office, which operated here from June 1912 through June 1961, was likely named after Major-General Sir Geoffrey Twining (1862-1920). Born in Halifax and a graduate of the Royal Military College in Kingston, he spent most of his military life away from Canada, returning for six years from 1893 to 1899 to teach military engineering at his alma mater. He served

with the Royal Engineers in East Africa, India and China, was mentioned in despatches seven times in World War I, and was ultimately Director of Fortifications and Works for the War office. He was knighted in 1919.

Two Hills (town)

73 E/12 - Two Hills
32-54-12 W4
53°42′40″N 111°44′15″W
Approximately 117 km east north-east of Edmonton.

The first post office in the area was named "Poserville" in 1908 and was changed to Two Hills in March 1913. The descriptive name refers to the two distinct hills south-west of the town. The other features take their names from the same hills. This town was incorporated 1 January 1955.

Two Hills County #21 (county)

73 E/12 - Two Hills
53 to 55-6 to 15-W4
53°40′N 111°35′W
East north-east of Edmonton.

(see Two Hills)

Two Hills Lake (lake)

73 E/9 - Marwayne
7-55-1-W4
53°44′N 110°07′W
Approximately 52 km north north-west of Lloydminster.

The name for this lake has been official since at least 1958 and is likely descriptive.

***Two Lakes** (former locality)

73 L/4 - Cache Lake
30-60-13-W4
54°13′N 111°49′W
Approximately 49 km north-west of St. Paul.

___
*denotes rescinded name or former locality.

The name for this former locality, whose post office operated from August 1937 through March 1943, is descriptive. The name was officially rescinded 10 November 1970.

Twomey (locality)

83 A/15 - Ferintosh
29-46-19-W4
52°59′N 112°44′W
Approximately 8 km east of Camrose.

The origin for the name of this locality on the Canadian Pacific Railway line from Saskatoon to Edmonton is unknown.

Tyler Lake (lake)

73 E/8 - Lloydminster
35-50-3-W4
53°21′N 110°20′W
Approximately 28 km west north-west of Lloydminster.

It appears that two Tyler families owned land in the vicinity of this feature, but it is unclear who named the lake.

* Ukalta (former locality)

83 H/16 - Willingdon
34-57-17-W4
53°58′N 112°27′W
Approximately 20 km south south-east of Smoky Lake.

The name was originally applied to the post office, which operated from January 1934 through December 1964. This former locality was settled by people from the Ukraine in the early part of the century, and the name is a combination of their former homeland and their new province.

Uncas (locality)

83 H/6 - Cooking Lake
15-52-21-W4
53°29′N 113°01′W
Approximately 30 km east of Edmonton.

The Canadian Northern Railway established a station here in 1909, and named it after the town of the same name in Oklahoma. James Fenimore Cooper introduces a character by this name in his novel *The Last of the Mohicans*. The post office operated from August 1925 through May 1968.

Unipouheos Indian Reserve #121

(Indian reserve)

73 E/16 - Frog Lake
33-56-2-W4
53°53′N 110°14′W
Approximately 66 km north north-west of Lloydminster.

The name for this Cree Indian reserve, established in 1879, is taken after Chief Unipouheos, the successor to Puckeechkeewin. Unipouheos means "standing erect." The English equivalent is "Stanley."

Upper Mann Lake (lake)

73 L/3 - Vincent Lake
31-59-10-W4
54°09′N 111°29′W
Approximately 22 km north-west of St. Paul.

The name for this lake has been official since 28 July 1945, but its precise origin is unknown.

Upper Stony Creek (creek)

82 O/15 - Sundre
24-34-8-W5
51°56′32″N 114°59′45″W

Flows north-east into Burnstick Lake, approximately 27 km north-west of Sundre.

(see Lower Stony Creek)

Upper Therien Lake (lake)

73 E/14 - St. Paul
33-57-9-W4
53°58′N 111°17′W
Approximately 4 km south of St. Paul.

(see Lower Therien Lake)

Usona (locality)

83 A/13 - Bearhills Lake
33-44-26-W4
52°51′N 113°43′W
Approximately 20 km south-west of Wetaskiwin.

A post office, which operated here from June 1905 through April 1952, took the name of a place in California. The name is the initial letters of United States of North America.

Val Quentin (summer village)

83 G/9 - Onoway
16-54-3-W5
53°40′N 114°23′W
Approximately 50 km south of Barrhead.

The origin of the name of this summer village, incorporated 1 January 1966, is unknown.

* Val Soucy (former locality)

83 H/14 - Redwater
4-58-21-W4
53°59′N 113°03′W
Approximately 53 km north north-east of Edmonton.

A post office operated here from May 1917 through June 1951 and was named after Joe L. Soucy, the first postmaster. Before the opening of this post office, mail for the area had to be brought in from Cookville, 15 kilometres away. The Soucy family came from Kankakee, Illinois, and later settled near Redwater.

* Vallejo (former post office)

72 M/15 - Monitor
9-35-7-W4
51°58'N 110°57'W
Approximately 36 km east south-east of Coronation.

The precise origin for the name of this post office, which operated from December 1909 through January 1913, is unknown. There is a Vallejo in California. The name was later changed to Loyalist. (see Loyalist)

Valley Lake (lake)

83 A/10 - Donalda
8-42-21-W4
52°36'N 112°59'W
Approximately 3 km south of Bashaw.

The precise origin of the name of this lake is unknown; however, it is likely descriptive, as another local name for this feature is "Long Valley."

Valley Lake (lake)

83 I/7 - Newbrook
6-62-18-W4
54°20'N 112°41'W
Approximately 28 km north north-west of Smoky Lake.

The descriptive name for this lake refers to its location in a valley. It is locally called "Briar Lake," because it lies in what is locally known as the "Briar Valley."

* Valleyview (former locality)

83 A/5 - Red Deer
SE-6-39-27-W4
52°19'N 113°52'W
Approximately 6 km north of Red Deer.

The subdivision plan for this settlement was registered at Land Titles Office in Edmonton in July 1960 as Valleyview. When County #23 decided to take advantage of a Hamlet Street Assistance Grant provided by Alberta Transportation & Utilities in 1979, the name for this place needed to be changed because there was already a town in Alberta of this name. The county was required to change the name in 1979, and it was changed to Linn Valley. (see Linn Valley)

* Vanesti (former locality)

73 E/2 - Grizzly Bear Creek
33-47-4-W4
53°05'N 110°31'W
Approximately 35 km south-east of Vermilion.

The origin of the name of this former locality, whose post office operated from July 1911 through March 1948, is unknown. The name was officially rescinded 18 January 1974.

Vega (locality)

83 J/8 - Shoal Creek
33-62-3-W5
54°24'N 114°23'W
Approximately 30 km north of Barrhead.

When the school district for the area was being organized in 1928, the trustees met at Charlie Anderson's home to choose a name. Two options were forwarded: the first, Viewpoint, was already taken; the second choice was suggested by Oscar Bonson, who noticed a Vega cream separator and suggested Vega. The post office, opened in August 1930, took the name of the School District.

Vegreville (town)

83 H/8 - Ryley
18-52-14-W4
53°29'35"N 112°03'00"W
Approximately 95 km east of Edmonton.

Father Valentin Vegreville, O.M.I. (1829-1903), served as a missionary in western Canada for fifty years, beginning in the early 1850s. Early residents chose his name for their new settlement as a tribute to him and in recognition of the help they received on many occasions from the Oblate fathers of St. Albert. Father Vegreville was an expert linguist in the Cree, Montagnais and Assiniboine (Stoney) languages. He had several manuscripts focussing on the many dialects of native languages. An opportunity arose at one time for some of his work to be published by the Smithsonian Institution. The original hamlet of "Old Vegreville" was in townships 51 & 52, R 15, W4M, approximately 7.2 kilometres southwest of its present location. Its first settlers included a group of French Canadians from Kansas, U.S.A. The post office opened in December 1895 under the postmastership of Eugene Poulin, one of the these first inhabitants. Vegreville later became a centre for Ukrainian settlement. Ironically, although it was named for Father

Vegreville, 1904

Vegreville, he never served in the immediate district of Vegreville. This town was incorporated 15 August 1906.

Veldt (locality)

73 D/5 - Alliance
7-38-14-W4
52°15′N 111°59′W
Approximately 40 km north-west of Coronation.

This former Canadian Pacific Railway station was named after General Botha, the famous Boer general. The name means "plain" in Boer, though the modern rendering of the word is *Velt*.

Venice (hamlet)

83 I/9 - Hylo
11-66-15-W4
54°42′N 112°08′W
Approximately 15 km south-west of Lac La Biche.

The first postmaster, J.O. Billos, was born in Venice, Italy, and came to the area in 1902. The post office operated from September 1916 through August 1970, and was named after his home town. A number of Italian families lived in the area by the year 1916.

Vermilion (town)

73 E/7 - Vermilion
33-50-6-W4
53°21′21″N 110°49′23″W
Approximately 57 km west of Lloydminster.

The original post office was named "Breage," after the village of Breage in Cornwall, England. The town takes its name from the Vermilion River on which it is situated. Shortly after 1800 the Hudson's

Bay Company and the North West Company both built posts on the north side of the North Saskatchewan River. These posts were known as Paint Creek House (or Fort Vermilion) and were abandoned in 1816.

Vermilion Lakes (lakes)

73 E/12 - Two Hills
32-54-12-W4
53°41′N 111°44′W
Approximately 10 km east south-east of Two Hills.

(see Vermilion River) Another native name for this feature is *kianiskkotiki*, descriptively translating "chain of lakes joining each other."

■ **Vermilion Park Lake** (lake)

73 E/7 - Vermilion
50-6-W4
53°22′N 110°54′W
Approximately 7 km north-west of Vermilion.

(see Vermilion River)

Vermilion Provincial Park

(provincial park)

73 E/7 - Vermilion
1-51-7-W4
53°22′N 110°54′W
Approximately 6 km west north-west of Vermilion.

This 767.19 hectare (1,895.79 acre) park was created by Order-in-Council No. 1211/78 and is named for its proximity to the Vermilion River and the town of Vermilion. (see Vermilion River)

Vermilion River (river)

73 E/9 - Marwayne
5-54-3-W4
53°38′N 110°25′W

Flows north-east into North Saskatchewan River, approximately 48 km north north-west of Lloydminster.

The name for this river is a translation of the Cree *wiyaman*. There are ferruginous beds in the vicinity of the lakes and at numerous points along the valley of the river. Many other features along its course take their names from the river.

Vermilion Valley and River, 1907

Vermilion River County #24 (county)

73 E/8 - Lloydminster
45 to 55-1 to 7-W4
53°19′N 110°30′W
North-west of Lloydminster.

(see Vermilion River)

* **Vermilion Valley** (former post office)

83 H/1 - Holden
14-49-16-W4
53°14′N 112°14′W
Approximately 47 km north-east of Camrose.

The post office operated here under this name from February 1904 through May 1907. The descriptive name referred to the ferruginous beds of clay in the area. The name was later changed to Holden in order

---

*denotes rescinded name or former locality.

to avoid confusion with nearby Vermilion. (see Holden)

Vernon Lake (lake)
73 D/13 - Sedgewick
10-46-11-W4
52°57′N 111°30′W
Approximately 27 km north-east of Sedgewick.

The name for this lake has been official since 1958, but its origin is unknown.

* Vetchland (former locality)
83 B/3 - Tay River
5-38-8-W5
52°14′N 115°06′W
Approximately 18 km south-west of Rocky Mountain House.

Vetch is a plant of the pea family and is used for forage. Wild vetch grows in abundance in this area, and the post office, which operated from April 1915 through April 1917, was named because of this fact. The name was changed to Strachan in 1917. The name "Vetchland" was officially rescinded 30 April 1976.

Veteran (village)
73 D/3 - Coronation
17-35-8-W4
52°00′20″N 111°07′00″W
Approximately 26 km east south-east of Coronation.

This was a Canadian Pacific Railway station on the same line as Consort, Loyalist, Throne, and Coronation. Each community was named in 1911, the coronation year of King George V, commemorating service to the Crown. It was formerly the "Wheatbelt" post office until 1 April 1913. This village was incorporated 30 June 1914.

_____

*denotes rescinded name or former locality.

Victor (locality)
82 P/16 - Farrell Lake
3-33-17-W4
51°48′N 112°20′W
Approximately 34 km north-west of Hanna.

The post office, which operated here from April 1910 through June 1920, was named after Victor Gay, a surveyor from Lloydminster.

Victor Lake (lake)
83 I/8 - Victor Lake
3-63-14-W4
54°25′N 112°03′W
Approximately 44 km north north-east of Smoky Lake.

The name for this lake was officially approved 3 June 1954, but its precise origin is unknown.

* Victoria (former locality)
83 I/1 - Smoky Lake
1-58-17-W4
54°01′N 112°23′W
Approximately 15 km south of Smoky Lake.

(see Pakan)

Victoria Lake (lake)
82 P/16 - Farrell Lake
33-32-16-W4
51°47′N 112°13′W
Approximately 20 km west north-west of Hanna.

The name for this lake has been official since 1958, but its precise origin is unknown.

Victoria Settlement (settlement)
83 I/1 - Smoky Lake
10-58-17-W4
54°00′N 112°26′W

Approximately 17 km south south-east of Smoky Lake.

This settlement was named by the Reverend George McDougall in memory of Queen Victoria (1819-1901). Mr. McDougall also choose this spot as a Methodist mission. There was a Hudson's Bay Company trading post established here in 1864. The name was then changed to Pakan in 1887 after the Cree Indian chief of the same name. For years the road from Edmonton to Pakan was known as Victoria Trail.

Vie Lake (lake)
73 E/7 - Lloydminster
16-50-6-W4
53°18′N 110°47′W
Approximately 4 km south south-east of Vermilion.

The name for this lake has been official since at least 1958, but its precise origin is unknown.

Viewpoint (locality)
83 A/15 - Ferintosh
15-45-20-W4
52°53′N 112°49′W
Approximately 15 km south of Camrose.

The name for the post office, which operated here from July 1930 through March 1941, is descriptive of the view.

Viking (town)
73 E/4 - Viking
36-47-13-W4
53°05′40″N 111°46′00″W
Approximately 70 km east north-east of Camrose.

The post office was established in July 1904 and was named by the early Norwegian settlers after their ancestors. The Vikings were Norsemen who raided the coasts of Europe during the eighth, ninth, and tenth centuries. This town was incorporated 10 November 1952.

Villeneuve (hamlet)
83 H/12 - St. Albert
18-54-26-W4
53°40′N 113°49′W
Approximately 27 km north-west of
Edmonton.

This hamlet, whose post office operated
from July 1900 through April 1970, was
named in honour of Frédérick Villeneuve,
who came to Edmonton from Montreal to
open a law office. He served for one term as
Conservative member of the Northwest
Territories Legislature for St. Albert, and
then returned to Montreal. The settlement
was previously known as "St. Peter's" or
"St. Pierre."

Vilna (village)
73 L/4 - Cache Lake
20-59-13-W4
54°07′10″N 111°55′10″W
Approximately 36 km east of Smoky Lake.

The Vilna district was first opened up by
homesteaders and squatters in 1918-1919,
and as many of the first settlers came from
Vilna in Galicia, the post office was named
for their home town. In the latter half of
1919 the Canadian Northern Railway laid
steel through the district and the hamlet
was named Vilna as opposed to "Villett."
The town of Vilna in Galicia went to
Poland from Austria-Hungary after World
War I. This village was incorporated 23
June 1923.

Vimy (hamlet)
83 I/4 - Westlock
33-58-25-W4
54°04′N 113°39′W
Approximately 17 km south-east of
Westlock.

A post office opened here in May 1917 and
was named at approximately the same time
the Canadian troops captured Vimy Ridge.

The battle was fought from 9 through 14
April 1917 during World War I. The long,
low ridge formed a key position linking the
Germans' new Hindenburg Line to their
main trench lines leading north from Hill
70 near Arras, France. The battle was
commanded by Lt.-Gen. Sir Julian Byng,
later Viscount Byng of Vimy. After careful
training and rehearsal, and supported by
almost 1,000 artillery pieces, the Canadians
attacked along a 6.4-kilometre front on 9
April 1917. It was the first time the Canadians had attacked together as a corps, and
they achieved a magnificent victory,
sweeping the Germans off the ridge. By 14
April they had gained more ground, more
guns, and more prisoners than any previous
British offensive had done. Canadian
casualties amounted to 10,602, of which
3,598 were killed (R.H. Roy, from *The
Canadian Encyclopedia*, 2nd edition, p.
2264: Hurtig Publishers).

Vimy Ridge (ridge)
73 D/11 - Hardisty
28-43-8-W4
52°41′55″N 111°04′35″W
Approximately 19 km east of Hardisty, in
the Wainwright Regional Training Area.

This feature was so named because of its
resemblance to Vimy Ridge in France
where many Canadians lost their lives in
World War I. The battle was, without
doubt, the greatest Canadian victory of the
war. Vimy Ridge is the only feature in the
Wainwright Regional Training Area that
has been given a name from the Great War.
(see Vimy)

Vincent Lake (lake)
73 L/3 - Vincent Lake
19-59-09-W4
54°06′N 111°20′W
Approximately 13 km north of St. Paul.

The name for this lake has appeared on the
survey returns of A.F. Cotton, Dominion

Land Surveyor, who made the original
survey in this district in 1884; however, the
precise origin for the name is unknown.

Violet Grove (hamlet)
83 G/3 - Blue Rapids
24-48-8-W5
53°10′N 115°02′W
Approximately 8 km south-west of
Drayton Valley.

The name for this hamlet, whose post office
operated from February 1934 through
January 1980, is descriptive of the many
violets found in the area.

Volmer (locality)
83 H/12 - St. Albert
32-54-25-W4
53°43′N 113°40′W
Approximately 25 km north-west of
Edmonton.

The tiny hamlet of Volmer had its beginning when the Canadian Northern Railway
pushed north of St. Albert to Athabasca in
1908, and a group of farmers petitioned the
company to have a siding established east of
the Ray Settlement. In compliance with this
request, the railway purchased the necessary land on SW4-55-25-W4 from Joseph
Vollmer and named the siding Volmer. In
1904, Joseph and Franzseska Vollmer left
their small village of Brenken, Germany, to
join other members of their community
who had emigrated to the St. Albert area
years earlier. Joseph, being a farmer at heart
and the second son, knew that he could not
establish a successful farm in his home
village. Joseph died in 1917, leaving
Franzseska with five children (from *The
Black Robe's Vision*).

Wabamun (village)

83 G/9 - Onoway
11-53-4-W5
53°33'40"N 114°28'35"W
Approximately 65 km west of Edmonton.

This village was named for its location on
the north shore of Wabamun Lake. The
post office opened in August 1903. This
village was incorporated 1 January 1980.
(see Wabamun Lake)

Wabamun Creek (creek)

83 G/8 - Genesee
25-51-3-W5
53°29'N 114°23'W
Flows south-east into North Saskatchewan
River, approximately 57 km west south-
west of Edmonton.

(see Wabamun Lake)

Wabamun Indian Reserve #133A

(Indian reserve)
83 G/9 - Onoway
29-52-3-W5
53°32'N 114°24'W
Approximately 60 km west of Edmonton.

(see Wabamun Lake)

Wabamun Indian Reserve #133B

(Indian reserve)
83 G/9 - Onoway
6-53-3-W5
53°33'N 114°26'W
Approximately 60 km west of Edmonton.

(see Wabamun Lake)

Wabamun Lake (lake)

83 G/10 - Isle Lake
1-53-5-W5
53°33'N 114°35'W
Approximately 70 km west of Edmonton.

This feature was listed as "White Lake" on
Palliser's map of 1865. The descriptive
name for this lake, which is very clear and
blue in colour, is the Cree word for
"mirror." The lake has a maximum depth of
11 metres and a mean depth of 6.3 metres.

Wabamun Lake, 1913

Wabamun Lake Provincial Park

(provincial park)
83 G/9 - Onoway
7-53-3-W5
53°34'N 114°26'W
Approximately 70 km west of Edmonton.

This park is named for its proximity to
Wabamun Lake. (see Wabamun Lake)

Wabash Creek (creek)

83 I/5 - Dapp
15-61-27-W4
54°15'15"N 113°55'00"W
Flows north-west into Pembina River,
approximately 15 km north north-west of
Westlock.

W~X~Y~Z

The name for this creek has been official
since at least 1958, but its precise origin is
unknown.

* **Waghorn** (former post office)

83 A/5 - Red Deer
14-39-27-W4
52°23'N 113°47'W
Approximately 12 km north of Red Deer.

The name for the post office, which
operated here from August 1891 through
October 1902, was taken after its first
postmaster, Walter Waghorn. The name
was later changed to Blackfalds. (see
Blackfalds)

* **Wahstao** (former post office)

83 I/1 - Smoky Lake
5-59-15-W4
54°04'N 112°14'W
Approximately 26 km east of Smoky Lake.

The name for the post office, which
operated here from November 1907
through June 1957, was suggested by Peter
Erasmus, a Hudson's Bay Company
employee. The name is a corruption of the
Cree word *wahsato*, meaning "spiritual
light."

Wainwright (town)

73 D/15 - Wainwright
31-44-6-W4
52°50'20"N 110°52'00"W
Approximately 75 km south-west of
Lloydminster.

Both a post office and a Grand Trunk
Pacific Railway station were established

---

*denotes rescinded name or former locality.

here in 1908, and were named after William Wainwright, 2nd vice-president of the railway. William Wainwright was born in England in 1840 and came to Canada in 1862, at the invitation of Sir Edward Watkin, a railway promoter, to be chief clerk in the accountant's office of the Grand Trunk Railway, and ultimately, became senior vice-president of the G.T.R., parent of the G.T.P. This town was incorporated 14 July 1910.

Wainwright (main street), 1916

Wainwright Municipal District No. 61

(municipal district)
73 D/15 - Wainwright
41 to 47-1 to 10-W4
52°50′N 110°40′W
South of Lloydminster.

(see Wainwright)

Wainwright Regional Training Area

(Canadian Forces Regional Training Area)
73 D/15 - Wainwright
44-6,7-W4
52°45′N 111°00′W
South-west of the town of Wainwright.

(See Wainwright)

---

*denotes rescinded name or former locality.

Wakinagan Creek (creek)

83 H/7 - Tofield
11-52-19-W4
53°25′N 112°39′W
Flows south-east into Beaverhill Lake, approximately 60 km east of Edmonton.

The name has been official since at least 1958, but its precise origin is unknown.

Wakomao Lake (lake)

83 I/4 - Westlock
5-60-24-W4
54°09′N 113°33′W
Approximately 20 km east of Westlock.

The name has been official since at least 1958, but its precise origin is unknown.

Wall Lake (lake)

83 A/2 - Big Valley
1-38-20-W4
52°14′45″N 112°44′20″W
Approximately 12 km south of Stettler.

The name for this feature, previously called "Ross Lakes," was officially changed 3 October 1991 to reflect current local usage of the descriptive name that is well-established in local usage. The lake has steep banks resembling walls.

Wallaby Lake (lake)

73 D/10 - Hughenden
17-42-5-W4
52°37′N 110°42′W
Approximately 27 km south south-east of the town of Wainwright.

The name has been official since 1958, but its origin is unknown.

Walter Lake (lake)

83 H/10 - Elk Island Park
31-52-20-W4
53°32′N 112°56′W
Approximately 41 km east of Edmonton, in Elk Island National Park.

The name has been official since at least 1958, but its precise origin is unknown.

Walton Creek (creek)

82 O/15 - Sundre
31-32-7-W5
51°47′30″N 114°59′30″W
Flows north into Bearberry Creek, approximately 17 km west north-west of Sundre.

The name was officially approved for this feature 16 March 1937, but its origin is unknown.

* Wanekville (former post office)

83 G/14 - Mayerthorpe
7-57-7-W5
53°55′N 115°02′W
Approximately 10 km south-east of Mayerthorpe.

The post office operated under this name from October 1912 through February 1921. It was named after the postmaster, R. Wanek, until the name was changed to Rochfort Bridge.

Wanisan Lake (lake)

83 H/7 - Tofield
8-52-20-W4
53°28′N 112°55′W
Approximately 37 km east of Edmonton.

The name has been official since at least 1958, but its precise origin is unknown.

Warburg (village)

83 G/1 - Warburg
36-48-3-W5
53°11′N 114°19′W
Approximately 50 km south-west of Edmonton.

The name for this village, whose post office opened in January 1916, is taken after an ancient castle in Sweden called Warberg. The spelling was incorrectly altered. Many of the early settlers were of Swedish origin. This village was incorporated 31 December 1953.

Ward Lake (lake)

83 J/9 - Flatbush
14-64-2-W5
54°31′N 114°10′W
Approximately 45 km north north-east of Barrhead.

The name for this lake has appeared on maps dated 1948, but its precise origin is unknown.

Ward Lake (lake)

83 I/10 - Boyle
19-66-17-W4
54°44′06″N 112°33′57″W
Approximately 40 km west of Lac La Biche.

The name for this lake appeared on a list of names submitted by C.P. Hotchkiss, Dominion Land Surveyor, on 21 January 1922. It was named after a draughtsman on his survey party.

Warden (locality)

83 A/7 - Stettler
12-38-20-W4
52°16′N 112°44′W
Approximately 8 km south of Stettler.

The Canadian Northern Railway established a station here in 1919. It was a junction of the railway's Battle River and Brazeau branches. The post office, which operated from November 1928 through July 1962, was known as Warden Junction. Warden is a village in Northumberland, England. Some residents maintain that this station was named after Bruce Ward, an early homesteader who lived nearby.

* **Warden Junction** (former post office)

83 A/7 - Stettler
13-38-20-W4
52°16′N 112°45′W
Approximately 8 km south of Stettler.

(see Warden)

Warspite (village)

83 I/2 - Waskatenau
10-59-18-W4
54°05′25″N 112°37′00″W
Approximately 10 km west of Smoky Lake.

This village was named after a British cruiser engaged in the Battle of Jutland, 31 May–1 June 1916. H.M.S. *Warspite* was completed in March 1915 and served in both world wars. She was the sixth ship in the Royal Navy to bear the name; the first *Warspite* was in service from 1596 to 1649. The name is believed to be a compound term from Elizabethan days, akin to *Dreadnought*, a name borne by at least ten English and British warships from 1573 onward. The 1915 battleship *Warspite* was sold for breaking up in 1947, but the "Old Lady," as some called her with affection, sank on her own while being towed to the breaker's yard and was spared the ignominy of becoming scrap metal. The name for the post office was changed from Smoky Lake Centre in September 1916. This village was incorporated 31 December 1951.

Warwick (locality)

83 H/9 - Mundare
31-53-14-W4
53°38′N 112°03′W
Approximately 14 km north of Vegreville.

A post office operated here from January 1904 through April 1970 and was named after S.R. Warwick, an early homesteader who settled in the area in 1899.

Wasagamu Lakes (lake)

73 E/16 - Frog Lake
11-56-3-W4
53°49′N 110°20′W
Approximately 40 km east south-east of Elk Point.

The descriptive name has been official since at least 1928 and is the Cree word for "clearwater."

Wasel (locality)

83 H/16 - Willingdon
2-58-15-W4
53°59′N 112°07′W
Approximately 31 km east south-east of Smoky Lake.

The post office, which operated here from August 1911 through June 1969, was named for its first postmaster and one of the earliest settlers, Wasel Hawreliak (1880-1973). He arrived in the area from Bukovina in 1898 and his emigration encouraged many others to follow. His last name was later spelled Hawrelak. His son, William (1915-1975), was mayor of Edmonton for a number of years.

Wash Lake (lake)

73 E/16 - Frog Lake
27-55-2-W4
53°46′N 110°12′W
Approximately 57 km north north-west of Lloydminster.

The name has been official since at least 1958, but its precise origin is unknown.

Washing Lake (lake)

83 H/3 - Bittern Lake
1-48-22-W4
53°12′N 113°05′W
Approximately 25 km north north-east of Wetaskiwin.

The name has been official since at least 1958, but its precise origin is unknown.

Washout Creek (creek)
83 G/3 - Blue Rapids
7-47-7-W5
53°03'00"N 115°00'15"W
Flows north-west into North Saskatchewan River, approximately 19 km south of Drayton Valley.

The name has been official since at least 1958, but its precise origin is unknown.

Waskasoo Creek (creek)
83 A/5 - Red Deer
8-38-27-W4
52°15'15"N 113°48'30"W
Flows north into Red Deer River, within the city limits of Red Deer.

The name for this creek is a rough translation for "red deer" or "elk." (see Red Deer River)

Waskatenau (village)
83 I/2 - Waskatenau
16-59-19-W4
54°05'40"N 112°47'00"W
Approximately 22 km west of Smoky Lake.

The descriptive name for this village, whose post office opened in August 1919, is the Cree term translating "opening in the banks." There is a cleft in the ridge through which the creek of the same name flows into the North Saskatchewan River. The village was incorporated 19 May 1932.

Waskatenau Creek (creek)
83 I/2 - Waskatenau
28-58-19-W4
54°07'N 112°47'W

Flows south into North Saskatchewan River, approximately 21 km west south-west of Smoky Lake.

(see Waskatenau)

Waskwei Creek (creek)
83 H/8 - Ryley
2-52-16-W4
53°27'N 112°14'W
Flows north-east into Vermilion River, approximately 7 km south south-west of Vegreville.

The name has been official since at least 1958, but its precise origin is unknown.

Wastina (locality)
72 M/11 - Youngstown
10-31-8-W4
51°39'N 111°03'W
Approximately 60 km east of Hanna.

A post office was established here June 1912, and was named after a school district. Wastina is a corruption of the Cree word *miwasin*, "pretty place."

Wat Lake (lake)
83 H/7 - Tofield
36-50-21-W4
53°21'N 112°58'W
Approximately 41 km east south-east of Edmonton.

The name has been official since at least 1958, but its precise origin is unknown.

Watelet Lake (lake)
83 H/4 - Kavanagh
11-47-26-W4
53°02'N 113°42'W
Approximately 24 km west north-west of Wetaskiwin.

The name has been in use since 1898 when an early Belgian settler applied it after himself.

Water Valley (hamlet)
82 O/10 - Fallentimber Creek
27-29-5-W5
51°30'15"N 114°36'00"W
Approximately 32 km south of Sundre.

The name for the post office, which opened in March 1937, is descriptive.

* **Waterglen** (former locality)
83 A/11 - Chain Lakes
21-43-22-W4
52°32'N 113°08'W
Approximately 17 km north north-west of Bashaw.

A post office operated here from March 1908 through July 1947. The name referred to the various lakes in the vicinity.

Waters Hill (hill)
82 P/16 - Farrell Lake
4-3-35-16-W4
51°58'15"N 112°12'45"W
Approximately 40 km north north-west of Hanna.

The hill is on land homesteaded by Ralph Waters. In the spring of 1910 Mr. Waters and his family moved from Ontario to the Alberta prairie south of Gadsby. Mr. Waters moved to Calgary in 1960 and died there in June 1963. The locally well-established name was officially approved in July 1986.

Waterstreet Lake (lake)
82 O/10 - Fallentimber Creek
21-30-5-W5
51°35'N 114°38'W
Approximately 24 km south of Sundre.

The name was made official in November 1937, but its precise origin is unknown.

* Watt Lake (former locality)
72 M/14 - Kirkpatrick Lake
14-34-10-W4
51°56'N 111°20'W
Approximately 22 km south of Coronation.

The precise origin for this name is unknown. (see Watts Lake)

Watt Lake (lake)
73 E/12 - Two Hills
36-54-14-W4
53°42'N 111°56'W
Approximately 13 km west of Two Hills.

(see Wattsford)

Watts (hamlet)
82 P/9 - Craigmyle
17-31-15-W4
51°40'N 112°05'W
Approximately 11 km west of Hanna.

The Canadian Northern Railway established a station here in 1914 on its Saskatoon-Calgary branch. The post office followed in October 1917 and operated until June 1960. It may have been named after an early resident.

Watts Lake (lake)
72 M/14 - Kirkpatrick Lake
22-34-10-W4
51°56'N 111°20'W
Approximately 20 km south of Coronation.

A post office named Watt Lake operated nearby from September 1923 through August 1933, but the precise origin for the name of either feature is unknown.

* Wattsford (former locality)
73 E/12 - Two Hills
20-54-13-W4
53°41'N 111°53'W
Approximately 10 km west of Two Hills.

The name for this former locality, whose post office operated from October 1914 through October 1928, was taken after Thomas Watt, the first rancher in the valley.

Waugh (locality)
83 I/3 - Thorhild
19-58-23-W4
54°02'N 113°25'W
Approximately 21 km west north-west of Redwater.

The name for this locality, whose post office operated from June 1905 through May 1969, was taken after W.J. Waugh, the first postmaster.

* Waybrook (former locality)
83 H/14 - Redwater
19-57-23-W4
53°57'N 113°24'W
Approximately 42 km north of Edmonton.

A post office operated here from September 1910 through November 1939, but the origin for the name is unknown.

Wayetenaw Lake (lake)
73 L/5 - Goodfish Lake
34-61-13-W4
54°19'N 111°51'W
Approximately 46 km north-east of Smoky Lake.

The descriptive name for this lake has been official since at least 1928 and is a corruption of the Cree equivalent of "deep hole," *wayetenau*.

* Wayward (former locality)
83 H/6 - Cooking Lake
4-52-24-W4
53°28'N 113°30'W
Within the city limits of Edmonton.

A post office operated here from July 1947 through December 1951. The name was likely taken after the first postmaster, F.D. Way. It is now subdivision #39 in Edmonton, near Westmount Shopping Centre.

Weald (locality)
83 F/7 - Erith
7-51-19-W5
53°23'N 116°47'W
Approximately 34 km south-west of Edson.

The name for this former Grand Trunk Pacific Railway station on the Coal Branch to Coalspur, Luscar and Cadomin, is the Old English term meaning "Wooded land." It is the name of a district in southeastern England lying between the North and South Downs and covering much of Kent, Sussex, southern Surrey and easternmost Hampshire. The post office operated here from January 1922 through May 1927.

* Wealthy (former locality)
73 E/6 - Mannville
28-51-9-W4
53°26'N 111°15'W
Approximately 31 km west north-west of Vermilion.

The name for this former locality, whose post office operated from July 1909 through February 1930, expressed the hopes of the first homesteaders for prosperity.

Weasel Creek (creek)
83 I/2 - Waskatenau
26-59-20-W4
54°07'N 112°52'W
Flows south-east into North Saskatchewan River, approximately 24 km west south-west of Smoky Lake.

The descriptive name for this creek refers to the large number of weasels that inhabited the area at the time of the feature's naming.

Weasel Creek (locality)

83 I/2 - Waskatenau
9-60-20-W4
54°11′N 112°55′W
Approximately 33 km north-west of
Smoky Lake.

The post office operated here from April
1927 through April 1969 and took its name
from the nearby stream. (see Weasel Creek)

Weed Creek (creek)

83 H/5 - Leduc
4-26-49-28-W4
53°18′15″N 113°59′30″W
Flows north-east into Willow Creek,
approximately 35 km south-west of
Edmonton.

The name for this creek is a shortened
translation of a native name found in Sir
George Simpson's *Narrative of a Journey
Round the World* (1847), where he and his
companions camped one night near the
atcheskapesekwa seepee, or "Smoking Weed
River."

Weed Creek (locality)

83 G/1 - Warburg
27-48-1-W5
53°10′N 114°04′W
Approximately 54 km south-west of
Edmonton.

The post office operated here from April
1927 through January 1935 and is a rough
translation of the native term
atcheskapesekwa, meaning "smoking
weed."

Weeks Lake (lake)

73 E/2 - Grizzly Bear Creek
34-48-7-W4
53°11′N 110°56′W
Approximately 65 km west south-west of
Lloydminster.

The name has been official since at least
1958, but its precise origin is unknown.

Welch Creek (creek)

83 B/9 - Rimbey
15-41-4-W5
52°32′N 114°29′W
Flows east into Medicine River, approximately 19 km south-west of Rimbey.

The name has been official since at least
1958, but its precise origin is unknown.

Well Hill (hill)

73 D/11 - Hardisty
22-43-8-W4
52°43′N 111°05′W
Approximately 18 km east north-east of
Hardisty.

The name has been official since 1958, but
its precise origin is unknown.

* Wellsdale (former locality)

73 E/10 - Clandonald
10-53-5-W4
53°34′N 110°44′W
Approximately 26 km north north-east of
Vermilion.

The post office here operated from April
1909 through February 1927, but its origin
is unknown. The name was changed to
Clandonald. (see Clandonald)

Wenham Valley (locality)

83 G/1 - Warburg
10-47-3-W5
53°03′N 114°20′W
Approximately 47 km south-east of
Drayton Valley.

The name for this locality, whose post
office operated from June 1911 through
August 1952, was taken after Mark
Wenham, the first postmaster.

* Wernerville (former locality)

83 H/6 - Cooking Lake
27-51-24-W4
53°26′N 113°27′W
Within the southeastern city limits of
Edmonton.

The precise origin of the name of this
country residence subdivision is unknown.

Wessex (railway point)

82 O/9 - Didsbury
26-29-1-W5
51°31′N 114°03′W
Approximately 7 km south-east of
Carstairs.

This Canadian Pacific Railway station was
established in 1910 and takes its name after
Wessex, England. This was originally a
tribal name, "the West Saxons." Wessex
was one of the seven kingdoms formed by
the Saxons in England.

West Baptiste (summer village)

83 I/13 - Grosmont
3-67-24-W4
54°45′43″N 113°34′02″W
Approximately 19 km west north-west of
Athabasca.

This summer village is beside the narrows
on the west shore of Baptiste Lake. (see
Baptiste Lake)

West Cove (summer village)

83 G/10 - Isle Lake
34-54-4-W5
53°42′00″N 114°30′01″W
On the west shore of Lac Ste Anne,
approximately 67 km west north-west of
Edmonton.

This summer village was incorporated 1
January 1963. Its name is descriptive of its
location on the west shore of the lake.

West Michichi Creek (creek)

82 P/10 - Munson
13-29-29-19-W4
From 51°31'00"N 112°39'00"W
to 51°42'55"N 112°37'50"W
Flows south into Michichi Creek, approximately 48 km south-east of Three Hills.

This creek was officially named in July 1986 for its proximity as a north-west tributary of Michichi Creek. (see Michichi Creek)

* **West Wingham** (former post office)

72 M/14 - Kirkpatrick Lake
25-32-11-W4
51°46'N 111°26'W
Approximately 36 km north-east of Hanna.

This former post office was named by its first postmaster, Neil Golly, who selected the name because it was west of Wingham, Ontario, from which the Golly family and many other early settlers had come. The post office closed in October 1959.

West Whitemud Creek (creek)

83 H/4 - Kavanagh
SE-36-47-26-W4
53°06'20"N 113°40'45"W
Within the southern city limits of Edmonton.

The Water Survey of Canada requested that the creek be officially named but did not submit a suggestion with the request. As there was no established local name uncovered during a field study, this name was made official 29 July 1986 for its proximity as a tributary of Whitemud Creek. (see Whitemud Creek)

Westcott (locality)

82 O/9 - Didsbury
35-30-3-W5
51°37'N 114°19'W
Approximately 15 km west south-west of Didsbury.

The name for this post office, previously known as Kansas, is the same as that of a place in Berkshire, England. The post office operated under this name from July 1908 through March 1968. (see Kansas)

Westerdale (former locality)

82 O/9 - Didsbury
14-32-3-W5
51°44'N 114°20'W
Approximately 15 km west south-west of Olds.

The name for the post office, which operated from August 1910 through February 1932, is taken from a parish of the same name in Yorkshire, England.

Westerose (hamlet)

83 A/13 - Bearhills Lake
9-46-28-W5
52°58'N 113°59'W
Approximately 40 km west of Wetaskiwin.

The name for this hamlet, whose post office opened in May 1907, was taken after Westerose, Sweden, the home town of John Norstrom and family. The name is derived from *Wästerås*, the Swedish term meaning "Western hilltop," or "flat-topped hill." The place in Sweden is now part of the outer eastern suburban area of Stockholm.

Westlock (town)

83 I/4 - Westlock
4-60-26-W4
54°09'15"N 113°51'00"W
Approximately 75 km north north-west of Edmonton.

The original settlement was located 6.5 kilometres east of here and its post office was named "Edison." In 1912 the present townsite was purchased from two settlers, Westgate and Lockhart, and was renamed Westlock, a combination of the two names. This town was incorporated 7 January 1947.

Westlock Municipal District #92

(municipal district)

83 I/4 - Westlock
57-63-24-27-W4
54°20'N 113°45'W
North north-west of Edmonton.

(see Westlock)

Westward Ho (hamlet)

82 O/15 - Sundre
33-32-4-W5
51°47'N 114°31'W
Approximately 16 km east south-east of Sundre.

The name for this hamlet, whose post office operated from April 1905 through February 1970, was taken after Charles Kingsley's novel, *Westward Ho!*, published in 1855. The name was suggested by Captain Thomas, a British army officer and early settler.

Wetaskiwin (city)

83 A/14 - Wetaskiwin
14-46-24-W4
52°58'15"N 113°22'18"W
Approximately 63 km south of Edmonton.

This city came into being circa 1891 as Siding 16, when the Calgary and Edmonton Railway was under construction. The name is a translation of the Cree word *wi-ta-ski-winik*, "place of peace." The Blackfoot call it *inuststi-tomo*, "peace hills," and the Sarcee term is *natzuna-atsi-klukee*. The name refers to the nearby Peace Hills.

According to C.D. Smith, the Cree and the Blackfoot made a treaty here in 1867, after an exhausting battle.

Wetaskiwin, 1898

Wetaskiwin County #10 (county)

83 A/13 - Bearhills Lake
45 to 47-22 to 7-W4&5
52°55′N 113°52′W
South-west of Edmonton.

(see Wetaskiwin)

* Wheatbelt (former post office)

73 D/3 - Coronation
17-35-8-W4
52°00′N 111°07′W
Approximately 26 km east south-east of Coronation.

At the time of the post office's opening in April 1911, the area appeared to have potential as a thriving wheat-bearing region. The name was changed to Veteran in April 1913. (see Veteran)

Whelp Brook (brook)

83 A/12 - Ponoka
7-41-26-W4
52°30′30″N 113°44′00″W

Flows north-east into Wolf Creek, approximately 10 km south-west of Ponoka.

The origin of the name of this watercourse is unknown.

Whiskey Creek (creek)

82 O/15 - Sundre
13-09-33-7-W5
51°49′20″N 114°54′50″W
Flows east into Walton Creek, approximately 18 km west north-west of Sundre.

The locally well-established name was officially applied to the creek 3 October 1991. The name was applied to this stream during Prohibition in the 1920s. Some bootleggers located their stills along the creek. Whiskey Creek was used for both making and storing the moonshine whiskey. Thirty years later, a quart sealer of moonshine was found intact and, reportedly, it still tasted the same as it had in the 1920s.

Whiskeyjack Lake (lake)

73 L/3 - Vincent Lake
32-59-10-W4
54°09′N 111°28′W
Approximately 22 km north-west of St. Paul.

The name for this lake has been official since 6 July 1950 and is taken after the Canada jay or whiskeyjack. The Cree refer to the bird as *weskuchanis,* meaning "little blacksmith."

Whispering Hills (summer village)

83 I/13 - Grosmont
34-66-24-W4
54°45′37″N 113°33′25″W
Approximately 16 km west of Athabasca, along the east shore of Baptiste Lake.

The precise origin of the name of this summer village, incorporated 1 January 1983, is unknown.

Whitby Lake (lake)

73 L/4 - Cache Lake
31-59-13-W4
54°08′N 111°55′W
Approximately 45 km west north-west of St. Paul.

The name has been official since 6 April 1950, but its precise origin is unknown.

White Creek (creek)

82 O/16 - Sundre
10-35-3-W5
51°59′00″N 114°20′12″W
Flows east into Little Red Deer River, approximately 22 km west south-west of Innisfail.

This feature was previously called "Spring Creek," and was later named for the two White brothers, Bert and Owen, who homesteaded here in 1902. Not long afterward, Bert was drowned trying to cross the Little Red Deer River. The White Creek district was named after White Creek. The name for this creek was officially approved 3 October 1991.

White Earth Creek (creek)

83 I/1 - Smoky Lake
6-59-15-W4
54°04′N 112°14′W
Flows south-east into North Saskatchewan River, approximately 15 km east south-east of Smoky Lake.

The name for this lake has been in use since at least 1814 when it appears on David Thompson's map as "White Earth Brook." The name is a translation of the Cree name *wapitanisk,* which is likely descriptive.

White Gull (summer village)

83 I/13 - Grosmont
11-67-24-W4
54°47′08″N 113°33′15″W

North-eastern shore of Baptiste Lake, approximately 19 km west north-west of Athabasca.

The precise origin of the name of this summer village, incorporated 1 January 1983, is unknown.

White Sands (summer village)

83 A/7 - Stettler
27-40-20-W5
52°28′19″N 112°48′33″W
Approximately 18 km north north-east of Stettler.

The descriptive name for this resort community, developed by Ernie Salt in the 1960s, refers to the light-coloured sand that covers the beaches nearby. The name was officially recognized 31 January 1980.

Whitebrush Lake (lake)

83 A/10 - Donalda
1-18-42-20-W4
52°37′N 112°51′W
Approximately 7 km east north-east of Bashaw.

The name for this lake is descriptive. The alkaline water killed the trees in the lake, causing them to turn white and lose their bark. The name is a translation of a native name, *kawapetegok*.

Whitecourt (town)

83 J/4 - Whitecourt
24-59-12-W5
54°07′20″N 115°39′10″W
Approximately 158 km west north-west of Edmonton.

The Cree name for this town is *sak-de-wah*, translating "where the waters come together," and it is from this name that the slogan "where even the waters meet" has emerged for the area. Walter White,

originally from Greencourt, 42 kilometres south-east, was the first postmaster at this place when the post office was established in June 1909. The name "Whitecourt" was derived from the combination of Mr. White's name and "court," to conform with Greencourt, his former home. This town was incorporated 20 December 1971.

Whitecroft (hamlet)

83 H/11 - Edmonton
23-52-23-W4
53°31′N 113°18′W
Approximately 15 km east of Edmonton.

The precise origin for the name of this hamlet is unknown.

Whitefish Creek (creek)

83 I/8 - Victor Lake
12-63-14-W4
54°26′N 111°59′W
Flows north into Amisk River, approximately 35 km south south-west of Lac La Biche.

The name has been official since at least 1958 and is likely taken after the fish.

Whitefish Creek (creek)

73 L/5 - Goodfish Lake
9-11-63-14-W4
From 54°26′07″N 112°00′00″W
to 54°23′03″N 111°51′04″W
Flows south into Whitefish Lake, approximately 33 km south of Lac La Biche.

This creek was named for its proximity to Whitefish Lake. (see Whitefish Lake)

Whitefish Lake (lake)

73 L/5 - Goodfish Lake
14-11-62-13-W4
54°22′00″N 112°53′56″W
Approximately 45 km south of Lac La Biche.

The descriptive name for this lake has been official since at least 1928, but likely dates from the late 1850s, when the native Methodist missionary Henry Bird Steinhauer, born on an Ojibwa reserve in Ontario, set up a mission at the lake. The name refers to the number of whitefish in the lake. It was previously called "Lac Poisson Blanc," the French term for "Whitefish Lake." The Cree refer to the lake as *atikameg sagahegan*.

Whitefish Lake Indian Reserve #128

(Indian reserve)
73 L/5 - Goodfish Lake
36-61-13-W4
54°20′N 111°48′W
Approximately 142 km north-east of Edmonton.

(see Whitefish Lake)

Whitemud Creek (creek)

83 H/12 - St. Albert
24-52-25-W4
53°30′15″N 113°33′15″W
Flows north into North Saskatchewan River within the city limits of Edmonton.

The name is taken after the hill of the same name and from which Hudson's Bay Company men obtained a white mud used as a whitewash at their posts.

Whitewater Lake (lake)

73 D/13 - Sedgewick
11-45-13-W4
52°51′N 111°47′W
Approximately 13 km north-west of Sedgewick.

The name has been in use since at least 1958, but its precise origin is unknown.

Whitewood Lake (lake)
83 G/10 - Isle Lake
20-53-4-W5
53°35′N 114°32′W
Approximately 67 km west of Edmonton.

The name has been official since at least
1958 and is likely descriptive; however, this
is unconfirmed.

Whitford (hamlet)
83 H/16 - Willingdon
30-56-15-W4
53°52′N 112°13′W
Approximately 32 km south-east of Smoky
Lake.

The name for this hamlet, whose post office
operated from July 1897 through June 1969,
was taken after one of the earliest family of
settlers on the lake. According to a letter
from A. Whitford, the second postmaster,
to R. Douglas, secretary of the Geographic
Board of Canada, dated 8 May 1916, "22
years ago there was a quite a large half-
breed population already here. Two thirds
of them were named Whitford. The others
were related to them in some way. However, they are nearly all gone now. Some of
them died and the others moved further on
the frontier. I could never get much
information as to their origin except that
the first one was a Hudson's Bay Company
man."

Whitford Creek (creek)
83 H/16 - Willingdon
20-55-17-W4
53°46′30″N 112°29′15″W
Flows north-east into Whitford Lake,
approximately 32 km south south-east of
Smoky Lake.

(see Whitford)

Whitford Lake (lake)
83 H/16 - Willingdon
26-56-16-W4
53°52′00″N 112°15′30″W
Approximately 33 km south-east of Smoky
Lake.

(see Whitford)

Whitney Lake (lake)
73 E/15 - Elk Point
17-56-4-W4
53°50′N 110°33′W
Approximately 23 km east south-east of
Elk Point.

The name has been official since at least
1958, but its precise origin is unknown.

* Wiesville (former post office)
83 A/5 - Red Deer
26-40-28-W4
52°27′N 113°56′W
Approximately 16 km west of Lacombe.

The post office, which was named after its
first postmaster, W. Wiese, operated here
from August 1907 through February 1916.
The name was later changed to Aspen
Beach. (see Aspen Beach)

* Wildhorse (former locality)
83 G/15 - Sangudo
17-57-4-W5
53°55′N 114°34′W
Approximately 38 km east of Mayerthorpe.

The descriptive name referred to the fact
that many wild horses were seen in the
vicinity by early settlers. The post office
operated by this name from September
1908 through November 1914, when it was
changed to Ballantine. (see Ballantine)

Wildmere (locality)
73 E/2 - Grizzly Bear Creek
12-48-6-W4
53°08′N 110°45′W
Approximately 56 km west south-west of
Lloydminster.

The name for this locality, whose post
office operated from May 1910 through
October 1955, may be descriptive. *Mere* is
an old English word for "pool" or "lake."

Wildwood (hamlet)
83 G/11 - Chip Lake
27-53-9-W5
53°37′N 115°14′W
Approximately 38 km south of
Mayerthorpe.

The name for this one-time village, whose
post office opened in November 1929, is
descriptive of the bushy area. It was known
as "Junkins" until 1929. An early resident,
Ruby Lord, suggested the present name.

* Wilhelmina (former post office)
72 M/16 - Grassy Island Lake
13-34-2-W4
51°55′N 110°09′W
Approximately 48 km south of Provost.

(see Altario)

Wilkins Lake (lake)
73 D/11 - Hardisty
9-42-8-W4
52°36′N 111°05′W
Approximately 15 km south-east of
Hardisty.

The name has been in use since at least
1958, but its origin is unknown.

Willesden Green (locality)
83 B/10 - Carlos
1-43-5-W5
52°41′N 114°35′W
Approximately 24 km west of Rimbey.

A post office operated here from October 1913 through February 1947 and was named after Willesden Green, London, England, the former home of the first postmaster, George Wager.

Williamson Lake (lake)

73 D/10 - Hughenden
36-43-7-W4
52°44'N 110°53'W
Approximately 15 km south south-west of the town of Wainwright.

The name has been in use since at least 1958, but its origin is unknown.

Willingdon (village)

83 H/16 - Willingdon
11-56-15-W4
53°49'40"N 112°07'00"W
Approximately 97 km east north-east of Edmonton.

The post office opened here in May 1928 and was named after Freeman Freeman-Thomas, first Marquess of Willingdon (1866-1941). This British statesman and colonial administrator was Governor-General of Canada from 1926 to 1931. He then served as Viceroy of India from 1931 to 1936. On his return to Britain he was given the largely ceremonial post of Constable of Dover Castle and Lord Warden of the Cinque Ports. This village was incorporated 31 August 1928.

Willow Creek (creek)

83 H/5 - Leduc
29-49-27-W4
53°15'15"N 113°54'15"W
Flows north-west into North Saskatchewan River, approximately 24 km west south-west of Edmonton.

The descriptive name for this creek refers to the willows lining its banks.

Willow Lake (lake)

73 D/10 - Hughenden
11-43-6-W4
52°41'15"N 110°45'30"W
Approximately 15 km south south-east of Wainwright.

The name has been in use since at least 1958 and is likely descriptive.

Willow Lake (lake)

73 L/8 - Cold Lake
10-61-2-W4
54°16'N 110°13'W
Approximately 20 km south of Cold Lake.

The name has been official since at least 1958 and is likely descriptive.

* Willow Trail (former locality)

73 L/7 - Bonnyville
6-64-6-W4
54°30'N 110°56'W
Approximately 26 km north of Bonnyville.

The name for this locality, whose post office operated from August 1933 through June 1954, was taken after the tree. The name was officially rescinded 10 November 1970.

Willowbend Reservoir (reservoir)

72 M/12 - Hanna
1-31-13-W4
51°38'N 111°44'W
Approximately 22 km east of Hanna.

The name for this feature is likely descriptive of the reservoir shape and common flora in the area.

Willowlea (locality)

73 E/8 - Lloydminster
18-52-1-W4
53°29'N 110°09'W
Approximately 25 km north-west of Lloydminster.

The name for this locality, whose post office operated from August 1917 through December 1956, was taken after the tree.

Wilson Creek (creek)

83 B/10 - Carlos
31-43-4-W5
52°44'N 114°34'W
Flows south into Medicine River, approximately 20 km west of Rimbey.

Pilot Officer R. Wilson was born in Gadsby and was educated in Stettler. He enlisted 10 April 1941 in the R.C.A.F. at Edmonton and, after completing his aircrew training, was awarded the Air Gunner's Badge. He proceeded overseas and was engaged in air operations, winning the D.F.C. He was reported missing on 23 August 1944, and subsequently presumed dead.

Wimborne (hamlet)

82 P/13 - Torrington
26-33-26-W4
51°52'N 113°35'W
Approximately 25 km west of Trochu.

The post office, which opened here in April 1909, was likely named after the town of Wimborne in Dorset, England.

Windfall (hamlet)

83 K/1 - Windfall Creek
18-60-15-W5
54°12'N 116°13'W
Approximately 28 km west north-west of Whitecourt.

---

*denotes rescinded name or former locality.

The name has been official since at least 1958 and is taken from Windfall Creek which flows nearby.

Windfall Creek (creek)
83 K/1 - Windfall Creek
19-60-15-W5
54°12′N 116°14′W
Flows north-east into Athabasca River, approximately 32 km west north-west of Whitecourt.

The name has been official since at least 1958, but its precise origin is unknown.

Windfall Lake (lake)
83 I/9 - Hylo
33-65-16-W4
54°40′N 112°21′W
Approximately 30 km south-west of Lac La Biche.

The name has been official since at least 1958 and likely refers to the quantity of timber blown down by high winds when two cyclones passed through the area, one in July 1921 and the other in June 1963. The common name for such an occurrence is "Windfall."

Windsor Lake (lake)
83 A/11 - Chain Lakes
10-42-22-W4
52°35′45″N 113°05′30″W
Approximately 7 km west of Bashaw.

The well-established name for this lake was made official 8 November 1978. The name was requested by Mel Kraft, regional fisheries biologist. John Windsor was the original homesteader on the land surrounding the lake.

Windy Lake (lake)
73 D/6 - Brownfield
9-40-9-W4
52°25′N 111°14′W
Approximately 23 km south of Hardisty.

The name has been in use since at least 1958 and is likely descriptive.

Windy Lake (lake)
73 D/6 - Brownfield
9-40-9-W4
52°25′N 111°14′W
Approximately 23 km south of Hardisty.

The name has been in use since at least 1958 and is likely descriptive.

Windy Lake (lake)
73 E/7 - Vermilion
31-49-4-W4
53°16′N 110°35′W
Approximately 34 km west of Lloydminster.

The name has been official since at least 1958 and is likely descriptive.

Windy Lake (lake)
83 I/10 - Boyle
1-65-18-W4
54°36′N 112°36′W
Approximately 46 km south-west of Lac La Biche.

The name for this lake is likely descriptive, and refers to the southwesterly winds that blow between the gaps of the hills south-west of the lake.

Winfield (hamlet)
83 B/16 - Winfield
18-46-3-W5
52°57′N 114°26′W
Approximately 47 km south-east of Drayton Valley.

This hamlet, whose post office opened in February 1927, is named after Vernor Winfield Smith (1864-1932), M.L.A. for Camrose, who, after the 1921 election victory of the United Farmers of Alberta, became Minister of Railways and Telephones. He had worked as an accountant and paymaster for various railway contractors before taking up farming at Camrose in 1915. He was a cabinet minister until his death.

* Winterburn (former locality)
83 H/12 - St. Albert
31-52-25-W4
53°32′N 113°41′W
Within the city limits of Edmonton.

The post office opened here in May 1904. Local tradition reports that the name could be derived from steam "burning" off the muskeg in winter. There are numerous Winterbornes and Winterbournes in England, most with a second name following. There is also a Winterburn in the West Riding of Yorkshire. It is also possible that the Alberta hamlet was named by someone who may have hailed from one of the foregoing places. The name (however spelled) is derived from the Old English *Winterburna*, "a stream dry except in winter" (Ekwall).

Winterburn (post office)
83 H/12 - St. Albert
31-52-25-W4
53°32′30″N 113°41′20″W
Within the city of Edmonton, west of the urban area.

Since annexation, this hamlet has been within the boundaries of the City of Edmonton. (see Winterburn, former locality)

Wiste (locality)

72 M/15 - Monitor
35-32-7-W4
51°48′N 110°53′W
Approximately 56 km north-west of Oyen.

The name for this locality is taken after the father-in-law of the first postmaster, C. Leaf. The post office operated from May 1910 through October 1932.

Withrow (hamlet)

83 B/7 - Rocky Mountain House
28-39-4-W5
52°23′15″N 114°30′15″W
Approximately 11 km north-west of Eckville.

This hamlet, whose post office operated from April 1937 through August 1961, was named after W.H. Withrow (1839-1908), editor of the *Canadian Methodist Magazine* for many years.

* Wittenburg (former post office)

83 B/9 - Rimbey
35-41-4-W5
52°35′N 114°29′W
Approximately 17 km west south-west of Rimbey.

A post office, named after a town in Germany, operated here from June 1907 through December 1917. The name was then changed to Leedale.

Wizard Lake (lake)

83 H/4 - Kavanagh
5-48-27-W4
53°07′N 113°55′W
Approximately 50 km south-west of Edmonton.

The name for this lake was recorded as early as 1898 when it was shown on field notes of A.C. Talbot, a Dominion Land Surveyor. The name is a translation of the Cree word, *seksyawas sagahegan*.

Wolf Creek (creek)

82 P/9 - Craigmyle
8-32-16-4
51°44′N 112°14′W
Flows east into Dowling Lake, approximately 12 km north-west of Hanna.

The name has been official since 1958, but its precise origin is unknown.

Wolf Creek (creek)

83 A/12 - Ponoka
4-41-26-W4
52°30′15″N 113°41′30″W
Flows north into Whelp Brook, approximately 6 km west south-west of Ponoka.

The name for this tributary of the Battle River has been in use since the 1860s. Apparently, when Piscan Munroe, a Métis of Scottish and Blackfoot descent, camped three times at this crossing, his camp was surrounded by an unusual number of wolves.

Wolf Creek (creek)

83 F/9 - Edson
34-53-16-W5
53°38′N 116°17′W
Flows north into McLeod River, approximately 12 km north-east of Edson.

The name has been in use since at least 1928 and is taken after the mammal.

Wolf Creek (creek)

83 G/3 - Blue Rapids
26-46-8-W5
53°00′15″N 115°02′30″W
Flows north into North Saskatchewan River, approximately 19 km south of Drayton Valley.

The creek is about 49 kilometres long, beginning about 32 kilometres north-east of Rocky Mountain House. The creek was previously known as "Rose Creek," but the name was changed in 1991 to reflect local usage.

Wolf Hill (hill)

82 P/16 - Farrell Lake
9-24-34-18-W4
51°56′05″N 112°24′50″W
Approximately 45 km north-west of Hanna.

The hill, when viewed from the right angle, apparently looks like a wolf's head and is a landmark for miles around. The locally well-established name was officially approved 29 July 1986.

Wolf Lake (lake)

73 L/10 - Marguerite Lake
NE-2-66-7-W4
54°42′10″N 110°57′20″W
Approximately 49 km north north-west of Bonnyville.

The local history of Lac La Biche entitled *Yesterday and Today* describes an incident in 1911 involving three wolves who chased a fur-buyer in his sleigh near this lake.

Wolf River (river)

73 L/11 - Pinehurst Lake
16-66-7-W4
54°42′00″N 111°00′15″W
Flows west into Sand River, approximately 55 km east of Lac La Biche.

The name has been official since at least 1958 and is likely descriptive.

* Wolyn (former locality)

83 I/7 - Newbrook
18-63-18-W4
54°27′N 112°43′W
Approximately 36 km north of Smoky Lake.

---

*denotes rescinded name or former locality.

The name for the post office, which operated here from September 1934 through August 1936, is taken after a region of the same name in Ukraine. The Polish spelling for the region was Wolyń; the Russian was Volyn. After World War II, it became the Volhynia region of Ukraine.

Wood Lake (lake)
83 A/3 - Delburne
29-37-22-W4
52°12′30″N 113° 06′00″W
Approximately 40 km east of Red Deer.

The name for this lake has been in use since at least 1906 when School District #1512 was established adjacent to the feature. The descriptive name refers to the abundance of dead timber in the water.

Wood Lake (lake)
83 B/8 - Sylvan Lake
12-40-4-W5
52°26′46″N 114°26′15″W
Approximately 48 km north-west of Red Deer.

This lake was previously called "Gabriel Lake," probably after Baptiste Gabriel, described by Palliser as "a first-rate trader and a smart little hunter." The feature was identified as "Gabriel's Hill Lake" on Palliser's map of 1859 and as "Gabriel Lake" on the Arrowsmith map. The nearby hill was the feature from which Hector, of the Palliser expedition, had his first view of the Rocky Mountains. The name was changed in September 1991 to reflect current local usage.

* Wood River (former locality)
83 A/11 - Chain Lakes
1-43-24-W4
52°40′N 113°21′W
Approximately 16 km east of Ponoka.

The post office operated here from August 1903 through March 1947 and was named after the home town of F.J. Bullock, the first postmaster. Since there is no river of that name close by, it is deduced that the name was taken after Wood River, a town in Hall County, Nebraska.

* Woodbend (former locality)
83 H/5 - Leduc
24-51-26-W4
53°25′N 113°41′W
Immediately west of Edmonton.

The post office operated here from June 1908 through September 1953. The original proposal was for the name "Woodbine," after the grade of flour milled in the vicinity. The post office authorities made the adjustment to the name.

Woodenpan Lake (lake)
83 H/6 - Cooking Lake
3-52-22-W4
53°28′N 113°09′W
Approximately 20 km east of Edmonton.

The name has been official since at least 1958, but its precise origin is unknown.

* Woodglen (former locality)
83 H/1 - Holden
2-47-16-W4
53°01′N 112°14′W
Approximately 29 km east of Camrose.

A post office operated here from March 1908 through February 1942 and was named after a town in Minnesota. The original suggestion, Glenwood, was a duplication, so the modification to Woodglen was made by postal authorities. At the time of naming, there were already Glenwood post offices in British Columbia, Ontario, New Brunswick, Nova Scotia and Prince Edward Island. In 1988, three post offices with this name remained, in Alberta, Nova Scotia and Newfoundland.

Woodgrove (railway point)
83 I/3 - Thorhild
3-20-58-21-W4
54°01′21″N 113°05′25″W
Approximately 62 km north north-east of Edmonton.

The name was officially approved 23 September 1991 and is taken from former School District #3143 and is descriptive. It was proposed by Canadian National Railways as an important historical name in the area. The elevator was built by the Alberta Wheat Pool.

* Worley (former locality)
83 H/4 - Kavanagh
21-51-27-W4
53°25′N 113°55′W
Approximately 28 km south-west of Edmonton.

(see Golden Spike)

Worm Lake (lake)
83 I/5 - Dapp
3-62-27-W4
54°20′N 113°58′W
Approximately 23 km north north-west of Westlock.

The name has been official since at least 1958, but its precise origin is unknown.

Worry Lake (lake)
73 L/3 - Vincent Lake
30-60-10-W4
54°13′N 111°28′W
Approximately 26 km north-west of St. Paul.

The name has been official since at least 1958, but its precise origin is unknown.

---

*denotes rescinded name or former locality.

Wostok (hamlet)
83 H/16 - Willingdon
16-56-17-W4
53°51′N 112°28′W
Approximately 76 km north-east of
Edmonton.

When the first group of settlers from
Galicia, a largely Slavic province of the
Austro-Hungarian Empire, organized
under the direction of Dr. Joseph Oleskow,
arrived at Strathcona early in May 1896, a
few of the families chose to settle to the
south-west in the Rabbit Hill area. The rest
of the group selected their homesteads
directly east of Limestone Lake settlement
in 56-18-4. *Vostok* is "east" in Russian;
Wostok may be a Polish or other Slavic
variation thereof. The following is taken
from *Pride and Progress*, Alberta Rose
Historical Society, 1982, Friesen Printers:
"They arrived in the area on May 22, the
Friday before Pentecost Sunday or as was
more commonly known as 'Green Holidays' ... On January 1, 1899, the post office
was officially opened with my father in
charge. It was located on his homestead."

Wyeclif (hamlet)
83 H/11 - Edmonton
19-52-22-W4
53°31′N 113°14′W
Approximately 17 km east of Edmonton.

The name of this hamlet is taken after the
Wye River Valley in England.

Yagraw Lake (lake)
83 I/16 - Plamondon
4-67-15-W4
54°47′30″N 112°14′00″W
Approximately 20 km west of Lac La
Biche.

The name has been official since at least
1958, but its precise origin is unknown.

Yak Lakes (lakes)
73 D/10 - Hughenden
14-43-7-W4
52°42′10″N 110°54′50″W
Approximately 12 km south south-east of
the town of Wainwright, in the Wainwright
Regional Training Area.

The precise origin of the name of these two
lakes is unknown.

Yankee Flats (flat)
83 B/1 - Markerville
16-36-2-W5
52°07′30″N 114°14′00″W
Approximately 35 km south-west of Red
Deer.

These flats are so called because of the
number of Americans who settled near here
around the turn of the century. The name
was officially approved 7 February 1983.

Yates (locality)
83 F/9 - Edson
32-53-16-W5
53°38′N 116°20′W
Approximately 9 km north-east of Edson.

The Grand Trunk Pacific Railway established a station here in 1911 and named it
after a chief clerk in the treasurer's office of
the railway. The post office operated here
from August 1913 through November
1953.

Yekau Lake (lake)
83 H/5 - Leduc
15-52-26-W4
53°29′N 113°44′W
Approximately 20 km west of Edmonton.

The name has been official since at least
1958, but its origin is unknown.

Yelling Creek (creek)
73 L/3 - Vincent Lake
14-60-9-W4
54°11′30″N 111°14′00″W
Flows north-east into Thinlake River,
approximately 25 km north north-east of
St. Paul.

The name has been official since at least
1958, but its precise origin is unknown.

Yellowstone (summer village)
83 G/9 - Onoway
9-55-3-W5
53°44′N 114°23′W
Approximately 63 km west of Edmonton,
near Lac Ste Anne.

The precise origin for the name of this
summer village, incorporated 1 January
1965, is unknown.

Yeoford (locality)
83 G/1 - Warburg
35-46-3-W5
53°01′N 114°19′W
Approximately 52 km east south-east of
Drayton Valley.

The name for this locality, whose post
office operated from September 1909
through July 1969, commemorates the
home village in Devonshire, England of the
first postmaster, Charles Marson.

Young Creek (creek)
73 D/5 - Alliance
26-38-13-W4
52°18′00″N 111°45′15″W
Flows north into Castor Creek, approximately 31 km north-west of Coronation.

The name has been in use since at least
1958, but its origin is unknown.

Youngstown (village)

72 M/11 - Youngstown
33-29-9-W4
51°31'40"N 111°12'25"W
Approximately 50 km east south-east of
Hanna.

This village was named after Joseph Victor
Young (?-1952), the original owner of the
land upon which the early townsite was
established. The post office opened in July
1912. This village was incorporated 31
December 1936.

* **Youngstown** (former post office)

73 D/13 - Sedgewick
SE6-45-13-W4
52°50'N 111°52'W
Approximately 20 km north north-west of
Sedgewick.

James M. Bickell was the first postmaster at
this site, and he named the post office after
the maiden name of his wife, the daughter
of Tran Young, a shoemaker. The post
office operated for only two years, from
February 1905 through February 1907.

* **Zawale** (former locality)

83 H/16 - Willingdon
6-56-16-W4
53°48'N 112°23'W
Approximately 75 km east north-east of
Edmonton.

A post office operated here from September
1910 through July 1947 and many of the
early Ukrainian settlers came from a town
of the same name in Galicia.

Zeer Lake (lake)

73 L/12 - Beaver Lake
12-64-12-W4
54°32'N 111°41'W

Approximately 33 km south south-east of
Lac La Biche.

The name was officially applied in 1951 and
commemorates Lance-Bombadier Edwin
Zeer, M.I.D., of Calgary, who was killed
during World War II.

Zeta Lake (lake)

83 G/4 - Zeta Lake
29-48-12-W5
53°10'N 115°44'W
Approximately 50 km west of Drayton
Valley.

The name been official since at least 1958.
Zeta is the sixth letter of the Greek alphabet; however, its association with this lake
is unknown.

* **Zoldovara** (former locality)

73 E/3 - Buffalo Creek
2-48-9-W4
53°07'N 111°14'W
Approximately 37 km south-west of
Vermilion.

The post office operated here from June
1912 through June 1928, but the precise
origin for the name is unknown.

---

*denotes rescinded name or former locality.

BIBLIOGRAPHY

Acme and District Historical Society. *Acme Memories*. Acme, Alberta: Acme and District Historical Society, 1979.

Adshead, Herbert B. *Pioneer Tales and Other Human Stories*. Calgary, Alberta: Albertan Job Press, 1929.

Ahlf, Marguerite. *Edson 75 Years – A History of the Town*. Edson, Alberta: M. Ahlf, 1986.

Akrigg, Philip and Helen. *British Columbia Place Names*. Victoria, British Columbia: Sono Nis Press, 1988.

Alix-Clive Historical Club. *Gleanings After Pioneers and Progress*. Alix, Alberta: Alix-Clive Historical Club, 1981.

Alix-Clive Historical Club. *Pioneers and Progress*. Alix, Alberta: Alix-Clive Historical Club, 1974.

Anderson, Anne. *Plains Cree Dictionary in the "y" Dialect*. Edmonton, Alberta: Anne Anderson, 1975.

Anderson, Roy F. *Pioneer Legacy: Memories of Yesteryear and Today for Tomorrow of Bowden and Districts*. Bowden Chamber of Commerce: Inter-Collegiate Press, 1979.

Andrew Historical Society. *Dreams and Destinies: Andrew and District*. The Society, 1980.

Atlas of World History. Rand McNalley and Company, 1957.

Baker, Edna. *Prairie Place Names*. Edna Baker, 1928.

Ball, Joe. *Memories of Central Alberta*. Botha, Alberta: Joe Ball, ca. 1975.

Barrhead and District Historical Society. *Trails Northwest: A History of the District of Barrhead*. Barrhead, Alberta: The Society, 1967.

Barrhead History Book Committee. *The Golden Years*. Barrhead, Alberta: Barrhead and District Chamber of Commerce, 1978.

Berry, J.P. *Clover Bar in the Making*. Clover Bar, Alberta: s.n., J.P. Berry, ca. 1931.

Berrymoor/Carnwood Historical Society. *Forests to Grainfields*. Berrymoor, Alberta: Berrymoor/Carnwood Historical Society, 1977.

Bond, Courtney C.J. *Surveyors of Canada 1867-1967*. In *The Canadian Surveyor* 20(5); special issue to honour our Centennial, 1967.

Bowes, Gordon E. *Peace River Chronicles*. Vancouver, British Columbia: Prescott Publishing Co., 1963.

Breton and District Historical Society. *The Ladder of Time: A History of Breton and District*. Edmonton, Alberta: Co-op Press Ltd., 1980.

Brown, Harriet C. (ed.). *Beaver Tales: History of Ryley & District*. Ryley, Alberta: Book Committee of the Ryley Ladies' Auxiliary, 1978.

Brownfield, Silver Heights, Talbot and Bulwark citizens. *Shadows of the Neutrals*. Brownfield, Silver Heights, Talbot and Bulwark citizens, 1967.

Byefield, Ted. *History of Alberta, Volume 2*. 1993.

Campbell, Jessie J. *Chatter Chips From Beaver Dam Creek: Castor & Her Neighbours, 1909-1974*. Castor, Alberta: Castor Old Timers' Association, 1974.

Campbell, Marie J. *Still God's Country: The Early History of Byemoor and Area*. Byemoor, Alberta: Byemoor History Committee, 1975.

Camrose Historical Society. *Early History of Camrose and District*. Camrose, Alberta: Job Press, 1947.

Canadian Almanac. Toronto: Copp Clark Publishing Co., 1908.

The Canadian Annual Review for 1973. Toronto: Annual Review Publishing Co. Ltd., 1914.

The Canadian Encyclopedia, 2d ed. Edmonton, Alberta: Hurtig Publishers Ltd., 1988.

Canadian Forces Sentinel. Ottawa: Directorate of Information Services, National Defence Headquarters, October 1971.

The Canadian Parliamentary Guide. Guide parlementaire canadien. Ottawa: R.G. Normandin, 1916.

Canadian Railway Guide, 1977.

Canadian Securities Handbook. London, England: E. Wilson, 1907.

Carter, Velma, and Wanda Leffler Akili (eds.). *The Window of our Memories.* B.C.R. Society of Alberta: V. Carter and W. Leffler, 1981.

Charuk, Myrtle (ed.). *The History of Willingdon: A Past That Guarantees the Future, 1928-1978.* St. Paul, Alberta: L.H. Drouin, 1978.

Chipeniuk, R.C. *Lakes of the Lac La Biche District.* Calgary, Alberta: D.W. Friesen and Sons Ltd., 1975.

Clark, Edith L. *Trails of Tail Creek Country.* [s.l.: s.n., 1968].

Cochrane and Area Historical Society. *Big Hill Country: Cochrane and Area.* Cochrane, Alberta: Cochrane and Area Historical Society, 1977.

Columbo, John Robert. *Columbo's Canadian References.* Oxford, England: Oxford University Press, 1976.

Concise Dictionary of American Biographies. New York: Scribner, 1964.

Concise Dictionary of Canadian Biography, 1901-1950.

The Conroy Club and the Yeoford Ladies Club. *Trail Blazers.* Winfield, Alberta: The Conroy Club and the Yeoford Ladies Club, 1973.

Cooke, Alan. *The Exploration of Northern Canada: 500 to 1920.* Toronto: Arctic History Press, 1978.

Coulton, Betty, et al. *The Great Lone Land: Consort's 50 Years of Progress, 1912-1962.* Consort, Alberta: B. Coulton, 1962.

Country Life, 6 February 1958.

County of Smoky Lake No. 13. *Waskatenau, 1867-1967.* Smoky Lake, Alberta: County of Smoky Lake No. 13, 1967.

Dau's Blue Book (for Toronto), New York: Dau's Blue Book, Inc., 1920.

Davison, Vi, and Ava Stephenson (ed.). *Spirit and Trails of Lac Ste Anne.* Alberta Beach, Alberta: Alberta Beach and District Pioneers and Archives Society, 1982.

Daysland History Book Society. *Along the Crocus Trail: A History of Daysland and Districts.* Daysland, Alberta: The Society, 1982.

Delia and District Historical Society. *The Delia Craigmyle Saga.* Lethbridge, Alberta: Southern Printing Co., 1970.

Dempsey, Hugh A. *A History of Rocky Mountain House.* Ottawa: National Historic Sites Service, National and Historic Parks Branch, Department of Indian Affairs and Northern Development, 1973.

Dempsey, Hugh A. *Indian Names for Alberta Communities. Occasional Paper No. 4.* Calgary, Alberta: Glenbow Alberta Institute, 1969.

Department of the Interior. *Alberta-Sundry Railways, Vol. III.* Ottawa: Department of the Interior, 1915.

Deville North Cooking Lake Historical Society. *Land Among the Lakes.* Deville, Alberta: The Society, 1982.

Dictionnaire et Grammaire de la Langue des Cris. Par le Rév. Père A. Lacombe, Montreal: Albert Lacombe, 1874.

Donalda & District History Committee. *Fifty Years on the Coulee Rim.* Donalda, Alberta: Donalda & District History Committee, 1963.

Doty, Arlynn. *Roads to Pipestone.* A. Doty, 1970.

Drive Publications for the Automobile Association, London. *AA Road Book of France,* 1970 ed.

Drouin, Eneric O. *Lac Ste Anne Sakahigan.* Edmonton, Alberta: Editions de l'Ermitage, 1973.

Eagle Hill Dorcas Ladies' Aid. *The Eagle Calls: History of Eagle Hill.* Olds, Alberta: Eagle Hill Dorcas Ladies' Aid, 1975.

Eckville and District Historical Society. *Homesteads and Happiness.* Eckville, Alberta: The Society, 1977.

Edberg Historical Society Book Club. *Trails, Trials and Triumphs of Edberg and Community*. Edberg, Alberta: Edberg Historical Society Book Club, 1981.

Edstrom, Sylvia, and Florence Lundstrom. *Memoirs of the Edberg Pioneers*. Sylvia Edstrom and Florence Lundstrom, 1955.

Elk Point and District Historical Society. *Reflections: A History of Elk Point & District*. Elk Point, Alberta: The Society, 1977.

Elnora History Book Committee. *Buried Treasures: History of Elnora Pine Lake and Huxley*. Elnora, Alberta: Elnora History Book Committee, ca. 1972.

Encyclopedia Britannica., 10th ed. Chicago, Encyclopedia Britannica.

Encyclopedia Britannica., 11th ed. 1910. Chicago, Encyclopedia Britannica.

Encyclopedia Britannica., 12th ed. Chicago, Encyclopedia Britannica.

Encyclopedia Canadiana. Toronto: Grolier of Canada, 1958.

Encyclopedia of Canadian Biography, Vol. 1. Montreal, Quebec: Canadian Press Syndicate, 1904.

Eskrick, Muriel E. *Road to Ya Ha Tinda. A Story of Pioneers*. Sundre, Alberta: M.E. Eskrick, 1960.

Eskrick, Muriel E. *The Norwegian Settlers: Eagle Hill and Bergen; Stories of the West Country*. Eagle Hill, Alberta: M.E. Esdrick, 1971.

Falun Historical Society. *Freeway West*. Falun, Alberta: The Society, 1973.

Filipenko, Laura (ed.). *From the Bigknife to the Battle*. Gadsby, Alberta: Gadsby Pioneers Association, 1979.

Fitzgerald, Walter P. *The Wheels of Time. A History of Rivière Qui Barre*. Walter P. Fitzgerald, ca. 1978.

Flatbush Silver Threads Fifty Plus Club History Book Committee. *Where Friends and Rivers Meet. Flatbush and Surrounding Districts*. Flatbush Silver Threads Fifty Plus Club History Book Committee, 1986.

Fleming, Freda, and Angie Edgerton. *The Days Before Yesterday: History of Rocky Mountain House District*. Rocky Mountain House, Alberta: Rocky Mountain House Reunion Historical Society, 1977.

Forgotten Echoes Historical Society. *Forgotten Echoes: A History of Blackfoot and Surrounding Area*. Winnipeg, Manitoba: Inter-Collegiate Press, 1982.

Fowler, Mrs. Gordon. *The Big Valley Story: Golden Memories, 1914-1964*. Stettler, Alberta: *Stettler Independent*, s.n., 1964.

Frater, Alexander (ed.). *Great Rivers of the World*. London, England: Hodder and Stoughton, 1984.

Gaetz, Annie L. *The Park Country: A History of Red Deer & District*. Red Deer, Alberta: Annie Gaetz, 1948.

Geographic Board of Canada. *Place Names of Alberta*. Ottawa: Department of the Interior, 1928.

Gibbons History Committee. *Our Treasured Roots: A History of Gibbons & Surrounding Areas*. Gibbons History Committee, 1982.

Globe & Mail
   24 March 1958 – "Columnist for 55 Years, J.V. McAree Dies" (obit.).
   15 December 1958 – "Belgian Fliers Leave Crash, Head for Depot."
   28 October 1961 – "Gay Adventurer Recalls Life" (book review by Leonard Brockington).
   19 November 1962 – "Prince, Wife Hurt."
   11 February 1963 – "War hero Built Sports Empire" (obituary for Brig.-Gen. Alfred Cecil Critchley in Sports section).
   9 March 1968 - "The Chateaux of Brussels Delight the Connoisseur."
   15 February 1969 – "Dr. Edmund Walker Entomologist at U of T, ROM, found ice-bug" (obit.).
   25 March 1969 – "Lawyer Served as Gallery Head" (article on H.C.Walker).
   27 October 1969 – "B.C. Mother Who Lost Sons to Lay Wreath."
   6 April 1974 – Obituary for A.A. Walker.
   21 December 1974 – "Walker Print Exhibit Timely Tribute," by Kay Kritzwiser.
   31 May 1975 – "J.V. McAree" (biography).
   7 August 1975 – Obituary for Mrs. A.C. Webb (last surviving child of Sir E., Walker).

18 August 1975 – Obituary for Miss Marjory A. Ford. *1990 Stylebook*

The Golden Trail. Compiled by the staff of the *Camrose Canadian*. Camrose, Alberta: *Camrose Canadian*, 8 August 1955.

Gore, L. Grace. *M.D. of Kneehill, 1904-1967*. L. Grace Gore, 1968.

Gratz, Humphrey (ed.) *Footprints on Mi-Chig-Wun: Memoirs of Sunnyslope Pioneers*. Linden, Alberta: Sunnyslope History Book Committee, 1973.

Guide to Sportfishing Regulations. Alberta Fish & Wildlife, 1985.

Halkirk Historical Society. *Halkirk Home Fires and Area*. Halkirk, Alberta: The Society, 1985.

Hambly, J.R. Stan. *A Light Into the Past: A History of Camrose. 1905-1980*. Camrose, Alberta: Gospel Contact Press, 1980.

Hambly, J.R. Stan. *Battle River Country: The History of Duhamel and Area*. New Norway, Alberta: Duhamel Historical Society, 1974.

Harmattan-Westward Ho Historical Society. *Links of Memory: A History of Harmattan & Westward Ho*. Olds, Alberta: The Society, 1983.

Hartnoll, Phyllis, et al. *Oxford Companion to the Theatre,* 1st ed. London, England: Oxford University Press, 1951.

History Committee of the Wheatsheaf Womens' Institute. *Pioneer Heritage of Kirriemuir, Altario and Compeer*. Wheatsheaf, Alberta: Women's Institute, 1971.

Holmgren, E.J., and Patricia Holmgren. *Over 2000 Place Names of Alberta*. Saskatoon, Saskatchewan: Western Producer Prairie Books, 1976.

Holt, Vera E. (ed.). *Land of Red & White*. Heinsburg, Alberta: Frog Lake Community Club Book Committee, ca. 1977

The House of Commons Parliamentary Guide, 1909.

Howe, Helen D. *Seventy-Five Years Along the Red Deer River*. Calgary, Alberta: D.W. Friesen, 1977.

Hughes, Neil. "Post Offices of Alberta, 1876-1986." Unpublished manuscript, 1986.

Independence Womens' Institute. *Decades of the Independence District*. Independence, Alberta: Independence Womens' Institute, 1981.

Innisfail & District Historical Society. *Candlelight Years: A History of Innisfail & District's Pioneers*. Innisfail, Alberta: Innisfail & District Historical Society, 1973.

Innisfail & District Historical Society. *Innisfail – 75 Years a Town, 1903-1978*. Innisfail, Alberta: Innisfail & District Historical Society, 1985.

Innisfree History Book Club. *Through the Years: A History of Innisfree and District*. Innisfree, Alberta: Innisfree History Book Club, 1986.

James, Jean. *This was Endiang*. Saskatoon, Saskatchewan: Modern Press, 1969.

Jensen, Bodil J. *Alberta's County of Mountain View – A History*. Didsbury (?), Alberta: Mountain View County No. 17, 1983.

Johnston, James B. *Place Names of Scotland*, 2d ed. Edinburgh, Scotland: David Douglas, 1903.

Jouan, Marion L. (ed.). *Tomahawk Trails*. Tomahawk, Alberta: Tomahawk Trails Book Club and Silver Tops Club, 1974.

Kilgour, Betty (ed.). *As the Years Go By*. Three Hills, Alberta: Three Hills Rural Committee Group, 1970.

The Kinette Club of Didsbury History Book Committee. *Echoes of an Era: History of Didsbury and District*. Didsbury, Alberta: The Kinette Club of Didsbury History Book Committee, 1969.

Kozma, Leslie S. "Railway Stations in Alberta: 1883-1930, Volumes I & II." Unpublished manuscript prepared for Alberta Culture, October 1976.

Lac La Biche Chamber of Commerce. *Lac La Biche – The Pow Wow and Fish Derby Town*. Ottawa: Lac La Biche Chamber of Commerce, 1967.

Lac La Biche Heritage Society. *Lac La Biche: Yesterday and Today*. Lac La Biche, Alberta: The Society, 1975.

Lacey, Robert. *Aristocrats*. Toronto: McClelland and Stewart, ca. 1983.

Lacombe and District Chamber of Commerce. *Lacombe, The First Century*. Lacombe, Alberta: Lacombe and District Chamber of Commerce, 1982.

Lacombe Rural History Club. *Wagon Trails to Hardtop*. Lacombe, Alberta: Lacombe Rural History Club, 1972.

Lamerton Historical Society. *Land of the Lakes*. Lacombe, Alberta: The Society, 1974.

Leslieville & Districts Historical Society. *From Hoofprints to Highways. Leslieville & Districts Commemorate Alberta's 75th Anniversary.* Leslieville & Districts Historical Society, 1980.

Levine, Allan. *The Exchange: 100 Years of Trading Grain in Winnipeg.* Winnipeg, Manitoba: Peguis Publishers Ltd., 1987.

Lin, Leslie. "History of Elk Island National Park." Unpublished manuscript, 1986.

Lindroth, Helen. *We Came and We Stayed: Accounts of the Pioneers, Their Descendants and Other Residents of Bawlf, Alberta*. Camrose, Alberta: Gospel Contact Press, 1980.

Lougheed Women's Institute. *Verdant Valleys in and around Lougheed*. Lougheed, Alberta: Lougheed Women's Institute, 1972.

Lubbock, Basil. *The Nitrate Clippers*. 1932.

Lynn, Esther. *Derbytown Echoes: A History of Rockwood, Lobley, Eagle Point & James River*. Youngstown, Alberta: Derbytown Book Club, 1975.

MacGregor, James, G. *Behold the Shining Mountains; Being an Account of the Travels of Anthony Henday, 1754-1755*. Edmonton, Alberta: Applied Arts Products, ca. 1954.

Macgregor, J.G. *Pack Saddles to the Tête Jaune Cache*. Toronto: McClelland and Stewart, 1962.

MacMillan World Gazeteer. Toronto: MacMillan, 1955.

Maloff, Greta. *Recollections of the Homestead Trails, 1900-1978: History of Bearberry & Sunberry*. Sundre, Alberta: Bearberry Wapitana Society of Bearberry, 1978.

Mardon, Ernest G. *Community Names of Alberta*. Lethbridge, Alberta: E.G. Mardon, 1973.

Masters, Kathy, et al. *Beautiful Fields*. Bashaw, Alberta: Bashaw History Committee, 1974.

McCarty, Tom. *As We Remember Big Valley*. Big Valley, Alberta: T. McCarty, 1974.

Mecca Glen Centennial Committee. *Mecca Glen Memories*. Ponoka, Alberta: Mecca Glen Centennial Committee, 1968.

Morgan, Henry J. *The Canadian Men and Women of the Time: A Handbook of Canadian Biography*. Toronto: W. Briggs, 1898 and 1912.

Nestow, Tawatinaw, Rochester Paerryvale History Book Committee. *Rolling Hills & Whispering Pines: A Peek at the Past. Volumes I & II.* Winnipeg, Manitoba: Inter-Collegiate Press, 1985.

The New Century Encyclopedia of Names. New York: Appleton-Century-Crofts, 1954.

Old Timers' Centennial Book Committee. *Open Memory's Door: A History of Coronation and District*. Coronation, Alberta: Old Timers' Centennial Book Committee, 1967.

Olds Old Timers' Association. *See Olds First: A History of Olds & Surrounding District*. Olds, Alberta: Olds Old Timers' Association, 1968.

Onoway Women's Institute. *The Pathfinders: A History of Onoway and District*. Onoway, Alberta: Onoway Women's Institute, 1978.

Owens, Brian M., and Claude M. Roberto. *A Guide to the Archives of the Oblates of Mary Immaculate*. Edmonton, Alberta: The Missionary Oblates, Grandin Province, 1989.

Phillips, Grace A. (ed.). *Tales of Tofield*. Tofield, Alberta: Tofield Historical Society, 1969.

Ponoka & District Historical Society. *Ponoka Panorama*. Ponoka, Alberta: The Society, 1973.

Prud'homme, Essie. *Yesteryears of the Hays Municipality*. Red Deer, Alberta: County of Red Deer No. 23 Centennial Project, 1967.

Red Deer East Historical Society. *Mingling Memories*. Red Deer, Alberta: The Society, 1979.

Redekop, Linda, and Wilfred Gilchrist. *Strathcona County, A Brief History*. Edmonton, Alberta: W. Gilchrist, 1981.

Reynolds, A. Bert. *Siding 16: An Early History of Wetaskiwin to 1930*. Wetaskiwin, Alberta: R.C.M.P. Centennial Committee, 1976.

Ricinius-Caroline History Committee. *In the Shade of the Mountains: A History of the Following School Districts: Chedderville, Clear Creek, Crammond, Crooked Creek, Dovercourt, Hazeldell, Pineview, Ricinius, Shilo, South Fork, Wooler*. Caroline, Alberta: Ricinius-Caroline History Committee, 1979.

Ross, Toni A. *Oh! The Coal Branch; A Chronicle of the Alberta Coal Branch*. Edmonton, Alberta: T. Ross, 1974.

Rumsey-Rowley Historical Society. *Pioneer Days: Book Two. Rumsey-Rowley*. Rumsey, Alberta: The Society, 1982.

Sangudo and District History Society. *The Lantern Era: A History of Cherhill, Rochfort Bridge, Sangudo and Surrounding School Districts*. Sangudo, Alberta: The Society, 1979

Sawatsky, A. "The Mennonites of Alberta." Edmonton, Alberta: A. Sawatsky, M.A. thesis, University of Alberta, 1964.

Schultz, Fred. *Pas-ka-poo*. Rimbey, Alberta: *The Rimbey Record*, 1962.

Shillinglaw, Merton. *The Early Devisers*. Forestburg, Alberta: Forestburg Historical Society Inc., 1973.

Smith, Bessie, and Joyce Gould (eds.). *The Sunny Side of the Neutrals: Stories of Consort and District in Alberta, Canada*. The Association of Consort and District Seniors, 1983.

Smyth, Alice Mary, et al. *Oxford Dictionary of Quotations*. London, England: Oxford University Press, 1941.

Spruce View School Area Historical Society. *Grub-Axe to Grain*. Spruce View, Alberta: The Society, 1973.

Stainton, Irene Hackett, and Elizabeth Course Carlsson (eds.). *Along the Victoria Trail: Lamont and Districts*. I.H. Stainton and E.C. Carlsson, 1978.

The Statesman's Year-Book. New York: St. Martin's Press, 1971-72.

Stony Plain Historical Society. *Along the Fifth – A History of Stony Plain & District*. Stony Plain, Alberta: Stony Plain Historical Society, 1982.

Stout, C.H. (ed.). *From Frontier Days in Leduc and District: 65 Years of Progress*. Leduc, Alberta: Representative Publ. Co., 1956.

Strome Senior Citizen's Club. *Lanterns on the Prairie; Strome Diamond Jubilee, 1905-1980*. Strome, Alberta: Strome Senior Citizen's Club, 1980.

Swettenham, John. *Valiant Men; Canada's Victoria Cross and George Cross Winners*. Toronto: Hakkert, 1973.

Sylvan Lake Historical Society. *Reflections of Sylvan Lake*. Sylvan Lake, Alberta: The Society, 1984.

Thompson, Don W. *Men and Meridians: The History of Surveying and Mapping in Canada*. Ottawa: Queen's Printer, 1967.

Three Trails Home: A History Of Mayerthorpe and Districts, Alberta, Canada. Winnipeg: Inter-Collegiate Press, 1980.

Toronto Star, 1 March 1980 – "Walker's Ice-bug Commemorated by Entomologists." David Jones in *Historical Toronto*.

Unrau, Henry. *Sherwood Park, The First Twenty-Five Years*. County of Strathcona No. 20: 25th Anniversary Committee, 1983.

Vancouver Sun, 30 November 1992 – "Britain's Richest Man: Sex, Real Estate, Wicked Combination for U.K. Billionaire."

Westerdale Willing Workers. *A Trail Grows Dim*. Westerdale, Alberta: Westerdale Willing Workers' History Committee, 1967.

Who was Who and Why. Toronto: International Press Ltd., 1914.

Who was Who in America. Chicago: A.N. Marquis Company, 1897-1963.

Who's Who in Canada. Toronto: International Press, 1916-28, 1936-37, 1958-60.

Willsie, Marie. *White Creek Echoes*. Innisfail, Alberta: Innisfail Booster, 1967.

Winterburn Women's Institute. *Memory Trails of Winterburn*. Winterburn, Alberta: Winterburn Women's Institute, 1975.

Within Our Borders (serial), 1966.

Women's Institute, Hughenden. *The Lantern Years: Buffalo Park to Neutral Hills*. Winnipeg: Inter-Collegiate Press, 1967.

Women's Institute, Majestic-Farrell Lake. *Harvest of Memories*. Lethbridge: Southern Printing Limited, 1968.

Wood, Kerry. *A Corner of Canada: A Personalized History of the Red Deer River Country*. Red Deer: Kerry Wood, ca. 1966.

PHOTOGRAPHS

Birch Lake   *Battle Lake*

Astotin Lake

Bonnie Lake   *Floatingstone Lake*

Blindman River

Garner Lake

Gull Lake

Hairy Hill

Kehiwin Lake

Moose Hills

Moose Lake

Moosehills Lake

Lower Mann Lake

Paddle River

North Saskatchewan River

Lac Ste Anne

Sylvan Lake

Pembina River at Sangudo

Vermilion Park Lake